D1270910

THE RESURRECTION OF THE

Romanovs

THE RESURRECTION OF THE
Romanovs

*Anastasia, Anna Anderson,
and the World's Greatest Royal Mystery*

Greg King
and
Penny Wilson

WILEY

John Wiley & Sons, Inc.

Copyright © 2011 by Greg King and Penny Wilson. All rights reserved

Published by John Wiley & Sons, Inc., Hoboken, New Jersey
Published simultaneously in Canada

Photo credits: pages 30, 36, 49, 50, 61, 68, 69, 81, 82, 115, 149, 154, 171, 178, 184, 200, 202 bottom, 203, 204 top and bottom, 205, 206 top and bottom, 224, 229, 230, 233, 240, 241, 244, 246 top and bottom, 279 top and bottom, 282, 298, 299, 306, and 307: Ian Lilburn Collection; pages 52, 260, 327, and 328: Katrina Warne; page 72: Staatsarchiv, Darmstadt; pages 80 and 280: Annelies Dogterom and Alex Uitvlugt; page 216: Michael Fulda Collection.

No part of this publication may be reproduced, stored in a retrieval system, or transmitted in any form or by any means, electronic, mechanical, photocopying, recording, scanning, or otherwise, except as permitted under Section 107 or 108 of the 1976 United States Copyright Act, without either the prior written permission of the Publisher, or authorization through payment of the appropriate per-copy fee to the Copyright Clearance Center, 222 Rosewood Drive, Danvers, MA 01923, (978) 750-8400, fax (978) 646-8600, or on the web at www.copyright.com. Requests to the Publisher for permission should be addressed to the Permissions Department, John Wiley & Sons, Inc., 111 River Street, Hoboken, NJ 07030, (201) 748-6011, fax (201) 748-6008, or online at http://www.wiley.com/go/permissions.

Limit of Liability/Disclaimer of Warranty: While the publisher and the author have used their best efforts in preparing this book, they make no representations or warranties with respect to the accuracy or completeness of the contents of this book and specifically disclaim any implied warranties of merchantability or fitness for a particular purpose. No warranty may be created or extended by sales representatives or written sales materials. The advice and strategies contained herein may not be suitable for your situation. You should consult with a professional where appropriate. Neither the publisher nor the author shall be liable for any loss of profit or any other commercial damages, including but not limited to special, incidental, consequential, or other damages.

For general information about our other products and services, please contact our Customer Care Department within the United States at (800) 762-2974, outside the United States at (317) 572-3993 or fax (317) 572-4002.

Wiley also publishes its books in a variety of electronic formats. Some content that appears in print may not be available in electronic books. For more information about Wiley products, visit our web site at www.wiley.com.

Library of Congress Cataloging-in-Publication Data:

King, Greg, date.
    The resurrection of the Romanovs : Anastasia, Anna Anderson, and the World's Greatest Royal Mystery/ Greg King and Penny Wilson.
       p. cm.
    Includes bibliographical references and index.
    ISBN 978-0-470-44498-6 (cloth); ISBN 978-0470-89086-8 (ebk); ISBN 978-0-470-89093-6 (ebk); ISBN 978-0-470-89106-3 (ebk)
    1. Anderson, Anna. 2. Anastasiia Nikolaevna, Grand Duchess, daughter of Nicholas II, Emperor of Russia, 1901–1918—Legends. 3. Anastasiia Nikolaevna, Grand Duchess, daughter of Nicholas II, Emperor of Russia, 1901–1918. 4. Princesses—Russia—Biography. 5. Romanov, House of—Biography. 6. Impostors and imposture—Case studies. I. Wilson, Penny, 1966– II. Title.
    DK254.A7K56 2011
    947.08092—dc22
    [B]
                                                                    2010016887

Printed in the United States of America

10 9 8 7 6 5 4 3 2 1

To Professor Doctor Eckhart Franz of the Staatsarchiv, Darmstadt, and Ian Lilburn for their generous assistance; and to the immortal memory of Dr. Louis Pedrotti

Contents

Authors' Note

The multitude of titles, styles, and linguistic complexities contained within this book need a brief explanation. Nicholas II ruled over the Russian Empire from 1894 to 1917. The formal title, adopted by Peter the Great in 1721, was *emperor*, although Nicholas preferred the older, more Slavic form of *tsar*. His wife, Alexandra, was *empress*, although she was widely referred to as *tsaritsa* in Russian; *tsarina*, familiar to some readers, does not exist in the Russian language. Their son and heir, Alexei, was properly titled *tsesarevich*, while Anastasia and her sisters were *grand duchesses*, meant to convey a higher rank than mere European princesses. Russians use two names: a Christian name, and a patronymic, derived from his or her father. The masculine form takes the father's name and adds *-vich* to the ending, indicating "son of." Nicholas II was thus Nicholas Alexandrovich—son of Alexander. The feminine form adds *-evna* or *-ovna* to the end of the father's Christian name; Anastasia was thus Anastasia Nikolaievna, daughter of Nicholas. With no disrespect, we have tried to escape, as much as possible, the often cumbersome and repetitious use of titles and, after initially introducing them in the pages of the book, have simply referred to many of the Russian actors in the Anna Anderson drama using their Christian names and patronymics. Readers may find it beneficial to refer to the cast of characters as an aid to keep names and relationships in order.

In transliterating Russian names, we have followed the Library of Congress system, with some exceptions. Christian names—and those names familiar to English-speaking readers—have been rendered in English: thus we have Nicholas rather than Nikolai, and Tchaikovsky in place of the unfamiliar Chaikovskii. But a whole host of issues arise in a book such as this, which begins in Russia and takes readers through Germany and to modern Poland, not the least of which is consistency in spelling. We have tried to obey German rules of grammar and spelling when dealing with a sometimes mind-boggling galaxy of witnesses, interested parties, and Romanov relatives in the Anderson case, but haven't attempted to cloak everything in an accurate veil; instead of referring to Empress Alexandra's brother Ernst Ludwig as grand duke von Hesse und bei Rhein—his correct German title—we've gone with the simpler grand duke of Hesse. Certain inconsistent spellings and usages, especially among Anna Anderson's relatives, are documented and explained in the notes rather than in the actual text.

In Russia, before the Revolution, the Julian calendar was in use; in the twentieth century, this lagged thirteen days behind the Gregorian calendar, used in the West. We have given dates according to the Gregorian calendar, but noted the use, in letters, of the Julian calendar by including the reference OS (for Old Style).

Acknowledgments

The poor, unfortunate friends and family of those of us who call ourselves authors have to endure absences, preoccupation, missed birthdays and holidays, and other turns of fate that can seem inexplicable, egregious, and dangerously selfish as we labor over laptops and try to reconcile gut instinct when telling a story with demonstrable fact. They put up with it all, and deserve to be noted.

For twenty-five years, Christopher Kinsman has been a true and constant friend; Penny Wilson thanks him for his longtime interest and support, and looks forward to many more Friday nights sinking beers at the Yardhouse or the Falconer. Penny Wilson works at Riverside City Gym in Riverside, California, the best little gym in the Inland Empire. Over the past few years, the staff there has undertaken extra hours and extra duties to accommodate the writing and research schedule of the resident author. For their unswerving support, Penny thanks Arthur Bruckler, Greg English, Carlos Mata, Tom Mishler, and Ed Gardner; the Perez family: Emilio Sr., Maricela, and Emilio Jr.; Wellington Porter, Madeline Pruett, Josh Sweeten, Cousin James, Tommy Gutierrez, and Allison Wondolleck. Special thanks to Jennifer Hawkins, who is never less than a complete inspiration. Penny also thanks members of City Gym who have given kind words and encouragement, including David Armstrong, Dr. Ron Bailey, Carlos and Laurel Cortes, David Edgin, Tom Foley, Michael "William" Grey, Francisco Guerra, Billie McWhorter, Mike Luvisi, Chad Trenham, Seton Williams, Raz Williams, Ali Yahyavi, and Donna Zeeb. The Internet has introduced the possibility of friendships with people one may never—or only seldom—meet. Simon Donoghue has provided much-needed stress relief, humor, perspective, and advice throughout the entire process of researching and writing this book, despite his own busy schedule directing theater productions, and Penny thanks him from the bottom of her heart. Mike Pyles has proven a wonderful friend and sounding board. Penny also thanks the members of

Planetsocks for their enduring good sense, wicked wit, and peculiar sort of wisdom. And finally, Penny's boss, personal trainer, personal friend, and body-builder extraordinaire, Oscar Shearer, has proven an excellent friend, mentor, and 5:00 A.M. philosopher; Penny looks forward to many more years of workouts, coffeehousing, and conversation.

Penny Wilson would also like to thank her family for their support: her parents, Edward and Mary O'Hanlon; her brother and sister-in-law, Peter and Lynne O'Hanlon; her sister Trisha O'Hanlon; nephews and their families, Jon and Jacquie Phillips, and Jamie, Lindsey, and Georgia Phillips; and not forgetting Bill Yonush. In addition, Penny would like to thank Paul and Barbara Wilson; Liz Wilson; and Peggy, Darren, Eric, and Ryan Cartwright. Tom Wilson still has Penny's love and Greg's gratitude for a few more years of technical and emotional support as we undertook yet another book project. Hopefully, he can retire on this one!

Greg King thanks Sharlene Aadland, Professor Joseph Fuhrmann, Chuck and Eileen Knaus, Angela Manning, Ceceilia Manning, Mark Manning, Susanne Meslans, Scott Michaels, Russ and Deb Minugh, Steve O'Donnell, Brad Swenson, and Debra Tate. A special thanks to Henderson's Books in Bellingham, Washington, the state's best source for obscure and antiquarian books, whose generosity has saved me from despair more than a few times.

And, as ever, Greg thanks his parents, Roger and Helena King, for their enduring support, generosity, and belief in this most peculiar career path.

Dorie Simmonds, of the Dorie Simmonds Literary Agency in London, has shepherded this book from idea to fruition with an unfailing sense of enthusiasm and a stream of sage advice. It wouldn't have been possible if not for her belief in us. And Stephen Power, our editor at Wiley, was instrumental in shaping the finished book. With a sure and certain eye and a knack for penetrating even the deepest layers of complexity, he's forced us to look at the story in different ways and through different eyes, making it possible to approach the Anderson saga with a renewed interest and sense of wonder that we trust our readers share.

In the acknowledgments for *The Fate of the Romanovs*, we noted that the project had begun long before we met, as each of us worked on our own separate Romanov research. The same can be said of this book, but there is something even more special about Anastasia: Anastasia's story, in the guise of Anna Anderson's claim, is what initially brought both of us to a study of imperial Russian history. Had there never been a claimant or a case, it's likely that the last imperial family of Russia would have sunk gently into historical obscurity. And it's often been the interest of various supporters—and for various claimants—that's forced continued research and historiography on the subject, a fact that sits uneasily with some who venerate the Romanovs as Orthodox saints. But as this book shows, the claim of Anna Anderson, at least, has become an integral part of the story of the last tsar and his family, and because of this, we extend our thanks first and foremost to the "Anastasians," a group of historians, authors, researchers, friends, interested parties, and the truly convinced who over the years have kept the story alive, who probed discrepancies in the case, and who continued—often in the face of ridicule and personal attack—to ask the troubling questions, the questions we have attempted to finally answer in these pages.

This book represents a massive undertaking, more than a decade of sifting through depositions and statements, letters and memoirs, and does not just rest on years of our own private interest and research, but also draws on work done for other projects over the years; never quite knowing if we would—individually or together—ever write about Anderson's case, we nevertheless took advantage of every opportunity that came our way, accessing materials and questioning those involved in the story when the chance came. Many of those who aided us in Russia, Germany, England, and North America as we researched *The Fate of the Romanovs* had an unwitting hand in this book, facilitating access to important collections and extending cooperation for a project not yet even envisioned.

We want to thank our good friends the members of Cold Harbor for their knowledgeable and often inspired debates and conversations on the subject covered in this book. We know some may find this a difficult road to travel, but we have done our best to make what is an essential journey as painless as possible for those who still believe that Anna Anderson was Anastasia.

In particular, for research, for generosity in sharing materials, and for answering a multitude of questions, we thank Patte Barham; Arturo Beeche; Prince David Chavchavadze; Robert Crouch; Dr. Richard Davis, curator of the Russian Archive at Leeds University in Great Britain; Annelies Dogterom; the late George Gibbes; John Godl; Coryne Hall; Andrew Hartsook; Gretchin Haskin; DeeAnn Hoff; John Kendrick; Marlene Eilers Koenig; the late James Blair Lovell; Laura Mabee; Professor Syd Mandelbaum; Dr. Terry Melton of Milotyping Technologies; Ilana Miller; Dr. Andre Moenssens, professor emeritus, University of Richmond, University of Missouri at Kansas City; Annette Nason-Waters; Ulrike Nieder-Vahrenholz; Julian Nott; Maurice Philip Remy and his entire staff at MPR Productions in Munich; Greg Rittenhouse; Bernard Ruffin; Dr. Stefan Sandkuhler; Marilyn Swezey; Alex Uitvlugt; Katrina Warne; Frances Welch; Colin Wilson; Dietmar Wulff; and Marion Wynne.

Especially instrumental in the completion of this book are some dedicated souls who uncomplainingly read—and reread—through several versions of the manuscript, enduring its messy and rambling beginnings as we struggled to find a correct format in which to convey the story. It was an embarrassment, the first draft, but the honest opinions that confirmed this helped us craft the story into something we hope is more satisfactory. Our thanks go to Janet Ashton, Lisa Davidson, Simon Donoghue, Jeannine Evans, Susan Grindstaff, Brien Horan, Mike Pyles, David Vernall-Downes, and Tim Welsh, and especially to Sarah Miller, who holds the singular and dubious distinction of being the only person to read every single version—all six of them— that came at her, fast and furious, over the course of eighteen months and whose opinions and advice were never short of miraculous.

On the Alexander Palace Time Machine, (www.alexanderpalace .org/palace/) we thank long-time posters and friends, as well as those who thoroughly challenged our opinions and views as they shifted and progressed in this case. There are few as knowledgeable about the domestic life of the last imperial family as Bob Atchison and Rob Moshein, and we sincerely thank them for their enduring friendship under difficult and sometimes contentious circumstances. Rob, especially, went out of his way to assist in research, and cheerfully accepted repeated requests for information even as he dealt with pressing family concerns. Both have our lasting thanks.

Pepsi Nunes helped fund much of the research that's ended up in these pages, and the late Marina Botkin Schweitzer and her husband, Richard, proved generous and understanding when circumstances often spiraled out of control. Lawyer and Anderson historian Brien Horan has been a constant source of advice, information, and assistance, a sure sounding board for theories who never let preconceptions affect his own responses. Michael Fulda, Lili Dehn's grandson, generously read portions of the manuscript and shared his knowledge and family history with us. Author and historian Robert K. Massie provided us with valuable materials collected during his own research into the Anna Anderson case. David Vernall-Downes investigated the contradictory threads in this story on our behalf, providing a multitude of rare books and antiquarian newspaper articles that helped elaborate the saga and made him a writer's dream. Dr. Michael Coble, formerly of the Armed Forces DNA Identification Laboratory and now Forensic Biologist at the National Institute of Standards and Technology in Gaithersburg, Maryland, and Dr. Daniele Podini of George Washington University, undertook new DNA tests on Anna Anderson hair samples. And Anderson's biographer our friend Peter Kurth has been supportive and generous with his time and his knowledge, even when we faced the daunting task of admitting that our book was taking an unexpected direction.

In the summer of 2000 we spent several weeks in London, undertaking research and probably making nuisances of ourselves in asking royal author Sue Woolmans to help us arrange this dinner party or that expedition. It was Sue who helped establish what—for a time, anyway—became Anna Anderson Central, renting a copying machine and having it delivered to our flat; ensuring that we were stocked with supplies; packing up boxes and boxes of books, collecting them, and shipping them back to America for us; and probably ignoring her long-suffering husband, Mike, in the process to help a couple of enthusiastic writers she'd never previously met. Because of Sue, we ended up with the means to tap into the single greatest Anna Anderson archive in private hands, that of Ian Lilburn. It was no accident that we took a flat a mere four houses down a leafy square from Ian's London residence: armed with the copying machine, we flew back and forth every day, amassing an extraordinary collection of documents that Ian freely and generously shared. Perhaps even more important was Ian's extraordinary memory: as the only person to have attended every session of the Hamburg appeal in the 1960s, and an almost unofficial member of Anderson's legal team, his recall makes him the acknowledged expert on her case, and we owe him a deep debt.

And finally, a word about Darmstadt. Our thanks go to Heiner Jerofsky, Direktor von Presse und Offentlichkeitsarbeit for the Darmstadt Police Archives, who allowed us unrestricted access to the files assembled on Anna Anderson in the 1920s following the investigation into her claim by Grand Duke Ernst Ludwig. We also thank Prince Moritz of Hesse for so graciously allowing us free access to the materials in the Staatsarchiv, Darmstadt, on the Anderson case, including personal family papers and letters, access facilitated, encouraged, and furthered by the extraordinary and generous Professor Dr. Eckhart Franz. As director of the Staatsarchiv, Professor Franz not only helped us at every turn, beginning in our momentous summer of 2000, but also did so in ways we never could have expected, ensuring not just that we could consult every single piece of documentation amassed over more than fifty years, but also that we were able to have our own copies of this unique assemblage. It was an unexpected gift, one made on behalf of a family that trusted us when they had every reason to be suspicious, especially after decades in which many of Anderson's supporters portrayed Grand Duke Ernst Ludwig of Hesse and his involvement in her case in the worst possible light. If nothing else, hopefully this book helps right some of the wrongs done by one of the twentieth century's most pervasive myths.

Cast of Principal Characters

THE IMPERIAL FAMILY

Nicholas II (1868–1918), last Russian emperor, reigned 1894–1917

Alexandra (1872–1918), empress and consort of Nicholas II, born Princess Alix of Hesse und bei Rhein

Alexei (1904–1918), tsesarevich and heir to the Russian throne, only son of Nicholas and Alexandra

Olga Nikolaievna (1895–1918), grand duchess and eldest daughter of Nicholas and Alexandra

Tatiana Nikolaievna (1897–1918), grand duchess and second daughter of Nicholas and Alexandra

Marie Nikolaievna (1899–1918), grand duchess and third daughter of Nicholas and Alexandra

Anastasia Nikolaievna (1901–1918), grand duchess and fourth and youngest daughter of Nicholas and Alexandra

THE HOUSE OF ROMANOV

Alexander Mikhailovich (1866–1933), grand duke, second cousin to Nicholas II, and husband to Grand Duchess Xenia Alexandrovna

Andrei Vladimirovich (1879–1956), grand duke, first cousin to Nicholas II; married (1921) former ballerina Mathilde Kschessinska, onetime mistress to Nicholas II; investigated Anderson's claim

Felix Felixovich Yusupov (1887–1967), prince, Rasputin's principal assassin; married (1914) to Princess Irina Alexandrovna (1895–1970), only daughter of Xenia Alexandrovna and Alexander Mikhailovich

Kirill Vladimirovich (1876–1938), grand duke, first cousin to Nicholas II; married (1905) Princess Victoria Melita ("Ducky"), divorced wife of Empress Alexandra's only surviving brother, Grand Duke Ernst Ludwig of Hesse; rightful heir to the Russian throne

Marie Feodorovna (1847–1928), dowager empress of Russia, widow of Alexander III, and mother of Nicholas II; born Princess Dagmar, daughter of King Christian IX of Denmark

Nina Georgievna (1901–1974), princess of Russia, eldest daughter of Grand Duke George Mikhailovich; married (1922) Prince Paul Chavchavadze, mother of Prince David Chavchavadze

Olga Alexandrovna (1883–1960), grand duchess, youngest sister of Nicholas II, favorite aunt of Anastasia; married Prince Peter of Oldenburg (marriage annulled); married Colonel Nicholas Kulikovsky

Xenia Alexandrovna (1875–1960), grand duchess, eldest sister of Nicholas II, wife of Grand Duke Alexander Mikhailovich, and mother-in-law of Prince Felix Yusupov

Xenia Georgievna (1903–1965), princess of Russia, youngest daughter of Grand Duke George Mikhailovich; married William Leeds (divorced 1930); married Herman Jud (1946); mother of Nancy Leeds Wynkoop; hosted Anderson in 1928 at her Long Island estate, Kenwood

ANASTASIA'S ROYAL RELATIVES

Ernst Ludwig (1868–1937), last grand duke of Hesse und bei Rhein, only surviving brother of Empress Alexandra; married Princess Victoria Melita ("Ducky") (1894, divorced 1901); married Princess Eleonore of Solms-Hohensolms-Lich

Irene (1866–1953), Princess Heinrich of Prussia, born Princess Irene of Hesse und bei Rhein, sister of Empress Alexandra, married to Prince Heinrich of Prussia, younger brother of Kaiser Wilhelm II

Sigismund (1896–1978), prince of Prussia, second son of Princess Irene and Prince Heinrich, married to Princess Charlotte-Agnes of Saxe-Altenburg, sister of Prince Friedrich of Saxe-Altenburg

Victoria (1863–1950), marchioness of Milford Haven (after 1917), born Princess Victoria of Hesse und bei Rhein, eldest sister of Empress Alexandra, mother of Lord Louis Mountbatten, grandmother of Prince Philip, duke of Edinburgh

MEMBERS OF THE RUSSIAN IMPERIAL COURT, SUITE, AND HOUSEHOLD

Buxhoeveden, Baroness Sophie (1884–1956), *kamer-freilina* (personal lady-in-waiting) to Empress Alexandra from 1913

Gibbes, Charles Sidney (1876–1963), English tutor to the imperial children

Gilliard, Pierre (1879–1962), tutor of the French language to the imperial children; married (1919) the imperial children's former nursery maid Alexandra Tegleva

Mordvinov, Colonel Anatole, former adjutant to Nicholas II

Sablin, Captain Nicholas, former officer aboard the imperial yacht *Standart*

Tegleva, Alexandra ("Shura") (died 1955), former nursery maid to the imperial children; married Pierre Gilliard in 1919

Volkov, Alexei (1868–1929), former valet de chambre to the empress

MEDICAL PROFESSIONALS

Barfknecht, Emilie, nurse at Dalldorf Asylum, Berlin

Bonhoeffer, Dr. Karl, treated Anna Anderson at the Mommsen Clinic, Berlin

Buchholz, Erna, nurse at Dalldorf Asylum, Berlin

Eitel, Dr. Theodore, specialist in internal medicine, treated Anna Anderson at the Stillachhaus Sanatorium at Oberstdorf in Bavaria, 1926–1927

Kastritsky, Professor Serge, former court dentist to Nicholas II

Malinovsky, Anna (Thea), later Chemnitz, nurse at Dalldorf Asylum, Berlin

Nobel, Dr. Lothar, director of Mommsen Clinic, Berlin

Rudnev, Professor Serge, Russian émigré tubercular specialist, treated Anna Anderson 1925–1926

Walz, Bertha, nurse at Dalldorf Asylum, Berlin

Willige, Dr. Hans, director of the Ilten Asylum near Hannover, treated Anna Anderson 1931–1932

LAWYERS IN THE ANNA ANDERSON CASE

Berenberg-Gossler, Dr. Gunther von (1901–2001), lawyer for Barbara, Duchess Christian Ludwig of Mecklenburg, in the Anderson civil trial and appeals

Fallows, Edward, Anna Anderson's American lawyer, 1928–1940

Krampff, Dr. Hans Hermann, lawyer for Prince Ludwig of Hesse in the Anderson civil trial and appeals

Leverkuehn, Dr. Paul, with Kurt Vermehren Anna Anderson's German lawyer, 1938–1960

Stackelberg, Dr. Baron Curt von, lawyer who headed Anna Anderson's 1970 appeal to the West German Federal Supreme Court

Vermehren, Dr. Kurt, with Paul Leverkuehn Anna Anderson's German lawyer, 1938–1962

Wollmann, Carl August, from 1962 lawyer for Anna Anderson's appeals

INTERESTED PARTIES

Auclères, Dominique, reporter for *Le Figaro*, covered the Anderson civil suit

Botkin, Gleb (1900–1969), youngest son of court physician Dr. Eugene Botkin, who was murdered with the Romanovs

Botkin, Serge (died 1945), first cousin to Dr. Eugene Botkin, president of the Office of Russian Refugees in Berlin

Botkin, Tatiana (1898–1986), only daughter of court physician Dr. Eugene Botkin, who was murdered with the Romanovs; married (1918) Konstantin Melnik

Burkhart, Susan (née Grindstaff), owner of Anna Anderson hair sample tested for DNA in 1994

Cecilie, crown princess of Prussia (1886–1954), married to Crown Prince Friedrich Wilhelm of Prussia, eldest son and heir of Kaiser Wilhelm II

Dassel, Captain Felix (died 1958), former patient in the Tsarskoye Selo hospital operated by Grand Duchesses Marie and Anastasia Nikolaievna during the First World War

Dehn, Lili von (1888–1963), close friend of Empress Alexandra

Friedrich Ernst, Prince of Saxe-Altenburg (1905–1985), distantly related to the Romanovs; acted as legal adviser for Anna Anderson from 1949; his sister Charlotte-Agnes married Prince Sigismund of Prussia

Grunberg, Inspector Franz, Berlin Police official, sheltered Anna Anderson 1922–1924

Hardenberg, Count Kuno von, former marshal of Grand Duke Ernst Ludwig's court

Horan, Brien Purcell, American lawyer and Anderson case historian

Jennings, Annie Burr, heiress who periodically sheltered Anna Anderson 1928–1930 in New York

Kleist, Baron Arthur von, former provincial police chief in Poland, periodically sheltered Anna Anderson 1922–1924 in Berlin, recorded her early alleged memories

Kleist, Baroness Gerda von, youngest of four daughters of Baron and Baroness von Kleist

Kleist, Baroness Marie von (née Grotthaus), wife of Baron Arthur von Kleist

Klemenz, Vera von, music teacher at Schloss Seeon in Bavaria

Knopf, Martin (born 1891), private bank detective in Berlin, hired by Count Kuno von Hardenberg on behalf of Grand Duke Ernst Ludwig to investigate Anna Anderson's claim, worked with the Scherl Press in Berlin

Kurth, Peter, Anna Anderson's biographer

Lavington, Faith, English tutor at Schloss Seeon

Leuchtenberg, Duke Georg Nikolaievich de Beauharnais (1872–1929), distantly related to the Romanovs; married (1895) to Princess Olga Repnin-Volkonsky (1872–1953); sheltered Anna Anderson at his Bavarian estate, Schloss Seeon, 1927–1928

Leuchtenberg, Duchess Elena (1896–1977), eldest daughter of Duke Georg of Leuchtenberg

Leuchtenberg, Duke Dimitri (1898–1972), eldest son of Duke Georg of Leuchtenberg, married (1921) Catherine (1900–1991)

Leuchtenberg, Duchess Nathalia (1900), daughter of Duke Georg of Leuchtenberg, married (1924) Baron Vladimir Meller-Zakomelsky

Leuchtenberg, Duchess Tamara (1901–1978), daughter of Duke Georg of Leuchtenberg

Leuchtenberg, Duke Konstantin (1905–1983), son of Duke Georg of Leuchtenberg

Lilburn, Ian, historian and expert on the Anna Anderson case

Lücke, Fritz, editor of the Scherl Press in Berlin, publisher of papers *Die Woche* and *Berliner Nachtausgabe*, worked with Martin Knopf to investigate Anna Anderson's claim

Ludwig, Prince of Hesse und bei Rhein (1908–1968), youngest son and only surviving heir of Grand Duke Ernst Ludwig and Anastasia's first cousin; voluntarily joined as a defendant in Anderson's civil suit against Barbara, Duchess Christian Ludwig of Mecklenburg

Manahan, John E. ("Jack") (1919–1990), married Anna Anderson in 1968

Mecklenburg, Princess Barbara of Prussia, Duchess Christian Ludwig of (1920–1994), granddaughter and adopted heir of Princess Irene, Princess Heinrich of Prussia, and daughter of Prince Sigismund of Prussia, principal defendant in Anderson's civil suit

Miliukov, Alexei, Russian émigré, friend of Gleb Botkin, chronicler of Anna Anderson's conversations in the 1960s

Mountbatten of Burma, Lord Louis (1900–1979), youngest son of Empress Alexandra's sister Victoria, first cousin to Anastasia; helped finance legal opposition to Anna Anderson's civil case

Osten-Sacken, Baron Vassili, deputy to Serge Botkin at the Office of Russian Refuges in Berlin

Peuthert, Marie Clara (born Meissen, 1871–1933), patient at Dalldorf Asylum, Berlin

Rathlef-Keilmann, Harriet von (1887–1933), sculptor by profession, looked after Anna Anderson 1925–1926, author of the first book on the claimant

Remy, Maurice Philip, German documentary producer, involved in 1993–1994 legal battle over testing Anna Anderson's tissue samples

Schwabe, Captain Nicholas von, former officer in Dowager Empress Marie Feodorovna's Cuirassier Life Guards Regiment, member of the émigré Monarchist Council in Berlin; he and his wife, Alice, periodically sheltered Anna Anderson 1922–1924

Schweitzer, Marina, née Botkin, daughter of Gleb Botkin; with her husband, attorney Richard Schweitzer, arranged and paid for the 1994 DNA tests on Anna Anderson's tissue samples

Schweitzer, Richard, husband of Marina Botkin Schweitzer; arranged and paid for the 1994 DNA tests on Anna Anderson's tissue sample

Spindler, Gertrude, friend of Harriet von Rathlef-Keilmann and Anna Anderson supporter; investigated her claim to have stayed in Bucharest

Tolstoy, Zenaide, aristocratic friend to the imperial family at Tsarskoye Selo

Wasserschleben, Agnes, former matron at Stillachhaus, tended to Anna Anderson at Schloss Seeon

Zahle, Herluf (1873–1941), Danish Minister in Berlin, temporary president of the League of Nations, 1928–1929

MODERN SCIENTISTS

Coble, Dr. Michael, formerly of the Armed Forces DNA Identification Laboratory, now Forensic Biologist at the National Institute of Standards and Technology in Gaithersburg, Maryland, helped identify the Romanov remains uncovered in 2007; conducted new DNA testing on Anna Anderson hair samples in 2010

Podini, Dr. Daniele, professor at George Washington University, conducted (with Dr. Michael Coble) new DNA tests on Anna Anderson hair samples in 2010

Gill, Dr. Peter, formerly of the British Home Office's Forensic Science Services Laboratory, head of the team that conducted 1993–1994 DNA tests on both the exhumed Romanov remains and on tissue and hair samples from Anna Anderson

Mandelbaum, Dr. Syd, geneticist who made first inquiry about Anna Anderson tissue samples; arranged for testing of Susan Grindstaf Burkhart's hair sample

Melton, Dr. Terry, with Dr. Mark Stoneking, conducted DNA tests on the Anna Anderson hair samples at Pennsylvania State University

Stoneking, Dr. Mark, with Dr. Terry Melton, conducted DNA tests on the Anna Anderson hair samples at Pennsylvania State University

Weedn, Dr. Victor, conducted privately commissioned DNA tests for Richard and Marina Schweitzer on the Anna Anderson tissue sample at the Armed Forces Institute of Pathology in Maryland

THE SCHANZKOWSKY FAMILY

Anton Czenstkowski (1842–April 13, 1912), Franziska's father; married Josefina Peek in 1890 (died 1892); married Marianna Witzke in 1894

Marianna Witzke (1866–December 20, 1932), Franziska's mother; married Anton Czenstkowski in 1894; married Herr Knopf in 1913

Martin Christian Czenstkowksi (born November 16, 1895, in Borowilhas, West Prussia), first child of Anton and Marianna, died in infancy

Franziska Anna Czenstkowski (later Schanzkowska) (born December 16, 1896, in Borowilhas, West Prussia), second child and first daughter of Anton and Marianna

Gertrude Czenstkowski (born November 12, 1898, in Zukovken, West Prussia), third child of Anton and Marianna; married (1926) August Ellerik; daughter Margarete Ellerik

Michael Czenstkowski (born December 16, 1899, in Zukovken, West Prussia), fourth child of Anton and Marianna, died in infancy

Valerian Czenstkowski (born April 25, 1900, in Glischnitz, Pomerania), fifth child of Anton and Marianna

Felix Czenstkowski (later Schanzkowsky) (born February 17, 1903, in Glischnitz, Pomerania), sixth child of Anton and Marianna; married Emma Mueller; daughter Waltraut von Czenstkowski

Maria Juliana Czentskowski (born April 30, 1905, in Schwarz Dammerkow, Pomerania), seventh child of Anton and Marianna; married Florian Zakowsky (Zagorski)

Maucher, Karl, son of Margarete Ellerik, grandson of Gertrude; donated blood sample in 1994 for DNA testing

ASSOCIATES OF FRANZISKA
SCHANZKOWSKA

Meyer, Otto, Franziska's teacher in Hygendorf, father of Richard Meyer

Meyer, Richard, son of Otto Meyer; childhood friend of Franziska; later burgomeister of Hygendorf

Schrock, Martha (later Borkowski, previously Reetz), childhood friend of Franziska in Hygendorf

Wingender, Anna (née Thewalt) (born 1867), Franziska's landlady on Neue Hochstrasse in Berlin; mother of Kathe, Doris, and Luise Wingender

Wingender, Luise (born 1907), youngest daughter of Anna Wingender; married a Herr Fiedler

Wingender, Rosa Dorothea (Doris) (born 1903), daughter of Anna Wingender; married (1936) Werner Rittmann

Wypyrczyk, Kathe (née Wingender) (born 1901), eldest daughter of Anna Wingender

HOSPITALS AND INSTITUTIONS

Berlin-Schöneberg Asylum (Franziska Schanzkowska: September 19, 1916–January 1917)

Dalldorf State Institute for Welfare and Care, Wittenau, Berlin (Franziska Schanzkowska: January 1917–May 19, 1917; Anna Anderson [as Fraulein Unbekannt]: March 28, 1920–May 30, 1922)

Elisabeth Hospital, Lützowstrasse, Berlin (Anna Anderson [as Fraulein Unbekannt]: February 17, 1920–March 28, 1920)

Four Winds Rest Home, Katonah, New York (Anna Anderson: July 24, 1930–August 1931)

Ilten Psychiatric Institute, Hannover (Anna Anderson: August 1931–June 1932)

Landesheilanstalt Neuruppin, Neuruppin (Franziska Schanzkowska: May 19, 1917–October 22, 1917)

Mommsen Clinic, Berlin (Anna Anderson [as Anastasia Tchaikovsky]: July 1925–spring 1926)

St. Mary's Hospital, Berlin (Anna Anderson [as Anastasia Tchaikovsky]: periodically 1922–1925)

Stillachhaus Sanatorium, Oberstdorf, Bavaria (Anna Anderson [as Anastasia Tchaikovsky]: June 25, 1926–March 1, 1927)

West End Hospital, Berlin (Anna Anderson [as Anastasia Tchaikovsky]: periodically 1922–1925)

Introduction

IN THE EARLY MORNING HOURS of Wednesday, July 17, 1918, muffled gunshots sounded from the basement of an ornate mansion in the Siberian city of Ekaterinburg. Twenty minutes later, a truck rumbled out of the courtyard, passing through the sleeping city and disappearing into a nearby dark forest. In the bed of the truck, hidden beneath a stretch of canvas, lay a grotesque and bloody jumble of corpses, the earthly remains of the last Russian Imperial Family and four servants, executed by the Bolsheviks.

The bullets that morning ended the 304-year-old Romanov Dynasty, which had ruled Russia from 1613 until the abdication of Tsar Nicholas II in March 1917. But the end of one chapter in history also marked the beginning of another, a chapter comprised of a new mythology that shrouded the events of that July night in a veil of intrigue. The fate of Nicholas II's youngest daughter, Grand Duchess Anastasia, became one of the twentieth century's greatest, most romantic, and most enduring mysteries. A mystery because, for most of that century, there were no Romanov corpses to prove their deaths, only a theory that the bodies of the victims had been chopped up, burned, and dissolved in acid by their executioners; a mystery because since 1918 there had been persistent rumors that one or more of the Romanovs, and specifically Anastasia, had somehow managed to escape death that night; and a mystery because, in 1991, when the previously unknown Romanov mass grave outside Ekaterinburg was finally exhumed, it was missing the remains of the thirteen-year-old heir to the throne, Tsesarevich Alexei, and one of his sisters, believed by American forensic experts to be those of Anastasia. And a mystery because, in 1920, a battered, psychologically damaged young woman had been rescued from a Berlin canal, a woman who later declared that she was Anastasia.

This was Anna Anderson. The claim invested her in a mantle of tortured enchantment, embodying the coming traumas of the twentieth century while evoking a vanished empire of pomp and privilege. She was not the first, nor would she be the last, royal claimant in history, but, uniquely, Anderson's claim transformed her into a living legend. Books, magazines, and newspapers diligently chronicled her adventures, offering the world a modern fairy tale gone horribly awry, a tragic princess who miraculously survived war, revolution, and the brutal execution of her family, only to be denied the most basic of all human rights: an identity. Grand dukes and duchesses, princes and princesses, aristocrats and courtiers—they all became embroiled in a mystery that cast son against mother, husband against wife, and caused deep divisions among Europe's remaining royal families. Actresses Ingrid Bergman, Lili Palmer, Julie Harris, Amy Irving, and Meg Ryan portrayed her onscreen and gave her voice, transforming the least important of Nicholas and Alexandra's children into the most famous of all Russian princesses, creating a myth so powerfully appealing to imagination that it persists today. Even President John F. Kennedy was so fascinated with her story that he once cornered the real Anastasia's cousin at a White House state dinner to grill her on the case. Anderson's claim and the fate of Anastasia, he said, was the "only aspect of Russian history" that he found interesting.[1]

The idea that Anastasia had miraculously survived the brutal execution in Ekaterinburg burst upon a world traumatized by a decade of tragedies that marked the passing of the old order: the sinking of the *Titanic*, the horrors of the First World War, the fall of dynasties, the Bolshevik Revolution, and the threat of communism. However unlikely, it spoke to natural human optimism, to the desire that somehow, Bolshevik bullets had failed to destroy an entire family. That for decades it captured international imaginations undoubtedly owed something to the almost unbelievable universe of opulent privilege that was, until 1917, the world of the Romanovs. In this sweeping epic, the public discovered a drama of mythological proportions: a glittering lost kingdom; the tragic love story of Nicholas and Alexandra; the young hemophiliac heir to the throne, destined never to reign; four beautiful young daughters in flowing white dresses and picture hats, frozen for eternity in haunting photographs and flickering newsreels; the malevolent peasant Gregory Rasputin; a tumultuous revolution; a brutal, bloody mass murder; and a former ruling family, scattered by war and struggling to adjust in an unfamiliar world. The narrative that emerged in the wake of Anderson's claim wedded the romanticism of a faded Edwardian past with the travails of the modern era, Greek tragedy and traditional fairy tale, transcending a realm of dispassionate fact to become legend.

Before the Revolution, Anastasia had been an insignificant princess, her life spent behind protective palace walls; her presumed death in 1918 wrapped her in a mantle of martyrdom, slaughtered at the hands of the Bolshevik regime. A surviving Anastasia, though, particularly for many of the highly impressionable émigrés who fled Russia after the Revolution, represented a figurative and literal rallying point for monarchist sentiments and hopes. Anderson's claim fell upon an audience left battered by upheaval and deprivation, loss of families, loss of positions, loss of fortunes, and loss of country—the very elements her tale so powerfully embodied. Those who accepted and those who rejected Anderson did so for many reasons, but all had been touched by the traumatic events in Russia. Those favorable often came filled with hope and saw her through eyes moist with influential, nostalgic tears; many on the opposite side denied the possibility that the ill and emotionally unstable woman could be Anastasia, and denounced her on the presumption that it was simply impossible for anyone to have survived the Bolshevik firing squad. The struggle of Anderson's claim reflected the struggle among the surviving Romanovs, royal relatives in Europe, émigrés, and the world at large to make sense of a complex tragedy, to find in the chaos of war and revolution some glimmer of hope, some hint of mercy, some proof that goodness still existed on the horizon of a new day.

The idea of miraculous survival from Ekaterinburg played upon this psychological need. Anna Anderson appeared at a moment in history when emotions were still raw and little was known. Silence by Soviet authorities, the fact that investigators never found any Romanov corpses, persistent rumors of escape and rescue—for Anderson all of it coalesced into a powerful alliance that surrounded her with an aura of plausibility. For most of the twentieth century, history had only a theory—and, as time proved, a largely erroneous one—of what had happened to the bodies of the imperial family. Conflicting reports, picked up and repeated by officers, foreign diplomats, and journalists, had the Romanovs evacuated from Ekaterinburg to Poland, to Germany, to the Vatican, or to the Far East; Alexandra and her daughters, it was said, were hiding in remote convents, or were prisoners in Siberia. Stories from those who believed that the Romanovs were dead were often equally absurd, including tales that Nicholas II's severed head was on display under a glass dome somewhere in the Kremlin. The paucity of fact, of actual, physical evidence, allowed imaginations to run wild. If, during her lifetime, Anderson and her supporters could never successfully prove that she was Anastasia, neither could her opponents prove that she was not. For most of the world, supporters and opponents alike, acceptance or rejection of her claim owed less to evidence than to the subjective intangibles of personal belief.

Perhaps some émigrés were so susceptible to the story because it not only echoed Orthodoxy's mystical belief in miracles but also events in Russia's past. Far from being a Western phenomenon, mysterious claimants and tales of royal survival peppered the pages of Russian history. At the beginning of the seventeenth century, three men appeared in quick succession, each claiming to be Dimitri, the youngest son of Ivan the Terrible. In 1591, nine-year-old Dimitri had died while under house arrest in an isolated Russian village; although officially he was said to have accidentally stabbed himself in the throat, many believed that Boris Gudunov, his uncle by marriage and regent for Dimitri's brother Feodor, had ordered the young prince killed to pave his own way to the throne. Soon enough, there were rumors that Dimitri, fearing for his safety, had faked his death and gone into hiding, waiting for the moment to return and lead the country.

The first of the False Dimitris, as this trio of impostors was called, appeared in 1600, two years after Boris Gudunov proclaimed himself tsar. The claimant, who was roughly the correct age and seemed to resemble the supposedly dead Dimitri, insisted that his mother had smuggled him to the safety of a remote monastery. Gudunov denounced him as a young monk named Gregory Otrepyev and ordered his arrest, but the alleged prince escaped to Poland. A few years later, backed by Polish and Baltic aristocrats, the self-proclaimed Dimitri invaded Russia at the head of an army. Gudunov died in 1605; in the chaos that followed, powerful boyars—members of Russia's aristocracy—murdered Gudunov's son and swore loyalty to the invader, proclaiming him Tsar Dimitri IV. The patriarch of Moscow, citing the young man's supposedly intimate knowledge of court life and regal bearing, blessed his cause, and even Dimitri's own mother embraced the impostor as her son. The new tsar, however, quickly alienated his supporters: attempts to strip the boyars of their power eroded their allegiance, and his marriage to a Polish Catholic woman named Marina Mniszech antagonized Orthodox Moscow. In 1606, Dimitri was overthrown and killed, his body burned, and his ashes fired from a cannon west, toward Poland.

The second False Dimitri appeared a year later. He seems to have been the son of a priest and, like his predecessor, impressed those whom he met with his knowledge of court life. In a truly bizarre twist, Marina Mniszech, widow of the first False Dimitri, promptly recognized the second as her dead husband, even though the two men bore no resemblance to each other. Drawing on a contingent of dissatisfied peasants and Cossacks, and financed by Polish and Lithuanian aristocrats, the new Dimitri laid siege to Moscow. When this failed and his foreign mercenaries revolted, Dimitri—with Marina in tow—fled to the town of Kostroma, where, in December 1610, he was killed by one of his guards. Fewer than four months passed before the third and last False Dimitri surfaced, declaring himself tsar in March 1612 with the support of Cossack troops. By this time, however, Russia had grown weary of such intrigues, and the newest Dimitri was arrested and executed in Moscow. Within a year, Russia was saved from such uncertainties when a group of boyars offered the crown to Ivan the Terrible's great-nephew by marriage. In July 1613, the sixteen-year-old boy was crowned as Tsar Michael, and the House of Romanov, which was to rule the country until the abdication of Nicholas II in 1917, was born.

More than a century later, Catherine the Great, who had come to the throne in a coup that deposed and killed her husband, Peter III, faced two impostors. In 1772, a young woman named Elizabeth Tarakanova appeared in Paris, claiming to be the secret daughter of Peter III's aunt Empress Elizabeth. Disturbed by her growing notoriety, Catherine dispatched Alexei Orlov, her former lover and one of the men involved in Peter III's assassination, to seduce and then kidnap her. Arrested in Italy, Tarakanova was hauled back to Russia, but died in prison before she could be tried.

Tarakanova caused little more than a ripple among cognoscenti of St. Petersburg's ruling elite, but the same could not be said for Emelyan Pugachev. The son of a Don Cossack, Pugachev took advantage of widespread discontent among Russian peasants and declared himself Peter III in 1773, claiming miraculous escape from the deadly machinations of his evil "wife." Although Pugachev looked nothing like the dead emperor, and was, in fact, illiterate, he convinced a great number of followers in his native Volga region, among them peasants, Cossacks, religious figures, and Orthodox schismatics known as Old Believers. His ever-expanding army swept through the countryside, terrorizing opponents and promising rewards of land, money, and freedom to those who aided his endeavor. Catherine launched an expeditionary force, and after several disastrous turns, Pugachev's own men handed him over. Taken to Moscow in a cage, he was publicly executed by being quartered the following year.[2]

And at the beginning of the nineteenth century, this penchant for intrigue, this taste for mystery, repeated itself in the tale of Feodor Kuzmich. In 1836, eleven years after the sudden death of the fatalistic emperor Alexander I, Kuzmich appeared in Siberia as a wandering religious pilgrim. He supposedly possessed an extraordinary knowledge of Catherine the Great, of life at the imperial court, of political affairs, and of the 1812 war against Napoleon, knowledge said to be beyond the capabilities of a humble peasant. At times, according to stories, letters arrived at his hut from the imperial court, along with important visitors from St. Petersburg; even before his death in 1864, it was whispered that he was, in fact, Alexander I, grown weary of the throne and responsible for faking his own demise. Rumor jelled into legend when Alexander I's tomb was supposedly opened and found to be empty.[3]

These stories shared some remarkably similar characteristics with the tale of Anna Anderson. Deaths were mysterious, corpses were missing, and intrigue surrounded their ultimate fates. Evidence was muddled, offering contradictory paths that seemed viable to both those who believed and those who did not. Much was often made of supposed aristocratic bearing and manner, while alleged intimate knowledge lent such claims a seeming patina of truth. Questionable "recognitions" were often accepted as evidence, despite the numerous difficulties they posed, and troubling issues were often dismissed.

Unlike her predecessors, Anna Anderson benefited by appearing at a time when her claim could be promoted on a universal scale, through magazines, books, newsreels, films, and documentaries. A legend was created, a complex, multilayered myth appealing to nostalgic sentiment, to romantic hopes, to imagination; a legend so compelling, so widespread that it became part of twentieth-century history and culture. "Whoever she was," wrote one Romanov relative, "Anna Anderson was no simple impostor."[4] And this was true; even those opposed to her claim had to acknowledge that there was something special about Anna Anderson. Anastasia or not, she managed something quite extraordinary: alone of all royal claimants, she became an almost inextricable part of the Romanov story, a shadowy character destined to forever haunt the tale of Nicholas and Alexandra, a figure of historical importance in her own right.

And unlike other pretenders who came and went, appearing in a burst of publicity, only to be unmasked as clumsy frauds, Anderson seemed to be a genuine enigma. Far from receding into obscurity, she became celebrated, the sheer persistence and duration of her claim lending it a special aura of plausibility. From the autumn of 1921, when she first declared that she was Anastasia, until her death in 1984 and beyond, Anderson's tale refused to die, a modern fairy tale enacted in grim hospital wards and private asylums, sprawling estates and ancient castles, across Germany and in America. Her legal battle to prove that she was the grand duchess spanned more than thirty years—the longest trial in German history—and stretched to include hundreds of witnesses and thousands of pages of testimony. Even Romanovs, European royalty, and former courtiers recognized her as Anastasia—an impressive array of supporters if she was merely an obvious fraud.

An obvious fraud she certainly wasn't, nearly everything seemed to declare. It was what made her claim so intriguingly possible: Anderson was the same height as the diminutive Anastasia and, like her, suffered from a foot condition called *hallux valgus*; then there were her eyes—"unforgettable blue-gray eyes," recorded one of her supporters, that reminded so many of Nicholas II.[5] When pulled from a Berlin canal in 1920, runs the history of her claim, Anderson's body was covered with "many lacerations" and numerous scars, including a triangular-shaped wound through her right foot, a wound said to match exactly the shape of the bayonet blades used by the Bolsheviks during Russia's Civil War—mute evidence, her supporters insisted, that she had been severely wounded during the Ekaterinburg massacre.[6] What impostor could be so lucky?

Or take languages, convincing, compelling evidence that Anderson was Anastasia, as the legend noted. She most often refused to speak Russian, though clearly she understood the language; yet she spoke it in her sleep "with good pronunciation," said a doctor, and her voice carried a "typical Russian accent."[7] Princess Xenia Georgievna, Anastasia's cousin and a woman who believed that Anderson was the grand duchess, was said to have called it "perfectly acceptable Russian, from the point of view of St. Petersburg society."[8] Under anesthesia, ran the stories, she "raved in English" and possessed what one lady described as "the clearest and best English accent."[9] And, recorded one journalist, "Her French pronunciation was perfect."[10] If she was an impostor, Anderson's supporters pointed out, she must have been a very skillful and carefully prepared impostor to manage such a linguistic feat.

How could an impostor amass the wealth of intimate details about Anastasia's life? people argued. Would an impostor know enough trivial details, as Anderson did, about former wounded officers who had convalesced in Anastasia's hospital at Tsarskoye Selo to not only answer questions, and answer them accurately, but also to correct deliberate inaccuracies and—impressively—to recall a nickname the grand duchess had once bestowed on an obscure colonel?[11] Would an impostor break into tears of recognition, as Anderson was said to have done, upon hearing an obscure waltz that had been played for the grand duchesses?[12] Or know the intricacies of imperial etiquette so well that she never made a mistake in behavior, never a lapse in manner? Or convince anthropological experts that she was Anastasia? Or handwriting experts? And on and on it went—this string of unlikely coincidences, if they could be called that, that peppered the history of Anderson's claim, that raised her from simple impostor to possible, plausible, even likely, said some, grand duchess.

This catalog of evidence reaches a kind of crescendo with the October 1925 encounter between Anderson and Grand Duchess Olga Alexandrovna, Anastasia's favorite aunt. After three days, Olga left Berlin, left, said one of the claimant's supporters, with words impossible to ignore: "My intelligence will not allow me to accept her as Anastasia, but my heart tells me that it is she. And since I have grown up in a religion that taught me to follow the dictates of the heart rather than those of the mind, I am unable to leave this unfortunate child."[13] And she followed this with letters—"You are not alone now, and we shall not abandon you," promised one.[14]

Wasn't this all convincing, compelling proof? The story of Anna Anderson's claim, the mythology that enshrouded her case, that gave birth to endless books and movies, seemed so heavily weighted in her favor, so clear, that it was nearly impossible to accept the denunciations of Romanov relatives and former courtiers who rejected the idea that she was Anastasia. In the 1960s, in the midst of her legal battle, Anderson's lawyers successfully appealed an earlier verdict by pointing out the double standard imposed by a German judicial tribunal in their ruling: the evidence of those who rejected Anderson or asserted the death of Anastasia in 1918 was received without objection, while those supporting her or questioning the Ekaterinburg massacre were subjected to rigorous examination. Outside of the court, though, it was just the opposite: so alluring was the myth, so pervasive the sympathetic renderings of her case, that—for much of the world—Anderson's opponents had to justify themselves before history, to explain again and again, and often not very convincingly, why they believed she could not be Anastasia. This is how her case came to the public, how it played out in twentieth-century media. And this is how the public preferred it: people were more interested in the possibility that Anderson was Anastasia than in hearing tedious arguments challenging such a popular piece of modern lore.

One might ask, Why another book on Anna Anderson? What more could be said? An enormous record documents her case; the problem is that very little of it has ever come before the public. What has appeared, unfortunately, has been incomplete, often selectively edited to support the myth—if presented at all. This much we found as we embarked on this study, a study that began many years ago from personal interest and that eventually took us past the magazines and books and into boxes of files and legal records crammed with previously unknown and untapped detail. And in these documents we found something extraordinary: decades of distortion, manipulation, and outright lies, a series of deliberate deceptions and innocent errors churned up, added to, and endlessly repeated in the history of this case. This isn't meant as a blanket indictment of those who have chronicled Anderson's story; many have simply accepted without question the integrity of the original written record—a record compiled and composed, published and promoted by those most sympathetic to her claim, those who truly believed that she was Anastasia. Unfortunately for history—and for the history of this case—much of what the public has been led to believe is simply wrong.

The real story of Anna Anderson's claim has never been told. It was a story we wanted to tell, but one that first we had to understand—understand what the evidence was, how her case grew into legend, how people came to believe and why they *needed* to believe, and ultimately who she was. And we eventually found the answers to these questions, and to a hundred others that have plagued her case for decades, that linger today as troubling contradictions and seemingly impressive rebuttals to her opponents. The answers were surprising, sometimes shocking, and made us reconsider nearly everything we thought we knew, nearly everything we—and history—had been led to believe was true in this case. Readers familiar with the tale may view this evidence skeptically, but they should be aware that we've been able to document the validity of what, until now, have always—at least in the usual accounting of Anderson's story—been considered unreliable or questionable sources: a 1927 investigation into her identity, funded by Anastasia's uncle Grand Duke Ernst Ludwig and carried out in the pages of a Berlin newspaper based on the word of a witness who'd been paid for her testimony, turned out to be far more convincing and surprisingly accurate than usually assumed, while former imperial tutor Pierre Gilliard, a man widely vilified as a pathological liar, proved—with one notable exception—to be one of the more reliable voices in the saga. Such discoveries meant not just a reassessment of the case, but also a new examination, starting from scratch, in an attempt to correct the historical record and inch ever closer to the devastating truth.

That truth was easier to find—"easier" being a relative word here—by returning to the original statements, depositions, affidavits, diary entries, letters, and reports that were woven together over the decades to create this most complex of modern myths. It meant wading through thousands of pages, in Russian, German, French, and English—a formidable task that consumed a decade of patient discovery, confusing assertions, and hopeless blind alleys. In the summer of 2000, we spent several weeks in London, working closely with Ian Lilburn, the acknowledged expert on Anderson's case and the only man who attended every session of her German legal appeal in the 1960s. We rented a flat adjacent to his house and, thanks to British royal author Sue Woolmans, stocked it with a copying machine and stacks of paper; day by day, Ian

shared both his memories and his vast collection, generosity that made
our task much easier. Back in America, Anderson's biographer Peter
Kurth added numerous boxes of materials from his own archives to our
growing collection, but the real coup came from an unexpected source:
the Staatsarchiv in Darmstadt. The Hessian Royal Family, including
Grand Duke Ernst Ludwig, had vehemently opposed Anderson's claim;
after the grand duke's death, his son Prince Ludwig had voluntarily
signed on as a codefendant when she brought suit in Germany for
legal recognition, in a trial resulting in dozens of bound volumes of
testimony. Assembled over the decades, the Darmstadt collection is an
extraordinary cache of letters, reports, statements, depositions, medical
opinions, and important testimonies, and we were the first historians
granted access to this unique archive. In a case noted for decades of
widespread publicity and international attention, it was an astonishing,
embarrassingly deep well of riches upon which to draw, a historian's
dream, and one that allowed us to investigate the story in ways that
constantly challenged our own opinions and the accepted mythology
of the claim.

   We have done our best to address some of the more perplexing
questions in Anderson's case, but fully admit that—as with most of
history—certain aspects of her claim are probably destined to forever remain lost; when she died in 1984, she took many secrets to
the grave. In some instances, we found the answers we were seeking;
in others, those explanations remain obscure, or are so buried in the
impenetrable layers of conflicting assertions that no one can now possibly resolve them. We've been careful to document everything and
never accept a single opinion as fact unless it can be bolstered by other
evidence, and have tried to keep theories to a minimum. But we've
learned along the way that much of what we—and presumably many
readers—took to be fact in Anderson's story rested on erroneous and
unreliable information. This book may shake preconceptions about
her case, but it does so based on a written record that's remained hidden
far too long.

   In the end, this is the story of a myth, of how a modern legend developed, of how people wanted to believe that Anderson was Anastasia,
and of how fate and coincidence came together in one of the twentieth
century's most extraordinary figures. No matter history's verdict on
Anna Anderson and the question of her identity, one thing is apparent:
she was an exceptional woman, a woman with exceptional talents and an
exceptional charm that enveloped her in an aura of believability that the
world could not ignore. When she stepped off a Berlin bridge in 1920
and into the pages of history, she laid the foundation for a modern fairy

tale so bewitching that she spawned magazine and newspaper articles, books, movies, cartoons, dolls—mute testament to the tantalizing power of her enigmatic story. This is the woman who haunts the pages that follow, and who continues to haunt history, a specter from a world long vanished, who in death—as in life—arouses violent passions and whose place in the story of Nicholas and Alexandra cannot be denied.

PART ONE

ANASTASIA

I

"My God, What a Disappointment!"

I T WAS AT THE HEIGHT of St. Petersburg's famous White Nights, when the sun barely disappeared for a few hours from Russia's capital, that the artillery thunder began. Night had come and gone in less than a few hours, leaving the sky over the placid Gulf of Finland awash in crimsons, blues, and pearls as dawn crept over the land. Alarmed by the crack of guns, crows cawed protests into the northern morning; a few early travelers, passing along a road fringed by a tall iron fence, also heard the echoes and momentarily stopped. On the other side of that fence sprawled the imperial estate of Peterhof. Here, sentries in blue uniforms patrolled through groves of pine, oak, and beech trees, holding tight to the reins lest their mounts become too restive or spooked by the noise. And along the edge of the water, rising against rows of reeds that gently waved in the soft wind, carriage wheels crunched over graveled drives leading to a rambling Italianate villa, where lights had burned since three that morning.

Those within the Lower Palace, as the building was called, already knew what those awakened by the guns firing a salute from the nearby naval base at Kronstadt did not: at six that morning—June 18, 1901— a fourth child had been born to Nicholas II, tsar of all the Russias, and his wife, Empress Alexandra. When the artillery count reached 101 shots, people paused; even those just starting their day twenty miles east in St. Petersburg could hear the thud of cannon. All Russia knew that the empress was expecting: after three imperial daughters—Olga, born in

15

1895, Tatiana in 1897, and Marie in 1899—everyone hoped for a son, an heir to the Romanov Dynasty, whose birth would be greeted by a thunderous 300 salvos. But on that morning there was no 102nd shot; the empress had given birth to yet another girl.

"My God, what a disappointment!" recorded Nicholas II's sister Grand Duchess Xenia Alexandrovna in her diary on hearing the news.[1] These words summed up the general feeling within the imperial family and across the Russian Empire. But if the parents were disappointed, they hid it well. In his diary, Nicholas wrote only of "a feeling of calm," and noted that his wife "felt quite cheerful."[2] It may have been unspoken, but both parents were keenly aware of the succession laws. Emperor Paul, who hated his mother, Catherine the Great, dictated that females could inherit the Russian throne only after all male members of the Romanov Dynasty. If Nicholas and Alexandra had no son, the crown would pass to his brother, Grand Duke Michael Alexandrovich, then to his uncles and to their sons, to great-uncles and to second cousins; only the deaths of all of these forty or so male relatives would allow for the succession of the new infant or her sisters.

The imperial couple temporarily set aside such worries twelve days after their new daughter's birth when, on a glorious summer morning, the infant was christened with all the pomp and ceremony demanded by her style of imperial highness and position as a grand duchess of Russia. A string of crimson and gold carriages, carrying members of the imperial family and their guests, rolled through the park at Peterhof, passing between rows of crisply drawn sentries and alongside fountains glistening in the morning light. At intervals rode scarlet-coated Cossacks and members of the Chevalier Garde in white tunics and silver-gilt cuirasses, their ranks interrupted by marching regimental bands and by courtiers adorned with orders and awards. Finally, after much anticipation, the gilded carriage bearing the new grand duchess appeared, its six white horses led by scarlet-and-gold-liveried grooms bedecked in powdered wigs; only the parents were absent from this spectacle, forbidden by Orthodox custom from attending the solemn rite.[3]

Empress Alexandra with the newborn Anastasia, 1901.

A fanfare of trumpets greeted the procession when it reached the eight-hundred-foot-long Great Palace at Peterhof; within, hundreds of aristocrats and courtiers crowded the elaborately decorated halls, medals shining against broadcloth tunics and jewels scintillating on gowns of silver tissue and velvet. Footmen and chamberlains, adjutants and ladies-in-waiting cleared the way for Princess Marie Golitsyn, the empress's mistress of the robes, who held the infant on a cushion and carried her along a ribbon of crimson carpet to the cathedral. As a choir chanted and fragrant smoke from incense curled toward the gilded dome, Father Ioann Yanishev, personal confessor to the imperial family, took the baby from the pillow, removing the white lace christening gown before dipping her into the font three times.[4] As if prompted by some unconscious glimpse of her future, Nicholas and Alexandra gave their new daughter a name that meant Resurrection, and she was christened Anastasia.

The imperial family after the christening of Anastasia, 1901.

"ONCE UPON A TIME . . ." runs the fairy tale. For Anastasia, the fairy tale began with this elaborate ceremony, which embodied all the splendid privilege of the Russian Court. Related by blood and marriage to the royal houses of Great Britain, Denmark, Romania, Germany, Spain, and Greece, she was born into a lavish world of palaces and liveried servants, gold-braided courtiers and sleek yachts, loving parents and a devoted family—everything necessary to the traditional, heartwarming conclusion. For Anastasia, though, there would be no happy ending; her fairy tale went horribly awry, its peaceful promise shattered by war and revolution. In its place arose a new tale that gave resonance to the meaning of her name, in which hope triumphed over despair, and desire transcended brutal reality. There was even a Prince Charming said to have come to Anastasia's rescue. It all coalesced to form a powerful myth, a modern legend, a new fairy tale that, in its traumas, seemed to encapsulate the turmoil of the twentieth century.

Looking back after a century, it is difficult to imagine the opulent life into which Anastasia was born. The almost barbaric, Byzantine splendor of the imperial court endowed her life with all of the fantastic elements demanded of any good fairy tale. Nicholas II was undoubtedly the wealthiest monarch in the world. He ruled a sixth of the land surface of the globe as autocrat, responsible to no one. Instead of one palace, he owned more than thirty; there were country estates in Finland, Poland, and the Crimea; huge timber and mineral reserves in Siberia and the Caucasus; five yachts and two private trains; hundreds of horses, carriages, and new motorcars; accounts stocked with gold bullion in Moscow, London, and Berlin; thousands of works of art, including important paintings by Van Dyke, Raphael, Rembrandt, Titian, and da Vinci; crowns, tiaras, necklaces, and a fortune in jewelry; and a priceless collection of objets d'art and Easter eggs by famed jeweler Peter Karl Fabergé. Cared for by a small army of cooks, maids, footmen, chamberlains, gardeners, chauffeurs, carpenters, grooms, and valets, tended by devoted courtiers who kissed their hands, and protected by thousands of soldiers and police officers, the Romanovs wanted for nothing.

And, at least at the beginning of Nicholas II's reign, there was every hope that he would rule Russia evenly and gently, in keeping with his placid character, steering it with wisdom and foresight through the unknown waters of the early twentieth century. The eighteenth ruler in a Romanov Dynasty that included such larger-than-life figures as Peter the Great and Catherine the Great, Nicholas was young, handsome, and exceptionally polite when he came to the throne in 1894 following the premature death of his father, Alexander III. The country was backward and already straining under modern pressures and expectations. The vast majority of the emperor's subjects were peasants, loyal but illiterate, consumed by the constant struggle to simply survive; then there were the workers, thousands of wretched beings who toiled in danger and misery in the great industrial factories. A small middle class had developed intellectuals and sent its sons to universities, where they readily found sympathetic comrades filled with their own horrible stories of hardship. And at the very apex of the country, separated by comforts and languages, ensconced in privilege and often more concerned with pleasure than with progress, stood the elite: the military officers, the bureaucracy, the hierarchy of the Russian Orthodox Church, the courtiers, the aristocracy, and the imperial family itself. Surely, people thought, this system could not last. The antiquated autocracy Nicholas II inherited survived only by force of character and by a tradition that insisted the emperor alone was responsible to himself and to God for governing this enormous cauldron of simmering discontent.

But then the shy, gentle, and polite Nicholas II did something that quite confounded those who hoped that such an educated, modern young man would recognize the impossibility of continued autocratic rule. Just a few months after taking the throne, he made it clear that he would never share his power with an elected assembly and that the pace of needed reforms would be miserably slow. Clinging to the idea that he had been ordained by God to rule according only to his own conscience, he

Nicholas II, about 1900.

saw himself as *batushka*-tsar, father of the Russian people, a benevolent and all-knowing schoolmaster suddenly confronted with a classroom of unruly pupils who needed his wisdom and his whip to maintain order. Ambition clashed with reality, and as the twentieth century began, the rumblings grew louder, the demands for reform more insistent, as the country careened from disaster to disaster: tsarist ministers and officials fell victim to a growing revolutionary movement; war between Russia and Japan ended in humiliating defeat; soldiers and sailors mutinied, peasants looted estates, and pogroms erupted with the tacit and often overt approval of the government; and by 1905, strikes and unrest had paralyzed the country. Faced with this tumult, Nicholas II reluctantly bowed to pressure and created a parliament, the Duma. This was a concession wrested rather than granted, and Nicholas could never reconcile himself to the idea that he had signed away his autocratic powers.

An uneasy peace settled over the country in these years after the turn of the century. Thoroughly disillusioned, Nicholas II increasingly withdrew from his public duties, finding comfort only in his wife and children. It was a passion shared by his wife, Empress Alexandra.

Empress Alexandra, about 1905.

Born a princess of the German Grand Duchy of Hesse und bei Rhein, and a favorite granddaughter of Queen Victoria, Alexandra—Alix, or "Sunny," as her husband called her—was a great beauty when they married in 1894; together Nicholas and Alexandra seemed to embody the very image of the prince and princess who would indeed live happily ever after. But beneath this veneer lay something unsuspected: excessively shy, serious, and high-minded, Alexandra possessed the steely character her husband lacked. She passionately believed in the Orthodox faith she embraced upon her marriage, but she found in its mystical doctrines justification for an increasingly extreme view of her husband's power; like Nicholas, she refused to acknowledge that the autocracy had ended, insisting that the emperor make no popular concessions. It was one of the great ironies of the tale: the granddaughter of Queen Victoria, the most powerful democratic monarch on the face of the earth, soon became even more convinced of a divinely mandated autocracy than her own husband.

Nicholas rarely protested his wife's interference and admonitions. Beyond the realm of politics, the imperial couple at least fully inhabited the roles assigned to them by the fairy tale: they were indeed hopelessly, devotedly in love with each other, their marriage a triumph over familial objections and circumstance. "Even after many years," recalled one relative, "they were like young lovers."[5] For each, this marriage became their principal comfort in increasingly uncertain times, but the warm and loving empress remained hidden, unknown to Russia. Instead, aristocratic St. Petersburg saw only a woman they deemed a humorless prig, someone who despised the empty social life and lavish balls that filled the long winter days; Alexandra never bothered to conceal her disapproval of this frivolity, and soon she alienated society and even most of her husband's extended family. Knowing that she was disliked and increasingly unwell, she led her husband into a cloistered world that insulated them from scandalous gossip and unwholesome thoughts but also isolated them from the realities of a changing world.

Alexandra's mysticism increased after 1904, when she finally gave birth to the long-awaited son and heir, Tsesarevich Alexei. The public rejoiced, but within six weeks his parents learned that he suffered from hemophilia, passed on to him by his mother, who had inherited the defective genes through Queen Victoria. This discovery cast a pall over the lives of Nicholas and Alexandra; rather than admit that their only son was prey to such a devastating illness, they kept Alexei's hemophilia a state secret. His sisters were told, as were a few servants, courtiers, and intimate family members, but most of Russia knew only that their future emperor was frequently unwell. There was no cure, and almost any bump or fall could result in a potentially fatal internal hemorrhage.

Hoping to prevent such incidents, the imperial couple charged two sailors, Andrei Derevenko and Klementy Nagorny, with keeping a constant watch over their fragile son, but the uncertainty took an emotional and physical toll on the parents, particularly Alexandra, who knew that she was unwittingly responsible for Alexei's suffering. In the absence of scientific hope, Nicholas and Alexandra turned to religion, seeking comfort in the ministrations of a series of questionable seers and holy men, desperate for a miracle. They found their miracle in 1905, when they first met the infamous Siberian peasant Gregory Rasputin.

Anastasia in Russian court dress for the christening of Tsesarevich Alexei, 1904.

The thwarted ambitions, strikes, wars, unrest, assassinations, aristocratic animosity, Alexei's illness—it all coalesced to drive Nicholas and Alexandra into retreat, to an idyllic world of bourgeois values and familial love carved from a privileged backdrop of imperial palaces. Fifteen miles south of St. Petersburg, cocooned within two dozen modestly decorated rooms in a wing of the yellow and white neoclassical Alexander Palace at Tsarskoye Selo, the Romanovs lived a confined, isolated existence. Sentries patrolled the perimeters of the imperial park, footmen stood at attention in the palace's marble halls, and courtiers bowed, yet somehow Nicholas and Alexandra created a life for their children that, in comparison with that of many of their European cousins, was almost stunning in its lack of artifice.

While pompous Russian aristocrats condemned the empress as a bourgeois German hausfrau, domestic cares ensured that her children were brought up in a warm and loving environment. She could be frustratingly obsessive and smothering, but Alexandra also was a tactile mother whose devotion to family life stood in contrast to the deliberate distance maintained by many royal women of the era. She kept her children's bassinets in her bedroom when they were infants, and bathed, changed, and nursed them herself. But her somewhat anachronistic attitudes, seriousness, and high-minded ambition often made it difficult for Alexandra to indulge her children's natural spirits, and most people agreed that with the exception of Tatiana, they all favored their father.[6] In her teenage letters to Nicholas II, Anastasia was effusive, calling him her "Golden, Good, Darling Papa," writing, "I want to see you so much," and signing, "I kiss you 1,000,000 times, your hands and feet."[7] Unfortunately, as one courtier recalled, "In ordinary times, the Tsar did not see much of his children. His work and the demands of court life prevented him from giving them as much time as he would have wished."[8]

Instead, with the empress often unwell and the emperor occupied with work, the children were largely brought up by a series of English nurses. For a time, Alexandra's former nanny Mary Anne Orchard supervised the imperial nurseries and selected the Russian women who served below her.[9] At the time of Anastasia's birth, Margarette Eagar was the principal nanny, but she left the court in 1905, and her position went to her colleague Alexandra Tegleva. Known to the children as "Shura," Tegleva—along with several Russian girls—saw to their daily needs, nursing them when they were unwell and pampering them with doting attention. Later, as her two eldest daughters matured, Alexandra appointed a young woman named Sophie Tiutcheva as their governess, although she eventually fell out with the empress over Rasputin's visits to the nurseries.[10]

Secluded and largely unknown, the four grand duchesses became ciphers, their appearances in public rare and often restricted to a select audience of courtiers and aristocrats. Their father's subjects saw their faces in formal photographs and souvenir postcards, but very few outside the insular universe of Tsarskoye Selo knew anything of their real lives. Denied friends and social opportunities, they existed in an artificial sanctuary that tended to magnify ordinary clashes and the insecurities of youth as they struggled to win approval and establish a sense of their own identities.

Olga, the eldest of the four daughters, was generally thought to be the most intelligent of Nicholas and Alexandra's children. A deeply religious, sensitive young woman, Olga possessed a stubborn streak and tendency to depression that occasionally led to clashes with her mother. In temperament and appearance she most resembled her father, whom she adored.[11] In contrast, Tatiana, the second of the girls, was closest to her mother, and her siblings nicknamed her "the governess." Naturally thin and elegant, Tatiana had her mother's refined features and unquestioning acceptance of their extraordinary privilege. Even so, she was essentially modest by nature, and while she enjoyed what little she was allowed to experience of society, she disliked the ceremonial etiquette that accompanied her rank: she once kicked a lady-in-waiting out of embarrassment for publicly referring to her as "Your Imperial Highness."[12]

Being closest in age, Olga and Tatiana formed a natural bond, and within the family they were informally called "the big pair," while the two youngest grand duchesses became "the little pair."[13] Marie, the third daughter, also was the most beautiful. Her thick golden hair and large blue eyes won her many admirers; her cousin Prince Louis of Battenberg—the future Lord Mountbatten—was so taken with her that until his 1979 assassination by the IRA, he kept a photograph of her beside his bed.[14] Unpretentious and simple in her tastes, Marie was content to dream of one day marrying and of raising a large family.[15]

The youngest of the four daughters and destined by history to become the most famous, Anastasia, said one courtier, was "quite unlike any of her sisters, with a type of her own."[16] Lili Dehn, one of the empress's closest friends, called Anastasia "pretty" but noted that "hers was more of a clever face."[17] Her hair was dark blond with a slight golden tinge, and her features "were regular and finely cut."[18] Above all else, it was her gray-blue eyes—"of great luminescence," as Tatiana Botkin, daughter of the imperial family's chief physician, Eugene Botkin, recalled—that attracted attention, vibrant "wells of intelligence," according to Dehn, that were constantly moving and glowed with mischief.[19]

This impression—that with Anastasia mischief was always lurking just beneath the surface—was one that the little girl herself cultivated from an early age. Perhaps, as the youngest of four girls and the least important of five children, she consciously grasped at opportunities—no matter how inappropriate—to assert her individuality, for she was certainly very different from her sisters in behavior and temperament. There was something altogether irrepressible about her spirited energy, as if she knew no boundaries and feared nothing. Her aunt and godmother Grand Duchess Olga Alexandrovna nicknamed her "Shvibzik" (Imp), and Anastasia fully lived up to the designation.[20] From an early age, said Dr. Botkin's youngest son, Gleb, Anastasia "undoubtedly held the record for punishable deeds in her family, for in naughtiness she was a true genius."[21]

Anastasia loved to disappear in the vast imperial park, hiding from concerned sentries until

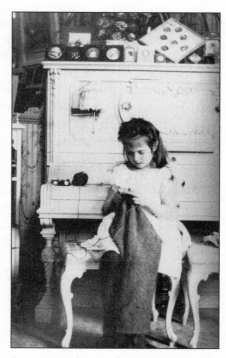

Anastasia in her mother's boudoir at the Alexander Palace, about 1910.

worry forced her out of hiding; she climbed trees to dizzying heights, refusing to come down until ordered to do so by her father, and she made faces at the stony-faced guards.[22] Visiting cousins feared her: one, Princess Nina Georgievna, declared Anastasia "nasty to the point of being evil," while her sister Xenia Georgievna called her "wild and rough," and remembered how she would "often scratch me and pull my hair" if she disliked the outcome of a game.[23]

It was all distinctly unroyal behavior, but Anastasia usually managed, through charm or through a startling frankness, to get away with such antics. They became an expression of personality within the rarefied and sheltered environment of the Russian court, a subtle rebellion against the regularity and oppressive strictures of life at Tsarskoye Selo. Tradition ruled in the Alexander Palace. Her father may have been the wealthiest sovereign in the world, but as soon as Anastasia outgrew the crib, she shared a bedroom with her sister Marie, an unpretentious chamber made comfortable with overstuffed furniture, chintz fabrics, and walls bedecked with icons, watercolors, and favorite photographs.[24] Like her sisters, she slept on a narrow, folding army camp bed, a tradition within the Romanov family dating back to the childhood of Alexander I and meant to instill character and guard against indulgence.[25] The same concerns dictated cold baths each morning, although the warm baths permitted at night took place in a solid silver tub engraved with the names of all the imperial children who had used it.[26] Anastasia and her sisters helped maids clean their rooms, and in a further effort to prevent them from being spoiled, servants and courtiers referred to them using their Christian names and patronymics—Anastasia Nikolaievna—rather than by their titles or styles.[27] Each month came a modest allowance, out of which Anastasia could purchase any gifts or personal items, including her favorite Coty perfume, Violette.[28] "In this way," recalled one courtier, "their mother hoped to make them realize the value of money, a thing that princes find hard to understand. But etiquette prevented their going into any shops but those of the stationers at Tsarskoye Selo and Yalta, and they never had any clear idea of the value and price of things."[29] It was all very simple, especially compared to many other royal households, but it also was very studied, an echo of the simplistic charade enacted by Marie Antoinette in Le Hameau at Versailles before the Terror swept the Bourbons from their throne.

Days passed with a comforting regularity at Tsarskoye Selo. If, beyond the protected confines of the imperial estate, Russia seethed with danger and discontent, here there were only smiling and obsequious faces. Aroused from slumber, the grand duchesses crept down the narrow wooden staircase connecting their rooms to those of their mother to bid Alexandra good morning before returning to their own apartments for breakfast. Nicholas would already be at his desk, and although he might join his children for a walk in the park, sometimes accompanied by the empress, the family often came together for the first time each day at four, when they all gathered for tea in Alexandra's famous Mauve Boudoir. This, too, was ruled by tradition: the regulations, set down in the reign of Catherine the Great, dictated the number and type of rolls, plates of bread, and pastries placed on the table. Alexandra complained that "other people had much more interesting teas," but that even as empress she was "unable to change a single detail of the routine of the Russian Court."[30] Alexandra poured, and handed around plates of tiny sandwiches and pastries; for the children there was cocoa and little vanilla-flavored wafers called *biblichen*. Nicholas smoked and read aloud, the empress and her eldest daughters embroidered, and Anastasia played games with Alexei on the sage-green carpet.[31]

These quiet scenes of domestic, thoroughly middle-class harmony were often repeated in the evening, usually with the addition of the empress's great friend Anna Vyrubova, a "sentimental and mystical," naive young woman whose devotion to Alexandra was rivaled only by her uncritical belief in the infamous Rasputin.[32] The family might listen to the gramophone—recordings of Wagnerian operas were a favorite— or to Nicholas as he read from Russian or English novels, the empress inevitably busy with needlework and the girls carefully pasting photographs they had taken with their Kodak box cameras into leather-bound albums.[33] On other evenings films would be shown in the palace's large semicircular hall: newsreels, something for the children, and perhaps an American or European silent comedy or serial. All were carefully screened to ensure that no offending scenes existed, although inevitably the censor missed a passionate kiss or meaningful glance that sent the imperial children into howls of laughter.[34]

For all of this apparent idyllic domesticity, one thing was missing: Anastasia had no real friends. As a young girl, she pathetically dragged around a well-worn, one-armed, one-eyed, bald-headed doll she had named Vera, and looked to her siblings and the family's pets for comfort.[35] In their isolation, the grand duchesses found comfort and companionship with each other, and with the courtiers and servants around them. Anastasia Hendrikova, a countess who served their mother, was a particular favorite, as was Baroness Sophie Buxhoeveden, who was appointed a lady-in-waiting to the empress in 1913 at age twenty-eight, but they could not take the place of real confidantes.[36] The grand duchesses, noted imperial tutor Pierre Gilliard, "by force of circumstances," learned "to be self-sufficient" in "a life deprived of outside amusements."[37]

The blame lay with the empress. Alexandra, Anna Vyrubova remembered, "dreaded for her daughters the companionship of over-sophisticated young women of the aristocracy whose minds, even in the schoolroom, were fed with the foolish and often vicious gossip of a decadent society."[38] There were, it is true, infrequent visits with the children of Nicholas II's eldest sister, Grand Duchess Xenia Alexandrovna; with Prince George and Princess Vera, the youngest children of Grand Duke Konstantin Konstantinovich, who lived at Pavlovsk, near Tsarskoye Selo; and with Princesses Nina and Xenia Georgievna, daughters of Grand Duke George Mikhailovich, second cousin to Nicholas II, but such occasions were sporadic and provided only momentary diversions rather than true companionship. Alexandra, said Vyrubova, "discouraged" even these innocent encounters, deeming many of her husband's relatives "unwholesomely precocious in their outlook on life."[39]

Recognizing the isolation of her nieces and their inability to enjoy any meaningful social life, Nicholas II's youngest sister, Grand Duchess Olga Alexandrovna, tried to step in and provide them with a modicum of diversion. Unhappily married to a homosexual prince, the rather plain and unassuming Olga Alexandrovna shared her goddaughter Anastasia's intense dislike of the rigidity of imperial life and the crushing etiquette of the Russian court. Her answer was to take the grand duchesses away for days at her palace in St. Petersburg, and to lunches with their grand-mother Dowager Empress Marie Feodorovna. Olga also organized small parties, teas, and dances for her nieces, and the grand duchesses looked forward to these Sunday afternoons, when they could mingle with other young men and women invited by their aunt, dance, and play games with carefree abandon.[40] They all, Olga Alexandrovna later recalled, "enjoyed every minute of it," especially Anastasia. "I can still hear her laughter rippling all over the rooms. Dancing, music, games— why, she threw herself wholeheartedly into them all."[41]

It was the only apparent flaw in the fairy tale, this lack of friends and influences outside the palace, this isolation imposed by the empress upon her daughters. In a very real way, the grand duchesses were prisoners in a gilded cage. "More than her sisters," recalled one courtier, "Anastasia chafed under the narrowness of her environment."[42] Still, little could be done. The same sentries, special details of police, sailors from the Garde Equipage, and members of the Cossack Konvoi Regiment who patrolled the palace grounds to ensure her safety also trapped her in this stifling universe. Such protections were unfortunate but necessary. The Russian throne was an unstable institution, the empire a place where discontent constantly threatened to erupt into violence. It had happened before, with unnerving frequency: Peter the Great had his son and heir Alexei tortured to death; Catherine the Great came to the throne in a conspiracy that resulted in the murder of her husband, Peter III; and Paul I was killed by a group of aristocrats. And it was not just the distant past: in 1881, when the future Nicholas II was just twelve, he had stood at the bedside of his grandfather Tsar Alexander II, watching as he bled to death from a terrorist bomb; less than a quarter century later, Nicholas's uncle and brother-in-law Grand Duke Serge Alexandrovich was literally blown to pieces by revolutionaries. There had already been half a dozen unsuccessful attempts to assassinate Nicholas II by the time Anastasia turned ten. At times, violent strikes and unruly riots left the imperial family confined to their estates; even when they left this protective cocoon and traveled across the vast Russian Empire, they did so in a heavily armored train of royal blue carriages shadowed by a second, identical string of railway cars designed to confuse any would-be revolutionaries.[43] This terrible uncertainty became the leitmotif of Anastasia's fairy tale, an unseen yet very real danger that lurked just beneath the glittering surface of her privileged world.

2

The Imp

ANASTASIA'S YOUTHFUL VIVACITY and eagerness for life, so pervasive in her early years, seemed to grind to a halt when she faced the ordeal of the classroom. She was never described as an intellectual, but the quality of her natural curiosity was especially engaging. "Whenever I talked with her," wrote General Count Alexander von Grabbe of the Cossack Konvoi Regiment that guarded the family, "I always came away impressed by the breadth of her interests. That her mind was keenly alive was immediately apparent."[1]

Early on, though, before she faced the formalized rigors of education, Anastasia seemed positively possessed by a desire to learn. Everything fascinated her, and she wanted to know who people were, how things worked, what words meant. In 1905, twenty-five-year-old, Swiss-born Pierre Gilliard, who had previously worked as a tutor for distant Romanov relation Duke Serge of Leuchtenberg, took a position at court instructing the older grand duchesses in French.[2] One day, he recalled, he had just finished a lesson with Olga Nikolaievna when a nearly five-year-old Anastasia burst into the classroom. "She carried beneath her arm a big book of pictures, which she ceremoniously placed on the table before me," he wrote, "then she gave me her hand and said in Russian, 'I would like to learn French, too.' Without waiting for my reply, she climbed atop a chair, knelt down, opened the book, and pointing to a picture of a huge elephant, asked, 'And what is this called in French?' Soon I was confronted with an entire Ark of names—lions, tigers, and every other animal pictured." Anastasia seemed intrigued not just by the exotic French language but also by this new addition to the imperial court, and she became a regular visitor to Gilliard's classroom, "running in" as soon as he was alone and "telling me all about the important incidents in her life. She had a child's picturesque turn of phrase, and the melodious Russian gave her voice a soft, almost coaxing tone. Occasionally she even got me to let her sit and listen as I taught one of the older girls. She preferred to sit on the carpet, watching everything in earnest silence for she knew that any interruption would lead to banishment from the schoolroom, which at that time she seemed to regard as a sort of forbidden paradise."[3]

This idea of the schoolroom as a paradise vanished as soon as it became a required destination. Anastasia began lessons when she was eight. Gilliard remembered that at first she possessed a "zeal for learning" and "remarkable memory," though her mind tended to move quickly from one subject to another as her attention waned.[4] She was not just a diffident pupil: she could also be a difficult one. Perhaps because her more outrageous behavior had largely been indulged, Anastasia seemed to approach lessons with a sense of amusement, as though they were simply obstacles requiring escape. Her usual approach, when confronted with difficulty, was simply to charm her way out of unpleasant situations. Once, after a particularly disastrous test, a tutor graded her accordingly; Anastasia left the classroom, returning a few minutes later and offering a large bouquet of flowers snatched from a nearby table if her marks were changed. When the tutor refused, she drew "herself up to the most of her small height" and "marched into the schoolroom next door," loudly and pointedly presenting the flowers to another teacher.[5]

Perhaps part of the problem for Anastasia stemmed from the unimaginative road her education followed, for like her sisters she was tutored by a string of instructors—of varying degrees of ability and psychological insight—in history, religion, arithmetic, geography, science, and literature, as well as dancing, drawing, painting, and music. In most, she did just well enough to achieve minimal marks or comprehension; she was never outstanding in any subject, and frequently below expectations in many areas, but then, she could argue, what really was demanded of her in life except that she one day marry some suitable prince and raise a family? The things she would need for such a position—especially if she married some distant European cousin—were languages. For Anastasia, this meant Russian, English, French, and, later, German. "Four languages is a lot," Alexandra wrote of her daughters, "but they need them absolutely."[6]

Anastasia was brought up in a mul-
tilingual household, speaking Russian
with her father, siblings, courtiers,
and servants, and English with her
mother.[7] "Grammar, alas, was never
her strong point, even in Russian,"
Gilliard wrote, and her written
essays and letters were always more
effusively enthusiastic than formally correct.[8] Because Anastasia
spoke English with her mother from
birth, many assumed that she carried
a very proper and precise aristocratic
English accent, as befitting a great-
granddaughter of Queen Victoria.
It was part of the fairy tale's charm
for much of the English-speaking
world, the idea that the ruling family of Russia spent their days talk-

Anastasia, in an informal photo taken during
a 1910 visit by the Russian imperial family
to Grand Duke Ernst Ludwig of Hesse in
Germany.

ing, joking, and whispering away in a language that somehow made
them seem less exotic. Yet this bit of mythology is almost certainly
wrong. While Nicholas and Alexandra may have been skilled lin-
guists and employed English, the casual proficiency and accents of their
children—at least in that language—left something to be desired.
In 1908, after thirteen years of daily speaking the language with
her mother, Olga Nikolaievna had what was termed a bad English
accent; Anastasia and Marie were even worse, and Alexei seems to
have spoken almost nothing of the language before 1914.[9] This led
Empress Alexandra to hire Charles Sidney Gibbes, a thirty-three-
year-old native of Yorkshire who taught English in St. Petersburg, to
tutor her children.[10] In time, and under Gibbes's tutelage, Anastasia's
spoken English vastly improved, though her spelling and grammar
left something to be desired.[11]

Gilliard took on the task of teaching French to Anastasia. Her early
curiosity and desire to learn the language, though, soon dissipated in
the classroom; still, of all the foreign languages she learned, it was
probably the one she liked best. Gilliard thought that Anastasia had an
"excellent" accent, but she never succeeded in mastering grammar and
had no real fluency; after seven years of instruction, he was forced to
admit that she "spoke French badly."[12]

In 1912, when she was eleven, Anastasia also began instruction in
German with tutor Erich Kleinenberg; this continued sporadically
until the Revolution.[13] By 1916, after four years of lessons, she was

The five imperial children in a formal photograph from 1910. From left: Tatiana, Anastasia, Alexei, Marie, and Olga.

writing German compositions in Gothic script, though—as with her other languages—spelling and grammar were often beyond her grasp.[14]

Gilliard noted that Kleinenberg had "great difficulty" in his lessons, "for the Grand Duchesses had no practice in German" beyond the classroom; what little they spoke, according to Gibbes, they did so "badly" and, as the Empress's Lady-in-Waiting Buxhoeveden recalled, with a "strong Russian accent."[15]

The end results of all of these lessons were negligible. Anastasia strained under the confines of the classroom. Gilliard thought that her behavior was often that of "a gifted child," but noted that she was only a very moderate pupil, with "little taste for learning."[16] In time, even this halfhearted dedication faded and she became, he thought, "distinctly lazy" in her approach. "In vain I tried to fight against the pronounced indifference she showed during lessons," Gilliard recalled, "but this only turned them into tearful scenes that

Anastasia in Russian court dress, 1910.

Anastasia during the imperial family's 1910 visit to Germany.

produced no results. To the end, she remained a lazy pupil."[17] The problem, thought her aunt Olga Alexandrovna, was not that Anastasia was lazy; rather, she believed that "books, as books, never said much to her."[18]

THE YEARS PASSED. The grand duchesses were maturing into young women; Tsesarevich Alexei, though he periodically suffered from a painful hemorrhage, was largely well—because of Rasputin's prayers, the empress thought—and the unrest plaguing the empire seemed to ebb. Anastasia was growing up, even if her mother continued to dress her two youngest daughters identically, as if they were matching porcelain dolls, and there was little opportunity to express personal taste or individuality. Olga was pretty if not beautiful, serious if not brilliant; Tatiana was lean and elegant; Marie was transforming into a stunning young woman; and Anastasia—well, Anastasia was fat, short, and dumpy, as if somehow the genetic gods had poured out all their bounty on her sisters and had nothing left for the youngest daughter. Her features, it is true, were good, but they seemed lost in a face that lacked refinement. She hated the way she looked: the fact that she was so short, the fact that she could never lose the pudginess that inevitably followed from her love of everything sweet.[19] Once, Dr. Botkin found her alone in a room, covered in sweat and hopping up and down on one leg. To his bemused look, she explained with all seriousness: "An officer on the yacht told me that to hop around a dining room table on one leg helps one to grow!"[20] She didn't even have the consolation of a few extra inches gained from wearing high heels, not that Alexandra would have favored the idea in any case, for Anastasia suffered from *hallux valgus*: her big toes curled inward, forming painful bunions that meant she had to wear specially designed, low-heeled shoes.[21]

But if Olga could be smart, Tatiana dignified, and Marie beautiful, Anastasia found that she could be practical, a young girl ambitious for everything in life except for lessons, with a zest for enjoying herself and making the most of her admittedly peculiar environment. "I never noticed in her the least trace of mawkishness or dreamy melancholy," recalled Gilliard, "not even at an age when girls fall prey to such tendencies. . . . She was very boisterous, and sometimes too temperamental. Every impulse, every new sensation was something she immediately had to indulge to the utmost; she glowed with animated life. Even at sixteen, she behaved like a headstrong young foal that has run away from its master. In her play, in realizing her wishes, in her schemes, in everything she did, there was the same impetuousness and youthful enthusiasm."[22]

Age brought a natural end to the most audacious of her practical jokes and tomboyish behavior, though Anastasia replaced them with an often reckless, acerbic wit. Her humor, sharp, pointed, and often unwelcome, honed in on humiliation and mockery, and she developed a keen sense of mimicry.[23] Relatives, courtiers, servants—no one was safe from her unstinting lampoons of personal foibles and flaws. "Ladies who came to see my sister-in-law," recalled Olga Alexandrovna, "never knew that, somewhere unseen in the background, their Empress's youngest daughter was watching every movement of theirs, every peculiarity, and later it would all come out when we were by ourselves. That art of Anastasia's was not really encouraged but, oh, what fun we had!" She especially recalled how adeptly her niece had acted the role of an obese countess who claimed to have suffered a heart attack on seeing a mouse; it was, Olga admitted, all "very naughty," though she had to admit that everyone thought Anastasia "was certainly brilliant at it."[24]

Aboard the imperial yacht *Standart* about 1911. From left: Tatiana, Marie, Olga, Empress Alexandra, and Anastasia.

These petty amusements perhaps hinted at something of greater concern, had Nicholas and Alexandra possessed a more discerning attitude, for all of their children tended, in varying degrees, to be somewhat immature. The imperial couple encouraged innocent little romances with young officers from their yacht or with members of the suite who partnered the girls in dancing and tennis matches but "continued to regard them as children," as Anna Vyrubova recalled.[25] "Even when the two eldest had grown into real young women," said one courtier, "one might hear them talking like little girls of ten or twelve."[26] It was as Alexandra wanted it: a family protected from the potentially dangerous and morally questionable world beyond the palace walls, but it left her son and daughters isolated from emotional influences that might have better helped steer them through the tumultuous years to come. Anastasia's own letters underscored not just the normalcy of her life but also the childish atmosphere in which she lived. "I am sitting picking my nose with my left hand," a twelve-year-old Anastasia wrote to her father. "Olga wanted to biff me one, but I escaped her swinish hand!"[27] A year later, again writing to her father, she noted how a nineteen-year-old Olga Nikolaievna was "hitting Marie, and Marie is shouting like an idiot"; even at a time when uncertainty and death hovered over the empire, Anastasia thought it funny that her eldest sister had led them all in mock battles using toy guns and in racing their bicycles through the palace rooms.[28]

Anastasia enjoyed this stream of happy games and laughter, and indeed, there was much to enjoy. Life settled into a quiet, pleasant routine: winters at Tsarskoye Selo; perhaps a few nights—when it was absolutely unavoidable—in St. Petersburg's immense Winter Palace; and, if possible, Easter in the Crimea. The isolated peninsula, jutting its rocky cliffs and beaches into the clear waters of the Black Sea, was a world unto itself, a tropical paradise of palm and cypress trees, rolling vineyards and lush roses. Here, at the imperial estate of Livadia, Nicholas and Alexandra built an Italianate palazzo, a sprawling white palace of loggias and sun-washed courtyards high above the crashing surf. Life at Livadia was deliberately informal, dominated by walks in the fragrant gardens, games of tennis, excursions to nearby picturesque villages, and afternoons spent swimming, though the waves that broke along the beach were particularly dangerous. Once, Anastasia was happily splashing about in the water when a breaker sucked her beneath the surface. Nicholas, watching from the beach, dove into the sea and barely managed to pull his youngest daughter to safety; shortly after, he had a canvas pool built atop the bluff so that his children could swim in safety.[29]

The warm climate in the Crimea was particularly beneficial for tubercular patients, and the empress used the fact to introduce her daughters to the idea of noblesse oblige. They sponsored hospitals and clinics in the surrounding hills, and regularly visited patients despite occasional protests. A courtier once objected to the practice, asking Alexandra, "Is it safe, Madame, for the young Grand Duchesses to have people in the last stages of consumption kiss their hands?"

"I don't think it will hurt the children," the empress replied, "but I am sure it would hurt the sick if they thought that my daughters were afraid of infection."[30] To aid these patients, Alexandra organized two annual events. The first, a charity bazaar, always took place along the quay in Yalta, and everyone contributed, the grand duchesses adding their needlework, small watercolors, and vases they had painted to the assemblage of knickknacks, souvenir postcards, furniture, and food that Alexandra and others sold from awning-draped booths along the pier.[31] But it was the Day of White Flowers that not only allowed the imperial siblings to make a meaningful contribution but also gave them a rare taste of freedom. On the appointed day, they left the protected confines of Livadia and freely roamed the streets of Yalta, holding long staffs decorated with clusters of white flowers. They entered shops, stopped motorcars, and engaged strollers in impromptu conversations, asking for donations in exchange for one of their flowers "as enthusiastically as though their fortunes depended on selling them all," remembered Anna Vyrubova.[32] On no other occasion, and in no other place than the

The Russian imperial family, 1914. From left: Olga, Marie, Nicholas II, Empress Alexandra, Anastasia, Alexei, and Tatiana.

Tsesarevich Alexei with Alexandra Tegleva ("Shura," later the wife of Pierre Gilliard).

Crimea, could Anastasia so freely meet and mingle with her father's subjects.

Time in the Crimea was pleasant and relaxed, but lessons, duties, and imperial obligations still managed to intrude. Real escape only came each June, when the Romanovs spent several weeks cruising through the Gulf of Finland aboard their yacht *Standart*. If, at Livadia, the routine of court life carried on in abbreviated form, summer cruises were true holidays, free of all cares. More than four hundred feet long and manned by some three hundred sailors, the *Standart* was a sleek, black-hulled vessel, with wicker furniture scattered over awning-shaded teak decks and comfortably appointed cabins decorated in chintz and mahogany.[33] All of the grand duchesses, recalled a courtier, "loved the sea," as well as the "intimacy with their beloved father, which was otherwise impossible. To be at sea with their father—that was what constituted their happiness."[34] Sailing through the Finnish Skerries, the yacht would anchor in some secluded cove, and the imperial family went ashore. Nicholas walked with the suite, rowed, and shot game; Alexandra read and did needlework; and the grand duchesses hunted in the forest for wild berries and mushrooms. When they returned to the *Standart*, there were teas on deck and dances for the grand duchesses, partnered by handsome young officers.[35]

With autumn came another move, this one to Poland, so that Nicholas could hunt at one of his country estates. In September 1912 they arrived excited and relieved at Spala: excited to once again temporarily abandon some of the intrusive pressures that came from life at court, and relieved because just two weeks earlier, Alexei had injured himself while jumping into a boat, but after a few days the crisis had luckily passed.[36] The lodge, a rambling wooden chalet so gloomy that electric lights burned throughout the day, sat in the middle of a thick forest of evergreen, fir, and pine fringed by the chilly waters of the Pilitsa River.[37] While Nicholas hunted, the grand duchesses roamed the woods collecting mushrooms, took carriage rides over the sandy roads, or played games of tennis on the clay court.

One day, thinking that the air would do him good, Alexandra took her eight-year-old son for a ride in the forest. As the carriage jostled over the uneven, sandy roadways, the swelling from the previous hemorrhage in Alexei's thigh dislodged, and the internal bleeding began anew. "Every movement of the carriage," Anna Vyrubova recalled, "every rough place in the road, caused the child the most exquisite torture, and by the time we reached home, the boy was almost unconscious with pain."[38]

The tsesarevich took to his bed in agony with a high temperature as the blood flowed from the upper left thigh into the abdomen, into an ugly swelling; the pressure was unbearable, but nothing could be done. Day and night, the tsesarevich's screams rang through the villa, terrible wails so heartrending that servants and members of the suite had to stuff their ears with cotton to continue their work.[39] It was all the more vivid, this sound track to an unraveling nightmare, as the silence of worry, of an urgent sense of despair, of impending death, descended over Spala.

This reality, that Alexei was desperately ill and his life in danger—Nicholas knew it, Alexandra knew it, the grand duchesses knew it, and a few members of the suite knew it—and yet dozens of others at Spala had no idea what was wrong, or just how serious the situation had become. A tragic charade, dictated by the imperial couple's decision to conceal their son's hemophilia, meant that life went on, said one courtier, "as if nothing were happening." An idea had been drummed into Anastasia and her sisters, the necessity of secrecy, of deception where their brother's health was concerned, an emotional struggle to maintain a facade of normalcy in the face of looming catastrophe. Even as their brother lay dying, recalled a member of the suite, the grand duchesses "never mentioned a word."[40]

For ten days, Alexandra rarely left her son's bedside; the only comfort she could offer him was her presence. She "never undressed," recalled Anna Vyrubova, "never went to bed, rarely even laid down for an hour's rest. Hour after hour, she sat beside the bed where the half-conscious child lay huddled on one side, his left leg drawn up. . . . His face was absolutely bloodless, drawn and seamed with suffering, while his almost expressionless eyes rolled back in his head. Once, when the Emperor came into the room, seeing the boy in this agony and hearing the faint screams of pain, the poor father's courage completely gave way, and he rushed—weeping bitterly—to his study."[41]

Only one other person at Spala truly understood what the empress suffered: this was her sister Irene, Princess Heinrich of Prussia, who had come to the lodge for a brief holiday with her sixteen-year-old son Sigismund, known as Bobby.[42] Married to the brother of Kaiser Wilhelm II, Irene—like Alexandra—was a hemophilia carrier, and had passed the disease to her two other sons, Waldemar and Heinrich.

Like Alexandra, she had endured the agonies of uncertain days and nights, watching helplessly as her sons suffered without relief; unlike the empress, though, she knew loss, for her son Heinrich had died at age four when, following a minor accident, he hemorrhaged to death.[43] This shared pain, this maternal guilt, created a bond between Alexandra and Irene that came to the fore at Spala that autumn, providing the desperate empress with an ally who shared her agony.

Day after day, life went on: Nicholas hunted, the grand duchesses walked and played tennis, groups of Polish nobles arrived for teas, and the imperial couple presided over "dinners in the company of their suite," full of the "same meaningless conversations," said a courtier.[44] One evening, in the midst of the crisis, Anastasia and Marie acted out two scenes from Molière's *Bourgeois Gentilhomme* for an audience of assembled guests. The two grand duchesses seemed happy and boister- ous, with Anastasia embracing the comedic role and enjoying the laughter that rang through the hall; yet Gilliard, watching from the wings of a makeshift stage, saw the empress in the front row, smiling and laughing one minute, only to excuse herself and flee in terror, face white and eyes wide, to answer the muffled screams of her son.[45]

Finally, despite their reluctance, the situation became so grave that Nicholas and Alexandra finally consented to the publication of medical bulletins; for the first time, Russia learned that its future emperor was gravely ill, though there was no mention of hemophilia. Prayers were said, and a priest administered the last rites of the Orthodox Church to the dying boy.[46] In despair, the empress sent a cable to Rasputin in Siberia, pleading with him to pray for the life of her son; his answer came the following morning: "The Little One will not die."[47] And suddenly, inexplicably, Alexei began to recover. Convinced that the peasant's prayers had saved her son, Alexandra's faith in Rasputin became unassailable as the peasant's shadow lengthened over the lives of the Romanovs.

IN 1913, RUSSIA celebrated three hundred years of Romanov rule. On a frigid late February morning, sparse crowds lined St. Petersburg's broad, snowy avenues, awaiting the string of carriages that conveyed the impe- rial family from the Winter Palace to a Te Deum at the Cathedral of Our Lady of Kazan. There were receptions and balls, theater galas and concerts, and carefully choreographed rituals of power designed to elicit loyal responses from an empire that had largely grown apathetic to its ruling family. In the sanctuary of their pastel palaces, aristocrats openly gossiped about Rasputin's friendship with the empress, wondering aloud

in French—for most would never con-
descend to speak Russian—if she was
quite sane, and shaking their heads in
frustrated resignation as the formerly
brilliant imperial court shrank away
into memory.

Anastasia, 1914.

Nicholas and Alexandra saw none
of it. That spring, they took their children and extended family on a tour
along the Volga, visiting river towns,
monasteries, and medieval fortresses;
watching from the deck of the steamer,
Olga Alexandrovna recalled "crowds
of peasants wading high in the water"
to catch a glimpse of her brother.[48]
On June 1 they arrived in Kostroma;
here, in 1613, a delegation from
the Zemsky Sobor in Moscow had
called upon sixteen-year-old Michael
Romanov, then hiding at the town's Ipatiev Monastery, and offered
him the Russian crown. Unlike the dismal reception in St. Petersburg,
here the Romanovs received a resounding welcome: thousands of
onlookers, held back by lines of smartly uniformed soldiers, cheered as
they passed through the town in open carriages, along streets bedecked
with flags and floral arches and resounding with patriotic songs from
peasant choirs and ringing church bells.[49]

Everything, watched with wide-eyed excitement by the cloistered
Romanovs, seemed to attest to their popularity, to the loyalty of the
nation, to the permanence of their rule. Flickering newsreels and
souvenir prints, sepia photographs and popular postcards captured it
all, freezing Anastasia, almost inevitably clad throughout the festivities
in white dresses and feathered hats, in the amber of time, a time that
finally seemed ripe with promise and stability. This is how Russia saw
her: Grand Duchess Anastasia, idealized and enshrouded in a careful mythology: for the public she was a delightful young girl, a para-
gon of virtue, an Orthodox princess who inhabited an ethereal plane
dominated by palaces and jewels, servants and balls. The Tercentenary
cloaked the imperial family in an aura of enchantment, a fairy-tale family in a fairy-tale world. Beneath this seductive surface, though, below
this impassively proud universe, a volcano was stirring, its molten fires
of revolt and revolution churning and simmering with an insistent,
increasing urgency that no one, in 1913, could have foreseen.

3

Into the Abyss

A T EIGHT O'CLOCK ON THE EVENING of August 1, 1914, Anastasia sat down with her mother and sisters in the dining room of the Lower Palace at Peterhof. The summer had begun happily, with a long, late holiday in the Crimea and a cruise to visit the king and queen of Romania, but then came June 28, and the assassination in Sarajevo of Archduke Franz Ferdinand of Austria-Hungary and his wife. Diplomatic tensions ran high as alliances formed in the chancelleries of Europe strengthened, armies mobilized, and ambassadors presented ultimatums.

The world stood poised on the edge of an abyss that August night as Alexandra and her daughters waited nervously, impatiently: Nicholas II was cloistered in his study, reading the latest dispatches and poring over telegrams. As the minutes passed and the usually punctual emperor failed to appear, the empress grew increasingly agitated. No one knew what was happening, though everyone feared the worst. The fears were confirmed when Nicholas entered the room: quietly, he told his family that Germany had just declared war on Russia. Hearing this news, Anastasia—like her mother—immediately burst into tears.[1]

The following day, a yacht brought the imperial family to St. Petersburg; only the tsesarevich, who had suffered a fall and could not walk, remained behind at Peterhof. The August sun shone over the imperial capital, washing its baroque palaces in the golden light of this last day of peace; cannons thundered from the Fortress of St. Peter and St. Paul, and bells pealed as the yacht slowly steamed up the shimmering Neva River, churning a ribbon of white foam in its wake. Every inch along the granite embankments brimmed with a nervous, excited, enthusiastic crowd that shouted and cheered the family on their progress. At the Winter Palace, a crimson carpet led them from sunlight to shadow, from heat into the cool and cavernous building: an impassive Nicholas, a strained Alexandra, and the four grand duchesses, clad in white and faces tense, joined within by a string of aunts, uncles, and cousins—nearly all of them, like Anastasia, born of unions between Russian men and German women, and now about to witness one country, one royal family, pitted against the other.

A crowd of aristocrats, officials, and courtiers crushed together in an immense hall; through windows opened to provide a welcome breeze came the continuous roar of thousands outside, still cheering and singing, hailing the beginning of what the Russians thought would be a sure and swift victory. "Hands in long white gloves nervously crumpled handkerchiefs," Grand Duchess Marie Pavlovna saw as she entered the hall, "and under the large hats . . . many eyes were red with crying. The men frowned thoughtfully, shifting from foot to foot, readjusting their swords, or running their fingers over the brilliant decorations pinned on their chests."[2] Standing before this crowd of five thousand, as priests chanted and incense floated across the room, Nicholas II formally declared war on Germany.

Empress Alexandra and her daughters, 1914. From left: Olga, Tatiana, Alexandra, Anastasia, and Marie.

Optimism overwhelmed reality in these early days, and people spoke of the massive Russian Army easily annihilating the kaiser's soldiers, of a quick victory that would restore the prestige of Nicholas II's crown and shower his reign with laurels. Enthusiastic patriotism overtook everyone: even the empress and her two eldest daughters threw themselves into the war effort, training as Red Cross nurses and working daily in a hospital they established at Tsarskoye Selo.[3] The boisterous and energetic Anastasia, though, found herself constrained: at thirteen, she was too young to undertake such work; instead, with her sister Marie, she sponsored her own hospital for officers injured in the war. Their committee commandeered an ornate, medieval-style building in a theatrical cluster of barracks, crenellated walls, and peak-roofed towers called the Feodorovsky Gorodok, just across a lake from the Alexander Palace, and founded Convalescent Home No. 17.[4] Several wards, filled with simple white metal beds, housed two dozen wounded officers; there was a small library of books and magazines, a common room with games of chess and checkers, and even a billiard table to keep the recuperating patients occupied.[5]

This hospital and its patients gave Anastasia a sense that she, too, could contribute something useful, could play some small role in fighting for her beloved "Papa"; that this also offered a temporary escape from the drudgery of her life must have had its own special appeal. With Marie, she visited these men several times a week, sitting at their bedsides,

The hospital for wounded officers operated by Marie and Anastasia at Tsarskoye Selo.

reading to them, writing letters for them, and playing games with them to help pass their long hours of convalescence.[6] She was curious about them, about their lives before the war, about their families, about their experiences fighting, about their wounds, and they, in turn, were fascinated by these privileged young women who paid them such attention, these daughters of their beloved and divinely inspired emperor. Perhaps they had seen them in newsreels or in postcards, the idealized family at the heart of its own national myth, but the reality was often startlingly, amusingly different. Anastasia kept her pockets stuffed with sweets, little, round, *crème brûlée*-flavored candies; she freely handed them out to the patients but also, recalled one, "ate them herself all the time." She was also watchful for any other treats that might come her way: visiting one patient, she found that someone had given him a box of sugared cherries and, soon enough—and with the man's permission—she was cramming them into her mouth "with great pleasure," although with sidelong glances across the ward lest she be caught in the act.[7] And still she charmingly and innocently moaned and muttered about the constant battle to control her waistline.

The hospital offered diversion, and it filled a void, but it also became yet another opportunity for Anastasia to understand and embrace the idea of noblesse oblige, which was so important to her position. While the empress and her two eldest daughters, according to their own wishes, were spared nothing in the operating room, from amputations to death on the table, the youngest grand duchesses had a less demanding role to fulfill. They knitted gifts for their patients, and arranged small entertainments to keep the men occupied. "Today we went to our hospital," Anastasia wrote in a 1915 letter to her father. "There was a concert. There were singers and then dancers, and then there were those who sang and danced. . . . I sat with some of your old officers. Everyone applauded at the end."[8] When the men were discharged, the grand duchesses provided them with watches, small souvenir medals with their initials, and other presents commemorating their encounters with the emperor's daughters.[9] Inevitably, though, Anastasia came face-to-face with a sad reality that these men knew only too well. "Two more poor things died," Anastasia wrote in a letter, "we sat with them only yesterday."[10] Such painful days became increasingly common as the conflict continued and the ravages of war took hold.

These men fought for her country, for her father, for her, sacrificing their lives in the name of holy, imperial Russia, an abstract idea that, for Anastasia, took on a more personal aspect in the summer of 1915. Soldiers had protected the Romanovs, patrolled the confines of their estates, lined the avenues they traveled; in turn, members of the imperial family all enjoyed close ties with the military, serving as honorary

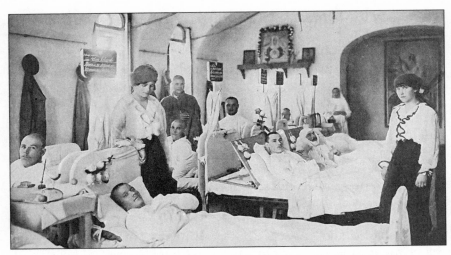

Marie (left) and Anastasia visiting patients in their hospital at Tsarskoye Selo, 1916.

colonels in chief of regiments—all, that is, except Anastasia, who had been deemed too young to receive such responsibility. It was, like her weight, an unending source of despair: officers aboard the *Standart* had teased her unmercifully over the situation, saying that Anastasia would be lucky to be named chief of some obscure fire brigade in St. Petersburg.[11] But her father came to the rescue. On June 18, 1915— Anastasia's fourteenth birthday—Nicholas II named his daughter honorary colonel in chief of the 148th Caspian Infantry Rifle Regiment.[12] Custom dictated a regimental parade, the presentation of colors, and a review on horseback by the new colonel in chief, all things Anastasia would undoubtedly have enjoyed, if not for the ceremonial aspects then at least for the opportunity to make herself the center of attention, but war denied her the experience. At the time, her regiment was off in distant Galicia, fighting German and Austro-Hungarian troops along the Dniester River; she had to wait two months before finally receiving the formal congratulations of Colonel Vassili Koliubakin, the regimental commander, at a short meeting in the Alexander Palace.[13] Still, she seized on every detail, receiving, as she proudly wrote, "a report about my regiment," and deeming it "all very interesting."[14]

In August 1916 the war entered its third year. Military setbacks, shortages of ammunition, and poor planning decimated hopes for a quick and decisive victory; instead there were disasters; retreats; and, on the home front, an increasingly discontented and restive populace. The previous summer, heavily influenced by a wife under the spell of an insistent Rasputin, Nicholas II had personally assumed command of the Russian Army—over objections of his government—and taken up semipermanent residence in the town of Mogilev, where the headquarters, or Stavka, was located, and where he was joined, when he was well enough, by Tsesarevich Alexei. Left in the imperial capital, which Nicholas had re-christened with the more Russian moniker of Petrograd, Empress Alexandra propelled herself to unfortunate notoriety as, egged on by Rasputin, she demanded that her husband replace ministers at a frenetic pace that left the government hopelessly crippled. Clouds were gathering, and even members of the Romanov family openly whispered of a possible coup d'état and revolution.

It was to be the last of Anastasia's carefree summers, these months divided between Tsarskoye Selo and visits to Mogilev with her mother and sisters. She missed her father and relished these reunions, when the imperial train pulled into a secluded siding on the outskirts of town and informality prevailed. In the mornings, the grand duchesses explored the surrounding countryside, walking through the forest and calling on surprised peasants and the children of railway workers, inevitably bringing little gifts of food and candy.[15] Each day, the empress and her daughters motored into Mogilev, to the Governor's House, where Nicholas and Alexei shared a room, joining them for luncheons and teas, followed by cruises along the Dnieper River or excursions across the sandy hills. The latter, recalled Baroness Buxhoeveden, could be real treks, "more of a pain than a pleasure," for Nicholas loved exercise, and he tended to ignore not just the more obvious boundaries but also the abilities of those who accompanied him. It was not uncommon for the emperor to set off at a rapid pace up and down hills, over fences, and across streams, leaving behind him a struggling, motley assortment of his children, his officers, and even his invited guests. More than once,

Anastasia on the balcony at the Alexander Palace.

these exhausted, breathless groups stumbled into the yard of some isolated dacha, surprising families sitting quietly drinking tea and who objected to the unwelcome intrusion; soon enough, though, most realized the illustrious identities of the intrepid wayfarers tromping across their lawns and clumsily stumbled over themselves to bow and present hastily plucked bunches of flowers to the giggling grand duchesses.[16]

These visits, "all too short" for the grand duchesses, said Gilliard, relieved some of the boredom of "their monotonous and austere lives."[17] Inevitably, though, military matters demanded Nicholas's attention, and forced the family back to Tsarskoye Selo, back—for Anastasia—to lessons, to the wards of her hospital, to the trivial events that filled the ebb and flow of her days. And those days, so relentless in their unceasing regularity, were about to veer into violent uncertainty.

Influenced by their mother, the grand duchesses had completely accepted the infamous Rasputin as a genuine religious figure whose prayers kept their brother alive. "All the children seemed to like him," Olga Alexandrovna remembered. "They were completely at ease with him."[18] Very early on, they learned from Alexandra to avoid mentions of the peasant and even to conceal his visits from curious servants, as their aunt Grand Duchess Xenia Alexandrovna noted. "He's always there, goes into the nursery, visits Olga and Tatiana while they are getting ready for bed, sits there talking to them and caressing them," she complained of Rasputin in 1910, deeming the situation "quite unbelievable and beyond understanding."[19] This bit of dissembling, like the secrecy

The four Grand Duchesses, seated in the Corner Salon of the Alexander Palace, about 1915. From left: Olga, Tatiana, Marie, and Anastasia.

imposed over Alexei's illness, led people to believe the worst. One nurse employed at the palace accused Rasputin of raping her and spread her story across St. Petersburg; it was taken up and carried into the ether of escalating rumor when governess Sophie Tiutcheva lost her position at court over the peasant's presence and complained of his malignant influence at Tsarskoye Selo.[20]

"Our Friend," Alexandra wrote of Rasputin to Nicholas, "is so contented with our Girlies, says they have gone through heavy 'courses' for their age and their souls have much developed."[21] Just ten days after this letter, on the night of December 29, 1916, Rasputin accepted an invitation to visit Prince Felix Yusupov at his Petrograd palace. Yusupov, the immensely wealthy, decadent, and debauched husband of Anastasia's first cousin Princess Irina Alexandrovna, gathered a group of conspirators, including Nicholas II's first cousin Grand Duke Dimitri Pavlovich, and poisoned, shot, and stabbed Rasputin in a highly melo-dramatic and mythologized murder before dumping his body into a frozen tributary of the Neva. Discovery of the crime, and of Rasputin's body, shocked the imperial family. Anatole Mordvinov, one of Nicholas II's adjutants, recalled how he had found the grand duchesses on a sofa on hearing the news, "huddled up closely together. They were cold and visibly, terribly upset, but for the whole of that long evening the name of Rasputin was never uttered in front of me. They were in pain, because the man was no longer among the living, but also because they had evidently sensed that, with his murder, something terrible and undeserved had started for their mother, their father, and themselves, and that it was moving relentlessly toward them."[22]

In killing Rasputin, Yusupov and the other conspirators had hoped to prevail upon Nicholas II to radically change his reactionary policies; with Rasputin gone, it was thought, an aggrieved empress would with-draw from political affairs altogether. But the murder of the peasant merely strengthened the imperial couple in their resolve to stand firm against any hint of concessions, any admission that public opinion mattered, any acknowledgment that the autocracy had ceased to exist when Nicholas II had granted the Duma in 1905. By March 1917, when Nicholas had returned to Mogilev, the country stood poised on the edge of an abyss, and strikes and bread riots in the capital quickly swelled into revolution.

As chaos erupted on the streets of Petrograd, Empress Alexandra remained isolated at Tsarskoye Selo. Not only was her husband away at headquarters, but also Olga, Tatiana, and Alexei had suddenly come down with serious cases of the measles, confined to their beds and nursed around the clock by Dr. Botkin and by their increasingly anxious mother.[23] Rumors about the disorders in the capital replaced fact, and no one knew quite what to believe as the empress anxiously awaited the return of her husband. Alexandra's friend Lili Dehn, who had come to Tsarskoye Selo, spent the evening of Tuesday, March 13, putting jigsaw puzzles together with Anastasia, an ordinary slice of life that played out in a palace isolated from the churning storm gathering beyond its walls. After sending her youngest daughter to bed, Alexandra turned to her friend, saying, "I don't want the girls to know anything until it is impossible to keep the truth from them, but people are drinking to excess, and there is indiscriminate shooting in the streets. Oh, Lili, what a blessing that we have here the most devoted troops. There is the Garde Equipage, they are all our personal friends."[24]

These guards became crucial the next day when a mutinous mob of soldiers decided to storm the Alexander Palace and take the empress and her son back to the capital under arrest. The emperor was expected back early the following morning, but that night his family prepared for an attack. Some fifteen hundred loyal men surrounded the building and huddled in the snowy palace courtyard around open fires awaiting the expected mob; the guards were armed with rifles and a massive field gun pointing out into the black night.[25] Warning her sick children that maneuvers were under way and that soldiers might be firing their guns close to the palace, Alexandra went out to the courtyard, accompanied by Marie, to speak to the remaining guards and thank them for their loyalty.[26] Looking down on this scene with Lili, Anastasia naively remarked, "How astonished Papa will be!"[27]

Marie remained with her mother through the nervous hours, and Lili Dehn took the grand duchess's camp bed in the room she usually shared with Anastasia. Throughout the winter night, a restless Anastasia tossed and turned, unable to sleep; occasionally, alarmed at the sound of gunfire, she jumped from her bed and raced to the windows, peering out into the darkness. By six the next morning, she waited with her mother in the Mauve Boudoir, expecting her father to return as promised; after several hours passed with no word, though, even the usually ebullient Anastasia sensed that something was terribly wrong. "Lili," she nervously confided to Dehn, "the train is never late. Oh, if only Papa would come quickly."[28]

Wednesday passed in growing anxiety, without word of the emperor and with increasingly ominous rumors from Petrograd. Entire regiments deserted, and increasingly angry mobs tore through the streets, looting shops and burning police buildings. By Thursday, the men guarding the Alexander Palace had abandoned their posts, and revolutionaries had cut its water and electricity, leaving its nervous inhabitants to await the unknown by candlelight.[29] That same day, at a railway siding in the town of Pskov, where his train had been diverted, Nicholas II bowed to the calls of his generals and abdicated the throne for both himself and his son. The 304-year-old Romanov Dynasty had come to an end.

ON MARCH 21, after her father's abdication, Anastasia began 483 days of captivity, first under the new Provisional Government and later under Vladimir Lenin's Soviet regime. Telephone lines were disconnected, all communications read, packages searched, and the Alexander Palace locked and ringed with soldiers guarding the imprisoned Romanovs.[30] Although most courtiers and servants abandoned their posts in the wake of the Revolution, nearly a hundred ladies-in-waiting, adjutants, valets, grooms, footmen, tutors, maids, nurses, and cooks remained—resembling "the survivors of a shipwreck," said Anna Vyrubova—to loyally share their captivity at Tsarskoye Selo.[31] This created a slightly surreal environment, where armed sentries patrolled the exterior of the palace, while inside, footmen in elaborate liveries still bowed and offered the prisoners vintage wines from the imperial cellars.[32]

Although there were petty annoyances—fruit was banned from the imperial table as a "luxury that prisoners could not be allowed"—life in the palace was not uncomfortable.[33] A modicum of normalcy descended as the imperial family settled into their new routine, and Anastasia resumed her lessons. Gibbes had not been at Tsarskoye Selo during the

The Romanov children, imprisoned at Tsarskoye Selo, taking a break from working on the kitchen garden in the grounds of the Alexander Palace, spring 1917. From left: Olga, Alexei, Anastasia, and Tatiana.

The five Romanov children, imprisoned in the Alexander Palace following their father's abdication. Their heads have been shaved following measles. From left: Anastasia, Olga, Alexei, Marie, and Tatiana.

Revolution and was denied access by the Provisional Government, but Gilliard remained and continued French instruction; to occupy his time, Nicholas taught Russian history; Mademoiselle Catherine Schneider, the empress's lectrice, took on Russian language; and Baroness Sophie Buxhoeveden stepped in for the absent Gibbes and gave lessons in English.[34]

It was when the prisoners left the palace that they faced the most insistent and unpleasant reminders of their changed status. For several hours each day, they were allowed to exercise in a corner of the park, always shadowed by armed soldiers and watched by a crowd gathered along the length of a nearby iron fence. These spectators included a handful of still-loyal former subjects along with the merely curious, anxious to see for themselves the family that had once ruled over them, but the most vocal were those who loathed the Romanovs; since the Revolution they had read the myths of a heartless tsar and his deranged wife who wanted her native Germany to crush her adopted homeland. Heads filled with gossip and exaggerations, these spectators jeered and shouted revolutionary slogans and obscenities, all in an effort to attract the prisoners' attention.[35] Men had previously bowed to the ground just to touch Nicholas II's shadow; now, soldiers guarding him turned their backs when he offered his hand in greeting, knocked him from his bicycle as he rode through the park, and insolently addressed him as "Mr. Colonel" as his family looked on helplessly.[36]

Eventually, after weeks of watching the prisoners, the revolutionary hatred displayed by most of the guards softened. When spring came, the imperial family started a kitchen garden, and these soldiers helped the four grand duchesses in moving earth and planting rows of vegetables.[37] Having been brought up since birth around members of the imperial guard, Anastasia and her sisters were soon at ease with the new soldiers, befriending them and chatting about their families; as a result of measles, the grand duchesses' hair had been shaved, and they even felt comfortable enough to remove their hats and be photographed—bald imperial heads shining in the sun—with their guards.[38] Even if attitudes softened, though, there were occasional unwelcome incidents. One hot summer night, Anastasia was sitting on an open windowsill, doing needlework as her father read aloud. Suddenly, soldiers burst into the room: a sentry patrolling the grounds had seen the prisoners signaling from the window with flashing red and green lights. The Romanovs professed ignorance, and investigation soon revealed what had happened: as Anastasia repeatedly leaned forward while doing her needlework, she had blocked and then uncovered two lamps burning behind her with green and red shades.[39]

This was how the summer passed for Anastasia, in occasionally amusing but petty annoyances, in lessons, in the new vegetable garden, and in uncertainty. No one expected the imprisonment at Tsarskoye Selo to last. There was talk of the Romanovs being allowed to live quietly at Livadia in the Crimea, but nothing came of the idea; plans to exile the prisoners to England also failed when King George V intervened and pressed his government to deny his Romanov cousins asylum. By late summer, Alexander Kerensky, head of the Provisional Government, was increasingly worried that the continued presence of the Romanovs so near to the capital would lead to disaster, and decided to transfer them away from potential danger. Warning that they would soon be leaving Tsarskoye Selo, Kerensky advised the prisoners to quietly pack what they wished to take with them. He refused to reveal their destination, but did say that they should bring warm clothing.

On the evening of August 12—Tsesarevich Alexei's thirteenth birthday—the imperial family gathered in a luggage-filled semicircular hall at the palace, anxiously awaiting word that the train ordered by Kerensky was at the station. In past, happier years, they had gathered here to watch films, the children giggling at the sight of some meaningful glance or the batting of a suggestive eyelash that had escaped the censor; now it had become a place of torment, as hour after agonizing hour passed without any news. The grand duchesses stood alone in one corner and "wept copiously" as morning approached.[40] Finally, as dawn broke over Tsarskoye Selo, the prisoners were ushered into a series of motorcars and, accompanied by an armed escort, driven to a nearby station, where a train, disguised with Japanese flags to confuse any revolutionaries bent on vengeance, took them east, toward Siberia.

A modern view of the Governor's House in Tobolsk, where the Romanovs were imprisoned during their Siberian exile from August 1917 to May 1918.

The journey took a week. "I will describe to you who [how] we traveled," Anastasia wrote in her imprecise English,

> We started in the morning and when we got into the train I went to sleap, so did all of us. We were very tierd because we did not sleap the whole night. The first day was hot and very dusty. At the stations we had to shut our window curtanse that nobody should see us. Once in the evening I was loking out of the window we stoped near a little house, but there was no staition so we could look out. A little boy came to my window and asked: "Uncle, please give me, if you have got, a newspaper." I said: "I am not an uncle but an anty and I have no news-paper." At the first moment I could not understand why did he call me "Uncle" but then I remembered that my hear [hair] is cut and I and the soldiers (which were standing next to me) laught very much. On the way many funy things hapend, and if I shall have time I shall write to you our travell father on. Good by. Don't forget me.[41]

The destination was Tobolsk, a small, remote town in Siberia; it was so remote that there was no railway link, and the prisoners had to make the last leg of the journey by river, aboard a steamer named *Rus*. During the voyage they sailed past the little hamlet of Pokrovskoye and saw Rasputin's native village in the distance, as the peasant had once predicted they would.[42] With the prisoners came their three pet dogs; forty-two courtiers and servants to attend to their needs; dozens of steamer trunks packed with clothing, photograph albums, paintings, and souvenirs; and a contingent of some three hundred armed soldiers under the command of Colonel Eugene Kobylinsky to guard them.[43] They also carried something else: more than $14 million worth of diamonds, pearls, sapphires, emeralds, rubies, and gold, carefully concealed in their belongings from inquisitive eyes, a fortune that would help ensure their well-being in the event that they were forced to leave the country.[44]

The Governor's House, where the Romanovs were imprisoned, was a large, two-story structure that the prisoners decorated and adorned with their favorite paintings, carpets, and possessions sent from the Alexander Palace.[45] The four grand duchesses shared a corner room on the second floor, "arranged all quite cozily," as Olga Nikolaievna wrote to Anna Vyrubova, sleeping in their camp beds beneath walls hung with icons, family photographs, and memories of happier days aboard the *Standart*.[46] Large as the house was, it could not accommodate more than a handful of the retinue that had followed the imperial family into exile; other courtiers and servants were given rooms in a large, ornate villa, the Kornilov Mansion, just across the street. When the imperial family casually visited them, though, some members of the special detachment guarding the prisoners objected, and Kobylinsky was forced to ring the Governor's House with a high stockade fence to placate his soldiers.[47] The Romanovs were now truly prisoners.

The arrival of the Romanovs in Tobolsk marked not only the end of their indulgent captivity but also, in many ways, an end to their tangible existence for many of their former subjects. It was not merely the fact that their faces and names, so well known, disappeared from newspapers and magazines. At Tsarskoye Selo, they had still lived largely as they had done before the Revolution, in a palace and surrounded by the trappings that had defined them as a ruling family. Their identity was still royal, their experiences not entirely unpleasant and certainly comfortable. Now, deprived not only of power, titles, and money but also of the privileged mise-en-scène that had set them apart from mere mortals, they disappeared into the vast Siberian landscape, into myth. The fairy tale had ended, replaced by a terrible, creeping nightmare that depicted Tobolsk as the first stage of the Romanovs' earthly Calvary.

At first life in Tobolsk was not unpleasant, although the house became incredibly cold as the Siberian winter took hold. Everyone agreed that "the inhabitants of Tobolsk were well disposed toward the Imperial Family," as Gilliard wrote. Citizens regularly gathered in the street outside the Governor's House, staring in curiosity, crossing themselves, and bowing if they saw any movement at the windows.[48] People collected donations and dispatched cakes, eggs, milk, fresh fish, candy, and other gifts for the prisoners.[49] An agreeable routine settled over the house. After breakfast, Anastasia had several hours of lessons: English with Gibbes when he finally arrived in Tobolsk, French with Gilliard, Russian and arithmetic with a young woman named Klaudia Bitner, religion with her mother, and history with her father.[50] At eleven, the prisoners usually went outside. There was no garden; for exercise, they could only walk back and forth along a section of roadway enclosed by the fence. Here, Nicholas and his children, assisted by retainers, took turns cutting logs with a twin-bladed saw; when the snow came and blanketed the compound, the grand duchesses pulled each other and their brother on sleds, and built an ice mountain for their toboggans.[51] Lunch, at one, generally consisted of four courses (soup, fish, an entrée, and dessert), while dinner, at eight, sometimes added a fifth course, of fruit.[52] In the afternoon, the imperial family took tea, and in the evenings the Romanovs and their retainers gathered in the drawing room to play cards or listen as Nicholas read aloud, just as they had done in the Alexander Palace; occasionally the grand duchesses—except for Tatiana, who remained with her mother—visited the rooms occupied by nurse Alexandra Tegleva and the empress's maids, exchanging jokes and playing games to pass the time.[53] There were, as Anastasia wrote to Anna Vyrubova, few diversions: "We often sit in the windows, looking at the people passing, and this gives us distraction."[54] The grand duchesses had merely exchanged the suffocating boredom of their lives at Tsarskoye Selo for a new kind of isolation.

That autumn Dr. Botkin's two children, nineteen-year-old Tatiana and seventeen-year-old Gleb, arrived in Tobolsk, sharing his lodgings in the Kornilov House. When they asked for permission to visit the grand duchesses and the tsesarevich, though, authorities refused, apparently on the pretext that they were not intimates and had never been invited to the palace.[55] From the windows of the Kornilov House, Tatiana and Gleb could catch only occasional glimpses of the prisoners, but Botkin's son found a novel way to amuse the youngest Romanovs. A talented artist, Gleb created an allegorical story about a group of aristocratic animals living through a revolution, illustrated with charming drawings. These he gave to his father, who smuggled them to Anastasia and Alexei for review; they would make suggestions about the stories, which Dr. Botkin conveyed back to his son.[56]

The winter passed. Anastasia, as her mother wrote, had now grown "very fat," and even at sixteen she stood just a little over five feet tall.[57] Kobylinsky called her "over-developed for her age . . . stout and short, too stout for her height," while Gibbes deemed her "ungraceful" and said, rather unkindly, that "if she had grown and lost weight she might have been the prettiest of the family."[58]

Monotony set in. To relieve the boredom, Gilliard and Gibbes organized small plays, acted and staged by Marie, Anastasia, and Alexei for the amusement of their parents and members of the household sharing their exile. One night, it was an English farce called *Packing Up*, in which Anastasia took the principal male role. As always, she relished the attention, and was doing a splendid job of it until the end, when she turned so quickly that her dressing gown flew up, exposing "her sturdy legs and bottom encased in the Emperor's Jaeger underwear," as Gibbes recalled. The audience collapsed in laughter as Anastasia, with no idea of what had happened, stood on the makeshift stage with a confused look on her face.[59]

Laughter was much needed in Tobolsk as life became more uncertain. The Bolshevik coup in November that replaced the Provisional Government marked the end of the rather indulgent treatment the Romanovs had thus far received. Over the months that followed, restrictions and personal freedoms tightened: new, coarse guards replaced the old, friendly soldiers who had been charged with security, and attendance at church services was denied. Money became tight: when Kerensky's regime ceased, so did government stipends for the prisoners' upkeep and pay for the men guarding them.[60] In the spring of 1918 the Romanovs were placed on ordinary soldiers' rations, and eggs, butter, and coffee disappeared from their diet, although occasionally sympathetic citizens in the town dispatched baskets of provisions.[61] Dinner now, Gilliard reported, without a hint of irony, "consisted of two courses, and this situation was difficult to bear for those who had been accustomed since birth to an entirely different manner of life."[62] Although the Romanovs possessed a fortune in jewelry that they had smuggled into exile with them—enough to bribe entire regiments of soldiers and escape—lack of imagination; a critical failure to recognize the mounting forces aligned against them; and, above all, a fatalistic approach to life all coalesced into a stunning sense of resignation. As winter turned to spring, the prisoners whispered of possible rescue plots, dreaming of a world of freedom that lay beyond the still-frozen Siberian plains.

The late April arrival of Vassili Yakovlev, a new commandant from Moscow, brought with it new worries. Relieving Kobylinsky of duty, he explained that he had come to immediately transfer the Romanovs from Tobolsk, although he refused to reveal their intended destination. Tsesarevich Alexei's precarious health, though, threatened the urgency of Yakovlev's mission: he found the thirteen-year-old in bed, suffering from a severe internal hemorrhage and unable to travel. When the commissar insisted on taking Nicholas II as planned, Alexandra was forced to choose between her husband and her sick son; after a terrible night that found the whole family in tears, the emperor and empress, together with Marie and a handful of servants, agreed to travel with

Yakovlev; the others would follow when Alexei had recovered. Just before dawn on the morning of April 26, Olga, Tatiana, and Anastasia stood on the steps of the Governor's House, "three figures in gray suits," as Tatiana Botkin saw them from her window, who "gazed for a long time into the distance" as the carts holding their parents and sister disappeared into the darkness.[63]

4

"How Little I Suspected That I Was Never to See Them Again"

FEARFUL AND ALONE, not knowing the reason why the mysterious Yakovlev had taken their parents and sister away nor where they had gone, the three grand duchesses and their brother remained in Tobolsk, uncertain and awaiting any news. "The sadness of death," recalled Alexei Volkov, elderly groom of the chamber to Empress Alexandra, "descended on the Governor's House."[1] There were suspicions that the mission involved a journey to Moscow; everyone in Tobolsk was therefore surprised and alarmed on learning that Yakovlev's train had been diverted to the city of Ekaterinburg, an industrial center and Bolshevik stronghold in the Ural Mountains.[2] There, the emperor, empress, their daughter, and servants had been imprisoned in a house commandeered from a wealthy local. "We were so terribly glad to receive news," Anastasia wrote to her sister Marie in Ekaterinburg, "we kept on sharing our impressions! Forgive me for writing so crookedly, I'm just being stupid. . . . I am always with you dears in my thoughts. It's so terribly sad and lonely. I just don't know what to do. The Lord helps and will help. . . . We played on the swing, that was when I roared with laughter, the fall was so wonderful! Indeed! I told the sisters about it so many times yesterday that they got quite fed up, but I could go on telling it masses of times, only there's no one left. In fact I already have loads of things to tell you. . . . I'm sorry of course for such a clumsy letter, you will understand that my thoughts keep racing ahead and I can't write everything down, I just grasp at whatever enters my noodle."[3]

There was another letter, this one dictated by Alexandra but written by her maid Anna Demidova, who had followed her to Ekaterinburg. Although she could say little about their new situation, the empress warned her daughters that on arrival all of their belongings had been searched, even their "medicines."[4] This was a code word meant to indicate that the grand duchesses should conceal their jewelry. Aided by Alexandra Tegleva, the young women spent several days quietly sewing diamonds, ropes of pearls, and other gems under the lining of undergarments, into the bands of hats and belts of dresses, and behind buttons covered with cotton wadding to escape the attention of the Bolsheviks.[5]

Worried that some monarchist group would manage to rescue the Romanovs remaining in Tobolsk, the Ural Regional Soviet in Ekaterinburg dispatched a contingent of reliable Bolshevik soldiers to surround the prisoners in the Governor's House.[6] With them came a new Bolshevik commissar named Nicholas Rodionov, a dour man who delighted in inflicting petty humiliations on the prisoners, including a daily roll call at which the three grand duchesses had to appear and answer to their names, "like so many inanimate objects," Tegleva recalled.[7] One day, he pulled Alexei Volkov aside and, "armed to the teeth," announced, "Tell the young ladies that they may not close the door to their bed-chamber at night." Volkov attempted to argue with the commissar, but to no avail as Bolshevik soldiers wandered freely through the house.[8]

The day before the prisoners were to leave, Tatiana Botkin sought out Rodionov. Her father had accompanied Nicholas and Alexandra to Ekaterinburg and shared their confinement, and she asked if she and her brother Gleb could join him. Rodionov first tried to dissuade her from this, saying it would be better if they remained in Tobolsk; when Tatiana pressed, the commissar warned her that, once transferred to Ekaterinburg, all of the Romanovs would either be imprisoned or, more ominously, "be shot." Although Tatiana quickly dismissed this threat, she and Gleb decided to stay in Tobolsk. That night, Gleb took to the street, hoping to catch a glimpse of the prisoners; he spied Anastasia smiling from a window, took off his cap, and gave a low bow, only to be chased from the street by armed soldiers.[9]

On May 20, Anastasia and her siblings left Tobolsk aboard the *Rus*, the same river steamer that had brought them into exile nine months earlier; in Tyumen they transferred to a train and, at two on the morning of May 23, finally arrived in Ekaterinburg, where a contingent of heavily armed soldiers mounted a guard outside their railway car-riage.[10] The following morning, as rain poured from the gray Siberian sky, an angry mob gathered at the siding, demanding to see the "bloodsuckers" as the grand duchesses nervously peered from the windows of their compartment. Soldiers struggled to hold the crowd back as it screamed, "Hang them!" The anger reached a crescendo when soldiers began to unload the baggage; the mob surged forward, tearing into the trunks and suitcases, ripping up clothing, and shouting, "Off with their heads!"[11] In those few tense moments, the petty humiliations and uncertainties endured by Anastasia and her siblings in the year since their father's abdication must have been replaced by the first very real fears for their lives.

Not until nine that morning did a string of carriages pull up alongside the train. Although twenty-seven courtiers and servants had followed the tsesarevich and grand duchesses from Tobolsk, authorities in Ekaterinburg arrested most of the group. Some were later executed, while others, such as Gilliard, Gibbes, Tegleva, and Buxhoeveden, were set free.[12] Armed guards hustled the prisoners off the train as the crowd screamed and jeered. First came Alexei, still unable to walk and carried by his sailor Klementy Nagorny, followed by Olga, Tatiana, and Anastasia; holding their suitcases and their three dogs, they slipped and struggled in the thick morass of mud before reaching the waiting vehicles. From the windows of his railway carriage, Pierre Gilliard watched Anastasia and her siblings disappear into the incessant rain. "How little I suspected," he later wrote, "that I was never to see them again."[13]

SURROUNDED BY WIDE, shallow lakes and deep birch forests, the Siberian city of Ekaterinburg stands on the eastern slope of the Ural Mountains, just fifty miles from the border dividing Europe and Asia. Named for Catherine the Great, by the twentieth century it had developed into a substantial industrial center, where miners grew wealthy from rich mineral deposits and workers toiled in a string of grim suburban factories. A tinderbox for revolution, the conflict between rich and poor, between prosperity and despair, erupted with the rest of Russia in 1917, and Ekaterinburg quickly acquired a proud reputation as a fiery Bolshevik stronghold, the "Center of the Red Urals." Here, in an increasingly uncertain and hostile environment, the Romanovs began the final months of their captivity.

On Voznesensky Prospekt, near the city center and sprawled along the edge of a steep hillside, stood an ornate, whitewashed mansion owned by engineer Nicholas Ipatiev. In April, the local ruling Ural Regional Soviet had evicted Ipatiev and commandeered the property; they ringed the structure with a stockade fence dotted with sentry boxes, and positioned machine guns on the balcony and in the attic.

г. Екатеринбургъ. № 32.
Сѣверо-западная часть города.

View of Ekaterinburg from Cathedral Square; the Ipatiev House is the building at the extreme left.

Windows were whitewashed and sealed, interior doors nailed shut, and workers drawn from local factories were given rifles and posted around the perimeter. Ominously, the Ural Regional Soviet rechristened the building "the House of Special Purpose."[14] This was the new prison Anastasia and her siblings entered on the morning of May 23, 1918. "What an enormous joy to see them again and to embrace them after the four week separation and uncertainty," Nicholas II wrote in his diary. "The poor things had endured a lot of personal, spiritual suffering both in Tobolsk and during the three day trip."[15]

The House of Special Purpose was not as large as the Governor's House in Tobolsk, and the Romanovs were given only eight rooms to use; these they shared with the handful of retainers remaining with them. Aside from Dr. Botkin, this included maid Anna Demidova; valets Alexei Trupp and Terenty Chemodurov; Klementy Nagorny; cook Ivan Kharitonov; footman Ivan Sednev; and Sednev's fourteen-year-old nephew Leonid, who helped in the kitchen. Increasingly ill and senile, Chemodurov left the house the day after Anastasia arrived, while the Bolsheviks arrested both Nagorny and Ivan Sednev on May 27 and, unknown to the Romanovs, executed them.[16] These servants slept on sofas or cots in the hallways, kitchen, and drawing room, while the imperial family took three rooms at the southern end of the house. Alexei had one bedroom (he later shared his parents' bedroom) and Nicholas and Alexandra another; the four grand duchesses slept on their camp beds in a former dressing room between the two chambers,

The Ipatiev House in Ekaterinburg, where the Romanovs were imprisoned and executed by the Ural Regional Soviet.

its walls hung with pink, red, and green floral paper and the ceiling adorned with a bronze Italian chandelier with colored glass shades.[17]

Behind these heavily guarded walls a new myth was born, one that replaced the former fairy-tale existence of the imperial family and that would last throughout the twentieth century. History, relying on reports of the White Army and on the memoirs of those who had known the Romanovs, would record the seventy-eight days spent by the imperial family in the Ipatiev House as a time of unrelenting brutality. British journalist Robert Wilton, who in 1920 produced the first published account of the Ekaterinburg period, thus asserted, "Before their death, the captives were subjected to ill-treatment, amounting to horrible torture, mental if not physical."[18] He described their guards as "coarse, drunken, criminal types," with "leering eyes," "loathsome familiarities," and "evil smelling bodies."[19]

This set the pattern for what followed, a chronicle of distortions depicting the Romanovs' time in Ekaterinburg as a long string of deliberate humiliations that culminated in their execution.[20] There was a clear political and religious value in such tales. The White Army, monarchists, and Russian émigrés scattered by the Revolution not only attained sympathetic martyrs in the imperial family but also gained in their deaths a piece of stunning anti-Soviet propaganda. An atheistic regime that maltreated and executed the sick tsesarevich and his four sisters offered a stark moral contrast to the vanished empire carried in the hearts and minds of Russian exiles; this position spoke less of reality than of attempts to ignore the factors that had led to the Revolution,

never hurt anyone." They were agreeable to this, but explained that they did not know how to do laundry. Avdayev went off to the local library in search of an instruction manual but could find nothing useful; he finally hired a man named Andreyev from a local factory who, christened with the absurd title of "Comrade Laundry Teacher to the House of Special Purpose," came to the prison to give the grand duchesses lessons in washing towels and sheets.[33]

Time passed slowly, the weeks marked with a string of family birthdays. Nicholas II turned fifty in the Ipatiev House; Alexandra, forty-six; Tatiana, twenty-one; Marie, nineteen; and, on June 18, Anastasia seventeen. It was a beautiful, warm Tuesday; the grand duchesses served their bread at lunch, and just after three that afternoon all of the family went into the garden for an hour. It was, Alexandra recorded in her diary, "very hot," though the air was scented with lilac and honeysuckle. That evening came a welcome surprise: with Avdayev's permission, nuns from a nearby convent began regular deliveries of milk, cream, and eggs for the prisoners.[34]

Seventeen found Anastasia, as one of her jailers recounted, "very attractive" and "very fat. She had rosy cheeks, and a quite lovely face and features." Of all the prisoners, she seemed "best adjusted to their position."[35] One guard deemed her "very friendly and full of life," while another termed her "a very charming devil! She was mischievous and, I think, rarely tired. She was lively, and was fond of performing comic mimes with the dogs, as though they were performing in a circus."[36] In time, these men sympathized with their prisoners, and the lines between captors and captives faded as the beautiful grand duchesses gave them smiles, teased them, shared stories of their former lives, and even showed them their photograph albums. "There were long conversations," remembered one guard, "in which they spoke of their hopes for the future and talked about living in England one day." Innocent flirtations developed, and several of the soldiers spent their off-duty hours making and hanging a wooden swing for the grand duchesses in the garden. At night, when off duty, some of the soldiers even confessed that they "would not mind so much if they were allowed to escape."[37]

Escape, in fact, was very much on the minds of the Romanovs as the summer of 1918 began. In early June, acting on orders from the Ural Regional Soviet, Bolshevik authorities in the town of Perm secretly executed Nicholas II's brother, Grand Duke Michael Alexandrovich, publicly claiming that he had escaped with the help of White Army officers. Just a week later, the imperial family in Ekaterinburg received the first of four letters, smuggled into the Ipatiev House and written in French, that promised their freedom.[38] They replied with details of their living arrangements, moved Alexei into the bedroom shared by his parents, and secretly spent several anxious nights fully dressed in their darkened rooms, awaiting a rescue that never came.[39] "The days passed and nothing happened," Nicholas confided in his diary. "The waiting and the uncertainty were very upsetting."[40]

Unknown to the Romanovs, the letters had been written by the Ekaterinburg Cheka in an effort to trap them in circumstances that could then be used to justify their execution. In anticipation of this, on July 4, the Ural Regional Soviet fired the lax and indulgent Avdayev and replaced him with a new commandant named Yakov Yurovsky; over the next few days, the old guards who had grown friendly with the prisoners were barred from duty within the Ipatiev House, replaced by a contingent of more reliable men.[41] Yurovsky forced the Romanovs to hand over any visible jewelry—watches, necklaces, bracelets, and rings—that they wore; he allowed Anastasia and her sisters to each keep a single gold bracelet each that they had been given by their parents and that they could not remove. He also changed the time of the prisoners' daily roll call, put a halt to the petty thievery of their belongings by the guards, and covered the only open window with a heavy grate.[42]

On Sunday, July 14, Yurovsky allowed two priests to celebrate a service for the prisoners at the Ipatiev House. They found the Romanovs and their retainers gathered in the drawing room, where a makeshift altar had been prepared. One of the priests, Ioann Storozhev, later recalled that Anastasia had worn a black skirt and white blouse, and had stood next to her father throughout the service, as Yurovsky watched from a corner of the room.

> It seemed to me that on this occasion, Nicholas Alexandrovich and all of his daughters were—I won't say in depressed spirits—but they gave the impression just the same of being exhausted. . . . According to the liturgy of the service it was customary at a certain point to read the prayer *Who Resteth with the Saints*. On this occasion, for some reason, the Deacon, instead of reading this prayer, began to sing it, and I as well, somewhat embarrassed by this departure from the ritual. But we had scarcely begun to sing when I heard the members of the Romanov family, standing behind me, fall on their knees. After the service everyone kissed the Holy Cross. . . . As I went out, I passed very close to the former Grand Duchesses and heard the scarcely audible words, "Thank you."[43]

Early the following morning, two nuns arrived from a local convent, bringing provisions for the prisoners; Yurovsky passed along a note from one of the grand duchesses, asking for some thread.[44] At ten-thirty, four women from the Ekaterinburg Union of Professional Housemaids arrived to clean the prisoners' rooms. The Romanovs were playing cards at the dining room table when they arrived. One woman, Maria

Starodumova, recalled that they were all "gay. The Grand Duchesses were laughing. There was no trace of sadness."[45] After greeting the women with "friendly smiles," said Eudokia Semyonovna, "the Grand Duchesses got up and went with us four into their bedroom to move their beds for us. As I remember it, they were neither in the least scared, nor in the least worried. Their eyes shone brightly with fun and high spirits, their short hair was tumbled and in disorder, their cheeks were rosy like apples. They did not dress like Grand Duchesses, but wore short dresses of black, with white blouses underneath and a bit of décolletage showed. The commandant Yurovsky was a snooper. For some time, he stood listening at the open door and would look in to glare at us when we exchanged jokes and pleasantries with the young Grand Duchesses. We were all cautious, and spoke in low voices after that. At one time, when Yurovsky withdrew his head from the room, the smallest Grand Duchess, Anastasia, turned to the doorway and made such a face at him that we all laughed, then she put out her tongue and thumbed her nose at his back."[46]

Tuesday, July 16, 1918, dawned overcast and humid in Ekaterinburg; by afternoon, the gray clouds had disappeared, replaced by a baking sun.[47] At seven that morning, the nuns arrived and left their provisions for the prisoners, and the day passed as usual.[48] Between three and four that afternoon, the prisoners took their walk in the garden; Alexandra remained inside with Tatiana. Then, at eight o'clock, as the prisoners were eating dinner, Yurovsky entered and told the young kitchen boy Leonid Sednev that he was to go join his uncle Ivan, who had been removed from the Ipatiev House six weeks earlier and who, unknown to the prisoners, had been executed. At ten-thirty, the Romanovs went to bed.[49] The White Army was fewer than twenty miles away, and everyone knew that the Bolsheviks would lose Ekaterinburg to them within a few days.[50] Through a single, open window in the bedroom shared by Nicholas, Alexandra, and Alexei, the prisoners could hear the distant echo of approaching artillery, a sound that must have beckoned to them with thoughts of freedom as, one by one, lights were extinguished and the dark July night overtook the Ipatiev House.

AT A LITTLE after two the following afternoon, guard Anatoly Yakimov reported for duty at the Ipatiev House. He recalled, "The door leading from the anteroom into the rooms which had been occupied by the Imperial Family was closed as before, but there was no one in the rooms. This was obvious. No sound came from there. Before, when the Imperial Family lived there, there were always sounds of life in their rooms: voices, steps. At this time there was no life there. Only their little dog stood in the anteroom, at the door to the rooms where the Imperial Family had lived, waiting to be let in. I well remember thinking at the time: You are waiting in vain."[51]

In vain, Yakimov said, because he had been told that just twelve hours earlier, the imperial family had been executed in the basement of the Ipatiev House. This same evening, the Ural Regional Soviet also ordered the execution of several Romanovs held prisoner in the Siberian town of Alapayevsk. Empress Alexandra's sister Grand Duchess Elizabeth Feodorovna, known as Ella, who had founded an order of nursing sisters after the 1905 assassination of her husband, Grand Duke Serge Alexandrovich, and five other members of the family were taken into a forest and thrown alive down an abandoned mine shaft. Yet ironically, the same Bolsheviks who deemed it politically expedient to kill the Romanovs were also responsible for the myth of their survival.

Just three days after the rumored carnage in Ekaterinburg, and with an irony fitting their later canonization by the Russian Orthodox Church, the Romanovs rose again from their presumed graves, resurrected in deceptive announcements by Soviet officials. The Bolsheviks admitted only to the execution of Nicholas II; the empress and Alexei, it was said, had been sent away from Ekaterinburg, while there was no mention of the grand duchesses. The Soviet government would not deviate from this position until the 1920s; it was meant not only to

Basement storeroom in the Ipatiev House, where the Romanovs were executed.

confuse the White Army but also to protect the reputation of the Soviet regime. Lenin was only too aware of how the world would view word of the slaughter of the empress and her innocent children.

Ekaterinburg fell to the advancing forces of the White Army and Czechoslovak troops on July 25, just eight days after the supposed execution. Rushing to the Ipatiev House, they found that its former inhabitants had vanished, the floors strewn with a few pathetic remnants of clothing and possessions, and a room in the cellar pocked with bullet holes and signs of blood. The only hint of what may have happened came in the Bolshevik announcement that Nicholas II had been killed; starting from this presumption, judicial and military investigators began a search for the missing imperial family. In January 1919, the third and last of the official White Army investigators, Nicholas Sokolov, was appointed to determine precisely what had become of the Romanovs and, building on evidence collected by his predecessors, developed a circumstantial case that all had perished. Sokolov produced what, for most of the twentieth century, history believed to be the truth about the end of the Romanovs; it was, however, only a theory, deeply flawed, riddled with conjecture, and often at odds with science, facts that led many to question his conclusions and fed the mythology of survival.

There was, to be sure, the bloodstained and bullet-marked basement room in the Ipatiev House, which certainly pointed toward some violence, particularly after the Romanovs disappeared, but it offered no definitive proof of their fate. More concrete was the discovery of a Bolshevik telegram

The area surrounding the Four Brothers Mine in the Koptyaki Forest outside Ekaterinburg, where the corpses of the Romanovs were taken following their execution.

Nicholas Sokolov, who headed the last White Army investigation into the fate of the Romanovs.

in which the Ural Regional Soviet had informed Moscow that the entire family had "suffered the same fate" as Nicholas II. Because Soviet authorities had already publicly admitted to the execution of the former emperor, this, too, suggested the worst, but the first real evidence of what had taken place in that ominous basement room in the early morning hours of July 17 came when several former Ipatiev House guards recounted that the imperial family had been killed. Altogether four men gave statements, although only one claimed to have actually seen the bodies.

Publication of these statements in 1920 gave the world its first glimpse at what was said to have happened to the imperial family. Yurovsky, according to these accounts, woke the prisoners sometime after midnight, saying that they would have to be immediately evacuated as the White Army approached Ekaterinburg. They dressed quickly, and Yurovsky led them through the house and down a staircase to the basement. Nicholas came first, carrying Alexei in his arms, followed by the empress, the four grand duchesses, Botkin, Kharitonov, Trupp, and finally Demidova, who carried a pillow concealing a box of jewelry.[52] At the southern end of the ground floor, Yurovsky ushered them into an empty room, directly beneath that used by the grand duchesses; chairs were brought for Nicholas, Alexandra, and the sick tsesarevich, and the commandant told them to wait.[53] When he reappeared, Yurovsky was accompanied by an execution squad armed with pistols and revolvers. "Nicholas Alexandrovich," he said to the emperor, "your relatives are trying to save you; therefore we are compelled to shoot you!"[54]

"What?" Nicholas asked.

"This is what!" Yurovsky said, ordering his men to open fire.[55] As the shots rang out, there were "loud cries" and screams.[56] "Death had been instantaneous," reported Robert Wilton, for Nicholas, Alexandra, the three oldest grand duchesses, Botkin, Kharitonov, and Trupp.[57] Alexei, said guard Paul Medvedev, "was still alive and moaned. Yurovsky went up and fired two or three more shots at him. The heir grew still."[58] Anastasia, still alive, "rolled about and screamed," Wilton wrote, "and, when one of the murderers approached, fought desperately with him till he killed her."[59] She finally fell, "pierced by bayonets."[60] Demidova was the last to die. The soldiers grabbed rifles from the corridor, chasing her back and forth across the rear of the cellar room and repeatedly stabbing her with bayonets as she screamed in vain.[61] All of the Romanovs, remembered Medvedev, were "on the floor, with many wounds on their bodies. The blood was running in streams."[62]

On learning of Bolshevik roadblocks and the comings and goings of soldiers in the nearby Koptyaki Forest immediately following the executions, investigators searched the area. In a clearing called the Four Brothers, they found easily recognizable artifacts near and in several disused mine shafts. Gilliard, Gibbes, Tegleva, and other former retainers who had survived the Bolsheviks readily identified these items as having belonged to the Romanovs. There were jewels—large diamonds, an emerald cross given to Alexandra by her mother-in-law, Dowager Empress Marie Feodorovna, pearls, and fragments of sapphires, rubies, and other gems that bore signs of having been subjected to sharp blows; scorched pieces of cloth, belt buckles, buttons, hooks, and eyes that had come from clothing and coats worn by the imperial family; burned bones, clasps, and stays of six corsets believed to have been worn by Alexandra, her four daughters, and Anna Demidova; three small icons and crushed glass vials for smelling salts carried by the grand duchesses; the gold frame of Dr. Botkin's pince-nez and his upper plate of dentures; a badge from the jubilee of Empress Alexandra's military regiment; and the corpse of the spaniel Jemmy, one of the three dogs the Romanovs had brought with them to Siberia.[63]

There were, though, no bodies. Intensive searches of the Four Brothers found only a severed finger, two pieces of skin, and some forty-odd chopped and burned bone fragments that could not even be established as human.[64] Eleven presumed victims had been killed in the Ipatiev House, but their bodies had simply disappeared. Even Sokolov was troubled by the lack of remains, saying, "They must be hidden somewhere."[65] He—and twentieth-century history—found an answer on learning that large quantities of sulfuric acid and gasoline had been delivered to the Koptyaki Forest following the executions;

from this, and from the evidence that jewelry and clothing had been subjected to chopping and burning, Sokolov developed a theory. The corpses, the public was told, had been taken to the forest and there hacked apart, doused with gasoline, and burned; whatever remained was dissolved in acid. This was the theory that filtered out of Siberia, first published in the *Times* of London in 1919 and quickly reprinted around the world as fact.[66] There was, declared Wilton, "not the shadow of a doubt as to what happened."[67]

But there were doubts, and they took wing even before the official investigations had ended. Conflicting rumors and the absence of any corpses soon gave rise to tales of escape and survival that spread first across Siberia and then throughout the world. Nicholas II, it was said, had been dragged away, bound in chains, aboard a mysterious train; Alexei supposedly died from fright after a bomb exploded at the Ipatiev House. Stories declared that the entire family had escaped to Japan; that Kaiser Wilhelm II or King George V had forced the Soviet government to hand over their crowned cousins; even that Pope Benedict XV had organized a rescue of the prisoners and granted them asylum in the Vatican. International journalists, military aides, heads of Allied missions in Siberia, intelligence operatives, and diplomats all eagerly seized upon and disseminated the latest rumors with few attempts at verification, creating an impenetrable web of innuendo that only hinted at some great, unknown mystery.

Rumors were kept alive not only by the possibility that one or more of the Romanovs might have escaped and by the absence of any bodies, but also by the appearance of the first claimants in the case. Princess Elena of Serbia, whose Romanov husband was one of those thrown alive down a mine shaft in Alapayevsk, confronted one early claimant in the autumn of 1918, when the Bolsheviks asked her to meet a young woman said to be a rescued Anastasia. Elena denounced her as a fraud, but this was merely the first of many such putative Romanovs.[68] Just six months after the presumed execution in Ekaterinburg, a woman hiding in a Siberian convent let it be known that she was really Empress Alexandra; the young boy and girl with her, she said, were Alexei and Anastasia. She attracted a fair amount of local attention before the Bolsheviks exposed her as an impostor.[69]

A year after the executions, a young man named Alexei Poutziado appeared in Siberia, claiming to be Tsesarevich Alexei. White Army officials at first ignored the story; after learning that collections were being taken on his behalf by worshipful crowds, however, they had him brought to the city of Omsk and arranged for Pierre Gilliard to confront him. "The door of the next room was opened a little," Gilliard recalled, "and I was able to observe, unknown to him, a boy, taller and stronger

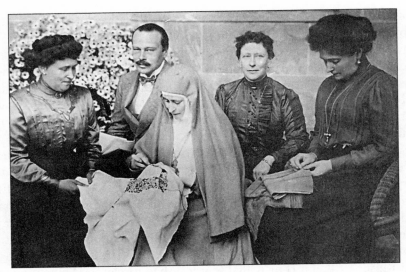

The five Hessian siblings during the 1910 visit to Germany. From left: Irene, Princess Heinrich of Prussia; Grand Duke Ernst Ludwig; Grand Duchess Elizabeth Feodorovna; Princess Victoria of Battenberg (later Marchioness of Milford Haven); and Empress Alexandra.

than the Tsesarevich, who seemed to me fifteen or sixteen years old. His sailor's suit, the color of his hair, and the way it was arranged, were all vaguely reminiscent of Alexei Nikolaievich but there the resemblance ended. . . . The boy was introduced to me and I put several questions to him in French: he remained silent. When a reply was insisted upon, he said that he understood everything I had said but had his own reasons for only speaking Russian. I then addressed him in that language. This, too, brought no results."[70] In the end, Poutziado confessed, to the surprise of no one, that he was not the tsesarevich.

Then there were stories that the Bolsheviks had evacuated the empress and her daughters to the Siberian city of Perm. Rudolf Gaida, who headed the Czechoslovak forces that took Ekaterinburg with the Whites in July 1918, launched his own inquiry into the Romanov case. This uncovered tales, often of Bolshevik origin, in which "witnesses" had encountered the empress and her daughters, caught fleeting glimpses by candlelight of supposed grand duchesses, and even a doctor who claimed that he had treated a battered Anastasia after she had been captured following an escape attempt.[71] None of this was deemed convincing by the White Army—which, after all, hoped to use the dead Romanovs as anti-Bolshevik propaganda—but it did contribute to the growing mythology that surrounded the disappearance and fate of the imperial family.

These early claimants, along with persistent rumors, tangled newspaper reports, and inaccurate diplomatic dispatches, all contributed to the air of uncertainty that hovered over the fate of the Romanovs. In June 1920, Count Paul von Benckendorff, former grand marshal of the imperial court, recorded in his diary, "I am still without definite news with regard to the fate of the Emperor, Empress and their children."[72] A few weeks later, noting the "legends and vague rumors," he reported the latest story that had the Romanovs hiding in the Vatican.[73] In 1922, the empress's friend Lili Dehn wrote in her memoirs, "From time to time reports of the safety of the Imperial Family have reached us, but the next moment we are faced with evidence that the whole of them have perished. God alone knows the truth, but I still permit myself to hope."[74] And a year later, Anna Vyrubova recorded similar sentiments in her own memoirs:

> It is certain that Nicholas II and his family have disappeared behind one of the world's greatest and most tragic mysteries. With them disappeared all of the suite and the servants who were permitted to accompany them to the house in Ekaterinburg. My reason tells me that it is probable that they were all foully murdered, that they are dead and beyond the sorrows of this life forever. But reason is not always amenable. There are many of us in Russia and in exile who, knowing the vastness of the enormous empire, the remoteness of its communications with the outside world, know well the possibilities of imprisoning in monasteries, in mines, in deep forests from which no news can penetrate. We hope.[75]

On July 25, 1918—just a week after the presumed executions—King George V attended a memorial service for his cousin Nicholas II in London. "I hear from Russia," the king wrote in his diary, "that there is every probability that Alicky [Alexandra] and four daughters and little boy were murdered at the same time as Nicky. It's too horrible and shows what fiends these Bolsheviks are. For poor Alicky, perhaps it was best so. But those poor innocent children!"[76] At the time, no one knew quite what to believe. "What has happened to that unfortunate, mistaken Alix, who was in *so* many ways cause of all your misfortune?" Queen Marie of Romania wondered that fall in a letter to Nicholas's sister Grand Duchess Xenia Alexandrovna. "And is little Alexei still alive? How and where are all the girls?"[77]

Even as circumstantial evidence of the mass executions accumulated, some relatives, not surprisingly, clung to hope. In the 1920s, wrote Xenia Alexandrovna's husband, Grand Duke Alexander Mikhailovich, he spent a good deal of time "exhausting my supply of logic and patience in talking to my wife, my sister-in-law, and my mother-in-law, who maintained with all the fervor of real devotion that their brother and son Nicky had been rescued."[78] Dowager Empress Marie Feodorovna, in fact, steadfastly clung to the idea that her son Nicholas II and his family had all escaped execution in Ekaterinburg, a position she held until she died.[79]

Alexandra's sister Irene, Princess Heinrich of Prussia, found news of the presumed executions particularly hard to accept. In a letter to Eleonore, second wife of her brother, Grand Duke Ernst Ludwig of Hesse, Irene noted the conflicting stories but seemed resigned to accept the worst. "I can only hope," she confided, "that the children and Alix died together and unmolested, as they were too beautiful."[80] No one in the empress's family, though, was more traumatized by the events of 1918 than Grand Duke Ernst Ludwig himself. An artistic, sensitive man, he had been emotionally scarred by the early deaths of his hemophiliac brother and of his mother; his first marriage, arranged by his grandmother Queen Victoria against his wishes, failed miserably and ended in a scandalous divorce; and his only daughter had died of typhoid at age eight while on holiday with Nicholas II and his family. A happy second marriage provided him with two sons, but the grand duke lost his throne in the revolution that drove his cousin Kaiser Wilhelm II into exile. For Ernie, as his family called him, the tumult in Russia brought not just the presumed loss of Alexandra and her children, but also of their sister Ella, Grand Duchess Elizabeth Feodorovna, a blow he shared with his remaining sisters but that fell upon a man whose spirit was already bowed by tragedy. So worried was his family about the effect of all this that his wife, Eleonore, conspired with servants and his relatives to deliberately keep devastating reports from Russia from him as long as they could.[81]

Others, though, reconciled themselves to the tragedy. In England, Victoria, Marchioness of Milford Haven, Alexandra's eldest sister, continued to hold out hope through the summer of 1918. Her son Prince Louis, the future Lord Mountbatten, recalled, "How very excited my mother was at the vaguest possibility of one of them having survived the assassination at Ekaterinburg."[82] After King George V told her that early reports confirmed everyone had perished, though, Victoria wrote candidly of her sister Alexandra, "Though her loss is pain & grief to me, yet I am grateful that I can think of her as being at peace now. She, her dear husband & children removed for ever from further suffering."[83] According to Mountbatten, the news, in retrospect, had seemed inevitable: "We were expecting it to take place, we had no reason to doubt it; and there may not have been any proof, but they in those days were not requiring proof. What else could we believe but the worst?"[84]

PART TWO

ANNA ANDERSON

5

Resurrection

DARKNESS CAME EARLY to Berlin on Tuesday, February 17, 1920. By the time Berliners spilled from bureaucratic offices and crowded factories and into the streets, the late winter night had already come to the city. The city was cold, though the seemingly incessant snow of the past few days had finally stopped, replaced by intermittent rain and sleet. It was the biting wind, a chill phantom that swept over the great squares and down urban canyons lined by apartment blocks, that seemed so cold, catching anyone unlucky enough to be out that evening in its determined and icy grasp.

Perhaps the cold somehow seemed more pervasive in light of the struggles through which Berlin had suffered. Just a little over five years had passed since that seemingly glorious, golden summer of 1914, when its two million citizens had enjoyed the sights and sounds of peace and prosperity as a rush of carriages, motorcars, and electric trams endlessly circled the city's broad avenues and magisterial monuments.[1] Bakeries and restaurants had spilled their enticing odors into the streets, where students in school uniforms pushed past fur-wrapped dowagers and top-hatted bureaucrats. Workers and merchants sat at the sidewalk cafés and dance halls of the Tiergarten, filling their stomachs with potatoes, sauerkraut, sausages, bread, and beer, or enjoying the newsreels and comedy shorts that flickered across cinema screens.

Then came August 1914, when Kaiser Wilhelm II declared war on Russia, and Berlin had been swept along in a sudden rush of patriotism. Jubilant crowds had thronged the streets, waving flags and handkerchiefs as troops paraded down the Unter den Linden to the strains of the national anthem. "Life in the Germany of today," recorded one witness, "seems to move to the rhythm of this tune. Every day troops pass by my window on their way to the station, and as they march along to this refrain, people rush to the windows and doors of the houses and take up the song so that it rings through the streets, almost like a solemn vow sung by these men on their way to death."[2]

The months passed, and as hopes for a quick victory faded, the inevitable effects of conflict had slowly, invidiously crept across the German capital. With winter came rationing of food, fuel, and even textiles, as a British naval blockade attempted to starve the Germans into submission and stores ran short of basic supplies. "A deep-seated discontent animated the masses of the population throughout the first winter of the war," recalled one member of the Reichstag.[3] One Berlin resident wrote that the city appeared to be "enveloped in an impenetrable veil of sadness, gray in gray, which no golden ray of sunlight ever seems able to pierce, and which forms a fit setting for the white-faced, black-robed women who glide so sadly through the streets, some bearing their sorrow proudly as a crown to their lives, others bent and broken under a burden too heavy to be borne."[4] Rationing took hold and strangled the city in increasing despair. First the bread ran out, then potatoes; people cut slabs from horses that had fallen from cold and exhaustion in the streets and fed the meat to their starving families. Electricity was inconsistent and heating was unreliable. Thousands stood in food lines through the night, through rain and snow, suffering from cholera and typhus that swelled into epidemics.[5]

After four agonizing years of war, Berlin had slid into chaos. By the autumn of 1918, streets were almost entirely devoid of motorcars for lack of fuel, and the sidewalks were filled with "heart-broken women," deprivation firmly etched in "faces like masks, blue with cold and drawn with hunger."[6] Strikes and demonstrations filled the great squares, eyed with unease by bands of mounted police who patrolled the city day and night.[7] The uncertainty and discontent had finally erupted the first week of November, as rioters took to the streets and shots rang out from barricades manned by both loyalists and by rebels sporting red flags.[8] Revolution was on every tongue. Having lost the support of his people and of his military, Kaiser Wilhelm II had abdicated, escaping to the relative safety of an exile in Holland to avoid the fate that had befallen his Romanov cousins in Russia earlier that summer.

The fragile Weimar Republic had managed to reestablish some semblance of order over a Berlin that swelled in these years with thousands of dispossessed and distraught Russian émigrés. In the years immediately following the Russian Revolution, and not without a bit of irony given the four years of intense hatred and armed conflict that had just ended, Berlin became home to some fifty thousand tsarist émigrés.[9] "At every step," recorded one historian, "you could hear Russian spoken. Dozens of Russian restaurants were opened—with balalaikas, with gypsies, pancakes," all the trappings expected of this bit of refugee St. Petersburg.[10] These émigrés worshipped in Russian Orthodox cathedrals and churches; read their own newspapers and periodicals; ran their own cafés, bookstores, and shops; distributed aid through their own charities; and mourned the passing of the old order in the privacy of their own clubs.[11]

An atmosphere of intrigue and hope dominated the Russian émigré community in Berlin. In their struggles, they keenly followed developments in Russia, and the latest stories concerning the fate of the imperial family. "All our conversation still turned around one subject—the past," recalled Grand Duchess Marie Pavlovna. "This past was like a dusty diamond, which we held to the light in the hope of seeing the sun rays playing through it. We spoke of the past, we looked to it."[12] Scattered from their homeland in a cataclysmic diaspora, former tsarist generals drove taxicabs, once-proud countesses served as maids, elegant courtiers waited tables in crowded cafés, and dispossessed princesses acted as tutors. Most accepted the loss of titles, positions, fortunes, and country with an almost disconcerting resignation, echoing the deeply ingrained Russian belief in *sudba*, an inescapable, inexorable fate. Yet many of these émigrés, even the most pragmatic, clung to their vanished past, convinced that soon all they had lost would be restored: that the fledgling Bolshevik regime would collapse; that once again they would live in their looted palaces and estates; and that their wealth and positions would be restored in a resurgent Russian Empire guided by the twin powers of Orthodoxy and monarchy.

But on that Tuesday night in February 1920, most Berliners, natives and émigrés alike, had gratefully retreated into their houses, apartments, or temporary hotel rooms, and by nine the snow-banked streets were largely deserted. A few trams rumbled along the main avenues, passing beneath the ghostly halos that ringed strings of streetlights stretching into the darkness, but Berlin was nothing if not a creature of habit, and those habits—prim, proudly Protestant, and dominated by the Prussian love of regularity and order—drove most of its citizens toward their beds. It was, after all, a typical winter weeknight, and a weeknight before the frenzied and cosmopolitan cafés and cabarets that became hallmarks of Weimar Berlin had taken hold.

A police officer, a certain Sergeant Hallman, happened to be on patrol that evening, on a route just west of the city center that took him to an area of darkened government offices. As he turned along the spidery length of the Landwehr Canal, he heard a splash. His light swept over the graceful, arched iron bridge spanning the canal and into the dark waters below, where it picked out a struggling figure. Hallman raced over the granite embankment and pulled a young woman to safety.[13] The sergeant quickly appraised the situation. The woman was small, with dark hair, and seemed to be in her twenties. She wore a black wool skirt, black stockings, a light-colored linen blouse, high black boots, and a heavy plaid wool shawl, all completely soaked, but a quick look revealed no obvious injuries.[14]

Hallman asked her name and what had happened, but the woman refused to speak. He could not leave her—he had no idea how she had ended up in the canal, and in any case, if she continued to sit out in the cold night she would undoubtedly freeze to death. The sergeant hurried her down the street and around the corner, to the Elisabeth Hospital on the Lützowstrasse, handing the young woman off to medical staff. Although doctors and nurses questioned her, she would say nothing. Examination showed that she was suffering from nothing more immediately serious than the cold, and after changing into a dry gown she was given a temporary bed for the night, booked into the common ward as "Fraulein Unbekannt," or "Miss Unknown."[15]

A contemporary view of the new Bendler Bridge over the Landwehr Canal in Berlin, where Anna Anderson attempted suicide in February 1920.

The Elisabeth Hospital, Berlin, where Anna Anderson was first taken following her February 1920 suicide attempt.

Over the days that followed, no one could get any information from Fraulein Unbekannt. She refused to give her name, age, or occupation; only reluctantly did she admit that she had tried to kill herself, but would not reveal what had led her to such a grave decision.[16] "Can you understand what it is suddenly to know that everything is lost," she would later say in her defense, "and that you are left entirely alone? Can you understand then that I did what I did?"[17] Her clothing was nondescript, bore no labels, and offered no clues to her identity, nor did the young woman carry any identification papers or even money.[18]

After much prodding, Fraulein Unbekannt finally declared that she had no family. She had, she insisted, no siblings and no parents; her father, she said, had only recently died. She was unmarried but, as one doctor discretely recorded, admitted to "sexual congress," though she refused to answer any intimate questions. Her last admission was that before her suicide attempt, she had been "a working woman."[19] To further questions, she would only say, "I have asked for nothing."[20] She apparently spoke in good, grammatical German, for there was no mention of any linguistic peculiarity aside from some mystery on the origin of her accent: there was talk of a Bavarian or Franconian accent, suggesting that she had perhaps come from southern Germany.[21]

Examination placed Fraulein Unbekannt at 5 feet 2 inches tall, and her weight at 110 pounds.[22] Not knowing where else to turn for clues to the patient's identity, the doctors noted that she had, at some point in the past, suffered from physical violence, though precisely what, and to what extent, later became a matter of some contention; in addition to older scars, it was said that her body bore "many

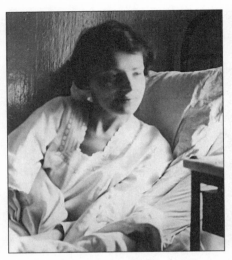

Fraulein Unbekannt at Dalldorf, 1920.

lacerations."[23] If she was indeed covered with "many lacerations," they must have been minor, as no examining physician thought them serious enough to record at any length. They may simply have been abrasions suffered in her suicide attempt and subsequent rescue.

But a legend later arose, one that portrayed Fraulein Unbekannt as severely battered and her body intensely scarred by violence when she was pulled from the Landwehr Canal. One doctor, Josef Knapp, spoke of "two distinct deepenings in the parietal bones" of her head, "one right on top and affecting both parietals, another on the left side." These he called "distinct artifacts," and speculated that they had been "caused by some accident or act of violence."[24] Author Harriet von Rathlef-Keilmann, who first marshaled and published evidence in Fraulein Unbekannt's case, insisted that the patient bore "a scar behind her right ear that doctors stated was due to a glancing bullet wound."[25] This, she said, was so deep that a finger could be inserted into the channel "when touching it."[26] Then there was Professor Serge Rudnev, who declared that the X-rays showed "cicatrized bone" in Fraulein Unbekannt's right frontal lobe or temple and in the right occipital or rear skull, damage he believed had been caused by heavy blows to the head and that had caused a hemorrhage.[27]

In fact, none of this was true, but it was all repeated endlessly until it became accepted fact. No other physician ever described the depressions recalled by Knapp, who made his statement four years after the fact and from memory; no medical report or X-ray recorded the extensive cranial damage suggested by Rudnev; and no doctor supported Rathlef-Keilmann's idea that a glancing bullet had left a deep channel behind the patient's ear.[28] The physical damage Fraulein Unbekannt had suffered was quite real, but it was not as severe as history has been led to believe.

In all, ten physicians who examined Fraulein Unbekannt in the first decade following her suicide attempt left some written record or comment on her physical injuries. This number included five German general practitioners: Dr. Winicke of the Elisabeth Hospital; Dr. Friedrich Reiche of Berlin's Dalldorf asylum; Dr. Karl Sonnenschein of Berlin's St. Mary's Hospital; Dr. Josef Knapp, who was in private practice; and a Dr. Graefe, who had some expertise in tuberculosis; a tubercular specialist and Russian émigré named Professor Serge Rudnev; two physicians, Lothar Nobel and Karl Bonhoeffer, of the Mommsen Clinic in Berlin; Dr. Theodor Eitel, a specialist in internal medicine at the Stillachhaus Sanatorium in Bavaria; and Dr. Hans Willige of the Ilten asylum near Hannover. Bonhoeffer, uniquely, had access to all of the early medical records that were later lost.[29] From these accounts, it is possible to finally establish the nature and extent of Fraulein Unbekannt's past injuries.

Contrary to the reports of Knapp, Rathlef-Keilmann, and Rudnev, the damage to Fraulein Unbekannt's skull was minimal. Friedrich Reiche reported no injuries to the top or rear of her skull; X-rays and further physical examination also revealed "no deformities and no gross external injuries or damage." Bonhoeffer could find no "serious external lesions to the skull," and pointed out that while personally inspecting her head he found "no deformation or any indication of scarring" along the top of the cranium. The only sign of previous injury to the skull, noted by Reiche and confirmed by Bonhoeffer, was a narrow scar of 2 to 3 centimeters (approximately 0.79 inch to 1.2 inches) behind her right ear, which left a "superficial furrow." This was so shallow that it did not appear in any X-rays, contrary to what Knapp, Rathlef-Keilmann, and Rudnev claimed.[30] This limited damage also was confirmed by physicians Lothar Nobel, Theodor Eitel, and Hans Willige. "The top of the skull seems to display no distinct impressions," Nobel reported.[31] Eitel noted "a superficial scar behind the right ear"; this, however, was the only wound he found on her skull.[32] And Willige recorded a scar "about 3 centimeters long" above and slightly behind the right ear, beneath which he thought he could "detect a slight depression in the bone."[33]

If there was no significant damage to the skull—no bullet channel, no deep impressions, no hemorrhage from fractures—Fraulein Unbekannt had suffered some heavy blow or blows to her face. The ethmoid bone, separating the nasal cavity from the brain, had been fractured, as had both her upper and lower jawbones.[34] Although the ethmoid bone is easily damaged, blows of considerable force would have been necessary to fracture both jaws. This blunt force trauma had likely done significant damage to her teeth. When she was pulled from the Landwehr Canal, Fraulein Unbekannt was missing eight teeth, five in her upper jaw and three in the lower jaw, and at least seven more were loose in the gums.[35]

There were other scars, some so minor that few of the examining physicians even bothered to report them. There was apparently a very faint scar on her forehead; a "small white scar" on her right shoulder blade; and a scar of some 2 centimeters on her middle left finger, which left it slightly stiff.[36] On the upper chest, in the middle of the sternum, was a small scar; Rudnev thought that this might have been caused by a stab wound, but in this he was challenged by Drs. Reiche, Graefe, Bonhoeffer, and Eitel, all of whom deemed it "the probable result of a tubercular bone fistula."[37] And just below this was an area of discoloration, "round bluish-brown marks" on Fraulein Unbekannt's upper stomach.[38] Rudnev suggested that this might be the result of a powder burn from a possible gunshot wound; Reiche and Bonhoeffer, though, believed it was a "compressive injury resulting in edema," as if the patient had been forcefully struck in the torso and hemorrhaged.[39]

Fraulein Unbekannt bore two final physical peculiarities. On the right foot was a scar of just over half an inch in diameter, visible on both the top and the sole.[40] This was a transpiercing wound, the clear result of some object having been driven through the foot. Later there were assertions that this left either a triangular or star-shaped scar; in fact, no medical report seems to have documented its appearance or suggested that it had any recognizable shape.[41] And, like Anastasia, Fraulein Unbekannt suffered from *hallux valgus*. Doctors described this as "a pronounced abduction of the big toe" on her right foot; it was also present, though to a lesser degree, on her left foot.[42] Only Rudnev, who had no expertise in podiatric issues, suggested this was so severe that it must have been present since childhood.[43]

Fraulein Unbekannt's scars, at least the damaged jaws, indicated that she had suffered violence in her past. No one, though, could convince her to talk about her experiences, and no one at the Elisabeth Hospital knew what to do with her. There was nothing particularly bizarre in her behavior beyond her apparent desire for anonymity, but observation seemed to indicate that the patient might be suffering from some form of mental illness. She spent her time sitting in her bed or staring vacantly out of the windows; when approached by hospital staff, she apparently turned to the wall or attempted to cover her head with a blanket. She simply wanted to be left alone.[44] All anyone knew was that Fraulein Unbekannt had appeared mysteriously, just one of many dispossessed in a chaotic city where most people were completely consumed with the exigencies of daily life, and refused to reveal her identity.

Near the end of March 1920, after six frustrating weeks, authorities at the Elisabeth Hospital decided to transfer Fraulein Unbekannt to the State Institute for Welfare and Care in northwestern Berlin's Wittenau district, commonly called Dalldorf.[45] This was a much larger hospital, with twelve hundred patients divided among separated brick buildings and wards according to their physical or mental needs. Doctors at Dalldorf described their new patient as "very haughty. Refuses to reveal her name, origins, age, or profession. Remained seated in a stubborn manner. Refuses to speak, indicating that she has reasons and already said everything at the Elisabeth Hospital. . . . The doctor could believe what he liked, but she would say nothing to him. When asked if she heard voices or saw things, she replied haughtily, 'Oh, I am sure you are much smarter than I am, doctor.' She acknowledged her suicide attempt, but refused to give her reason or offer any explanation." Provisionally diagnosed with "a depressive mental illness," she was given a bed in Ward B, where fourteen other patients deemed to be nonaggressive also were housed.[46]

The appearance of one mysterious, unknown, and distinctly uncooperative young woman in this large, unstable city was cause for little attention, but authorities did attempt to investigate. On April 28, 1920, the Berlin Police Office of Missing Persons released three photographs of Fraulein Unbekannt along with particulars of her case; these were sent to various hospitals and asylums in the belief that she may previously have been treated in the city. The only response came from an asylum near Spandau, but further inquiries proved fruitless.[47] Based on a suggestion that the patient's voice bore some trace of a Slavic accent, several Polish families with missing relatives met Fraulein Unbekannt, but with no results.[48]

On June 17, police again questioned Fraulein Unbekannt and collected what little information authorities at Dalldorf had gathered. The patient was fingerprinted and made to pose for two more photographs, one full face and one in profile. This she tried to resist: Fraulein Unbekannt could only be photographed when warders held her in place, and even then she tried to distort her features before the camera lens.[49] It is likely that this represented an attempt to thwart any identification, particularly given what happened next. Already missing eight teeth when admitted to Dalldorf, Fraulein Unbekannt complained to Dr. Gorz, the asylum dentist, of constant pain. Gorz found that her lower incisors, which had been allowed to grow in at an acute angle, were loose, as were another five teeth: in all, seven teeth, deemed too damaged or rotted to be saved, were extracted.[50] Inexplicably, though, Gorz complied with her request that an upper incisor, which was apparently healthy, also be removed, in what one nurse believed was a deliberate attempt to alter the appearance of her mouth.[51] This left Fraulein Unbekannt with sixteen missing teeth, including nearly all of those in her upper front jaw, and slightly distorted the shape of her mouth, something that led her to habitually cover her lips with a handkerchief when speaking.[52]

At some point, after several months of investigation and inquiry, the Berlin police seem to have washed their hands of an apparently unsolvable case. Fraulein Unbekannt was left alone, isolated at Dalldorf, her identity as much a mystery as when she had been pulled from the Landwehr Canal.

+   +   +

FOR ALMOST NINETEEN months, Fraulein Unbekannt lay in her bed at Dalldorf, silent about her name or former life, largely unresponsive, and communicating only occasionally with members of the staff. She remained an enigma to all who encountered her, a physically and presumably psychologically damaged young woman whose situation confounded those tending to her welfare. It was not, those treating her thought, that she did not know who she was, but rather that for some unknown reason she simply refused to reveal her identity. Anna Malinovsky, a twenty-three-year-old native of Kulm in what is today Poland, began working at Dalldorf on July 21, 1921, a year after the arrival of Fraulein Unbekannt.[53] Malinovsky, who went by the name of Thea, later spoke of the patient's "restraint. She kept mainly to her bed, usually covering her face with the blankets. She rarely spoke to anyone." Malinovsky recalled that she, like the other nurses on duty, had been asked to "carefully listen to anything she said that might indicate her identity." Attempting to describe the patient's behavior, the former nurse declared that she had "acted always as an educated lady," someone who was "very, very polite," who "behaved decently to everyone" despite her reserve.[54] She was left, she explained, with the impression of "a lady of the highest class of society."[55]

These conversations took place in German. According to Malinovsky, Fraulein Unbekannt spoke "impeccable German." Malinovsky also recalled, "I often spoke Polish to her, especially to tell jokes and chat. Of course, she did not answer me, but I could tell from her attitude and my impressions that she understood me." She thought that the patient spoke with what she termed a "very light" Slavic accent.[56]

More intriguing were claims that while at Dalldorf Fraulein Unbekannt spoke Russian with numerous members of the nursing staff and doctors.[57] The evidence, however, does not support such a conclusion. Nurse Bertha Walz recalled, "I never heard that Fraulein Unbekannt spoke Russian"; nurse Emilie Barfknecht said, "To my knowledge Fraulein Unbekannt spoke no Russian," though in her sleep the patient had mumbled in a language other than German; and Malinovsky stated that not only had she never spoken Russian with the patient but also that "I never heard from anyone else that Fraulein Unbekannt had spoken Russian."[58] In fact, only one nurse, Erna Buchholz, claimed to have conversed with Fraulein Unbekannt in Russian during her stay at Dalldorf.[59] Buchholz was a Latvian from the town of Libau; Latvia, like the other Baltic provinces, had formed part of the Russian Empire. She spoke of an encounter with the patient that she placed from memory sometime in the summer of 1920: "I asked her if she also knew how to speak Russian. She replied, 'yes,' and thereafter we spoke Russian together. She did not speak broken Russian, but rather she spoke without restraint, in complete, commanding and coherent sentences."[60] But Buchholz then added something confusing: according to her, the patient "scarcely spoke Russian like a native, nor yet like a foreigner who had learned Russian."[61] This certainly suggests that Fraulein Unbekannt bore a peculiar accent, though it is telling that Buchholz thought that her Russian was not that of a native speaker at a time when so much speculation swirled over her possible Eastern origins.

When not sleeping or sitting silently in her bed, Fraulein Unbekannt spent her days at Dalldorf reading. She liked to read. Patients had access to the institute's library, which contained a number of books, illustrated magazines, and newspapers.[62] A review of the asylum records showed that she read "newspapers and books" and that even from her hospital bed she "followed political events with some interest."[63] Malinovsky also remembered that Fraulein Unbekannt "read often," including the works of several Russian authors that the nurse herself brought for the patient.[64] And a fellow patient at Dalldorf recalled that although she would speak only German, Fraulein Unbekannt often asked for and received books in English and French, again presumably brought in for her by members of the asylum's staff.[65]

The details of what happened next became a matter of some confusion. Later, none of the four Dalldorf nurses could quite recall exactly when Fraulein Unbekannt began to hint about her alleged identity or what had been said. It was a magazine that led to the intrigue, the October 23, 1921, issue of the popular German weekly periodical *Berliner Illustrirte Zeitung*. From the cover stared a ghostly echo of Russia's recent troubled past, a large photograph of Grand Duchesses Tatiana, Marie, and Anastasia Nikolaievna, all beautifully fragile and smiling wistfully for the camera of Pierre Gilliard shortly after the Revolution. "*Lebt eine Zarentochter?*" (Is One of the Tsar's Daughters Alive?) the caption asked dramatically. Within, an account of the imperial family's captivity and execution in Siberia ended with a dramatic flourish: "To this day, it has not been possible to definitively establish if, during the massacre, one of the Grand Duchesses, Anastasia, was not merely severely wounded, and if she remained alive."[66]

One day, Bertha Walz showed the magazine to Emilie Barfknecht and to Fraulein Unbekannt. When the patient looked at the photographs, Walz said, her "behavior became quite altered." The nurse pointed to one of the grand duchesses pictured, which one she could not recall, commenting on rumors that she had survived; but the patient "corrected me" and indicated that it was a different imperial daughter who had escaped.[67] A photograph taken in Tobolsk, Barfknecht recalled, provoked Fraulein Unbekannt to comment that "in that house, the Tsar's family had always been watched by soldiers, who very often were rough and displayed a lack of discipline."[68] Even more intriguingly, the patient showed Erna Buchholz an image of the Romanovs, saying, "I knew all of these people."[69]

But it was Thea Malinovsky who heard the full story, or as much of it as Fraulein Unbekannt was willing to reveal. One night in the autumn of 1921, Malinovsky sat at her desk in Ward B. After the other patients had fallen asleep, she spotted Fraulein Unbekannt sitting up in her bed, staring at her. Suddenly the patient crept across the ward, took a chair beside the desk, and began to talk, slowly at first, mentioning nothing of particular importance, until she finally declared that she wanted to show the nurse something. "She went back to her bed and from beneath the mattress pulled out a copy of the *Berliner Illustrirte*," Malinovsky remembered. "There was a picture of the Tsar's family on the cover." Fraulein Unbekannt handed the magazine to the nurse "and asked if I was struck by anything in the picture. I looked carefully at the picture, but had no idea what she meant. On closer examination, I noticed that Fraulein Unbekannt bore a certain resemblance to the Tsar's youngest daughter. But I was careful not to indicate this to her."[70]

Dissatisfied with this, Fraulein Unbekannt again pointed at Anastasia, urging Malinovsky to look more closely, but the nurse professed confusion. "Don't you see any resemblance between the two of us?" the patient demanded. When Malinovsky admitted to this, Fraulein Unbekannt suddenly grew "very excited." Uncertain what to do, the nurse asked if she was the grand duchess. The patient said nothing. It was, Malinovsky recalled, "as if she was stuck," and uncertain what to say next. Then Fraulein Unbekannt's "entire body shook" and her face "turned red with agitation" as she rewarded

The October 23, 1921, issue of the *Berliner Illustrirte Zeitung*.

Malinovsky with a rush of details. Fraulein Unbekannt spoke of the murder of her family, of losing consciousness, and of waking in the back of a peasant cart, badly injured. A Polish soldier had saved her and spirited her out of Russia to Romania, selling pieces of jewelry concealed beneath her clothing along the way to pay expenses. At some point this man had brought her to Berlin, where she had been found in the Landwehr Canal. She was, she announced, the youngest daughter of Tsar Nicholas II, Grand Duchess Anastasia.[71]

6

Fraulein Unbekannt

ANASTASIA: THAT WAS what Fraulein Unbekannt had said. It was a stunning, dramatic turn in the intrigue over this mysterious young woman's identity. And one that might have remained a secret, as the patient wished when she swore the Dalldorf nurses to secrecy, but for the admission of a certain Marie Clara Peuthert to the asylum on December 18, 1921. Her thirty-three days at Dalldorf forever altered the course of Fraulein Unbekannt's life and propelled her claim into the pages of history.[1] A highly strung, emotional woman of fifty, Peuthert, having suffered an attack of nerves, swept into Dalldorf trailing an air of intrigue and mystery in her wake.[2] Although German, she had lived in Russia, letting it be known that before the Revolution she had been employed in Moscow by the aristocratic Novikhov family as a house dressmaker.[3] While she had indeed once lived in Russia, there was some doubt about her real history, including claims that she had worked for German intelligence during World War I.[4] Peuthert soon befriended Fraulein Unbekannt and spent hours sharing intimacies with her in Dalldorf's Ward B. Precisely what next occurred remains a mystery. Although the usual story has Peuthert confronting Fraulein Unbekannt and insisting that she has recognized her, this is not what happened, at least according to Peuthert. When prompted, she said, Fraulein Unbekannt "did not answer my questions as to her real name or descent," though she did often speak about the Russian imperial family. She, too, showed Fraulein Unbekannt the October 1921 issue of the *Berliner Illustrierte Zeitung*, leafing through the pages and listening as she commented on the images from Tobolsk and Ekaterinburg.

"In further conversations," Peuthert recalled, "Fraulein Unbekannt dropped some hints that finally led me to believe that she was a rescued daughter of the Tsar."[5]

Peuthert was excited over this apparent discovery, recalled nurse Emilie Barfknecht, but Fraulein Unbekannt seemed distressed.[6] Peuthert mentioned no name, at least at this time. Barfknecht, though, thought Fraulein Unbekannt most resembled one grand duchess in particular; when she showed the photograph to the mysterious patient, Fraulein Unbekannt readily identified her as Anastasia.[7] But when Peuthert was released from the asylum on January 20, 1922, she began insisting that she had discovered a rescued Grand Duchess Tatiana. Sure that she had solved a great mystery, Peuthert was determined to find someone—anyone—who could confirm her beliefs.

A few months later, one Sunday afternoon, an émigré named Nicholas von Schwabe stood in the forecourt of Berlin's Russian Orthodox cathedral on Unter den Linden, selling anti-Semitic pamphlets, when "an elderly, dark-haired, very poorly dressed woman" approached him. It was Peuthert. She eyed his collection of booklets and postcards before whispering that she possessed sensitive information on the Romanovs. After von Schwabe assured her that as a former staff captain in the Cuirassiers Life Guards Regiment of Dowager Empress Marie Feodorovna he was completely trustworthy, Peuthert confessed, "In a Berlin lunatic asylum a person called Fraulein Unbekannt is kept, who greatly resembles Grand Duchess Tatiana. I am personally convinced that she is so."[8]

Von Schwabe was sufficiently intrigued to pursue the matter, and after another meeting with Peuthert and a discussion with a friend named Franz Jaenicke, the trio visited the asylum. It was Wednesday, March 8. When they approached the bed in Ward B, Fraulein Unbekannt pulled the sheet up to her face and turned to the wall; she was largely silent, insisting that she could not speak Russian. "She asked what I wanted," von Schwabe recalled. He tried to befriend her, offering a copy of his magazine, but when shown a photograph of Dowager Empress Marie Feodorovna, she "looked at it a long time," then declared, "I do not know that lady."[9] Later, said Emilie Barfknecht, Fraulein Unbekannt commented that the visitors had "shown her a picture of her grandmother."[10]

Despite these uncertainties, von Schwabe went straight to the Supreme Monarchist Council, alerting them to the possibility that a rescued Grand Duchess Tatiana was a patient at Dalldorf.[11] Formed in 1921 by Nicholas Markov, a former deputy in Russia's parliament, the Duma, the Supreme Monarchist Council in Berlin acted as a center for émigré life and assistance; von Schwabe himself helped

edit the council's virulently anti-Semitic, promonarchist journal
Dvouglavy Orel (Double Eagle) and other tracts alleging Masonic plots
and a Jewish ritual murder of the Romanovs.[12] These publications,
widely distributed and avidly believed within the émigré community,
reflected the burgeoning mythology that wrapped the Romanovs in
a mantle of martyrdom. For some, the idea of a grand duchess who
miraculously survived the massacre in Ekaterinburg conflicted with
anti-Soviet propaganda that portrayed the Bolsheviks, to a man, as
ruthless and savage murderers. Others, though, were more receptive
to the notion. According to tsarist law, Nicholas II's daughters could
only inherit the throne after all male members of the dynasty; in
1922 there were more than two dozen such male Romanovs who had
survived the Revolution and escaped Russia. But what was in force
before 1917 might, some speculated, no longer be valid; at the very
least, within émigré circles filled with nostalgia for their martyred
tsar and lost empire, a surviving grand duchess offered a sentimental
figurehead around whom the community could rally, someone who,
even if she held no actual power, certainly would wield enormous
influence over political affairs and the social life of Russian exiles.

    This was the dilemma now faced by the Supreme Monarchist
Council in Berlin. In the end, though, filled with hope, and their emotions still raw from the tragedy of the Revolution, officials took Peuthert
seriously, contacting Zenaide Tolstoy, an aristocratic lady who had lived
at Tsarskoye Selo and been friendly with the imperial family. On Friday,
March 10, accompanied by Schwabe and several others, Tolstoy called
on the patient at Dalldorf, who greeted her visitors with a repeat performance of her earlier behavior, turning to the wall and attempting
to conceal her features behind a sheet. When, eventually, she showed
her face, Tolstoy thought that she detected some resemblance between
the eyes of the patient and those of Nicholas II. Fraulein Unbekannt
was agitated throughout the encounter, and when Tolstoy showed her
postcards of the imperial family, signed photographs of the grand duchesses, and letters from the Romanovs, she apparently began to cry.[13]
Tolstoy left the asylum saying she had recognized the patient as the
second of Nicholas and Alexandra's daughters. Later, though, once it
became clear that Fraulein Unbekannt insisted that she was Anastasia,
Tolstoy changed her mind, insisting that she now recognized her as the
youngest grand duchess; after several months she abandoned even this
position, rejecting her altogether, only to express doubts later.[14]

    As the second week of March 1922 began, word of Tolstoy's recog-
nition of a rescued Grand Duchess Tatiana at Dalldorf quickly spread
through the Russian émigré community in Berlin, and the Supreme
Monarchist Council had no reason to doubt her veracity. On March 11

they dispatched a former officer north to Kiel, where Empress Alexandra's sister Princess Irene and her husband, Prince Heinrich of Prussia, lived at their estate, Hemmelmark. Also living here was Baroness Sophie Buxhoeveden, Alexandra's former lady-in-waiting who had escaped the Bolsheviks and eventually made her way to Europe. Just four years had passed since Buxhoeveden had last seen the grand duchesses during the journey from Tobolsk to Ekaterinburg, making the baroness one of those best placed to render a verdict on the claimant, and Princess Irene asked her to go to Berlin and assess the young woman at Dalldorf.[15]

Peuthert somehow learned of the visit and ran to Dalldorf, shouting warnings. By the time the baroness arrived, Fraulein Unbekannt was nervously peering out from behind the sheet she held to her face. She turned to Peuthert and whispered a few questions in German. "I attempted to attract the young woman's attention," Buxhoeveden later said, "caressing her hair and speaking to her in English." She called her "Darling" several times, but the claimant "made no reply, and I saw that she did not understand a word of what I had said," nor was there "anything in her eyes to indicate that she had recognized me," Buxhoeveden declared. She showed her an icon commemorating the Romanov Tercentenary in 1913, as well as a ring that had once belonged to Empress Alexandra, but "none of these things seemed to evoke in her the slightest recognition. She remained completely indifferent." Attempting to save the situation, Peuthert stepped in, whispering to the patient, showing her photographs of the imperial family and prompting her rather obviously, "Tell me, isn't that Mama?" But Fraulein Unbekannt seemed oblivious to these efforts, refusing to talk and redoubling her attempts to conceal her face.[16]

Finally, in exasperation, Buxhoeveden grabbed the sheets and pulled them back so that she could fully examine the patient's face. "There was some resemblance in her eyes and forehead to Grand Duchess Tatiana," she recorded, "but this disappeared as soon as her full face was revealed." She thought that the shape of the face and the features were wrong. "Her hair was lighter in color, some of her teeth were missing, and the ones that remained did not resemble those of the Grand Duchess."[17] Despite repeated requests, Fraulein Unbekannt refused to leave her bed so that the baroness could judge her height. Finally, Buxhoeveden simply grabbed her and pulled the claimant to her feet. "Rather stupidly," wrote Lord Mountbatten, Buxhoeveden then declared, "You can't be Grand Duchess Tatiana, who was much taller than me. Only Grand Duchess Anastasia was shorter than me."[18]

With this, Buxhoeveden left Dalldorf. The claimant's supporters later insisted that the baroness had rejected her too quickly, and that had she remained longer and studied her face she would have recognized the patient as Anastasia. This Buxhoeveden refuted, insisting that the claimant "did not in the least physically resemble" the youngest grand duchess.[19] Fraulein Unbekannt later complained that the encounter had been "dreadful"; she explained that she had refused to show her face or to speak because she was "ashamed of my past experiences."[20] Buxhoeveden made no public statement; unaware of her rejection, many émigrés in Berlin considered the matter open, and soon the curious, the concerned, and the convinced flocked to Dalldorf to see for themselves the woman who might be their emperor's daughter. At all times of the day, Malinovsky recalled, there was a constant crush of visitors around Fraulein Unbekannt's bed, attempting to question her, staring at her, and showering her with candy, flowers, and books.[21]

Among these visitors were Russian émigrés Baron Arthur von Kleist and his wife, Marie, alerted by their friend Madame Tolstoy to the possible grand duchess at Dalldorf. Before the Revolution, von Kleist had been an unimportant Tsarist bureaucrat, chief of a provincial police district in Poland.[22] They came to Fraulein Unbekannt with gifts and sat by her bed in Ward B to keep her company. At first, the baroness thought, the claimant was "very frightened," and rarely spoke; when she did talk, it was in German, "with a somewhat foreign accent, Russian, or perhaps Polish," said the baroness, "but it struck me as being more Russian than anything else." In time, Fraulein Unbekannt seemed to trust the baroness, and the two women spent hours looking at the latest magazines, discussing the newest fashions.[23]

Fewer than two weeks after Tolstoy's first visit to Dalldorf, the von Kleists had requested that Fraulein Unbekannt be discharged into their care, "out of humanitarian reasons," the baron explained, adding that he would see to her needs "according to my means."[24] In the spring of 1922, word somehow reached Fraulein Unbekannt that officials were considering moving her from the protective cocoon she had established at Dalldorf to another asylum, in Brandenburg; panicked, she sent for von Schwabe and asked if she might live with the von Kleists.[25] Everyone was in agreement, although the baroness recalled that on hearing this, one asylum official "asked us if we knew what we were undertaking." The baron assured the man that they believed in her identity and would assume responsibility for her expenses. On May 30, 1922, after 792 days, a "happy, radiant" Fraulein Unbekannt, as the baroness recalled, left Dalldorf and moved in with the aristocratic couple.[26]

The von Kleists had never met Grand Duchess Anastasia, but they were certain that the young woman they welcomed into their home was indeed the youngest daughter of Nicholas II. Their luxurious apartment, which occupied the entire fourth floor of a building at 9 Nettelbeckstrasse in the Charlottenburg district of Berlin, now became home to the enigmatic young woman from Dalldorf.[27] The von Kleists provided Fraulein Unbekannt with her own room, in a household staffed with servants, and clothing borrowed from their two married daughters, Frau Irmgard Freund and Frau Anna Reim (the two youngest von Kleist daughters, Irina and Gerda, still lived with their parents). At first Fraulein Unbekannt was largely left alone to do as she pleased, although soon enough an endless succession of Russian émigrés, former tsarist officers, dedicated monarchists, and the simply curious plagued the apartment, intent on seeing for themselves the supposed grand duchess.[28]

From the first, the claimant despised such attention, often refusing to leave her bedroom if a crowd had assembled to see her; she even took most of her meals in private, and only rarely would she join the family at the dinner table.[29] Despite these tensions, she at first found life with the baron and his family quite tolerable. They bought her new dresses from Berlin's most fashionable stores, and took her on outings to museums and to the Hohenzollern palaces in nearby Potsdam.[30] The numerous émigrés also brought her magazines, newspapers, and books about her presumed Romanov family, along with souvenir albums, photographs, and postcards, all of which she greatly treasured.[31] Nicholas von Schwabe recalled that she "constantly asked me to bring her photographs of the Imperial Family."[32] Her compilation stretched to include Romanov aunts, uncles, and cousins, and also Empress Alexandra's Hessian relatives and members of European royal families, all of which Fraulein Unbekannt kept in careful order. She could often be found sitting alone, these images spread out around her, as she studied faces for hours, although when visitors entered the room she would often shove the images beneath a blanket.[33]

Gerda von Kleist, the baron's youngest daughter, later commented that even in these early days the claimant "paid absolutely no attention" to actively advancing her case.[34] This was quite true. Her only concession was to clarify her asserted identity—a necessity given Peuthert's belief that she was Tatiana. At the end of her first week with the von Kleists, the baron pressed the issue, handing her a paper on which he had written the names of all four of Nicholas and Alexandra's daughters and asking who she was. She took a pen and underlined the name "Anastasia"; a few weeks later, she repeated this to the baroness.[35] This resolved one issue, but no one knew precisely what to call her—"Fraulein Unbekannt" no longer seemed appropriate, but neither did "Your Imperial Highness." The claimant resolved the issue, asking that the von Kleists "not observe" the etiquette her alleged position as a grand duchess would have demanded, and settled on temporarily being called "Fraulein Annie."[36]

Fraulein Annie offered little proof to support her claim in these early days, though occasionally odd little incidents seemed compelling. One day, it was later said, Zenaide Tolstoy was visiting the von Kleist apartment, sitting at the piano in the drawing room and idly playing a waltz. The claimant, on hearing the tune, was said to have reacted in "shock" and erupted into tears; Tolstoy's brother had composed the song and she herself had often played it for the grand duchesses at Tsarskoye Selo before the Revolution. Tolstoy took this as convincing evidence that the claimant was Anastasia, for who else would have recognized such an obscure tune?[37]

The "Piano Story" soon became famous in the mythology of the claimant's case, yet as a piece of evidence it was seriously flawed. In her own affidavit on the case, Tolstoy made no mention of this supposedly pivotal incident, a curious omission if it had actually revealed what she took to be the claimant's intimate knowledge.[38] In fact, it was Baroness Marie von Kleist who repeated the story, apparently secondhand from her husband, several years after it supposedly occurred. In her statement, she recorded simply, "Frau Tolstoy sat at the piano and played waltzes from the old days. After this, Frau Tolstoy told me she was convinced that 'Fraulein Unbekannt' was Grand Duchess Anastasia."[39] There was nothing here of the claimant's reaction, and no indication that she had recognized the tune.

There were other curiosities, things that seemed somehow just a bit suspect. Early in her stay with the von Kleists, Fraulein Annie asked the baron to inform her relatives in Paris of her survival. "I pointed out to her," he recorded, "that it would be better not to notify her relatives in Paris, for in my opinion, it would be proper first to inform her relatives who were in Denmark."[40] The baron thought it odd that Anastasia would not immediately think of her grandmother Dowager Empress Marie Feodorovna in Copenhagen, or even of Empress Alexandra's siblings in Germany. She also asked him to contact Nicholas II's sister Grand Duchess Xenia Alexandrovna: "I liked this aunt best," she told him, "and I am sure she will recognize me better than any other aunts." Xenia Alexandrovna, she declared, had called her "Astouchka." "When reminded of this," she told the baron, "she will have no doubt as to my identity."[41] Von Kleist wrote to the grand duchess mentioning this assertion, but Xenia Alexandrovna quickly replied that she had never referred to her niece by such a nickname and that the word meant nothing to her.[42] It was even more curious given that Xenia's sister Olga Alexandrovna had been closest to her nieces and had actually been Anastasia's godmother. On another occasion, the von Kleists invited their doctor to dinner, but did not introduce him to the claimant; when Gerda von Kleist later asked Fraulein Annie if she recognized him as someone "very important in your life," the claimant first insisted that he was a stranger, only to admit, "I do know him, of course. I just cannot recall if he is a duke or a prince."[43]

Even more peculiar was Fraulein Annie's reluctance to speak Russian. "We always tried to get her to speak Russian," recalled Gerda von Kleist, "but she never would."[44] At first, Fraulein Annie said that "although I know Russian," speaking it "awakens in me extremely painful memories. The Russians did so much harm to me and my family."[45] Her supporters largely accepted this, though soon she also blamed her injuries, saying that her memory was impaired. "If you knew how terrible it is," she once declared. "Most dreadful of all, I do not find the Russian again. All forgotten."[46] In June 1922, Fraulein Annie, suffering from both anemia and the early onset of tuberculosis, collapsed. The von Kleists summoned their family physician, T. A. Schiller, who treated the claimant throughout the summer. "In her sleep," he noted, "she speaks Russian with good pronunciation; mostly inessential things."[47] It is not known, however, precisely who determined this; it was certainly not Schiller, for on the margin of the report he wrote, "Supposed to have done so."[48] Then there were reports, all rather unsatisfactory, that during her stay with the von Kleists the claimant had cried out in both Russian and Polish.[49] On the other hand, Fraulein Annie clearly understood Russian; when questioned in the language, she provided correct replies, albeit in German.[50] Because she complained of an inability to concentrate and a damaged memory, the baron took to reading aloud to his guest from the numerous books and magazines with stories about the Romanovs; these were in both Russian and in German. She understood when von Kleist read the Russian texts, but all discussions took place, at her request, in German.[51]

Fraulein Annie settled into life at the von Kleist apartment and very soon the family discovered just how apt the warnings from the Dalldorf official had been, for she was a distinctly odd guest. One moment, she might be sitting quietly, staring at her growing collection of photographs and postcards of the Romanovs, or conversing politely, only to suddenly erupt in tears and flee to the security of her bed; attempts at amiability alternated with displays of temper that left the family aghast at her rude manner.[52] Her moods were variable, and she seemed to alternate between aristocratic disdain and curious bursts of distinctly unregal behavior. Gerda von Kleist, who was just sixteen when Fraulein Annie came to live with them, despised the claimant and was convinced that the woman was no grand duchess. She later described her as an ill-mannered young woman completely lacking in any social abilities, "someone without any culture," she insisted, who had once darted beneath the dining table to wipe her nose.[53]

This emotional volatility and rapidly accumulating mass of contradictory evidence resulted in numerous scenes and an increasing tension that traumatized the household and pitted members of the von Kleist family against each other. The baroness always remained an adamant supporter, but the baron, who initially believed that his guest was Anastasia, later backed away from this position, and no one could quite agree if he was hero or villain. "He went to immense trouble to solve the mystery," one contemporary declared, "and made no secret of his first conviction that the alleged Grand Duchess was genuine. It is, however, true that he may have possessed ulterior motives, as was intimated within the émigré community. Should the old regime ever be restored in Russia, he hoped great benefits would arise from having cared for the young woman."[54] As for the claimant herself, she later accused the baron of being interested in only two things. The first was the money he thought she could bring him; the second, or so she declared with what always seemed to be her rather prurient interest in such matters, was her body, for she hinted that he had crept into her bedroom one night with an idea to seducing her.[55]

Whatever the truth, it took just nine weeks for this tension to erupt. On the morning of Saturday, August 12, 1922, the baroness asked her guest if she would like to go shopping; Fraulein Annie excused herself, saying that she was too tired. Because of her suicide attempt in 1920, the von Kleists had never left the claimant alone, but on this morning the baron was at his office and the daughters were away. Baroness von Kleist reluctantly left the apartment; a few hours later, when she returned, Fraulein Annie was gone.[56]

Suspecting that her guest had run off to visit Clara Peuthert, whom the baroness distrusted and had barred from her apartment, the von Kleists alerted the Berlin police, who in turn filed a report on the missing woman.[57] That evening, the von Kleists and detectives arrived at Peuthert's rather seedy apartment in a building at 1 Schumannstrasse; when questioned, Peuthert professed ignorance, and a thorough search of the premises by the police indeed proved that the claimant was not there.[58] Later, Peuthert would insist, contrary to this, that Fraulein Annie had indeed been with her and had never left her apartment, a demonstrably false assertion, given the police inspection.[59]

On August 16, Franz Jaenicke, a friend of Nicholas von Schwabe, discovered the claimant by accident, wandering through the Berlin Zoo in the Tiergarten, and took her back to his apartment.[60] She was adamant that she would not return to the von Kleists, while the baroness, for her part, told Jaenicke that the young woman "was no longer welcome in our home." The next day, though, Marie von Kleist came to see her. She found Fraulein Annie suddenly, inexplicably overwhelmed when she entered the room. "She was not wearing any of the clothing we had given to her," the baroness recalled, "and sat in silence in the drawing room; she hung her head and would not say a word." When the baroness pressed, the claimant collapsed in tears, sobbing, "I feel so dirty! I cannot look you in the eye!"[61] Although the baroness agreed to take her back in, Jaenicke arranged for Fraulein Annie to stay temporarily with his friend Franz Grunberg, an inspector with the Berlin Police Department.

It was the beginning of a restless, peripatetic phase in Fraulein Annie's life: over the next few years she was passed from one émigré household to another, at times returning briefly to the von Kleists, only to flee to Captain Nicholas von Schwabe and his wife, Alice; to the Berlin apartment of Schwabe's friend and fellow monarchist Franz Jaenicke; to the dingy flat of Clara Peuthert; or to the protection of Berlin police inspector Franz Grunberg, either at his city apartment or at his country estate at Funkenmühle, near Zossen.[62]

She remained very much an enigma, and acceptance or rejection of her claim owed less to evidence than to desire, to the beliefs of those who came to see this damaged young woman who might be their late emperor's only surviving child. Many of those who opposed her suspected that Fraulein Annie was some sort of pawn, and that a second party must have influenced her and prepared her for this astonishingly difficult role. In the years immediately following the Bolshevik Revolution and her appearance in Berlin, many simply assumed that she was some kind of Soviet plant, promoted to cause dissention within the émigré community.[63] Others in the émigré community whispered and pointed fingers at each other, believing that some unscrupulous fellow exile was using her to lay claim to a rumored Romanov fortune in European banks. But these ideas were absurd: had either the Soviets or some group of disaffected monarchists wished to pass off a false grand duchess, would they really have selected a candidate as emotionally volatile and uncooperative as Fraulein Annie proved to be? It was one of the most compelling arguments advanced in her favor.

And so she wandered in and out of Berlin, in and out of houses and apartment blocks, drifting through the consciousness of the émigré community as a living specter of their vanished past, living in a faded dream that whispered of hope and unaware of what the future held.

7

A Story of Escape

I T WAS IN THE SAFETY of the von Kleist apartment that the claimant first revealed what she said was the tale of her rescue from the massacre in Ekaterinburg. She was always reluctant to discuss the subject; when she did so, it was with emotion and what seemed to be obvious distress, as she often burst into tears. "I have passed through everything," she would say, "dirt and all, everything!"[1] The story came in fragmented form, a few sentences uttered over the weeks and months to her early supporters, principally Baron von Kleist, who, as his wife noted, "carefully wrote down everything she said" during their hours of conversation.[2] Zenaide Tolstoy and Clara Peuthert added details, all of it pieced together in an attempt to provide a cogent narrative.[3] Her supporters excused the often improbable, fragmented, and contradictory narrative as evidence of the trauma they believed she had endured, while her opponents dismissed it as a complete fabrication.

Fraulein Annie offered few details of the time in Ekaterinburg, saying that life in the Ipatiev House had been "Hell itself," where "the soldiers were like wild animals toward us."[4] The executions had come quickly and without warning. "When the carnage began," she told Baron von Kleist, "I hid myself behind the back of my sister Tatiana, who was killed immediately. Then I received some blows and lost consciousness."[5] To another supporter, however, she was just as adamant in stating, "I can remember that I was standing beside my sister Olga, and sought shelter behind her shoulder."[6] To Peuthert, she said that she had been wounded in the shooting before she was "beaten to the floor" and finally fainted.[7] A few years later, she added, "I fainted, everything was blue, and I saw stars dancing and had a great rushing in the ears."[8] She also gave differing accounts of her alleged wounds. "I received some shots and lost consciousness," she once said.[9] To Peuthert, she declared that she had "received injuries to her hand and behind the ear, then was knocked to the floor, upon which she fainted."[10] She even insisted that she had been shot "in the neck," despite the fact that she bore no such wound.[11]

When she awoke, the claimant said, she found herself in the care of a soldier named Alexander Tchaikovsky. "I cannot recall," she told one supporter, "having seen this Tchaikovsky among the soldiers of the guard during the time we were at Ekaterinburg."[12] A few years later, though, she changed her story. "Many attentions," she declared, "were shown to me while in Ekaterinburg by one of the young guards." On numerous occasions, she said, "we talked together and hoped to see each other under different circumstances."[13] This was the man she identified as Alexander Tchaikovsky. Her rescuer, she said, was apparently Russian, the son of a convict exiled to Siberia, although his family had once belonged to the Polish nobility.[14] He was, she said, "about twenty-six years of age and handsome," with "black hair."[15]

According to her tale, Tchaikovsky had taken a wounded Anastasia to the home of his family, supposedly situated in a small settlement near Ekaterinburg, where his mother, Maria, sister Veronica, and brother Serge helped care for her and tended to her wounds.[16] When the Ekaterinburg Bolsheviks learned that Anastasia was missing, the claimant said, Tchaikovsky feared capture and, together with his family, took her to Romania by cart. She remembered "Lying on a heap of straw in a wagon. I did not know who the people were that I could hear talking. I only felt that, as the wagon jolted, my head ached terribly, that it was swathed in damp cloths, and that my hair was matted with blood."[17] New horses and carts were purchased along the route and expenses paid by using the jewelry she said was sewn into her clothing.[18]

She could recall almost nothing of her supposed journey across Siberia and the Ukraine to Romania. "I cannot say that I was conscious," she later offered to explain the enormous gaps in her story; she only spoke of "weeks, perhaps months" in which she lay in the back of a cart, suffering from her injuries. "We came through such lonely districts; we had to rest in forests, and we traveled on many roads. . . . There were times, when we had traveled for too long a period over unfrequented roads, that we had no water, and our provisions ran out. Soft, black bread was placed in my mouth so that I should not starve."[19] At some point during the journey, she said, she discovered that she was pregnant with Tchaikovsky's child. "She told me she had been raped," recalled Gerda von Kleist.[20] The claimant seemed very forgiving of the alleged attack. "A peasant," she told one supporter, "is a man of a different nature from ours. Often he does not know what he is doing. I do not wish to judge him too harshly, nor think of him with bitterness. He saved me."[21]

Sometime in the autumn of 1918, Fraulein Annie said, the group crossed an unnamed river, possibly the Dniester, and went to Bucharest, taking refuge with a Tchaikovsky relative who worked as a gardener and lived in a small house in the city.[22] "I was ill all the time," Fraulein Annie declared. "I cannot remember much about it."[23] The house, she thought, had been near the main train station; it seems to have been Zenaide Tolstoy, hearing this tale, who first suggested that the street might have been called Swienti Voyevoda.[24] The claimant herself apparently never volunteered any street name, saying several times that she could not recall such a minor detail.[25]

The uncertain time frame in the rescue tale became critical when the claimant apparently told Baron von Kleist that she had given birth to a son in Bucharest on December 5, 1918.[26] This date was a problem, as it placed conception—even for a premature birth—before the executions in Ekaterinburg. She soon insisted that von Kleist had invented the date and that she had no idea when her child had allegedly been born.[27] Given the fragmented manner in which her tale was pieced together, perhaps the baron was simply mistaken; but the claimant so frequently altered details of her story that it is equally possible that von Kleist correctly recorded her remark. To von Kleist, Peuthert, and a police inspector, she declared that the child had been named Alexei.[28] Later, for inexplicable reasons, she refuted this minor point, claiming that all three had invented the detail and that "the child is called like his father, Alexander."[29]

It was this pregnancy and birth, Fraulein Annie explained, that had prevented her from approaching Nicholas and Alexandra's first cousin Queen Marie of Romania when the group arrived in Bucharest. "How could I?" she asked. "At first I was very ill, then when I began to get better I was horrified to find that I was going to have a child. How could I present myself in this shameful state to the Queen?"[30] She was forthright in declaring that she had "never wanted" the baby and "had no interest in it," saying that she had given the baby to Tchaikovsky's family and "did not care" what became of him.[31]

The damage was done. The problems inherent in the story aside, it sent immense shock waves through the Russian émigré community in Berlin. The idea that an alleged Russian grand duchess had been raped by a common soldier—and an apparent Bolshevik, at that—and given birth to an illegitimate child whom she had then abandoned and whose whereabouts were unknown was simply too much for many of her supporters to stomach. Thus Zenaide Tolstoy summed up the position of many when she coldly declared, "A Grand Duchess cannot have a child by a private soldier."[32]

Of one date, Fraulein Annie said she was reasonably certain: according to what she told Baron von Kleist, she had married Alexander Tchaikovsky on January 18, 1919; she first said that she had been married under the name "Anna Romanska," although she later insisted that she had used "Anastasia Romanova."[33] It had, she said, been a Catholic ceremony, held in a church in Bucharest whose name she could not recall, and conducted by a priest she did not remember. She had, she admitted, converted to Catholicism during this period, and had her son baptized in this faith before giving him away.[34]

At some point, the claimant said, Tchaikovsky supposedly found an unnamed apparatus that she then used to successfully alter the appearance of her mouth and nose; she later dropped this assertion from her story.[35] Although uncertain of most dates, she told Peuthert that she thought that she had lived in Bucharest for nearly two years before her presence was discovered.[36] One day, she said, Alexander Tchaikovsky was attacked in a Bucharest street, shot in some kind of altercation by suspected Bolshevik agents sent to find her, and died three days later, being buried in a Catholic cemetery in the city. Her details were never consistent: to Baron von Kleist, she said he had been killed in August 1919; to Zenaide Tolstoy, however, she claimed it had happened in 1920.[37]

Following this, Fraulein Annie declared, she left her son with Tchaikovsky's family in Bucharest and made her way north.[38] At first she said she had used money gained from the sale of her last remaining piece of jewelry to pay for the journey; later, however, she offered up the unlikely claim that Alexander Tchaikovsky's brother Serge had gone to Queen Marie of Romania in January 1920, explained her situation, and traded her jewels for a small amount of cash to finance a trip to Germany.[39] According to what she later told a supporter, she had gone from Romania to Hungary, then made her way through Austria, all without any papers or passport, which necessitated secretly crossing borders and dodging customs officials.[40] She claimed variously to have crossed into Germany on foot or aboard a train.[41] Peuthert recalled that the claimant told her she had first gone to Paris in search of a Russian aristocrat, chased by Bolshevik agents along the way, and only later journeyed on to Germany.[42] According to what she told both Zenaide Tolstoy and Baron von Kleist, however, she had traveled directly to Berlin, arriving sometime in the middle of February 1920.[43]

According to von Kleist, Fraulein Annie twice stated that she traveled to the German capital alone, although she later claimed that she had been accompanied by Serge Tchaikovsky.[44] Arriving in Berlin, she told Zenaide Tolstoy that she took a room in a small boardinghouse on Friedrichstrasse, close to a train station, but could not recall the name of the establishment, although to others she would later claim to remember nothing of her time in the city.[45] "I intended," she told Baron von Kleist, "to live hidden for fear of the pursuers, and to earn a living by working."[46] She had hoped, she would later say, to somehow gain an audience with Princess Irene of Prussia.[47]

It was either on that first evening in Berlin or a week later (she insisted upon both as correct) that Fraulein Annie made her suicide attempt.[48] She usually admitted to this, calling it her "greatest folly."[49] She told one doctor that as she lay alone in her hotel room, the enormity of her hopeless situation overwhelmed her and she feared going to see Princess Irene because then "everyone would know her shame, that she had borne her common rescuer's child, and that he was somewhere in Romania." This, she declared, led her to throw herself into the Landwehr Canal.[50] But if Peuthert is to be believed, the claimant told her that soon after arriving in Berlin, she realized she was being followed. One night, she was pulled into a passing car and drugged; those who kidnapped her removed her clothing and dressed her as a worker before pulling alongside the Landwehr Canal and casting her, half conscious, into the water.[51]

Such was the rescue tale Fraulein Annie related, a complex tangle of fantastic elements and contradictions that did nothing to advance its credibility. Seemingly implausible, it gained an aura of possibility when, shortly after passing through the émigré community and appearing in print, rumors and assertions emerged that apparently supported the tale. Starting in the late 1920s, the claimant's supporters marshaled statements and gossip suggesting that Anastasia had survived the massacre. Franz Svoboda, an Austrian prisoner of war in Ekaterinburg at the time of the executions, said that he happened to be passing the Ipatiev House early on the morning of July 17, 1918, when he heard muffled gunshots; running into the courtyard, he "saw a soldier turning over a woman's body; she screamed, and the soldier struck her on the head with his rifle butt." Svoboda said that the young woman was not dead and ran for help; along with two unnamed friends, he bundled the injured girl—Anastasia—into a cart and spirited her to a house down the avenue.[52] Another man, Heinrich Kleibenzetl, picked up the tale, later saying that he had seen a wounded Anastasia shortly after the execution, being cared for by his landlady near the Ipatiev House.[53]

Then there were stories from those who had been in Siberia, and from Soviet officials, that one or more of the grand duchesses had escaped; according to one man, the rumors "never ceased to circulate" in

Ekaterinburg.[54] Several people later alleged that Bolshevik authorities in Ekaterinburg had conducted a house-to-house search, looking for a missing imperial daughter, and told of posters offering a reward for her capture.[55] Arthur Rohse, a lieutenant in the White Russian Army, recalled "special orders" from the military command to prepare "four fully manned and armored railway carriages," to be sent across Siberia to find and save a rescued grand duchess.[56] In addition to Princess Elena of Serbia, who was shown an early Anastasia claimant by the Bolsheviks in the autumn of 1918, Count Carl Bonde, chief of the Swedish Red Cross in Siberia, recounted how one day in 1918 his private train was "stopped and searched for Grand Duchess Anastasia, daughter of Tsar Nicholas II. The Grand Duchess was not aboard the train, however, and no one seemed to know where she had gone."[57]

It was an intriguing, seemingly impressive body of evidence that lent credence to what even many of Fraulein Annie's supporters admitted was a less than credible tale. Somewhat more ambiguous was the claimant's rescuer, the mysterious Alexander Tchaikovsky. Although no one by this name had served in the guard at the Ipatiev House, the claimant's supporters assumed that this was a pseudonym. Eventually, they suggested that a Pole named Stanislav Mishkevich—who had indeed been a guard in Ekaterinburg with his brother Nicholas—was the enigmatic Tchaikovsky.[58] After Fraulein Annie's tale was published along with pleas for corroborating information, a man named Constantine Anastasiou came forward, claiming that a Bolshevik soldier from Russia named Stanislav had approached him in Bucharest in the autumn of 1918, saying that he had rescued one of the grand duchesses when the bodies were being transported to the Koptyaki Forest. She had been injured and needed medical treatment, but he was fearful of taking her to any hospital.[59] Although this story contradicted the tales of Svoboda and Kleibenzetl, the claimant's supporters seized upon it as further evidence in her case. Then there was a certain Sarcho Gregorian, who said that on December 5, 1918—the same date on which the claimant supposedly gave birth in Bucharest—several people led by a man fitting Mishkevich's description had crossed the Dniester River; he remembered this, he said, because he had been told one of them was a rescued grand duchess, and he had been paid for his services with money received from the sale of a string of pearls.[60] The Germans occupied Bucharest until the autumn of 1918; many years later, several former intelligence officers testified to hearing secondhand stories of a rescued Anastasia hiding in the city, supposedly under German protection.[61]

This story took an even more bizarre turn in the spring of 1925 when a man whom one of the claimant's supporters rather too conveniently described as "a Russian soldier by appearance" arrived at

Dalldorf asking about "Fraulein Unbekannt." Someone directed him to Clara Peuthert, and on seeing a photograph of the claimant, he was said to have burst into tears and exclaimed that she was Anastasia. He left a letter stating that her child had been placed in an orphanage in Romania, and on the back of the photograph wrote, "Anastasia Nikolaievna . . . Alexandereva . . . Ivan . . . Alexev . . . Shorov . . . geb [born] Pittersburg [Petersburg]." The claimant's supporters suspected that the man was Serge Tchaikovsky, brother of her alleged rescuer and the person said to have accompanied her from Bucharest to Berlin. He disappeared, though, before he could be questioned, and was never seen or heard from again.[62]

These rumors, stories, and curious twists—it all seemed intriguing, and in January 1926 the claimant's supporters in Berlin sent a woman named Gertrude Spindler to Bucharest to investigate the story. Her mission was extraordinarily broad: Was there any documentation that Tchaikovsky, Mishkevich, or anyone fitting his description had crossed the Romanian border singularly or with other travelers in 1918 or 1919? Was there any evidence, anecdotal or otherwise, that the claimant or her alleged rescuers had lived in Bucharest between 1918 and 1920? Was there any religious or civil record of the alleged marriage between the claimant and Tchaikovsky in January 1919? Was there any evidence that her alleged child had been born and baptized in Bucharest? Was there any indication—stories, records, or even press reports—of a man being wounded and killed in a street battle in late 1919 or early 1920, as Fraulein Annie claimed Tchaikovsky had been? And was there any record of Tchaikovsky's alleged burial in the city? M. V. Pokloevsky-Kozell, the former Russian ambassador to Romania, met Spindler and offered his full cooperation in her quest; additionally, he contacted the Romanian minister of the interior and the director of the State Police, briefed them on the story, and won from them the complete cooperation of the government. A detective was assigned to assist Spindler, and she was given a police motorcar and driver to facilitate her quest. Even the press cooperated, publishing the claimant's story in the national papers and asking for witnesses or anyone else with information to come forward to aid in the investigation.[63]

Spindler spent weeks roaming through Bucharest and the surrounding countryside, searching through records and wandering along narrow lanes, from obscure churches to the most impoverished hut, interviewing officials, priests, police, doctors, nurses, and anyone who might offer any evidence supporting Fraulein Annie's story. She had the advantage of unlimited resources, the cooperation of the government, and of being on the ground just a few years after the claimant's supposed stay in Bucharest. But in the end, she uncovered nothing.

There was no evidence of any border crossing; nothing to suggest that the claimant or anyone who fit the description of her alleged rescuers had ever been in Bucharest; and no records supporting the claimant's story of her alleged marriage, the birth and baptism of her alleged son, or the death and burial of her alleged rescuer. Spindler's only positive achievement came in locating the Bucharest street apparently first suggested by Zenaide Tolstoy as the possible place were the mysterious Tchaikovsky family had lived. This was Sventi Voyevoda, a narrow lane that ran behind a former aristocratic villa in the city.[64] But of the Tchaikovskys, the Mishkevichs, the claimant—indeed, anyone who had supposedly lived on the villa's grounds—Spindler could find nothing.

The Romanian royal family, crowned relatives of the Romanovs, treated rumors about a rescued Anastasia in their capital quite seriously. Queen Marie of Romania took a personal interest in the claimant's tale and asked that everything be done to accommodate Spindler in her quest.[65] And her daughter Princess Ileana told lawyer Brien Horan, "The family did everything within their power to find out if there was any veracity to her claim, but were unable to find any trace of her."[66]

And this is how it stood throughout the claimant's life. Grand Duchess Olga Alexandrovna deemed the story "palpably false. I was convinced then, as I am now, that it is so from beginning to end. Just think of the supposed rescuers vanishing into thin air, as it were! Had Nicky's daughter been really saved, her rescuers would have known just what it meant to them. Every royal house in Europe would have rewarded them. Why, I am sure that my mother would not have hesitated to empty her jewel box in gratitude. There is not one tittle of genuine evidence in the story."[67]

There had, of course, been dozens of rumors about the fate of the Romanovs, second- and thirdhand tales about their presumed executions, stories of their whispered movements aboard mysterious trains, alleged witnesses to their secret captivity in isolated convents, and questionable claims of their miraculous rescue by one or another of their crowned relations. From Siberia, these stories spread across Russia, to the German-occupied Ukraine, to Romania, and to elsewhere in Europe, a seemingly impregnable web of intrigue. There was talk of a rescued grand duchess, yet it could not be confirmed; a few people recalled the Bolsheviks openly searching for a missing imperial daughter, yet this occurred at a time when the Soviets were actively engaged in deceptive announcements; there were claims of posters warning of an escaped Anastasia, yet no one could ever produce one or even prove that they existed; and there were those who claimed knowledge of Anastasia's presence or that of her alleged rescuer in Bucharest, yet such accounts emerged only after the claimant's story was publicized and pleas for information printed in newspapers. There was no proof that Alexander Tchaikovsky ever existed; that he was in fact Stanislav Mishkevich; that he or anyone fitting his description had lived or died in Bucharest; nor that the claimant had wed her alleged rescuer and had his child baptized.

It all seemed so unlikely, but unlikely was not impossible. If no one could discover definitive evidence to support the claimant's story, neither could her opponents find any conclusive proof that it had not happened. Unknown rescuers, tales of searches, stories from those both apparently credible and mysterious—in the end the claimant's account came down to a simple question of belief in her integrity and in her asserted identity. Fraulein Annie's tale of miraculous survival thus soon transcended the realm of objective fact, weaving its threads into the tapestry of myth enshrouding her claim.

8

A Ghost from the Past?

DESPITE THE FREQUENTLY implausible twists and turns it contained, the claimant's rescue story did achieve one thing: she now gained a new name. In place of the ambiguous "Fraulein Unbekannt" and the even more peculiar "Fraulein Annie" adopted by the von Kleists came Frau Anastasia Tchaikovsky, derived from her presumed Christian name and the surname of her supposed rescuer and temporary husband. This is how the world first came to know the woman who became Anna Anderson, as her story took hold and spread in the pages of newspapers, magazines, and books as the 1920s progressed.

Just a week after her August 1922 disappearance from the von Kleist apartment, Frau Tchaikovsky found herself a guest of Berlin police inspector Franz Grunberg at his country estate at Funkenmühle outside the city. She arrived armed with her packets of photographs and growing collection of books on the Romanovs, her actual identity as much of a mystery as it had been on the night she had been pulled from the Landwehr Canal. To this point, she had confined her conversations to German, yet one of Grunberg's relatives, Konrad Wahl, insisted that during this period she more often spoke in English than in German.[1] This was the first mention of the claimant using English, yet it is not entirely convincing. Wahl, who had been a child at the time, apparently waited more than fifty years before volunteering this important bit of information, and may have harbored imprecise memories. It is certainly a problematic piece of evidence, for if such conversations actually took place, why did Inspector Grunberg not mention them in his own detailed report on her case?[2] Surely, had Frau Tchaikovsky actually been conversant in English, someone—anyone—around her at this time would have noted the fact, especially given the immense controversy over her linguistic abilities. In fact, the idea was contradicted by Serge Botkin of the Office of Russian Refugees in Berlin, who flatly asserted, "She did not speak English during her stay in Berlin."[3]

The omission of such a critical piece of evidence favorable to Frau Tchaikovsky's claim, if it actually occurred, is all the more inexplicable given that Grunberg apparently believed she was the rescued grand duchess.

> Anastasia is no adventuress, nor, in my opinion, is she merely the victim of a delusion that she is the Tsar's daughter. After living with her for a number of months, I have become firmly convinced that she is a lady accustomed to intercourse with the highest circles of Russian society, and that it is likely she was born to a regal rank. Each of her words and movements reveals such a lofty dignity and commanding a bearing that it is impossible to claim she learned these characteristics later in her life.[4]

Grunberg held to this view even though he witnessed what, on the surface, seemed to be an apparently compelling rejection of Tchaikovsky's claim. The inspector contacted Anastasia's aunt Princess Irene, assuring her that the case was still unresolved and imploring her to come to Funkenmühle and judge the claimant herself. Just five months earlier, Irene had dispatched Baroness Sophie Buxhoeveden to meet the young woman at Dalldorf in an encounter whose negative result seemed definitive. Yet Irene apparently remained uncertain, perhaps hoping that the former lady-in-waiting had been too rash. Now, at Hemmelmark, the estate near Kiel she shared with her husband, Prince Heinrich of Prussia, Irene agonized over the situation. The actual fate of the Romanovs was still unknown, the belief that they had all been killed merely a theory that was constantly challenged by a perpetual stream of rumor. Someone from the family had to resolve the issue. Victoria, marchioness of Milford Haven, eldest of Empress Alexandra's surviving siblings, lived in England, while Grand Duke Ernst Ludwig of Hesse was so distraught by events in Russia that putting him through the emotional ordeal of meeting the claimant was apparently never considered.[5] And so it fell to Irene—sensible, good-natured Irene—to face the ghosts of the past in the young woman claiming to be her niece.

Princess Irene, who had seen Anastasia regularly on family holidays until 1913, arrived at Funkenmühle accompanied by Eleonore von Oertzen, her lady-in-waiting; Grunberg agreed to keep Irene's identity a secret, and at dinner introduced her to the claimant under an assumed name. The princess, Grunberg recalled, "was placed opposite Anastasia, so as to be able to observe her carefully." Her first impression was not favorable: "She did not think," Grunberg recorded, "she could recognize her, but admitted to having seen the Imperial Family for the last time ten years ago."[6] Irene herself declared:

> I saw immediately that this could not be one of my nieces. Although I had not seen them for nine years, the fundamental traits of the face could not have changed to such a point, particularly the position of the eyes and ears. At first sight, one could perhaps find a certain resemblance to Grand Duchess Tatiana. I remained with the unknown woman, at the first with Fraulein von Oertzen, and then alone, but I could find no sign that she had recognized me. In 1912 and 1913 I had lived with my niece for many weeks, and myself had changed very little.[7]

Before Irene left Hemmelmark, her husband, Heinrich, had told her that if she was in any way uncertain, she should bring the claimant back with her so they could further investigate her story.[8] At some point during the visit, as Fraulein von Oertzen later recalled, the princess may have followed her husband's directive and extended such an invitation.[9] But after a few uncomfortable minutes of silence, Frau Tchaikovsky suddenly jumped up and fled to her bedroom. Grunberg implored the princess to follow her; they found the claimant huddled in her bed, her back turned to her visitors in a display that even the sympathetic inspector termed a "disgusting" display of lèse-majesté.[10]

"In vain," Irene recorded, "I spoke to her using the intimate language of the past, reminding her of previous events, using nicknames, speaking of people we would both know, but none of it made any impression. Neither did she reply when I urged her to give any sign that she had recognized me." Finally, "not wishing to neglect any possibility," the princess said, "Don't you know your Aunt Irene?" Anderson, however, refused to speak, and finally the princess left, armed, she said, with "the firm conviction that the unknown woman was not my niece. I no longer had the slightest doubt on the subject. We had formerly lived in such intimacy that the smallest sign or unconscious movement would have sufficiently awakened in me a convincing familial feeling."[11]

Attempting to explain away this adamant rejection, Frau Tchaikovsky later insisted that she had been insulted to have her "aunt" presented to her under a false name.[12] "I was ill," she declared, "had to get up, the room was dark, and then a lady came. I knew the voice, and was listening to the voice, but did not know because the name was different. Then, at table, the face was familiar to me, but I did not know, was not sure. Then I recognized Aunt Irene."[13] Yet not even the favorably inclined Grunberg suggested that the claimant had recognized her visitor.

Irene, Grunberg recalled, was "profoundly revolted" at the encounter and "wanted nothing further to do with the whole matter."[14] But Frau Tchaikovsky was not content to let the matter rest. "Dear Aunt," she wrote to the princess, "you will probably remember how you came to Funkenmühle. . . . I have certainly recognized you at the time, but was so upset that you made out before me to be somebody else that in the first moment I was terribly hurt. . . . Please be so kind as to call on me again as soon as possible so that I can tell you all and that you can see I am really Anastasia."[15] A few weeks later: "Dear Aunt Irene, Must implore your forgiveness that then at Funkenmühle I did not speak. It was all so unexpected and you were introduced to me as a strange lady so I had lost all courage, I entreat you to bring me somewhere, else they have the intention to put me into an asylum or hospital, love and kisses, your Anastasia."[16]

These communications produced no response, and finally Frau Tchaikovsky appealed to Clara Peuthert to intercede. The message Peuthert dispatched was unlikely to win over anyone at Hemmelmark, for she began her long, ungrammatical letter by saying that she had not wanted to write on "Anastasia's behalf" because "I consider myself too good to be thought of by everyone as stupid or a liar or worse crazy." All the claimant wanted, Peuthert declared, was for her "Aunt Irene" to provide "some little corner" in which she could live out her last days, before she "passed from this world."[17] This was too much, they thought at Hemmelmark, for within two weeks Prince Heinrich's secretary wrote to Baroness von Kleist, who had herself tried to intercede with Irene on the claimant's behalf: "His Royal Highness requests me to inform you that he, as well as his wife—after the visit of the latter to your protégé—have reached the unshakable conviction that she is not one of the Tsar's daughters, especially not Grand Duchess Anastasia. Prince Heinrich considers the matter, as related to himself and to the Princess, as clarified and settled, and insists that you refrain from further communications or requests of him or of the Princess."[18]

This was the end of Irene's involvement, at least publicly, though privately she is said to have wavered. Prince Friedrich of Saxe-Altenburg, whose sister married Irene's son Prince Sigismund, once confronted the princess over her rejection. Irene listened patiently to his argument in favor of the claimant before finally insisting, "I couldn't have made a mistake, I couldn't have made a mistake!"[19] According to Prince Friedrich, the princess finally admitted, "She *is* similar, she *is* similar, but what does it mean if it is not she?"[20] A few years after Irene's death, Grand Duke Andrei Vladimirovich, in a letter to his cousin Grand

Duchess Olga Alexandrovna, declared that the princess had admitted—to whom he did not say—that "she might have made a mistake, and that it probably is Anastasia."[21] This is possible, especially if Irene later tried to reconcile a single traumatic encounter and rejection against the apparently compelling evidence that favored Tchaikovsky's claim. Such apparent struggles to accept decisions made under intensely emotional circumstances plagued those on both sides of the case, reflecting the air of uncertainty that lingered over the claim.

Those Russian émigrés who disputed the claimant presumed that the apparently negative encounter with Princess Irene, coming just a few months after the denunciation by Baroness Buxhoeveden, would end the matter, but they were wrong. People whispered of doubt: for every rejection and piece of contrary evidence there seemed to be some-one who believed that Tchaikovsky was Anastasia, and some intriguing and inexplicable fact that weighed in her favor. It was this irresolvable conflict that fed the mystery, for no one could satisfactorily explain away the opinions of Irene and Buxhoeveden nor the accumulating evidence supporting the claimant's case. It all remained a tantalizing enigma.

Despite the tensions that existed, the von Kleists remained convinced, at least in these years, that their occasional guest was Anastasia. That autumn of 1922, they arranged for the claimant to meet two former courtiers, Captain Nicholas Sablin and Admiral Federov, both of whom had served aboard the imperial yacht *Standart*. These men had known Anastasia well; in 1912, the thirty-two-year-old Sablin also had been appointed an adjutant to Nicholas II, and saw the imperial family not only on their annual cruises but also throughout the year while on duty at Tsarskoye Selo and on their holidays in the Crimea, when he often accompanied the grand duchesses on walks and partnered them in games of tennis.[22] At the meeting, over dinner in a Berlin restaurant, Sablin and Federov openly reminisced, in Russian, about the imperial family, annual cruises in Finland, holidays in the Crimea, and about the Romanovs and their courtiers, ostensibly to see if the conversation sparked any reaction from the claimant. "After some time," Sablin recalled, he asked "which of the young women present" claimed to be Anastasia; when she was pointed out, Sablin said he "found no resemblance" to the grand duchess. "We talked with the Admiral about walks, trips, parties, and many events well known to the Grand Duchesses and, although we did so loudly, the person in question showed no sign of interest." At the end of the evening, Sablin again declared that the claimant was not Anastasia, insisting that "not a single feature of her face reminded me of the Grand Duchesses, nor of any of the Imperial Family."[23]

Sablin had known Anastasia as well as anyone outside of her family, and his rejection was problematic for those who believed the claimant was the grand duchess. There would later be insinuations against Sablin—and others who, like him, rejected Frau Tchaikovsky—that he may have done so from ulterior motives. With Sablin, it was a case of his behavior in 1917, when following the Revolution he—like many courtiers—had deserted the Romanovs. "It was a fact Sablin never lived down," wrote Peter Kurth, "and something a daughter of Nicholas II might not have forgotten."[24] Was this meant to suggest that Sablin refused to recognize the claimant as Anastasia because he feared she would then turn around and condemn him for his previous actions? If that was the theory, it made little sense for Sablin to have agreed to a meeting in the first place, but whispers and hints of intrigue would pepper the case, carefully, cautiously insinuating duplicitous motives to those who failed to acknowledge Frau Tchaikovsky as Anastasia.

And what of Federov? According to Sablin, the admiral shared his opinion: the claimant was not Anastasia.[25] Yet Baroness von Kleist recorded that Federov told her that "had she spoken Russian to him, or had she spoken with him of any shared memories, or had she awoken any memories in himself, then he would have been prepared to recognize her as Anastasia."[26] Was Federov uncertain, but leaning toward acknowledging her as the grand duchess, as her supporters believed? Or was he merely offering a list of the reasons why he had been unable to recognize her as Anastasia?

Frau Tchaikovsky was a restless, lonely figure in these years, valued only for what the ambitious could envision winning from her claim and shuffled from one émigré to another like an unwelcome burden.

Anna Anderson in St. Mary's Hospital, Berlin, 1925.

Her health was deteriorating and forced her into extended stays at various Berlin hospitals. That she was truly ill no one could doubt: even by the spring of 1922, when she left Dalldorf, she was already suffering from the early effects of tuberculosis; serious infections came and went, along with bouts of anemia and persistent headaches. In the autumn of 1922 she was admitted to Berlin's West End Hospital, a Catholic-run institution at Charlottenburg, under the name of Anastasia Tchaikovsky and treated for the tubercular infection on her chest.[27] She came and went from the hospital over the next year as her health improved or worsened; by the summer of 1925 she was again a patient, this time at Berlin's St. Mary's Hospital.[28]

Fortunately, finally, a disparate trio had stepped in and begun to tend to Frau Tchaikovsky's interests in an organized fashion. Serge Botkin, president of the Office of Russian Refugees in Berlin, was a cousin of Dr. Eugene Botkin, who had been murdered in Ekaterinburg with the Romanovs. Assisted by his deputy Baron Vassili Osten-Sacken, Botkin collected and distributed funds among the émigré community, organizing their feeble efforts at cohesion and offering a single channel through which the human flot-

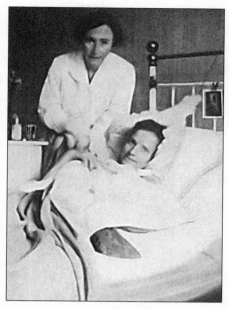

Anna Anderson in a Berlin hospital, tended by Harriet von Rathlef-Keilmann, 1925.

sam of the Russian Empire could appeal for official papers and needed aid.[29] Witnesses and depositions, claims and counterclaims all flowed through Botkin's office in these years, making him one of the best-informed people in Berlin on the case. He was seemingly impartial in his conduct, and never publicly offered an opinion on her identity; privately, however, he was favorably disposed to her claim.[30]

Herluf Zahle, the Danish minister to Berlin, was the second member of this triumvirate. A future temporary president of the League of Nations, Zahle began his involvement with the case innocently enough, exposed to the increasing rumors in the German capital; in time, however, he assumed a much larger role in the saga.[31] Those involved with the claimant eventually came to view Zahle strictly in terms of black or white. For those who supported Tchaikovsky's claim, he was a noble and honest diplomat, attempting to navigate a fine line between impartiality and his own eventual belief that she was Anastasia; those who opposed her claim, however, charged him with naive partiality, pointing out that he did all in his power to advance her case.[32]

The last of the trio arrived on the scene in June 1925. This was a middle-aged woman named Harriet von Rathlef-Keilmann, who soon became Frau Tchaikovsky's principal caretaker, most ardent supporter, dedicated chronicler, and the person who, more than any other, propelled her case into legend. Born into a wealthy Jewish family in

Riga—then a Russian province—Rathlef-Keilmann converted to Catholicism, married, had four children, and escaped to Germany after the Revolution, where—following her 1922 divorce—she established herself as an illustrator and sculptor of some repute. She was brought into the case by Dr. Karl Sonnenschein of St. Mary's Hospital, who at the time was treating the claimant for a recurrence of tuberculosis.[33] Opinions of Rathlef-Keilmann varied greatly, though no one doubted that she was absolutely dedicated to the claimant. Those who believed Tchaikovsky was Anastasia were convinced that Rathlef-Keilmann was absolutely honest, while opponents accused her, generously, of naïveté, and more often asserted that she deliberately distorted and suppressed information that undermined the claimant's case. The latter, at least, was the opinion of former imperial tutor Pierre Gilliard, who at first believed Rathlef-Keilmann to be "an exalted person whose imprudent zeal threatened" her integrity.[34] Even some of those who supported the claimant were at times troubled by what Zahle termed Rathlef-Keilmann's "fixed ideas" and her "partiality" in investigating the supposed grand duchess and ignoring contrary evidence.[35]

By 1925, and after more than three years of intrigue over her claim, Frau Tchaikovsky remained very much an enigma. No one could quite agree, not only on her identity but also on her personality. Having observed her in the privacy of their Berlin apartment, both Nicholas von Schwabe and his wife, Alice, were less than impressed with the alleged grand duchess in whom they had first believed. Alice, in particular, was "persuaded that Frau Tchaikovsky was neither Russian, nor Orthodox."[36] Yet Dr. Ludwig Berg, who met her at St. Mary's Hospital in Berlin, recorded that "in every circumstance she showed proof of altogether distinguished manners, and her conversation and her attitude were those of a person of good education."[37] These conflicting impressions underscored the claimant's complex personality, her frequent changes of mood, her ability to appear completely charming one minute and storm into uncontrolled rages the next. Rathlef-Keilmann offered a knowing and not altogether flattering description of her character. Frau Tchaikovsky, she recorded, was "unable to understand actions that were genuinely intended for her welfare. Often she suspected those who were unselfishly working on her behalf."[38] The claimant "knew well how to sulk. She is sulky. In such periods of ill humor she even upbraided me, and asserted that I grudged her everything. With all her charm it is sometimes very difficult to get on with her, as she is irritable and oversensitive; for days at a time, she sulks and says nothing. She sulks and mopes, and displays with the utmost arrogance the consciousness of her social superiority. . . . Despite her sensitiveness, her mistrust, and her willfulness, she is a person of great charm, with whom it is impossible to be angry for long, and whom everyone who learns to know must love."[39] This says something of the claimant's innate charm, that even those who suffered her fits of temper regarded her with loyalty.

Frau Tchaikovsky remained isolated in these years, confined to a succession of Berlin apartments and hospital wards, but her notoriety spread through Berlin and elsewhere in Germany and Europe. Even among members of Europe's royal families it had become a subject of considerable allure and intrigue. Crowned uncles, aunts, and cousins took opposing views of this seemingly enigmatic case. Shortly after arriving on the scene, Rathlef-Heilmann dispatched a woman named Amy Smith to Darmstadt to plead the case with Grand Duke Ernst Ludwig of Hesse. Smith carried a dossier of reports, affidavits, and photographs supporting the idea that Tchaikovsky was the grand duke's niece. The grand duke, though, was less than impressed: his sister Irene had met with and rejected the claimant, and he had no reason to doubt her. Count Kuno von Hardenberg, the grand duke's former marshal of the court, told Smith that "it was impossible that Anastasia or any member of the Imperial Family" could have survived the executions in Ekaterinburg.[40] Privately, the grand duke suspected that the case was driven by Soviet agents "hoping to lay their hands" on any tsarist money in Europe.[41]

Yet others were more amenable to the idea that the claimant might just be Anastasia after all. Princess Martha of Sweden, who later married the future King Olav of Norway, came to Berlin in the 1920s and asked to meet Frau Tchaikovsky. When told how notoriously difficult the claimant could be over such encounters, she settled on viewing her from a distance. "That's Anastasia!" the princess is said to have exclaimed, according to a later secondhand story, though how she could reach such a decision, especially given that she had last met Anastasia when the latter was still a child, is not known.[42] One royal reaction without

Dowager Empress Marie Feodorovna, in her last years in her native Copenhagen.

question came from former crown princess Cecilie, married to Kaiser Wilhelm II's eldest son and herself the daughter of a Russian grand duchess. She, too, visited Frau Tchaikovsky in Berlin; though she had only a passing familiarity with Anastasia, she thought that the claimant bore some resemblance to members of the imperial family, particularly to Nicholas II and to his mother, Dowager Empress Marie Feodorovna. Her efforts at conversation failed. "She remained completely silent," Cecilie recalled, "either from stubbornness or from confusion—which I could not decide." The princess eventually left without forming a definite opinion.[43] Nevertheless, she was interested enough to raise the issue with her sister-in-law Viktoria Luise, the kaiser's only daughter; when Viktoria Luise, in turn, discussed the case with her mother-in-law, Thyra, duchess of Cumberland, things took a dramatic turn, for Thyra was a sister to Nicholas II's mother.[44]

Recent events had not been kind to Marie Feodorovna. Long alienated from her daughter-in-law Empress Alexandra, the dowager empress had lost all three of her sons: George from tuberculosis in 1899, and Nicholas II and his brother Grand Duke Michael Alexandrovich, both victims of Bolshevik firing squads in 1918, while the presumed massacre in Ekaterinburg had taken the lives of five of her grandchildren. She had escaped Russia in 1919 with her daughter Xenia Alexandrovna (her other daughter, Olga Alexandrovna, fled the country separately), eventually settling in her native Denmark; here she lived outside Copenhagen in a villa called Hvidøre with Olga; Olga's second, morganatic husband, Nicholas Kulikovsky; and their two sons. At the time, Nicholas II's first cousin King Christian X sat upon the Danish throne; though his aunt Marie Feodorovna held fast to the idea that none of the imperial family had been killed, he listened to the stories of the claimant told by Thyra and by the dowager empress's brother Prince Waldemar of Denmark, who was intrigued with the case. Apparently with the king's blessing, Waldemar asked Herluf Zahle in Berlin to begin a private investigation into her case.[45] Waldemar also asked Zahle to discreetly step in and pay the young woman's expenses until the issue of her identity could firmly be settled.[46]

The Hessian royal family, relatives of Empress Alexandra, had taken an early interest in the case and at least made efforts to satisfy themselves about her asserted identity, but not a single Romanov had yet expressed any curiosity in the mysterious young woman. This finally changed when Zahle reported back to Copenhagen that the claimant might be Anastasia. Prince Waldemar apparently spoke with Grand Duchess Olga Alexandrovna, and the latter agreed to send former courtier Alexei Volkov to Berlin to meet the young woman and report his findings.[47] If she was a fraud, the issue was to be considered as settled; if, however, he was uncertain, the matter would be further investigated.[48]

Volkov, Empress Alexandra's former groom of the chamber, had accompanied the Romanovs when, in 1917, they had been exiled to Siberia. He had spent nine months at Tobolsk with the prisoners, only to be arrested in Ekaterinburg and thrown into the city jail. After the execution, he and several other courtiers, transferred to Perm, were taken from their cells one September morning and led into a field; suspecting what was about to happen, Volkov ran for a nearby forest and managed to escape the bullets that killed his companions. After arriving in Europe, he had eventually gone to Copenhagen, where the dowager empress gave the elderly man a position in her household.

What precisely happened when Volkov visited the claimant became, like so much of Frau Tchaikovsky's case, a matter of some contention. He arrived at St. Mary's Hospital in Berlin at the beginning of July 1925, but on the first day could only observe the claimant from a distance as she sat in the garden. After closely examining her the following day, though, said Rathlef-Keilmann, he found no resemblance to Anastasia. "The Grand Duchess had a much rounder face," Volkov declared, "and had a fresher complexion. The features I now see do not remind me of the Grand Duchess." For her part, Tchaikovsky remained curiously silent; after he left, she insisted that she had recognized him, but could not give his name, saying, "My brain simply will not work."[49]

Volkov did not speak German, and used Russian throughout his visits; although the claimant understood him, and answered his questions, she would do so only in German, with Rathlef-Keilmann serving as translator. Volkov asked if she could name the two attendants who had looked after Tsesarevich Alexei; if she could identify Tatischev as one of Nicholas II's adjutants; where the grand duchesses had kept their jewelry in the last days of their captivity; and if she recognized photographs of the dowager empress and Grand Duke Ernst Ludwig of Hesse.[50] Although she accurately answered the elderly man's inquiries, the claimant soon grew tired of the questioning and, turning to Rathlef-Keilmann, declared that she would make no further effort to prove her identity.[51]

Volkov himself left an account of the meeting quite different from that given by Rathlef-Keilmann. He asked the claimant "whether she recognized me." According to Volkov, "She answered negatively." He agreed that she had answered some questions correctly but, opposed to Rathlef-Keilmann, also insisted that "to other questions I asked, she gave unsatisfactory answers," without indicating what these might have been. The end result, he asserted, was negative: "I can affirm in the most categorical manner that Frau Tchaikovsky has nothing in common with

Grand Duchess Anastasia Nikolaievna. If she has any knowledge of the life of the Imperial Family, she has imbibed it exclusively from books; her knowledge for the rest is quite superficial. One can prove this by the fact that she was not able to cite a single detail outside those which had appeared in the press."[52]

Questions remain over how the visit ended. In a statement made immediately after the visit, Rathlef-Keilmann contended that Volkov had told the claimant, "Don't cry! Please don't cry, I don't want you to cry!"[53] Three years later, though, in her book on the case, she had him confessing dramatically, "Just think of the position I am in! Supposing I were to say that it is she, and others later on maintain that it is not, what would my position be then?"[54] One would expect Rathlef-Keilmann's first statement to be the most reliable; why, then, would she omit from it the telling words she later ascribed to Volkov? But this is not the only variation: in her book, *Anastasia: The Survivor of Ekaterinburg*, she also claimed that Frau Tchaikovsky had peppered Volkov with questions, mentioning incidents that had greatly impressed the former courtier.[55] These differences, though, remained unknown, hidden in Rathlef-Keilmann's notes, statements, and papers; instead, the public was left only with her carefully crafted and convincing book, where such discrepancies were nowhere to be found.

After Volkov's death in 1929, Professor Serge Ostrogorsky, who also had served at the Russian court, asserted that the former groom had not been entirely certain in his denunciation. "On the one hand," Ostrogorsky wrote, "he denied her identity. On the other, he told me that his interview with the invalid had moved him deeply, that he had been crying, and had kissed her hand, which certainly he would never have done if someone other than the Grand Duchess had been standing before him." Asked about this discrepancy, Volkov, according to Ostrogorsky, broke down in tears and cried, "It is true, I believe that she is the Grand Duchess, but how can the Grand Duchess speak no Russian?"[56]

Pierre Gilliard with Olga and Tatiana on the terrace at Livadia, 1913.

What did this mean? Volkov could have found the meeting

A luncheon during the Romanov Tercentenary trip down the Volga River in 1913. From left: Count Paul von Benckendorff, Grand Marshal of the Imperial Court; Marie; Tatiana; Anastasia; and Alexandra Tegleva ("Shura," later Alexandra Gilliard).

an emotional ordeal that, regardless of the claimant's identity, reawakened painful memories of the Romanovs and of his own perilous time in Siberia. If he was not as favorably inclined as Rathlef-Keilmann suggested, neither did he seem convinced that Frau Tchaikovsky was not the grand duchess, as he later insisted. This ambiguity was confirmed when Volkov returned to Copenhagen and delivered a report that did nothing to clarify the situation. He could not—or would not—confirm or deny that the young woman was Anastasia. And there was more: that summer of 1925, the claimant casually mentioned the word "Schwibes," a variant of "Schwibzik," the nickname bestowed on Anastasia by her aunt Olga Alexandrovna.[57] When Olga heard this, she confessed herself "astonished."[58] She immediately dispatched an urgent letter to former nursemaid Alexandra Tegleva, who in 1919 had married Pierre Gilliard and settled with him in Lausanne after the pair escaped Russia: "I beg you to leave without delay for Berlin with M. Gilliard to meet the unfortunate woman. What if it should *really* be the little one? God knows! And it would be so sinful if she is alone in her misery, if it is true. . . . I pray you, I pray you, leave at the very earliest moment: you better than anyone else in the world can tell us the truth of the story. . . . God help you! I embrace you with all of my heart. If it is really she, telegraph me; I will join you in Berlin."[59]

This letter alone indicates that Volkov's report was indecisive enough to require further investigation. Now, at Olga Alexandrovna's request, the Gilliards traveled to Berlin to meet the claimant. Frau Tchaikovsky was still at St. Mary's Hospital, seriously ill with a tubercular infection on her left elbow, gaunt, and in so much pain that doctors plied her with a constant stream of morphine.[60] This is how Gilliard found the woman claiming to be his former pupil when he arrived on July 27. He later recalled, "I asked her several questions in German, to which she muttered some vague monosyllabic answers. In the long silences, we studied her face with great attention, but could not find the least resemblance with the one who had been so dear to us. The patient has a long, upturned nose, a very large mouth, and full lips; Grand Duchess Anastasia, on the other hand, possessed a short, straight nose, a small mouth, and thin lips; nor was the shape of the ears consistent, nor the expression, nor the sound of her voice. Aside from the color of the eyes, we found nothing that made us believe that the patient was Grand Duchess Anastasia, and we had the keen impression of being in the presence of a stranger."[61]

The following morning, the couple returned to the hospital and found the claimant more alert. Alexandra Gilliard asked to examine the patient's feet; seeing that she suffered from *hallux valgus*, as had Anastasia, she told Rathlef-Keilmann of the similarity.[62] When Gilliard attempted to question Tchaikovsky, though, the few answers she gave were evasive. Pointing to his wife, Gilliard asked the patient if she did not recognize her; according to the former tutor, Frau Tchaikovsky stared at the nursemaid for a long time and finally answered in German, "It is my father's youngest sister," meaning Grand Duchess Olga Alexandrovna.[63] Zahle, who was present, apparently agreed that this had indeed happened, as did Rathlef, although she insisted that the claimant had been delirious.[64]

The Gilliards met with Rathlef and Zahle at the Danish Legation in Berlin that evening. Although Gilliard would later say that he had found no real reason to suspect that the patient was Anastasia, he described himself as burdened "by the great responsibility" of making any decision after so brief a visit and when the young woman had been unwell.[65] He decided it would be best to return to Berlin at some later date, when the claimant had improved. Before leaving, however, he did ask that she be moved from St. Mary's Hospital to a private clinic where she would receive better treatment.[66] The next morning, Frau Tchaikovsky was duly transferred to Berlin's private Mommsen Clinic, where she would remain for the rest of the year.[67]

The former tutor and his wife left Berlin without expressing an opinion on the claimant's identity. Although Gilliard's initial impressions had been unfavorable, he could not definitely state that the young woman was not Anastasia. Zahle and Rathlef both argued that injuries to her head and face might well have altered her appearance, something Gilliard accepted; he even granted that possible blows to the head might explain her apparent inability to speak Russian. Afraid "of making an irreparable mistake," he was willing to evaluate her again at a later date.[68] As for Alexandra Gilliard, she was even less certain, overcome, her husband confided, "with hope that perhaps, after all, the invalid was the girl she had loved so much."[69] Zenaide Tolstoy had recognized the claimant; Baroness Buxhoeveden had rejected her; Princess Irene, too, had been unconvinced, although she may have harbored doubts. Now, neither Volkov nor the Gilliards could offer a definitive verdict. Something had to be done to resolve this dilemma, this living enigma, this open, emotional wound on the hearts of Romanov relatives and Russian émigrés. That task fell to Grand Duchess Olga Alexandrovna. Her visit that autumn to the young woman in Berlin would become the single most contentious and legendary episode in the claimant's case.

9

Encounter in Berlin

THE YOUNGEST SISTER of Nicholas II, Grand Duchess Olga Alexandrovna, had been one of the few Romanovs allowed into the intimate life of the imperial family at Tsarskoye Selo, and had done her best to provide her sheltered nieces with some semblance of a social life beyond the palace walls. World War I, though, brought separation, and she had last seen Anastasia during an hour-long 1916 visit by Nicholas II and his children to Kiev, where Olga had established a hospital. That same year, her unhappy first marriage was annulled and she promptly wed an army officer, Colonel Nicholas Kulikovsky, in a morganatic union that produced two sons. Olga knew that her mother, Dowager Empress Marie Feodorovna, among many other relatives, disapproved of this second marriage, which left the grand duchess something of a black sheep within the Romanov family. Still, Olga had dutifully followed her mother out of Russia after the Revolution and to Copenhagen, where she, her husband, and their children shared the dowager empress's roof and were largely dependent on her largesse to survive in this new and uncertain world.

While insisting that none of the Romanovs had been killed in Ekaterinburg, the dowager empress made it clear that she regarded the young woman in Berlin as a fraud.[1] But after the ambiguous meetings with Volkov and the Gilliards, and their inability to offer any clear opinion, Olga Alexandrovna wasn't at all certain that the claimant was an imposter; distressed by the idea, uncertain of the secondhand stories she heard, and surprised at the young woman's knowledge, she thought that the only way to resolve the issue was to visit Berlin and see for herself. Word of her intention caused a panic: both her mother and her sister Xenia Alexandrovna first protested and then finally attempted to prevent her trip. "We were all apprehensive," Xenia recalled, "about the wisdom of her going, but only because we feared it would be used for propaganda purposes by the claimant's supporters."[2] It is also possible, given her morganatic marriage, that both the dowager empress and her eldest daughter harbored doubts about Olga Alexandrovna's own judgment. Olga, though, refused to be put off and, accompanied by her husband, arrived in Berlin on October 27, 1925.

It was the beginning of the most extraordinary and confusing turn in the claimant's case. What took place—or more precisely, what was said to have taken place—over the three days of Olga Alexandrovna's visit did more to elevate Frau Tchaikovsky's story into the realm of mysterious, modern myth than any other single event. Her encounters with the claimant, as well as those of the Gilliards, who had come from Lausanne to join her, would be seized upon by both supporters and opponents, each side marshaling the contrasting evidence and shifting versions to bolster their own absolute convictions. In many ways, the reality of what actually occurred became less important than the perceptions of what it meant, of what lay unsaid, unacknowledged, hidden just beneath the surface of acceptance or rejection.

Word of the impending visit, said Frau Tchaikovsky's supporters, had been kept from her so that she had no opportunity to prepare for or anticipate her callers.[3] Not so, countered Olga Alexandrovna and Pierre Gilliard. According to the grand duchess, the claimant "had been warned of my visit" and had even been told, "Someone is coming from Denmark," from which she believed the claimant could easily have guessed her identity.[4] To this point, Gilliard produced a letter from Zahle in which the minister had warned that it had proved "simply impossible" to keep word of the impending visit from the claimant, whose "thoughts are concentrated on this visit and especially on that of you and your wife."[5]

Pierre Gilliard was the first to call on Frau Tchaikovsky in her room at the Mommsen Clinic in Berlin. He found her thin and ill; she had recently undergone an

Grand Duchess Olga Alexandrovna.

invasive operation to save her arm from a tubercular infection, and still suffered from a persistent fever and pain that required regular injections of morphine.[6] "I found her sitting in bed, playing with a cat that had been given to her," he wrote. "She held out her hand to me and I sat down beside her. From this moment on, she looked at me steadily, but I must insist that she said nothing to me, in the course of my visit, which made me suppose that she had recognized me." He attempted to question her, but to no avail.[7]

"Please chat with me a little," Gilliard said. "Tell me all you know of your earlier life."

"I don't know how to chat!" Frau Tchaikovsky suddenly and angrily replied. "I know nothing about which I could chat with you!" Gilliard, perplexed by this turn of events, soon left the room.[8]

When Olga Alexandrovna arrived a few hours later, the controversy really began. The claimant later insisted that the grand duchess "immediately recognized me, and treated me in a most familial manner during her repeated visits."[9] Journalist Bella Cohen, writing for the *New York Times*, insisted that as soon as Olga entered the room Frau Tchaikovsky sat up in her bed and shouted, "Oh, my dear aunt!"[10]

This was nonsense: not even Rathlef-Keilmann, always eager to publicize any evidence favorable to the claimant, made such an assertion.

In fact, there seems only to have been extreme caution from all of those present. When Olga entered, Gilliard wrote, the claimant "made none of those spontaneous movements of tenderness that one would have expected from her if she had really been Grand Duchess Anastasia."[11] "I was deeply moved," Olga admitted, writing of "a tender feeling" that the claimant inspired in her.[12] But she seemed to be confused—at least initially—by the claimant's appearance, remarking, said Rathlef-Keilmann, that she looked more like Tatiana than she did Anastasia.[13]

Apparently, though, the more she looked at the claimant, the less resemblance Olga could find. "My niece's features could not possibly have altered out of all recognition. The nose, the mouth, the eyes were all different."[14]

Olga spoke in Russian, and the claimant replied in German; she understood—"with difficulty," Gilliard said—Russian but "would not speak it."[15] When Frau Tchaikovsky did speak, Rathlef said, she peppered the grand duchess with questions, asking, "How is Grandmama? How is her heart?"[16]

Out came photographs—of palace rooms, of the Crimea, of the Romanovs, of the Tercentenary tour in 1913—and Olga and Gilliard watched to judge her reaction. Frau Tchaikovsky occasionally pointed at figures and identified faces; with other images, though, she evinced no interest or recognition.[17] And then, after this disappointment, an apparent surprise: according to Rathlef-Keilmann, the claimant, after identifying Alexandra Gilliard by the nickname "Shura" she had used with the imperial children, motioned to a bottle of perfume and asked that she moisten her forehead. This, Rathlef-Keilmann said, had been one of Anastasia's favorite rituals with the nurse, though she offered no evidence to corroborate the point.[18] Gilliard, according to Rathlef-Keilmann, was so moved, so overwhelmed, that he had stumbled from the room, crying, "How horrible! What has happened to Grand Duchess Anastasia? She is a wreck, a complete physical wreck! I want to do everything I can to assist the Grand Duchess."[19]

At the end of the visit, Olga Alexandrovna, according to Zahle, seemed agitated, confused. "I can't say that's it her," she told him, "but I can't say that she isn't."[20] Rathlef-Keilmann, though, portrayed events in a different light. The grand duchess, she insisted, had pulled her aside and whispered, "Our little one and Shura seem very happy to have found one another again. If I had any money, I would do everything for the little one, but I haven't any and must earn my own pocket money by painting." And a bit later, Rathlef-Keilmann said, she added, "I am so happy that I came, and I did it even though Mama did not want me to. She was so angry with me when I came. And then my sister wired me from England saying that under no circumstances should I come to see the little one."[21]

Was this recognition on Olga's part? Rathlef-Keilmann suggested as much. And there was more: Gilliard and his wife, she said, acted as if "they plainly admitted to the possibility" that the claimant was Anastasia; the former tutor, she said, had even "spoken about the patient" as if he were speaking about Anastasia during this visit.[22] And then, of course, there had been, she said, Gilliard's emotional outburst, "What has happened to Grand Duchess Anastasia?"[23]

Later, Gilliard admitted only that both the grand duchess and his wife were "deeply troubled" over "strange revelations" made by the claimant, revelations such as her mention of the word "Schwibs," suggesting that she possessed intimate knowledge of life within the imperial family. Both women, he said, were consumed with "the pity that this unhappy creature inspired in them and, above all else, the haunting fear that they would commit an irreparable error. For them, these were terrible, anguished days." But while this anguish played itself out, Gilliard excused himself, disappearing with Olga's husband, Kulikovsky, to interview several Russian émigrés in Berlin who had been involved with the claimant. He insisted that talks with Captain Nicholas von Schwabe and his wife, Alice, had been "a veritable coup de théâtre."[24] From the couple, who by now had turned against the claimant, came accusations that she had studied books and magazines about the imperial family; had learned details of court life from her numerous callers; had collected and memorized photographs and postcards—in short, a convenient answer to how Frau Tchaikovsky had come by her knowledge and managed to seem so convincing.[25]

And there was more, for von Schwabe explained just how Frau Tchaikovsky had learned the mysterious word "Schwibs" that so perplexed Olga Alexandrovna. Before one of his visits to the patient at Dalldorf, von Schwabe said, a former officer—either Serge Markov or Paul Bulygin (von Schwabe named both in his statement)—had come to him, suggesting that he ask her if she recognized the word; Olga Alexandrovna had given the officer the term, to use as a code if he secretly contacted the imperial family during their Siberian captivity. The man wrote it inside a Bible, which von Schwabe duly presented to the claimant; when confronted with this, though, she seemed confused, and Alice von Schwabe helped her with the pronunciation and explained its significance.[26]

As far as Gilliard was concerned, these were the answers he had needed, and Kulikovsky as well, for the latter insisted that his wife meet the Schwabes that evening and listen to their stories.[27] There followed, recalled Olga Alexandrovna, a "horrible dinner" hosted by Zahle at the Danish legation.[28] "Horrible" presumably because the meal quickly devolved into a shouting match between Gilliard and Zahle, the one apparently convinced that he had discovered the solution to the mystery of the claimant's "strange revelations," the other just as firmly convinced that she was Anastasia and was about to be abandoned based on what he believed to be lies. Gilliard tried to explain what he had heard, only for Zahle to interrupt him, complaining that the former tutor "had gone beyond the role of neutral observer" to conduct an unnecessary investigation. The conversation became "so violent," Gilliard later wrote, that the dinner ended quite abruptly, "in great embarrassment for all."[29]

The effect of these stories, these talks with Berlin émigrés, and the traumatic evening at the Danish legation was quite clear the following morning, when the group returned to the Mommsen Clinic for their final visit. The behavior of the Gilliards toward the claimant, Rathlef-Keilmann saw, was "noticeably different."[30] Everyone seemed tense, on edge; even Frau Tchaikovsky sensed that something had changed, for she "cried and cried," recalled Olga, "saying that everyone was going to abandon her."[31]

The visits ended on decidedly ambiguous notes. Alexandra Gilliard was in tears. "I used to love her so much, so much!" Rathlef-Keilmann recorded her saying. "Why do I love this girl here so much?"[32] As this was taking place, Gilliard pulled Zahle aside, confiding that neither he nor his wife could find "the slightest resemblance" between the claimant and Anastasia.[33] But then, confusingly, said Rathlef-Keilmann, he departed with the curious remark, "We are going away without being able to say that she is *not* Grand Duchess Anastasia."[34]

Olga Alexandrovna echoed this apparent uncertainly in her parting words to Zahle: "My intelligence," Rathlef-Keilmann quoted her as saying, "will not allow me to accept her as Anastasia, but my heart tells me that it is she. And since I have grown up in a religion that taught me to follow the dictates of the heart rather than those of the mind, I am unable to leave this unfortunate child."[35]

It was an extraordinary statement, an admission of uncertainty from the grand duchess. And this was reflected, at least initially, in a letter Olga sent to Zahle on leaving Berlin. Referring to the claimant as "our poor little friend," she declared, "I can't tell you how fond I got of her—whoever she is. My feeling is that she is not the one she believes— but one can't *say she* is not as a fact—as there are still many strange and inexplicable facts not cleared up."[36]

And, thought Rathlef-Keilmann, for Zahle and for those who believed the claimant was Anastasia, it was reflected in five short letters Olga Alexandrovna dispatched to Frau Tchaikovsky over the next few months. "I send you all my love," ran one, "and think of you all the time. It is very sad to go away, knowing that you are ill and suffering and alone. Don't be afraid. You are not alone now, and we shall not aban- don you."[37] In others, written in Russian, she gave news of her sons and continued to ask after the claimant's health; all were signed simply "Olga" or "With love, Olga." With them came a number of small gifts, including a silk shawl; a sweater Olga Alexandrovna had knitted; and, most peculiarly, one of her family photograph albums, containing personal pictures of her brother Grand Duke Michael Alexandrovich and cap- tioned in her own hand, certainly a curious present for a woman the grand duchess would later claim had been an obvious and complete stranger when they met.[38]

The telling remarks recorded during the visit by Rathlef-Keilmann, the fact that neither the Gilliards nor Olga Alexandrovna had openly rejected the claimant, the curious letters and intimate gifts—for Frau Tchaikovsky's supporters it all suggested impending recognition of her as Anastasia. As late as December 1925, Alexandra Gilliard was writing to Zahle's wife, " How is the invalid? My long silence might make you think that I have lost interest in her. That is definitely not the case. I think about her very often, and her tragic situation. . . . Tell her, I pray you, that not a day passes but I think of her and send her my most affectionate greetings."[39]

Then, suddenly, without warning, the story took a dramatic turn. On January 16, 1926—ten weeks after the visits to Berlin—the Copenhagen newspaper *National Tidende* carried a story that, while not attributed to the Romanovs, clearly originated with them and carried their blessing. "We can state," it reported, "with approval from the most authoritative source, that no common identifying characteristics exist between Grand Duchess Anastasia Nikolaievna, daughter of Tsar Nicholas II, and the lady in Berlin known by the name Tchaikovsky." For the first time, Olga Alexandrovna's visit to the claimant was made public. The article declared, rather inaccurately, that "neither she, nor anyone else who had known the Tsar's youngest daughter, could find the slightest resemblance" between Anastasia and the claimant; pointed how that at first it had been said that the young woman was a surviving Tatiana; curiously asserted that the claimant spoke with "a Bavarian accent"; and ended by describing her as a "sick and highly strung" young woman who "believes in her story."[40]

This had come directly from Olga Alexandrovna, channeled via her mother's private secretary Prince Dolgoruky to the editor of the paper.[41] Some two months later, Frau Tchaikovsky's supporters publicly fired back, in a *New York Times* article written by journalist Bella Cohen that was picked up by wire services and printed around the world. Drawing heavily on information from Rathlef-Keilmann, this offered up a sympathetic—and wildly inaccurate—rendering of the October 1925 meetings that left readers in little doubt that Olga Alexandrovna and the Gilliards had indeed recognized the claimant as Anastasia.[42] These two warring narratives, set out before a curious public, cemented a conflict that raged throughout the twentieth century: did the grand duchess and the Gilliards believe that Frau Tchaikovsky was an impostor, as they publicly asserted? Or, as Rathlef-Keilmann and the claimant's supporters argued, had they recognized her as Anastasia, only to later callously reject her? Seemingly irreconcilable, the opposing views enshrouded Frau Tchaikovsky's case with an air of intriguing, unfathomable mystery.

Adding to the legend were stories of what one relative termed Olga Alexandrovna's "anguished indecision," of how she had been forced to reverse her initial recognition of a woman she knew to be her niece.[43] Olga, said her cousin Princess Margaret of Denmark, had returned to Copenhagen uncertain; in the end, she had rejected the claimant because of "the influence of others."[44] The "others" here were popularly believed to be the Romanovs in exile, and more specifically Dowager Empress Marie Feodorovna, Grand Duchess Xenia Alexandrovna, and Olga's husband, Nicholas Kulikovsky. The latter, it was whispered, was anxious not to upset the precarious balance within the Copenhagen household, where he and his family lived dependent on the charity of Marie Feodorovna, who insisted that the claimant had to be a fraud, given her belief that no executions had ever occurred. It was said that the trio all regarded a surviving Anastasia as a stumbling block to their efforts to benefit financially from any tsarist funds discovered in foreign banks; there were allegations that the imperial family turned their backs on a woman they knew to be Anastasia because of her shameful admission of rape and having given birth to a bastard son whose whereabouts were unknown; and then there were assertions that consideration for her mother's beliefs and fragile health had led Olga to denounce the claimant.[45] To this last point, Tatiana Botkin added a piece of fourthhand information from former courtier Major General Alexander Spiridovich, who told her that after the meeting in Berlin, Olga Alexandrovna had confided to a friend, "Poor Mama! How am I supposed to tell her? It will kill her."[46]

After speaking to King Christian X of Denmark and his wife, Olga's cousin Grand Duke Andrei Vladimirovich wrote that "although there are some people who influence her by presenting everything as a story invented after the event, she is very troubled." He referred to "great pressure" exerted "to stop her from believing in the sick girl's identity. Although the Grand Duchess bows to this pressure, sending letters stating that she does not believe in the patient, this does not correspond at all with her inner feelings and morally she is suffering greatly because of it."[47] As to the Gilliards, or so the theories ran, they had gone along with this cruel deception in exchange for either money or in an attempt to curry favor with the remaining Romanovs and their relatives.

These ideas, given life in newspapers, magazines, and books that chronicled Frau Tchaikovsky's story, became an integral part of the mythology of her case. Yet the mystery is not without a solution, and that solution can be found not in answering the question Was the claimant Anastasia? but rather in the more complex Did Olga Alexandrovna and the Gilliards, as the evidence suggests, ever believe that she might be?

How else, for example, to explain Rathlef-Keilmann's contention that the Gilliards' behavior during the visit led her to believe that they "plainly admitted to the possibility" that the claimant was Anastasia? This might be put down more to opinion than to demonstrable evidence, but then there was the former tutor's startling outburst on his visit, "How horrible! What has happened to Grand Duchess Anastasia? She is a wreck, a complete physical wreck! I want to do everything I can to assist the Grand Duchess."[48]

This is more than suggestive; it is compelling. But is it true? Zahle read Rathlef-Keilmann's manuscript and said that her version "agrees with my memories and notes."[49] Yet he contradicted himself.

According to the minister, what Gilliard had in fact said was, "Oh, the poor grand duchess," a remark that he may have meant to indicate Olga Alexandrovna's difficult position.[50] And then Rathlef-Keilmann added to the confusion because the effusive words she attributed to Gilliard in her book—his reference to the claimant directly as "Grand Duchess Anastasia"—was missing from her earliest statements and letters concerning the visits. In a March 1926 statement, she quoted Gilliard as saying, "It's terrible, so terrible. I want to do everything I can to help the Grand Duchess." There was no mention of the name Anastasia here. That addition seemed to first appear in the pages of Rathlef-Keilmann's 1928 book.[51] The closest she came was an oblique line in an August 1926 letter to Serge Botkin, stating that Gilliard "spoke about the patient as about Grand Duchess Anastasia," but she recorded no words in which Gilliard had allegedly referred to the claimant directly as "Anastasia."[52]

With Zahle challenging Rathlef-Keilmann's precise words—and in this case the precise words attributed to Gilliard carried great significance—the only apparent confirmation for her published account was given after the fact by Professor Serge Rudnev, the tubercular specialist treating the claimant. But Rudnev had his own problems: he provided inaccurate descriptions of Frau Tchaikovsky's wounds that were disputed by every other doctor; he may have insisted—depending on whether one believed Rudnev or Rathlef-Keilmann was telling the truth, for each claimed the other was wrong about the issue—that he had treated Anastasia in 1914; and described a 1914 encounter in Moscow with Anastasia—"on the day war was declared," he said—when she had been in St. Petersburg with the imperial family.[53] In fact, as Gilliard recalled, Rudnev had not even been present when the conversation supposedly occurred; Frau Tchaikovsky's supporters who insisted that Gilliard was lying might have dismissed this but for one inconvenient fact: Gilliard first described the doctor's absence during the visit in the summer of 1926, before Rathlef-Keilmann had published a single line about the encounter and before the former tutor presumably knew of the need to challenge the professor's veracity.[54]

But in arguments over what was said—or supposedly said—one curiosity was lost, a curiosity that should have raised serious questions about Rathlef-Keilmann's version of events. According to her, Gilliard had gone through his first and second meetings with the claimant at St. Mary's Hospital in July 1925 without expressing an opinion on her identity; in October he had spent a morning at her bedside in the Mommsen Clinic, again without revealing anything. Then, suddenly, as he left the room, said Rathlef-Keilmann, he had been overcome—inexplicably—by some epiphany in which he adamantly recognized the claimant as Anastasia. And it had come without any discernible change, any intriguing revelation—bursting from the former tutor as if he had just encountered a ghost from the past for the first time. Rathlef-Keilmann never bothered to address what supposedly prompted this alleged and extraordinary outburst, rendering her account even more unlikely.

When Gilliard first heard Rathlef-Keilmann's claims he was furious, insisting that he had never referred to Frau Tchaikovsky as "Her Imperial Highness" or as "Grand Duchess Anastasia." Such claims by Rathlef-Keilmann, he wrote, were "knowingly false," calling them "words never uttered" but used "to create with readers the impression that I had been convinced and later changed my declaration."[55] Gilliard seemed to be on solid ground, given that even Zahle disputed the words Rathlef-Keilmann recounted, but the former tutor published a January 1926 letter in which Rathlef-Keilmann had assured him that any assertion he "had recognized the patient as the Grand Duchess is certainly untrue."[56] Gilliard later burned the letter—along with the rest of his files on the case, including evidence he had amassed against her—after a 1957 court ruling against the claimant, when he assumed they would no longer be needed.[57] The entire affair, including numerous public accusations from Rathlef-Keilmann and others that they had lied about recognizing the claimant, he explained, had been so painful that when the 1957 ruling came, he wanted nothing to remind him of Frau Tchaikovsky.[58] But since the letter no longer existed, some of Frau Tchaikovsky's supporters either ignored it or suggested, without evidence, that Gilliard was simply lying.[59] But tellingly, Rathlef-Keilmann never challenged the letter's 1929 publication, its attribution to her, nor its authenticity, suggesting that she had indeed written the damaging message.

Even Rathlef-Keilmann inadvertently offered evidence that undermined her contention that the Gilliards had recognized the claimant as Anastasia. On the last morning of the visit, as she noted, both had been "noticeably different" in their behavior toward the patient than on previous days; surely this change coincided with stories told by the von Schwabes and others asserting that Frau Tchaikovsky had acquired her knowledge of the Romanovs from books, photographs, and meetings with émigrés, which for the visitors apparently helped explain away some of the more troubling questions over her claim. That last morning, Gilliard had even told Zahle that he and his wife could not find "the slightest resemblance" between the claimant and Anastasia. But then, what of his parting words—"We are going away without being able to say that she is *not* Grand Duchess Anastasia"—which indicated uncertainty? It is likely that they stemmed not from confusion but rather from deference to Olga Alexandrovna; it was not that the Gilliards were unable to take a position on whether the claimant was Anastasia, but that they felt they could offer no opinion before the grand duchess did so, as the former tutor confided to one émigré that December of 1925: despite his "firm conviction that she is not Grand Duchess Anastasia Nikolaievna, I have not been authorized to make any official declaration."[60] Less than a week later, Alexandra Gilliard echoed this caution in a letter to the Danish legation in Berlin, asking, "Have they made a decision about her in Copenhagen? What are they going to do?"[61]

Even so, Gilliard remained in regular contact with Zahle, Rathlef-Keilmann, and members of the Russian émigré community in Berlin, probing the case. "I have not concealed from you, since my second visit to Berlin, that my investigation has only brought negative results, but out of duty I thought I should impartially and conscientiously continue to examine new facts as they appear, to give the patient every possible chance and to not overlook a single detail, however insignificant it might at first appear. Since my first visit to Berlin, all of the facts you have communicated from the patient were either matters of common knowledge—and thus not surprising that they were known to her—or if they were intimate in nature, without exception contained errors that Anastasia Nikolaievna would never have made."[62]

What of Alexandra Gilliard? Frau Tchaikovsky's supporters believed, as Grand Duke Andrei Vladimirovich asserted, that she "certainly did recognize Anastasia during the visits to the hospital."[63] But Andrei Vladimirovich had not been present during the encounters in Berlin, and his declaration rests on nothing more than the opinions of Rathlef-Keilmann and of Zahle; he never even spoke to Alexandra Gilliard about the issue. Still, people assumed the worst—that Alexandra Gilliard could not, as Peter Kurth wrote, "admit" to having recognized the claimant "because she was Mme. Pierre Gilliard."[64] Thus, the claimant's supporters were convinced, Alexandra Gilliard was forever silenced by her husband. She was forced, they held, to conceal her true feelings; Gilliard, they believed, never allowed her to express a single opinion on the case. They were wrong.

For the former nurse, the wife of Pierre Gilliard, the woman whom Zahle declared had a heart "stronger than her head," did indeed offer her opinion on Frau Tchaikovsky's asserted identity.[65] The encounters in Berlin—evoking, as they did, the ghosts of a painful past—were fraught with anxiety and emotion, something her husband fully admitted. But Alexandra Gilliard's parting words, as recorded by Rathlef-Keilmann, her reference to the claimant not as Anastasia but rather as "this girl here," suggest not recognition but rather the pity of which her husband later wrote. Three months after the meeting in Berlin, Madame Gilliard wrote frankly to Rathlef-Keilmann, "Though I have not found anything in her features or her ways that remind me of Anastasia Nikolaievna, I am ready to help you in your researches. . . . The letter of the invalid is touching and has moved me, but I have not found in it Anastasia."[66] This seems decisive enough, but there was more: in January 1927, Alexandra Gilliard signed her name to a formal statement rejecting the claimant as Anastasia. There was, she admitted, "a common malformation of the feet" shared by Frau Tchaikovsky and the grand duchess, and "a vague resemblance, more to Grand Duchess Tatiana Nikolaievna than to Anastasia Nikolaievna," but "any similarity" to the youngest of Nicholas II's daughters "vanished on prolonged physical inspection." According to Alexandra Gilliard, Frau Tchaikovsky was not Anastasia.[67]

If evidence does not support the pervasive myth that the Gilliards recognized Frau Tchaikovsky as Anastasia, it is even less compelling in the case of Olga Alexandrovna. She may well, as Gilliard wrote, have been "deeply troubled" over Frau Tchaikovsky's "strange revelations," and confused over certain aspects of the case; after all, she had last seen a fifteen-year-old, pudgy Anastasia for an hour in 1916, and in Berlin faced an emaciated young woman in her twenties. But much of the supposed evidence of her recognition—the very evidence that helped transform the case into a modern myth—is at best questionable and often demonstrably wrong. Take, for example, the heartwarming conversation at the Mommsen Clinic that Rathlef-Keilmann noted in her statement, in which Olga had spoken of "Our Little One" and "Shura" being "happy to have found one another again." Surely this was proof that she believed Frau Tchaikovsky to be Anastasia. And yet, if this took place, why did Rathlef-Keilmann omit such a critical and highly revealing piece of information from her book on the case? It is yet another conflict between what she claimed privately and what she published, another shifting of Rathlef-Keilmann's stories. Perhaps she simply eliminated an exaggerated conversation from her book because, prior to publication, she asked Olga Alexandrovna to read the manuscript; according to Zahle, the grand duchess only examined those passages in which her visit was mentioned, and she had agreed that they were "correct" in their "depiction" of what had occurred.[68] But coupled with other discrepancies in her accounts, contradictions from Zahle, from Gilliard, and from her own writings, it undermines Rathlef-Keilmann as a completely credible voice in the case.

It seems likely, especially given her parting words—whatever they may have been—to Zahle, that Olga Alexandrovna left Berlin troubled, perhaps still uncertain, but without having recognized Frau Tchaikovsky as Anastasia. She may, though, have harbored some uncertain hope, something hinted at in the letter she sent to Zahle on leaving Germany, a letter that had included such lines as "whoever she is" and "my feeling is that she is not the one she believes," but that also ended with the ambiguous "one can't *say she* is not as a fact." From this it is apparent that Olga was unable or unwilling to immediately make a final decision, although she clearly doubted that the claimant was her niece. Just a few weeks later, she reiterated this position to John Prince, an envoy at the American embassy in Copenhagen, saying that neither she nor the Gilliards "could establish an identification," though Prince noted that the grand duchess "did not absolutely deny this woman's identity. . . . She is convinced that she is not consciously simulating, as she was given many opportunities to give false answers which she did not avail herself of, but neither could she give correct ones. Grand Duchess Olga left Berlin without being able to give any definite answer as to the identity of Frau Tchaikovsky, although she is almost sure that the claimant cannot be Anastasia."[69]

But if this was true, why did Olga Alexandrovna send all of those letters to Frau Tchaikovsky, all of those intimate gifts, including a personal photograph album? These, the claimant's supporters suggested, were proof that Olga had indeed recognized her as Anastasia and only later changed her mind, ignoring the fact that her own farewell letter to Zahle undermined any such contention. Later, Olga justified her actions, declaring, "I know I should never have done so, but I did it out of pity. You have no idea how wretched that woman looked."[70] While the grand duchess may have acted rashly in dispatching letters and gifts, she almost certainly did so, as she insisted, out of compassion rather than recognition. Indeed, in none of the letters did she address the claimant as "Anastasia," indicate that she accepted any family relationship with her, nor sign herself as "Aunt Olga." In writing to Frau Tchaikovsky in Russian, she employed the formal form of "you," addressing her not as an intimate but as a stranger.[71]

These letters, though, may have served a hidden agenda. Olga Alexandrovna was awaiting word of Gilliard's ongoing investigations into the more perplexing aspects of the case before making any public statement. There were, she frankly admitted, "many remarkable things" that the claimant seemed to know, and that needed to be resolved, but she asked Gilliard to continue his investigation in Berlin, seeking possible answers from the émigré circles in which Frau Tchaikovsky had moved.[72] Until these questions could be answered, Olga may have hoped that the apparently friendly gestures would ensure the temporary silence of Tchaikovsky and her supporters, for there was constant worry that Rathlef-Keilmann was about to go public with her version of events.[73] Zahle, for his part, reported in an official memorandum what seems to have been the truth of the affair, a truth that—despite his claims that Rathlef-Keilmann's book was correct—contradicted the legend. Olga Alexandrovna, he explained, had been unable to give a definitive answer to the question of the claimant's identity during the visit, but after receiving more information from Berlin and answers from Gilliard's investigation, she was able to reject the possibility that the woman was her niece.[74]

And if this was true, what of all the stories of Olga's private doubts, of her anguished indecision over the affair? Nearly all were based on second-, third-, or fourthhand information, and many were spread by Andrei Vladimirovich, who, despite receiving assurances from Olga that she had not recognized Frau Tchaikovsky as Anastasia, reported quite the opposite, seizing upon every rumor because he fully believed in the integrity of Rathlef-Keilmann and Zahle. Rendering the situation even more confusing, Andrei—after diligently circulating and repeating all rumors to the contrary—later insisted that he did not believe Olga Alexandrovna had ever been "entirely convinced" that the claimant was Anastasia.[75] And whatever uncertainly Olga may have had evaporated over those autumn months of 1925. At the beginning of December, she wrote to Anatole Mordvinov, former adjutant to her brother Nicholas II, "All of us tried very hard to get her to reveal something new, but she merely spoke of happy trivialities. When we asked her about some aspect of the past, she would fall silent and cover her eyes with her hands. There's no resemblance, and she is without doubt not Anastasia, but still it is a remarkable thing, and she is completely convinced that she is Anastasia. . . . I left deeply moved. . . . It's a very sad tale, and I'm terribly sorry for this confused girl. . . . Mama isn't interested at all and opposed my trip, but I had to go for the sake of the family."[76] And to Princess Irene of Prussia she wrote, "There is no resemblance at all. . . . She was unable to answer one of the many intimate questions asked. It was pitiful to see how the poor creature tried to convince us she was Anastasia. . . . Her head had been stuffed with all these stories, she has been shown a lot of photos, etc., and, one day, she astonished the world with her 'memories.' Mr. Gilliard, his wife, my husband, and above all, old Volkov, all saw and spoke with her, and none believe she is our Anastasia. But it is said that we all recognized her and later had orders from Mama to say she is not Anastasia. This is a huge lie! I suspect blackmail, though many people, who never knew Anastasia, seem to believe it. During the four days we spent in Berlin, Mr. Gilliard and my husband saw all the Russians with whom she had lived formerly, and they thus learnt many things that are of great importance. . . . It is always possible to find explanations for this case, if one takes the time to do so."[77]

Olga Alexandrovna never officially wavered from this position, and she repeated it in a series of letters over the next few years. "No matter how much we tried," she wrote to Tatiana Botkin, "none of us were able to recognize either of my nieces Tatiana or Anastasia in this patient; in fact, we were convinced of the opposite."[78] Soon enough, though, Olga learned of the intimations, of the rumors, and of the outright declarations asserting that she had indeed recognized Frau Tchaikovsky and later rejected her. "Everyone," she wrote, "is assailing me from all sides over this affair. Letters come from all over about her—it's simply horrid! No one wants to believe that we didn't recognize her, and we hear such unkind things being said. She herself is very nice, but those around her all lie."[79] And, a few months later, "I am so tired of this Berlin business! Letters and telegrams without end come from the world over—even California. People accuse us, out of self-interest, of not recognizing her. What an idiotic thing to believe! God be with them! But we're not going to issue any more denials."[80]

The idea that Olga Alexandrovna had recognized and then rejected Frau Tchaikovsky as her niece became central to the mythology of the case, but it haunted the grand duchess for the rest of her life. There was, it is true, a certain ambiguity in her statements and in her behavior that led many favorable to the claimant to suspect the worst; later there came tales that in her waning years Olga was again overwhelmed with doubt, that she had confided to a friend in Toronto that she had indeed recognized the claimant as Anastasia. Ultimately, according to this story, she had been forced to deny her owing to "family pressure."[81] Whether this was true or not, whether it reflected a momentary lapse or a more pervasive and lingering question, Olga despised any hint that she had in any way been uncertain, and like many others in the case she began to recast her history with the claimant, depicting the meeting at the Mommsen Clinic in increasingly adamant and contradictory statements designed to conceal any initial doubt.

In 1959, a reluctant Olga Alexandrovna gave a deposition to a visiting German judge in the court case the claimant had brought for legal recognition as Anastasia. In this encounter at the West German consulate in Toronto, Olga explained her letters and small gifts to Frau Tchaikovsky as "friendly acts toward a sick person," not as indications of recognition.[82] Then there was the issue of a cable Olga was said to have received from her sister Xenia during the Berlin visit, instructing her not to acknowledge the claimant as Anastasia. Though such a cable has never come to light, its existence was largely accepted as fact by the claimant's supporters.[83] "I swear to God," Olga Alexandrovna said during her testimony at the consulate, "that I never received, either before or after my visit to Berlin, any telegram or letter from my sister Xenia advising me not to acknowledge the claimant. This is simply not true."[84] When asked about the October 31, 1925, letter to Zahle

in which she had said, "one can't *say she* is not" Anastasia "as a fact."
However, Olga began to obfuscate. At first, she denied that any such
letter existed; when shown a copy, she insisted, not at all convincingly, that
she had not written the message. When someone dared to point out
her signature at the bottom of the letter, she finally snapped, saying,
"If I wrote that letter, I cannot say today why I used these words, as it
was certainly my opinion that the person was not Anastasia!"[85] Clearly
unwilling to admit that she had ever harbored even the most minimal
of doubts, Olga Alexandrovna became increasingly agitated, her replies
"curt and evasive" when they were given at all; finally, she became so
hysterical that officials summoned a doctor, but she prematurely ended
the evidentiary dilemma by declaring the deposition at an end and
storming out of the consulate.[86]

At the time, Olga was working with writer Ian Vorres on her memoirs;
like her deposition, these were reshaped to eliminate any hint of uncertainty about the claimant's identity and included assertions and incidents
at variance with other evidence. When her memoirs finally appeared in
1964, four years after her death, they represented less a factual accounting
of the grand duchess's experiences than they did efforts to minimize
her own initial doubts. Thus she insisted that on entering the patient's
room, the claimant had said in German, "*Ist das die Tante?*" (Is this the
aunt?). "That," Olga said, "at once took me aback."[87] No one else present, not even Gilliard, mentioned any such remark, and had it occurred,
surely the former tutor would have included it as damning evidence
against Frau Tchaikovsky. She insisted that the claimant "did not seem
to understand a word of Russian," although just five weeks after the
encounter she had written to Anatole Mordvinov quite the opposite,
saying, "She appears to understand Russian, but would only answer in
German."[88] Then there was her adamant statement, "As soon as I had
sat down by the bed in the Mommsen Nursing Home, I knew I was
looking at a stranger. The spiritual bond between my dear Anastasia
and myself was so strong that neither time nor any ghastly experience
could have interfered with it. I don't really know what name to give to
that feeling—but I do know it was wholly absent."[89]

Clearly, though, Frau Tchaikovsky bore some minimal resemblance
to Anastasia, or acquitted herself well enough, or seemed to know per-
plexingly intimate details about the Romanovs that Olga—like Volkov
and the Gilliards—could not immediately and automatically dismiss.
She needed further visits, further evidence, before she could satisfy
herself that the claimant was not her niece. Had the grand duchess
really been confronted with so obvious a fake as she later insisted, why
did she then return to her bedside for two further, extended visits?
Faced with such objections, Olga's son Tikhon asserted that his mother

"saw immediately" that the claimant was not Anastasia "and was ready to go home," but had remained in Berlin out of pity, "tricked because of her unusually kind heart." Zahle, he asserted, had "insisted" that Olga Alexandrovna remain "just a few days more, because the poor sick woman was anticipating the meeting for a long time; it would be cruel to just disappear."[90]

But not everything could be blamed on Zahle. As much as she later refused to admit it, Olga Alexandrovna had harbored—even if only for a day or two—uncertainty over the identity of the young woman claiming to be her niece. By concealing this temporary doubt, the grand duchess added fuel to the conspiratorial fires that enveloped the claimant's case. In the adamant denials of her own history, she unwittingly fed the intrigue that transformed Frau Tchaikovsky into a living legend.

10

"If the Imperial House of Russia Wants to Let One of Its Own Die in the Gutter . . ."

ANASTASIA TCHAIKOVSKY FLOATED through these momentous
months, largely unaware of the increasing intrigue surrounding
her claim and still hopeful that fate would turn in her favor.
She seemed curiously detached from her claim, uninterested in attempts
to prove that she was the youngest daughter of Nicholas II. "She does not
want, and is not striving for, recognition," wrote Serge Botkin's deputy
Baron Osten-Sacken in 1926. "Nobody could give her back her peace
of mind, in any event; the mental anguish is so unbearable. . . . She
wants under no circumstances to return to Russia, and then she doesn't
understand either why it is necessary to establish her identity, which
even her near relations are contesting."[1]

It was one of the hallmarks of Tchaikovsky's claim, and most
curious behavior for someone condemned by her opponents as a fraud.
Wouldn't any impostors, almost by definition, seek to prove their
alleged identity? Wouldn't they cooperate in attempts to win recognition?
Even Tchaikovsky's most vociferous critics acknowledged that she was different, that she confounded expectations, and that her disinterest alone
invested her claim with an aura of plausibility. She would meet with
those who came to see her, but she never sought them out; she would
often freely and spontaneously speak of her alleged past, but when
pressed by others to do so she usually refused; the nonchalance with

which she treated the most serious of issues, as if it was all beneath her, all too humiliating and painful, simply elevated her to a mythic realm no other royal claimant ever entered. But while she remained unwell and isolated in her bed, a storm was building outside the Mommsen Clinic.

The January 1926 article in Copenhagen's *National Tidende* denouncing Frau Tchaikovsky and the realization that Olga Alexandrovna and the Gilliards had rejected her shocked the claimant's supporters in Berlin. Zahle immediately returned to Denmark and attempted to intercede with Olga Alexandrovna; he was, she confided to Gilliard, "more convinced than ever" that the claimant was Anastasia.[2] She now blamed Zahle for all the intrigue, "the author of this present, complete chaos. No one asked him to meddle in this affair and to cause such a furor. He's stubborn and imagines that he has found a protégé, that she will make him famous, that his name is now linked with a quite extraordinary bit of history."[3]

Olga Alexandrovna found a sympathetic ally in Gilliard. "I am persuaded," he wrote, "that M. Zahle undertook this investigation impelled by the most honorable sentiments. But instead of keeping to a serious examination of the evidence, he let himself be fooled by appearances. He threw himself body and soul into this adventure, and has tried to move heaven and earth when he faced obstacles. Before our second visit to Berlin he had already gone and agitated the entire Danish Court and asked the advice of the Danish and German Foreign Ministries. . . . And because he did not see his error in time, his position has been completely compromised. Events of the last few months have convinced me that M. Zahle is determined to prove that he is not mistaken; already, he imagines himself to be in jeopardy. To save himself, the patient in Berlin *must* be Anastasia."[4]

Influenced by Rathlef-Keilmann, Zahle, in turn, made no secret of his belief that Olga Alexandrovna and Pierre Gilliard had knowingly turned their backs on a surviving Anastasia. While he was circumspect in referring to the grand duchess, he had no such hesitation when discussing the former tutor, asserting flatly that Gilliard's version of events in Berlin was inconsistent with fact.[5] After Olga's rejection at the beginning of 1926, King Christian X abruptly terminated Zahle's investigation. Fearing that he might be constrained from further involvement by Copenhagen, Zahle drew up a list of theoretical questions concerning his knowledge of the case that were written so as to answer themselves. Although the persistent mythology of Tchaikovsky's case painted them as telling, there was nothing particularly revelatory in the list: Zahle suggested that during the October 1925 visit neither Olga Alexandrovna nor the Gilliards had explicitly declared that the claimant was not Anastasia; that Nicholas and Alice von Schwabe had negatively influenced the trio against the claimant; that von Schwabe and Gilliard had been in communication with representatives of Grand Duke Ernst Ludwig of Hesse; that Zahle believed the grand duchess had "given the appearance" of having recognized the claimant, only to later reject her; that Gilliard had dismissed his uncertainty in an effort to "secure the approbation of the surviving members of the Romanov Family"; that the claimant had clearly understood Russian when it was spoken but had answered in German; and that Tchaikovsky suggested Baroness Buxhoeveden had betrayed the imperial family in Siberia and had rejected her because she feared exposure.[6]

Zahle is said to have summed up his eventual position on the claimant in a comment made to her supporter Prince Friedrich of Saxe-Altenburg: "All I want is that my Royal House of Denmark be blameless in the eyes of history in this affair. If the Imperial House of Russia wants to let one of its own die in the gutter, then we can do nothing."[7] By 1927, he had apparently come to believe that Rathlef-Keilmann had used him and abused his trust by distorting evidence in the case. In January of that year, he spent several days in Darmstadt with Grand Duke Ernst Ludwig, arguing evidence and details in the case. "We had hard discussions," wrote Ernst Ludwig, "because he arrived with the idea that we knew hardly anything, and would follow his advice. But slowly I got him round for we were able to show him that he had also been lied to." The grand duke allowed Zahle to read his own files on the claimant, files that included voluminous correspondence with Rathlef-Keilmann as well as his detailed replies to her queries, and to compare them against what Rathlef-Keilmann had told the minister. This revealed numerous instances where Rathlef-Keilmann had either withheld information or had edited the grand duke's replies to make it appear as if he was lying about the facts in the case. Zahle, Ernst Ludwig wrote, "was very much taken aback at this," convinced as he had been that Rathlef-Keilmann was completely honest and had provided him with nothing but accurate information. "He wants to get out of this affair now, as he is sick of it," the grand duke recorded. By the end of the visit, Zahle told Ernst Ludwig that he "sees that he has been lied to" and that he wanted to quietly excuse himself from further involvement with Rathlef-Keilmann, though he asked the grand duke not to reveal this decision.[8]

True to his word, Zahle began to extricate himself from Rathlef-Keilmann's circle, though not from the claimant, with whom he remained friendly and in whose asserted identity he continued to believe. After meeting with Grand Duke Ernst Ludwig, said Serge Botkin, for the first time he detected in Zahle "a note of doubt" about Frau Tchaikovsky's identity, as if "he knew something, but he would not tell me what.'"[9] By this time, though, the damage had largely been done. Zahle and Serge Botkin had worked closely with Rathlef-Keilmann to advance the case, and Rathlef-Keilmann was now the accepted authority on Frau Tchaikovsky, the person who cared for her and arranged her life, who granted access and kept the suspicious at bay, who recorded her memories and publicized her case. By 1926, she had a new protégé: Grand Duke Andrei Vladimirovich, first cousin to Nicholas II and Olga Alexandrovna and a graduate of St. Petersburg's Alexandrovsky Military Judicial Academy. Andrei had followed the case with interest, and began his own investigation into Frau Tchaikovsky's claim, hoping, he said, "to establish the truth, no matter what it may be," based on an analysis of "all materials, whether favorable or otherwise."[10] The dowager empress and Olga Alexandrovna, reported Zahle, had "authorized" the grand duke "to represent them in this matter."[11] Zahle was wrong. "Rumors reached me," Andrei admitted to Serge Botkin, "indicating that Dowager Empress Marie Feodorovna and Grand Duchess Olga Alexandrovna were against this inquiry, and that efforts to resolve the situation would be met with disapproval from that quarter."[12] After he explained his interest, Olga told her cousin that while she did not believe the young woman was Anastasia, neither her mother nor herself "could forbid" his private inquiry.[13]

Grand Duke Kirill Vladimirovich, Andrei's elder brother and the rightful heir to the former Russian throne, was firmly against this investigation. In the highly uncertain and politically charged émigré universe, the brothers often battled over Andrei's alliances with questionable parties and his tendency to gravitate to intrigue; Andrei, said one official, was too "easily influenced."[14] For the moment, though, Kirill did nothing, and Andrei launched his inquiry. With so many conflicting claims and the pervasive swell of rumor, Frau Tchaikovsky's claim carried just enough evidence to endow it with an aura of plausibility, but it was already becoming a morass of contradictions, and Andrei's involvement did nothing to clarify matters. Most of his information on the case came from Zahle, who had received it from Rathlef-Keilmann herself, and it was this evidence—much of it of questionable integrity and almost all of it favorable to the claimant—that Andrei examined.

Grand Duke Andrei Vladimirovich.

Thus he came to believe that his cousin

Olga and the Gilliards were lying about the encounters in Berlin, accepting Rathlef-Keilmann's contention that they had recognized the claimant as Anastasia.

Not surprisingly, when Gilliard learned of the grand duke's investigation he began to flood him with letters, warning that he was being used and was relying on prejudiced materials. By this time, the former tutor had become Rathlef-Keilmann's dedicated enemy and Frau Tchaikovsky's most vociferous critic; in the fall of 1925, he had begun actively working with Count Kuno von Hardenberg, Grand Duke Ernst Ludwig's former marshal of the court, in collecting evidence against the claimant. Soon enough, Gilliard was pompously calling himself "the Representative of the Grand Duke of Hesse."[15] Now, with all the fervor of a religious crusade, Gilliard attempted to persuade Andrei to drop the matter; when the grand duke swept aside the former tutor's objections, Gilliard dropped any pretense of being polite. As the grand duke confided, Gilliard "wrote me a letter so impertinent that I decided it was best not to answer him. In the end he has unmasked himself as a petty man who is capable of lying."[16] Gilliard, in turn, eagerly believed the worst of the grand duke. He openly accused Andrei Vladimirovich of "collecting and believing documents, many of Bolshevik origin," supporting the claimant, and of ignoring evidence against her case.[17] What these alleged Bolshevik documents were, or what they said, Gilliard never explained, and there is no proof that they ever existed. But Gilliard's rather too heated advocacy destroyed any hope that the stubborn grand duke would prove receptive to his version of events, for soon he was writing, "I must note with regret that all that Gilliard has written about the Berlin meeting is quite far from the truth."[18]

Adamant and erroneous assertions from those on both sides of the case flew about in these years, creating a tangled web of claims and counterclaims that shrouded Frau Tchaikovsky in a growing legend, but the young woman at the center of the storm remained aloof from the intrigues. By the spring of 1926, as an increasingly large universe of interested parties battled each other over her identity, she had finally, after nearly two years of constant hospitalization, sufficiently recovered to be discharged from the Mommsen Clinic. She had nowhere to go, however, and Zahle finally arranged for her, accompanied by Rathlef-Keilmann, to travel to the Swiss resort of Lugano. Their extended stay at the Hotel Tivoli was a holiday paid for by Prince Waldemar of Denmark, who, despite his niece Olga Alexandrovna's negative opinion of the claimant, was still willing to ensure the mysterious young woman's well-being.[19] Her supporters thought that this reflected continued uncertainty over her identity; it may, though, have been yet another attempt—like the letters and gifts from Olga Alexandrovna—to control the claimant. As long as some Romanov relative was tending to her financial needs, the expectation may well have been that she would remain isolated and that Rathlef-Keilmann, about whom rumors of publishing contracts constantly swirled, would remain silent.

At first, things went well, but soon enough Frau Tchaikovsky's volatile and difficult temperament surfaced. She was depressed, "completely embittered," said Rathlef-Keilmann, "and she distrusted everybody, even those who were good and kind to her. This may be partly explained by the fact that she was completely without any understanding of human nature. She believed most in those who constantly flattered her and were servile towards her."[20] Frustrated and angry, she increasingly lashed out at Rathlef-Keilmann, blaming her for every misfortune; by the third week of June, after endless days of abuse, Rathlef-Keilmann had had enough, and returned to Berlin. "She's either crazy or truly wicked," she declared of the claimant.[21] But Frau Tchaikovsky could not be left alone; she was not responsible enough to care for herself, and Serge Botkin dispatched his assistant Baron Vassili Osten-Sacken to Lugano to make other arrangements for her. The baron's solution was to have the claimant admitted to the Stillachhaus Sanatorium at Oberstdorf in the Bavarian Alps.[22] Complaining that this was an "attempt to lock her up in an insane asylum" but with nowhere else to go, she reluctantly entered the clinic on June 25, 1926; here she would remain until the spring of 1927.[23]

Stillachhaus in the Bavarian Alps, where Anderson spent the winter of 1926–1927.

The new patient at Stillachhaus was a living enigma. Those who had treated her in Berlin, tubercular specialist Dr. Serge Rudnev and Professors Lothar Nobel and Karl Bonhoeffer, and the two doctors who tended to her at Stillachhaus, Chief Physician Professor Saathof and his deputy, a young intern specializing in internal medicine named Theodor Eitel, all left intriguing and occasionally contradictory assessments of her complex personality in these years. According to Rudnev, the claimant was "convinced that everything was useless, and she was only waiting to die." Tchaikovsky was often depressed, and always suspicious of unknown faces and surroundings. In drawing out her feelings, Rudnev found that she "regarded everyone around her as hostile." When he finally convinced her to speak about her alleged childhood at the Russian court, though, Rudnev believed that the details "could only have been known to the closest relatives of Nicholas II's family."[24]

Dr. Lothar Nobel of the Mommsen Clinic offered a more comprehensive analysis. He noted that while she could be "friendly and polite," Frau Tchaikovsky possessed a "unique timidity and troubled reserve," particularly when questions of the past were raised, to which she most often responded with silence. He called her character "variable; at times she seems to be in good humor, at others, she is melancholic in nature." He observed her frequent feelings of "apathy and impotence," bouts of depression during which she kept to her bed, "declaring that she wished to die," a situation undoubtedly exacerbated by her illness. She spoke in vague terms of her past, describing her existence as so "terrible" that she had tried to kill herself in an effort to "forget the horrible things" she had experienced." She also often expressed a "fear of being discovered"; this, her supporters suggested, stemmed from worry that Soviet agents would track her down and kill her, while opponents thought she merely feared exposure of what they believed to be her real identity.[25]

Nobel concluded that the claimant exhibited no "signs of mental deficiency, nor any evidence of suggestion or influence." He deemed her to be sane, though highly strung. Then, like Rudnev, he abandoned his professional analysis and ventured into the realm of speculation. "It seems to me impossible," he wrote, "that the numerous and apparently trivial details she recalls cannot be attributed to anything other than her own experiences. Also, from a psychological point of view, it seems unlikely that anyone engaged for whatever purpose in acting the part of another would behave as the patient does in displaying so little initiative in achieving her aims."[26]

Professor Karl Bonhoeffer, too, noted Frau Tchaikovsky's depression and morbid preoccupation with death. At times she was "a kind and courteous person, who expressed her gratitude for small favors," although he also noted that "she could also appear somewhat overbearing." It was,

Bonhoeffer declared, "extremely difficult to obtain a definitive portrait of her personality" owing to her reticence and to conflicting impressions. She gave the appearance of "having come from good circles," of being "an aristocratic lady," though at the same time there were clear indications that "she suffers from mental impairment." Like Nobel, Bonhoeffer was adamant in declaring that the claimant "is not suffering from mental disease in the usual sense," though he described her as "possessed of a psychopathic condition" that manifested itself in depressed, emotional instability and frequent changes of mood. He also denounced the idea of any hypnotic influence or "deliberate fraud."[27]

Professor Saathof supervised the facility at Stillachhaus and left most of Frau Tchaikovsky's care to his staff. In evaluating her case, Saathof—as he freely admitted—relied on impressions gathered from his infrequent talks with the claimant as well as a review of her records, and the idea that she was Anastasia certainly seems to have influenced his views. He wrote of her "distinctive character" that occasionally manifested itself in displays of "ingratitude." Saathof asserted, "To view Frau Tchaikovsky as an intentional fraud is, to my mind, quite out of the question," citing her lack of cooperation with those who sought to advance her case. He believed that it was "impossible that this woman originated from the lower ranks of society. Her entire character is so distinctive, so completely cultivated, that even if nothing be known with certainty about her origins, she must be viewed as the descendant of an old, cultured, and I feel extremely decadent family."[28]

For his part, Eitel described Frau Tchaikovsky as "reticent, nervous, pleasant, and very restrained." At first he accepted Bonhoeffer's diagnosis of a psychopathic condition shaped by the patient's apparently intentional will to forget her past, largely because Eitel had only a passing familiarity with psychiatric matters. He noted the apparent gaps in her memory, as well as the fact that when comfortable in her surroundings, she would often speak spontaneously and at great length of her alleged childhood at the Russian court. This Eitel took as evidence that "the patient actually experienced the events she described." In time, and despite his own lack of psychiatric training, Eitel criticized the opinions offered by Nobel and Bonhoeffer, insisting that he observed no "symptoms of mental derangement, and no conclusive indications of a psychopathic state." Rather, as he came to believe that the claimant was Anastasia, he wrote of her "noble nature" and his belief that she had been "exposed since birth to the highest circles." Citing as evidence the personal opinions of several convinced supporters, Eitel thus reported, "It is possible to conclude that Mrs. Tchaikovsky is, in fact, Grand Duchess Anastasia."[29]

This psychological portrait, like so much in Frau Tchaikovsky's case, was subject to interpretation. Everyone agreed that she could be polite and cooperative; at other times she was depressed, and would erupt in sudden displays of temper. The doctors all believed her to be sane, though highly strung and often emotional. She could be charming and callous at the same time, friendly and yet imperious. No one—not in these years or through-out the decades that followed—could ever really say that they knew her, for she erected a protective wall and care-fully guarded her innermost thoughts. There was undoubtedly an aura of

Anderson, 1926.

tragic vulnerability about her, something so seemingly helpless and desperate that led many to excuse her worst excesses, a childlike quality as if she needed to be cared for and cosseted against the uncertainties of the world.

The chief interest in these accounts, though, is in some surprising revelations about Frau Tchaikovsky's mental acumen and memory. She and her supporters always contended that the injuries to her head made recall a difficult and painful process, and that it was a constant struggle for her to remember details of her life. This explanation excused much—her refusal or inability to converse in Russian, in English, or in French, her apparent reluctance to answer queries about her past, her battle to recall names and faces and dates when pressed. She declared that she had forgotten how to tell time or count; that although she often played solitaire, she could not differentiate between the numbers; that she had to constantly remind herself how to dress; and even that the ability to write evaded her. Everything—languages, words, memories, and daily tasks—required extraordinary efforts and "constant practice, or else she forgets."[30] It was all further evidence, ran the story, that she must actually be Anastasia, for how could an impostor, a woman so physically and psychologically damaged, ever successfully commit to memory the multitude of trivial details about the life of the imperial family that Frau Tchaikovsky revealed?

But was this true? The reports of Nobel and Bonhoeffer chal-lenged this widely believed interpretation. Nobel noted that Frau Tchaikovsky asserted, quite falsely, that she had never read any books or magazines with stories about the Romanovs, something contradicted by the historical record. When she spoke of her alleged past as Anastasia, Nobel recorded, she did so "slowly, and with hesitation"; much of the time, however, she attributed her inability to answer questions to headaches or to her poor health. Nobel thought that she suffered from a diminished memory, saying, "Only concerning recent events is her recall normal." Yet he contradicted this, recording how she often spoke spontaneously and in great detail about life at Tsarskoye Selo, cruises aboard the imperial yacht *Standart*, holidays in the Crimea, and about her time in Berlin. She possessed extraordinary recall of her stay at Dalldorf; according to Nobel, she recounted her experiences "correctly and without hesitation," replete with such complex details as the names of the nurses and doctors who had cared for her; the names and illnesses of specific fellow patients; and even the dates on which certain events had occurred at the asylum. And there was something else: Nobel could find no organic cause for her apparent loss of memory or impaired abilities; rather than the result of physical trauma, he believed that such apparent difficulties were simply "a question of will."[31]

Bonhoeffer, too, noted that Frau Tchaikovsky could accurately recall "the names of her hospital wards, the names of her nurses, and even the names of some individuals" from her stays at the Elisabeth Hospital and at Dalldorf, along with numerous childhood memories. When pressed, though, she "often evades detailed questions by saying that it is too painful to discuss her memories, or that she is too ill to express herself." She insisted, again quite falsely, that she could not read German, certainly an odd claim given all of the evidence to the contrary. He could find "no organic basis" for the apparent lapses in memory or in her recall of languages, writing that "none of the other expected symptoms that would accompany an injury to the cranial centers of communication are present." He speculated that this reticence was mental rather than physical in nature, a deliberate, though he believed perhaps unconscious, ploy on her part, reflecting a desire to "suppress unpleasant experiences."[32]

What did this mean? If Nobel and Bonhoeffer were correct, the injuries to Frau Tchaikovsky's head—injuries never as severe as portrayed by her supporters—played no role in her apparent inability to convincingly speak Russian, English, or French, or to recall certain memories. With this contention, at least, Eitel also agreed, for he, too, could find no physical impairment to her mental faculties and nothing in the injuries to her head that would affect her memory.[33] If it was merely a question of "will," as Nobel thought, was Frau Tchaikovsky consciously feigning difficulty with her memory, or was she genuinely plagued with some unknown mental condition that hampered her abilities? Supporters and opponents alike saw in this exactly what they expected to find—a damaged Anastasia or a deliberate fraud.

These perceptions constantly hovered over Frau Tchaikovsky in these uncertain months, for no one around her really knew what to believe of her claim. The claimant herself was lonely, unhappy at Stillachhaus, believing that she had been abandoned by everyone, but she might have remained here, secluded and cared for, had not Gilliard again intervened. In the spring of 1927, he persuaded Count Kuno von Hardenberg to seek Frau Tchaikovsky's expulsion from Bavaria, asserting that she was a criminal impostor.[34] When Zahle learned of this, he appealed to Duke Georg of Leuchtenberg, a Russian émigré related to the Romanovs who lived in Bavaria, to intercede and protect her interests. The duke agreed, inviting the claimant to stay at Schloss Seeon, his country estate; his goal, he explained, was "to give her a refuge with a friendly Russian family" until her case could be resolved.[35]

It took some negotiation before Frau Tchaikovsky agreed to this plan.[36] "The Leuchtenbergs! What are the Leuchtenbergs?" she exclaimed on first hearing the suggestion, although Rathlef-Keilmann later insisted that she had immediately recognized the name and launched into a detailed genealogical recitation, something unsupported by the evidence.[37] Although she was unhappy at Stillachhaus, she had endured a rootless existence, shuffled from one émigré to the next, from one hospital to another; she was tired, alone, and not at all certain what to expect of life at Seeon. Would she be left alone, cared for, and allowed to do as she wished? Or, as had happened during her time with the von Kleists, would she be put on show, questioned and queried by a constant stream of inquisitive, skeptical émigrés? But with threats of possible legal action, and nowhere else to go, she had little choice. Just after nightfall on the evening of March 1, 1927, she stepped from a train at the little village of Prien on the Chiemsee, where the duke of Leuchtenberg waited in the shadows. Sitting silently in the rear of a somewhat battered open touring car, she bounced and bumped as they sped over the frozen countryside, up low hills and down narrow country lanes before Schloss Seeon, its walls ghostly white in the moonlight, loomed out of the darkness, an uncertain sanctuary in the tumultuous uncertainty that was her life.

I I

"A Sort of Weird Charm"

Seeon, Frau Tchaikovsky would later say, "is the loveliest place in Germany."[1] Originally a Benedictine monastery founded in the tenth century, the white-walled, red-roofed complex sprawled serenely on a tree-shaded island at the edge of the alpine waters of the Klostersee. There were actually two churches here: the Chapel of St. Walburg, set in its own walled cemetery, and the large Church of St. Lambert, its sanctuary adorned with Renaissance frescoes and its two towers crowned with onion domes distinctive to both Bavaria and to imperial Russia. At the height of its eighteenth-century glory, Seeon witnessed frequent visits by Mozart, who composed several pieces dedicated to the abbey, but in 1803 the monastery was dissolved and the property was eventually purchased by the Leuchtenberg family. Over the years, the former monastic buildings were transformed into something resembling a comfortable country house.[2] It was all a curious jumble of courtyards and cloisters, where large, impressive halls decorated with stucco reliefs and elaborate frescoes nestled side by side with rooms so crowded with bits of cast-off furniture and incongruous bric-a-brac that according to one visitor they resembled those in "a cheap German boardinghouse."[3]

If Frau Tchaikovsky worried that at Seeon she would be under constant surveillance and subject to relentless questioning, she must have been relieved to find that the Leuchtenberg family expected nothing from her. She stayed in room 20, at the top of a staircase guarded by a stuffed brown Siberian bear; she even took most of her meals in private.[4] Her new hosts, wrote one visitor, were so "typically Russian" that they "could well have walked out of the pages" of some novel by Gogol or Chekhov.[5] A tall and handsome man with a gray mustache and a rather disconcerting lisp, Georg Nikolaievich de Beauharnais, duke of Leuchtenberg, was a great-grandson of Tsar Nicholas I and a descendant of Napoleon's stepson Eugene de Beauharnais.[6] Born in Rome in 1872, Georg had served in the Russian Imperial Guard and, in 1895, married Princess Olga Repnina-Volkonsky. After inheriting Seeon, the duke had moved his family to Bavaria, although they patriotically returned to Russia when war erupted in 1914; when the Revolution broke out three years later, they fled to Germany, living at Seeon on the edge of perpetual financial disaster despite their regal surroundings. With their money gone, they raided Seeon, selling a different jeweled Napoleonic sword or dusty volume from the library every month to keep the seemingly endless parade of creditors at bay.[7]

The duke, recalled one acquaintance, gave the "impression of a very kindly but fidgety and rather timid man." In contrast, Duchess Olga was a short, forceful woman, armed with seemingly unlimited energy and the personality of a "sergeant," who confusingly, given their ordeal in Russia, seemed attracted to revolutionary politics.[8] This curious couple lived at Seeon with their five children: Duke Dimitri (called Dima) and his wife, Catherine; Duchess Elena; Duchess Nathalia and her husband, Baron Vladimir Meller-Zakomelsky; Duchess Tamara; and Duke Konstantin.[9] Despite his ties to the Romanovs, the duke had not been an intimate of Nicholas II, and his encounters with the imperial family had been infrequent; his wife had only rarely observed them from a distance at court ceremonies.[10]

Frau Tchaikovsky, by her own choice, had little interaction with the Leuchtenberg family. The only member she saw with anything bordering on regularity was the duke, and even this was infrequent; at one point she refused to receive her host for more than a week.[11] Not until June 18—Anastasia's birthday—did she consent to join the family for a regular meal, and this was a rare exception.[12] Four women at Seeon stepped in and acted as companions to the claimant: Agnes Wasserschleben, former matron from Stillachhaus, and three others who worked for the Leuchtenberg family: the English tutor Faith Lavington; music teacher Vera von Klemenz; and Maria Baumgarten, an elderly Russian émigré. Over the course of her eleven-month stay, the temperamental Frau Tchaikovsky succeeded in alienating all four with her constant changes of mood and frequent accusations of betrayal.[13]

Aside from accidental encounters in the corridors, Tchaikovsky saw the entire family only twice in her first hundred days at Seeon, when she attended a church service and joined them for the Easter liturgy.

This brought with it new controversies. For a Russian Orthodox grand duchess, the claimant had expressed surprisingly little interest in matters of faith, explaining not very convincingly that since the execution of the Romanovs she had been struggling with her conscience. In December 1925, during her stay at the Mommsen Clinic, she had for the first time attended services at the Russian Orthodox church on Berlin's Nachodstrasse, joined by Rathlef-Keilmann; émigré writer Lev Urvantsov, who chaired a committee promoting her claim; and his sister-in-law Gertrude Spindler, who searched for evidence of her stay in Bucharest.[14] After the service, Nicholas Markov, the head of Berlin's Supreme Monarchist Council, quickly asserted that the claimant had crossed herself from left to right, in the Catholic rather than the Orthodox manner.[15] On hearing of this, Rathlef-Keilmann, Urvantsov, and Spindler—all three supporters—protested, saying that the claimant had crossed herself correctly according to Orthodox practice.[16]

No one knew quite what to believe or expect, and when Frau Tchaikovsky finally did join the family for services, everyone saw, in the end, confirmation of their own opinions. According to the duke of Leuchtenberg, after services a Russian priest with the rather unfortunate name Father Jakshitsch told him that the claimant was "definitely Orthodox" from her confession and behavior.[17] The priest, however, deemed some of her religious "mannerisms" peculiar; this the duke explained away as an example of "the homely—one might say rustic—way

Seeon.

in which the rites were administered in the Tsar's household."[18] After the service, Frau Tchaikovsky excused any errors she had made, recalled the duke, by saying that she had "found it very difficult to follow the service" owing to her ill health.[19]

Others, though, were more skeptical. Baroness Nathalia Meller-Zakomelsky said that the claimant "appeared to struggle through the ritual. At times she seemed very knowledgeable about Orthodox rites, while at others her worship seemed to be a combination" of Orthodox and Catholic practices.[20] Dimitri Leuchtenberg and his wife, Catherine, on the other hand, asserted that Frau Tchaikovsky had seemed "bewildered" during the service and had crossed herself "numerous times" in the Catholic manner.[21] And Maria Hesse, widow of the former commander of the palace at Tsarskoye Selo, also observed the claimant during services at Seeon and declared, "She did not know at which prayer one should kneel. . . . In approaching for Holy Communion, she was completely lost; the priest had to prompt her to kiss the chalice and to make the sign of the Cross." She added that the claimant had crossed herself throughout in both the Catholic and Orthodox manners.[22]

It was not the only curiosity, for questions over Frau Tchaikovsky's linguistic abilities reemerged during her stay at Seeon. Evidence of her familiarity with Russian was elusive. It was not a question of whether she could understand it—this much nearly everyone seemed to agree on—but that she would not speak it. There was, it is true, the statement from Dalldorf nurse Erna Buchholz that she had conversed with the claimant in the language in the summer of 1920; stories that she had called out in Russian while staying with the von Kleists, including the rather confusing secondhand account given by Dr. Schiller; and in December 1925 writer Lev Urvantsov said that she had replied to one of his comments in Russian, although the six words she used had parroted his own.[23]

During her stay with the von Kleists, complaining of her damaged memory, Frau Tchaikovsky, it was said, had practiced her Russian with the baron and worked at writing out the Cyrillic alphabet.[24] Something similar apparently happened at Lugano. "When I first came to know her," Rathlef-Keilmann insisted, "she could neither write nor read."[25] This was clearly wrong: the records of her stay at Dalldorf, the statements from the nurses there, from the Schwabes, from the von Kleists—even from Clara Peuthert—all confirmed that the claimant had eagerly read numerous magazines, newspapers, and books.[26] If this was all suspicious, what happened next seemed—at least to those skeptical of Frau Tchaikovsky's claim—entirely too convenient. During their stay at Lugano, Rathlef-Keilmann spent her days helping the claimant study the Russian language, reading books and practicing the Cyrillic alphabet.[27]

Whether or not she was Anastasia, Frau Tchaikovsky was thus able to learn—or as her supporters believed, relearn—the language most important to her claim.

And people were convinced that the claimant *had* to be Russian: Bonhoeffer reported her "Russian accent," while Nobel described "a foreign accent, most probably Russian," though these statements may have reflected perception more than fact.[28] And then there was Dr. Theodor Eitel, who in 1926 had noted the claimant's "typical Russian accent."[29] This fit perfectly with the idea that Frau Tchaikovsky was Anastasia, but the evidence wasn't nearly as compelling as the legend suggested. Eitel's remark on her "typical Russian accent" seemed intriguing, but it was, as the doctor admitted later, an error on his part. "In my understanding," he clarified in 1959, "her speech had an eastern cast. 'Typically Russian' was something I heard said often of it, but then, I spoke no Russian myself and thus could not say."[30] And Nobel may have believed that she carried a Russian accent, but he also believed that it was not her native language. He noted that while she could understand Russian when it was spoken, she seemed to go through "a laborious mental process" in translating phrases in her head to find the German expressions before she could offer any meaningful replies.[31]

It all seemed just a little too ambiguous, too conflicted, to appear entirely convincing one way or the other. The duke of Leuchtenberg insisted that "She understands Russian quite well."[32] Yet he reached this judgment after hearing nothing more than a few isolated words scattered over a few months. There was, for example, the occasion when she said to Duchess Olga, in decidedly ungrammatical Russian, "Thank you very much, all was very good."[33] Although Dimitri Leuchtenberg later asserted that during her time at Seeon the claimant "did not speak or understand Russian," this was clearly not correct on either count.[34] Dimitri's brother Konstantin offered what was probably a more reliable summation of her capabilities in saying, "She cannot even speak Russian properly."[35]

German remained Frau Tchaikovsky's language of choice. Until 1925, everyone—doctors, nurses, supporters, and detractors—all agreed that Frau Tchaikovsky spoke good German. In 1921 Malinovsky had called it "impeccable German," Rathlef-Keilmann deemed it "very well chosen and formal German," and Nobel flatly stated, "She speaks good German."[36] In the summer of 1925, when Alexei Volkov visited her at St. Mary's Hospital, he was perplexed by not only her refusal to speak Russian but also, as Rathlef-Keilmann noted, her "exceptionally good German." It was so good, Rathlef-Keilmann explained—"complete with the inflections unique to Berlin"—because "for the past five years she has lived in the city."[37]

And then, suddenly, in the aftermath of Volkov's visit and the concerns he had voiced over Frau Tchaikovsky's proficiency in the language, something strange happened: overnight the claimant's German became atrocious.[38] Ludwig Berg of St. Mary's Hospital recalled that she "spoke German, but slowly, and she often had to search for her expressions. Her sentences were not always of German construction."[39] A year later, one supporter deemed her German "grammatically incorrect and of unusual construction," while Eitel contended that she "spoke poor German, always in short sentences and with simple, one-syllable words and many grammatical errors."[40] The duke of Leuchtenberg insisted that her German was "so faulty that it is obviously not her native tongue," while Faith Lavington, the English tutor at Seeon, insisted that the claimant "can only comprehend quite childish German."[41]

What did this mean, this sudden outburst of bad, ungrammatical German? How could it be that not a single person before 1925 noted any peculiarities in her German if she indeed spoke it so badly? Surely someone would have recorded this fact at the Elisabeth Hospital or at Dalldorf, particularly when active attempts were under way to determine her identity. It was only one curiosity among many in her case.

Evidence of Frau Tchaikovsky's English, too, remained elusive. Aside from the later, problematic claim that she had regularly used the language while staying with Inspector Grunberg's niece and an almost casual mention by Franz Jaenicke, thirty years after the fact, that she had supposedly conversed in English, no one hinted at any familiarity with English until 1925. In her first few weeks with the claimant at St. Mary's Hospital, Rathlef-Keilmann tried to practice English with her: "I wrote some English words down for Frau Tchaikovsky," she noted. "She read them and was silent. I asked the significance of the words. She was silent, but I could see that she understood them but was afraid to pronounce them." Rathlef-Keilmann bought her a copybook and worked with her to practice the language.[42] How proficient Frau Tchaikovsky may have been—or how far such lessons went—is not known; that fall, during her stay at Mommsen, according to Professor Serge Rudnev, the claimant had "raved in English" while under anesthetic.[43] Although a number of assistants presumably attended Rudnev during the operation, none was ever questioned on this point, nor did anyone step forward to confirm the assertion. Rudnev himself, as he frankly admitted, spoke no English, and couldn't confirm what he had heard.[44] Serge Botkin challenged these stories, stating, "She did not speak English during her stay in Berlin."[45] Only thirty-three years after Rudnev's statement did someone offer confirmation, when French journalist Dominique Auclères heard thirdhand that a certain Frau Spes Stahlberg—who happened to be a relative of Baron von Kleist—insisted that she had been at the surgery and heard the claimant "speaking English incessantly" while under anesthetic.[46] Evidence on the point might be more compelling if it rested on something beyond a thirdhand account delivered three decades after the fact, and if Rudnev was not prone to demonstrably untrue exaggeration in his attempts to support the claimant's case. But assuming it to be true, it is possible that Frau Tchaikovsky, after working on lessons with Rathlef, did indeed mutter in a language that had occupied her waking hours and thoughts.

As with Russian, Rathlef-Keilmann made sure that Frau Tchaikovsky, while at Lugano, had been able to practice her English—"every day," she noted.[47] It wasn't just lessons with Rathlef-Keilmann, either; an English lady in Lugano also spent time working with the claimant, according to Baron Osten-Sacken.[48] Even so, Frau Tchaikovsky's fluency in the language, thought Eitel later that year, amounted to only a few "isolated words."[49] Things improved at Seeon. Frau Tchaikovsky began to read English books and newspapers, and to have them read aloud to her as well.[50] Was this simply the effect of the lessons, or was the claimant finally remembering the English she said had been lost? The duke of Leuchtenberg insisted that she could "read, speak, and even think" in English.[51] Yet just a few weeks after he wrote this, Faith Lavington found that when she spoke to the claimant in English, Frau Tchaikovsky—though she seemed to understand what was said—"could not manage" to reply in the same language.[52] German, she wrote, "is really the only thing she can speak."[53]

Lavington now picked up where Rathlef-Keilmann had left off, beginning English lessons with Frau Tchaikovsky at Seeon. "In order to get her to talk," Lavington wrote, "I took a nursery rhyme book with me, with very gay colors, and by asking her questions about these pictures I got her to speak quite a lot and could see quite well that she does know English very well, but the trouble is to get her to speak. She also can write, for she copied a line today very clearly, in a trembling but entirely educated handwriting, which is rather a triumph." During the course of these lessons, Lavington would ask questions in English about the stories, and Frau Tchaikovsky answered in German. "It really is very interesting to see how, when she does not think at all, she can say quite a lot of English words—but ask her to repeat a thing that she has to think over, and she is lost." Still, Lavington, as Frau Tchaikovsky's supporters were quick to point out, said that the claimant spoke with "the clearest and best English accent."[54]

Or did she? In fact, these words, often quoted as proof that Frau Tchaikovsky always knew and spoke impeccable English, offer a misleading impression of Lavington's actual experience. One night, she wrote in her diary, she went to the claimant's room, and Frau Tchaikovsky greeted her with, "Oh, please do sit down," before reverting to her usual German. It was these five words—and these five words only—"Oh, please do sit down"—that Lavington described as having been spoken with "the clearest and best English accent."[55] Agnes Wasserschleben honestly admitted that while she "often spoke English" with the claimant, "this means that I spoke English, and she answered me in German."[56]

There were similar stories about Frau Tchaikovsky's musical abilities. At Seeon, she was said to have readily played the piano, indicating a talent that had, to this point, been unsuspected, but that was fully in keeping with Anastasia's music lessons. The reality, though, was not quite as compelling. One day, the claimant told Fraulein Vera von Klemenz that she would like to again play, but explained that she had "forgotten all the notes." Klemenz played for her as Frau Tchaikovsky carefully watched; after a few more days of such observation, she accepted von Klemenz's invitation to "practice with her."[57] The pair began with a simple children's song; at first, von Klemenz recorded, "she found it difficult. I had the impression that she could not see well, and could not distinguish the individual keys. Then suddenly, she repeated the song without the music, by ear."[58] The next day, von Klemenz noted, "She is playing better and better, and, in this connection, I have noticed that, when she is taking trouble, she is generally not able to place her fingers on the keys correctly; but, when she plays quite automatically, without thinking much about it, she does very well."[59] After twenty-five days of such lessons, von Klemenz concluded, "It is quite clear to me that she has known how to play."[60]

Has she played before? Perhaps, but Frau Tchaikovsky also struggled with these efforts. She was able to repeat a simple children's tune only after carefully watching Fraulein von Klemenz; there was no evidence that she mastered this ability or that she could read music. Here, though, she at least had a valid excuse: because of a tubercular infection, she could not fully extend her left arm, and could play the piano with only one hand. It required exceptional effort, and after a few months, she abandoned the practice, saying that she found it too painful to continue, a real possibility but also a convenient one.[61]

In her months at Seeon, Frau Tchaikovsky thus succeeded in offering evidence seemingly favorable to her claim and at the same time revealing facts that damaged it. If the legend surrounding her case was not quite as compelling as history has been led to believe, nor was there solid evidence that she was an impostor. This enigma tore the Leuchtenberg family apart. Duke Dimitri and his wife, Catherine, as well as Duke Konstantin, were all convinced that she was an impostor, and a clumsy one at that; Duchesses Elena and Nathalia seem to have believed that she was Anastasia; and Duchess Tamara wavered between these two positions.[62] The duchess of Leuchtenberg also offered contradictory opinions, occasionally based less on the evidence than on the undoubted difficulties involved in playing host to this temperamental houseguest. She frequently argued with the claimant—Faith Lavington forthrightly insisted "the Duchess hates her"—yet at the same time she seemed torn by the question of her identity.[63] Once, Olga confided that she was "pretty confident" that Frau Tchaikovsky "was not an imposter," explaining that she "carried herself just like her grandmother in Denmark."[64]

As for the duke of Leuchtenberg, he proved himself to be a less than discerning judge of character. His wife apparently thought him gullible, and the duke clearly let his belief in and sympathies for the claimant override any critical appraisal of the evidence.[65] Even Frau Tchaikovsky thought so: she later declared, rather thoughtlessly, that although the duke "was always very kind, I had to take him in hand."[66] A few months after the claimant first came to Seeon, the duke fell ill, suffering the first effects of a brain tumor that was to kill him within two years.[67] One visitor to Seeon in 1927 described him as "on the verge of a nervous collapse."[68] This illness may have impeded his judgment, for he certainly demonstrated a propensity for wishful thinking, a habit of deliberately ignoring unfavorable events and developments, and of recounting experiences in ways at considerable variance with the known facts. He also occasionally asserted incidents unsupported by evidence, including claims that he had repelled numerous attempts to kidnap and poison Frau Tchaikovsky during her stay under his roof.[69]

The duke of Leuchtenberg never made an overt public declaration that he believed the claimant was Anastasia, explaining that his brief encounters with the real grand duchess had not left him in a position to make an educated judgment.[70] Privately, he seemed to oscillate between acceptance and rejection.[71] To his daughter Nathalia, he once confessed that "deep down in his innermost conscience," he did not believe the claimant was Anastasia, at the same time confusingly adding that he was "ninety-five-percent certain" that she was the grand duchess.[72] "My father agreed to receive Mrs. Tchaikovsky in Seeon," wrote Dimitri Leuchtenberg, "because, as he told us, 'If she is the Grand Duchess, it would be a crime not to help her and if she is not the Grand Duchess, I do not commit a crime by giving shelter to a poor, sick, persecuted woman, while making investigations regarding her identity.'"[73]

In Russia, before coming to the imperial court, Pierre Gilliard had worked as a tutor for one of the duke's relatives, which gave him some familiarity with the Leuchtenberg family. It also gave him a certain ability to approach Georg Leuchtenberg with a particular frankness. In 1928, the former tutor called on the duke at his castle and spoke to him at length about Frau Tchaikovsky's claim. Gilliard fully admitted to what he termed the duke's "goodness" and kind heart, but as he tried to lay out what he believed to be the evidence against her, he found Leuchtenberg less than receptive. In the end, according to Gilliard, the duke dismissed Gilliard's concerns for the same reason he once gave to Faith Lavington, a reason that would seem out of place except in this most convoluted and confusing of cases: "How can you be satisfied that she isn't Anastasia Nikolaievna," the duke asked Gilliard bluntly, "when three clairvoyants have told us that she is?"[74]

Spiritualists assuring exiled aristocrats, well-intentioned ladies attempting to awaken memories of languages presumably lost, suspicious eyes diligently watching to see how she crossed herself—thus passed Frau Tchaikovsky's days at Seeon. People continued to believe or to deny, but as Faith Lavington learned firsthand, one thing was abundantly clear: no one could pretend to understand how Frau Tchaikovsky's mind worked. She had, Lavington thought, "a sort of weird charm" about her, something that attracted despite the claimant's "very bad character" and "complete lack of the most elementary gratitude."[75] There was Frau Tchaikovsky's "atrociously high opinion of her own importance" and her "towering and quite ill-directed pride."[76] At times she found the claimant pleasant; then, without warning, something would set Frau Tchaikovsky off and her screams would upset the entire household. "Another day straight from Dante's *Purgatory*," Lavington recorded in her diary, after the claimant was "wild all day, and finished up in a screaming gale of passion." Although Lavington pitied her, it was, she said, "impossible to really like her, she has no winning charms, nothing to attract."[77] "I only know one thing," she added presciently, "that wherever she is or in what circumstances she is, her unhappy character will always bring grief and pain upon the people surrounding her."[78]

12

The Making of a Myth

A S THE BAVARIAN WINTER OF 1927 turned to spring, Frau
Tchaikovsky remained largely isolated in her small suite on the
second floor of Schloss Seeon. Seven years had passed since
her leap into the Landwehr Canal, years fraught with seemingly endless
arguments over languages and memories, over scars and manners.
With contradictory assertions flying back and forth, she remained very
much an enigma, a damaged, unlikely Anastasia, perhaps, but one still
wrapped in a veneer of plausibility.

And then there were the recognitions and denunciations, often
subjective, frequently flawed, occasionally compelling, but all mute
testament to Frau Tchaikovsky's unique status in the pantheon of royal
claimants. Anastasia's Romanov and Hessian relatives, former courtiers
and servants, acquaintances and the merely curious, friend and foe—
they all continued to shake their heads over a woman they believed to
be an impostor, or blazed with fury that a miraculously rescued grand
duchess was being denied her rightful name. On the opposing side,
former nursemaid Margaretta Eagar, who had last seen a four-year-
old Anastasia in 1905, rejected Frau Tchaikovsky after looking at
photographs of the presumably twenty-six-year-old claimant, as did
Madeleine Zanotti, Empress Alexandra's principal lady's maid, and
Alexander Conrad, who had given the grand duchesses music lessons.[1]
"There is," Conrad asserted, "not the slightest resemblance with my
dear little pupil."[2]

Given the passage of time—particularly with Eagar—and the reliance
on photographs, these negative judgments were somewhat less than

compelling. Similarly problematic were the opinions offered by Maria von Hesse, widow of the former commander of the imperial palaces at Tsarskoye Selo, and her daughter Darya, Countess Hollenstein. Although her relations with the grand duchesses had been rather formal, Maria von Hesse was adamant in rejecting Frau Tchaikovsky. "I was struck by the lack of resemblance in her vulgar features and gestures to either Grand Duchess Anastasia Nikolaievna or to any other member of the Imperial Family," she insisted. She thought that the mouth and lips were too large, adding that the claimant "wore high-heeled shoes, which Grand Duchess Anastasia could not do on account of the problem with her foot."[3] Darya had known the older grand duchesses a little better, having taken dancing lessons with them, and she showed Faith Lavington a number of their letters to her, though she most certainly had not, as she insisted, "lived with the Grand Duchesses" and "known them as real friends all my life until I married."[4] After visiting the claimant in her room at Seeon, Darya told Lavington that she could find "no earthly resemblance to the real Anastasia." She mentioned several childhood incidents but said that the claimant showed "absolutely no sign of recognition." "This creature," she told Lavington, "is laughing at us all for being so simple—you can see it in her eyes."[5]

Always eager to insinuate himself into any potential excitement, Prince Felix Yusupov arrived at Seeon to judge Frau Tchaikovsky, despite the fact that he had scarcely known Anastasia; indeed, his contact with her had been limited to a few meetings in the Crimea and some rare court functions. Yusupov, though, had heard too many stories and wanted to see this enigmatic woman for himself. With him came Professor Serge Rudnev, who went off to convince Frau Tchaikovsky to receive her visitor; according to Yusupov, Rudnev quickly returned, saying that the claimant had shouted with excitement, "Felix, Felix! What a joy to see him again! I will dress and go down at once! Is Irina with him?" To Yusupov, "this joy at seeing me appeared to be exaggerated," but he spent some thirty minutes with her. "I spoke to her in Russian, but she answered in German, seeming not to hear either the French or the English in which I had first attempted to converse." She answered some of his questions while, to others, she was silent—"she feigned a lack of understanding,"

Prince Felix Yusupov.

Yusupov insisted. "From the first disastrous impression," the prince declared, "I understood that this affair was simply that of a comedienne badly playing her part. Even at a distance, nothing in her resembled any of the Grand Duchesses, neither her carriage nor her appearance."[6]

Yusupov was a melodramatic man, given to sweeping theatrics, and he certainly encapsulated something of this in a letter to Grand Duke Andrei Vladimirovich, denouncing Frau Tchaikovsky as "a sick hysteric and frightful play-actress," a "frightful creature" from whom anyone would "recoil in horror."[7] But Frau Tchaikovsky could be equally melo-dramatic. On learning of his arrival, she supposedly ran to Duchess Olga of Leuchtenberg in hysterics, shouting, "Yusupov is here! Felix . . . Yusupov!"[8] It was, at least, a more convincing reaction from a presumed Anastasia, given Yusupov's role in murdering Rasputin, a man whose prayers the Romanovs believed had kept Tsesarevich Alexei alive. Later, though, she insisted—in a bizarre flight of fancy—that during the meeting Yusupov tried to kill her and that she had run screaming down a hall to escape death at his murderous hands.[9]

These denunciations were of varying significance, given reliance on photographs and, with the Hesses and Yusupov, little personal experi-ence with Anastasia on which to base their opinions. Someone who had known Anastasia well, though, did arrive at Seeon that spring of 1927 to see Frau Tchaikovsky; this was Nicholas II's former adjutant Colonel Anatole Mordvinov, invited by the duke of Leuchtenberg to meet her and offer an opinion. Having served at court for many years, Mordvinov knew the grand duchesses well and was presumably able to render a reliable opinion; he came, despite having been told by Olga Alexandrovna that the claimant was not Anastasia, because, as he said, "I hoped that the Grand Duchess was miraculously saved."[10]

Before the meeting, the duke pulled Mordvinov aside and warned him that injuries and the passage of time might well have altered the claimant's features "so greatly that she is unrecognizable" as Anastasia. This certainly lowered expectations, but Mordvinov had not changed, and "placed great importance on being recognized by the patient." He spent three days with Frau Tchaikovsky; at his request, she was not told of his identity. Apparently, when confronted with her visitor, she was perplexed, and attempted to wrest clues from those around her. "Who is he?" she asked after the first meeting. "A Russian or a German? What is his family name?" No one would tell her, though eventually she did learn that the man was Russian. Mordvinov attempted to question Frau Tchaikovsky using both Russian and German; she provided few if any answers, at first appearing agitated, then alternately smiling and cover-ing her mouth with a handkerchief. He was puzzled at what he deemed her "complete lack of similarity" to Anastasia. The only resemblance, he said, was that the claimant shared Anastasia's blue eyes.[11]

At their last meeting, when finally told the name of her visitor, Frau Tchaikovsky showed no recognition. Mordvinov thought that she lacked "the innate simplicity that was characteristic of the real Grand Duchess. The enigmatic patient seemed to be so imbued—almost excessively so—with notions of her own noble origins that I think she had grown into the idea. Her manner of speech, of talking about the past, her sorrows and joys, her point of view—all was that of a person entirely different to the Grand Duchess."[12] During this final encounter, Mordvinov purposely toyed with a cigarette holder that the four grand duchesses had presented to him shortly before the Revolution; they had

Anastasia with Colonel Anatole Mordvinov, her father's adjutant, in the park at Tsarskoye Selo, about 1913.

something of a running joke with the frequently careless adjutant, asking each time they saw him if he had lost their gift. But Frau Tchaikovsky seemed uninterested, and Mordvinov left Seeon convinced that the claimant was "a complete stranger to me, physically and morally."[13]

Frau Tchaikovsky later insisted, as she had done before, that she had recognized her visitor but had been unable to recall his name, yet this seems unlikely.[14] Faced with such an apparently categorical rejection, some of her supporters insinuated that the former adjutant had denied her only to protect himself and salvage his reputation, for after the Revolution he—like many former courtiers—had deserted the imprisoned Romanovs. But Mordvinov's actions were well known before he met the claimant, and he was on friendly terms with Nicholas II's sister Olga Alexandrovna, who did not hold his behavior in 1917 against him. As such, the arguments rang hollow.

But not every meeting was negative. It was at Seeon that Frau Tchaikovsky won from former Russian soldier Felix Dassel what was, according to the mythology surrounding her case, one of her most compelling recognitions as Anastasia. In autumn 1916, Dassel—a captain in Grand Duchess Marie Nikolaievna's 9th Infantry Regiment of the Kazan Dragoons—was shot in the leg and evacuated to Tsarskoye Selo, where he recuperated at the hospital founded by Anastasia and her sister; here he remained from September until late February (according to the Julian calendar) 1917, seeing Anastasia a few times a week when she visited the patients. After the Revolution, Dassel made his way to Berlin, where he worked as a journalist for several émigré publications. Although he admitted to learning of the claimant in 1923, Dassel said he had no interest in Frau Tchaikovsky's case until 1927, when it received intense coverage in the press.[15]

In September 1927, Dassel traveled to Seeon to meet Frau Tchaikovsky. What happened during this visit soon slipped into legend. Before the meeting, Dassel—who as a special adjutant to the grand duchesses had come to know them well—wrote an account of his time in the hospital at Tsarskoye Selo containing "details that only the real Anastasia" would know. He "sealed the notes in an envelope" and handed them to the duke of Leuchtenberg, who put the sealed envelope in a safe to preclude the possibility that the claimant could see them. "He then met and questioned the claimant, making deliberate mistakes to discover whether or not she would correct them. The claimant passed the test with flying colors." This included correcting "Dassel's deliberate error of placing the billiard table" at the hospital on the wrong floor and accurately refuting Dassel's assertion that the grand duchesses had come to the hospital every day and had often brought their brother, Alexei, with them. "The clincher for Dassel came when the Duke of Leuchtenberg referred to an old Russian colonel" in a photograph, and the claimant erupted into sudden laughter, exclaiming, "The Man with the Pockets!" This, Dassel said, had been a nickname bestowed upon the officer by Anastasia herself, owing to the colonel's habit of always speaking to the grand duchesses with his hands thrust into his pockets, in defiance of imperial etiquette. "Abruptly I recognized her," Dassel said. "I was convinced."[16]

This sounds compelling, for who but Anastasia would know such obscure information or identify by nickname an otherwise unknown colonel? Such things surely couldn't be put down to coincidence or lucky guesses, and Dassel's recognition has stood as one of the most convincing pieces of evidence that Frau Tchaikovsky was indeed the youngest daughter of Nicholas II. Unfortunately for history, though, much of what has been said about this encounter is at best contradictory and at worst simply untrue.

Dassel initially wrote to the duke of Leuchtenberg about the claimant, saying he had known Anastasia and suggesting that he ask Frau Tchaikovsky if she could identify "Mandrifolie." "The Duke," Dassel later said, "told me that the patient had looked at him for a long while as if in shock, and then remarked that her sister Marie had many nicknames."[17] Dassel deemed this correct, although he seems to be the only source to suggest that Marie Nikolaievna ever bore such a nickname, for it is mentioned nowhere else. But this was enough, Dassel said, to convince him to travel to Seeon.

The former captain arrived on the evening of September 14, 1927, accompanied by a friend named Otto Bornemann, but there were immediate problems, for Frau Tchaikovsky—having been warned of a visitor from her past—refused to receive him. Maria Baumgarten, Vera von Klemenz, and the duke had been working hard to change her mind, but told Dassel that if he was presented, he needed "to be patient, and not press her too quickly with questions."[18] Baumgarten finally won her over, but spent the rest of the evening, as both the duke and Dassel later admitted, helping Frau Tchaikovsky "prepare" for the meeting. And this wasn't simply a matter of bolstering her courage; almost incredibly, Baumgarten sat with the claimant, poring over a souvenir photograph album of Anastasia's hospital at Tsarskoye Selo. If, before this, Frau Tchaikovsky had no idea who her visitor was or what his connection to Anastasia had been, she certainly knew he had been involved with the hospital by the time she retired for the evening.[19] But no one knew of this crash course, for Dassel omitted it from his later accounts.

The next morning Baumgarten overtly confirmed to Frau Tchaikovsky that her visitor was a former Russian officer and patient in the hospital at Tsarskoye Selo. Then, suddenly, she reversed her earlier decision to meet him. "She only kept repeating that she wished to be spared of the past, that she could no longer stand such reminiscences," Baumgarten said. Hoping to convince her, Dassel gave Baumgarten two photographs, asking that she show them to the claimant: one showed Dassel, in his dressing gown, sitting on his hospital bed between Marie and Anastasia; the other showed the grand duchesses and a group of officers standing at the hospital entrance, which Dassel purposely mis-identified as a church. He wanted to know if the claimant recognized the church. When shown the image, Frau Tchaikovsky corrected the error, though this was not surprising, given that her commemorative album bore the same photograph along with numerous other depictions of the hospital exterior.[20]

Not until September 16 did Frau Tchaikovsky finally agree to receive Dassel for ten minutes. Escorted by the duke and accompanied by Bornemann, Baumgarten, and Vera von Klemenz, Dassel was taken to the claimant's sitting room on the castle's second floor. They found her reclining on a sofa, peering nervously from behind a blanket that she had pulled up to cover most of her face.[21]

"I've brought you a former Dragoon," the duke announced. "Don't worry, we won't stay very long." Frau Tchaikovsky said nothing; she dropped the blanket, only to conceal her mouth behind a handker-chief as Dassel approached. "On a sudden impulse," Dassel recalled, he clicked his heels together, saluted, and said in Russian, "Your Imperial Highness! Captain Dassel of the Dragoon Regiment of Her Imperial Highness Grand Duchess Marie Nikolaievna!" Frau Tchaikovsky remained on the sofa but extended her hand; when Dassel leaned forward to kiss it, he tried to examine what he could see of her face.[22] Frau Tchaikovsky had agreed to the meeting only on the condition that she not be asked about the past, which made any questions pointless; instead, the conversation turned on her health, the weather, and other trivialities. Dassel spoke in Russian, while the claimant replied only in German. Dassel was not impressed; "the face said nothing to me," he wrote, and in general he thought it was "too difficult" to detect any resemblance to Anastasia.[23] That evening, Frau Tchaikovsky had Baumgarten ask Dassel if he had received the medal given by the grand duchesses to all of their former patients when discharged from hospital; the previous year she had seen one of the medals at Stillachhaus.[24] But the Revolution, Dassel said, had erupted before his discharge.[25]

The next morning, Dassel watched the claimant pass down a corridor; for the first time he detected some resemblance to Anastasia, not in her features but in the way she walked.[26] He was still not convinced. "It was impossible for me to be at peace without having definitively resolved this enigma," he recorded. Contrary to his later versions, it was at this point—and not before arriving at Seeon—that Dassel, "after discussing the plan with the Duke," wrote down his memories of the hospital and handed the envelope to Leuchtenberg.[27] The duke and Baumgarten, privy to the questions, now began to confront her with Dassel's memories. Baumgarten first asked if she recalled Nicholas II's tattoo.[28] This, the claimant insisted, was nonsense. She had, she declared, often seen her father rowing, with his shirtsleeves rolled up, and "Papa had nothing on either arm. No, no, that I can say for sure. He had nothing whatever."[29] But she was wrong. In 1891, during a visit to Japan while still tsesarevich, Nicholas had a dragon tattooed on his right arm, a design so large and colorful that it had, as he recorded in his diary, taken seven hours to complete.[30] Why, if Frau Tchaikovsky was Anastasia, would she make such an obvious mistake?

Another test came when Dassel mentioned his regret that he had not received "the watches and sabers presented to the other officers" in the military hospital. This was a "deliberately false statement," Dassel later wrote, and the claimant corrected his error.[31] Yet what actually happened was quite different. According to Vera von Klemenz, when the claimant was told of this she apparently said nothing. Later, though, Frau Tchaikovsky remarked, "I know we gave presents, but I do not recall any longer what they were. It is so long ago. I cannot picture it. Watches, yes, but I do not think sabers. I don't know. Sabers? Sabers?

Perhaps this was done in my mother's hospital. But if he says it, then it must be so."[32] Not only was there no correction here, but also Frau Tchaikovsky ended by agreeing that Dassel's "deliberately false" statement was true.

More questions and "deliberately false" statements came on the last day of the visit. Dassel declared that the grand duchesses had visited the hospital every day. "No, not every day," the claimant rightly corrected him.[33] Then there was his question of the hospital billiards table: according to Dassel, he erroneously insisted that it had been in an upstairs room. The claimant objected, saying, "No! Billiard table was downstairs!"[34] But Faith Lavington, who also was present, recalled the question differently. Dassel, she wrote in her diary that night, insisted that he had "quite frankly forgotten" where the billiards table was located, suggesting that he "had an idea" that it had been on the second floor but making no definitive statement.[35] Aside from this, though, and to further questions and erroneous statements, Frau Tchaikovsky, as Dassel recounted, "made us understand that she does not remember anything."[36]

On the last afternoon Dassel closely studied the claimant's face, attempting to compare what he saw with his memory of Anastasia. As he looked, he perceived "the same eyes" as the real grand duchess, "the Emperor's eyes." Finally he said, "I knew. I recognized Grand Duchess Anastasia."[37] With this, Dassel left Seeon. "Based on a great deal of detailed observation," read his statement the next day, "I was able to come to the conviction that the patient is Grand Duchess Anastasia, despite the fact that she has changed a great deal externally and is suffering a great lack of memory."[38]

The eyes, the same eyes, "the Emperor's eyes"—for Dassel, this was apparently what convinced him, for he admitted that the claimant's general appearance was different. But how well had Dassel really known Anastasia? From a few weekly visits to patients spread out over six months? Even the apparently intimate knowledge Dassel found so convincing wasn't quite as convincing as the mythology suggests. Frau Tchaikovsky's recognition of the nickname "Mandrifolie" would have been more convincing if there was any reference to its use independent of Dassel. She knew about the commemorative hospital medallions, but then, she had discussed them with a friend a year earlier. She had studied photographs of the hospital and its patients before facing Dassel or his questions; she had not actually corrected his deliberate error regarding gifts of sabers; and she had erroneously insisted that Nicholas II had no tattoo. Maybe it was all compelling, or seemed so, but it is also clear that elements of the legend relied on variations, omissions, and incorrect information.

And the same is true of what has always been taken to be the single most intriguing aspect of Dassel's recognition, the famous "Man with the Pockets" story. This took place a few weeks after Dassel's first visit. While showing Frau Tchaikovsky photographs of the hospital patients and staff, the duke of Leuchtenberg pointed to one man and apparently asked if she recalled his name. She did not, but said, "Great big officer, I remember—always used to put his hands in pockets, always forgot it, was not nice." This, Dassel said, was indeed correct: contrary to etiquette, the man in question, a Colonel Sergeyev, had often addressed the grand duchesses with his hands thrust into his pockets.[39] But where, in this, did the claimant burst out with a laugh and exclaim, "The Man with the Pockets!" as the legend insisted? Dassel made no such claim in his book, and Frau Tchaikovsky apparently did little more than remark on the officer's bad habit. Still, how would she know such an insignificant detail? Perhaps the photograph actually showed the man with his hands thrust into his pockets and she merely commented on what she saw, but for those who believed that she was Anastasia it was a convincing piece of evidence in her favor.[40]

Those opposed to Frau Tchaikovsky's claim, though, pointed out that Dassel was working as a journalist and soon produced an account of his meeting, as if this mere fact was sufficient to cast aspersions on his honesty. Dassel admitted to learning of Frau Tchaikovsky's case while living in Berlin in 1923, but insisted—rather curiously, for someone who carried such vivid and apparently treasured memories of his encounters with Anastasia at Tsarskoye Selo—that the question of her identity had not been of any interest. And with this, at least, Dassel's credibility crumbled, for he had been a frequent visitor to the von Kleist apartment during the claimant's stay. He later spoke of Baron von Kleist as "someone who inspired in me little confidence" and noted that the circle of émigrés around him "seemed to harbor hopes that they could benefit from the claimant in some financial way," suggesting that he possessed more than a passing familiarity with the baron.[41] Gerda von Kleist recalled seeing Dassel numerous times at her parents' apartment.[42] Frau Tchaikovsky's supporters rejected this idea, saying that Gerda was unreliable and had refused to swear to this fact, but it was confirmed by a surprising source: Baroness von Kleist, who fully believed that the claimant was Anastasia and thus had little reason to undermine her case. She recalled, "Herr Dassel came to us more and more in this time, and through us he learned who 'Fraulein Unbekannt' was supposed to be. He let it be known that he had seen Anastasia in her hospital, and thus knew her well from Russia."[43]

The implication was ugly: that Dassel had met and discussed his memories with Frau Tchaikovsky and that the encounter at Seeon had been a charade, enacted for a gullible audience to provide a convincing mise-en-scène for his recognition of the claimant as Anastasia. Had this been true, though, would he really have waited four years to arrange a definite meeting with Tchaikovsky? Yet if such a proposition seems unlikely, troubling questions remain. Dassel certainly seems to have visited the von Kleist apartment and expressed enough interest in the claimant to speak of his time in the hospital at Tsarskoye Selo; why, then, did he later insist that her identity had been of no interest to him at the time? It is possible that Frau Tchaikovsky learned certain details innocently enough, passed along to the von Kleists during these visits. Neglected in such arguments, though, is one startling fact: in April 1927, Dassel had published an extensive article in a German magazine on his experiences in the hospital at Tsarskoye Selo, discussing memories of his stay, his fellow patients, and his interaction with the grand duchesses—an article that may certainly have come to Frau Tchaikovsky's attention in the months before she met the former patient that fall at Seeon.[44] No matter the connections, what the legend often portrayed as the claimant's uncannily intimate knowledge as confirmed by Dassel turns out to be somewhat less than compelling and even occasionally wrong.

Dassel's acceptance of Frau Tchaikovsky as Anastasia may have turned a few heads, but it was her recognition by Tatiana and Gleb Botkin, children of Dr. Eugene Botkin, that renewed interest in her claim and halted what had, until that time, been an increasingly negative progression of opinions. In the summer of 1926, Zenaide Tolstoy approached Tatiana Botkin, expressing guilt over her rejection of the claimant. "I don't know, I don't know!" she cried. "It's horrible. I don't know what to think. One instant I am absolutely convinced, and then again am plagued with complete doubt. I cannot decide."[45] Tatiana had, of course, heard of the claimant. Her uncle Serge Botkin had marshaled evidence and coordinated efforts to help Frau Tchaikovsky, and she knew of the controversies and disparate claims. But she had never taken the story seriously, believing that Anastasia had perished by the same Bolshevik bullets that had presumably killed her father in Ekaterinburg. Yet Tolstoy seemed genuinely torn, and Tatiana, imbued with a sense of duty toward the martyred imperial family,

Tatiana Botkin at Unterlengenhardt, 1960.

thought that she owed it to the memory of the Romanovs to meet and judge the claimant for herself.

Tatiana visited Frau Tchaikovsky at Oberstdorf in August 1926. Baron Vassili Osten-Sacken first had to convince Frau Tchaikovsky to receive her caller, though despite her repeated pleas he refused to reveal her identity; if only she would try to guess, he said, he would tell her the name of her caller. Frau Tchaikovsky refused, and finally Osten-Sacken confided that the young woman's father had served Nicholas II very closely.[46] On first seeing her from a distance, Tatiana noted "a resemblance to the manner and movements of the eldest Grand Duchesses, Olga and Tatiana Nikolaievna," but nothing particularly reminiscent of Anastasia in the claimant.[47]

The following morning, according to Osten-Sacken, Frau Tchaikovsky seemed agitated, saying that she knew her visitor's face but could not recall her name. Had Serge Botkin sent her? Apparently it was an innocent question; even Tatiana thought it unremarkable, writing, "As the Baron acted as my uncle's deputy and I had arrived in his company, it was only natural that she would make such a connection."[48] But Osten-Sacken was sure Frau Tchaikovsky was dropping broad hints: "You promised to tell me her name if I guessed, and I did not name Botkin in vain," she told him. "Now who is she?" This was enough for the baron, who broke down and confessed that Dr. Botkin's daughter Tatiana had come to see her.[49]

"When at first I saw her face up close, and particularly her eyes, so blue and filled with light, I immediately recognized Grand Duchess Anastasia Nikolaievna," Tatiana later wrote. "She was much thinner, had aged, and was therefore somewhat changed; the mouth has changed and noticeably coarsened, and owing to her thinness her nose seemed more prominent than before." In continuing her examination, "I noticed more and more the resemblance." She was struck by "the height, the form, and the color of her hair," which reminded her of Anastasia, as well as the same "roguish" appearance when she laughed. Above all, she wrote, "her unforgettable blue-gray eyes had exactly the same look in them as when she was a child."[50]

That afternoon, over tea, Frau Tchaikovsky was showing her visitors some images taken at Lugano when Tatiana said, "I also have photographs" and produced a souvenir album of the hospital at Tsarskoye Selo. After a quick glance, the claimant slammed the cover shut, crying, "This I must see alone!" She ran from the room, followed by a worried Tatiana. Then something truly peculiar happened: although Osten-Sacken had already told the claimant her visitor's name, when Tatiana gently asked, "Do you not know me?" Frau Tchaikovsky insisted that though she recognized the face, she needed to rest before the name would come to her. Unaware of this contradiction, Tatiana later helped her prepare for bed, remarking, "I'll undress you as my father did when you were ill."

"Yes, with measles," Frau Tchaikovsky replied. It was all the confirmation Tatiana needed, for Dr. Botkin had indeed tended to Anastasia when she was ill with measles at the time of the Revolution. "This fact," Tatiana insisted, "had not been published and apart from my father I was the only one to know of it."[51] She may have believed this to be true, but Tatiana was wrong. The claimant already owned several books, including the German edition of Gilliard's memoirs, that recorded Dr. Botkin's attendance on the grand duchesses during the nights preceding the Revolution; Tchaikovsky had even discussed this fact with Rathlef-Keilmann a year before she met Tatiana.[52]

"It is Grand Duchess Anastasia Nikolaievna," Tatiana told Osten-Sacken. "I have recognized her. She is the same person I used to know, only the lower half of her face, her mouth, has changed."[53]

After this encounter, Tatiana dispatched a hasty cable to Olga Alexandrovna in Copenhagen, explaining her recognition and begging the grand duchess to reconsider the issue. To this, however, Olga replied, "We took the matter very seriously, as shown by the visits paid by old Volkov, two visits by M. Gilliard and his wife, and those of myself and my husband. . . . Despite our repeated efforts to try to recognize the patient as either Tatiana or Anastasia, we came away quite convinced of the reverse."[54]

Tatiana's recognition of Frau Tchaikovsky as Anastasia earned her the lasting wrath of many Russian émigrés. Those who sided with Olga Alexandrovna and other opponents took Tatiana's acceptance of the claimant as a betrayal of the Romanovs and callously accused her of dishonoring their memory and that of her father. Even her own Uncle Peter once dismissed her identification by insisting that at the time of the meeting his niece had been "suffering from the hallucinations common to a pregnant woman."[55] Yet despite the social consequences and persistently mean-spirited insinuations against her, Tatiana remained absolutely convinced that Tchaikovsky was Anastasia. Uniquely, in a case often populated with dubious assertions and exaggerated stories, no one—not even the surviving Romanovs—ever accused Tatiana of duplicity or doubted her obvious sincerity.

The same, unfortunately, could not be said of Tatiana's brother Gleb. It was 1925 or 1926, he recalled, when, working as a journalist in New York, he first saw an article on Frau Tchaikovsky. Her features, he said, "vividly reminded me of a mixture of Grand Duchesses Tatiana and Anastasia." Even so, he noted that there "had always been many rumors" about the escape of one or another member of the imperial

Gleb Botkin, about 1930.

family, and that he had "never paid any attention to them, so certain had I been that they had all perished."[56] This certainly, though, changed when Tatiana twice wrote to her brother, assuring him that Frau Tchaikovsky was indeed Anastasia.[57] Hoping to clarify this confusing situation, Gleb contacted Gilliard, asking his opinion; the reply, tinged with a bit of hysteria, denounced Frau Tchaikovsky as "a miserable creature" and asserted that the entire affair was "Bolshevik propaganda."[58] In April 1926, the North American Newspaper Alliance in New York agreed to fund Gleb's trip to Germany to meet the claimant in exchange for a story about the encounter.[59]

When Botkin arrived at Seeon, Frau Tchaikovsky first refused to see him, and he had to content himself with observing her as she passed down a corridor. "I knew the moment I caught sight of Mrs. Tchaikovsky," Gleb later wrote, "that I was standing before Grand Duchess Anastasia. She was, it is true, changed in body and in features . . . . Her face seemed elongated, and the nose more prominent, perhaps owing to her thinness." He was particularly struck by "her eyes, which retained their unique, great charm," adding that "her traits, her voice, inflection, carriage, and certain manners" were all identical to those of Anastasia.[60]

Like his sister Tatiana, Gleb honestly admitted that the claimant physically differed from Anastasia in several respects. She was, it is true, the same height, and had the same blue eyes, but he noted his feeling that her face had changed, that her nose was more prominent than that of the grand duchess he had known, and that the shape of her mouth appeared different.[61] Nothing suggests Gleb was not sincerely convinced that Frau Tchaikovsky was Anastasia, but aside from her eyes and her height, he based his recognition on subjective intangibles, including her manner, her carriage, and her voice. Perhaps knowledge that his sister had already done so helped convince Gleb to accept the claimant as genuine.

Throughout, he recalled, Frau Tchaikovsky spoke German, and he alternated in Russian and in German. She understood Russian and, he said, "substituted one Russian word for a German one" when speaking to him.[62] In fact, as Gleb clarified, she had done just that—provided a single Russian word as he was telling a story and forgot the German term for squirrel. "Oh, I know," the claimant interrupted. "*Belka* is *Eichhörnchen* in German."[63] Yet from this single Russian word, Gleb concluded that "not only did she have a perfect command of Russian, but she had also preserved that unique accent which I have never heard outside of her own family."[64] Aside from this single word, though, he admitted, "I do not remember that the Grand Duchess spoke Russian with me or in my presence."[65]

But the most compelling aspect of the encounter once again involved Frau Tchaikovsky's revelation of startling and intimate information that, her supporters contended, only the real Anastasia would have known. One day, she asked if Gleb had brought "his funny animals." Everyone but Gleb was puzzled, and he quickly produced a batch of the drawings he had done to illustrate his allegorical stories peopled by animals; some of the images were new, while some dated from his stay in Tobolsk—the same drawings that his father had smuggled into the Governor's House to amuse Anastasia and Alexei. These the claimant readily identified.[66]

Surely this was proof: who but Anastasia would know of the images, or be able to point out which drawings dated to the stay in Tobolsk? Yet the story was not quite as convincing as this account suggests. Contrary to what Gleb wrote in his 1938 book on the case, Frau Tchaikovsky never asked about his "funny animals" or offered any evidence that she was aware of their existence. It was, in fact, Gleb who first raised the issue, as he confirmed on three separate occasions: first to Rathlef-Keilmann, then in his 1931 book on the Romanovs, and finally in his affidavit on the claimant's case; only later did he change his story.[67] He had mentioned the drawings, he said, "to break the ice," "to ease the conversation."[68] It was not, though, really a question of who first raised the subject but rather the claimant's apparent ability to detect the older images from those done more recently, "the painful feelings that overwhelmed her" on seeing those done in Tobolsk, and her comment "You did them then, in Siberia" that seemed so powerful.[69] It has been suggested that she simply guessed which pictures had been done in Siberia, as "at least some" bore dates at the bottom.[70] This is unlikely, as very few of the drawings were dated.[71] For those who did not believe that Frau Tchaikovsky was Anastasia, though, there was a simpler possibility: that when looking through the drawings the claimant may simply have made some vague comment, a general remark about Siberia, that the impressionable Botkin interpreted in a way most favorable to the idea that she was the grand duchess.

This seems possible, especially given Botkin's somewhat questionable assertions, willingness to dismiss contrary evidence, and alterations to his stories—facts that did nothing to enhance his reputation with the émigré community. Where his sister Tatiana was merely scorned over the case, Gleb took an overt pride in the numerous enemies he made; he even accused his sister of treachery. To Gleb, everyone who had met and rejected Frau Tchaikovsky as Anastasia was guilty of deceit, of denying a surviving grand duchess her name and identity. His was a mystical rather than a practical nature, and it allowed him to embrace such charges in the service of what he believed was a just cause. He cast himself in the role of champion, and Frau Tchaikovsky never had a more convinced—and ultimately damaging—supporter than the man who believed that in aiding her he was continuing his father's service to the imperial family.

13

"A Gruesome Impression"

B Y THE BEGINNING OF 1928, and after nearly a decade of intrigue, Frau Tchaikovsky's claim to be Anastasia had grown into a confusing enigma. The previous year, much against the claimant's wishes, Rathlef-Keilmann published a series of articles on the case: for the first time, the public read of the controversies over recognitions and denunciations, scars and languages, memories and manners. It was a tragic fairy tale come to life, replete with royal intrigue and a compelling air of mystery. In Berlin the claimant's haunted face stared from newspapers and magazines arguing and analyzing her case; and it was not just Berlin that followed her tale with rapt attention—all of Germany seemed fascinated, along with the rest of Europe and even America.[1]

Intrigue seemed inseparable from the story as it continued to develop. Opinions and assertions hardened on both sides amid a constant swell of rumor and conflicting reports. The newspaper headlines chronicling the case were remarkably consistent if only in their inconsistency: one day, they announced that Frau Tchaikovsky had been exposed as a Bolshevik agent; the next, that she had "confessed" to being a Romanian actress; one month, she had been "unmasked" as a Polish factory worker; the next, she was said to be the fiancée of a well-known Baltic gangster.[2] There were threats of lawsuits, retractions, and demands that Frau Tchaikovsky be arrested. Faced with this growing uncertainty, Gleb Botkin thought it best that the claimant leave Europe. A New York socialite named Margharita Derfelden, whose late husband had served in the dowager empress's personal escort, contacted Botkin after

Anna Anderson, dressed in her new winter white wardrobe, in America, 1928.

he returned from Seeon; she also was friendly with Princess Xenia Georgievna, the real Anastasia's second cousin, who lived on Long Island, and eventually arranged a meeting so that Botkin could inform her of the case.[3]

Xenia Georgievna's uncle Prince Christopher of Greece happened to be present at her Long Island estate Kenwood when Botkin arrived and unraveled his tale of having recognized the claimant as Anastasia. Botkin's "sincerity," wrote the prince, "was obvious as he described his visit to her." After hearing this story, Xenia Georgievna "burst into tears" and suddenly exclaimed, "We must bring her over to America! I will pay all the expenses and she can live with me!"[4] "I thought that if I took her in," Xenia Georgievna later said of the claimant, "publicity surrounding the case could be avoided. This seemed so simple to me, and I was certain that when I was sure in my own mind I could then approach important members of my family." Above all, she declared, "I felt if she was separated from people of doubtful intent who were accused of suggesting memories and facts to her that I would be able to obtain a true picture of her personality and identity. If she was indeed an impostor, it would save my family much unpleasantness, and if she really was Anastasia, it was terrible to think that nothing was being done for her."[5]

On Saturday, January 28, 1928, Frau Tchaikovsky left Seeon, armed with an expensive new winter wardrobe in white. "There is a universal feeling of compassion for poor little Princess Xenia," wrote Faith Lavington, "who has no idea what she has landed herself into."[6] She traveled to Cherbourg to board the liner *Berengaria* for New York, accompanied by Agnes Gallagher, Scottish nanny to Princess Xenia's daughter Nancy. During their stop in Paris, Gallagher recalled, the claimant had ordered breakfast for them both, and in French—the first recorded instance that she possessed any familiarity with the language. Gallagher spoke no French herself, so had no idea what Frau Tchaikovsky had actually said, though a waiter duly delivered breakfast to their table. But it was an exception, an aberration, not to be repeated for another three decades; in fact, as Gallagher recalled, she spoke English with the claimant throughout the trip. Not that Frau Tchaikovsky answered in kind, for she continued to speak only German. Eventually, necessity resulted in "increasing fluency"; by the time they reached New York, said Gallagher, Frau Tchaikovsky "was talking English perfectly."[7]

The *Berengaria* steamed into New York Harbor on February 9, greeted by a curious and enthusiastic mob, prying newsreels, exploding flashes from cameras, and the shouted questions of more than fifty reporters who crowded the Thirteenth Street Pier as the liner slowly drew near, all hoping for a glimpse of the young woman who just might be the only surviving daughter of Russia's last tsar. Chaotic as the scene was, it was somehow entirely fitting to this tangled tale and its relocation to the New World, amid rumors that "Anastasia" would soon be off to Hollywood to star in a motion picture based on her story.[8] Princess Xenia Georgievna was on holiday in the West Indies when the claimant arrived, so Frau Tchaikovsky temporarily stayed as the guest of elderly New York socialite and Standard Oil heiress Annie Burr Jennings at her luxurious apartment on East Seventieth Street, attending cocktail parties and being feted by the city's elite.[9] New York, with its congested streets and modern skyscrapers, was an entirely new universe, one far removed from the tranquility of Seeon, yet Frau Tchaikovsky found it all fascinating. "For two weeks," she recalled, "the newspapers talked about me," an indication that she was soon caught up in the excitement surrounding her visit.[10] The *New York Herald Tribune* rather appropriately summed up the enigmatic nature of the tale by writing, "Historians and enthusiasts produce their mountains of proof; but one never really knows, and one is never quite sure that one would want to."[11]

After a few weeks, Princess Xenia Georgievna returned from holiday and the claimant finally took up residence at Kenwood, her sprawling estate at Oyster Bay on Long Island. Born in 1903, Xenia Georgievna had only occasionally seen Anastasia, most often in the Crimea when they were both children.[12] Along with her mother and elder sister Nina, Xenia left Russia in 1914 to live in England and thus escaped the Revolution; her father, Grand Duke George Mikhailovich, was not as lucky, being executed by the Bolsheviks. In 1921, Xenia wed William Leeds, son of widowed American gilded age socialite Nancy Leeds, who, in a confusing twist, had the previous year married Xenia's uncle Prince Christopher of Greece.

"Fourteen years had passed since the spring of 1914, when I had last seen Anastasia in the Crimea," Xenia later said, but she believed herself "competent to distinguish between a member of my own family" and an impostor. Over the next five months, Xenia Georgievna gradually formed an opinion on her guest's identity, a quest made somewhat difficult by what she termed the claimant's "frequent agitation, volatile emotions, and changes of mood." In time, however, she became convinced that Frau Tchaikovsky was Anastasia. "I should not say," Xenia Georgievna declared, "that even after prolonged exposure, I recognized the claimant visually. My recognition was based on an intuitive impression of a family resemblance, especially to her mother's relatives. One of the most convincing aspects of her personality was a completely unconscious acceptance of her identity. At all times she was herself, and never gave the impression of acting a role." According to Xenia, the claimant "never, no matter the pressure, ever made an error that would have shaken my growing conviction and final complete embrace in her identity."[13]

At Frau Tchaikovsky's request, Xenia Georgievna largely avoided questioning her about her alleged past or recalling incidents in Russia; and yet, rather than discuss innocuous subjects such as courtiers or servants, holidays in the Crimea, or rooms in the imperial palaces, the claimant "many times," Xenia recalled, raised her supposed survival of the massacre of her family and escape across Siberia, and her alleged time in Bucharest.[14] Perhaps she simply wished to avoid her alleged childhood owing to difficulty in remembering, or to escape the inevitable feeling that she was being scrutinized, but Frau Tchaikovsky's apparent willingness to relive what would have been the most brutal period in Anastasia's life was altogether odd.

Yet if this seemed strange, there also were those inexplicable turns, things that suggested—as they had so often in this case—that Frau Tchaikovsky might very well be Anastasia. Xenia had agreed to the claimant's request not to arrange any confrontations or meetings with relatives, but one day her cousin Prince Dimitri Alexandrovich came to Kenwood to play tennis with a friend. A mesh fence overgrown with vines separated the tennis court from the claimant's window, so that she could hear the game but not see it being played. As Xenia recalled, Dimitri and his friend were playing, calling out the score and yelling back and forth to each other in English. When Xenia entered the claimant's room later that day, Frau Tchaikovsky was furious. "You lied to me!" she screamed. "You promised not to bring them here!" When Xenia pressed, the claimant cried, "I know his voice! It's one of the cousins!"[15]

Who but Anastasia, Xenia Georgievna was convinced, could identify some minor Romanov cousin merely by hearing his voice? No one seems to have actually questioned the implicit implication: that a surviving Anastasia possessed such extraordinary recall that she could accurately recognize the voice of a cousin whom she had not seen for more than a decade. Yet a more mundane answer suggested itself to Frau Tchaikovsky's opponents. Although she couldn't see the players, the claimant had heard and followed their conversation as they shouted back and forth; it doesn't seem unreasonable to assume that names were used that provided Frau Tchaikovsky with the identity of at least one of the men.

And, as usual, there were renewed controversies over languages. Stories asserted that during her stay at Kenwood, Frau Tchaikovsky had occasionally and unintentionally lapsed into Russian. A visiting Margharita Derfelden later recalled that once, when walking through the garden, the claimant had "talked of the flowers in Russian, calling them by their quaint Russian names."[16] More famously, Xenia Georgievna once supposedly walked into the claimant's room while the latter was playing at the window with her two pet parakeets. "Look!" Frau Tchaikovsky said in Russian. "They are dancing on the windowsill!" From this, Xenia declared that the claimant spoke "perfectly acceptable Russian from the point of view of St. Petersburg society."[17]

Convincing? As relayed in numerous accounts favorable to Frau Tchaikovsky's claim, yes; in truth, no. Derfelden did indeed declare that the claimant had spoken of flowers at Kenwood using Russian names; but she—and not Xenia Georgievna—also was the source for the parakeet story. In the early 1970s, Xenia Georgievna's nephew Prince David Chavchavadze told case historian Brien Horan that he had often heard the parakeet story from his mother, Princess Nina Georgievna, who said that she, in turn, had heard it from Xenia herself. The remark about the quality of the claimant's spoken Russian also originated with Chavchavadze; the words frequently quoted were thus not those of Xenia Georgievna but, at best, a thirdhand version of what she may have said.[18]

Yet even this is problematic. In 1959, Xenia spent two days answering questions about the claimant at the West German consulate in New York. When asked specifically about Frau Tchaikovsky's languages, she declared, "From the beginning the claimant and myself communicated only in English. Her English accent was good, but she was somewhat out of practice, in that sometimes she could not find the correct expression. However, we never spoke Russian together, despite the fact that one day I said to her, 'It's a pity that we don't speak Russian, our mother tongue.' The claimant explained on this and other occasions that she did not want to hear Russian."[19]

So Xenia never heard the claimant speak Russian during her stay at Kenwood. Was the parakeet story merely a bit of lore, filtered through the family, until it assumed a veneer of truth? Perhaps it all originated with Derfelden, who told it to Xenia, who told it to Nina, who told it to her son David Chavchavadze; what is clear, though, is that the reality behind the myth wasn't as compelling as everyone was led to believe. Xenia said that she spoke to Frau Tchaikovsky in English throughout her stay, although as she admitted, while her accent was "excellent," she occasionally had to search for the right words or expressions. Yet Xenia's sister Princess Nina Chavchavadze met the claimant and came away with quite a different impression. Frau Tchaikovsky, she was convinced, was not Anastasia, though she believed her to be "a lady of good society."[20] The claimant's linguistic skills, though, stunned her: "My God, what English she spoke! I didn't even have to be told that she was an impostor by the way she spoke English. . . . We all spoke Russian in the family. But I've heard her [Grand Duchess Anastasia Nikolaievna] speak English. She used to speak English with her mother, and it wasn't that sort of English, I assure you."[21]

In the end, Xenia Georgievna, as she fervently declared in 1959, was "convinced that the claimant is in fact Grand Duchess Anastasia of Russia."[22] She never wavered from this view, but the decision caused her nothing but grief. Visiting America at the time, Grand Duke Alexander Mikhailovich, brother-in-law and second cousin to Nicholas II, and Xenia Georgievna's uncle, was repeatedly hounded by a persistent gaggle of reporters who were interested only in the enigmatic young woman's identity. With his typical flair for the mystic, the grand duke asserted that Anastasia's "spirit has returned to this world, and incorporated itself into another body. She knows so much about the intimate life of the Tsar and his family that there is simply no other explanation for it; and of course it wouldn't be the first time that a spirit has returned to earth in new physical form."[23] But the Romanovs took aim not at Alexander Mikhailovich but at Xenia. "Xenia's irresponsible statement should be somehow refuted," one relative declared. "We know she left Russia in 1914, aged ten-years-old; I also know that Nina and Xenia never saw Uncle Nicky's family very often, and when they did see them that was when they were very young."[24]

The claimant's stay with Xenia Georgievna spread over five highly charged months, during which time the princess's marriage, already disintegrating, crumbled under the strain of caring for her difficult guest. There were frequent arguments, and Frau Tchaikovsky's unpredictable moods and volatility infected the already fragile household.[25] Xenia foolishly promised the claimant that she would somehow arrange a meeting with the dowager empress in Copenhagen, an assurance she could not keep.[26] But it was not just the claimant's behavior, a broken promise, or a fractured marriage that led to the break. Xenia's real mistake was in allowing Gleb Botkin unrestricted access to Frau Tchaikovsky. Much of the animosity and misunderstanding that arose at Kenwood over these months, at least as far as Xenia Georgievna was concerned, was due solely to his persistently stubborn and invidious intervention.

The problems began on Botkin's return to America from Seeon, as he published a series of articles about the claimant. Interest in her story was so high, particularly in the United States, that, as Gleb recalled, he was "swamped with requests for articles," and a good deal of possible income was bandied about to tempt him. He was at first guarded, even refusing offers that would have considerably enriched him personally.[27] Over time, however, his reliance on Rathlef-Keilmann, and presumption that she had provided an accurate accounting of events, led to exaggeration. The duke of Leuchtenberg personally protested one of Gleb's articles, insisting that he had been extensively misquoted, a point that Botkin apparently conceded.[28] But being successfully challenged did nothing to stop what many came to see as Botkin's increasing recklessness. After one such story, Grand Duke Andrei Vladimirovich complained, "The tone of the last part of the article is absolutely unwarranted. . . . Gleb is no longer relying here on facts but on notoriously untrue gossip. Has Gleb really not got enough feeling and tact to understand how inappropriate, even harmful, it is for a Russian to sling mud at his own people in the columns of the foreign press? His insinuations against the Grand Duke of Hesse I find equally distasteful. . . . He is completely ruining the invalid."[29]

But Gleb saw enemies everywhere, and he felt certain that the Romanovs were simply denying the claimant so they could obtain any money deposited in Europe by Nicholas II. With an eye to protecting what he thought were her rights, Gleb became increasingly strident in pushing Frau Tchaikovsky to make a claim on the reputed Romanov fortune. At first his visits to Kenwood and to the claimant were cordial, though he disagreed with Xenia Georgievna's cautious approach in advancing the case; soon he apparently complained to the claimant that the princess did not have her best interests at heart. In her suspicious state, Frau Tchaikovsky was always susceptible to any slight, whether real or perceived, and began to vent her anger on her luckless hostess. The situation quickly devolved into shouting matches among the trio, with Xenia accusing Gleb of hoping to exploit the claimant for publicity, and Gleb charging Xenia with keeping her a virtual prisoner at Kenwood on orders from the Romanovs. There were absurd, dueling press conferences and statements among the warring parties that helped no one, least of all the claimant.[30] Gleb later insisted that at one point Xenia had told him that Grand Duchesses Xenia and Olga

Alexandrovna, aware that the claimant was their niece, were willing to give her a large financial settlement and provide for her if she would consent to drop her claim and thus pave the way for them to obtain any funds deposited by Nicholas II in Europe.[31]

This, Xenia Georgievna insisted, was a lie, nonsense. "I would never, never have said such a thing," she later declared. "The attitude of my aunts was too negative to imagine them proposing such a thing."[32] Few actually believed Botkin's version of events, but the damage was done. He continued to poison the claimant against her hostess, and soon enough, the situation at Kenwood reached the breaking point. Whether it was Xenia Georgievna or her husband, William Leeds, who finally asked the claimant to leave, or if it was Frau Tchaikovsky's own rash decision, in August she fled the estate with Gleb. "You know," Xenia later said, "she isn't normal."[33]

Frau Tchaikovsky didn't go far, checking into the Garden City Hotel on Long Island on August 10, 1928. To evade any curious reporters, Botkin registered the claimant as "Mrs. Eugene Anderson"; soon this evolved into "Anna Anderson."[34] A porter named Walter Ruch was deputized to tend to her needs, as he could speak to her in German; this suggests that her fluency in English was still less than satisfactory. As opposed to those who had deemed her German atrocious, Ruch found that she spoke "very good" German, though he noted that she seemed to carry "a foreign accent."[35]

And it was Gleb Botkin who now tried to rescue her from the legal and financial limbo that had dominated the previous decade of her life.

Edward Fallows, the first lawyer to take on Anderson's case.

He retained Edward Fallows, a corporate lawyer from New York City, to pursue the claimant's possible financial interests. Ten years had passed since the executions in Ekaterinburg, and Gleb suspected that surviving Romanovs might attempt to lodge inheritance suits against any potential European funds. Contrary to what many elected to believe, Botkin urged this path not because he was personally avaricious and hoped to profit should any such accounts be found but rather from genuine concern over the claimant's future. He himself had little money and could not afford to care for her, yet some provision had to be made for her security. When

Fallows drew up a will for Anderson that summer, she named—without their knowledge—Gleb and his sister Tatiana as her principal beneficiaries; Gleb somehow got wind of this and had Fallows draft a document naming the American Red Cross as recipient should he receive any money through the claimant.[36]

The money issue: from this point forward, it hung like a millstone around Anderson's neck, confirmation—to those who suspected her of fraud—that the claim was nothing more than an unseemly attempt to lay her hands on the mythical Romanov fortune. Whatever money had existed in Russia before the Revolution was gone—on that much everyone agreed—but what of Romanov funds deposited abroad? There had been money, a commingling of both governmental and private assets—a distinction lost on the autocratically minded Nicholas and Alexandra—in the Bank of England, the Mendelssohn Bank in Berlin, and probably other institutions, at least in 1914. The funds in Germany were frozen, and those in England, at least according to the Romanovs, were patriotically brought back to finance the war effort; in fact, money remained in the Bank of England, as the British ambassador to Russia, Sir George Buchanan, frequently delivered large sums to the empress.[37]

But the questions of what if anything remained—and in which institutions—became as enigmatic as the claim of Anna Anderson. She told Fallows that Nicholas II had deposited 5 million rubles for herself and each of her three sisters in the Bank of England, to be used as dowries, something she said she had told Olga Alexandrovna during her visits.[38] Discovery of this supposed fortune, so many of Anderson's supporters held, had led the avaricious Romanovs in exile to deny that she was Anastasia.[39]

"It was all fantastic and terribly vulgar," said Olga Alexandrovna. "Would my mother have accepted a pension from King George V if we had any money in England? It does not make sense."[40] Yet her sister Xenia Alexandrovna at least wondered if it might be true, to the extent that she hired two lawyers to seek out any deposits made by her late brother that could then be claimed.[41] No one, on either side, ever found any fortune hidden in the Bank of England or any other British bank, but, as with so much in Anderson's case, it was belief rather than fact that continued to fuel the conspiratorial fires. Gleb Botkin's determined and overt pursuit of this mythical fortune on behalf of the claimant seemed, to many, at best unseemly and at worst deeply suspicious. Gleb, who so frequently and freely hurled libelous insults and accusations at those he deemed "Anastasia's" enemies, thus gave the impression that he was some Machiavellian character intent on using Anderson for financial gain. Such assumptions were erroneous, but great damage was done when Fallows organized the Grandanor

Corporation that summer of 1928; in exchange for large financial contributions to fund the claimant and pay her legal fees, those who donated received a certain number of shares in the corporation. If and when the rumored Romanov fortune was found, these shareholders would be duly rewarded according to their contributions.[42] To many, this reduced the presumed struggle of a damaged young woman's sincere efforts to reclaim a lost past to the unfortunate appearance of a treasure hunt.

And it was this—the possibility that Botkin and Fallows would attempt to force the issue in a court of law—that drove Princess Xenia Georgievna to write a desperate letter to Empress Alexandra's sister Victoria, marchioness of Milford Haven, begging her to assume financial responsibility for the claimant and thus prevent such an unseemly circus. To this, though, Victoria replied, "I have given much thought to what you have written about the situation of A (as I also shall call her in this letter), and the action you suggest I should take, and have also discussed the question with Irene. . . . I am quite unable to look upon her as being really my niece, and I assure you solemnly that I should have rejoiced if I could have thought otherwise, for I really loved my poor sister Alix's children, whom I saw nearly every year before the war and met for the last time at its outbreak. Not lightly nor with prejudice have I come to my conclusion. . . . The question of supporting A by money or otherwise in order to save us from much possible unpleasantness—a danger you warn me of, has to be considered. I have come to the conclusion that I cannot follow your suggestion and must face any risks this refusal may entail. People claiming to be one or the other member of that martyred family are certain to continue turning up. . . . I cannot myself nor advise any of my relatives to take up the burden of responsibility for A's future life and actions."[43]

Nothing happened, and neither side seemed willing to force the issue of Anderson's identity until the autumn of 1928. That October, Dowager Empress Marie Feodorovna died in Copenhagen. Within twenty-four hours, the Romanovs in Denmark as well as former grand duke Ernst Ludwig of Hesse in Darmstadt issued a statement that had obviously been prepared in advance. Citing the negative opinions of Grand Duchess Olga Alexandrovna, Baroness Sophie Buxhoeveden, and Pierre and Alexandra Gilliard, it categorically rejected the claimant, declaring, "It is our firm conviction that the woman who calls herself Mrs. Anastasia Tchaikovsky, and who is at present in the United States, is not Grand Duchess Anastasia Nikolaievna." It was, the statement said, "very difficult and painful for us, the nearest relatives of the Tsar's family, to accept the idea that not a single member of that family survived. We would willingly believe that one at least escaped from their murderous extermination in 1918. We would heap on the survivor that love of ours which has had no object on which to expend itself all these years. And with our great love we would drown our great sorrow that it has not been our lot to be able to protect the pure in heart, these models of goodness and love, from the slanderous tongues of their enemies. But our sense of duty compels us to state that as far as the woman in question is concerned, her story is a pure invention. Our memory of the dear departed must not be doubted by allowing this fantastic tale to be spread abroad and gain substance." Thirteen members of the Romanov family signed the Danish version: Grand Duchess Olga Alexandrovna; her sister Grand Duchess Xenia Alexandrovna and her husband, Grand Duke Alexander Mikhailovich; their six sons, Princes Andrei, Feodor, Nikita, Dimitri, Rostislav, and Vassili Alexandrovich; their daughter, Princess Irina Alexandrovna, and her husband, Prince Felix Yusupov; and Grand Duke Dimitri Pavlovich and his sister Grand Duchess Marie Pavlovna, first cousins to Nicholas II. The version issued in Darmstadt carried the additional signatures of Grand Duke Ernst Ludwig of Hesse and his two sisters, Victoria, marchioness of Milford Haven, and Princess Irene of Prussia.[44] But of this roster, only three—Olga Alexandrovna, Princess Irene of Prussia, and Prince Felix Yusupov—had actually met the claimant.

Gleb Botkin took this statement as a declaration of war, a "revolting" gesture "without provocation" that, he declared, left him "disgusted."[45] In response, apparently unbidden and without consulting anyone, Gleb very publicly struck back. To Grand Duchess Xenia Alexandrovna he wrote:

> Twenty-four-hours did not pass after the death of your mother . . . when you hastened to take another step in the conspiracy against your own niece. . . . It makes a gruesome impression that even at your mother's deathbed your foremost worry must have been the desire to defraud your niece, and it is appalling that you did not have even the common decency of waiting if only a few days before resuming your ignoble fight. . . . The manner in which your statement was published is obviously calculated to mislead the public. . . . The statement is accompanied by the usual absurd lies so characteristic of the whole campaign of vile slander which you are leading against your unfortunate niece. . . . But permit me for the moment to disregard that malicious nonsense and come down to facts well known to you. These facts in short are that there exists a considerable fortune in both money and real estate belonging to the late Emperor and his heirs, including personal funds of Grand Duchess

Anastasia, all of which should now rightfully belong to her; that you are trying for years by fraudulent methods to gain possession of that fortune; that much of the information concerning the Emperor's fortune came into your possession only after it had been disclosed by Grand Duchess Anastasia; that your sister Grand Duchess Olga practically acknowledged Grand Duchess Anastasia in 1925 upon the assurance of physicians that she could not live longer than for one month; and finally, that as soon as Grand Duchess Anastasia began to recover and you could no longer hope for her immediate death, you and your sister began to denounce her as an imposter. . . . I refuse to believe that you are actually convinced that Mrs. Tchaikovsky is not Grand Duchess Anastasia. You know very well that she remembers the slightest details of her childhood, that she possesses all her physical signs including birth marks, that her handwriting is at present the same as it had been in her youth. . . . You also know that she has been fully acknowledged by many people of unquestionable truthfulness who had known her in her childhood, as well as by several members of the Russian Imperial Family. You further know that all physicians who had ever treated her unanimously agree that it would be a scientific impossibility for her to be anybody but who she claims to be. Finally, you know that all the so-called evidence pretending to disprove her identity consists of nothing but fabrications, falsifications, perjured statements of bribed witnesses and malicious and stupid fiction. . . . That you personally are convinced of the real identity of Grand Duke Anastasia Nikolaievna is evident enough from the fact that in the course of your whole fight against her you have never made a truthful statement nor mentioned a single fact, but resort exclusively to the vilest slander and most preposterous lies. Before the wrong that Your Imperial Highness is committing, even the gruesome murder of the Emperor, his family, and my father by the Bolsheviks pales! It is easier to understand a crime committed by a gang of crazed and drunken savages than the calm, systematic, endless persecution of one of your own family . . . Grand Duchess Anastasia Nikolaievna, whose only fault is that, being the only rightful heir to the late Emperor, she stands in the way of her greedy and unscrupulous relatives.[46]

This, Botkin insisted, had been a carefully considered response, intentionally designed to "make it a grave libel if untrue." If left unanswered, he asserted, American authorities would inevitably accept the Copenhagen statement as evidence that the claimant was a fraud. By deliberately provoking Xenia Alexandrovna, he said, he hoped that she would threaten legal action against the claimant and thus force a courtroom confrontation that would turn on the evidence supporting her identity. And yet Gleb admitted that he found it "impossible to restrain myself" when writing the letter, and that in composing it he had "poured all the indignation and bitterness" over what he apparently believed to be a callous rejection of a surviving Anastasia by members of her own family.[47]

Intentions aside, Botkin's actions caused irreparable harm. Not only did he send his insulting letter to Xenia Alexandrovna but he also compounded the damage by releasing it to the media, who, quick to grasp the sensational story, published it in full in newspapers around the world. Even Gleb's sister Tatiana was horrified. Although she described the move as typical of her brother's "impulsive manner," his "miserable letter," Tatiana thought, now "made it impossible for the Romanovs to recognize Anastasia."[48] Exasperated by such behavior and deeply suspicious of Fallows and his Grandanor Corporation, Tatiana said that she would no longer support her brother or his actions. To this, Gleb responded in typical fashion, openly accusing his sister of deceit.[49] He even suggested that she, too, was part of what he termed a "truly medieval cabal" set on depriving the claimant of her rightful name and inheritance.[50] He publicly denounced Grand Duchesses Xenia and Olga Alexandrovna as "monsters" who, along with Gilliard, "decided to ruin" a woman they knew to be "their own niece" so they could steal her inheritance.[51] And yet Gleb professed amazement that he had been "deserted by all my relatives and friends in Europe, and do not expect to hear from any of them again until the day of Anastasia's final rehabilitation."[52]

Anderson, for her part, avoided these intrigues, this storm created on her behalf by the well-intentioned, ever loyal, and hopelessly reckless Gleb Botkin. She left the Garden City Hotel at the beginning of 1929 and returned to Annie Burr Jennings, throwing herself into the soirees, teas, and dinners her hostess staged to show her off to New York society.[53] Soon, though, and despite the expensive new clothes her hostess provided, Anderson grew weary of the spectacle. She was quite willing to sleep in her hostess's bed, explore the city in her hostess's chauffeur-driven limousine, shop along Fifth Avenue using her hostess's credit accounts, and eat the food prepared by her hostess's chef, but her dislike of strangers and of being put on display led to the familiar pattern of sudden outbursts, displays of temper, changes of mood, and wild accusations. Increasingly paranoid, she began to complain that people were spying on her; that the telephone lines were bugged; and that Jennings was alternately keeping her a prisoner or was attempting to steal her inheritance.[54]

The situation came to a head in the summer of 1930. On the evening of July 14, Anderson accidentally stepped on and killed one of the two pet parakeets that Xenia Georgievna had given her; she spent the entire night alternately sobbing and then screaming, mourning the loss of her pet, then demanding another. No one in the Jennings apartment slept that night, and no one knew quite what to expect when morning came. Mercurial as ever, Anderson left the apartment, having decided that the best way to overcome her grief was to spend more of her hostess's money, but when she attempted to charge a new purchase, she learned that Jennings had that morning cut off her guest's credit. Infuriated, Anderson returned to the apartment and to another storm, continuing the screams and accusations of the previous night; after attempting to physically attack the servants, she was chased, naked, onto the roof, only to be dragged screaming back into the apartment.[55]

Something had to be done; over the next few days, Anderson stood in the middle of a crowded department store, shouting abuse and accusations in her broken English at Jennings; sat at the window of her hostess's apartment, tossing busts and objets d'art at unsuspecting pedestrians below; threatened the servants with physical violence; and declared that she intended to kill herself.[56] Although Anderson was no stranger to depression and unpredictable moods, her behavior in New York was outrageous even for her, and signaled a serious nervous breakdown. Using her money and connections, Jennings found three doctors who, without benefit of examination or even a face-to-face meeting, were willing, for a fee of $1,250 (approximately $64,000 in 2011), to declare that the claimant was delusional and required hospitalization. Armed with the necessary medical opinions, Jennings had a New York Supreme Court judge sign commitment papers declaring that the claimant was suffering from a persecution complex and was "dangerous to herself and others," and on the night of July 24, a nurse and two orderlies manhandled Anderson out of the Jennings apartment and into a car that took her off to the posh Four Winds Rest Home in Katonah, New York, where she would remain—at Jennings's expense—for more than a year.[57]

14

A Tale of Two Books

ANASTASIA TCHAIKOVSKY, Anna Anderson, had disappeared, secluded somewhere behind the walls of the Four Winds Rest Home, but the world outside remained fascinated, unconcerned that the heroine in their tale had been locked away against her will in an asylum. Opinions hardened in these years: to some she remained a mystery, but as she slipped into obscurity, supporters and opponents alike had embraced their beliefs with a religious certainty. And foremost among those who laid claim to the truth, who revealed and publicized the warring elements and conflicting evidence, were two diametrically opposed actors in her drama, two equally insistent, adamant voices: Harriet von Rathlef-Keilmann and Pierre Gilliard. It was no accident that this pair, dogmatic and determined, each despising the other and freely hurling accusations of deceit, took their battle public, onto the pages of newspapers and between the covers of two rival books that chronicled Anderson's case and cemented her reputation as a living legend.

The Romanovs, so Rathlef-Keilmann believed, fired the first shot in this public relations war when in January 1926 Olga Alexandrovna allowed Copenhagen's *National Tidende* to publish word of her visit to and rejection of the claimant. Rathlef-Keilmann's reply came some two months later, in the form of journalist Bella Cohen's article in the *New York Times*—two diametrically opposing versions of Anderson's case that only confused the issue of her identity. Everyone feared Rathlef-Keilmann's voluminous dossier on the claimant, not so much for its content but rather for what she might do with it: there had been constant rumors since the October 1925 visits that she was actively seeking a publisher for a manuscript on the case, a book no one on either side of the argument wanted to see published. Even the claimant herself had warned Rathlef-Keilmann not to publicize the story. Supporters and opponents alike begged her not to take the issue to the press, knowing that such actions would result in the airing of ugly accusations and bring angry recriminations. But no amount of pleading could dissuade Rathlef-Keilmann, and in February 1927 the newspaper *Berliner Nachtausgabe* began her series on the case, a string of articles all overtly favorable to the claimant and highly critical of those who had denounced her.

This burst of publicity, with its insinuations of nefarious royal goings-on, did not go unnoticed. Barely two weeks passed before Ernst Ludwig's former court marshal Count Kuno von Hardenberg, working with Gilliard, issued a rebuttal. On March 7, the *Königsberg Allgemeine Zeitung* published a thorough, if often inaccurate, story essentially penned by Darmstadt: "The mystery of the false daughter of the Tsar, which has lately generated much talk in the press, seems now to be nearing resolution, as it is now definitely established that 'Fraulein Unbekannt' who, on February 22 [sic] of 1920 was pulled from the Landwehr Canal beneath the Bendler Bridge by Berlin police is not one of the Tsar's daughters. A long list of confrontations, inquiries, and careful examination of statements made by the alleged Grand Duchess Anastasia has finally resulted in this conclusion." The statement spoke mysteriously of an "anthropological comparison of the ears of Frau Tchaikovsky and Grand Duchess Anastasia" that revealed discrepancies, and asserted, quite erroneously, that "the deformities of the feet recalled by all of those who had known Grand Duchess Anastasia are not found in the claimant." Only those who had not known the real Anastasia thought that the claimant bore "a striking resemblance" to the grand duchess. "The closest relatives of the Tsar's family, as well as the tutor Gilliard and his wife, and the lady of the court Baroness Buxhoeveden all absolutely deny this alleged resemblance. Nor was Frau Tchaikovsky able to recognize Grand Duchess Anastasia's relatives and acquaintances when they visited her. Medical examination has revealed, contrary to assertions, that blows from a rifle butt to her jaw and skull have not resulted in any considerable alteration in her appearance. Nor, as has been alleged, was a heavy blow from the butt of a rifle responsible for the loss of numerous teeth in Frau Tchaikovsky's mouth; rather, a dentist at Dalldorf Asylum extracted them. An examination of the handwriting of Tchaikovsky and Grand Duchess Anastasia shows that they are two different people. The greatest enigma, however, is that Frau Tchaikovsky speaks only German and has forgotten both English and Russian, while Grand Duchess Anastasia barely spoke German but conversed in English and in Russian." Turning to her alleged knowledge and memories of life at court, the statement declared, "Frau Tchaikovsky, it must be noted, is not as mentally deficient and troubled as her supporters would lead us to believe, and she has long been acquainted with books and journal articles on the Tsar's family and also freely associated with many monarchist émigrés in Berlin. This last group, naively believing that she was actually the Grand Duchess, unwittingly helped fill in gaps in her memory through stories and gifts of books and photographs. And thus it happened that her statements, which in the beginning were vague and halting and often incorrect, became by degrees more assured and accurate, as can be proved. In summation, her statements are without value, and Frau Tchaikovsky knows only what contemporary literature and Russian emigrants know of the Tsar's family and court; she knows nothing intimate of the family, no sentiments or traditions, no nicknames, and no current relationships."[1]

It was precisely as Rathlef-Keilmann had been warned: take the case to the press and expect the battle over the claimant's identity to become fodder for public controversy. Her articles continued, answered throughout the summer by Pierre Gilliard now, who for the first time publicly denounced the claimant in Swiss, French, and English magazines and newspapers; Rathlef-Keilmann replied in the press that autumn, calling Gilliard a liar who "victimizes this poor, helpless invalid at every turn."[2] But she saved most of her venom for what almost everyone had feared and suspected: her book on the case, which arrived the following years in a burst of international publicity.

Anastasia: The Survivor of Ekaterinburg, by Harriet von Rathlef-Keilmann, was a book whose very title boldly declared its conclusions. She was, she admitted, determined "to secure recognition for the person whose cause I am attempting to take up."[3] Here was Anderson's case as Rathlef-Keilmann saw it, as her supporters saw it, and as history would largely see it, full of favorable evidence and inexplicable knowledge, a tale, proclaimed the author, of "extraordinary tragedy and romance," in which the "tortures of hell itself were meted out" to the claimant in her struggle to reclaim her lost identity.[4] Scars, memories, stories from those who said they knew Anastasia had been saved, had been taken to Bucharest—it all spilled across the pages of Rathlef-Keilmann's book. Baroness Buxhoeveden and Princess Irene had been too confused, the claimant had been too ashamed, for their negative encounters to hold any meaning; the visits of Volkov, the Gilliards, and Olga Alexandrovna, on the other hand, were recalled in dramatic—and questionable—re-creations that left the reader with no doubt as to their initial, favorable opinions. And Rathlef-Keilmann served up the recognitions by Princess Xenia and Tatiana and Gleb Botkin, along with a string of mysterious, unnamed alleged witnesses who attested to Anastasia's survival. It was all a compelling, convincing tapestry of evidence that Nicholas II's youngest daughter was indeed alive.

The Romanovs, though, saw things differently. Olga Alexandrovna had initially been content to let the matter drop, to rest her case for history with the *National Tidende* article and in the statement issued on the death of the dowager empress, but these declarations had no effect on the public, and on a belief—now stoked by Rathlef-Keilmann—that she and others had first recognized the claimant as Anastasia and later rejected her. With Olga's approval and full cooperation, and working with Count von Hardenberg, Pierre Gilliard now prepared to answer Rathlef-Keilmann in depth and very publicly, in his own book on the case. He had wanted to do so much earlier—had in fact been working with Konstantin Savitch, former president of the Court of Assizes in St. Petersburg, on collecting evidence against Anderson—but not until Rathlef-Keilmann's book did the idea win royal and imperial approval.

Twelve months after Rathlef-Keilmann's book came Gilliard's *La Fausse Anastasie*, a book filled with statements and declarations from the claimant's opponents, including Baron von Kleist, Baroness Buxhoeveden, Princess Irene, and others. For a man so determinedly eager to denounce Anderson, Gilliard adopted a surprisingly benign tone when discussing her. Perhaps she believed that she really was Anastasia, though Gilliard doubted this; she was, he admitted, a "pitiful creature" who "awoke in all who met her tender sympathies."[5] Convinced that she was too unstable to have engineered what he believed to be a false claim, to have learned the multitude of detail about Anastasia's life she seemed to possess, he pointed fingers at everyone surrounding the claimant, suggesting they had victimized her and filled her head with stories to advance her case.[6] Just as Gilliard served as Rathlef-Keilmann's chief villain, so, too, did the former tutor accuse his nemesis of blatant deception. "All of the facts she presents," he wrote, "are so distorted—when they are not simply made up out of whole cloth—that it becomes difficult for the reader who is not forewarned not to believe in the extraordinary adventure which is told."[7]

These two books offered the public two wildly irreconcilable views of Anderson's case. Other claimants came and went, appeared to great fanfare, and then disappeared, but their tales weren't debated by principal actors, in public, in the pages of newspapers and magazines, and in dueling books. It was Rathlef-Keilmann, published in Germany, Great Britain, and North America, widely distributed and promoted, serialized in magazines and newspapers, who won the publicity battle: Gilliard's book, published only in French, quickly came and went, disappearing from stores soon after its printing. Thus it was Rathlef-Keilmann's version of events that the public came to know, that captivated imaginations and left readers indignant over ."Anastasia's" callous rejection by her surviving relatives. And Rathlef-Keilmann had an unseen ally on her side: desire. Ten years had passed since the presumed execution, and still there were no bodies, no actual evidence that the Romanovs had all been killed, merely assumptions of what had happened and theories regarding the destruction of their remains. The veil of plausibility with which Rathlef-Keilmann's book thus wrapped the claimant offered the public an appealing alternative to the shocking and bloody end in a grim Ekaterinburg cellar, a story that—for all of its twists and heart-wrenching developments—still somehow seemed redolent of the power of the human spirit to triumph over evil.

But if Gilliard's book fell into obscurity, it—or more correctly, descriptions of it by those sympathetic to Anderson—assumed a pivotal role in her case, advanced as evidence that the former tutor was nothing short of a fraud himself, a man who repeatedly lied about the claimant. In typical fashion, Gleb Botkin thus declared that Gilliard's book was filled with "deliberate untruths," that he had used "retouched photographs and other faked or planted evidence," and had done it all as a paid agent of Grand Duke Ernst Ludwig of Hesse.[8] The anger stemmed from Gilliard's attacks on several dozen of the claimant's asserted memories, as related to him in Rathlef-Keilmann's letters and in the latter's book, errors he contended revealed that she could not be Anastasia. Those sympathetic to Anderson's case took Botkin's lead: Gilliard's "vicious, vituperative" book was filled with "gross errors" and "inventions" designed to "put an end" to her "career."[9]

But what, precisely, was Gilliard supposed to have done in his "vicious, vituperative" book? Three issues were central, three of Anderson's alleged memories as recorded by Rathlef-Keilmann, three claims that Gilliard completely rejected. "There was a palace at home," Rathlef-Keilmann quoted the claimant, "the windowsills and columns of which were made of malachite."[10] Gilliard dismissed this as "nothing but pure fantasy."[11] Anderson's supporters stumbled over themselves to point out the famous Malachite Hall in the Winter Palace, as well as another, similarly decorated room in the Grand Kremlin Palace. Why, they asked, did Gilliard lie?

In fact, he hadn't. On January 1, 1926, Rathlef-Keilmann sent him notes of her conversations with the claimant, notes that quoted Anderson as saying, "In several rooms at Tsarskoye Selo, the sills of the windows were of malachite."[12] This, Gilliard correctly replied, was wrong: there were no rooms in any of the palaces at Tsarskoye Selo with malachite-decorated windows. But when Rathlef-Keilmann reproduced the notes in her book, she edited out the claimant's reference to Tsarskoye Selo, replacing it with the less definitive "at home."

It wasn't the only such contradiction. Anderson told Rathlef-Keilmann that she had been awarded her own infantry regiment and named honorary colonel in chief when she was fifteen. She could not remember the name of the regiment, just that that the soldiers wore dark blue uniforms, that she had reviewed them on horseback, and that the review had been held at Tsarskoye Selo.[13] Anastasia, of course, had indeed been named honorary colonel in chief of the 148th Caspian Infantry Rifle Regiment by her father when she turned fourteen, in 1915, but perhaps the claimant simply misremembered the year.[14] Rathlef-Keilmann sent these details to Gilliard; within a day, she wrote, he had replied confirming that everything the claimant had said was "quite accurate."[15]

Really? Not according to Gilliard, who had the documentation to prove it. On receiving Rathlef-Keilmann's letter, he asked Colonel Vassili Koliubakin, former commander of the regiment, about the claimant's statements and learned that the unit had been posted to Galicia at the time and that no review—at Tsarskoye Selo or elsewhere—had taken place. Later, Koliubakin alone had offered his congratulations, on behalf of his men, to Anastasia in a room at the Alexander Palace. There had been no other delegations, no blue uniforms, and no parade, facts also confirmed by General Michael Repiev, who had commanded the infantry divisions to which Anastasia's regiment belonged.[16] This is what Gilliard communicated to Rathlef-Keilmann. And, as happened with the claimant's erroneous description of a room at Tsarskoye Selo adorned with malachite windowsills, Rathlef-Keilmann again edited her notes to erase Anderson's mistake before publishing them in her book. Now there was no mention of blue uniforms, or of a review at Tsarskoye Selo, though for some reason she retained the claimant's statement "I myself took charge of the parade on horseback."[17] Gleb Botkin insisted, not very convincingly, that it all must have been Rathlef-Keilmann's mistake, that the claimant had meant to say that the uniforms bore blue piping.[18] Later, French journalist Dominique Auclères, who passionately believed in Anderson's claim, apparently insisting that Gilliard had lied over the issue, swooped in to deliver what she believed to be the coup de grâce: the widow of a former regimental commander, she said, remembered that her late husband had recalled the ceremonial review on horseback—of "the Blue Regiment," no less—that Anderson described. Unfortunately for Auclères, this source insisted upon a different year—1916; a different season—autumn, not summer; and a different place—Peterhof, not Tsarskoye Selo—none of which confirmed Anderson's story except perhaps to those willing to reject the statements of the regimental commanders in an effort to embrace anything that supported her case.[19]

It was Auclères, too, who tried to take Gilliard to task over the issue of a samovar. "The park at home," Anderson said, "was so beautiful: it was like a forest. When it rained and the weather was bad, I liked the chimney corner, the samovar on the table, and drinking tea with good things to eat."[20] This Gilliard attacked as "all very poetical" but untrue, writing that no samovar was ever used in the Alexander Palace. "It might seem curious, but it is nonetheless true," he said.[21] Auclères found a photograph showing a samovar in use at Mogilev when Nicholas II lived there during the First World War, proof—or so the theory ran—that Gilliard had lied.[22] Yet Anderson hadn't been discussing Mogilev at all, but Tsarskoye Selo, a point that seems to have escaped the notice of the French journalist.

And this was essentially it—Anderson's supporters and generations who stumbled upon her tale branded Gilliard a liar because he correctly pointed out there were no palace rooms at Tsarskoye Selo whose windowsills were decorated with malachite, because officers he contacted refuted her erroneous statements regarding Anastasia's regiment, and because he said—without contradiction—that no samovar had been used in the Alexander Palace. In none of these points did he lie; if anyone was deceiving the public here, it was Rathlef-Keilmann, who so selectively presented information and edited out errors from the claimant's narrative. And because people assumed that Rathlef-Keilmann was reliable, because her notes remained unpublished, because her work won the battle of the books, and because *La Fausse Anastasie* disappeared from print, most of the public never knew what Gilliard had actually said.

But the conflict between these two books echoed a larger issue: what of the asserted memories Anderson relayed, memories so convincing, so intimate, her supporters believed, that they surely proved her identity? Thus Gleb Botkin said that there was "not a single impossible or obviously erroneous statement" made by the claimant, "while all her verifiable statements invariably proved to be correct in every detail."[23]

"It was pointless, in the end, for anyone to argue about the substance of Anastasia's memory," wrote Anderson's biographer Peter Kurth. "Reams of paper were wasted in a quarrel over detail."[24] This was fair enough, given the vagaries of childhood recall and the fact that many of the claimant's utterances were subject to interpretation. But this was, to a large extent, a case built upon minor details, and some of Anderson's statements, some of her asserted memories and declarations, were clearly wrong, and in a case often built minor detail upon minor detail by her supporters, such things mattered. The public might have been surprised, but they never knew: many of Anderson's errors were obscure, recorded in notes by Rathlef-Keilmann and in the statements of others, buried, hidden—sometimes deliberately suppressed—in documents that were never published.

"I noted down all her utterances," Rathlef-Keilmann recorded of the claimant, "in the hope that the material thus compiled would induce those most closely concerned to interest themselves in the fate of the unknown woman and to acknowledge her."[25] Anderson's supporters eagerly seized on every verifiable fact revealed, every hint of intimate knowledge, but dismissed any errors—as had Gleb Botkin with the issue of the "blue" regimental uniforms—by blaming Rathlef-Keilmann, charging her with inaccuracies in recording the claimant's words. But there were too many such instances, too many bizarre statements made to many others, to impose such a double standard, to lay the blame on anyone but Anderson herself.

There were the errors Rathlef-Keilmann recorded in her notes and edited out of her eventual manuscript, details about malachite windowsills at Tsarskoye Selo and Anastasia's regiment, of course, but others as well. Anderson claimed that as a child she had visited England "several times" when, in fact, Anastasia had made only one such trip, in 1909.[26] At Tsarskoye Selo, Anderson told Rathlef-Keilmann, "We lived upstairs: my two big sisters were together. I had a room next to that of Marie; there was no door between them, but a portiere."[27] But Anastasia had always shared a bedroom with her sister Marie, not only at the Alexander Palace but also in every other imperial residence; Gilliard pointed this out to Rathlef-Keilmann, who eliminated the reference from her published book.[28] Once, eager to see her reaction, Inspector Grunberg had played the Russian national anthem on the piano in the claimant's presence. She gave no sign of recognition. Puzzled by this, Grunberg finally stopped and asked her what he had been playing. "I don't know," she replied. "I haven't listened."[29] Not surprisingly, Rathlef-Keilmann—who recorded the incident—elected not to publish the story.

Some things, though, did make it into Rathlef-Keilmann's book, things just as perplexing to the notion that Anderson was indeed Anastasia. Who, Zahle had asked the claimant, was "Aunt Ella"? It was an easy request, the name used within the imperial family for Empress Alexandra's sister Grand Duchess Elizabeth Feodorovna, yet the claimant refused to answer—not, she explained, because she couldn't, but rather because it was a "secret"; only after considering her reply overnight did she finally volunteer the information.[30] Anderson said,

erroneously, that Empress Alexandra had preferred her daughter Marie
Nikolaievna as a companion when in fact she was famous for having
favored her second daughter Tatiana Nikolaievna; that Anna Vyrubova
had "such red hair," when in fact it had been almost black; that although
she recalled the Crimean palace of Grand Duke Peter Nikolaievich
quite well, unbelievably, she couldn't "remember just what ours was
like"; and that Nicholas and Alexandra had separate bedrooms when in
fact they always shared a room.[31] Sometimes even Rathlef-Keilmann
was incredulous at the things Anderson said and tried to convince her
that she was wrong, as when the claimant insisted that Mademoiselle
Catherine Schneider, the empress's lectrice, "was with us until the last
day, in the last night" at Ekaterinburg, when in fact she had previously
been arrested and never set foot in the Ipatiev House.[32]

And, Rathlef-Keilmann aside, Anderson continued the litany of
erroneous assertions. In 1928, on her way to America, she told Agnes
Gallagher that "in 1916," Trotsky had come to the Alexander Palace
and had "been very rude" to her father. Trotsky, she explained, had
"helped himself " to the family's jewelry before leaving.[33] During her
stay in New York, Gleb Botkin arranged a publishing contract, so that
Anderson could write her "memoirs." After several lengthy interviews
the idea was dropped—because the details she gave were simply too
uninteresting for general readers, wrote Peter Kurth, but more likely
because her lawyers and Botkin realized that much of what she said was
so demonstrably wrong that publication would only hurt her cause.[34]
Among her false statements, Anderson said that the imperial family had
visited Romania in 1914 aboard their yacht *Polar Star*, when in fact they
had gone aboard their yacht *Standart*; she adamantly insisted, "I never
met the Kaiser," a statement untrue for Anastasia; insisted wrongly that
Grand Duchess Olga Alexandrovna had been "horribly hurt" during a
1888 train accident at Borki; that Alexander III had been "poisoned"
by his doctors; that Grand Duke Paul Alexandrovich "died in Russia
before the War," when in fact he was executed by the Bolsheviks, and
that his first wife was "a Russian, a Princess Palovna," when she had
actually been Princess Alexandra of Greece; and that there had been no
bathroom in the Ipatiev House.[35]

But the public never learned of such things; they knew only of the
frightened, thin young woman, nervous and excited, protective of herself
and her identity. She riveted attention, captivating with her blue eyes
and her expressive face that seemed, to her supporters, to embody all of
the tragedy of Russia's recent past. There was something so fragile about
her, an almost palpable sense of pain that lent credence to her tale and
often made even her most vitriolic enemies fall temporary victim to her
charm. This was the woman who in 1931 walked out of the Four Winds

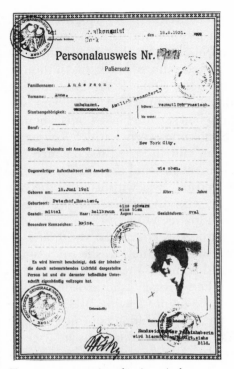

Temporary passport issued to Anna Anderson on her return to Germany from America, 1931.

Rest Home, quietly boarded a liner, and, accompanied by a nurse, returned to Germany, slipping into the nearest thing she would ever know to a happy life. Anastasia Tchaikovsky, the young, delicate phantom from the past who haunted magazines and books and captivated the world, was gone, replaced by Anna Anderson, who disappeared into obscurity; she would not reemerge from the shadows for a quarter century, when the possible princess had become a middle-aged hausfrau wrapped in dowdy clothes and snapping angrily at friend and foe alike.

On arriving in Germany, she had been shuffled off to the Ilten Psychiatric Institute near Hannover, a stay paid for—like her time at Katonah—by Annie Burr Jennings. Hans Willige, the chief psychiatrist at Ilten, had no idea that the woman named "Anna Anderson" was actually the famous Anastasia claimant. On being admitted, Willige recalled, she "showed no signs whatsoever of being mentally unbalanced. Rather, she gave the impression of someone very shy and suspicious." Having reached this determination, Willige told her that she was free to go, but the patient declared that she would remain, "as here she felt safe." He became the last psychiatrist to examine Anderson, and offered his views only after reviewing her files from various Berlin institutions and from Stillachhaus. He was particularly critical of previous views that she suffered from any diminished memory, rejecting theories by Nobel, Bonhoeffer, Eitel, and Saathof that she had simply suppressed unpleasant events. After a year, Willige concluded that her "powers of observation and recall" were undamaged. She "frequently declined to give us information when it did not suit her," he said, and at other times "she knowingly made false statements, quite consciously and willingly." Thus, while he reported that she was "not insane" and "bore no symptoms of mental disease," he deemed Anderson "a peculiar personality" marked by fears of persecution, "obstinacy," "an unhealthy willfulness," "unrestrained emotional impulses," "a highly egocentric outlook," and an "internal haughtiness," all of which manifested themselves in a complex and confusing composition.[36]

Anderson's June 1932 release from Ilten marked another restless, nomadic period in her life. She shuffled from place to place: from Ilten she briefly went to Bad Liebenzell in the Black Forest, then to stay with Frau Spes Stahlberg, a relative of Baron von Kleist; a sojourn with a family in Eisenach ended when she reconciled—perhaps out of necessity—with Rathlef-Keilmann, now forgiven for her 1928 book that Anderson had initially condemned as a betrayal. For a time the pair lived in Berlin, attending concerts and parties; then, in 1933, Rathlef-Keilmann collapsed and died of a burst appendix.[37] Once again, Anderson was alone, an itinerant wandering through her own uncertain life, always dependent on the generosity of others. And it would be like this for the next sixteen years: small rooms in crowded apartments, lavish suites in castles, dingy chambers in squalid residential hotels, airy country estates flanked with gardens—nothing definite, nothing permanent.

In 1936, the claimant was back with Frau Stahlberg, staying at her Pomeranian estate of Gut-Retzow when she met newspaper owner Paul Madsack and his wife, Gertrude; the couple was so taken with the claimant that they asked her to live with them, first at Deisterwald bei Barsinghausen and later in Hannover, where they provided her with a series of apartments.[38] Here she remained through most of the Second World War, living through the uncertainties and food shortages and nightly air raid sirens that regularly sent her scurrying in terror. One night, an Allied bomb fell on her apartment house, erupting in a "sudden explosion and clouds of dust and rubble" that exploded around her. When she looked up, Anderson saw that the windows were shattered, the doors all blown off their hinges; she ran past "white-lit rooms" where people were "screaming and shrieking" as flames swept through the building; on the street, she abruptly stopped when she found her neighbor's head, dead eyes staring. "The streets were on fire," she recalled, "it was all black, but on fire, and I was running through burning streets."[39] Anderson barely escaped this conflagration, but her apartment was lost, and like others left homeless by the war, she slept where she could, in temporary shelters, in houses where friends of the Madsacks offered respite, and finally in the relatively isolated Schloss Winterstein, a Thuringen castle belonging to Princess Louisa of Saxe-Meiningen. But the arrival of Soviet troops near the end of the war sent her into a panic, and one night she secretly fled, running through forests and crossing rivers with the help of a friend until she reached the safety of a French-occupied zone.[40]

Unterlengenhardt, the Black Forest village that became Anderson's home in 1949.

Not until 1949 did Anderson finally obtain a home of her own. This was a single-story, ramshackle hut formerly used as a barracks by German soldiers, a few miles outside of the Black Forest village of Unterlengenhardt near Bad Liebenzell. Purchased and given to her by a supporter, this required extensive repairs before it could be occupied, and limited finances meant that only one room could be heated, but for the first time the woman whose claim had captivated the world had some measure of personal security. She quickly set about turning this haphazard assemblage of rooms into her own zealously guarded miniature kingdom: windows were boarded up to preclude the possibility that she could be spied upon; a tall batten-board and chain-link fence topped with barbed wire that shielded the compound from the adjacent road arose; and, in a final effort to protect her privacy, she adopted four immense wolfhounds, christened with unlikely names such as "Baby"

Anna Anderson, with Prince Friedrich of Saxe-Altenburg, on the day she moved into her converted barracks at Unterlengenhardt.

and "Naughty," and set them loose to patrol the grounds.[41] Within, a succession of elderly aristocratic keepers and friends, including Baroness Monica von Miltitz and Frau Adele von Heydebrandt, cared for her daily needs, and Baron Ulrich von Gienath took charge of her financial affairs.[42] It was a curious place: although one supporter had presented Anderson with an impressively carved bed that had once belonged to Queen Victoria's family, she refused to sleep in it. The bed was given over to her dogs and to an ever-increasing swell of cats, while the claimant slept on a sofa in her sitting room, whose walls were adorned with portraits of Nicholas II and Empress Alexandra. There was clutter everywhere: piles of unopened and unanswered letters from the curious public; stacks of magazines and newspapers; dangerously uneven stacks of books that swayed on the uneven floor; and mountains of discarded clothing heaped upon bags of debris that eventually seeped out and permeated the little house with a rank odor.[43] Within a decade, the hut had become a health hazard, and a new, prefabricated chalet was erected nearby for the claimant in 1960. Soon enough it, too, had become a crowded repository for the flotsam and jetsam of her fabled life.

Visitors to the hut at Unterlengenhardt were never welcomed and rarely let inside, even when they were the claimant's most dedicated supporters. "Although the interest of the people was mostly friendly and curious," recalled Baroness von Miltitz, "they began to throng around her. Thousands of sightseers invaded our little village, anxious for a glimpse of the 'mysterious Grand Duchess.' Many motorists disregarded the sign outside the entrance forbidding traffic on this part of

The new chalet at Unterlengenhardt into which Anderson moved, 1960.

Anderson in her garden at Unterlengenhardt.

the road, and large buses came full of passengers who got out to stare at her grounds. They climbed trees, pressed against the fence, tried to vault the gate, peered through gaps in the hedge, threw stones, whistled, and called for her to come out."[44]

They came—and would continue to come—because by this time, Anna Anderson was indeed a living legend, her claim an enigma promoted or denounced in numerous books and even motion pictures. The first film had come in 1928, during her stay in America, a sixty-minute silent feature produced in Hollywood and called *Clothes Make the Woman*. Starring Eve Southern as a surviving Anastasia, this followed Anderson's tale only as far as the execution and her alleged rescue by a sympathetic soldier; more interested in appealing to imagination, the film then spun off into a true Hollywood twist, with a surviving Anastasia off to Los Angeles to portray herself in a new movie about her family's murder.[45] That same year brought a German production, *Anastasia: Die Falsche Zarentochter* (*Anastasia: The Tsar's False Daughter*), apparently rushed onto screens to take advantage of the publicity over Rathlef-Keilmann's book and the press furor over the claimant, and two more films followed in the 1930s: *Secrets of the French Police*, which offered up a poor Parisian flower girl as the victim of a sinister Russian general attempting to pass her off as the grand duchess, and *Kampf und Anastasia*, an unlikely German comedy short very loosely based on Anderson's tale.[46]

The story fell victim to the more pressing concerns of the Second World War, but in 1954 it returned with a renewed and persistent vengeance that would last for the rest of her life. It all began with a play, a simple, three-act piece by French writer Marcelle Maurette titled *Anastasia*. The plot was straightforward: an amnesiac

Anderson at Unterlengenhardt.

Anderson at Unterlengenhardt.

young woman named Anna is rescued from a suicide attempt in Berlin by a former White Russian general, Prince Sergei Bounine, who plans to fill her head with tales of the imperial family and pass her off as a surviving Anastasia to gain access to the Romanov fortune. Soon the destitute Anna is transformed into a woman of regal bearing, with a sure command of Anastasia's life, including facts she seems to recall spontaneously. When meetings with former courtiers and aristocrats produce no definitive opinion, Bounine convinces Dowager Empress Marie Feodorovna to receive his protégée. In the play's emotional highlight, Anna casually recalls a terrible storm during a cruise aboard the imperial yacht; it is enough for the dowager empress, who embraces the young woman as her lost granddaughter.[47]

Guy Bolton translated and adapted the play, and Sir Laurence Olivier's London production premiered to great acclaim; soon *Anastasia* moved to New York City, and a successful Broadway run with Viveca Lindfors as Anna and Eugenie Leontovitch as Dowager Empress Marie Feodorovna. The public was again fascinated by the story, and Hollywood, quick to recognize the romantic potential in the mysterious story of a lost princess, announced plans for a major motion picture. Hearing this, Dr. Kurt Vermehren, one of Anderson's lawyers, took the unprecedented step of negotiating with a German studio and director Falk Harnack to produce a rival film on the claimant's life. *Anastasia: Die Letze Zarentochter* (*Anastasia: The Last Tsar's Daughter*) abandoned the fictional premise of Maurette's play, offering a narrative history of the story that included such real-life characters as Grand Duchess Olga Alexandrovna,

Anderson, in the wild garden surrounding her chalet, surrounded by her dogs.

Harriet von Rathlef-Keilmann, Clara Peuthert, the duke of Leuchtenberg, and Gleb Botkin. Her performance as Anna Anderson won Lili Palmer a Best Actress Award at the 1957 Berlin Film Festival, but within a few months of its release it sank into obscurity, dwarfed by the steamroller that was Twentieth Century-Fox's 1956 Technicolor epic *Anastasia*.[48]

Starring Helen Hayes as the dowager empress, Yul Brynner as Bounine, and Ingrid Bergman in the title role, Anastasia was a lavish, $3 million rendering of the Maurette-Bolton play, as much an unlikely love story between the claimant and her muse as it was the story of her struggle for identity. The film, which gave Bergman her second Best Actress Oscar, was an enormous sensation; even Olga Alexandrovna enjoyed it, deeming the movie "well done and quite exciting."[49] Exciting it certainly was for most people, and once again the narrow lanes of Unterlengenhardt were overrun with curious tourists, whose buses whisked them past Anderson's ominous-looking compound to shops stocked with books on the Romanovs, pictures of the claimant, and even postcards of her little residence labeled "Anastasia Haus."[50] When

Anderson at Unterlengenhardt, 1960.

two men arrived from *Life* magazine, Anderson—in exchange for a small fee—reluctantly granted an interview and posed for photographs in her impossibly crowded sitting room, but she found the experience disturbingly intrusive. The men, she complained, had been "like mice in every corner," poking through her hut and constantly asking her to smile for their pictures.[51]

It was all, Anderson said, "like in a prison. I am a good business attraction for them—that Anastasia is living here means for all these cold business men good money, for it is very interesting for strangers to see the poor ape in the barrack. More I am not for nobody."[52] Yet her self-imposed seclusion only stoked public interest: Who, really, was this enigmatic, middle-aged woman? Had surviving Romanov relatives knowingly rejected a surviving Anastasia? What languages did she really speak? How had she come by her scars? And if not Anastasia, how did she know so many obscure, intimate details about imperial life? This was the power of the myth laid down by Rathlef-Keilmann, a myth that had been challenged but that remained intact, a myth that the public refused to surrender. Too many words, photographs, and films had seeped into imaginations; for much of the world, whether proved or not, Anna Anderson had now become Anastasia.

15

Émigrés at War

I T WAS BUILDING, slowly building, in these years, the intrigue over Anderson's claim, an intrigue renewed by the books and films and new onslaught of unwelcome attention. And still Romanov relatives argued and fought, not just about her identity but also about how to deal with her claim and with each other. Only two members of the family had actually met and accepted her as Anastasia: Princess Xenia Georgievna and Grand Duke Andrei Vladimirovich, both in 1928. The grand duke, immersed in his own inquiry, had met the claimant at the Palais Hotel in Paris before she sailed for America. Alexander Spiridovich, former head of Nicholas II's Court Chancellery, saw Andrei stumble from the room, greatly agitated, "upset, and profoundly moved. He had tears in his eyes. For him, there was no doubt."[1] He seems to have based his opinion merely on observation, for at their first meeting Anderson apparently refused to speak or to answer any of Andrei's questions, hiding her face behind a sheet for most of the encounter; only later, as he bid her farewell, was the grand duke rewarded with a few German sentences.[2]

"I had the opportunity," Andrei reported to Serge Botkin, "to observe and judge the invalid closely over two days, and I can categorically state that there is no doubt in my mind that she is Grand Duchess Anastasia. It is out of the question not to recognize her. Naturally, the years and her suffering have left their mark, though not as much as I had imagined. Her face is profoundly sad, but when she smiles, she is, without doubt, Anastasia."[3] And to his cousin Olga Alexandrovna he wrote, "I recognized her immediately, and further observation only confirmed my first impression. I really have no doubt on this: she is Anastasia."[4] By this time, though, the grand duchess had long abandoned any initial hint of ambiguity, and she rejected Andrei's pleas to meet the claimant again. Anderson's opponents complained that Andrei was in no position to offer such a definite opinion on the subject, that as Nicholas II's cousin his contact with Anastasia had been minimal, and that too many years had passed; her supporters countered by pointing out that the grand duke had served as a personal adjutant to the tsar and thus had regularly been on duty at Tsarskoye Selo throughout the First World War. In truth, both sides were correct. Andrei had seen a teenaged Anastasia roughly a dozen times in the last few years before the Revolution, many times in passing, and rarely when he was asked to join the imperial family for luncheon, tea, or dinner. Did this limited and periodic exposure leave him in a position to adequately assess the claimant? Apparently not, at least according to the grand duke himself, who had initially rejected the idea of meeting her by explaining to Tatiana Botkin, "I can't trust my personal impressions. I wasn't close enough to the tsar's children to be able to identify Anastasia."[5]

Perhaps by 1928 the grand duke's own investigation had led him to abandon his previous caution, or in embracing Rathlef-Keilmann's evidence he was ready to be convinced. He made no statement, though the public learned of his opinion when the duke of Leuchtenberg published a private letter Andrei had sent him describing the favorable meeting in Paris. When Rathlef-Keilmann's book was published, it also included a lengthy letter Andrei had written to her editor, printed as a preface that outlined all points in Anderson's favor. "Her reminiscences, so far as I have been able to examine them," he declared rather inaccurately, "yield a description, clear in every respect, of actual facts. Everything that she recalls is an absolutely accurate description of the life of the Imperial Family, including details that have never appeared in the Press. My own opinion is that the things that the patient remembers are such as only the Grand Duchess herself could recall." He noted a "striking similarity" physically between the claimant and Anastasia, as well as what he called "the general family resemblance, which is in some respects of almost greater importance than a personal likeness."[6]

So infuriated was Grand Duke Kirill Vladimirovich by these developments that he immediately summoned his brother and demanded an explanation. Andrei admitted to recognizing the claimant, whom Kirill had branded "an adventuress," but apparently denied that he had in any way authorized publication of any of his private correspondence. "Obviously," Kirill wrote, "my brother was used."[7] Whether this was true or not, Kirill ordered his brother to stop his investigation; by this time, Andrei had grown disgusted with Gleb Botkin's tactics and readily bowed out, never uttering another public word about the claimant. In 1955, though, just a year before his death, he wrote a curious letter to his cousin Olga Alexandrovna: "I had always believed you to be angry with me owing to the Tchaikovsky Affair. This would have saddened me even more. My love for you is too great to cause any such pain. . . . As things now stand, I have never formally stated my opinion on the matter, because I have never entirely been convinced. . . . The mystery remains unsolved. . . . I'm incapable of resolving this question."[8]

Andrei's son Vladimir commented that the grand duke "had been struck by a clear family resemblance. Sometimes, however, the detailed investigation, with its occasionally contradictory elements, did make him have doubts, and I can attest that in his files there is nothing that would prove one way or another whether the unknown woman is the daughter of Emperor Nicholas II. My father could never have sworn an oath either way in this case, being convinced that, like anyone, he could be mistaken."[9] But Prince Friedrich of Saxe-Altenburg, one of Anderson's most loyal supporters, thought that such revisions were merely attempts "to heal the quarrel" between Andrei and Olga over the claimant. He told case historian Brien Horan, "I saw Uncle Andrei shortly before his death and from the way he spoke about her, I had the impression that he still believed in her. I think his true opinion was his recognition of Anastasia after their rendezvous in 1928. It was a completely straightforward recognition based entirely on his personal impressions and on his research, and it was as yet uninfluenced by outside forces, such as his brother Kirill's order to withdraw from the case."[10] And Kirill's daughter Princess Kira recalled that before his death, her Uncle Andrei "had tried to convince me that she was Anastasia."[11]

Kira wasn't convinced. Only seven at the time of the Revolution, she had no real memories of Anastasia; when she finally met Anderson in 1952, she said, rather snobbishly, that she "was not a lady." Her English, she said, "was not the English that was spoken in the family," but rather seemed heavily accented—either Slavic or Polish, Kira thought. The idea that they might be cousins, Kira said, was "repulsive."[12] But it was true, insisted Kira's mother-in-law. This was Crown Princess Cecilie of Prussia, a woman with her own ties to the Romanovs: her mother, Grand Duchess Anastasia Mikhailovna, was a second cousin to Nicholas II and sister-in-law to his sister Xenia Alexandrovna. Cecilie first met Anderson in the 1920s; although she thought there was some vague resemblance, she hadn't really known Anastasia, and besides, all of the relatives seemed so sure that she wasn't genuine. But she followed the case in the press with some interest, and in 1952 visited Anderson at Unterlengenhardt. After several meetings, she said, "I am convinced that she is the Emperor's youngest daughter. Now that she is a mature woman, I can occasionally detect in her the features of her mother. But more pointedly, her behavior and cordial manner suggest to me an intimate familiarity and past association that bonds those of common origin together."[13]

Kira later suggested, not very helpfully, that her mother-in-law had been mentally unstable, but it was a pointless exercise to ascribe recognitions in Anderson's favor as the manifestation of some undiagnosed psychosis shared by her supporters, as some of the more unkind critics insinuated.[14] People seized upon the slightest coincidence—Marianne Nilov, widow of the imperial yacht's captain, apparently thought the claimant had the same eyes as Nicholas II, the same way of laughing as Anastasia, while two of her husband's former officers on the *Standart*, Baron George Taube and Vassili Woitinsky, found nothing at all in her to remind them of the grand duchess.[15] And many were genuinely convinced, and their conviction rested not on some imaginary delusion or elusively subjective factor, but rather on what they took for Anderson's inexplicable knowledge. Such was the case with Ivan Arapov, a former patient in Anastasia's hospital at Tsarskoye Selo. After reading of Anderson's claim, he suggested that her American lawyer Edward Fallows ask if she recalled his name. "Does he limp?" Anderson asked. When Fallows said no, she insisted that the only Arapov known to her had limped; when Arapov heard this, he explained that he had been shot in the leg and had indeed limped during his stay in the hospital at Tsarskoye Selo. Later Arapov met Anderson in Berlin and pronounced her genuine.[16]

Many others seemed genuinely conflicted. How else to explain the experience of Princess Vera Konstantinovna of Russia? Daughter of Grand Duke Konstantin Konstantinovich, she had occasionally played with Nicholas and Alexandra's youngest children, and her 1943 meeting with Anderson was fraught with confusing impressions. "I found a certain similarity," she declared. "It is said that every person has a twin. Even the possibility of a Romanov or Hessian transgression flashed through my mind."[17] Many years later, though, this seemingly favorable impression had been forgotten, as the princess offered ambivalent and contradictory statements on the claimant's identity.[18]

It was all too familiar, this decision to recognize or reject, this certainty that supposedly evaporated with the passing years, leaving only contradictory and impossibly tangled assertions that shrouded Anderson's case in impenetrable layers of intriguing mystery. And that mystery deepened in 1932, with one of the most legendary episodes in the entire claim. The second son of Princess Irene of Prussia and a first cousin to Anastasia, Prince Sigismund had seen the Romanovs on family visits in Germany and in Russia, the last time in the autumn of 1912,

212 THE RESURRECTION OF THE ROMANOVS

Prince Friedrich of Saxe-Altenburg.

when he and his mother had stayed with them at the Polish hunting lodge of Spala. Sigismund, who relocated to Costa Rica after the First World War with his wife, Princess Charlotte-Agnes of Saxe-Altenburg, initially had little interest in Anderson's case. Irene, after all, had met with and rejected her in 1922, and Sigismund had no reason to question his mother's judgment. But after the story broke, after rumors of familial indecision, after Rathlef-Keilmann's book and its compendium of seemingly convincing evidence, Sigismund was intrigued enough to draw up a list of eighteen questions for the claimant, questions about "certain incidents that took place before the War," he said, questions so obscure, so trivial that only the real Anastasia could answer them because both he and his brother-in-law Prince Friedrich of Saxe-Altenburg "had determined that they had not been mentioned in any memoirs or in the literature concerning the period."[19]

Prince Friedrich met Anderson during a 1932 visit to Germany and presented her with the list. Both Sigismund and Friedrich refused to reveal these eighteen questions, apparently in the belief that Anderson's opponents would somehow accuse them of having given her the answers in advance.[20] Yet three of the questions eventually leaked out. Sigismund wanted to know when he had last seen Anastasia. Anderson said that it had been in 1912. Where had they last met? Sigismund asked. At Spala in Poland, she declared. And, Sigismund asked, where had he stayed during the visit? In the rooms of Count Vladimir de Freedericksz, the minister of the imperial court, she replied. These answers, said Prince Sigismund, were not only correct but also, he insisted, "Could only have been given by the Grand Duchess herself. This, as well as everything I have since learned, convinced me that Frau Tchaikovsky is, without any doubt, Grand Duchess Anastasia."[21]

This is the stuff of which Anderson's legend was made. How could an impostor know such unimportant yet convincing detail? Who but Anastasia could accurately answer these eighteen questions? These facts, coupled with the secrecy that enshrouded the questions and answers, made it all seem so compelling. Yet the truth is not nearly as convincing as history has been led to believe.

First, the questions: only three have been known—until now. The eighteen questions Prince Friedrich handed Anderson were:

1. In autumn 1912, who was visiting Spala from Germany? Which people?
2. What was the name of the governor or *Staathalter* at Spala, the Polish man who was there?
3. Did this person have a son there?
4. Was the latter an officer?
5. Were these two men loyal to Russia and to the emperor's family, or did they have Polish leanings?
6. When one stood in front of and facing the lodge at Spala, on which story and in which side (right or left) were the rooms of Count de Freedericksz?
7. Which guest lived in these rooms during Count de Freedericksz's absence?
8. What was the name of the river at Spala?
9. Who was Beilosielsky-Bielosevsky?
10. What kinds of English-language magazines were lying in the emperor and empress's drawing room, or, what war did they generally refer to (pictures and cartoons were probably there as well)?
11. In which room did they usually say good night to the suite, including the priest?
12. Did the windows of this room lay toward the front or the rear of the lodge?
13. Were excursions into the forest made by carriage or by automobile?
14. Where was the train station?
15. Was the road to the train station in good or bad condition?
16. In which city was the imperial train kept?
17. Did one go to the station by carriage or by automobile?
18. What was the name of the emperor's adjutant?[22]

Prince Friedrich told Anderson that the questions had come from Prince Sigismund, and related to his experiences at Spala in 1912. Contrary to the legend, she didn't volunteer the obscure information that Sigismund had lodged in Count de Freedericksz's suite; rather, she had been asked who had stayed in these rooms. This was a rather obvious—if unintentional—clue pointing her to the correct reply, particularly as she knew the questions concerned Sigismund's visit. Questions 4 and 5 themselves answered question 3, but there was more: despite what Sigismund and his brother-in-law believed, answers to two thirds of the questions had already appeared in print, in the memoirs of Anna Vyrubova and former courtier Alexander

Spiridovich, and perhaps in other works as well. She certainly had the first book, as she had read it at Seeon; given her large collection of Romanov memoirs, it would be odd if by 1932 she did not have Spiridovich's 1928 memoirs.[23]

Still, how was Anderson able to correctly answer all of the other remaining questions? The simple answer is that, contrary to what history has been led to believe, she didn't; according to Sigismund, she provided only "enough correct answers" to satisfy him that she was Anastasia.[24] Unfortunately, Sigismund never revealed just how many of the questions she answered correctly; how many she answered incorrectly; and how many she may not have answered at all. Even more revealing, though, is the way in which the answers came. When Prince Friedrich first presented her with the list, she looked at it, pondered the questions, and declared that she could answer them but insisted that she needed time to think. She kept the list for five days; only at the end of the week did she finally offer her replies.[25] Was this simply, as her supporters often held, a struggle to overcome her damaged memory? Or did this interval allow the claimant time to seek out the answers to the prince's queries?

Though Sigismund was convinced, he did not meet Anderson until 1957, when he finally came to visit her at Unterlengenhardt and after three days restated his belief that she was his cousin.[26] Not knowing the content of the eighteen questions, critics turned on Sigismund himself. His cousin Lord Mountbatten confessed himself "astonished" to learn of this recognition, saying that the prince "knew Anastasia even less well than I did."[27] And there was something else: Sigismund also was firmly convinced that an elderly Dutch aristocratic lady calling herself Marga Boodts was, in fact, his cousin Grand Duchess Olga Nikolaievna, despite the fact that she had been unmasked decades earlier. "We spoke of so many familiar matters that an outsider could not have known about," he explained, "because they were things that had happened between us two."[28] But no one else believed her claim, at least no other Romanov relative, and Anderson's opponents were convinced that Sigismund was simply unreliable. "So much for the value of his testimony!" Lord Mountbatten once commented.[29]

But Sigismund's recognition also brought his brother-in-law Prince Friedrich of Saxe-Altenburg aboard the claimant's case. Friedrich had never met Anastasia, though he had peripheral ties to the Romanovs: son of the last duke of Saxe-Altenburg, his mother was a cousin of Dowager Empress Marie Feodorovna, and another relative, Elisabeth, had married Nicholas II's distant cousin Grand Duke Konstantin Konstantinovich. Anderson's answers to Sigismund's questions apparently convinced Friedrich that she was Anastasia.[30] He became one of her most dedicated and long-suffering supporters, alternately cherished and then abused by the ever-temperamental claimant, though his belief never wavered despite her mercurial treatment.

Equally sure of his opinion was Charles Sidney Gibbes, former English tutor to the imperial children. In 1926, on hearing of Anderson's claim, he wrote an urgent and excited letter to Alexandra Gilliard: "This news has greatly astonished me, and I don't know whether it is true or not." He implored her, "Please, tell me how far I may believe the news that Anastasia Nikolaievna has been found. If it is so, please give her my most heartfelt greetings."[31] This must have been astonishing indeed, for Gibbes later insisted, "I have never doubted that Grand Duchess Anastasia perished at Ekaterinburg."[32]

Apparently the Gilliards assured Gibbes not to worry himself over an impostor, for he waited nearly thirty years to meet the claimant. When they finally came face-to-face, he said, Anderson "looked at me suspiciously over the top of a newspaper, which she continued to hold on all occasions in front of her face so that only her eyes and hair were visible. This tactic she continued to use every time I saw her and never permitted me of her own will to see the whole of her face. From behind the newspaper she stretched forth a hand and gave me the tips of her fingers to shake. Such features as were visible did not correspond in any way with those of the Grand Duchess I had known and I consider that, even bearing in mind the years that had passed between 1918 and 1954, the Grand Duchess Anastasia whom I knew could not have become anything like the woman now calling herself Grand Duchess Anastasia. It is true that her hair had been dyed, but nevertheless the texture of her hair was extremely coarse and fuzzy, whereas the hair of the real Grand Duchess Anastasia had been very fine and soft. The so-called Grand Duchess Anastasia expressed no pleasure at meeting me again, made no recognition of me, made no conversation, asked me no questions, but merely answered questions I put to her. . . . I showed her six photographs that I had taken with me. She looked at each and shook her head and indicated that they meant nothing to her. These pictures actually were of the rooms in which the Grand Duchess Anastasia had lived, of the pet dog with which she had played, and of the teachers who had taught her. I did not show her any pictures or photographs of the Imperial Family, as she would probably have recognized them. I understand she had a collection of 2,000 postcards and photographs. On the last time I saw the so-called Grand Duchess to say goodbye to her, I was able to approach nearer to her and look over the top of the paper, and saw her whole face and in particular her right ear. Her right ear does not in any way resemble the right ear of the true Grand Duchess Anastasia, as I have a photograph that clearly displays the ear and its peculiar shape. She in no way resembles the true Grand Duchess Anastasia that I had known, and I am quite satisfied that she is an imposter."[33]

By this time, Gibbes had become an Orthodox priest, habitually clad in sweeping robes and sporting a long white beard, so perhaps it wasn't altogether unexpected that a surviving Anastasia would fail to recognize Gibbes nor, after thirty-six years, he her. Gibbes asserted, after this meeting, that "it was clear that she knew no English."[34] This was clearly wrong; by 1954 English had joined German as Anderson's language of choice. Why she apparently refused to speak it with the former English tutor, though, was an entirely different, speculative issue. But Gibbes found something else odd: in the 1920s, Anderson had told Rathlef-Keilmann that Gibbes was "altogether different from Mr. Gilliard, but we were very fond of him, too. He always held his head slightly to one side; one side of his body was deformed, and he rather trailed one foot."[35] She later repeated this, saying that Gibbes had "a limping leg."[36] This Gibbes rejected: "Had I been dead," he said, "it might have been difficult to prove, but being yet alive and happily in full possession of both my legs, I am able to say that I limp only in the imagination of Mme. Tchaikovsky."[37]

And balanced against the compelling rejection by Gibbes was the compelling recognition by Lili Dehn. As one of Empress Alexandra's closest and most trusted confidantes, Lili often had spent time with the imperial family and knew Anastasia well. In 1957, Prince Sigismund visited her in Caracas, showing her photographs of the claimant and insisting she was genuine. At his urging, Dehn traveled to Unterlengenhardt that autumn to judge for herself.[38] She had last seen a fifteen-year-old Anastasia at Tsarskoye Selo forty years earlier; she now faced a middle-aged woman peering nervously over the top of a blanket held up to her face. "Should I know you?" she asked her visitor. "You remind me somehow of my mother."

Lili Dehn in old age.

Lili looked at her, at "her poor, pale, aged little face. My first impression was terribly sad, but as soon as I heard her voice, I knew: it was so familiar to me, so real—it was the voice of Grand Duchess Anastasia. No one can imitate the voice or manner of speech of a stranger." She noticed her hands: Anderson's hands, Lili said, were "exactly like those of the Empress, with all three middle fingers being of the same length." When Anderson finally asked, "We were together . . . near the end?" it was all the evidence Dehn needed: "It was clear that she had recognized me," she declared. They spoke in English—"very good English" was how Lili described Anderson's speech. The claimant refused to speak Russian, and Lili did not press her; she did note, though, that she pronounced the names of various courtiers "in the best Russian manner," which to Dehn was "evidence that Frau Anderson could both speak and understand the language."[39]

If initial impressions had convinced her that Anderson was Anastasia, it was, for Lili, what followed over the week at Unterlengenhardt that cemented this belief, when the claimant "impressed her with her inexplicable and intimate knowledge" of life within the imperial family.[40] It was a lengthy and seemingly impressive list: the claimant, said Lili, spoke of Nicholas Sablin and knew that he had deserted the Romanovs after the Revolution; remembered Anastasia's hospital at Tsarskoye Selo; knew the nickname for Lili's son; recalled certain events Lili had witnessed with Anastasia at the Alexander Palace during the Revolution; could describe the color of the carpets in the empress's private apartments; had "mentioned one occasion" witnessed by Lili and by Anastasia when the empress had been "angry" with Anna Vyrubova; mentioned that governess Sophie Tiutcheva had left her post at court amid a scandal; and correctly identified the color of a dress worn by the empress in a black-and-white photograph.[41]

"Don't bother to tell me that she had read these things in books," Lili declared.[42] Like Prince Sigismund, Lili believed Anderson had revealed intimate knowledge only Anastasia could have possessed. Like the prince, though, she was wrong, for by 1957 a wealth of information about the Romanovs had been published, including the decoration of their rooms in the Alexander Palace. Anderson was well aware of Sablin, whom she had met in 1922 in Berlin; had discussed the hospital at Tsarskoye Selo with both Tatiana Botkin and Felix Dassel, and owned the latter's memoirs as well as a souvenir album of the facility; and Lili had detailed her experiences with Anastasia during the Revolution in her own 1922 book, which also had revealed her son's nickname.[43] Anderson had asked Dehn if she recalled "that ill-mannered governess," whom she identified as Tiutcheva when prompted. Numerous books, including Lili's own memoirs, had chronicled the governess's disagreements over Rasputin's presence in the palace, but when pressed for details Anderson said, "You know exactly why she was sent away!"[44] Details of a temporarily strained relationship between Empress Alexandra and Vyrubova also had appeared in numerous works. Anderson was vague on the issue, as Dehn admitted: aside from mentioning some disagreement between the pair, she could not recall when or where the argument had taken place, or even what it had concerned; it was enough, Dehn insisted, "that Frau Anderson remembered it at all."[45] The color of the empress's dress? It was mauve, Anderson said correctly, but then, a skeptic might have suggested, it was well known that this had been Alexandra's favorite color. And the fact that Anderson's middle fingers were of the same length, "exactly like those of the Empress"? Lili may have believed this to be true, but it was not: X-rays of Alexandra's hands, preserved in the Russian State Archives in Moscow, show that she had long, tapering fingers of noticeably different lengths.

But for Lili there was no doubt that Anderson was Anastasia. "I have recognized her both physically and intuitively," she declared.[46] The claimant's supporters took it all as definitive evidence in her favor; even the judges during Anderson's lawsuit for recognition as Anastasia accorded Dehn special weight, writing that her opinion merited "special consideration, given her intimacy with the Imperial Family."[47] Anderson's critics, on the other hand, suggested that too many years had passed for Dehn to physically recognize Anastasia in the claimant, and that her decision relied more on emotion than on reason. Dehn, though, was adamant; despite unfounded rumors that she had later wavered in her opinion, Lili remained—as her family confirms—completely convinced that Anderson was Anastasia.[48]

What more could be done? Who else could come forward and offer a definitive opinion? "I did contemplate going to see the claimant," Lord Mountbatten wrote to his cousin Prince Ludwig, son of Grand Duke Ernst Ludwig of Hesse, "but on the advice of my mother never went for, after all, I was only twelve-years-old the last time I saw Anastasia as I missed seeing her in 1914 when we could all have been together but for the war. Although I was very fond of Anastasia I do not think my evidence would be of any value since we were both such children the last time we had met."[49] The one person who knew Anastasia far better than Mountbatten, Olga Alexandrovna, Princess Irene of Prussia, Princess Xenia Georgievna, or the Botkins unfortunately never saw Anderson. From shortly after the turn of the century until 1917, when she was removed from the Alexander Palace, Anna Vyrubova had seen the imperial family nearly every day. She spent hours with the empress and her children at Tsarskoye Selo, joining the Romanovs on their annual cruises, and traveling with them to the Crimea and to Poland on holidays. But amazingly, no one—on either side of the issue—ever sought her opinion, for Vyrubova, who had escaped to Finland and eventually became an Orthodox nun, was best known as one of Rasputin's most ardent disciples. "We decided not to bring Madame Vyrubova into the case because of her involvement with the Rasputin clique, and its many intrigues," Tatiana Botkin explained. "This whole Rasputin group had a very bad reputation, and it was believed that Madame Vyrubova's involvement in the case could only have hurt."[50] And despite suggestions from some who believed that Anderson simply feared such a meeting, the claimant's opponents shared the same concerns: Lord Mountbatten and Prince Ludwig of Hesse briefly considered asking for Vyrubova's opinion but, in the end, elected not to do so, fearing that this would introduce the specter of Rasputin into the case.[51]

And so it seemed destined to remain a perpetual enigma. Decades of conflicting assertions and contradictory recognitions and denunciations, books, films, a legend that seemed increasingly plausible—and still there was no answer. There was no going back—and now the only way forward, the only hope that this most extraordinary of modern mysteries would ever be resolved, lay in what was to become the most extraordinary of modern trials: Anna Anderson's monumental, mammoth lawsuit to finally prove that she was Grand Duchess Anastasia of Russia.

16

The Trials

I N THE END, and fulfilling the fears of Anna Anderson's supporters, her quest for recognition as Anastasia all came down to money. In 1906, Nicholas II had deposited 2 million rubles (approximately $20 million in 2010 figures) in Berlin's Mendelssohn Bank; frozen at the beginning of the First World War, the money remained forgotten, and economic depression and inflation reduced its worth to a mere $105,000 (in 2011 currency). Then, in 1933, the Central District Court in Berlin, on the assumption that the imperial family was dead, awarded certificates of inheritance for the money to seven collateral Romanov heirs: Nicholas II's sisters Grand Duchesses Xenia and Olga Alexandrovna; his sister-in-law Nathalia, Countess Brassova, morganatic wife of his murdered brother Grand Duke Michael Alexandrovich; Michael and Nathalia's son George; and Empress Alexandra's remaining three siblings, Grand Duke Ernst Ludwig of Hesse, Victoria, marchioness of Milford Haven, and Princess Irene of Prussia.[1]

No one collected any shares, though, at least not in 1933. The Mendelssohn Bank, presumably hoping to prevent distribution, contacted Anderson's lawyer Edward Fallows, suggesting that he protest any payments based on his client's claimed identity. As an American, Fallows could not pursue the matter, but two German lawyers, Paul Leverkuhn and Kurt Vermehren, took Anderson's case and lodged a petition to halt distribution with the Central District Court in Berlin. The arguments and appeals that followed set in motion Anderson's mammoth, thirty-seven-year legal battle to prove that she was Anastasia.

And mammoth it certainly became. Although the Mendelssohn funds were eventually paid to the subsidiary heirs, Anderson's lawyers filed repeated motions seeking revocation, and the courts repeatedly rejected the petitions. The Second World War brought a temporary halt to legal proceedings, but in 1956 the case finally came before the Landesgericht, the High Court in Berlin. Their review was cursory: after accepting the conflicting evidence into the record, the court heard only one witness, a former prisoner of war in Ekaterinburg of dubious reputation named Hans-Johann Mayer. With a flourish, Mayer produced a collection of captured Bolshevik documents confirming the deaths of all of the imperial family.[2] The court accepted Mayer's evidence and rejected Anderson's appeal; only later was it learned that Mayer had forged his apparently impressive dossier.[3]

Leverkuhn and Vermehren were set to appeal this decision when they decided to change tactics. Rather than contest the inheritance, they would sue one of the beneficiaries in civil court, charging that Anderson, as Anastasia, had been financially defrauded.[4] They needed a defendant, someone who had profited from the distribution of the Mendelssohn funds, and a German defendant at that, to keep the case within national borders. Eventually they settled on Barbara, Duchess Christian Ludwig of Mecklenburg, a woman born two years after the presumed executions in Ekaterinburg and someone who had never met the claimant. As the granddaughter of Princess Irene, she had received a small share of the Mendelssohn monies, something that made her a convenient legal target, but there seems to have been something more cynical at work here. Barbara was the daughter of Prince Sigismund of Prussia and niece of Prince Friedrich of Saxe-Altenburg, two of Anderson's greatest supporters. In suggesting her as defendant, the two apparently believed that Barbara lacked the fortitude to endure a lawsuit and the attendant publicity, and that she could be pressured into reaching a settlement with the claimant.[5]

Barbara, though, was not so easily bowed, and she did the one thing Sigismund, Friedrich, and Anderson's lawyers had avoided: she brought Ernst Ludwig's only surviving son, Prince Ludwig, into Anderson's case. Ludwig also had received Mendelssohn funds, but none of Anderson's proponents wanted him involved, for the Hessian royal family had, in the past, demonstrated a willingness to oppose—and very publicly oppose—Anderson's claim by funding their own investigations into her case. Prince Ludwig's decision to join Barbara as a voluntary codefendant in the civil suit was, for the claimant's supporters, ominous enough; but it also brought the British royal family into the struggle, in the person of Lord Mountbatten, first cousin to Anastasia and uncle to Queen Elizabeth II's consort, Prince Philip, duke of Edinburgh. "It is completely out of the question," Mountbatten wrote to his cousin Prince Ludwig, "that any of us would not have acknowledged Anastasia with the greatest of ease if we had had the remotest hope that she were not a fake. . . . The honor and memory of Aunt Irene and of course of your father and mother, and my mother, and indeed all of us are at stake in this case. The suggestion that for some unworthy pecuniary or prestige motives we would be unwilling to acknowledge, and of course, receive into our midst someone of whom we were as fond of as Anastasia is quite unthinkable and I am sure that this unworthy suggestion must be fought to the bitter end."[6] Armed with the financial resources Barbara and Ludwig lacked, Mountbatten now stepped in and funded their opposition to Anderson's claim.[7]

The civil suit of Anna Anderson against Barbara, Duchess Christian Ludwig of Mecklenburg, opened in March 1957 before a three-judge tribunal at the Hanseatic Landesgericht Court, the High Court, in Hamburg. It shifted the burden of proof to the claimant: it was up to Anderson's lawyers to prove that she was Anastasia. Misfortune seemed to dog Anderson's legal team. Fallows had died, exhausted and impoverished by working on her case, in 1940, and Leverkuhn died in 1960 during the civil trail. Two years later, when Vermehren was fatally injured in a car accident, Carl August Wollmann assumed

Grand Duke Ernst Ludwig and his family, 1912. From left: Prince Ludwig, who became a codefendant during the Anderson civil trial, Grand Duchess Eleonore, Prince Georg Donatus, and Ernst Ludwig.

responsibility for her case. Hans Hermann Krampff acted as counsel for Prince Ludwig, but responsibility for the defense rested with Gunther von Berenberg-Gossler, a highly tenacious, thirty-six-year-old lawyer who, declared one of Anderson's supporters, "looks like an out of work play-boy. His appearance in court is theatrical, which may sometimes suit the superficial public, but his harangues are shallow."[8] Berenberg-Gossler never met Anderson, only glimpsing her in passing during a temporary court session at Unterlengenhardt, but to Michael Thornton, a young English barrister who held her power of attorney in Great Britain, he warned, "She will win you over. I know enough about her to assure you that she has the greatest degree of suggestive power over other people that I have ever encountered in all my years as a lawyer."[9] After his brief, silent encounter with the claimant, Berenberg-Gossler insisted rather snobbishly that "she resembled a house maid, not at all of royal blood," with "an unattractive, peasant-like face" that "reminded me of a charwoman."[10]

The trial became a nearly four-year spectacle, during which hundreds of witnesses took the stand and offered testimony, providing a mass of conflicting claims that eventually filled dozens of bound volumes. On May 15, 1961, the Hanseatic Landesgericht Court rejected Anderson's claim to be Anastasia, deeming the contention to be "unfounded." Her lawyers, read the tribunal's opinion, "failed to offer sufficient proof that the plaintiff is one of the Imperial children."[11] In response, Wollmann petitioned the Hanseatic Oberlandesgericht, the High Court of Appeals in Hamburg. Not only had the Hamburg tribunal, he declared, rejected testimony solicited from its own experts, but also the lawyers believed that the court had imposed a double standard on witnesses. Those who refuted the idea that Anderson was Anastasia, or who supported the deaths of the entire imperial family in 1918, had rarely been questioned, and the tribunal had simply accepted their evidence; those who had recognized Anderson as Anastasia, on the other hand, had been subjected to judicial cross-examination and their opinions disputed. After reviewing the case, the Oberlandesgericht Court found that the Hamburg tribunal had evaluated the evidence in a prejudicial manner, and allowed Wollmann to challenge the verdict. This appeal, which opened in April 1964 before a three-judge tribunal of the Hanseatic Oberlandesgericht Court in Hamburg, became, in essence, a second trial, in which all of the evidence was again examined.[12]

And it all took place without Anderson's cooperation. "She has never taken any interest or part in the efforts made on her behalf to establish her identity," said a supporter.[13] This apparent disinterest lent an aura of authenticity to her claim; surely, even the skeptics

Anderson lawyer Carl August Wollmann, with journalist Dominique Auclères.

thought, a pretender would do all within her power to prove her case. "I know perfectly well who I am," Anderson once declared. "I don't need to prove it in any court of law."[14] It was, said one of the ladies who looked after her at Unterlengenhardt, "a matter of pride" to ignore the proceedings.[15]

In her place came two determined and dedicated supporters who were, for all practical purposes, unpaid members of Anderson's legal team. The first, Ian Lilburn, was an assistant at the Royal College of Arms in Great Britain; as a keen genealogist and amateur historian, he became fascinated with her case and attended every session of her appeal in Hamburg. Though he believed absolutely in her claim, Lilburn found that dealing with Anderson was often fraught with difficulties. "It is impossible to persuade her with logic," he noted, "and it is useless to tell her that she 'must' do anything (she only becomes more stubborn and wants to show who is the boss)."[16] The second figure, French journalist Dominique Auclères, had initially been assigned to cover the case for Le Figaro; convinced that Anderson was Anastasia, she chased down favorable witnesses; collected asserted evidence; and, as Peter Kurth noted, "maintained only the professional appearance of neutrality" in offering her readers an increasingly partisan series of articles about the claimant.[17]

The two Hamburg trials offered up weeks of arguments over Anderson's asserted memories, and on the contentious issues of recognitions and denunciations. The question of Anastasia's possible survival from the executions in Ekaterinburg was, at the time, at least a historical plausibility, and the courts heard evidence from those who had heard rumors of rescue and testified that the grand duchess had supposedly stayed in Bucharest following her escape from Russia. There were, though, more objective attempts to resolve the claimant's identity. In 1963, Ian Lilburn purchased nine of the imperial children's school exercise books at auction; two had belonged to Anastasia, and he hoped that they might still contain her fingerprints.[18] The Oberlandesgericht Court received them into evidence, and experts examined the books for any latent prints but could find nothing of use; several smudges seemed promising, but at the time authorities did not possess the means to retrieve any prints without completely destroying the documents.[19]

Anastasia's two exercise books, though, did take center stage when the question turned to Anderson's linguistic capabilities. This was a morass of conflicting and questionable assertions, spanning her knowledge of Russian, English, French, and German. Anderson refused to set foot in the courtroom, but she correctly answered questions posed in Russian by an expert, although she did so in English; however, nothing—not even when one of the judges attempted to sing to her in Russian—could convince her to speak the language.[20] Berenberg-Gossler called in graphologist Georg Dulckeit, who examined several notes the claimant had written in the 1950s in Russian and found fault with her composition and grammar, suggesting that her understanding of the language was superficial and tenuous at best.[21] This, though, was not particularly convincing, given that Anastasia's own Russian essay book for 1913, received into evidence by the court, was full of grammatical and spelling errors.[22]

Arguments about the claimant's capabilities in Russian and in English did nothing to establish the truth of what were, after all, decades of conflicting assertions. Then there was the question of French: Anastasia had certainly learned it, though not very successfully, as Gilliard had admitted, but aside from the single instance of ordering breakfast for herself and Agnes Gallagher in Paris in 1928, Anderson had demonstrated no familiarity with the language.[23] Not until 1960 did a second episode occur, during a meeting with Dominique Auclères and Tatiana Botkin. Auclères wrote that Anderson had spontaneously spoken the language and that "her French pronunciation was perfect." But what had the claimant said? Auclères had poured tea and asked, *"Du lait d'abord?"* (Milk first?) To this Anderson replied, *"Oh, oui, merci."*[24] These two words, whether pronounced perfectly or not, scarcely offered any evidence that the claimant was familiar with the French language.

But most of the court's time was taken up with the question of German. If Anderson's supporters sometimes offered tenuous and unreliable assertions regarding her linguistic knowledge, her critics were just as guilty of attempting to rewrite history to disguise Anastasia's familiarity with German, especially when it became apparent that this was the language in which the claimant seemed most comfortable. Thus Grand Duchess Olga Alexandrovna later insisted, "My nieces knew no German at all," adding, "German was never spoken in the family."[25] This was wrong, but it was insignificant compared to the contradictory statements offered by those who had met and rejected Anderson.

In 1922, Baroness Buxhoeveden declared that Anastasia "hardly knew any words of German, and she pronounced them with a strong Russian accent."[26] Six years later, though, and in the midst of controversy over Anderson's claim, Buxhoeveden changed her story, now insisting that when it came to German, Anastasia "did not know it at all."[27] The same thing happened with tutor Charles Sidney Gibbes. In 1919 he recalled that all of the grand duchesses had spoken "German, but badly."[28] After meeting Anderson, though, he insisted that German "was a language the true Grand Duchess Anastasia could not speak."[29]

The worst offender was Pierre Gilliard. If he had not filled his *La Fausse Anastasie* with blatant lies and inaccuracies, as many of Anderson's supporters charged, he—more than anyone else—was responsible for the linguistic mess that the Hamburg tribunals had to sort through. In his first book, *Thirteen Years at the Russian Court*, published in 1921, before he knew of Anderson's claim, Gilliard insisted that the children "never had German lessons."[30] He may have done so for political reasons, as the last quarter of the book advanced the novel and quite untrue theory that Germany and German agents had been behind the executions of the imperial family. He corrected the error in *La Fausse Anastasie*, reporting Anastasia's German lessons with tutor Erich Kleinenberg, but then confused the issue by insisting, some fifty pages later, that Anastasia "did not speak German at all."[31] He soon abandoned even this contradictory position, declaring in newspaper articles that Anastasia "spoke German not at all," and insisting in interviews in his last years that the grand duchess had known "not one word of German."[32]

The exercise books purchased by Ian Lilburn resolved this dilemma. Item 8 was a thirty-two-page book labeled "A. Romanova, February 6, 1917, Tsarskoye Selo," in which Anastasia had continued the German lessons begun with Kleinenberg in 1912, practicing the language in Gothic script. These lessons continued, without Kleinenberg, at Tobolsk.[33] And there was more: though Gilliard had denied Anastasia's German, the Oberlandesgericht Court discovered timetables in his possession for her lessons at Tobolsk, which indicated that she had continued to work on the language through the beginning of 1918.[34]

Still, this linguistic nightmare did nothing to resolve the issue of Anderson's claim. Attempting to explore more relevant concerns, the courts tried to address the question of the claimant's scars, and precisely what they indicated, but here they were thwarted not only by the loss of most of the original documentation during the Second World War but also by Anderson herself. She absolutely refused repeated judicial requests to submit to new physical examinations by independent experts, something that might have clarified the nature of her injuries, and a position that drove her supporters to despair. "Your refusals to undergo such an examination," Gleb Botkin wrote to her in November 1963, "however justified, give the court a pretext for refusing to rule in your favor and allow your enemies to declare that you are afraid of such examinations."[35] Ten months later he tried again, saying that "however irksome, it is but a minor unpleasantness. I beg, nay, beseech you, therefore, to agree to that examination."[36] But she was unbending, and the courts were forced to rely on expert analysis of the remaining medical reports.

The catalog of Anderson's injuries had been argued and used to bolster her claim for more than forty years when the Oberlandesgericht Court took up the issue. There was the damage to her skull, the alleged depression behind her ear that Rathlef-Keilmann had insisted was "due to a glancing bullet wound."[37] But no medical documentation supported anything other than a single, minor scar above the ear, one that no doctor ever attributed to a bullet. There was a small scar—so minor no doctor bothered to mention it—on Anderson's forehead, the result, the claimant said, of a childhood fall and the reason why Anastasia had worn her hair in bangs.[38] Anderson said a small white scar on her right shoulder blade had come when a mole was cauterized so that she could wear a Russian court gown.[39] Journalist Bella Cohen insisted that Alexandra Gilliard confirmed that Anastasia bore such a scar, but this was not true; Rathlef-Keilmann quoted the former nurse as saying that she "could not remember" any such mark.[40] Instead, Rathlef-Keilmann wrote that former officer Nicholas Sablin recalled the scar, then confusingly provided no evidence to support this.[41] The Oberlandesgericht Court found no confirmation that Anastasia had any such scars.

Then there was the scar on Anderson's middle left finger, another childhood accident, she said, when a servant had shut a carriage door too quickly.[42] Was this true? Rathlef-Keilmann had asked Alexandra Gilliard. The former nurse said it sounded familiar, but she could not recall which of the grand duchesses had suffered such an injury, although Cohen once again insisted—contrary to Rathlef-Keilmann— that the former nurse had confirmed it all.[43] The judges examining Anderson's case heard from several émigrés who related second- and thirdhand tales of such an accident.[44] But Olga Alexandrovna rejected this. In 1925 she had written to Princess Irene of Prussia, "It was Marie who had pinched her finger, and some one who thought it was Anastasia must have told her that."[45] This was later confirmed by former imperial page F. van der Hoeven, who placed the incident about 1909; in her memoirs, Olga essentially repeated this, adding only that it had occurred aboard the imperial train.[46]

And the scar on Anderson's right foot, the transpiercing wound: this, her supporters held, matched exactly the triangular (or star—both were insisted upon) shape of the bayonet blade used by Bolshevik soldiers during Russia's Civil War.[47] It was an important piece of circumstantial evidence in her favor; proof, as Peter Kurth wrote, that she "had been stabbed in Russia."[48] No doctor who examined the claimant, though, ever seems to have described this wound as bearing a particularly recognizable and distinct shape; Faith Lavington, who saw it at Seeon, called it a "round mark right through the foot."[49]

Arguments over the state of the claimant's teeth were equally vague and contradictory. Serge Kostritsky, one of the former dentists to the imperial family, survived the Revolution and lived in exile in Paris. He never personally examined the claimant's teeth, as Rathlef-Keilmann admitted, because her supporters and the doctors treating her believed that the damage she had suffered to her jaws would have made any comparison impossible.[50] But the duke of Leuchtenberg had plaster casts made of Anderson's jaws and teeth and dispatched them to the dentist, whose only reply was a dismissive, "As if I would have left the teeth in such a condition!"[51] This avoided the issue, for the claimant was missing sixteen of her teeth and her jaws had been fractured, but Kostritsky declared, "These two plaster casts, in the placement of the teeth and in the shape of the jaws, bear no resemblance whatever to the placement of the teeth or the shape of the jaws of Grand Duchess Anastasia Nikolaievna." He also found something interesting: Hutchinson's incisors, a peculiar development of the teeth indicating that the claimant had been born with congenital syphilis, inherited from one or both of her parents.[52] Kostritsky relied, as he admitted, on memory in making this assessment, for he had left all of his records in Russia, but still he seemed convinced.[53] He told Victoria, marchioness of Milford Haven, that "the build of the jaw and the teeth, such as remained, were radically different" from those of Anastasia.[54] The judges hearing Anderson's appeal appointed a specialist, Dr. Volker Krüger, to analyze all of the dental evidence; after reviewing the plaster casts and the reports, Krüger stated that it was impossible to determine when and how her teeth had been damaged.[55]

And this was the problem with all of Anderson's scars: too much time had passed, and too many medical records and X-rays had been lost, for any modern review to conclusively establish how she had been wounded. The best that could be done was sort through the decades of often erroneous claims about her injuries—and the nature of her injuries—and determine which scars she actually bore. Their meaning, though—as with so much of Anderson's case—was subject to interpretation.

Lacking the opportunity to compare Anderson's fingerprints against those of Anastasia, the courts turned to photographic comparisons and to handwriting analyses. Pierre Gilliard had arranged the earliest photographic studies between the claimant and Anastasia, asking Professor Marc Bischoff, director of the Criminal Sciences Department at the University of Lausanne, to undertake three different analyses in 1927. Bischoff, who two years later founded the International Academy of Criminology in Lausanne with forensic science pioneer Edmond Locard, selected three photographs of Anastasia, one taken at Tsarskoye Selo in 1914, one taken in 1917 after the Revolution and showing the four grand duchesses and Tsesarevich Alexei after their heads had been shaved following measles, and one taken in 1918 at Tobolsk, and three photographs of the claimant, taken in 1920, 1921, and 1922. Bischoff admitted that the photographs did not depict "identical representations" and did not repeat the same angles and lighting conditions, but cavalierly suggested that these differences "posed no obstacle" to accurate comparisons. He compared the profiles, the shape of the right ears, and the facial features and their relationship to one another and found significant differences in the widths of the foreheads; in the shape of the eyes, eyebrows, noses, mouths, and chins; and in the contours of the ears. "It is impossible," Bischoff declared, "that Mrs. Tchaikovsky could be Grand Duchess Anastasia."[56]

Bischoff undertook two further photographic comparisons, using additional images. The first was another analysis of the ears, which he

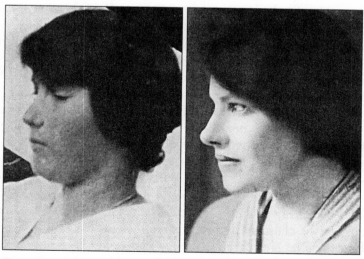

Comparisons for the civil trial in Hamburg of the profiles of Anastasia at Tobolsk (left), winter 1918, and Anna Anderson in the 1920s in Berlin.

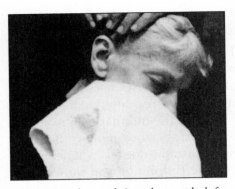

Anderson's right ear being photographed for comparisons during the Hamburg trials.

again deemed negative, while the second appraised any physical similarities between the claimant and Grand Duchesses Olga, Tatiana, and Marie Nikolaievna, to preclude the unlikely possibility that Anderson was not Anastasia but rather one of her sisters. This, too, was described as completely negative in outcome.[57] In her book, Rathlef-Keilmann contended that Gilliard had purposely misidentified Anastasia in the 1917 photograph depicting her with a shaven head; after showing the image to Prince Felix Yusupov, Maria von Hesse, Gleb Botkin, and, though an intermediary, Olga Alexandrovna, all four insisted that the figure Gilliard called Anastasia had actually been Olga Nikolaievna. She described this as "monstrous," contending that "in order to prove the lack of resemblance between the invalid and the real Grand Duchess Anastasia," Gilliard had lied.[58] When this accusation was published, Maria von Hesse flatly contradicted Rathlef-Keilmann, calling the assertion that she had refuted Gilliard's identification "pure invention" on Rathlef-Keilmann's part.[59] In fact, and despite what Rathlef-Keilmann insisted, Gilliard had correctly identified Anastasia in the photograph.[60]

Shortly after Bischoff conducted his first study, Grand Duke Ernst Ludwig of Hesse asked a Sergeant Riesling of the Darmstadt Police to also undertake a photographic comparison of the claimant and Anastasia. This focused exclusively on the ears. According to Empress Alexandra's sister Victoria, Anastasia's ears "closely resembled those of my father's brother, and were unlike the ordinary ones. Both Irene and my brother are in agreement with me in this opinion. Now it is an acknowledged fact that the modeling, especially of the curl over and lobe of an ear, remains unaltered from the day of birth of a person until death."[61] And Ernst Ludwig contended that he "remembered precisely" the shape of his niece's ears, "which had on their upper portion a deformity" consisting of a flat and long edge to the lobe.[62] The police examined photographs and plaster casts of the claimant's ears against images showing Anastasia's ears, and reported "no similarity" between the claimant and the grand duchess.[63]

The courts received into evidence and reviewed six further photographic studies of the claimant, conducted over four decades: four refuted the idea that Anderson was Anastasia, while two supported her claim. In March 1940, as part of their petition for revocation of the Mendelssohn inheritance certificates, Leverkuhn and Vermehren commissioned Professors V. Müller-Hess and F. Curtius to undertake a photographic analysis of the claimant and Anastasia. Known in the records of the Hamburg tribunal as "Study M," this concluded that Anderson was not Anastasia, citing in particular "distinct differences in the thickness and turn of the right earlobes."[64] A year later came "Study F," when as part of the proceedings Dr. Eugen Fischer, former director of the Kaiser Wilhelm Institute for Anthropology, Human Genetics, and Eugenics, submitted his own photographic comparison. Fischer did examine, measure, and photograph the claimant in person, attempting to replicate angles and lighting conditions in archival images of Anastasia. He cited a disparity in the philtrums—the thin indentation running from the middle of the top lip to the bottom of the nose—observed in the grand duchess and the claimant. He also found substantial variation in the shape of the noses and in the two profiles, though it was later found that he had used a profile photograph of Grand Duchess Marie rather than one of her sister Anastasia, which invalidated at least a portion of his negative conclusion that "Frau Anderson cannot be Grand Duchess Anastasia."[65] In 1955 came "Study C," commissioned from Professor Karl Clauberg, an anthropologist specializing in hematology. He, too, found against the claimant, citing a number of factors. Clauberg noted a significant difference in the philtrums and in the shapes of the mouths of the two women, particularly in the width of Anderson's upper lip; he also found that the bridges of the two noses varied in their curve when viewed in profile.[66]

In July 1958, Baron Egon von Eickstadt, professor of anthropology at the University of Mainz, together with his partner Dr. Werner Klenke, submitted to the Hamburg tribunal an extensive photographic study of the claimant and Anastasia, commissioned by Leverkuhn and Vermehren. They faulted the previous negative studies of the claimant with Anastasia, citing a variety of reasons ranging from "insufficient photographic materials" to the assertion that these professors had "only been looking for differences, and ignored similarities between the two women." Interestingly, they concluded, "no external injuries had altered the claimant's face, ears, or distinctive characteristics," which conflicted with the belief of many of her supporters that physical trauma had altered her features and thus led to difficulties of recognition. After examining 301 photographs, they noted "some similarity" in the ears of the claimant and Anastasia, though not enough to be deemed of importance. They did, however, declare an "unmistakable similarity in the shape of the face, in the root of the nose, in the bridge of the nose, in the cheekbones, in the width of the mouth, in the position of the lips relevant to the chin, and in the eyes" in the two women. They asserted, "Examination has revealed such a number of similarities that we must speak of a thorough physiognomic correspondence between Frau Anderson and Grand Duchess Anastasia. It is not only possible that we are dealing with the same identity but, in our opinion, it is the only acceptable conclusion."[67]

Hoping to resolve the conflict, in 1958 the Hanseatic Landesericht Court appointed its own independent expert, anthropologist and blood specialist Professor Otto Reche. Reche spent some six months collecting and examining hundreds of photographs of Anastasia and the imperial family, as well as her Hessian relations; to make adequate comparisons to Anderson, he traveled to her Black Forest home in Unterlengenhardt, where the usually uncooperative claimant allowed herself to be photographed in poses, at angles, and under lighting conditions matching archival images of Anastasia.[68] "For one year, at the rate of fourteen hours a day," Reche said, "I studied hundreds of these photographs." In his report he declared, "Frau Anderson is Grand Duchess Anastasia." He based this judgment on four points: the width of the cheekbones; the relationship of the lower jaw to the cheekbones; the position and size of the eye sockets; and the width of the forehead. From these he asserted, "Frau Anderson is identical to Grand Duchess Anastasia. Such coincidence between two human faces is not possible except when they are the same person, or identical twins."[69] Hoping to counter these results, Berenberg-Gossler again called upon Professor Karl Clauberg, who had produced a 1955 study, to offer a new analysis to the court. Not surprisingly, Clauberg simply echoed what his earlier examination had found: there was no resemblance between the claimant and Anastasia.[70]

With no consensus on the issue of photographic and anthropological analyses, the courts turned to various handwriting comparisons by trained graphologists. Darmstadt had commissioned the first of these studies in the 1920s from handwriting expert Lucy Weiszäcker, a member of the Cornelius Institute of Graphology in Prien. The majority of the historical samples from Anastasia dated from before the First World War, at a time when the grand duchess was still a child and her handwriting had not yet fully formed characteristic patterns, although some exemplars from her teenage years also were included. In comparing these samples to those written by the claimant, Weiszäcker concluded, based on a convergence of stylistic formation, that the claimant was Anastasia. Weiszäcker submitted her report, but authorities in Darmstadt, not wishing to reveal any evidence in the claimant's favor, apparently suppressed the results; they became known only when Weiszäcker came forward and volunteered them to Anderson's lawyers.[71]

The Hamburg courts commissioned several new tests. One, conducted by Maurice Delamain, former president of the French Society of Graphologists, concluded that the claimant was most probably Anastasia, but the most apparently compelling study was the handwriting comparison by Frau Minna Becker for the Hanseatic Landesgericht Court.[72] Becker had recently helped authenticate the diaries of Anne Frank. After comparing documents written by Anastasia with samples of the claimant's handwriting, Becker asserted 137 congruent points in samples from the two women. This, she said, was not only extraordinarily high, but also it led her to believe, "with a probability bordering on certainty," that the claimant was Anastasia.[73]

There was one further issue that consumed the courts, particularly the Hanseatic Oberlandesgericht Court: this was what came to be called the *Hessenreise*, Anderson's allegation that in 1916 Grand Duke

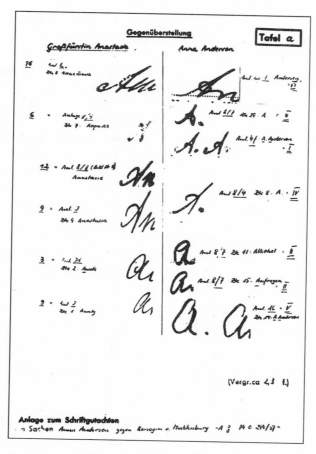

Comparison of handwriting samples from (left) Anastasia with those from (right) Anna Anderson as submitted during the trials in Hamburg.

Ernst Ludwig of Hesse had secretly visited Russia, hoping to arrange a separate peace with his brother-in-law Nicholas II. She first made this claim in 1925 to Rathlef-Keilmann, who conveyed it, through an emissary named Amy Smith, directly to Count von Hardenberg in Darmstadt.[74] When he heard this, Smith recalled, Hardenberg exploded. It was, he declared, "a terrible libel" against the grand duke, made by "a shameless creature" who was exposing herself to potential legal action if she persisted in "such derogatory and reckless accusations."[75]

This marked the beginning of Darmstadt's concerted efforts, through Hardenberg, against Anderson; her supporters believed that not only had she revealed one of the grand duke's secrets but also that, in her careless remark, lay further evidence of her inexplicably intimate knowledge of the imperial family. The alleged visit, said to have taken place in February 1916, became a central point in the case before the court of appeals. Statements were received into evidence and witnesses heard on the question, though only one, Prince Dimitri Golitsyn, claimed actually to have seen the grand duke at the Alexander Palace, and only then because he had been told his identity.[76] Still, there was a fairly impressive list of aristocratic and royal witnesses, none with actual firsthand knowledge, who repeated second-, third-, and fourthhand rumors of the alleged mission.[77] Among the more intriguing offerings were assertions from former Crown Princess Cecilie of Prussia, Kaiser Wilhelm II's daughter-in-law, and his stepson Prince Ferdinand of Schoenaich-Carolath, who said they had learned about the journey from the former monarch himself.[78] Something of the kind had been discussed, said Fritz von Unruh, tutor to Ernst Ludwig's two sons. He helped plan the route for such a trip, he declared, though he didn't know if it had actually occurred.[79]

"The suggestion that Uncle Ernie went to Russia during the middle of the First World War for political reasons," wrote Lord Mountbatten to his cousin Prince Ludwig of Hesse, "is absolutely ludicrous. My family, and especially my mother, would of course have known all about it. Certainly after the war, there would have been no object whatever in keeping such a visit secret in intimate family circles."[80] Ernst Ludwig denied it; Baron Fabian von Massenbach, his adjutant at the time, denied it; and Kaiser Wilhelm II's only daughter, Viktoria Luise, insisted that though there had been proposals, her father had never said anything to her of such a trip.[81] During the Hamburg appeals historian Professor Egmont Zechlin took the witness stand. He suggested, as had Princess Kira, that Crown Princess Cecilie of Prussia had not been entirely sane when she had made her statements supportive of Anderson, and that in exile Wilhelm II had often exaggerated and lied to members of his family in attempts to excuse his lack of action during the First World War and inability to save the Romanovs. Zechlin's coup, though, was in offering Ernst Ludwig's diaries and letters to his wife from the period in question, as evidence that he had been with the army in France. Anderson's lawyers countered that the documents were vague and contained anomalies that allowed for the possibility that the trip had indeed taken place.[82] After reviewing all of the statements and documents, the appeals court eventually ruled, "Evidence by witnesses on the subject of the alleged Hessian trip is without merit. The trip did not occur."[83]

Whether such a trip actually took place mattered little to Anderson's claim; rather, it was the contention that her allegation revealed intimate knowledge that was pivotal. Her supporters may have believed this to be true, but it was clear from the parade of witnesses that far from being some kind of privileged secret, rumors of such a trip were widespread, at least within aristocratic and émigré circles. Given her exposure to such influences after leaving Dalldorf, it was at least possible that Anderson encountered the story while living with the von Kleists or Nicholas von Schwabe.[84] In short, her knowledge of the rumors—whether true or not—went no farther than to show that Anderson had been exposed to gossip surrounding the issue.

On February 28, 1967, after three years of testimony, the Hanseatic Oberlandesgericht Court delivered its verdict. The claimant's appeal was rejected: she had not met the burden of proof imposed by her suit and provided convincing evidence that she was Anastasia. Wollmann, who declared his intention of taking the case to the West German Federal Supreme Court in Karlsruhe, particularly objected to two points in the ruling, for the court had apparently inexplicably commissioned and then ignored the anthropological and handwriting studies conducted by Otto Reche and Minna Becker, studies entirely in the claimant's favor. In fact, the court rejected all of the anthropological studies, not merely those suggesting that Anderson was Anastasia. They did so, as they explained, because the end results were too contradictory: seven studies produced five opinions against the claimant and two in her favor. None could establish who she actually was to a degree of legal certainty.[85] Even Eickstadt and Klenke acknowledged the subjective nature of the photographic comparisons, describing the results as "degrees of estimated probability" that render "only a possible approximation within a certain latitude of error."[86] Such studies offered the court only collected—and often contradictory—opinion based on individual analyses, and analyses confined to the often crude technology available at the time, which largely—as in Reche's work— consisted of simply cutting and pasting one photograph atop another and trying to match features visually.

And as evidence, the handwriting comparisons, the court ruled, fell into the same category—suggestive but too contradictory to be of legal value. The problem with the modern analyses done by Dulckeit, Delamain, Becker, and others, the court wrote, was that the samples examined had been insufficient and of poor quality.[87] It was an opinion shared by Delamain, who had complained that all of the tests were too limited to allow for any absolute verdict. The experts were often forced to work from photocopies, and original documentation, which was necessary to accurately analyze pressure and stroke formation, was too often missing from the materials made available to graphologists.[88]

By January 1970, when it finally reached the West German Federal Supreme Court, Anderson's case had become the longest legal battle in German history. The Supreme Court took the case, now argued for the claimant by Dr. Baron Curt von Stackelberg, as a judicial review. The purpose was not to relitigate the accumulated evidence, but rather to determine whether the ruling by the Hanseatic Oberlandesgericht Court had been free of judicial error. The verdict finally came on February 17, 1970, the fiftieth anniversary of Anderson's leap into the Landwehr Canal. The Hanseatic Oberlandesgericht Court, the Supreme Court found, had ruled appropriately on the question of rejecting its own experts. Such a matter, they wrote, "was a matter of responsibility entirely within the realm of the judges. When confronted with an opposite interpretation of such evidence, or should they be subject to any doubt, the judges were legally obligated to deny the case if conscientious examination of the assertion renders individual certainty of the truth impossible."

The Supreme Court noted that Anderson "has had sufficient opportunity, independent of the burden of proof and unfettered by any procedural rulings of the civil law, to clarify her identity." Rather than so doing, however, they ruled that "she has refused, in an astonishing manner, to contribute to the clarification of her identity." Despite what they found to be "the plaintiff's broad and entirely favorable access to the German legal system," Anderson, for reasons the Supreme Court found "incomprehensible," had "repeatedly evaded any attempts to discover her identity and refused explanations" that would clarify her origins. They specifically noted her "persistent refusals" to answer important questions that would resolve her case.

"An examination of the scars from wounds allegedly received during the massacre," the court noted, "has not substantiated their nature, their origin, or their cause." Medical documentation failed to "establish any physical link to Grand Duchess Anastasia," while "those remaining physical characteristics which lend themselves to reliable comparison yield no definite criteria" to support the claimant's contention. In particular, the Supreme Court noted that "the plaintiff has refused to cooperate with court-imposed attempts to clarify the extent and nature of her scars," which made it impossible to validate the assertions made about them.

Reviewing the collected statements and depositions advanced by Anderson's lawyers as evidence of her intimate knowledge of the life of the imperial family, the Supreme Court declared that these "lose all persuasive power" if, as was nearly always the case upon close examination, "they can be traced to another source to which the plaintiff had access." In assessing many of her asserted memories, the court noted that it was impossible, "owing to the lack of extensive and convincing data available to the public," to adequately confirm or deny Anderson's statements. "Her early and spontaneous statements," the decision read, "contained nothing beyond those subjects covered in numerous published materials known to have been made available to her with the von Kleist and von Schwabe families; later, she had even more materials at her disposal."

Addressing frequent declarations from Anderson's supporters that what they deemed to be her refined manner was evidence that she was Anastasia, the court rather scathingly declared, "The plaintiff's general behavior offers no definitive proof one way or the other for her claim. Certainly she has exhibited no lapse in behavior since the presumed age of twenty, but this in itself provides no evidence of high birth. Further, it must be noted that there are significant facts related to the plaintiff's activities in the early years of her claim that cannot be ignored. Favorable opinions of her behavior originate from a period when the plaintiff lived among émigré supporters of means and rank, a time when through careful observation she could absorb the subtle behaviors suited to royal rank."

Although not within their specific purview, the Supreme Court did examine the issue of Anderson's languages. "The plaintiff," it judged, "has not succeeded in proving that her linguistic abilities match those of Grand Duchess Anastasia." Anderson, the court declared, "possesses an understanding of the Russian language, but has consistently refused to provide the court with proofs of conversational ability." The ruling noted that Anderson's "knowledge of Russian, even at a time immediately following her alleged rescue, did not accord that which would be expected from Grand Duchess Anastasia." As to the German language, the Supreme Court corrected decades of misinformation from Gilliard and others that Anastasia was given no lessons in the language and that she did not speak it, noting that the grand duchess was given special lessons in the language periodically from 1912 until 1918. But, the court ruled, "The plaintiff's knowledge of

German, even in her early years, exceeded that of Grand Duchess Anastasia." The issue of languages, the ruling declared, "does not provide any compelling evidence to indicate the plaintiff's identity with the youngest daughter of the Tsar."

"The appeal of the plaintiff," the court ended, "has been rejected as groundless." They found no procedural errors in her case and noted that under German law the burden of proof had rested with her. Anderson and her lawyers, through "the collected evidence presented for judicial consideration in four successive legal venues," had failed to "definitively prove that the plaintiff is the Tsar's youngest daughter." If she could not prove that she was Anastasia, though, neither could her opponents prove that she was not, as the Supreme Court was careful to record; the death of Anastasia in 1918, the ruling declared, was not a matter of historically established fact.[89]

It was over, but Anderson, as usual, expressed nothing but disinterest. By the time the final verdict came, she had gone from Germany, the faded dreams of her youth abandoned as she slipped into the twilight years of her legendary existence.

17

"How Shall I Tell You Who I Am?"

I N T H E T H I R D W E E K of October 1963, a new issue of *Life* magazine appeared in millions of American mailboxes and on newsstands. A sepia photograph of the five children of Nicholas and Alexandra stared out from the cover, bearing the intriguing caption "The Case of a New Anastasia." The story within recounted the claim of a woman named Eugenia Smith, who had lived in obscurity near Chicago before a small New York publisher purchased her reputed memoirs. She offered a manuscript detailing how a sympathetic soldier named Alexander had rescued her after the executions in Ekaterinburg and spirited her across Russia to Romania, a story line clearly influenced by Anderson's claim. Smith passed a lie detector test, but photographic, handwriting, and anthropological analyses all refuted her claim, as did Princess Nina Georgievna, who met and promptly declared Smith an impostor.[1]

In the chalet at Unterlengenhardt, news of Smith's claim sent Anderson into an indignant fury. She believed that Smith had been invented and funded by Lord Mountbatten to distract attention from her own coming appeal in Hamburg. "All this dirt going round me," she once wrote, "the dirt what [sic] a creature of the Battenberg [Lord Mountbatten] is publishing!"[2] From America, Gleb Botkin assured her that Smith "bears not the slightest resemblance to Your Imperial Highness."[3] This new "Anastasia" soon fizzled when it was found that she had been born in Romania in 1899, but her very public

Anderson with her dog Baby, Unterlengenhardt.

debut was symptomatic of the intense interest engendered by Anderson's story. In the wake of 1956's triumphant film *Anastasia* came new books arguing or disputing Anderson's claim; new magazine articles chronicling her legal battles; and an NBC Television revival of the Maurette play starring Julie Harris as the would-be grand duchess. In 1965 Constance Towers and Lillian Gish took the stage in *Anya*, a new Broadway musical based on Anderson's story, and in 1967 Sir Kenneth MacMillan opened his famed ballet *Anastasia* in London. That same year saw the publication of Robert Massie's international best seller *Nicholas and Alexandra*, a work that, more than any other, popularized the story of the last tsar and his family and marked their shift from shadowy history to modern popular culture. "Who is this Massie?" Anderson quizzed Prince Friedrich of Saxe-Altenburg. When Prince Friedrich explained and gave her a copy of the book, though, she erupted in anger. "I don't want this book!" she yelled. "I don't need this book! I don't want to read it! That book, take it away!"[4]

Her vehement reaction may have stemmed from the publicity the book received, something she apparently linked—probably correctly— to the sudden reappearance of cars and busloads of unwelcome tourists who again crowded the streets of Unterlengenhardt and tried to peer over her garden wall to see for themselves this possible grand duchess, this woman portrayed by Ingrid Bergman, this solitary and mysterious figure at the center of one of the century's greatest enigmas. Even the rejection of her legal appeal in 1967 did nothing much to dampen public interest or enthusiasm; no one could satisfactorily explain her scars, or account for her apparently intimate knowledge, or sufficiently refute the favorable photographic and handwriting comparisons, or explain away the seemingly compelling recognitions by Grand Duke Andrei Vladimirovich, Princess Xenia Georgievna, the Botkins, or Lili Dehn. And still it continued, this slow accumulation of intriguing detail that drop by drop created a modern legend. In July 1965 Ian Lilburn arranged for the usually reluctant claimant to meet Prince Alexander Nikitich Romanov, grandson of Grand Duchess Xenia Alexandrovna. Alexander had never known Anastasia, but after spending two hours with Anderson in her garden, he confessed to Lilburn that he believed she must be the grand duchess, as she so closely resembled his grandmother and his aunt Princess Irina Yusupov.[5] Something similar took place in 1967, when a reporter interviewed elderly ballerina Mathilde Kschessinska at her home in Paris. The former mistress of Nicholas II before his marriage, and morganatic wife and now widow of Andrei Vladimirovich, she had seen Anastasia only from a distance on a few rare public occasions, but her husband introduced her to Anderson in 1928 as she passed through Paris on her way to America. Even after thirty-nine years, the former ballerina declared, "I am still convinced it is she. You understand, when she looked at me with those eyes, well, that was it, they were the emperor's eyes, the same exact look that the emperor had."[6]

Perceived resemblances to elderly relatives, the memory of a former lover's eyes after seventy years—it was all so vague, so reminiscent of the intangibles that had convinced people such as Tatiana and Gleb Botkin, and Princess Xenia Georgievna. But to Anderson none of it mattered. It was all too late to make a difference in a life winding toward its close. If she had ever been interested in legally pursuing her claim, she lost all interest after the Hanseatic Court of Appeals ruled against her. While her lawyers prepared to argue the case before the West German Federal Supreme Court, Anderson divorced herself from further involvement. She was—if Anastasia—sixty-six when the verdict came, and faced a future as uncertain as anything in her tumultuous past. Completely reliant on the generosity of supporters and on the ministrations of a succession of elderly ladies who looked after her, Anderson had nothing—not even a legally recognized identity—to call her own. The aristocratic luxury of the von Kleist apartment, of Seeon, and of Xenia Georgievna's Long Island estate now receded into

Anderson inside her chalet, 1960.

an increasingly distant past, her realm reduced to the small chalet and its overgrown garden at the edge of the Black Forest, reduced to a reluctant tourist attraction, a living historical curiosity, a tantalizing question mark to be fought and argued over by a world fascinated by her existence.

There was, it is true, some brief diversion in these years, in the form of a Russian émigré named Alexei Miliukov, who arrived in Unterlengenhardt armed with a recommendation from Gleb Botkin. Miliukov provided Anderson with an irascible sparring partner as the two discussed her life and argued for hours about her case. Soon, Miliukov asked permission to tape their conversations for the sake of history, and surprisingly she agreed. These talks, in English, with a smattering of German, only occasionally dealt with issues substantive to her claim, but her comments were by turns amusing, outrageous, and unintentionally reflective. "You know," she told Miliukov, "I'm not very pleasant, not very sugary."[7] She spoke with reluctance of her early years, though she would happily prattle off the names and tangled connections of various German aristocrats and offer running moral commentaries on their lives as she followed their exploits in the press. When Miliukov pressed her on events in Ekaterinburg, she almost always refused, saying, "Please not, please, not dirt!"[8] At times, though, she said some startling things: she chastised Miliukov when he referred to her suicide attempt in 1920, declaring, "I never jumped into that canal!" and even told him proudly, "I own a bank."[9] She once referred to Kirill Vladimirovich's wife, Grand Duchess Victoria Melita, as "a pig, a true swine," and condemned her daughter Kira—who had come out publicly against her claim—by saying, "She has the mind of a waitress!" Most of her scorn, though, was reserved for "my mortal enemy" and "that Battenberg creature," as she termed Lord Mountbatten. She seemed to blame him not only for Eugenia Smith but also for Massie's book, for the loss of her court case, for all of those who had rejected her as Anastasia, even for the busloads of tourists who came to Unterlengenhardt; it was all, she insisted, a "plot" against her, to exhaust her, to drive her crazy.[10]

Enemies, probably sent by Mountbatten, she was sure, were all around her. She trusted no one at Unterlengenhardt. Anderson probably never had two more devoted supporters than Prince Friedrich of Saxe-Altenburg and Baroness Monica von Miltitz, one of the ladies who lived with her and attended to her needs, but to Miliukov she expressed nothing but scorn for the pair, constantly belittling them and warning that neither was to be trusted. The prince, she warned, "constantly plots against me," and she made a point of swearing Miliukov to secrecy over her letters and plans because the dedicated Friedrich "is not to be trusted with anything ever!"[11] As for Baroness von Miltitz, nothing she ever did was good enough for Anderson; if she distrusted Prince Friedrich, she seemed to positively loathe the baroness, calling her "a snake" and "an abuser."[12]

"Botkin is the only friend," Anderson rather sadly told Miliukov. "Only Botkin I trust, not any other."[13] Although Gleb regularly corresponded with her, the pair had not seen each other since 1938. That same year, he had finally abandoned established religion for one of his own making, the Church of Aphrodite. Mystical by nature, at one point in his youth Gleb had seriously considered becoming a priest; in his first book, a 1929 novel called *The God Who Didn't Laugh*, he told an essentially autobiographical story of a young Russian seeking religious fulfillment and eventually turning to the cult of Aphrodite.[14] Certain that men had been responsible for all of the modern world's misfortunes, he saw his new Church of Aphrodite, over which he presided as self-appointed archbishop, as a celebration of feminine truth and an expression of hope that the horrors of the twentieth century lay behind him. It was a pagan church, certainly, with its worship of a goddess and embrace of sensuality and nature, but the Church of Aphrodite, for all of its bizarre peculiarities, was firmly rooted in the Russian sectarian tradition, drawing on rituals and beliefs inspired by that country's Old Believers.[15]

In 1965, Gleb and his wife, Nadine, moved to Charlottesville, Virginia, where their daughter Marina lived with her husband, attorney Richard Schweitzer, and their children. He described his new home to Anderson in lyrical terms. "It reminds me of Tsarskoye Selo," he wrote, "because of the many lovely Eighteenth Century buildings it contains."[16] He told her how the city nestled "in a hollow" surrounded by green mountains, and how it was filled with "friendly and well-mannered" people of mainly "British stock."[17] Slowly, surely, Gleb was laying the foundation for a suggestion that soon took concrete form: that Anderson abandon Germany and move to America—and to Charlottesville—permanently. In truth, there were sound reasons for his campaign. Convinced that nothing good would come of her remaining in the Black Forest, he was worried not only about her disintegrating living conditions and welfare but also about the financial security of a woman he adamantly believed to be Anastasia. Her supporters—her true supporters, who suffered her mercurial temperament and cared for her, who paid her bills and protected her from the world beyond Unterlengenhardt—were growing old; what she needed was certainty, an assurance that she would be looked after and provided for in her last years. People who accused Gleb of financial interests in backing her claim failed to understand just how tenuous his own situation was: often, Gleb could barely provide for his own family, his wife was seriously ill, and he himself was exhausted and in poor health. If he died, Gleb worried, who would step in and selflessly see to Anderson's needs?

This concern led Botkin to Dr. John Eacott Manahan, a well-known and much-liked Charlottesville figure. The son of the former dean of the University of Virginia's School of Education, Manahan, called Jack by his friends, possessed multiple degrees from the institution, a love of history, which he had formerly taught, and a passion for genealogy. More importantly, he was armed with a considerable fortune and, intrigued by the mystery of Anderson's identity, he agreed to finance what was portrayed as an extended visit to America. Gleb once described him as "quite a bit of a tornado," and Manahan tended to match Anderson in eccentricities.[18] He dispatched regular letters to her, whose contents even she occasionally found disturbing, so enthusiastic and convoluted were his rambling missives. "Mr. Manahan," she confided to Miliukov in 1967, "has written such a strange letter that I am afraid to go to America."[19] It took another year before Botkin finally assured her that she would be safe in Manahan's care.

The increasingly deplorable situation at Unterlengenhardt undoubtedly eased Anderson's decision. In the third week of May 1968, town authorities warned Prince Friedrich that the claimant would have to clean up both her chalet and its wild garden, in which Anderson had taken to burying her deceased dogs and cats in shallow graves.

Jack Manahan with Gleb Botkin and Botkin's wife Nadine, Charlottesville, 1966.

The smell was atrocious, and the inside of the chalet not much better. On hearing this news, though, Anderson locked everyone out of the chalet and barricaded herself inside the house, refusing to admit anyone. For three days, Prince Friedrich stood at the door, listening to her harangues as she accused him of betraying her; on the fourth day, there was no answer to his knock. Worried, he summoned the town fire department, and the door was axed open. They found Anderson on the floor, dehydrated, emaciated, and nearly unconscious. She was carried off to a hospital at Neuenburg, where she would remain in room 85 for seven weeks. During her absence Prince Friedrich swept through the chalet, which, as Ian Lilburn recalls, had "been completely devastated by her cats." There were more than sixty of them altogether, inbred and ill, the house reeking so badly that it took a week for the smell to dissipate. Prince Friedrich had the cats put to sleep, along with Baby, the last of Anderson's enormous and fierce dogs, and had the rotting animals in the garden dug up and carted away. By the time the smell within the chalet had faded enough for Prince Friedrich and Lilburn to work inside, they were astonished at what they saw. "It was incredible," Lilburn remembers, "signed photographs of the Emperor and Empress, letters from the Crown Princess of Prussia, a handkerchief that had belonged to Empress Alexandra—the most extraordinary mementos scattered haphazardly about the floors, lost in a wasteland of dog and cat mess and rotting food." Lilburn salvaged what he could, packing up boxes of Anderson's belongings, trying to salvage the physical history of her storied life.[20] When Anderson learned of all this, she deemed it to be Prince Friedrich's ultimate betrayal, and she refused to see or speak to him for ten years.[21]

With her animals gone and the sanctity of her house, as she saw it, invaded, Anderson agreed to Botkin's suggestion that she go to America. On July 13, 1968, accompanied by Miliukov, she very reluctantly boarded an airplane and flew from Frankfurt to Washington, D.C. It was the first time she had ever flown, and she was none too enthusiastic about it: airplanes, she told Miliukov, were "unnatural," and she cursed them as "devils" even as she disappeared across the Atlantic.[22] And it was the first time Anderson had set foot in America since being unceremoniously shuttled from the Four Winds Rest Home back to Germany nearly four decades earlier. She liked the United States, liked the people, the landscape, the national spirit, and she happily fell in with Manahan's plans as he took her to sites in Washington, D.C., and in Virginia as the summer wore on. Soon, though, they were in Charlottesville, visiting Gleb Botkin and his family and touring Manahan's nearby 660-acre Fairview Farm.

Anderson in America.

Anderson was happy, unencumbered by the constant pressure of having to prove that she was Anastasia, and after an initial burst of publicity documenting her arrival, the press largely left her alone. But this tranquility was shattered in August, when one of the most notorious names from Russia's imperial past emerged from the shadows amid a deliberate glare of publicity. This was Maria Rasputin, daughter of the infamous Gregory Rasputin, who arrived in Charlottesville to meet the claimant. Maria had, at best, met Anastasia on a few isolated occasions before the Revolution, though as she told journalist Patte Barham, who had accompanied her, Anderson seemed to recall many incidents from the past, incidents that she herself had forgotten. In everything she did, Maria told Barham, Anderson reminded her of "the regal manners" of the Romanovs.[23] This was somewhat less than compelling and seemed positively opportunistic when, after Anderson refused to return with her to Los Angeles to promote the recognition, Maria cynically reversed her opinion and declared that the claimant was not Anastasia.[24]

But the most unlikely development came that winter, when on December 23, 1968, Anderson married Jack Manahan at the Albemarle County Courthouse, in a hastily arranged ceremony proudly watched over by best man Gleb Botkin. At forty-nine, Manahan was nearly two decades younger than his new bride, but he was a millionaire and could offer her financial security. "If you ask her," he told a reporter, "she'll say she married me because she wanted to live in America and her six-month visa expires."[25] This may have been true, but after decades

Maria Rasputin.

of uncertainty, it was an arrangement that ensured Anderson would be provided for. It also brought her something else besides security: for the first time in her adult life, she had an indisputable, legally recognized name: Anastasia Manahan.

Had Gleb's own health not been so poor, and his financial stability so uncertain, he might well have married Anderson himself, for he was a widower by this time, but in Manahan he had found someone willing to assume the burden of caring for her and ensuring her future. But the introduction of a third party disrupted the previously intimate relationship between Botkin and Anderson. Previously she had looked to Gleb as her most trusted adviser, someone upon whom she could rely to see to her interests; now, Manahan stepped into that position, and gradually but inevitably Botkin's influence waned. And he had other problems as well, for throughout 1969 his health seriously declined. Just after Christmas 1969 he suffered a fatal heart attack.

There was something extremely odd yet somehow fitting in the existence that now enveloped the twentieth century's most famous living mystery. "Mr. Jack," confided Manahan's butler James Price, "well . . . he just never done growed up." As childlike as his new wife, he loved to show her off, as if she were "a sort of prize," remembers frequent visitor Bernard Ruffin, describing her "as a barker would describe a carnival freak."[26] She and Jack divided their time between his Fairview Farm and an elegant little Palladian house on Charlottesville's tree-shaded University Circle. Jack's circle of friends became her circle of friends, though she was social only on her own terms, that is, infrequently, reluctantly, and often angrily if her husband pushed, for she disliked being dictated to; still, when she found herself in convivial or sympathetic company, she could be charming, head lowered, a smile on her mouth, eyes raised to take in everything around her. It was Jack who shopped for her clothes, an increasingly curious and outrageous assortment of plaid pants, polyester suits, and garishly colored plastic raincoats and hats; it was a dramatic change from the fashionable figure who had arrived in New York in 1928 with her expensive white winter wardrobe, but she seemed to no longer care about such matters. She had few interests: she "ate very little," remembers her biographer Peter Kurth, "and usually with objections," preferring a largely vegetarian diet. She neither smoked nor drank, though she often pressed visitors into accepting a glass of wine; her one vice was coffee, which she drank from the time she arose until she retired.[27]

"Anastasia!" Jack would yell. "You have visitors!" Soon enough, she usually appeared, a "striking looking old lady," recalls Ruffin, "slender, with a beautiful, unblemished white complexion," "thick, closely cropped hair, usually bleached blonde," a "long, sharp, high-bridged nose," and "beautiful, sparkling blue eyes."[28] And following in her wake was an inevitable stream of animals—several dozen cats and upward of twenty dogs, and "none of them apparently housebroken."[29] She disliked those who greeted her with shouts of "Your Imperial Highness" or referred to her as "Grand Duchess," or even as "Anastasia." She wanted to be called simply "Mrs. Manahan."[30] She chatted amiably if she felt her visitors wanted nothing of her; when pushed, though, she usually became angry or simply ignored the flow of questions. "What does it matter if he thinks I am not me?" she once asked of a skeptic as she ate dinner. "Who cares? Maybe I am not me. Maybe not. All I care about is let's eat this ice cream!"[31]

The Manahans spoke in English, at least in the first years of their marriage. By now, after so many years of living in Germany and being surrounded by her coterie of German ladies, the claimant's English had deteriorated, though it had never been particularly impressive. She spoke in an accent no one could accurately place, a thick, guttural flow of words peppered with anachronistic idioms and phrases haphazardly thrown together in distinctly ungrammatical sentences. Soon, though, the Manahans took to using a mixture of English and German, and then, when alone, almost exclusively German, so that her grasp of English only faded with the passing years. To Manahan, she was "Anastasia," drawn out flatly in his genteel southern accent, while she took to calling her husband "Hans," a diminutive of the German "Johann" or "John."[32]

And of Russian there was nothing. In 1973, lawyer Brien Horan, who had become fascinated by her case, arranged for the claimant to meet Prince David Chavchavadze, son of Princess Nina Georgievna. The prince's mother had met and rejected the claimant, while his Aunt Xenia had accepted her as Anastasia, so he was intensely curious about the frail-looking woman he now encountered. Thinking to test her knowledge of Russian, he repeated, very slowly and deliberately, the story that had been passed down in his family of how the claimant had once spoken the language accidentally, when referring to her pet parakeets. She had, in the past, clearly followed conversations in Russian, even if she elected to reply in German, but hearing Chavchavadze now she seemed completely bewildered and stared at her visitor.[33] Horan and the prince left convinced "that she had not understood" what Chavchavadze said.[34]

At first it all seemed unlikely but interesting, this alleged grand duchess who now drove through the streets of Charlottesville with her husband. People were fascinated, but the public appearances began to devolve into startling and uncomfortable scenes. The couple were prominent figures—the *most* prominent figures—in Charlottesville, and though people largely left the claimant alone, it became difficult to ignore some of her more spectacular appearances. The Manahans belonged to the exclusive Farmington Country Club, and liked to dine in its restaurant, if "dine" is the correct word for what often took place, for while Jack enjoyed his meals, his wife merely picked at her food, waiting patiently for him to finish, then out came her purse, and rumpled bits of tinfoil that she spread on the table to receive the contents of her plate. Anything that was left went into her purse—treats for her cats and dogs. One Charlottesville local recalled the strange sight of this presumed grand duchess carefully pouring her tea into the saucer and then sipping it from the plate.[35] Manners aside, it was her occasional outbursts that seemed to most unnerve the refined country club set; if Manahan lingered too long over his food, if he said something she disliked, if she felt that he had slighted her in any way, out came the accusations, loud, shouted insults in a mixture of English and German that had heads turning and waiters coughing uncomfortably. Eventually it all became too much for the denizens of Farmington, and the club let Jack know that it would be best if he let his membership quietly lapse.[36]

Reporters who came to interview the alleged grand duchess were shocked on approaching the couple's once elegant house on University Circle: as Manahan aged and grew more eccentric, trees obscured windows, the remaining grass went uncut for years, and traps of banana peels, firewood, and sacks of garbage—set by the claimant to ward off unwanted visitors—encircled the little brick building. Other sacks of garbage had been tossed out windows or doors and left to rot.[37] Two British journalists who called on the couple in 1974 described the living room as "an extraordinary muddle. In the center, incongruously, is a huge tree stump; on the walls old pictures recalling the glories of Imperial Russia contend in cramped space with bric-a-brac and childish daubings; over everything hangs the pervasive smell of cats. The balcony, which should be a pleasant place to contemplate the view, is piled high with a mountain of potatoes, which have overwhelmed their container, a large plastic bath. All this, says Manahan, is how Anastasia chooses to live."[38]

And this visit took place when the house was still in relatively good condition. By the end of the 1970s, the situation at 35 University Circle had grown dangerous. "There is a great smell emanating from this property," declared one neighbor. "The odor can only be described as a stench."[39] Manahan put up with his wife's eccentricities: she refused to have any of her pets put to sleep, and when they died she generally cremated them herself in the living room fireplace. By 1978, neighbors reached their breaking point and swore out warrants against the Manahans for failing to maintain "clean and sanitary premises."[40] During a hearing on the issue, Mrs. Manahan sat stiffly in the last row of the courtroom, refusing to answer questions from the judge. "Anastasia," her husband explained, "feels she is not subject to American law." Although Jack insisted, rather improbably, that there was nothing unsanitary about his residence, the judge fined Manahan some $1,750 and ordered that he clean up the property.[41]

Still the reporters came, willing to add their own chapter to this most enduring of historical enigmas. The claimant cooperated one day, only to refuse to see someone the next. "I am ill of this dirt," she once declared. "I will not read this dirt. I am ill of the constant, constant questions."[42] To one television crew, she offered up the appropriately enigmatic: "How shall I tell you who I am? In which way? Can you tell me that? Can you really prove to me who you are? You can believe it or you don't believe it. It doesn't matter in any way whatsoever."[43] Things took an intriguing turn in 1976, when a book called *The File on the Tsar* appeared; a lengthy chapter presented the claimant's case in a highly favorable light, but quoted her as remarking of Ekaterinburg, "There was no massacre there, but I cannot tell the rest."[44]

Although she condemned the book as "a put together mess," Mrs. Manahan seemed to adopt some theories in *The File on the Tsar*, including the notion that the empress and her daughters may not have been murdered in Ekaterinburg.[45] Until then, she had been consistent—on the rare occasions when she could be coerced to speak of it—in repeating her story of the executions in the Ipatiev House, though the version she first gave in the 1920s took a lurid turn in her later life when she claimed that the Bolsheviks had repeatedly gang-raped the imperial family before shooting them.[46] But the stories now became more bizarre. In 1976 she claimed that the imperial family had all possessed doubles, who acted for them in public on dangerous occasions, and that these unlucky actors had somehow willingly maintained a charade that led to their executions in the Ipatiev House.[47] A few years later, this took an odd turn when a retired Richmond, Virginia, dentist stepped forward and claimed that his Uncle Herschel Meistroff had been Nicholas II's double and was shot in his place.[48] Hearing this, however, Mrs. Manahan dismissed it as "nonsense," while her husband added, rather unfortunately, "No Jew would have helped the Tsar."[49]

Soon, though, even this peculiar theory was eclipsed when Mrs. Manahan related that none of the Romanovs had been killed; instead, she insisted, they had all escaped from Russia to Warsaw, aboard a train that they somehow themselves operated. Nicholas II, she said, had died in Denmark in 1928, while Tsesarevich Alexei was still alive and in hiding.[50] The extraordinary historical revision reached a kind of zenith when the claimant insisted not only that the imperial family had not been killed, but also that they had all left Russia before World War I. Empress Alexandra and her daughters, she said, had moved permanently to Germany in 1911, while Nicholas II and Tsesarevich Alexei joined them in 1913.[51]

What to make of such tales? Was Mrs. Manahan merely entertaining herself with increasingly mischievous remarks, each more absurd than the next? Was she attempting, in so confusing the details of her case, to finally wrest back control of her own life? Or did all of these outrageous, conflicting stories reflect a mind falling victim to senility? Several of those who knew her in these years believe that it was Jack rather than his wife who was responsible for most of these theories. Manahan, recalls Ruffin, "was forever trying to put words in the mouth of his taciturn spouse. He had a detrimental effect on Anastasia's credibility. His wife's peculiarities were abetted and magnified by his even greater eccentricity, especially as he encouraged her penchant to repeat stories."[52] Jack was fascinated by conspiracies, claimants, and royal intrigues, and loved few things more than feeling that he had stumbled upon previously hidden historical mysteries. More to the point, it was Manahan, not his wife, who repeated these bizarre tales, eagerly sharing with newspapers and magazines his latest "discoveries"; his wife usually sat in silence, occasionally nodding if prompted—if she was present at all, for Jack liked to present his own ideas as a kind of shared revelation.[53]

On August 20, 1979, after several days of serious illness, Mrs. Manahan collapsed in pain and was rushed to Charlottesville's Martha Jefferson Hospital. "She obviously needed to be operated on," recalled Dr. Richard Shrum, "but she was in such bad shape I was scared that we'd kill her giving her an anesthetic." Finally, though, Shrum was forced to act: he found an ovarian tumor that had blocked her intestine and resulted in a dangerous case of gangrene. He removed the tumor and nearly a foot of the infected bowel tissue.[54] Although the wound itself healed, Mrs. Manahan never really recovered; suffering from severe arthritis, she was soon confined to a wheelchair, increasingly retreating into a world of confused infirmity.[55]

Unable to walk, she still insisted on joining Jack as he drove back and forth across Charlottesville on his innumerable errands. She would sit in the front seat of their rather battered station wagon for hours at a time, seemingly impervious to the discomfort; occasionally, though, when she felt well and thought that her husband had been gone too long, she poked her head out the window, screaming, "Hans! Hans!" in her weakened voice until he returned. Passersby stopped and stared, uncertain what to do; even when they had returned home, she often continued to stubbornly sit in the car, shouting at Jack. To the concerned questions of neighbors, though, Jack usually offered a shrug and a smile. "Oh, you know those Russians!" he would say. "They're never happy unless they're miserable."[56]

"I have lived much too long," she once told Ruffin. "It is time to leave this shell. I hope that the next time you come here, poor Anastasia will be cold. And when you hear that poor Anastasia is no more, think of me as happy, because then I will suffer no more." The last time he saw her, she whispered, "Pray, pray very much for my death."[57] After a lifetime of turmoil, she was simply worn out, but the miserable conditions in which she lived became increasingly dangerous. By the fall of 1983, living conditions in the house on University Circle had deteriorated so badly that the authorities once again stepped in after both of the Manahans fell ill, unlikely victims of Rocky Mountain spotted fever. A hearing in a Charlottesville circuit court found Manahan incapable of sufficiently caring for his wife, and the judge appointed a local attorney, William Preston, as her legal guardian. Preston found Mrs. Manahan's mental state so alarming that on November 28 he had her committed to the psychiatric ward of the Blue Ridge Hospital for observation.[58]

The captivating fairytale of the tragic, lost princess was but a distant memory, but the story was still not yet finished, for the very next day Manahan abducted his frail wife from the hospital, launching a media frenzy about the "missing grand duchess" and a multistate police search for the pair. It took four days to find them, living in their broken-down station wagon off a country road, and a dehydrated and confused Mrs. Manahan was returned to the hospital ward.[59] It was to be the last adventure in a lifetime of almost unbelievable twists of fate. A court found that while Mrs. Manahan was most likely suffering from senile dementia, she could not legally be kept in a psychiatric facility, and so Preston placed her in a privately run nursing home. The woman whose story had intrigued the world and spawned countless books and motion pictures was a mere shadow of her former self, emaciated and confused, her weight barely sixty pounds, her once-vibrant blue eyes clouded as she slipped into a haze of the unknown.[60]

Manahan visited her daily, decorating her room with photographs of the imperial family, but on January 28, 1984, a possible stroke sent her to Martha Jefferson Hospital.[61] Just two weeks later, at 11:40 A.M. on Sunday, February 12, 1984, she died, at peace, the years of intrigue finally behind her. Manahan later insisted that his wife had been murdered, claiming that either members of British intelligence or operatives from the KGB had disconnected her oxygen tube.[62] In fact, she had died of pneumonia. Her death certificate duly recorded her name as "Anastasia Nikolaievna Manahan," born June 5/18, 1901, at Peterhof in Russia; listed her parents as Tsar Nicholas II and Alexandra of Hesse-Darmstadt; and gave her occupation as "Royalty." In death, the commonwealth of Virginia granted her the identity she had claimed for sixty-three years.[63]

Many years before, when she was still lucid, the claimant decided that she wished to be cremated, and this was carried out on the afternoon of her death at a nearby funeral home. Two days later, her memorial service took place at the Chapel of the University of

Anderson's death certificate.

Virginia in Charlottesville. Some three hundred friends, neighbors, and supporters crowded the structure, which Manahan had decorated with Romanov photographs and brass altar candelabra bedecked with imperial double-headed eagles. Although she had long before abandoned organized religion, an Episcopal clergyman conducted the service, though it was the widower who commanded most attention, offering up what he termed "historical comments" on the Romanovs and on his late wife.[64] Like so much of her storied life, even the memorial quickly became a circus as Jack railed against those he termed her "former friends" in Europe who had abandoned her and against the Romanov family, for "rejecting Anastasia"; and, in a truly odd twist, blamed Queen Elizabeth II for his wife's misfortunes, proclaiming that the British monarch was "an international drug dealer."[65]

For a few months, Manahan kept his late wife's ashes in an urn. He faced some difficulty in carrying out her final wish, that her ashes be interred at Seeon. In 1934, the Nazi government forced the Leuchtenberg family to sell the estate to authorities in Berlin, though they preserved burial rights to the small, enclosed yard surrounding the Chapel of St. Walburg. Here, beneath a tomb he himself had designed before his death in 1929, rested Georg, duke of Leuchtenberg, joined by his wife, Olga, in 1953. Duchess Catherine of Leuchtenberg, widow of Duke Dimitri, protested the claimant's interment. Neither she nor her husband had ever believed she was Anastasia, and did not want a woman they regarded as an impostor buried alongside exiled members

Anderson's grave in the churchyard of the Chapel of St. Walburg at Seeon.

of Russia's aristocracy. Then, too, she objected that cremation was contrary to the teachings of the Orthodox Church.[66] It was left to the ever-loyal Prince Friedrich of Saxe-Altenburg to see to the details, and not until he provided a sworn statement offering assurances that Duchess Olga had personally granted permission did the Catholic officials who maintained the churchyard agree to Manahan's request.[67]

Monday, June 18, 1984, was a beautiful, warm, late spring day at Seeon. Snowcapped Alps glistened in the distance, and a gentle breeze from the Klostersee kissed the shading elms as a contingent of cars approached the former abbey. The procession halted at the high walls overgrown with wisteria and honeysuckle surrounding the small Chapel of St. Walburg, and a group of black-clad mourners left their cars, passing the open wrought-iron gates to enter the cemetery. It was a curious assemblage: Jack, looking confused and sobbing as he clutched a small, heart-shaped locket containing his late wife's hair; Prince Friedrich of Saxe-Altenburg; Princess Ferdinand von Schoenaich-Carolath, widow of Kaiser Wilhelm II's stepson; Ian Lilburn; Brien Horan; and a small group of German aristocrats bearing titles made obsolete in the aftermath of the First World War. The service coincided, not by accident, with what would have been Grand Duchess Anastasia's eighty-third birthday. The mourners gathered in a semicircle around a small depression set against the cemetery's eastern wall, heads bowed in prayer. No priest presided, and when a few words had been said, the group left the burial ground, strolling past its lines of marble monuments and wrought-iron crosses peeking from fragrant clusters of roses. Behind them, decorating the wall above the space where the box of ashes had been interred, was a memorial plaque adorned with a Russian Orthodox cross and an inscription selected by Prince Friedrich: "Our Heart Is Unquiet Until It Rests With You, Lord."[68] Here, beneath a tombstone emblazoned with the name Anastasia, the most famous royal claimant in history rests for eternity.

PART THREE

FRANZISKA

18

The Fairy Tale Crumbles

T HE MYSTERY LINGERED, it deepened; with Anastasia Manahan's death in 1984, it passed from the shadows of modern myth to legend, the solution to her true identity beyond the reach of man. She now belonged to a realm of unsolvable intrigue, forever destined to remain a historical question mark. The courts could not resolve her claim, but a few months before her death author Peter Kurth published his biography *Anastasia: The Riddle of Anna Anderson*, a book that did more to enshroud her case in a gauzy veil of probability than any other, such was its popularity and acclaim. And the case Kurth presented, to be sure, was inarguably compelling, though he later added a comment that must have echoed the views of many: "In a way, however, I am glad that Anastasia's case has never been proved past dispute."[1]

And so it seemed destined to remain. Then, in April 1989—five years after Anna Anderson's death—a Moscow newspaper published a story that shocked the world: a decade earlier, a trio of Soviet investigators had obtained a statement by Yakov Yurovsky, leader of the squad that had presumably executed the Romanovs. In it, he described not only the horrific massacre at the Ipatiev House but also how, contrary to what Sokolov and twentieth-century history had believed, the victims' bodies had not been chopped apart, burned, and dissolved in acid, but instead had been buried. The mass grave, in the old Koptyaki Forest, had been found a decade earlier, but not until the advent of Mikhail Gorbachev's glasnost had the men dared to reveal their sensational discovery.

Memorial marker at the Romanov mass grave in Pig's Meadow outside Ekaterinburg.

Two years passed, years filled with questions and speculation as wild as anything in the Anderson saga, before the grave was finally exhumed. And then, a surprise: there were remains: shattered bones, fragmented skeletons, and hollow-eyed skulls with gaping bullet holes, but only for nine of the eleven victims who had presumably been executed that summer night in 1918. Russian and American forensic and anthropological experts all agreed that thirteen-year-old Tsesarevich Alexei was clearly missing from the grave, as was one of his four sisters. Which sister, though, was a matter of controversy. Most Russian scientists insisted, based on photographic comparison of archival photographs to the terribly damaged, reconstructed skulls, that Marie had not been found; forensic, dental, and anthropological evidence, though, convinced two American teams that Anastasia was missing. Suddenly, the most persistent of twentieth-century royal legends again danced across the world's imagination, the decades of hope and belief propelled into the realm of undeniable probability.

The controversy over which grand duchess was missing would never be settled, but other mysteries in the Romanov case were gradually peeled away as it became increasingly clear that the Koptyaki remains were indeed those of five members of the imperial family and the four retainers who had perished with them. The final proof came when femurs recovered from the grave were subjected to genetic analysis by an international team lead by Dr. Peter Gill of the British Home Office's Forensic Science Service Laboratory. Humans carry two types of DNA: nuclear, and mitochondrial or mtDNA. Derived in equal measure from both parents and unique to each individual, nuclear DNA is considered the most reliable and stable of genetic indicators, being able to conclusively establish or refute identity. Mitochondrial DNA, on the other hand, is shared within families, passed through the maternal line from mothers to their children in a genetic chain unbroken for centuries; while it can exclude a genetic relationship, it can only confirm, with varying degrees of probability, common descent. A blood sample was donated by Prince Philip, duke of Edinburgh: scientists found that he, as a direct matrilineal descendant of the empress's mother, Princess Alice, and of her grandmother Queen Victoria, shared the same mitochondrial DNA pattern found in the remains of Alexandra and three of her daughters. The remains of Nicholas II were identified by comparing genetic samples donated by several relatives who shared his same matrilineal descent, and also by comparing his profile to that of his younger brother George, who had died in 1899.[2]

The science of DNA had solved one of the century's greatest mysteries—what had happened to the Romanovs—but could it solve another? Could it finally establish the true identity of Anna Anderson? The prospect seemed unlikely: genetic material would be needed, and her body had been cremated following her death in 1984. Syd Mandelbaum, a Long Island geneticist, took the first steps toward solving the conundrum. "I had the idea that anyone who lived in one town," he says, "would have needed to go to the hospital there. I thought perhaps the hospital in Charlottesville might therefore have biological material they could share, that would allow for DNA testing." On learning of the 1979 operation to remove a bowel obstruction, Mandelbaum contacted Martha Jefferson Hospital; his inquiries, though, met a dead end when a representative told him that the hospital held none of the claimant's genetic material.[3]

Others, too, shared Mandelbaum's idea, and soon enough the administration at Martha Jefferson Hospital was sorting through inquiries from several fronts; this burst of interest apparently spawned a more thorough search of the facility's holdings. Penny Jenkins, director of medical records for the hospital, soon found that Martha Jefferson did indeed possess pathology specimens taken during Mrs. Manahan's 1979 operation: five inches of the gangrenous bowel tissue, preserved, sectioned into one-inch segments, treated with formalin, and sealed inside paraffin blocks. Assigned an anonymous patient number to preserve medical privacy, the samples had been stored in the hospital's pathology archives.[4]

Discovery of the samples spawned an intense and bizarre legal battle over their potential genetic testing, a development entirely in keeping with the decades of controversy over the claimant's case. Jack Manahan died in 1990, but author James Blair Lovell received legal authority over the tissue from one of his cousins.[5] Objecting, on behalf of German producer Maurice Philip Remy, was a man named Willi Korte: Remy was making a documentary on the claimant and wanted to commission his own DNA tests.[6] Korte hired a Washington, D.C., legal firm to oppose Lovell's petition, and joined forces with the Russian Nobility Association, an émigré group based in New York that insinuated itself into the case.[7]

Illness forced Lovell out of the suit, and in the fall of 1993 retired international finance lawyer Richard Schweitzer, married to Gleb Botkin's daughter Marina, became involved in the case. "For us," he explained, "having known Anastasia and Jack Manahan all those years, it is a matter of family honor to try our utmost to fulfill her lifelong wish to have her identity as the Grand Duchess legally recognized."[8] Schweitzer, who wanted Gill to test the samples, filed a petition with the Sixteenth Judicial Circuit Court of Virginia on behalf of his wife, asking that the tissue be released to Gill's facility for genetic testing.[9] Six months of legal arguments followed; nothing was more bizarre, though, than the petition lodged by an Idaho woman calling herself Ellen Margarete Therese Kailing-Romanov, who insisted that she was the product of a 1937 liaison between Anderson and Prince Heinrich of Reuss. She wanted access to the tissue to validate her own claim, a claim that—like so much in the story—came in a haze of publicity and disappeared just as quickly.[10]

In May 1994 the court awarded custodianship of Anderson's tissue to a third party suggested by Schweitzer, and Botkin's daughter and son-in-law arranged for testing. On June 19, 1994, Dr. Peter Gill arrived in Charlottesville to collect a sample from the tissue. British producer Julian Nott, filming a television documentary on the case, recorded the process as five small segments were cut from the tissues preserved in paraffin blocks, transferred into sterile containers, and sealed. To avoid any contamination or challenges to the chain of custody, the samples remained with Gill until he placed them in protective storage at the Forensic Science Service Laboratory in Great Britain.[11]

While legal arguments had temporarily entangled the disposition of the Charlottesville tissue sample, another source of the claimant's genetic material came to light. In September 1990, a North Carolina woman named Susan Grindstaff Burkhart learned that a Chapel Hill bookstore, the Avid Reader, had purchased much of John Manahan's library following his death. Passionately interested in the Anastasia case since age twelve, she was looking through the boxes of books in the store's basement one afternoon when she found several samples of Mrs. Manahan's hair. One large clump, apparently collected from a hairbrush, was tucked inside an empty wine box packed in a box of books; other strands, cut locks of hair, were found in several of the books, held in tiny florist card envelopes inscribed by Manahan with "Anastasia's Hair" and various dates. She purchased the volumes containing the envelopes, along with some of the large clump of hair, for $20; the remaining hair was sold to Lovell. When Grindstaff Burkhart closely examined the larger hair sample, she found that some of the hair still had roots attached, as if it had been pulled out of the head when being brushed. She discussed this with her husband, who worked in a DNA research laboratory, wondering if it would be possible to extract a usable genetic profile from the follicular strands; with this idea in mind, she carefully preserved the samples under sterile conditions in a safety deposit box. When the genetic identification of the Koptyaki remains was under way, royal genealogist and author Marlene Eilers put Grindstaff Burkhart in touch with Anderson's biographer Peter Kurth, who arranged for the hair to be tested. Kurth traveled to Durham, North Carolina, in September 1992 to personally receive the hair sample, which Grindstaff Burkhart recalls was "prepared under strict procedures by a DNA researcher" at the lab where her husband was employed. Several strands of hair were taken to Dr. Gill at the Forensic Science Service, and six other strands were sent to Syd Mandelbaum; Mandelbaum, in turn, arranged for these strands to be tested by Dr. Mark Stoneking and Dr. Terry Melton of Pennsylvania State University.[12] "My only hope in all of this," Grindstaff Burkhart recalls," was to help prove Anna Anderson's claim."[13]

Over the next few months, three independent scientific institutions analyzed samples of Anderson's genetic material. In the United Kingdom, Dr. Gill and his colleagues at the Forensic Science Service Laboratory tested two tissue samples derived from different paraffin blocks preserved at Martha Jefferson Hospital, as well as strands of the claimant's hair from the large sample found by Susan Grindstaff Burkhart. The tissue samples were degraded, but Gill and his colleagues obtained usable profiles; testing established that they had come from a female. The profile of the tissue also matched that of the hair, confirming all had come from the same person. Now the question turned on whether Anderson matched the Koptyaki remains. Gill and his team derived a nuclear DNA sequence for the bowel tissue through the use of short tandem repeats, or STRs, to determine parentage. But when this profile was compared with that found in the remains of Nicholas II and Empress Alexandra, and confirmed in those of their three recovered daughters, it differed in four places; a difference of only two genetic loci excludes the possibility of descent. This mismatch, Gill's team noted, was "inconsistent with the hypothesis" that Anderson was a child of Nicholas II and Empress Alexandra.[14]

Next, the scientists analyzed the mitochondrial DNA profile derived from the bowel tissue and the hair sample against the mitochondrial DNA sequence of the duke of Edinburgh that had been found in the exhumed remains of Alexandra and three of her daughters. This revealed six discrepancies between the Hessian sequence and Anderson.[15] These two results were definitive. Nuclear DNA excluded the possibility that Anderson was a child of Nicholas and Alexandra, while deviations in the mitochondrial profile of the tissue and hair samples from the Hessian sequence precluded matrilineal descent from the empress. Scientifically, the woman known as Anna Anderson could not have been Anastasia.

Concurrent with the tests at the Forensic Science Service Laboratory, Syd Mandelbaum arranged for Dr. Mark Stoneking of Pennsylvania State University, assisted by his colleague Dr. Terry Melton, to test six strands of the clump hair discovered by Susan Grindstaff Burkhart.[16] Only mitochondrial DNA testing was done on these samples; the genetic profile for the clump hair, down to the same six mismatches, was identical to those found by Gill. These tests again precluded the possibility that Anderson had been Anastasia.[17]

The Armed Forces Institute of Pathology in Maryland, under the direction of Dr. Victor Weedn, performed a third test, commissioned, like the work of Gill, by Richard and Marina Schweitzer. This was meant to provide additional genetic reinforcement in the case and to ensure that all of the profiles derived remained consistent from facility to facility. Weedn examined new slices from the bowel tissue at Martha Jefferson Hospital and compared their mitochondrial DNA profile to that derived by both the Forensic Science Service Laboratory and by Pennsylvania State University. This new sequence matched those previously established for the tissue and for the two different hair samples. Again, the six mismatches, consistent in all of the samples, precluded any possibility that Anna Anderson had been Anastasia.[18]

After half a century of arguments, of contradictory recognitions and denunciations, of warring photographic comparisons and handwriting analyses, these DNA tests conclusively and damningly overturned popular belief: Fraulein Unbekannt, Anastasia Tchaikovsky, Anna Anderson, Anastasia Manahan—whatever name the world's most famous royal pretender had answered to, the one to which she had absolutely no claim was that of Grand Duchess Anastasia Nikolaievna of Russia. The bowel tissue examined by Gill and his colleagues genetically matched different samples examined by Weedn; the follicular hair from the envelopes found in the books was identical to the clump hair from the wine box; and the profile for the two different hair samples matched that derived for the bowel tissue. The three laboratories, working independently and relying on different samples, had achieved a uniform genetic profile for Anderson, one that excluded the possibility that she had been a child of Nicholas and Alexandra.

But if not Anastasia, who had she really been? Since the late 1920s, there had been rumors, assertions, accusations, and declarations—all rejected, mocked, ignored, or dismissed by Anderson's supporters—that she was actually a woman named Franziska Schanzkowska, described as a Polish factory worker who had gone missing in Berlin sometime at the beginning of 1920. Some of her opponents had taken it all quite seriously: in his *Fausse Anastasie*, Gilliard simply described it as accepted fact, but the stories that trickled out to the public were unconvincing, the evidence in favor of this unlikely solution so contradictory that even many who completely rejected the idea that Anderson was Anastasia refused to consider this a viable possibility. "Whoever she is," commented Princess Nina Georgievna, "she is no Polish peasant."[19]

However unlikely it seemed, though, Franziska Schanzkowska was the only actual identity—other than Anastasia—that had ever been ascribed to Anderson. Knowing this, producer Julian Nott located members of the missing girl's family and obtained a blood sample from her great-nephew Karl Maucher. This was sent to Gill's team: if Anderson failed to match the profile for Anastasia, a comparison with the Maucher sample might conclusively confirm or refute the Schanzkowska story. When the first results showed no match to the Hessian profile, therefore, the Forensic Science Service Laboratory analyzed the Maucher sample against that found in the Anderson tissue and hair. Maucher was the son of Margarete Ellerik, daughter of Franziska's sister Gertrude; as such, he and the missing Polish factory worker would share the same mitochondrial DNA profile. And this is exactly what Gill and his team found: five identical matches between the sequence established for Anderson's tissue and hair samples and the blood donated by Maucher. While two such mismatches could refute a genetic relationship, mitochondrial DNA could not prove identity; the most that Gill could say was that "Karl Maucher may be a maternal relative" of the claimant.[20]

Working independently of these scientists for German producer Maurice Philip Remy, Dr. Charles Ginther of the University of California at Berkeley obtained and sequenced a blood sample donated by Margarete Ellerik, Maucher's mother. The resulting mitochondrial DNA profile proved identical to that of her son and to that found in the Anderson tissue and hair samples.[21] But, with a genetic link established, the question of just how likely it was that Anderson had in fact been Schanzkowska came down to a statistical analysis contrasting the obtained profile against sequences collected in genetic databases. The profile shared by Anderson and Maucher, Gill found, was extremely rare—so rare that it did not appear in any database they examined. This rarity strengthened the odds that the two were indeed related. The tests undertaken by Stoneking and Melton of Pennsylvania State University established that the hair sample they examined matched the hair analyzed in Great Britain; the profiles for these samples of hair, as they now found, also matched the Maucher and Ellerik blood sequence, as did the bowel tissue tested by Weedn at the Armed Forces Institute of Pathology. Gill estimated the probability of a random match between Anderson and the Maucher profile at "less than one in three hundred" and placed the odds that the woman known as Anna Anderson had been Franziska Schanzkowska at roughly 98.5%.[22]

In a case filled with extraordinary twists of fate, this was the most extraordinary of all, this genetic turn, this intrusion of modern science into the Edwardian fairy tale. There was the bowel tissue, it was true, but alone it offered only a single compelling strike against Anderson's claim: it was the hair discovered by Susan Grindstaff Burkhart that, in many ways, provided the final, undeniable proof. "I was devastated when the results came back," she recalls. "This was not how the fairy tale was supposed to end."[23] Those who had known the Manahans in Charlottesville had deplored the disintegration of their house, the accumulation of clutter, Jack's well-known habit of saving anything and everything connected to his wife as a historic artifact. And yet, in the end, his diligence had unwittingly helped solve one of the twentieth century's greatest mysteries.

The world learned the news, learned that a few millimeters of preserved tissue and loose strands of hair had destroyed the most enduring of royal legends. But in the aftermath of scientific certainty, a certainty that contradicted nearly everything the world had been led to believe about Anderson's case, came the questions: Who was Franziska Schanzkowska? How had she managed to seem so convincing? How had she apparently fooled so many people who had known the real Anastasia? How had she come by her impressive roll of asserted memories, her linguistic skills, her scars? The DNA verdict did nothing to address these issues. The questions would remain unanswered.

Until now.

19

A Girl from the Provinces

A COLD, FROZEN LANDSCAPE stretched out as far as the eye could see: meadows green six months earlier and dotted with apple and cherry trees now blanketed in snow; forested hills rising against the dark sky; lonely, reed-rimmed lakes fringed by the white-frosted spikes of fir and pine trees. Now, this December evening, the northern edge of the Lippusch Forest, straddling the border of Pomerania and West Prussia, was still, unwelcoming, silent but for the wild boar and deer that crept over the marshes and bogs, nosing through the drifts to lap at the icy rivers trickling into the glassy lakes.[1]

Spidery wisps of smoke, fueled by peat burning in open hearths, curled over the cluster of little farmhouses and huts—sixteen in all—comprising the "noble village of Borowilhas," a tiny hamlet of 117 that clustered along a single road, muddy in spring and fall, dusty in summer, and now nearly impassable with snow.[2] And yet figures moved about, harnessing horses and oxen in the bitter cold, for this was Thursday, December 24, 1896—Christmas Eve—and the people who lived in Borowilhas, conservative and Catholic, were off to celebrate. It was a measure of their devotion, for this was a real trek: Borowilhas had no church, and attending Mass meant a journey over the frozen countryside to the little town of Borek, three miles to the north.

And, at one farmhouse, the activity, anticipation, excitement—it was all magnified. It was an old sod building, weathered and worn, divided in two, where "pigs, sheep, and hens," as a later visitor found, lived under the same thatched roof as the inhabitants. There were no comforts: a worn, dangerously crumbling hearth offered the only warmth to stave off the northern winter.[3] Here, just eight days earlier, on Wednesday, December 16, a rotund, middle-aged man and his hard-faced wife had greeted the birth of their first daughter. They may have been Catholic, but the couple, like their neighbors, were first and foremost Kashubians, descendants of Baltic Slavs who had settled in the area sometime in the Middle Ages. This heritage infused nearly every aspect of life: Kashubians kept to themselves, formed their own communities, celebrated their own festivals, practiced their own crafts, sang their own songs, and even spoke their own language.[4] They also knew and respected the centuries-old superstitions, knew that unseen evil lurked in the surrounding forests and must be battled at every turn. Following custom, the new baby would have been wrapped in one of her mother's aprons and a rosary placed around her neck to ward off any goblins or vampires waiting outside the house, and the heart of a freshly killed black cat hung in the fireplace to counter any hexes cast by a witch.[5]

Kashubian tradition also dictated that a new infant be baptized on the first Sunday following his or her birth, lest the child fall victim to

Birth registry for Franziska Schanzkowska.

the nefarious influences waiting to corrupt the innocent.[6] But the deep snow of 1896 made this an impossibility, and the parents, despite the superstitions, waited until this Christmas Eve to do their religious duty. And so they bundled themselves up and set out with their neighbors across the frozen countryside to Borek's seventeenth-century Church of St. Mary. Here, as candles burned and the congregation sang, the baby was christened after the fourteenth-century St. Frances of Rome, received into the Roman Catholic faith as Franziska Anna Czenstkowski.[7] Thus, in circumstances far removed from the glittering pageantry that welcomed the 1901 christening of Grand Duchess Anastasia Nikolaievna, began the adventures of Franziska Schanzkowska, Anna Anderson, the most famous royal claimant in history.

PRINCESS NINA GEORGIEVNA was correct in one respect: Franziska Schanzkowska was no Polish peasant. The place of her birth, today called Borowy Las, sits squarely in modern Poland, but in 1896 the entire region belonged to Germany: Borowilhas lay in West Prussia, just a few miles east of the border with the German province of Pomerania. Polish forces had occupied the land, as had Russian settlers, the Teutonic Knights, and invading Prussian and Swedish soldiers before Berlin finally seized control in the late eighteenth century.[8] The Czenstkowski family, as Franziska's ancestors spelled their name, did, though, have ties, however tenuous, to the old Polish kingdom. In 1683, King Jan III Sobieski had raised several members of the family to the *drobna szlachta*, or petty Polish nobility, after they helped his

The countryside around Borowilhas.

army repel forces of the Ottoman Empire at the Battle of Vienna.[9] The reward was not uncommon, but it gave the family certain rights not enjoyed by ordinary peasants and later allowed them to use the honorific "von" before their surname as a mark of their status. With the raise in rank came a minor grant of land in the area then known as Kartuzy, the marshy countryside that in the nineteenth century edged the borders of Pomerania and West Prussia.[10]

Did these past noble trappings somehow influence Franziska in later making her claim? Was it all some misguided attempt to capture what had been lost? For lost it had been: by the time of her birth, whatever privileges had once enveloped the von Czenstkowski family were gone. They still had the thirty-acre farm in Borowilhas, originally given to them by the king when they were ennobled, along with its sod house in which Franziska was born, but not much else.[11] Since his birth in 1842, her father, Anton, had struggled, struggled in Borowilhas, struggled during his mandatory three years with the Prussian Army, struggled to find a place for himself. Embittered by his lot in life, said to have harbored a passing interest in socialism, he had dropped the honorific "von" from his surname as an unwelcome reminder of just how far the family had fallen.[12]

Anton married late: he was fifty-four when Franziska was born. His first wife, Josefina Peek, died in 1892 after two years of marriage; in 1894, he wed twenty-eight-year-old Marianna Wietzke.[13] As far as anyone could tell, it was a marriage of convenient practicalities, for aside from a shared Kashubian heritage, Franziska's parents had little in

Kashubian farmers using a cow to plough their field, turn-of-the-century postcard.

common. Anton was gregarious and carefree, a man who disliked work but enjoyed drinking to excess with his friends; Marianna, in contrast, was an abrasive woman who seems to have left vivid and unfavorable impressions on those she encountered.[14]

Like Anastasia, Franziska grew up with four siblings. She was not her parents' first child: a son, Martin Christian, had been born in November 1895, but he died in infancy, as did another son, Michael, who arrived on Franziska's third birthday, in 1899. Of the others, a second daughter, Gertrude, was born in 1898; Valerian in 1900; Felix in 1903; and Maria Juliana in 1905. Franziska's early life was nomadic, defined by an unsettled restlessness, a succession of gruesome and grueling farms and villages where the family struggled to eke out a living. In 1897, they left Borowilhas, settling in the West Prussian village of Zukovken (now Treuenfelde), some ten miles to the north, where Anton worked as a *tageloehner*, or daily agricultural laborer, just one of the many desperate and dispossessed driven by poverty to indenture themselves to ensure that their families were housed and fed.[15] It was a brutal existence, recorded one critic, ruled "with the rod and the whip," where "drunkenness, theft, idleness, and the most degrading forms of immorality" were common.[16] In 1900, Anton signed a three-year contract with a Pomeranian agricultural estate at Glischnitz, bringing his family with him to work and live; in the spring of 1905, they were in the Pomeranian city of Schwarz Dammerkow (now Czarna Da'brówka); and by 1906 they were working at Gut-Wartenberg, an agricultural estate just outside the Pomeranian town of Bütow (now Bytów).[17]

Then, in 1906, Anton inherited the ancestral thirty-acre holding in Borowilhas; this he sold, purchasing a farm in the Pomeranian town of Hygendorf (now Udorpie), a few miles south of Bütow.[18] At the beginning of the twentieth century some five hundred people lived there, in modest little wood or brick houses set in gardens leading to flat meadows and long, low barns. At one end of the village stood two schools, Catholic and Lutheran churches, an inn, and the usual assortment of markets, bakeries, butchers' shops, blacksmiths, stables, and taverns; at the other sprawled two sawmills that planed trees from the surrounding forests, and a furniture manufacturing plant. The streets—all three of them—were still unpaved as the century began: in summer, clouds of dust swelled in the wake of horses and carts, and in winter they became a muddy morass. Farmers drove herds of cattle through town to pasture, leaving streets clotted with piles of manure rotted until the rains swept them away. The house where Franziska lived is gone now, but it would have followed traditional Kashubian design: a single-story structure of pine logs, the rooms—simply decorated with carved, brightly painted furniture and cheap lithographs—clustered around a massive central chimney. Electricity and running water were unknown; lighting came from candles or oil lamps, while water was carried in from a nearby pump.[19]

How different this all was from the Alexander Palace, from the heritage Franziska later attempted to claim as her own. The farm in Hygendorf erased some of the earlier deprivations, but for Franziska life was still simple, still lean: fields had to be turned and planted in spring for the coming fall harvest; animals had to be fed and watered; the garden tended; water pumped and carried to the house; baskets of logs brought from the woodpile; fires stoked; oil lamps filled, wicks trimmed, and candles replaced; laundry done; the farmhouse cleaned—a dozen little, daily chores comprising Franziska's universe. And at night, like every other Kashubian girl, she would have learned the elaborate, colorful needlework that adorned bodices and shirts—a skill her supporters later took as evidence that she must have been brought up in aristocratic circles for—presumably—who else but an idle aristocrat could devote time to such pursuits?[20]

Such ideas—that hers had been a world defined by few opportunities and even fewer abilities—extended to Franziska's education. It all stemmed from misguided attempts to reconcile preconceptions—sometimes snobbish preconceptions—about the woman erroneously described in the wake of the DNA tests as "a Polish peasant" and the legendary figure of Anna Anderson. A "Polish peasant," or so this reasoning often went, must by definition be incapable of assimilating the myriad of information the claimant revealed over the years. Even her sister Gertrude quarreled with this simplistic mischaracterization: "Franziska," she declared, "wasn't stupid." Even in grammar school she far outshone the rest of her family. "Her reports were better than mine and those of my other siblings," Gertrude added.[21]

Later, much would be made of a single comment by Otto Meyer, one of Franziska's teachers in Hygendorf. She had been, he said, "rather more limited than intelligent."[22] This was certainly descriptive, but was it accurate? Franziska began her education in 1902, at a grammar school in Glischnitz where her family was then living; continued when her parents moved to Schwarz Dammerkow; and ended her primary education at the village school in Hygendorf.[23] Then, in autumn 1908, she entered the equivalent of seventh grade at Hygendorf's Upper School, following the usual regimen of arithmetic, composition, German, German history, natural sciences, and religion. Here, as Otto Meyer's own son Richard recalled, Franziska "always did very good in school. She spoke well, and learned everything she could. She often received recognition for her performance from the School Rector."[24] Another schoolmate, Charlotte Meyer, remembered her as "an extremely good student," while her sister Gertrude related that Franziska had "learned quickly," that her school reports "were excellent," and that she continued her education in autumn 1910 on entering the Abbey School at Tannen-bei-Bütow, half a mile north of Hygendorf. Franziska was such a good student, in fact, that she completed her ninth-grade studies in fewer than six months, winning a certificate of graduation far ahead of her classmates.[25]

It certainly wasn't proof that Franziska was particularly brilliant, but her continued education, the memories of her sister and her classmates, and her early graduation all undermine Otto Meyer's description of her as more "limited than intelligent." Without doubt she possessed a good memory and—more important to her later claim—a clear aptitude for languages. Her first language was Kashubian, used by 90 percent of those in the areas around Borowilhas and Hygendorf.[26] Kashubian was a linguistic peculiarity: passed down from the Baltic Slavs who had settled in Pomerania, it was part of the Western Slavic Group of languages but had been heavily influenced over the centuries by inclusion of German, Swedish, and Polish words and phrases, a mixture that made it distinct and often unintelligible to outsiders.[27] Was it Kashubian that German-speakers later heard Franziska mutter in her sleep, the strange, Slavic-sounding language that some took for Russian?

"Polish," the duke of Leuchtenberg once insisted of Anna Anderson in a letter to Olga Alexandrovna, "she absolutely does not speak, nor can she understand it."[28] But, as with so many other things concerning the claimant, the duke was wrong, for Polish was Franziska's second language. This wasn't surprising for the area in which she lived; indeed, given that 80 percent of Kashubians in the area spoke Polish as their second language, it would have been extremely odd had Franziska not been among them.[29] Kashubians, noted a nineteenth-century ethnographic study of the region, easily understood Polish, and regularly read Polish newspapers and magazines.[30]

Franziska, recalled two of her siblings, learned Polish early, though her brother Felix thought that she had spoken very little of the language.[31] A few childhood friends later said that she had been fluent, while in 1927 her mother, Marianna, was using Polish as her everyday language.[32] Franziska clearly knew the language. In 1921 Dalldorf nurse Thea Malinovsky joked and chatted in Polish with Fraulein Unbekannt: rather confusingly, she thought that the patient both understood "some of what I said" and "did not speak the language." If the latter was true, why did Malinovsky continuously use the language with Franziska?[33] Then there were stories, none terribly compelling, that during her stay with the von Kleists Franziska had cried out in Polish.[34] It became a point of contention with those who supported Franziska's claim to be

Anastasia, this familiarity with Polish, presumably in the belief that it explained her understanding of spoken Russian and her inability to reply in the language.[35]

Then there was German, Franziska's third language. She spoke, said her brother Felix, "good German." At first this was Plattedeutsch, or Low German, the common German spoken by most middle and lower classes. In school, though, she learned Hochdeutsch, or High German; this was the more refined German employed in Berlin and throughout the provinces in official institutions. In the early years of her claim, at least, Franziska impressed everyone—Malinovsky, Nobel, Rathlef-Keilmann—with her "impeccable," "very well chosen," "formal," and "good" German.[36] Only later, when it became apparent that Anastasia had not been nearly as fluent in the language, did Franziska's capabilities in German suddenly and inexplicably deteriorate.

Franziska's secondary education, unique in her family, was not the only curiosity in these years. Anton, recalled Richard Meyer, doted on Franziska, spoiled her openly, and "treated her differently" than her siblings, and even his own wife. It was a bit of indulgence so obvious that even the neighbors whispered of it. Marianna and the other children wore clothing she made; Franziska, though, had pretty dresses, hats, and shoes. "All of her things," said Meyer, purchased by Anton, were from "the better shops" in Bütow.[37] Franziska, her sister Gertrude recalled, hated the regular agricultural work—plowing, planting, and harvesting—imposed by farm life, so Anton simply excused her from the tasks he expected of his other children. Thus free, she would disappear with a book. "I often saw her reading," Gertrude said.[38]

It all took a toll within the family. Franziska, Richard Meyer remembered, confused her siblings; she was somehow alienated from them, and they in turn "treated her as an oddity."[39] Anton, Meyer noted, "Did no work. Rather, he was always in the taverns, carousing and getting drunk."[40] He was inebriated so often, apparently, that his neighbors in Hygendorf openly referred to him as the *Dorftrinker* (village drinker).[41] And increasingly Marianna seemed to despise her husband, and her eldest daughter, Franziska, too; there were loud arguments accompanied by Marianna's hysterical, screamed accusations, scenes so nasty, so frequent, and so public that village children greeted her appearance with cries of "Witch!"[42]

This blatant indulgence of Franziska, the alcoholic father, the embittered wife and resentful mother—what did they all mean? Hygendorf was no different from any other small village: neighbors delighted in gossip, and rumors spread through the streets like mud in the heavy spring rains. And the rumors that later surfaced hinted at possible incest.[43] There was, to be sure, nothing definitive, though a weighty and terrible collection of circumstantial evidence lends some support to such a grim hypothesis. Incest often occurred in provincial families with lower economic and educational opportunities. Most abusers were fathers preying on their eldest daughters. The fathers were often alcoholics, believed themselves marginalized by society, and shared little intimacy with their wives, who tended to be the dominant marital partner. Abuse most often occurred well into a marriage, after the wife had given birth to multiple children and came to be viewed as less sexually desirable than her younger daughters. Fathers who abused often favored and indulged their victims, seeking to win compliance and affection through manipulation; mothers, on the other hand, often had fractured relationships with their abused daughters, as if blaming them for their own victimization.[44]

This catalog of circumstances echoes the few known facts of the highly charged emotional triangle among Anton, Marianna, and Franziska, and there was more. Victims of incest often become reclusive, abandoning previous friendships and suffering significant changes in personality and behavior as they struggle with profound emotional wounds. With the most sacred bonds of trust shattered, and unable to escape a hostile and brutalizing environment, victims may withdraw, attempting to dissociate themselves from traumatic experiences. The creation of a "safe place," a new, alternative reality promising eventual salvation, brings temporary comfort, though years of guilt, shame, anger, and repression often later surface and plague adult survivors in the form of severe emotional disorders.[45]

And this, at least, is precisely what happened with Franziska in these years. Not only was there the inexplicable favoritism by her father, and a growing strain with her mother, but also her entire personality abruptly changed. Soon, recalled her friend Martha Schrock, Franziska distanced herself from her former circle of acquaintances; she took no interest in their usual pursuits, in dances at the village grange, in flirtations with the sons of local farmers. Instead, Schrock said, "she displayed a pretentious manner" in the way she acted, as if she were no longer part of this ordinary world.[46] "She had nothing in common with the young people of the village," remembered Richard Meyer; the differences were so noticeable, he said, that even her friends and neighbors used to talk about it, and "wondered why such a person as Franziska was born to such a family."[47] Her behavior, he added, "was affected, though without any impression of grace."[48] It became a common theme running through the few descriptions of the teenaged Franziska: she wanted nothing to do with her family or with her former friends, and seemed focused on isolating herself, on envisioning herself in "better circles," on escaping the world around her.[49] Gertrude later took issue with such ideas. "I wouldn't say that Franziska was especially stuck up," she declared, "or that she put on airs." She termed her "a girl, like all other girls."[50] Yet even Gertrude qualified this with the word "especially," suggesting that others had been correct in their assessments.

This was the strange young woman, withdrawn, at odds with her mother, an anomaly to her siblings, consumed with escape, who became an enigma even to those who knew her in Hygendorf. Whatever the truth about the ugly whispers, whatever circumstances shaped her personality, whatever problems plagued her, Franziska was a lonely, confused, and conflicted figure: at best, she was caught between the world of her birth and her aspirations, between the realities of Hygendorf and the possibilities her education revealed. She seemed disconnected, apart, at war with the arrogance and fragility that later dominated her character.

Then, in 1911, just as Franziska completed her secondary education, Anton fell ill. Whether this was a relief or a worry, the practicalities were the same, as he took to his bed, unable to walk, increasingly unable to breathe. It was tuberculosis, the same disease later to plague Franziska.[51] On April 13, 1912, Anton died in Hygendorf at age seventy.[52]

Franziska was just fifteen when Anton died. The widowed, forty-six-year-old Marianna now had to care for the farm and for the three youngest children. Perhaps the situation between mother and daughter had already deteriorated beyond repair, or perhaps it was what happened next that irrevocably shattered any last familial feelings. For by now there was a second change in Franziska: provincial Hygendorf, remembered Richard Meyer, now condemned her as "fast," a girl with a forward reputation.[53] Whatever the causes—an improper sexuality or Franziska simply straining against the confines of village life as she matured into a young woman—the result was the same. Meyer termed her "a vulgar, insolent girl," someone he deemed "a man's woman," with all of the insinuations that accompanied such a turn of phrase. "You could," he said on learning of her claim to be Anastasia, "imagine her ending up in the gutter, but between satin sheets? Never!"[54]

This change, this forward manner, reached a crisis in the autumn of 1913 when, after a respectable, year-long period of mourning, the widowed Marianna married a local man named Knopf.[55] A conflict had been simmering between Franziska and her mother, over bitter feelings, over Anton's indulgence of his eldest daughter; with rumors sweeping Hygendorf, Marianna may have worried that Franziska was too closely following in her wayward father's footsteps. That a certain chill, a certain resentment, existed, is clear: there had, Marianna later said, "been enough talk about Franziska" among her neighbors in Hygendorf.[56] The animosity between mother and daughter finally seems to have erupted when Herr Knopf entered the farmhouse. Was Marianna simply tired of Franziska's antics, of her reputation? Or was she perhaps, as was later quietly hinted, worried about the security of her domestic life, about the abilities of either her new husband or her headstrong daughter to withstand temptation?[57]

Within a few months, some accumulated worry, some confluence of events led Marianna to send Franziska away from Hygendorf. It was not Franziska's decision. She may have welcomed the chance to escape provincial life, but there also may have been a sense of exile, of rejection, as if, no matter what had actually happened between Franziska and her father, between Franziska and Herr Knopf, no matter what the perceived threat, no matter the truth of her "fast" reputation, she was being punished, condemned. She had never before left the area surrounding Bütow. Now Franziska was suddenly sent to live in distant Berlin, a naive seventeen-year-old provincial girl with little practical experience or money. She had no relatives, friends, or acquaintances in the German capital, knew no one, in fact, as she anticipated the unknown. On February 2, 1914, she stepped from a third-class train carriage at Berlin's Ostbahnhof, the first steps that would carry her into the pages of history.[58]

20

The Polish Factory Worker

A SINGLE PHOTOGRAPH OF FRANZISKA before 1920 survives. It appears to be an informal scene, snapped against the background of some bucolic woodland. Probably taken in 1916, it shows not a dowdy peasant from the provinces, but a pleasant young woman, slender and petite, with her dark, auburn hair styled around a distinctive face. She wears a print dress adorned with a black bow at the neck, hands clasped in her lap, eyes bright and the hint of a smile on her lips. It is an image of a young woman seemingly full of confidence, her face optimistic, free of any hint of the tragedies that would soon befall her.

Franziska disappeared into the anonymity of metropolitan Berlin, just one of the capital's numerous *minderbemittelte Frauen* (women of meager means).[1] Little is known of her life here; like others armed with more ambition than money, she presumably rented a room in one of Berlin's grim working-class apartments, squalid tenements crowded with impoverished families.[2] Franziska first worked as a maid in a wealthy Berlin household; she soon took a job as a waitress in a *Konditorei*, a local bakery that also offered meals.[3] She went to work, came back to her lodgings, and, when time and money allowed, spent hours at the cinema, watching newsreels and short features produced in Germany or imported from England, France, or America.[4] And she did it all with a new name. Since birth, Franziska had carried the Czenstkowski surname of her ancestors; now, in Berlin, she adopted the more Germanic, feminized, and grammatically incorrect Schanzkowska, perhaps in an effort to abandon her Eastern background. (This change was inconsistent, in that Franziska used the feminized form of her surname, ending with "a," something

278

done in Poland and in Russia but not in Germany. The variations in spelling and confusion over proper usage meant that Franziska's brother Felix was usually referred to by the surname Schanzkowsky, while his daughter, conversely, reverted to von Czenstkowski.) The First World War came, and Berlin began its slow, torturous slide into despair as the British navy attempted to starve the Germans into submission. And in the midst of this daily struggle, Franziska was saddled with a new responsibility: looking after her sixteen-year-old sister Gertrude, who in 1915 had been sent to join her. A Frau Peters rented the sisters a room in her apartment at 17 Neue Hochstrasse, a grim, gray street in north-central Berlin where, as one reporter noted, "simple people live, passing the days of their lives in eternal sameness."[5]

The only known pre-1920 photograph of Franziska Schanzkowska.

Late that summer, Franziska's fortunes improved considerably when she obtained a position at Allgemeine Elektrizitäts Gesellschaft, or AEG (later AEG Farben), a factory in Berlin.[6] Mass conscription and the endless months of fighting had left Berlin's factories undermanned, and women were quickly encouraged to enter the industrial arena. "Every German woman," the state declared, "is a soldier in this economic war."[7] More than three million German women took such industrial jobs in the midst of the First World War, seizing the opportunity for steady employment at a time when insecurity had become a constant companion.[8] Work in munitions factories was one of the

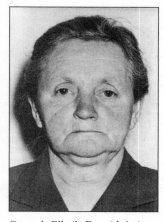

Gertrude Ellerik, Franziska's sister.

few jobs with guaranteed wage increases; steady employment; and, perhaps most important, special ration privileges—extra coupons for flour, meat, and fat at a time when daily life in the city was beginning to fall apart.[9]

The AEG factory where Franziska worked still stands in Berlin, a massive concrete and glass building at 71 Ackerstrasse, not far from the apartment on Neue Hochstrasse; ironically, much of the complex—built atop the remains of a slaughterhouse—had been designed by Peter Behrens, one of Grand Duke Ernst Ludwig's favorite architects.[10] Before the war, the factory produced dynamos and electrical motors; now it manufactured military matériel, including field telephones, airplane motors, machine guns, and munitions.[11] Franziska worked on an assembly line, polishing live grenades, a potentially lethal occupation under often inadequate safety regulations: daily she was exposed to explosives and hazardous chemicals, in an environment where industrial accidents and even deaths were increasingly frequent.[12]

Then came the spring of 1916, "so warm and so bright," recalled one Berliner, that it somehow seemed "out of tune and out of place" in a city "that still thinks it necessary to send hundreds of men each day to their deaths."[13] Franziska had met one of these men, a young

A contemporary view of the former AEG factory in Berlin, where Franziska Schanzkowska worked and where she had her industrial accident in 1916.

soldier training in the German capital, and, accelerated by the urgency of uncertainty, romance soon gave way to an engagement—an engagement perhaps marked by the single photograph of Franziska—before deployment separated the couple.[14] The name of the fiancé is lost to history, but not so his fate. He was sent to fight, not on the Western Front, as has previously been reported, but rather to the Eastern Front, joining in Germany's Galician campaign. In the early summer of 1916, he died after being wounded in combat.[15]

It was a time of war, and such a blow cannot have been unexpected, but the death may have coincided with a crisis of more pressing and personal concern: sometime before 1920, Franziska was pregnant. This much she admitted, though she insisted that she had given birth to Alexander Tchaikovsky's son after he raped her following the Ekaterinburg massacre, a story she may have invented to explain why a surviving Anastasia was no longer a virgin. In 1951, a gynecological examination in Germany revealed a distortion in the shape of her cervical opening; this change occurs naturally when a woman gives birth, but can also stem from a late-term miscarriage or abortion, or from an early, invasive abortion.[16]

Franziska's family later insisted that she had never been pregnant or given birth, something true enough up to February 1914. Circumstantial evidence, though, suggests Franziska may have been pregnant in the summer of 1916, a period coinciding with her only known romantic relationship. There was a sudden and violent break with her sister Gertrude at the time, some argument serious enough that Franziska abruptly moved out of their shared room at 17 Neue Hochstrasse.[17] Gertrude later tried to downplay the incident, admitting only to her sister's sudden departure. "I don't know why she moved," Gertrude insisted, suggesting that perhaps Franziska "thought the rent was too high."[18] This isn't convincing. The sisters had shared a room at Frau Peters's for more than a year; both were employed by AEG at the time; and nothing suggests that Franziska was in any financial difficulty.

The decision was even more curious since Franziska didn't even leave the building. Anna Wingender, the building manager, had a fourth-floor apartment where she lived with two of her daughters, thirteen-year-old Rosa Dorothea, known as Doris, and nine-year-old Luise (the oldest daughter, Kathe, lived elsewhere at the time).[19] Later described as a "loving, maternal type," Anna Wingender now came to the rescue. "I always felt sorry for Franziska," she said, attempting to explain how the young woman from Hygendorf first came to live with her.[20] Even after the move, relations between Franziska and Gertrude were strained; although only three floors separated them, Gertrude never once called on her sister.[21]

Doris Wingender, photographed during the Hamburg civil trial.

And this was all the more inexplicable because, as Gertrude later explained, Franziska suddenly fell ill. She was sick, weak, suffering from fainting spells and an inexplicable case of blood poisoning—symptoms certainly suggestive, first of a possible pregnancy and then of an invasive abortion.[22] It isn't a difficult scenario to envision: Franziska was alone, in the middle of an ongoing war, and facing an uncertain future. It wasn't merely the stigma of being an unwed mother, for by 1916 the public largely viewed all potential mothers as burdensome, unproductive drains on scarce resources; limited rations, it was argued, were best saved for those actively engaged in the war effort.[23] Pregnant women also lost their jobs, and losing a job at AEG meant the loss of privileged ration status as a munitions employee at a particularly desperate time. If Franziska was indeed pregnant, such considerations may have pushed her toward an abortion, a common enough occurrence in the Berlin of 1916 owing to wartime liaisons. Such a theory, at least, reconciles the evidence of her pregnancy with her sudden break with Gertrude, with her inexplicable move to the Wingender apartment, and with her illness and blood poisoning. And this fits in with what Franziska told Doris Wingender: that she had fallen out with her sister because Gertrude had been "telling tales" about her behavior to their mother back in Hygendorf.[24]

That August of 1916, ill, on edge, Franziska returned to work, laboring over grenades to kill Russian soldiers even as, a thousand miles east, Anastasia was busy at Tsarskoye Selo tending to her wounded officers. Then, on August 22, disaster struck. Franziska was on the line polishing a grenade when, suddenly ill, she fell to the concrete floor in a faint. The grenade rolled a short distance; when it hit the foot of the line foreman, it exploded, killing him in a shower of gore.[25]

Later, Franziska would call the Ekaterinburg massacre "an accident, a very bad accident." This was an odd choice of words to describe brutal executions, but an apt depiction of the horror at the AEG factory in 1916, suggesting an inadvertent weaving of personal history with imagined fiction. "I fainted," she said, "everything was blue, and I saw stars dancing and had a great rushing in the ears . . . my dresses were all bloody. All was full of blood."[26]

Was this 1916 accident how Anna Anderson came by the scars she bore in 1920 when pulled from the Landwehr Canal? This, at least, is what her critics believed. Franziska's family, though, contended that she had received no "scars," no "distinguishing marks," no "fractured skull," "no head wounds," and "no injury of any sort" during the explosion.[27] In this they were very nearly correct, for Franziska had been fortunate: in fainting and falling to the floor, she protected herself from the worst effects of the explosion. An internal report on the incident, issued by AEG authorities on August 29, noted that Franziska had suffered only a few superficial cuts from flying shrapnel, to her head and extremities.[28] This much was later confirmed by Gertrude, who could recall only that her sister had been struck "by shrapnel" on her feet, perhaps "on her heels."[29] The wounds observed on Anna Anderson in 1920 stemmed from another, previously unknown incidence of violence.

Though she had been cleared of any intentional responsibility for the accident, Franziska was let go from her job at AEG.[30] Perhaps what next happened was inevitable, a mere continuation of that catastrophic summer of 1916, for Franziska suffered a nervous breakdown. Authorities reportedly found her confused, wandering the streets of Berlin, and took her into protective custody.[31]

Thus began a pattern she would repeat in 1920 following her suicide attempt, for at first Franziska refused to give her name, age, profession, or any details that would clarify her identity. When she finally did submit to questioning, doctors found her suffering from hysteria, depression, and an apparent inability to care for herself. Declared insane on September 19, 1916, and designated a ward of the German state, Franziska was committed, at government expense, to the Berlin-Schöneberg Asylum on the Hauptstrasse in the southwestern quarter of the city, where she would remain through the end of the year.[32]

This 1916 declaration of insanity reveals little about Franziska's actual state of mind. At the time, she was clearly unable to cope with the accumulated tragedies that fell upon her already fragile shoulders. Her life as Anna Anderson was marked by depression, anxiety, hysteria, narcissism, unpredictable changes of mood, and feelings of persecution, a collection of symptoms suggestive of one or more behavioral disorders unknown to the psychiatric world of 1916. In particular, there are indications of a borderline personality struggling with what today might be classified as post-traumatic stress disorder, two conditions also observed with some regularity in adult survivors of incest.[33] But while

Franziska certainly suffered from and displayed a variety of psychological traumas, it is unlikely that she was actually clinically insane, as such a diagnosis would today be applied.

But even if her autumn 1916 breakdown was temporary, Franziska had real reasons for maintaining a certain mien of helplessness. By that winter, daily life for members of Berlin's working class had become an ordeal. Rations were again cut, turnips replaced potatoes, and desperation drove people to cut slabs from horses that had died in the street and feed the meat to their starving families. Electricity was inconsistent, heating unreliable, and cholera and typhus raged through the city.[34] The stay in the hospital relieved Franziska of such worries, and she was not alone: so many people claimed mental illness to win food and shelter that the government repeatedly set up review boards to protect the welfare system from such abuse.[35]

At the beginning of 1917, Franziska was transferred to the State Institute for Welfare and Care in Berlin's Wittenau district, Dalldorf, where she would return in 1920.[36] She stayed for four months. On May 19, 1917, authorities transferred Franziska to Landesheilanstalt Neuruppin, a state asylum some thirty miles northwest of Berlin.[37] Here she was treated for what was officially described as "nervous shock"; her records from Neuruppin recorded her as "quiet." She spent most of her time, the staff noted, sitting silently in her bed and occasionally reading; when confronted by doctors or nurses, however, she often turned to the wall, or tried to cover her head with a sheet, refusing to answer their questions—behavior she repeated at Elisabeth Hospital and at Dalldorf in 1920.[38] Still, there seemed to be nothing particularly wrong with her—she was highly strung and prone to violent changes of mood, but keeping Franziska locked away indefinitely served no point. On October 22, 1917, she was released from Neuruppin into the care of her sister Gertrude, discharged as "incurably mad, but harmless," a determination as equally problematic as the initial declaration of her insanity.[39]

Caring for Franziska, though, was beyond Gertrude's concern or capabilities, and in December 1917 she took her back to Hygendorf. Nearly four years had passed since Marianna had sent her eldest daughter to Berlin; the Franziska who returned had been declared insane and committed against her will in three asylums, an emotionally volatile, damaged young woman. Whatever circumstances had led Marianna to exile her daughter, whatever bitterness had existed, now suddenly came rushing back. Franziska, Marianna later commented, "always thought she was too good for work" and had come home to "put her hand in our pocket again."[40] Rather than care for a clearly damaged Franziska, she instead, as Gertrude recalled, "sent her back out to work," her "incurably mad" daughter, to labor in the chill winter on a nearby agricultural estate. It proved too much, and Franziska soon quit but, presumably out of necessity imposed by her mother's dictates, she took a job as a waitress at the Herrschen Brewery in Bütow, an establishment patronized by German soldiers fighting on the Eastern Front against Russia.[41] This meant a daily walk of thirty minutes from Hygendorf, through the January snow, but was at least preferable to agricultural work.[42] During this job Franziska accidentally caught her hand in the coils of a dishwashing machine, a deep wound that sliced her middle left finger open. Although the wound healed, she was, as her mother recalled, left with a deep scar—the scar that she would later insist had come when a servant slammed a carriage door on her hand at Tsarskoye Selo.[43]

Exiled from the farmhouse to Berlin, exiled from the farmhouse to work—there was something altogether disturbing in Marianna's overt lack of sympathy for her daughter, as if her mere presence was an unwelcome burden. Relations with her mother had always been difficult, but the four months Franziska spent at Hygendorf in 1918 must have reawakened every past bitter feeling between them as the last familial bonds fell away. When Franziska declared her intention to return to Berlin, Marianna made no effort to stop her, to step in and care for her damaged daughter.[44] Although she would occasionally dispatch letters, Franziska never again returned home.[45]

By April 8, 1918, Franziska was again at work, this time as a laborer on the agricultural estate of Gut-Friederikenhof in the northern German province of Schleswig-Holstein.[46] Here, Franziska worked in the asparagus fields, living in a brick dormitory on the estate along with other female laborers.[47] Despite her dislike of such intensive labor, Franziska did well here; her manager remembered her as "an active and energetic employee."[48] She spent her days in the fields, working under the vigilant eyes of armed German soldiers—a necessity, for the estate also served as an internment camp for Russian prisoners of war seized in hostilities along the Eastern Front and forced to join the agricultural laborers. Over the next five months, Franziska labored alongside these tsarist soldiers for ten hours a day, six days a week, and some relationship developed, a relationship significant enough that Franziska later mentioned it to the Wingenders.[49] Perhaps Franziska's familiarity with Polish allowed her to understand some of their conversations; but continued exposure over the course of the summer may well have left her with a rudimentary Russian vocabulary, a vocabulary she later built upon in her claim as Anastasia.

And then, one day that early autumn of 1918, violence erupted. Franziska was working in the fields when, for reasons unknown, one of the tsarist soldiers attacked her using some farming tool.[50] This previously unreported assault at Gut-Friederikenhof is the missing link in Franziska's case, bridging the gap between the minor wounds she received in the 1916 AEG explosion and the more serious injuries observed when she was pulled from the Landwehr Canal in 1920. Such an attack—with a pitchfork, hoe, or shovel—could certainly have left her with fractured jaws, teeth loosened from blows to the face, and the scar above her ear, and account for the sharp object that had been driven through her foot. It also resolves the dilemma of reconciling the testimony of Franziska's family that she bore no visible scars with the mute evidence observed on Anna Anderson, for she never told her mother or siblings of this attack, as Gertrude's later statements made clear.[51] Why she remained silent is not known. Perhaps her decision owed something to whatever led to the incident, or perhaps it stemmed from her mother's unsympathetic reception when she had returned home in the fall of 1917. Apparently unable or unwilling to turn to her family for help, Franziska did the only thing she could: she returned to Berlin, to the Wingender apartment, to Anna Wingender, the one person who had at least provided her with care and a semblance of maternal affection.

The young woman who in just three years would claim to be Anastasia was almost twenty-two now. She had, recalled Anna Wingender's daughter Doris, "a Slavic face, with a thick nose, especially prominent, pouting lips, and reddish-brown hair." Doris thought that Franziska had been "heavy and awkward," and somewhat larger than herself, though she admitted she could not precisely recall her weight or height.[52] She added that Franziska seemed "rather dirty, and she seldom bathed."[53] Anna Wingender especially remembered Franziska's hair: "She had beautiful brown hair with a natural wave, and in the sunshine it glowed with an auburn sheen. She was very proud of her hair."[54]

There were, Doris noted, wounds on the Franziska who reappeared in their apartment that autumn of 1918, especially "the one to her head." Franziska, she said, "constantly complained of headaches, and my mother used to go out and get her powders from the pharmacy."[55] Franziska must have been miserable and in a great deal of pain, for Anna often found her alone, rubbing her temples and face and crying, "All the time my head hurts me so much!"[56] Then there were her teeth, loose and damaged—presumably from the blows to the face she apparently received at Gut-Friederikenhof; Franziska, said Anna's daughter Luise, was "very self-conscious" of her damaged teeth, especially those in her upper front jaw, black and at jagged angles.[57] Both Doris and Luise recalled the curious way Franziska spoke, holding up her hands or a handkerchief in an attempt to hide her mouth, as she would do after her rescue from the Landwehr Canal.[58] Doris even thought that Franziska was so embarrassed by this that she bought a partial set of false teeth to disguise the noticeable gaps when she opened her mouth.[59] Doris did remember the scar on Franziska's finger, and Kathe Wypyrzyk, the eldest of the Wingender daughters, spoke of a mark on her shoulder—the same mark Franziska later insisted had come from a cauterized mole.[60] And Franziska, like Anastasia, had *hallux valgus*. Franziska, Anna Wingender said, "always tried to hide her bare feet," which she recalled as "small, but ugly," with "pronounced bunions that gave her a great deal of pain."[61] The condition was so bad, said Doris, that "it caused her shoes to become misshapen," and even Franziska's sister Gertrude remembered that the "joints of her toes had perhaps been a bit big."[62]

Franziska spent most her time alone. There was, Doris said, "something reclusive" about her: "If she ever had any close, personal friends, I never knew of them. She seemed close only to my mother." She "always seemed depressed. She was very devout, and often prayed, but she was someone who seemed burdened with grief. She usually dressed in black, heavy clothing, even in summer."[63] Franziska borrowed books from Doris and her sister Luise—"novels and romances," said Anna Wingender, which she "often read late into the night," but this seemed to be her only interest.[64] Most of the time, though, Franziska "lay in her bed, her head turned to the wall," Doris remembered, saying that she was usually "very bad tempered" and silent. "When we tried to speak to her, she refused to answer."[65]

Only Anna Wingender could penetrate this self-imposed barrier, though she, too, admitted that Franziska "could be so terribly difficult. Often, she would sit for hours beside the window, listening to me but refusing to answer any of my questions. She seemed lost, and I could see the pain in her eyes. And then, her personality would suddenly change, and she would try to behave properly, even attempting to anticipate all of my wishes." Sometimes, though, Franziska spoke about her dreams: "She was always talking about how she wanted to be someone grand," said Anna, "someone important." And there was a curious air of affectation about her: Franziska spoke "unusually slowly and softly, and with great deliberation," according to Anna. "Her speech and her accent were very strange." It was so soft, Doris recalled, that Franziska's voice was "almost a whisper." Her German was "good, free of error," though Doris, too, noted the strange accent, which she thought was "either West Prussian or Pomeranian." This strange way of speaking, this curious accent, caused endless confusion when Franziska was pulled from the Landwehr Canal, with officials, doctors, and nurses variously referring to it as Slavic, Bavarian, North German, Polish, Russian, or Franconian.[66]

Later, there would be many questions about this period in Franziska's life, not the least of which was how she managed to avoid being turned out into the streets. "When she lived with us," Doris recalled, "she was essentially dependent on Mother's charity." "Little Mother Wingender," as one newspaper later dubbed her, proved so accommodating, in fact, that she turned her young daughters Doris and Luise out of their room, forcing Doris to sleep in a chair and Luise on a sofa or mattress in the sitting room so that Franziska could have a private room.[67] Though she later insisted that she had felt sorry for Franziska, sympathy only extends so far.

Doris remembered the Franziska of this period as "promiscuous and vulgar," a woman who "had many boyfriends."[68] And yet, according to Doris, Franziska rarely left her room, and even more rarely the apartment. She had no friends, but she was "promiscuous and vulgar," and "had many boyfriends," and all within the privacy of the Winger apartment, the privacy of her bedroom? Doris never used the word "prostitute," but she may as well have done so.

The Berlin of autumn 1918 was a desperate place, the sidewalks filled, said one resident, with "heartbroken women," deprivation firmly etched in "faces like masks, blue with cold and drawn with hunger."[69] In October, there were riots in the streets; by November, Kaiser Wilhelm II had abdicated and the country was in chaos. And in the midst of this, there was nothing unusual in occasional prostitution: war widows, the unemployed, struggling workers, and young mothers all proved susceptible to the decision, which postponed starvation or life on the streets. Later rumors hinted that Franziska may have occasionally resorted to prostitution.

Was this why Franziska needed the privacy of her own bedroom? Was this how she managed to remain in the Wingender apartment without any apparent financial resources?

By the spring of 1919, Franziska was back at Gut-Friederikenhof, where she remained working through the autumn.[70] The seasonal work ended in November: on the twentieth of that month she went to a local police station and filled out an *Abmeldung*, the personal identification card the government required of all citizens; this listed her name, age, and place of birth, and gave the Wingender apartment at 17 Neue Hochstrasse as her permanent address.[71] Later it would be erroneously reported that Franziska had returned to Pomerania; Gertrude, however, was clear that none of Franziska's family ever saw her again after she left for Berlin in the spring of 1918.[72]

By 1920, twenty-three-year-old Franziska had lived a life of alienation and hardship. The young girl from the provinces who had been indulged and allowed an education, who had developed grandiose airs and envisioned a life of opportunity, had become a woman immersed in tragedy. She had endured a nomadic childhood, an alcoholic father, a distant mother, and a swirl of unpleasant rumors in Hygendorf; sent away to Berlin, she had lost her fiancé, inexplicably become ill, accidentally killed a man, suffered a breakdown, and been involuntarily committed and declared insane. When she returned home in 1917 her mother seemed to want nothing to do with her; attempts to make her own way at Gut-Friederikenhof apparently ended in a violent assault; and despair may have driven her to prostitution. She had no friends, no hope, and no future; events spiraled out of control, each crisis heaping emotional burdens atop an already fragile personality as she became a helpless witness to the strange and brutal dance that had become her life.

All of the elements were in place: the shattered, fragmented personality, the scars, the gift for languages, the sharp mind, the grandiose airs and belief in her abilities, and the overwhelming despair—the elements that Franziska carried with her that February day in 1920 when she left the Wingender apartment, when she wandered the streets of Berlin until darkness came. Standing atop the Bendler Bridge that night, she plunged into the waters of the Landwehr Canal, attempting to forever bury her tortured past.

21

The Myth Unravels

ND SO, WITH HER LEAP into the Landwehr Canal, Franziska
Schanzkowska disappeared, emerging from the waters as
Fraulein Unbekannt and the central figure in one of the twentieth century's most extraordinary myths. And the questions begin in
earnest: Why were authorities in Berlin unable to identify her? Why did
she make her claim? Was she responsible for her actions? How did she
manage to assimilate so much seemingly impressive knowledge? How
did she convince so many who had known Anastasia that she was the
grand duchess? In short, how did Franziska Schanzkowska, this humble
provincial farm girl, this "insane" factory worker, this "Polish peasant,"
transform herself into so believable a claimant, so compelling a legend?

First, though, her silence: at both Elisabeth Hospital and at Dalldorf,
she refused to reveal her name and, when questioned by doctors, turned
to the wall or tried to cover her head—an echo of her behavior on being
involuntarily committed to the Berlin-Schöneberg Asylum. In 1920, she
admitted only to being a worker, tellingly adding that her family was
dead.[1] The Franziska who had tried to kill herself had no real life and
no future. Now, again under state care, and as long as her real identity
remained a mystery, she ensured her care: she did not have to labor for
hours, did not have to worry about standing in the cold for hours to
obtain food, did not have to concern herself with the exigencies of life in
a tumultuous postwar Berlin. The birth of Fraulein Unbekannt echoed
Franziska's own desperate desire to escape the squalid reality of her life.

Why did Franziska's true identity remain a mystery? The Wingenders
waited twenty-two days to report that she had gone missing; perhaps

she had come and gone before, but something in this prolonged absence eventually led Anna Wingender to search her room. What she found was alarming: Franziska's purse, an odd item for her to have left behind, and in it her health insurance card, No. 1956, dated April 8, 1918—the same day on which she had begun her job at Gut-Friederikenhof—her work permit, and her identification card, issued in November 1919. On March 15, Doris Wingender went to the local police precinct and reported Franziska missing.[2] Even then, no one could agree on the details—a point of some contention later, when Anderson's supporters suggested that her identity as Franziska Schanzkowska had simply been invented. At first, Doris thought that her mother's boarder had gone missing on January 15, then later amended this to February 15, and finally, and with suspect precision, to 11:55 A.M. on February 17, the day upon which Franziska had thrown herself into the Landwehr Canal. Later, Doris explained that she had determined the correct date only after looking at the unused coupons in the ration book Franziska had left behind; she never clarified her error with police, she said, as "things were chaotic and took too long."[3] Her sister Luise, just twelve in February 1920, was, perhaps not surprisingly given her youth, even less certain, suggesting that Franziska had disappeared several weeks later, sometime in March, though she later admitted that she was mistaken.[4] The police collected these details and noted in their report that Franziska had "left for parts unknown.[5]

Sometime before her suicide attempt, Franziska mailed a birthday card to her brother Felix; his birthday, curiously, fell on February 17—the same day on which Franziska jumped into the Landwehr Canal. She apologized that it was late, and Felix later thought he had received it two weeks after his birthday; if Franziska was Fraulein Unbekannt, under observation at Elisabeth Hospital since February 17, how then had she mailed the card? Although her supporters suggested this as evidence that Anderson was not Franziska, Felix was only guessing; he had not kept the envelope, and only seven years later did he try to recall precisely when he had received what was, at the time, simply an unremarkable birthday message.[6] Franziska's family only learned that she was missing at the end of March. "Mother was very upset," Gertrude remembered. "No one knew where Franziska had gone."[7]

The Berlin Police never managed to identify Franziska as Fraulein Unbekannt because, contrary to stories of a widespread and determined investigation, they actually seem to have put little effort into pursuing the mysterious patient's identity.[8] Nor, for that matter, did the city's hospitals and asylums seem to take much notice of the police bulletins, at least not if Dalldorf was any example. Franziska had spent four months at Dalldorf in 1917, yet in 1920 no one was able to identify her as a former patient. Does this suggest that Franziska wasn't Fraulein Unbekannt? In fact, the answer to this apparent conundrum is surprisingly simple: with a dozen buildings, multiple wards, a rotating staff of hundreds, and more than fifteen hundred patients at any one time, no one in 1920 remembered Franziska, and why would they? In 1917, she had been just another unimportant patient; no one had any reason to recall her or the months she spent there. But her 1917 stay at Dalldorf lays waste to the idea that the Berlin Police were thorough in investigating Fraulein Unbekannt's identity; clearly no one even bothered to search the records of the city's largest asylum. Nor, for that matter, did the Berlin Police treat the matter as a priority; by the middle of March 1920, they already had in their files a report on the missing Franziska Schanzkowska, a report they apparently never bothered to consult. Had they done so, they would undoubtedly have learned Fraulein Unbekannt's identity.[9]

But there was something more here, another aspect to this inability to identify Fraulein Unbekannt that perhaps offers some insight into why she tried to kill herself. No one ever came forward to claim the mysterious patient; even the friendly "Little Mother Wingender" waited three weeks to report Franziska missing. She had no friends to miss her, no friends to identify her, not even former coworkers or mere acquaintances—evidence of just how little impression Franziska had made in anyone else's life. She had existed on the very edges of society, unremarkable and unimportant. To Franziska, suicide was more attractive than another day of uncertain, dispossessed anonymity in a life filled with pain.

And this same need to escape her former life, this desire to find at least some brief respite, drove Franziska into silence, into the safe persona of Fraulein Unbekannt and, finally, to her claim. The genesis of such an extraordinary modern myth, the forces that shaped her decision to declare that she was Anastasia—surely there was some monumental, telling moment of personal epiphany to neatly explain it all? The idea apparently first came to her at Dalldorf, in the institution's library, when she found the newspapers that, as Malinovsky recalled, were full of stories about the Romanovs and their presumed executions.[10] And then she found the magazine that changed her life, the October 23, 1921, issue of the *Berliner Illustrirte Zeitung*, with its extensive article on the last days of the imperial family and haunting photographs of the beautiful grand duchesses, its rumors that Anastasia had survived, and speculation that she had been spirited out of Russia.

Perhaps at first it was mere interest that drove her to take the magazine out of the library and keep it beneath her mattress, but interest soon turned to obsession as she read of this tantalizing mystery, this bewitching saga of romance and revolution, love and death. It must have been powerfully evocative to a mind seeking diversion that autumn of 1921, and diversion is almost certainly how it began, for, as unlikely as it might seem, Franziska apparently wanted nothing more than a few extra attentions, a few privileges granted to a woman who might be a grand duchess, and the nurses at Dalldorf responded, bringing her little gifts and books, and treating her "humanely and attentively," as Malinovsky recalled.[11] For presumably the first time in her life, Franziska was the center of attention, viewed as someone special and treated with respect, though it was a lie she attempted, in pledging the nurses to silence, to confine to the undemanding parameters of her ward at Dalldorf. In these early days, no one pressed her for particulars, and who at the asylum could definitively refute her?

It all came from Franziska's imagination and from Franziska's imagination only, despite later assertions that Clara Peuthert had somehow engineered the entire claim.[12] Such views presumably stemmed from misconceptions about Franziska: that as a crude "Polish peasant" she lacked the education to absorb information and learn languages; that as a provincial farm girl she was entirely lacking in the manners needed to appear convincing; that as an "insane" factory worker she didn't posses the mental acumen to sustain what became a lifelong charade. But both Thea Malinovsky and Emilie Barfknecht recalled that Franziska had confided her "secret" to them before Peuthert's admission to Dalldorf.[13] Nor, for that matter, was there any truth in another idea, that Franziska, inspired by the issue of the *Berliner Illustrirte Zeitung*, first claimed to be Tatiana and only later insisted that she was Anastasia after Baroness Buxhoeveden commented that she was too short to be the second of Nicholas and Alexandra's daughters.[14] The article detailed extensive rumors only of a surviving Anastasia, while Peuthert insisted that she had discovered Tatiana at Dalldorf. Had the two women colluded, surely they would have gotten their stories straight and both followed the narrative laid down in the magazine; for that matter, given that the magazine played a pivotal role in shaping Franziska's claim, why would she ignore its talk of Anastasia? The accusations, such as they were, made no sense.

Franziska may have had little knowledge of precisely how many Russian émigrés were in Berlin, or how many of Anastasia's close relatives were alive in Europe, but she must have been aware that people did exist who could presumably end her little adventure if the story gained circulation. Peuthert destroyed her attempts to limit the claim to Dalldorf, and the parade of visitors seeking to identify her threatened constant exposure, hence her behavior in turning to the wall or trying to hide her features when faced with those who had known Anastasia.

Yet she was also intrigued by the attention: after von Schwabe visited her, Franziska sought out nurse Emilie Barfknecht. "With great excitement," Barfknecht recalled, "she asked whether she really resembled one of the Tsar's daughters."[15] Perhaps this suggested the choice she made, for what was the alternative? Admitting to her identity, and returning to a future of hard labor, a dingy room with the Wingenders, rejection by her mother, the uncertainty of life in Weimar Berlin—these were the very things that had led to her suicide attempt.

And so Franziska declared that she was Anastasia, and moved in with the von Kleist family, into a luxurious apartment where servants catered to her needs and her hosts provided her with clothing, food, and medical care. For the first time in her life, she didn't have to worry about immediate concerns; as long as her claim generated interest, as long as her actual identity remained a mystery, she would be cared for and insulated from the brutality of her former subsistence. She occupied the center of a fragile universe of her own construction, a world so precariously balanced on deception that any misstep could irrevocably end her scheme. What had seemingly begun as nothing more than a lark, a ploy for attention, had spiraled into a complex tissue of lies. With every encounter, every false declaration, every insistence on her identity as Anastasia, Franziska was trapping herself in an inescapable reality. At any moment, her charade might be exposed, her gambit revealed, her real identity brought to light.

And for those looking back at her claim, seeking some moment of personal epiphany, some time when Franziska made a clear and conscious decision to spend the rest of her life living a lie, that moment came in the summer of 1922, when she fled the von Kleist apartment one August morning and disappeared for four days. Because it is the pivotal moment in her claim, and an incident that later played a key role in exposing her, it is worthwhile to revisit the events of those days armed with Anna Anderson's real identity.

Franziska left the von Kleist apartment sometime on the morning of Saturday, August 12, 1922.[16] Baroness von Kleist suspected that she had run off to see Clara Peuthert, but a police inspection of the latter's seedy apartment revealed no trace of the claimant, and Peuthert insisted that she hadn't been there.[17] Peuthert later insisted that Franziska had been with her at the time, had never left her apartment in these three days, an assertion picked up and repeated by Rathlef-Keilmann despite the fact that it was demonstrably untrue.[18]

In fact, Franziska had, for some inexplicable reason, returned to the Wingender flat at Neue Hochstrasse. Perhaps she had been drawn back to the apartment because it represented the only refuge she had known during her time in Berlin, and Frau Wingender had showed her kindness where others had regarded her with indifference. At about ten that Saturday morning, Doris Wingender answered a knock on the door and was startled to find Franziska standing on the threshold; no one had seen her since her sudden disappearance in February 1920. Franziska seemed well, and wore new and expensive clothing, "like a lady," Doris said.[19] But Franziska was confused and upset; in 1920, she said, she had met a wealthy gentleman; sometime later, a family of Russian émigrés took her into their Berlin apartment as they "mistook her for someone else," someone important. It had, Franziska said, become too oppressive, so she had escaped; in her purse she carried roughly 150 marks (approximately $26.50 in 2011 currency), an envelope with postcards of the Russian imperial family, and a small gold swastika.[20]

Franziska spent that Saturday night at the Wingender apartment, although her movements over the next two days remain somewhat murky, and she may indeed have gone to visit Peuthert during this time.[21] She finally left the Wingender flat on Monday afternoon, but not before asking Doris for some clothing to wear as a disguise. Doris gave her a dark blue skirt and matching jacket, and a hat adorned with yellow flowers; in exchange, Franziska left behind a mauve-colored dress, a camel hair coat, and some underwear that had been sewn with the initials AR.[22]

Later, this all became immensely important for those seeking to link Anna Anderson to Franziska Schanzkowska, and accusations and inconsistencies flew back and forth from supporters and opponents alike. Doris couldn't quite recall when Franziska had returned, at first apparently suggesting it had been in early summer 1922; later this was supposedly altered to the less definitive "summer of 1922" to better coincide with the claimant's disappearance from the von Kleists.[23] The clothing involved became central to the issue: in 1927, when the items Franziska had left with Doris were shown to the von Kleists, the baron recognized the camel hair coat he had purchased for the claimant at Israel's Department Store in Berlin. The baroness, too, identified the clothing, saying, "That's the underwear I monogrammed myself," a statement later confirmed by one of those present.[24] Although the baroness supposedly later backed away from this identification, her sworn affidavit makes no mention of this, recording only that when Franziska was found after her disappearance "she was not wearing any of the clothing we had given to her."[25] Later, during the Hamburg trials, Doris Wingender submitted a photograph of herself in the clothing Franziska had left behind; on examination, the court discovered that she had erased a figure and drawn in buttons and a belt, though investigation determined that the alterations had probably been innocent and that it was "unlikely" that Wingender had knowingly submitted falsified evidence.[26]

"I feel so dirty!" Franziska had said, sobbing, to Baroness von Kleist when she was found. "I cannot look you in the eye!"[27] "So dirty" because she had run away? Almost certainly not. The most likely answer is that the usually self-possessed Franziska had become overwhelmed at the magnitude of her charade. She must have recognized that hers was an extraordinarily tenuous position, that mystery was her greatest ally. Every confrontation, every question threatened the possibility that she could live in relative obscurity in a netherworld of uncertainty, where no one pressed to resolve her identity and she could remain an intriguing enigma. More than this, though, her remark to the baroness suggests that Franziska not only felt trapped in the situation she had created but also was ashamed of the knowing deception. It was a rare moment of self-reflection, an unspoken acknowledgment of the enormity of what she had done and its implications in the lives of those touched by her claim.

These four lost days in 1922 sealed Franziska's fate. Here is the personal epiphany, the deliberate decision, the embarkation on a careful and controlled deceit that was to last the rest of Franziska's life, for rather than own up to the charade, she now began a concerted effort to transform herself into a believable Anastasia. From her leap into the Landwehr Canal emerged the consoling light of a new identity, a second chance that her fevered brain seized as her only lifeline. In the Romanovs, a psychologically injured Franziska apparently discovered what her parents, her siblings, and the attentions of Anna Wingender could not provide: an idyllic family. Psychologically injured she certainly was, though the depression, morbidity, feelings of persecution, and extreme changes of mood in these years likely stemmed from the traumatic fusion of two warring identities, as Franziska willingly shed her previous life and struggled to achieve an emotional balance in her new role as Anastasia. One thing is clear: Franziska, as every doctor who examined her in these years agreed, was sane, if highly strung, and she knew exactly what she was doing. Yet those who condemned her as a mere "adventuress" failed to recognize just how desperately she needed to identify with her new persona, to embrace what, if true, would have been a horrendous past precisely because, for Franziska, it replaced a reality far worse than having survived the massacre in Ekaterinburg.

Continuation of the lie may have rescued an admittedly fragile young woman from the abyss, but it also trapped Franziska within a web of deceit from which she could never escape. And this, of course, explains what otherwise has seemed so inexplicable: her lack of cooperation with thus attempting to publicize her claim, to push for her asserted identity as Anastasia. No one stood to lose more than did Franziska if it was all revealed; she didn't want meetings with former courtiers, didn't welcome visits by even the most sympathetic of Anastasia's acquaintances. In 1926,

Dr. Nobel recorded that she often expressed a "fear of being discovered," a confusing concern for a surviving Anastasia whose case had already received publicity, but a very real peril for Franziska Schanzkowska.[28] Fear of revelation became a constant companion, ruling her actions and attitudes for the rest of her life.

Still, she *did* try, if not to prove that she was Anastasia, then at least to surround herself with an aura of plausibility. If she didn't want to push for recognition, neither did she want to sink back into the misery that had been her former life. What she apparently wanted to create was not certainty, but rather enough intrigue that her actual identity remained a tantalizing mystery, intrigue that would ensure her continued care by those who supported her cause. Armed with this determination, she launched on her deliberate transformation, a transformation that brings us to the most intriguing questions of all: How did Franziska gain her impressive knowledge? How did she avoid revealing her humble origins, especially to her aristocratic hosts? How did she convince so many people who had known the real grand duchess that she was Anastasia? In short, how did she create an illusion so believable that it propelled her into legend? The answers are almost stunning in their simplicity. Beginning in 1922, in the aftermath of her temporary disappearance, and continuing on through the 1960s, Franziska undertook what literally became the role of a lifetime, a part that required constant study; her early aptitude as a student, love of reading, and capacity for absorbing information coalesced into a powerful weapon to advance her charade, along with considerable charm and an ability to channel her painful past into an aura of tragic believability.

She began by relying on her memory, a memory she cunningly insisted was so damaged, so shattered, that she couldn't read or write, couldn't remember names, dates, faces, and places, couldn't find "her" Russian or English. And cunning it certainly was; for all the talk of this struggle to remember, she revealed the lie to Nobel and Bonhoeffer, both of whom not only could find no organic cause for the alleged gaps in her memory, but who actually recorded just how good—in recalling precise names of doctors, nurses, and patients at Elisabeth Hospital and at Dalldorf—it really was.[29] She fooled nearly everyone; the duke of Leuchtenberg thus gullibly insisted to Olga Alexandrovna that she couldn't possibly possess the "dedication, comprehension, and perfect recall" he thought an impostor needed, although even he admitted—as the doctors confirmed—that she had "an extensive memory."[30]

It began at Dalldorf, with the materials in the asylum library, with the newspapers that Malinovsky said were "full" of stories about the Romanovs, with the illustrated magazines that carried rumors of survival.[31] Franziska, the asylum records noted, spent most of her days "reading newspapers and books," following "political events with interest."[32] Malinovsky, too, brought her books—principally Russian literature—that she "read often."[33] This all would have been woefully short of intimate information on the Romanovs, but Franziska's access to materials dramatically improved when she moved into the von Kleist apartment. The baron and his family, as well as the constant stream of émigré visitors, supplied her with books, memoirs, newspapers, souvenir albums, and illustrated magazines on the Romanovs—natural enough gifts for a young woman thought to be Anastasia, but invaluable sources for a claimant attempting to grow into the role. This included German editions of Gilliard's memoirs; Nicholas II's diary; the extensive wartime correspondence between the emperor and the empress; a copy of the *Almanach de Gotha*, a comprehensive register of royal families in Europe; a German translation of Tatiana Botkin's memoirs; the English edition of Anna Vyrubova's book; a number of special illustrated magazines and newspapers devoted to the Romanovs, their Siberian exile, and their assassination; pamphlets on the imperial family written by former courtiers; and even a romantic German novel whose plot involved the rescue of one of the grand duchesses from the Ipatiev House by a sympathetic guard.[34] Then, too, Baron von Kleist often read aloud to her from various Russian books and émigré publications; armed with her knowledge of Polish and perhaps some rudimentary vocabulary picked up from the tsarist soldiers at Gut-Friederikenhof, she was clearly able to follow the main points, although all discussion of the contents took place, at her request, in German.[35]

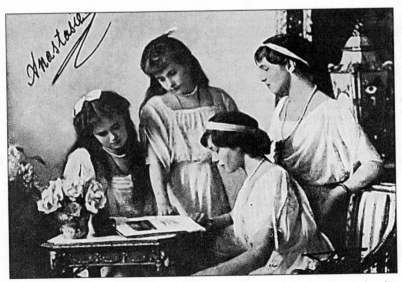

The four Grand Duchesses, 1914, photo signed in French by Anastasia and reproduced in Gilliard's first book, and later used by Franziska to copy her signature.

Franziska added to this assemblage of knowledge month by month, year by year, with more books, more magazines, and a growing collection of images: souvenir photographs, postcards, and varied illustrations of the imperial family, Empress Alexandra's Hessian relatives, and other European royalty. She could often be found sitting alone, photographs spread out around her as she studied what was an impressive visual tool that gave her a growing familiarity with the faces of those whom she would be expected to know.[36]

And Franziska used the accumulated information to bolster her claim, plunging forward with deliberate calculation, as revealed by one particular incident in 1925. That year, before they had rejected her, the Gilliards received a Christmas card signed "Anastasie" by the claimant. "It is quite true," Gilliard wrote to Rathlef-Keilmann, "that the signature greatly resembles that of Grand Duchess Anastasia when she was fourteen or fifteen years old. It is important to ascertain if the patient has seen the Grand Duchess's signature on cards or in books."[37] Rathlef-Keilmann, though, insisted that not only had the claimant "never copied the signature of the Grand Duchess," but also that she "had never even seen it."[38] This wasn't true: in June 1925, Franziska had filled the margins of a magazine with random "A's" and attempts to duplicate Anastasia's signature, presumably from a signed photograph in Gilliard's book, in which the grand duchess had used the French variant of her name.[39] And in the autumn of 1925, Zahle lent Rathlef-Keilmann a signed photograph of Anastasia that Alexandra Gilliard had let him borrow so she could show it to the claimant.[40]

Franziska's practice efforts at copying Anastasia's signature shown in No. 80.

Or take her rescue story: without doubt, Franziska derived all of the initial details from the October 23, 1921, issue of the *Berliner Illustrirte Zeitung*. Not only did it provide an account of the imperial family's captivity in Tobolsk and Ekaterinburg, as well as what was then believed of their executions, accompanied by numerous photographs, but also the magazine laid out, in a startling manner, precisely the tale Franziska offered: Anastasia, wounded during the shooting and fallen in a faint; a sympathetic soldier who discovered that she was still alive and rescued her; persistent rumors of Anastasia's escape across Russia; and the jewelry sewn into the grand duchesses' clothing that Franziska insisted had been used to finance her flight. And the article reported the case of a certain Mademoiselle Berditch, probably the first Anastasia claimant, who arrived in Paris in 1920 declaring that she was the grand duchess, wounded in the shooting, rescued by a soldier, and smuggled in a cart across Siberia into Europe.[41]

This is very nearly the story Franziska confessed to Malinovsky and to others, down to the inclusion of Paris as a destination—a detail, like the claim that Alexander Tchaikovsky had found some unnamed apparatus that she used to alter her appearance—that she later dropped from her tale. It also set the perimeters she would be forced to follow, often in the face of not only lack of evidence but also her own continuous amendments: had she envisioned the claim as anything more than mere diversion to pass her time at Dalldorf, Franziska certainly would have managed a more cogent and believable narrative that did not repeatedly contradict itself. Perhaps the rescue story also drew on Franziska's own life: haste and lack of foresight may have led her to the name "Tchaikovsky," but its similarity to her own surname suggests an inadvertent mingling of fact and fiction, as was her description of her alleged rescuer as the scion of minor Polish nobility—something certainly true of her own family.[42]

Information also came innocently to Franziska, from those who met the claimant, aristocrats, émigrés, former courtiers, and the merely curious. The simple human desire to assist a young woman many took to be a traumatized grand duchess almost certainly led many to become conduits of information as they spoke of the past, relating stories of life at the Russian court in misguided attempts to aid what she declared to be her shattered memory; this much Nicholas von Schwabe recalled during Franziska's stay with him.[43] Sometimes the efforts were overt, as when Peuthert, during the visit by Baroness Buxhoeveden, tried to prod the claimant, whispering in German and actually identifying figures in photographs for her. Other occasions required nothing of Franziska, as happened when she met Nicholas Sablin and Admiral Federov, when the two men openly reminisced about the Romanovs, their holidays, and various courtiers; it was a primer on the intimate life of the imperial family that required nothing of Franziska but her silent attention.

Franziska undoubtedly benefited from presumptions: only an aristocrat, it was presumed, would have her imperious manner and sense of entitlement; only an aristocrat would act in so ungrateful and uncooperative a manner with those attempting to help her; only an aristocrat would evince any interest in reading; only an aristocrat would know more than a single language (ignoring the fact that even as a young girl Franziska knew three); only an aristocrat would know how to play the piano (despite the fact that Franziska never demonstrated any real musical ability); only an aristocrat would know how to embroider (something Franziska undoubtedly learned, like all Kashubian girls); in short, only an aristocrat would behave as Franziska did. Shaped by class prejudices such views may have been, but still, how did Franziska manage to evoke a mien of aristocratic privilege? It is unlikely that she was an ill-mannered young woman, completely lacking in social skills, but how could the von Kleists or the duke of Leuchtenberg fail to spot the inadvertent gesture, the inexplicable lapse, that would have revealed the game?

As with so much of Franziska's story, the answer is simple, for it is a misconception that, from the first, she played her role every hour, every day, for weeks, months, and years on end, and all under the harsh, unforgiving light of scrutiny. She was, to be sure, a keen observer of people and circumstances, with a talent for absorbing information and adopting it as her own, but she was careful to limit her exposure to potentially dangerous situations. In her months living with the von Kleists, for example, she rarely joined the family for meals, preferring to eat in the privacy of her bedroom—a pattern she repeated with the von Schwabes, at Seeon with the Leuchtenbergs, and at Kenwood with Princess Xenia Georgievna. Consider her request to Baron von Kleist that his family "not observe" the etiquette demanded of her presumed position; this undoubtedly alleviated some of the pressure upon her, and when she did join her hosts, she was silent more often than not, perhaps taking in behaviors around her and adjusting her own responses accordingly. Then, too, she could excuse herself from uncertain situations using the pretext of her ill health before committing any visible and obvious errors.

What of those who met Franziska? How to explain away all of those apparently compelling recognitions? There was, in her approach, something so simple yet so brilliant that few took notice of it, for she had an undoubted skill in immediately evaluating those she met. Those deemed sympathetic were usually granted extended interviews that allowed her to respond to perceived desires; those suspected of posing a threat, though, were most often met with silence, and by her complete withdrawal from the situation. When she faced encounters deemed too challenging, Franziska frequently drew upon her fragile health, excusing herself from attempting to answer questions and thus preventing disaster. She could speak or maintain her silence as circumstance dictated. And when faced with unknown visitors, she consistently attempted to ferret out names and information from those around her, as happened in the encounters with Tatiana Botkin, Anatole Mordvinov, and Felix Dassel.

The problem is that none of the recognitions of Franziska as Anastasia were particularly compelling. Discount those who never met the claimant and only judged her based on examination of photographs or from anecdotal information to reject her, such as former nanny Margaretta Eagar and piano teacher Alexander Conrad; discount those who never had any real involvement with Anastasia and rejected her, such as Princess Kira of Prussia and Prince Felix Yusupov; and discount those who had at best fleeting or distant encounters with the real grand duchess and accepted the claimant, such as Crown Princess Cecilie of Prussia, Maria Rasputin, and former ballerina Mathilde Kschessinska—do this, and we're left with a fairly weighty and impressive list of rejections: Baroness Buxhoeveden; Princess Irene of Prussia (despite allegations that she later had second thoughts); Grand Duchess Olga Alexandrovna; Princess Nina Chavchavadze, sister of Princess Xenia Georgievna; Princess Vera Konstantinova; the Gilliards—*both* of them, as we now know; tutor Charles Sidney Gibbes; Maria von Hesse and her daughter Darya, Countess Hollenstein (who undoubtedly *had* known Anastasia better and seen her more often than someone such as Crown Princess Cecilie); and former courtiers Nicholas Sablin, Admiral Federov, Anatole Mordvinov, Baron George Taube, and Vassili Woitinsky. Missing from the list is Alexei Volkov, whose supposedly contradictory impressions and views render his opinion problematic.

Fifteen names. There were, of course, others, but these fifteen all had varying personal interactions over a period of time with Anastasia, and all met and rejected Franziska. And, on the opposite side of the spectrum, we find Grand Duke Andrei Vladimirovich; Princess Xenia Georgievna; Prince Sigismund of Prussia; Madame Lili Dehn; Madame Zenaide Tolstoy; Tatiana Botkin; Gleb Botkin; and the two wounded officers from the hospital at Tsarskoye Selo, Felix Dassel and Ivan Arapov. After the DNA results, the question is no longer, did these nine individuals know Anastasia better than those who opposed the claimant? but rather, what convinced them that Franziska was Anastasia?

That a certain emotional dynamic was at play here cannot be denied—take the shifting views of Zenaide Tolstoy, for example, who first believed the claimant was Tatiana. Under ordinary circumstances, at home in Russia, as a visitor to the Alexander Palace and before the trauma of the Revolution, Madame Tolstoy would certainly have been able to accurately distinguish between Tatiana and Anastasia. Like so many other émigrés, though, she had passed through tumultuous circumstances to find herself in a foreign country, called upon after the passage of time to render an emotional verdict in a heartrending case, and at a time when rumor and hope prevailed over events in Ekaterinburg. There was, among many devastated and dispossessed émigrés, desperation for the old order that made them particularly susceptible to the idea of a miraculously rescued member of the imperial family. They came to Franziska wounded and scarred, relying on subjective memories often governed by a desire to find in her a living remnant of what had been lost in the wake of the Revolution. Is this how one explains the opinion of Grand Duke Andrei, who admitted, in words that impeach the value of his recognition, "I can't trust my personal impressions. I wasn't close enough to the tsar's children to be able to identify Anastasia"?[44] Or the views of Princess Xenia Georgievna, who viewed the claimant through a fog of memory and who took eight years of studied manners, languages, and accumulated knowledge to be indications that she was indeed Anastasia?

Dassel and Arapov may well have been convinced that Franziska was Anastasia, though they certainly hadn't known her better than Olga Alexandrovna, Gilliard, or Baroness Buxhoeveden. They seem to have taken anecdotal information as evidence—something particularly problematic in Dassel's case, given the publication of his memoirs of life at the hospital five months before he even met the claimant. Accumulated information, too, played a role in recognitions by Lili Dehn and by Prince Sigismund, even though two thirds of the answers to the latter's famous eighteen questions could be found in a mere two books, and it took Franziska five days to provide the answers—and even then she didn't get them all right, contrary to the mythology that developed around her claim.

What of Tatiana and Gleb Botkin? Both freely admitted that they were never intimates of the grand duchesses, their personal interactions restricted to a few meetings over a five-year period.[45] Given their limited personal involvement with Anastasia, they both relied on intuitive belief, perceived physical similarities, and what they took as intimate knowledge in recognizing Franziska; even so, both admitted that they were *forced* to search for physical similarities, as the claimant simply looked different, particularly around the mouth and nose, from Anastasia.[46] Both had lost their father in the Ekaterinburg massacre, a circumstance that may have shaped the emotional prism through which they hopefully viewed any purported survivor, but nothing suggests that either was not genuinely convinced that Franziska was Anastasia. They simply happened to be wrong.

There was no simple, single formula to Franziska's efforts; rather, her success stemmed from her natural abilities and talents, from her desire to secure a future for herself, from her interest in surrounding herself with just enough intrigue that she could forever exist in the ether of perpetual uncertainty. With her deft mind and, when she elected to use it, winning, fragile charm, she emerges not as a gifted actress or a mere adventuress, but rather a determined woman of exceptional gifts, gifts she used to deceive everyone in her life but that carried Franziska into the pages of history.

22

Into the Pages of History

ONE MARCH EVENING in 1927, Doris Wingender sat in a
café on Berlin's Hausvogteiplatz, sipping coffee and flipping
through a month-old copy of the popular illustrated paper
Die Woche when she spotted a small photograph. It was of dubious
quality, a bit grainy, but the face staring back at Doris, the face of
the woman who said she was Grand Duchess Anastasia, was clearly
that of Franziska.[1] Excited, Doris rushed back to the apartment on
Neue Hochstrasse and woke her sister Luise. "She showed me the newspaper story, and asked if I recognized the person in the picture," Luise
recalled. "As soon as I saw the photograph, I knew it was Franziska."[2]
At the time, Anna Wingender lived in Gleiwitz, and the following day
Doris rushed to her mother, newspaper in hand. Anna, too, immediately recognized the claimant as Franziska, as did her eldest daughter,
Kathe Wypyrczyk.[3]

Ever sharp for financial opportunities, Anna Wingender urged
Doris to approach the editors of the Scherl Press in Berlin, which
published *Die Woche*, and find out how much they would pay for an
exclusive story unmasking their now famous former boarder.[4] It was
either March 13 or 14, editor Fritz Lücke later recalled, when Doris
arrived at his offices. Saying that she had recognized the claimant from
the photograph in *Die Woche* and knew her real identity, she boldly
asked what her story would be worth to the paper. "I sensed disaster,"
Lücke said. "If she went to one of our competitors down the street with
her story it would have been catastrophic. We had to keep her, and so
I offered her 1,500 Marks, on condition that she proved her story and

agreed to an encounter with the claimant." Wingender accepted; the contracts were signed on March 15, and Doris began to tell Lücke all she knew of the curious Franziska; of how she had simply vanished one day without explanation; and how she had just as suddenly reappeared in the summer of 1922, saying that she had been living with a Russian family "who apparently mistook her for someone else."[5]

Then a curious twist: the Scherl Press also owned the *Berliner Nachtausgabe*, whose publication of Rathlef-Keilmann's articles on the claimant had brought protests from Ernst Ludwig's former marshal Count von Hardenberg in Darmstadt. Lücke now answered their concerns with word of Wingender's recognition, and Darmstadt offered the services of Martin Knopf, a private bank detective in Berlin, to assist in the investigation.[6] In fact, it was Knopf who now took charge; to fund the inquiry, as Lücke later admitted, Darmstadt sent the Scherl Press between 20,000 and 25,000 marks (approximately $140,000–150,000 in 2011).[7]

Armed with a name, Knopf searched Berlin for records of the young woman from Hygendorf.[8] He found the registry card from November 1919, listing Franziska's address at 17 Neue Hochstrasse, and Darmstadt commissioned a handwriting comparison with a sample written by the claimant; this concluded, rather problematically, given that it rested exclusively on the formation of a single letter, that the handwriting was identical.[9] A few long-standing tenants in the building on Neue Hochstrasse identified photographs of the claimant as Franziska, and Knopf met with the von Kleists, who, he said, "had both immediately recognized" the articles of clothing the claimant had left with Doris Wingender in 1922 as items they had purchased for Frau Tchaikovsky.[10]

Events now moved quickly. Knopf discovered that Franziska's family was still alive, and on March 22, he arrived in Hygendorf.[11] At the time, Gertrude, Valerian, and Maria Juliana all lived with their mother, Marianna, and her second husband. The *Berliner Nachtausgabe* gave a dramatic— and occasionally inaccurate—accounting of this meeting to its readers: "The widow Schanzkowsky lays listlessly in her crude bed . . . seriously ill. The two sisters, Gertrude and Maria, enter. They have heard nothing of Franziska since February of 1920, when she disappeared without any word. The dying mother's eyes light up when shown a photograph of the claimant Frau Tchaikovsky. 'Yes, that is my daughter,'

Maria Juliana, Franziska's youngest sister.

she says. 'But she has probably been dead many years.' The sisters also immediately recognize Franziska."[12] Knopf later confirmed the identifications, as did Gertrude, though the detective found Franziska's mother "oddly cold" on learning that she was still alive. "We don't need her back here," Marianna told him. It was clear, Knopf noted, that the mother "wanted nothing to do" with her infamous daughter.[13] "We were so happy," Gertrude said, "to think that Franziska was still alive."[14] Yet Knopf couldn't convince any of the family to travel to Seeon to meet her; they did, though, hand him a photograph, the image of Franziska said to have been taken in 1916.[15] By the time it was reproduced in the *Berliner Nachtausgabe*, it had been "heavily retouched," recalled one reporter. "The Chinese white on the light parts was thick; the mouth had been retouched thickly, almost to the point of encrustation, so that the mouth appeared heavy and wide."[16]

Unmasked! screamed the headline in the Tuesday, April 5, 1927 edition of the *Berliner Nachtausgabe*. Investigation into the claimant, the paper declared, "Has brought sensational results. Without prejudice, and beyond all doubt, our research has answered the question, 'Is she Anastasia or not Anastasia?' finally and for all time." She was, the article announced, "the worker Franziska Schanzkowska." With this discovery, the *Nachtausgabe* declared, "One of the greatest enigmas of our time has finally been brought to an end."[17] Over the next ten days, the paper laid out the case: Franziska's background; her time with the Wingenders; the 1922 disappearance; and handwriting and photographic comparisons.[18] "It is a tragedy all the greater," the paper editorialized, "as we can now see the artful game this woman has played; we now know that this woman is a liar."[19]

Letter from Anna Anderson to Herluf Zahle, with a superimposed example of "Borowilhas" written on her November 1919 registry card, and used to compare the formation of the letter *s*.

The paper arranged a confrontation between the claimant and Doris Wingender, who arrived at Seeon with Knopf and Lücke on the same cold, rainy Tuesday morning that the *Berliner Nachtausgabe* broke the story.[20] Told to expect an old acquaintance, the claimant was reclining on a sofa when the visitors entered her room.[21] "Good day, Franziska," said Doris.[22] With "a horrified look," Franziska bolted up, covering her face with a handkerchief and screaming "in a wild rage," *"Das soll rausgehen! Das soll rausgehen!"* (That must go out! That must go out!)[23]

For a moment, Doris stood silent, uncertain what to do as Franziska continued to scream; Doris finally left the room, declaring that she had recognized "without any doubt" the claimant as her mother's former boarder.[24] Everything about her was the same: the same face, the same peculiar accent, the same habit of hiding her mouth—in short, "nothing distinguished her from the Franziska I had formerly known."[25]

Now it was Knopf's turn. "Good day, Fraulein Schanzkowska!" he said to the claimant, who sat in stunned silence as the duke of Leuchtenberg and Lücke looked on. He had gone to Hygendorf and met her family, he told her; her sisters and her mother, who was sick, had identified her photograph. And Knopf had a message from Anna Wingender: Franziska was welcome to return to the apartment in Berlin, she had told the detective; they had even kept her few meager belongings. Franziska seemed frozen, nervously watching Knopf as he spoke.[26]

"Wingender . . ." Franziska finally offered. "I . . . do . . . not . . . know . . . that . . . name!"[27] Then, suddenly, her shock apparently gave way to the crushing reality of what had occurred that morning. A few unexpected minutes shattered her artificial universe and destroyed all her efforts. Franziska had spent five years carefully re-creating herself as a plausible Anastasia; her rewards were tangible, her needs tended to, and she lived in a Bavarian castle as the guest of an aristocratic Romanov relative. For five years she had done her best to avoid dangerous encounters such as the one that played itself out that Tuesday morning. What would now happen? Would she be cast off, forced back into the despair of her hopeless former life? Or worse, would authorities charge her with fraud?

Franziska must have been convinced that her charade was at an end, for she turned to the duke and asked in a low voice, "And did you really believe that you had given shelter to the daughter of your Tsar?" It was a devastating admission of her deliberate fraud, but the duke followed this confession with something even more unbelievable: "Even Franziska Schanzkowska," he told her, "may stay at my house. I have never known for certain if you are the Tsar's daughter or not. I have only treated you with the sympathy one should have for a sick person." Hearing this, the *Nachtausgabe* reported, Franziska suddenly gave "a small, ironic smile," safe in the knowledge that the duke of Leuchtenberg would continue to protect her.[28]

Seeon was in an uproar. Faith Lavington, ruminating on the claimant's outburst on seeing Wingender, recorded in her diary, "This was a queer thing, to say the least, for one would scarcely greet an unknown person in such a fashion." While waiting for Lücke and Knopf, Doris sat in the drawing room, sipping a cup of tea from a samovar and speaking to Duchess Olga of Leuchtenberg. "Please tell her to return to us," Doris said to the duchess. "She still has a room and her clothing ready, and we would be very happy to have her back with us again." To the duchess's daughter Nathalia, Doris explained, "You know that Franziska always imagined that she was someone better than she really was. She was always very careful to keep her appearance, and took pride in her small, beautiful hands." Looking at the photograph of Franziska in the *Nachtausgabe*, Nathalia confessed to Lavington, her "heart sank, for the likeness is unmistakable."[29]

And then an even more bizarre scene was enacted: the duke now joined the group, and despite the claimant's admission, he was more convinced than ever that she really was Anastasia. Doris insisted that there wasn't any doubt, but Leuchtenberg interrupted, saying that he was sure his guest was the grand duchess because she knew how a samovar was used. This was too much for Knopf: turning to Doris, he asked if she, too, could work the contraption. When she answered that she could, the detective said, "So, Your Highness, she must also be a Grand Duchess!"[30]

This bit of mockery made no impression on the duke, who was soon publicly insisting that the confrontation with Wingender "had resulted in no evidence against the invalid; quite the contrary, it convinced me that she was not the missing Schanzkowska."[31] To Rathlef-Keilmann he declared that the results of the encounter "were absolutely negative. The witness Wingender stared at the invalid, who was lying in bed, in silence and bewilderment, as it is only possible to look at a stranger whom one sees for the first time. She quite obviously neither recognized her nor addressed her by name."[32]

This wasn't just wrong, it was inexplicable; his refusal to admit that Doris had actually identified the claimant, correctly or not, renders the duke a singularly unreliable witness. His denials may have given Franziska some temporary comfort; with such supporters—not merely the willfully naive but also those who blatantly lied about the particulars of her case—she may have hoped to ride out the "unmasking" storm, thinking it would all soon be forgotten. And then, as had happened when Peuthert carried her tale through Berlin, those who believed she was a grand duchess continued to force the issue. This time, it was Rathlef-Keilmann, intent on exposing what she believed to be an elaborate hoax engineered by Gilliard, the Wingenders, Lücke, and Knopf on orders from Grand Duke Ernst Ludwig of Hesse to discredit the claimant. She found Franziska's brother Felix, who was working as a miner at Ammendorf-bei-Halle in the Ruhr Valley, and asked him to meet the claimant; he had not seen Franziska since the winter of 1917–1918, and it took some persuasion before he agreed to Rathlef-Keilmann's proposal. He would come, he said, only if he wouldn't be held responsible for his sister's actions or her care; even so, he would say only what his mother had directed him to say.[33]

And what did his mother tell him to say? No evidence suggests that Franziska's family knew of her claim, or even that she was alive, before Martin Knopf appeared in Hygendorf. Saying that he believed he had found the missing Franziska, Knopf first asked Marianna and her daughters to simply identify photographs of the claimant; only when they had done so did he reveal that Franziska claimed to be Anastasia.[34] Unsophisticated and unaware, having already identified the claimant as her daughter, Marianna now for the first time learned of her charade. After the story broke in the *Berliner Nachtausgabe*, Hygendorf was overrun by inquisitive journalists, and the entire village was caught up in Franziska's escapades: by the second week of April, reporters had descended on the little hamlet and, as a neighbor recalled, "the driveway of the Schanzkowsky house was filled with autos." Journalists peered in windows, stopped people on the street to ask about Franziska, and knocked on Marianna's door day and night.[35]

One of the visitors was Fritz Schuricht, a private detective hired by Rathlef-Keilmann to investigate the *Nachtausgabe* story. He found Marianna "much vexed and agitated over the case," and at first she refused to speak to him, saying that she "wanted nothing to do with it at all." Finally, however, she relented. When shown photographs of the claimant, Marianna now insisted she wasn't her daughter, and she refused to let Schuricht speak to Gertrude, Maria Juliana, or anyone else. Midway through the interview, a car pulled up outside the farmhouse, and Marianna's second husband stormed in; after the couple exchanged a few words in Polish, he grabbed a pitchfork and waved it at Schuricht. "I came to the conclusion," Schuricht noted with ironic under-statement, "that there was no point in staying to ask any more questions, and Frau Schanzkowska [sic] assured me that it was best if I left. It was clear that the man was very annoyed with the whole business."[36]

What had changed? What caused this abrupt and unconvincing reversal? Franziska had become famous; supporters had paid her medi-cal expenses and provided for her in the belief that she was a grand duchess; she had lived with aristocrats, even a Berlin police inspector. Would her family now be held responsible, not just for her care but also for any legal action, for any charge of financial fraud? Lies had been told, lies by Franziska that could result in legal action; now Marianna added to the lie, scared to admit that Germany's most famous living enigma was her daughter. "It was from this point forward," remembered one of Franziska's friends in Hygendorf, that Marianna "began to tell everyone that her daughter was dead."[37]

This, presumably, was what Marianna told Felix to say, to deny that the claimant was his sister, to insist that she was most likely dead. When, on the afternoon of May 9, 1927, Rathlef-Keilmann and her lawyer Wilhelm Voller met his train, Felix said, "I don't think that my sister could still be alive, because Franziska was very fond of me, and I am sure that she would have written."[38] The trio drove to the village of Wasserburg-am-Inn, some twenty miles northwest of Seeon, where a meeting had been arranged in the beer garden of the Bridge Brewery; soon Franziska, accompanied by the duke of Leuchtenberg, his son Dimitri and daughter-in-law Catherine, and his two daughters Nathalia and Tamara, arrived in several cars.[39] As the claimant entered the beer garden, Voller turned to Felix Schanzkowsky, asking, "Who is this lady?"

"That's my sister, that's Franziska," he replied without hesitation.[40]

Seeing her brother, recalled the duke's two daughters, Franziska became "very agitated, and her jaw trembled through the whole of the meeting." Both Nathalia and Tamara thought that "the likeness" between the pair "was unmistakable, the same height, coloring, features, and particularly the mouth."[41]

"Well, go and speak to your brother!"[42] It was the duke of Leuchtenberg who broke the unnerving silence. The notoriously obstinate claimant meekly obeyed without any protest, her action confirming her brother's identification. The pair, remembered Dimitri Leuchtenberg, spoke "beyond our earshot" for some minutes, something confirmed by his wife, Catherine, though what was said is not known.[43]

After some thirty minutes, a silent Franziska returned to Seeon; the duke of Leuchtenberg, as willfully obtuse as ever, admitted only that Felix thought the claimant "might be his sister."[44] And Felix? "My sister's hair was different, my sister's figure was different, my sister's hands were different, but that's my sister," he said as she left the beer garden.[45] He sat with Rathlef-Keilmann and Voller, looking at an affidavit, drawn up in advance, in which he admitted that the claimant was Franziska. Suddenly, inexplicably, he changed his mind: the claimant wasn't his sister after all.[46] He did, though, sign a second affidavit, stating that while there was "a great resemblance" between the two, the claimant's "speech and manner of speaking" were different from those of his sister. The claimant, ran the affidavit composed by Voller and Rathlef-Keilmann and signed by Felix, "gave no sign that she knew who I was. From the look on her face, it was plain that she did not know me at all." Instead, she had treated him "as nothing more than an unknown person who had come to see her."[47]

It was all at odds—extraordinarily so—with what had just taken place, what the seven witnesses had just seen. Rathlef-Keilmann, of course, was quite willing to suspend disbelief and dismiss contrary evidence, but why had Felix Schanzkowsky made such a clumsy and unconvincing reversal? Perhaps he had arrived at Wasserburg prepared to follow his mother's directive, only to falter when he came face-to-face with his sister. If so, he must surely have realized that his immediate recognition could lead to disaster, for in lying to Schuricht, Marianna had set in motion a web of deceit that had to be maintained. If Felix clung to his immediate recognition, he may have feared that he exposed his mother to prosecution, his family, assurances to the contrary, to legal action and financial turmoil. To save his mother, he had to deny his sister, and this was the likely message he conveyed to Franziska when they spoke in the beer garden. In 1920, Franziska had insisted that her family was dead; now, in the spring of 1927, Marianna began telling people that Franziska was dead. After years of antipathy and uneasy relations, mother and daughter finally seem to have come to agreement: neither wanted anything to do with the other ever again.

For Franziska's supporters, though, Felix's ultimate rejection was enough; they ignored his immediate recognition in favor of his later repudiation. Soon the duke of Leuchtenberg was at it again, erroneously insisting that "throughout the confrontation" the claimant and her brother "each showed clearly that there was no previous relationship between them."[48] Gleb Botkin's dismissal of the entire episode bore an equally tenuous relationship to the truth. He declared that there was "not the slightest resemblance" between the photograph of Franziska and the claimant, and asserted that the entire story "was concocted by Knopf and Gilliard" based on the statements of Doris Wingender, whom he maliciously and erroneously called a prostitute.[49] Botkin reserved most of his scorn for Gilliard, writing that the former tutor had sold "his reputation as a loyal and honest man" to "our chief enemy, the Grand Duke of Hesse," to deny the claimant her rightful name.[50]

And then there was Rathlef-Keilmann, who refused to accept any of what she termed "the Schanzkowsky Myth."[51] She advanced a number of increasingly bizarre theories to explain it all away: the real Franziska, she first insisted, had fallen victim to a criminal gang in Berlin and could not, therefore, possibly be the claimant, a position she soon had to retract when challenged on the evidence.[52] Next, she contended that Doris Wingender was simply wrong, that she had once visited the same apartment building where Clara Peuthert lived, there encountered the claimant, "who must have had a certain similarity" to Franziska, and mistaken the two women—an ingenious theory but one unsupported by the evidence.[53] And Franziska? Rathlef-Keilmann now declared that she had fallen victim to Berlin serial killer and cannibal Georg Grossmann, a loathsome man who slaughtered upward of fifty young women in the years after the First World War; the bits of flesh he hadn't consumed were sold to unsuspecting butcher shops and ended up in the stomachs of a desperate city. Before he committed suicide in 1921, police found Grossmann's diary, a registry of barbaric horrors that included, among his victims, the name "Saznovski," which Rathlef-Keilmann suggested was the phonetic rendering of Schanzkowsky.[54] The Berlin police, however, rejected this would-be identification.[55]

Rathlef-Keilmann, though, wasn't about to let anything like investigations by the Berlin police change her determined mind, and in the autumn of 1927 she once again took her case to the press, publishing a series of articles in the *Tägliche Rundschau*. She openly attacked the *Berliner Nachtausgabe* and its investigation, asserting that the "Schanzkowsky legend" had been a plot against the claimant, "this poor, helpless creature, who is tormented and victimized at every turn," she declared. Doris Wingender had been paid for her story and she—well, Rathlef-Keilmann's conspiratorially minded readers could fill in the blanks. No one, Rathlef-Keilmann insisted—not a single member of Franziska's family, nor anyone else who had known her in Hygendorf or in Berlin—had recognized the claimant as the missing factory worker.[56]

And, as with so much of the evidence in the case, Rathlef-Keilmann was wrong, this time willfully wrong. By the summer of 1927, eleven people had identified the claimant as Franziska: Otto Meyer, her former teacher in Hygendorf; his son Richard; her childhood friend Martha Schrock; Anna Wingender and her three daughters Doris, Luise, and Kathe Wypyrczyk; her sisters Gertrude and Maria Juliana; and her mother, Marianna, and her brother Felix, even if the last two had abruptly and unconvincingly reversed themselves.[57]

But if Rathlef-Keilmann was willing to ignore this accumulated evidence, officials were not. Martin Knopf turned in his investigative reports, witness statements, and photographic evidence to Count von Hardenberg, who in turn presented the Darmstadt police with an edited version of the dossier, along with a letter stating that the claimant's identity as Franziska Schanzkowska had been definitively established. This the Darmstadt police passed on to the Berlin police, urging that they officially rule on the issue. After a short investigation, the Berlin police found that the claimant was Franziska and closed their files on her case.[58]

The game was over. Except that it wasn't, for fate once again came to Franziska's rescue. Amazingly, people still wanted to believe that she was Anastasia, that the story Rathlef-Keilmann told was true. Amazingly, the reality of the "unmasking" faded in the face of desire, ignored, distorted, and dismissed by her supporters until it was reduced to an absurdity, a mere footnote to her story.

Felix Schanzkowsky slunk away, back into the shadows, but he, too, had now become part of the story: as soon as he reversed himself and signed a statement denying his earlier recognition of the claimant as his sister, he, too, became enmeshed in his mother's conspiracy to subvert the truth. Each declaration buried the family deeper within a legal nightmare dominated by fear of collusion and prosecution. It was even worse, because privately he continually admitted he'd lied. He told Gertrude that he'd gone to meet Franziska in a place "where queens walked in the park," presumably a reference to Seeon; he'd recognized her, but denied it in his statement.[59] He confessed the same thing to his wife, Emma Mueller; to their daughter Waltraut; and to his niece, adding that "for the sake of the family" he'd changed his initial identification.[60]

It all died away, at least for a time, and a public fascinated by the myth of a surviving Anastasia quickly forgot "the Schanzkowsky legend." Not so officialdom, and not so the most unlikely player ever to enter the tangled tale: Adolf Hitler, whose Third Reich now wanted the issue resolved.[61] In 1937, a representative from the Ministry of the Interior in Berlin called on officials in Hannover, where Franziska then lived, and demanded a new confrontation with the Schanzkowsky family. The initiative was at least partially arranged by a former Russian general named Vassili Biskupsky, who had replaced Serge Botkin as head of the Russian Émigré Office in Berlin; Biskupsky, in turn, was closely allied to Grand Duke Vladimir Kirillovich, son and heir of Grand Duke Kirill Vladimirovich.[62]

And so, on order from the Reichschancellery, Nazi officials tracked down Franziska's family. Marianna Czenstkowski Knopf had died of pneumonia on December 20, 1932, in Hygendorf at age sixty-six.[63] Valerian still worked the farm in Hygendorf; Gertrude had married a coachman named August Ellerik and lived with him and their daughter Margarete on the outskirts of the village, near her sister Maria Juliana and her husband, Florian Zakorski; only Felix had fled the area to work in Ammendorf in the Ruhr Valley as a miner.[64] All were shown photographs of the claimant: Gertrude readily identified her as Franziska,

Felix thought she looked "too different," and both Valerian and Maria Juliana insisted that they'd scarcely known Franziska when she had lived with them, and that too much time had passed for them to offer a reliable opinion.[65]

But Berlin forced the issue: on July 9, 1938, Franziska obeyed a summons to appear at police headquarters in Hannover. She arrived with lawyers Edward Fallows and Paul Leverkuhn, Gertrude Madsack, and Gleb Botkin, and Criminal Police Commissioner A. W. Paar ushered her into a small room. Her four siblings, watched over by an intimidating representative from the Reich Ministry in Berlin, waited in another room. "Now we have a chance to see our sister again," Maria Juliana commented to Gertrude, "and make a decision if we recognize her or not." Suddenly the door opened and Franziska came face-to-face with her siblings. No one said anything; Criminal Police Commissioner Paar asked Franziska to walk back and forth as her siblings watched. At first, Gertrude struggled to reconcile the fashionable hairstyle and expensive clothing with her memories of Franziska; the claimant's voice, she thought, was somehow different from Franziska's, and she remembered her sister as larger—fatter—than the woman in front of her.[66] After studying her face and movements, though, "everything fell into place, and it was clear that she was my sister."[67] Maria Juliana looked Franziska over for a few minutes, then recognized her, saying, "Don't you know your sister?" Valerian apparently thought that the claimant looked "too different" from his sister, though he couldn't state "as fact" that she wasn't Franziska, while Felix thought she didn't even look like the woman he had met a decade earlier at Wasserburg; like Valerian, he, too, declared that he couldn't make a definitive statement. "That's the truth," he insisted.[68]

"Of course it's Franziska!" Gertrude suddenly insisted to her siblings. The other three whispered among themselves. Now Maria Juliana announced, "I have no real memory of Franziska. I can't say if this woman is my sister." This, apparently, was too much for Gertrude, who erupted in a sudden rage. Fists hammering on the table and face red with rage, she shouted, "You are my sister! You are my sister! I know it! You must recognize me!" The others tried to calm her; the siblings must have feared the consequences, for the louder Gertrude became, the more they insisted that the claimant was not their sister. Gertrude would have none of it. "Admit it! Admit it!" she shouted at Franziska, jumping from her seat, grabbing her by the collar, shaking her, and pulling the hat from her head. "She became more agitated as the minutes passed," Commissioner Paar noted. Felix, Valerian, and Maria Juliana insisted that while the resemblance between their sister and the claimant was "very strong," she was not Franziska. Gertrude, though, would have none of it: "I did so much for her!" she wailed. "I was so good to her! She must admit it!" Her siblings requested a private conference; when it ended, Gertrude, too, was now inexplicably filled with doubt; despite her adamant declarations, she—like her three siblings—refused to sign any statement admitting that the claimant was Franziska.[69]

What had happened? First Gertrude recognizes Franziska when shown pictures of the claimant, while her three other siblings insist they cannot do so, that they didn't really know Franziska well, that too much time has passed to offer any definite opinion. Maria Juliana is confused, first insisting the claimant isn't Franziska, then changing her mind, only to revert to her initial assessment after speaking with her brothers. And the trio whisper to Gertrude, trying to convince her that she is wrong. Perhaps Valerian and Maria Juliana really were confused, unable to recognize their sister in the woman they met that day, though the latter had been sure enough ten years earlier when she identified Franziska from photographs of the claimant; even Gertrude admitted that Franziska now seemed thinner, with a different hairstyle and expensive clothing. Yet it's difficult not to suspect that all of the whispers concealed a family desperately trying to present a unified front: Marianna might be dead, but Felix—who had, after all, signed a sworn statement in 1927 declaring that the claimant wasn't his sister—was right in the middle of this latest intrigue. He'd lied in a legal document, and the old worries about charges of fraud and prosecution must have been revived in that police station. And so Maria Juliana quickly backed away from her recognition, and everyone tried to convince Gertrude to do the same—and no one would sign anything definitive one way or the other about Franziska's identity. After years of lies, it was all the family could do to protect themselves, to protect Felix. And, as had happened after the confrontation at Wasserburg, Felix was soon admitting that he had indeed recognized the claimant as his sister. "He told me he had no doubt that it was Franziska," Gertrude later said.[70] He said the same thing to his wife, Emma, and to his daughter Waltraut; "circumstances" had forced him to deny that the claimant was Franziska.[71]

Franziska again emerged from the encounter unscathed; her supporters dismissed it, memories faded, and the public was led to believe that it had all been a pointless farce. But "the Schanzkowsky legend" would surface one last time, during the Hamburg trials, when the possibility that the world's most famous royal claimant was actually a former factory worker briefly took center stage. The courts heard of the alleged match that had been made between the claimant's handwriting and that on Franziska's November 1919 residency card, and received a report by graphologist Maurice Delamain, who studied the card and asserted, "Frau Anderson absolutely cannot be the Polish peasant Franziska Schanzkowska."[72] And Otto Reche weighed in after comparing the single photograph of Franziska to pictures of the claimant, declaring, "Frau Anderson is not Franziska Schanzkowska."[73]

The court also heard from those who, like Rathlef-Keilmann with her story that the real Franziska had been killed by Georg Grossmann, claimed to know what had happened to the missing factory worker. There was a certain Bruno Grandsitzki, who thirty-eight-years after the fact claimed that he had met Franziska in July 1920 in Danzig, at a time when she was actually a patient at Dalldorf. According to this story, she had found employment as a servant and was sailing for England with several other young women aboard a ship called *Premier*. Grandsitzki was nothing if not remarkable in his alleged recall of a thoroughly unremarkable and brief encounter with a woman whom he did not know and had no reason to remember, for he volunteered that she had even specified to him that her new employers lived in London, on Bedford Road.[74] A thorough investigation into this tale, which, as the German magazine *Der Spiegel* noted, "has become increasingly tall with the passage of time," yielded no results.[75] The ever-hopeful Dominique Auclères, stepping into the gullible void vacated by Rathlef-Keilmann, pursued this tale with a vengeance: she checked passenger manifests of ships that had operated out of Danzig; combed through registry ledgers; and pored over immigration files in Great Britain. None, not surprisingly, contained any reference to Franziska Schanzkowska.[76]

Then there were three former nurses, who emerged from the shadows to briefly take the witness stand in 1966. Charlotte Janus, Margarete Binner, and Emma Bezug all said that they had worked at an asylum in Herrenprotsch near Breslau, and claimed to have recognized a newspaper photograph of Franziska as a woman who, they insisted, had been incarcerated in their institution from 1929 to 1934—a time when she was actually in America and then at Ilten near Hannover. Like the tale woven by Grandzitski, no evidence ever emerged to support this rather contradictory claim.[77]

Such stories became commonplace in Franziska's saga, evidence not of some mysterious fate but rather[78] of the hold her claim held for a fascinated public. People not only wanted her tale to be true, they also wanted—no matter how contradictory or absurd their accounts—to be part of it themselves, to affix themselves to the greatest living mystery of the twentieth century. "If he can be considered part of her story," *Der Spiegel* presciently commented of Grandzitski, "he can become a part of history. Lie would be the wrong word for it all."

But the Hamburg courts weren't quite so easily taken in, or as forgiving as most of the public. In their 1961 verdict, the Hanseatic Landesgericht Court not only ruled against the plaintiff's claim to be Anastasia but also on a counterclaim brought by Berenberg-Gossler that she was, in fact, Franziska Schanzkowska. This last contention, they said, had also not been sufficiently established, though they thought it "seems highly probable."[79] It hadn't been sufficiently established because, in truth, Berenberg-Gossler hadn't really tried very hard to prove it, as an examination of the evidence now makes clear; instead, he spent most of his time in court attempting to refute those who claimed to have seen a rescued Anastasia in this or that province or country, or arguing against Franziska's contention that Grand Duke Ernst Ludwig had secretly visited Russia in 1916.

And Franziska's family? They did their best to avoid the entire spectacle. By the time of the Hamburg trials, Maria Juliana had died, and Valerian, though still living on the family farm, was inaccessible in Soviet-controlled Poland. In 1959, Hans Hermann Krampff, opposition lawyer in the case, wrote to Gertrude, "Research conducted in the interval confirms that you were not alone in recognizing Frau Anderson as your sister Franziska at the 1938 encounter. Your brothers and sister did so as well, but refrained from admitting this so as not to obstruct your sister's career. . . . There is nothing to be feared if you now tell the truth, as the term for any judicial punishment has passed."[80] And so Gertrude repeated her story, told of how she had recognized Franziska, but not so Felix, who, perhaps bound by the lie to which he had committed himself in his 1927 sworn affidavit, continually ignored legal requests that he participate in the court proceedings. Attempting to convince him, Gertrude's daughter Margarete Ellerik wrote to Felix, "It's not everyone who can say he has a full-blooded sister whom powerful and important people have mistaken for decades as the Tsar's daughter!"[81] But nothing would change Felix's mind, and he never gave any formal statement during the trials.

The lies, the silence, the reversals, the refusal to commit, it all played into Franziska's hands. She'd been unmasked, recognized, identified—even admitted that she was a fraud—and still, amazingly, she managed to survive it all. It is a remarkable testament to the extraordinary power of this most romantic of twentieth-century myths and to Franziska's extraordinary capabilities. People wanted to believe, and believe they did—even in the face of all evidence to the contrary. In the end, for much of the world, Franziska Schanzkowska, this former "peasant," this farm girl from the provinces, this "insane" factory worker, became Anastasia.

Epilogue

A FTER SO MANY DECADES of apparently compelling evidence in Anna Anderson's favor, so many recognitions, asserted memories, and minute details supporting her claim, the 1994 DNA results shocked many who had believed that she was Anastasia. It was simply impossible, Gleb Botkin once insisted, to "mistake a Polish peasant for a Grand Duchess."[1] Marina and Richard Schweitzer, his daughter and son-in-law, echoed the sentiment: although they never questioned the integrity of the scientists or the actual genetic tests, they rejected the conclusions. The bowel tissue tested, Schweitzer insisted, "did not come from the body of the Anna Anderson we knew. It had to be tampered with." It was not so much the claimant's exclusion as Anastasia that they protested, but rather the suggestion that she had been Franziska. "For all of us who knew her," Schweitzer said, "there's no way she could be a Polish peasant. That didn't match the rational human experience of the people who knew her."[2] The idea that she had been Franziska Schanzkowska, he declared, was "devastating," "an insult."[3]

Perhaps the identification of Anna Anderson as Franziska Schanzkowska seemed so unlikely because, like most apparently extraordinary things, people expected the solution to the mystery to be as fantastic as her claim. The DNA results and their stark scientific conclusions did nothing to address the lingering questions: How, the claimant's supporters asked, did a rural farm girl randomly embody so many elements that seemingly pointed to her identity as Anastasia?

What were the odds that she would be lucky enough to be the correct height to match the diminutive grand duchess, and share not only her hair and eye color but also the *hallux valgus*? How could she amass such seemingly intimate knowledge of the imperial family and life at court? How did she apparently develop a talent for languages, or learn to play the piano? How could she convincingly present herself as a person of refined character, allegedly versed in the intricacies of etiquette? How, Anderson's supporters asked—and continue to ask—could almost seventy-five years of such accumulated evidence refuting the idea that she had been Franziska Schanzkowska suddenly be cast aside in favor of a string of genetic codes? Was every contradiction to be ignored? Every recognition of the claimant as Anastasia ruled a mistake? Coincidence, they suggested, had its limits, and this tangled case couldn't be put down to mere chance.

But there were assumptions at play here, erroneous assumptions, resting on decades of erroneous information. People believed that the recognitions were compelling, that she'd simply known too much— "The Man with the Pockets," all of the answers to Prince Sigismund's questions—not to believe that she was Anastasia; people believed she possessed impressive linguistic abilities, that she'd convinced too many experts who studied her handwriting and her photographs, to think it was all a mistake. And people believed that a "peasant" such as Franziska was incapable of learning languages, of assimilating information; there was no way to reconcile her family's statements that she'd never been pregnant and hadn't been wounded during the AEG accident with the woman rescued from the Landwehr Canal. It was all wrong, of course, on both sides, but no one knew the truth, a truth that lay hidden, ignored, and suppressed as the myth took shape and swelled into a lasting cultural phenomenon.

People seized on contradictions: Franziska supposedly wore larger shoes than the claimant, she was taller, fatter, her hair color different, assertions never established in court, subjective memories advanced as reasons to dismiss the DNA results.[4] And there were other tests, they insisted, that stood in direct opposition to the 1994 verdict. In the 1970s, for example, after the ruling by the West German Federal Supreme Court rejecting Franziska's appeal, Dr. Moritz Furtmayr conducted two photographic studies of the claimant. The first, utilizing a system he developed called the "Personen-Identifizierungskartei" or "P.I.K. Method," a kind of early Identikit, measured what Furtmayr said were cardinal points on the face—the depth and distance of certain features whose relationship never altered over time.[5] According to Furtmayr, the claimant was Anastasia; the P.I.K. Method, he said, was accepted as valid scientific evidence within the West German legal system.[6]

Furtmayr also compared photographs of Franziska's right ear with that of the grand duchess. He identified seventeen points of concordance between the two women, five more, he said, than required by West German law to establish identity.[7]

This was clearly a problem. In a 1930 letter to Princess Xenia Georgievna, Empress Alexandra's sister Victoria, marchioness of Milford Haven, wrote:

> One insuperable obstacle to my acceptance of the question of identity is that A's ears were not the same shape as Anastasia's, which I remember very well and which my sister Alix and I used to say were a case of atavism as hers closely resembled those of my father's brother and were unlike the ordinary ones. Both Irene and my brother are in agreement with me in this opinion. Now it is an acknowledged fact that the modeling, especially of the curl over and lobe of an ear, remains unaltered from the day of birth of a person until death.[8]

Ernst Ludwig agreed, as did Victoria's son Lord Mountbatten, who again raised this objection in a letter to his cousin Prince Ludwig of Hesse.[9] Michael Thornton broke news of Furtmayr's tests to Lord Louis Mountbatten. "As he read it, his face was a picture of doubt and confusion," Thornton remembered. "But this isn't possible!" Mountbatten finally declared. "No impostor could be as lucky as that!"[10]

On the surface there were two immediate objections to Furtmayr's tests. He believed that previous photographic comparisons of the claimant utilized an image wrongly printed in reverse; when corrected, he found that her ear matched that of Anastasia.[11] In fact, the image in question—a profile photograph of Franziska taken at Dalldorf in 1920—had not been reversed, rendering his claims of a match problematic. Then, too, he used a photograph of Marie Nikolaievna, not Anastasia, in declaring a match with the claimant's ear.[12] Furtmayr, now deceased, is a bit of a shadowy figure. He worked as a carpenter, then a cook, then a lumberjack before taking a course through the International Detective Training Institute, a correspondence school in Washington, D.C., that regularly advertised its services to "train at home" and "earn big money" in the back of popular magazines and was apparently unaccredited by any organization.[13] Furtmayr's credentials are not known, but the problems in his study raise serious concerns about its results.[14]

Or take a 1994 test conducted by Professor Peter Vanezis of the Forensic Department of London's Charing Cross and Westminster Medical School. Vanezis and five colleagues studied six photographs of unidentified ears against an archival image of Anastasia. Five of the six men believed that Franziska's ears were the "most likely" match to those of Anastasia, though there was one dissenter. Even so, as Vanezis pointed out, this was "a possibility" but not one that could be considered definitive identification. Vanezis noted that these results were "based on the assumption" that individual human ears were unique and retained their characteristics from birth to death—the reasoning argued by Victoria, marchioness of Milford Haven, and echoed by Furtmayr.[15] And assumption it certainly was, for it lacks any scientific basis. Andre Moenssens, a legal professor specializing in forensic anthropological evidence, notes that the assumption of ear individuality "has never been empirically established. There is not a single published scientific study that establishes that ears are, in fact, different and distinct and that such individuality can be verified through comparisons."[16]

Nothing, in the end, was particularly compelling, and these tests were refuted, as ever in this case, by others. In 1994, British producer Julian Nott commissioned a number of studies—including that of Vanezis—for his documentary on Anna Anderson. Geoffrey Oxlee, a British specialist in facial comparisons, conducted a simple computer comparison of the only known pre-1920 image of Franziska and the claimant, superimposing the two to correlate their features. There was, he noted, variation in the ears, but suggested that if the two images represented different individuals, the disparity should be much greater. He found the evidence "consistent" with the belief that the claimant was Franziska. Dr. Peter French, a forensic phonetician of London's City University, analyzed Franziska's speech patterns as recorded in the 1960s by Alexei Miliukov. Of a definitive Russian accent there was no conclusive proof, though the way in which she pronounced the letter r suggested a Slavic, not German, origin, but, French added importantly, this same sound was "the standard pronunciation" in the area where Franziska had been brought up. And David Ellen, former head of Scotland Yard's Questioned Document Section, compared the claimant's handwriting to that of Anastasia. He concluded, "I find no evidence that Anna Anderson was in fact Grand Duchess Anastasia. When I say no evidence, I mean essentially that the writings are different in a number of respects, significantly different."[17]

It was all so like the Hamburg trials, with experts arguing opposing points in what was largely a subjective game. And what of the DNA, the crushing results that contradicted so much of what history had been led to believe? Three independent laboratories—Forensic Science Services, Pennsylvania State University, and the Armed Forces Institute of Pathology—tested biological materials from the claimant. Nuclear DNA testing of the bowel tissue by Forensic Science Services excluded any possibility that the claimant had been a child of Nicholas and Alexandra; mitochondrial DNA tests on three separate slices of the

Charlottesville tissue by Forensic Science Services and by the Armed
Forces Institute of Pathology excluded the possibility that she had
been a matrilineal descendant of Empress Alexandra; and the mitochondrial DNA profile derived by Forensic Science Services and by
Pennsylvania State University from two different samples of the claimant's hair also excluded any genetic relationship to Empress Alexandra.
But four additional tests had confirmed her genetic relationship with
the Schanzkowsky family. The mitochondrial DNA profiles derived
by Forensic Science Services for both the bowel tissue and for the hair
matched that established for Karl Maucher; the Armed Forces Institute
of Pathology, working with a different slice of bowel tissue, discovered
an identical mitochondrial DNA sequence matching the Maucher profile;
and Pennsylvania State University also obtained an identical mitochondrial DNA profile confirming a genetic link between the claimant and
Franziska's great-nephew.

Could any of this be challenged or dismissed? In 1994, Forensic
Science Services analyzed six short tandem repeats, or STRs, in their
nuclear DNA comparisons that had excluded Franziska from being a
child of Nicholas and Alexandra; within a few years, the science had
evolved—and continues to evolve—to more reliable ten-, twelve-, and
twenty-point tests. Does this invalidate the 1994 results? No. Analysis
of additional points might increase the odds of a genetic relationship,
but nothing will ever change the four mismatches Gill's team found,
not just with the emperor and the empress but also with the remains of
the three grand duchesses exhumed from the Koptyaki grave. Franziska
matched none of them, a scientific impossibility had she really been
Anastasia. The four mismatches remain immutable regardless of the
number of points analyzed.

Producer Maurice Philip Remy obtained a glass slide of Franziska's
blood taken on June 6, 1951, by hematologist Dr. Stefan Sandkuhler
with the idea of seeing if she had been a hemophilia carrier; half of the
slide was sent to Dr. Charles Ginther at the University of California
at Berkeley and half to Drs. Bernd Hermann, Jens Rameckers, and
Susanne Hummel at the Georg-August Institute for Anthropology at
the University of Göttingen in Germany.[18] This was compared against
blood samples given by Princess Sophie of Hannover, sister of Prince
Philip, duke of Edinburgh, and by Margarete Ellerik, Karl Maucher's
mother and Gertrude's daughter.[19] The profile for Princess Sophie
matched that of her brother, while that of Margarete Ellerik matched
that of her son; but the profile the German scientists obtained from
the slide—and sent to Ginther—matched neither sequence.[20] Did this
mean that Franziska wasn't related to the Schanzkowsky family? No.
The slide, which bore the name "Anastasia" scratched onto its surface,

had been stored without any protective covering, leading to a corrupted sample.[21] So the results meant nothing, but analysis of Princess Sophie's mitochondrial DNA profile confirmed that of her brother, while the blood sample from Margarete Ellerik established without question the Schanzkowsky profile found in Karl Maucher.

How about the chain of custody for the samples tested? Was it, as some of Anderson's supporters suggested, so legally questionable that the tests would be thrown out of any court?[22] No. To avoid any such challenges, Gill never allowed the samples out of his possession until he arrived at the Forensic Science Services Laboratory in Great Britain, and the Armed Forces Institute of Pathology employed similar safeguards in collecting and conveying a different section of bowel tissue from Martha Jefferson Hospital to their own laboratories.[23] Susan Grindstaff Burkhart preserved the hair she found in sterile conditions in a safety deposit box; the samples tested by Forensic Science Services and Pennsylvania State University were prepared by a trained lab technician, sealed in protective containers, and delivered to the laboratories by hand and by documented courier.[24] The chain of custody, the documentation of the samples during their collection, transfer, and analysis—at least according to American and European standards of legal admissibility—is pristine and presents no judicial difficulties.[25]

If not changes in methodology, conflicting results from a blood slide, or issues over the chain of custody, how about contamination? Could the results simply be wrong because the samples were corrupt? No. The uniformity observed in the samples precludes such a possibility. The mitochondrial sequence derived by Gill's team from the bowel tissue matched that derived from a separate section of bowel tissue analyzed by the Armed Forces Institute of Pathology; the profile from the hair sample tested by Gill matched that obtained by Pennsylvania State University. Contamination would have meant not just variation from facility to facility but noticeably corrupted profiles, sequences that would have been of no use for genetic comparison. The fact that the hair samples came from a different source than the bowel tissues yet all matched proved not only common origin but also demolished any contention that contamination had taken place.[26]

This leaves only one avenue: conspiracy, an idea fully in keeping with decades of erroneous claims that the Romanovs had recognized then rejected Franziska to seize tsarist funds, that Grand Duke Ernst Ludwig had invented the entire "Schanzkowsky legend" to discredit a woman he knew to be his niece, that Gilliard had repeatedly lied to undermine her claim. Such a theory presumably imagines some nefarious royal plot—by the Hessians? by the Windsors?—to subvert the truth, some shadowy figure who tampered with the genetic material prior to testing. Was this possible? No. Had someone accessed the tissue sample at Martha Jefferson Hospital and somehow injected it with mitochondrial DNA drawn from a living Schanzkowsky relative, the end result would have been a completely useless sequence of disparate genetic codes matching no one. How about someone substituting the claimant's sample with tissue derived from a member of Franziska's family? Again, no. The five-inch Anderson bowel tissue was gangrenous and came from a living female patient whose mitochondrial DNA matched that of Karl Maucher and his mother, Margarete Ellerik. So what mysterious, living female Schanzkowsky relative suffering from a gangrenous bowel obstruction had willingly donated five inches of her lower intestine? For that matter, how did a conspirator even find the Anderson tissue sample? It was stored in the hospital's pathology archives, listed only by patient number, and the identities behind those numbers were kept in a different registry. That nothing of the sort took place became clear in 1993, when the hospital discovered slices of the bowel tissue, sectioned after the 1979 operation and preserved in slides, separately from the bowel tissue, in its histology department. Comparison of the slides to the bowel tissue showed that they were identical.[27]

But the real nail in the conspiratorial coffin was the hair. The samples owned by Susan Grindstaff Burkhart had no association with Martha Jefferson Hospital. They had been stored in a safety deposit box since 1990; this was a year before the Koptyaki grave was exhumed, a year before anyone knew that two bodies were missing, and three years before scientists established a DNA profile for the Romanov remains. Grindstaff Burkhart even had an additional test privately performed, analyzing hairs from the large clump—from which Forensic Science Services and Pennsylvania State University had derived their genetic profiles—against the cut hair she discovered in one of the small florist envelopes tucked into several of John Manahan's books: the hairs proved to be identical, indicating a common source.[28] When did this conspiracy to tamper with the samples begin? In 1990? In 1989? The logistics demanded of such a conspiracy are matched only by its absurdity. Perhaps more to the point, what are the odds that in the Berlin of 1927, in a city of millions where thousands had gone missing, Grand Duke Ernst Ludwig's conspiratorial agents would just happen to pick the *one* missing woman whose mitochondrial DNA—some seventy years later—would exactly match that of the claimant? If the chances that something went wrong with the DNA are nonexistent, so, too, is the likelihood that Franziska Schanzkowska was plucked at random from obscurity and coincidentally ended up sharing Anna Anderson's genetic sequence.

But decades of earnest belief die hard, particularly when fed by whispers of conspiracy and rumors of nefarious royal goings-on. Even if the 1994 DNA results seem conclusive, doubts about their validity linger. The only way to offer definitive resolution is new testing, using the most up-to-date technology and taking into account the advances made in genetic science—and here is where this extraordinary story takes a final, unexpected turn. In October 1990 author Greg King received strands of Anna Anderson's hair from the same clump discovered by Susan Grindstaff Burkhart the previous month and tested in 1994. In an unexpected and generous turn, Dr. Michael Coble, formerly of the Armed Forces DNA Identification Laboratory and now Forensic Biologist at the National Institute of Standards and Technology in Maryland—and a man involved in the identification of the Romanov remains—suggested that the hairs King had received be tested. Professor Daniele Podini of George Washington University agreed to work with Coble on this new sequencing: if a genetic profile was derived, it could then be tested against those found in the Romanov remains and that established for Franziska's great-nephew Karl Maucher.

Coble and Podini selected five hairs to use, one of which included follicular tissue; these were cleaned to remove any possible external contamination. The results were replicated multiple times to ensure that there was no mistake. The nuclear DNA profile obtained by Coble and Podini matches that established by Gill and his colleagues from the Anderson bowel tissue and samples of her hair. Coble and Podini tested fifteen STR markers, of which eight provided reproducible—and thus reliable—results. All eight are incompatible with the idea that Anna Anderson was Anastasia—the Federal Bureau of Investigation requires only two exclusions for definitive results in criminal cases. "We can absolutely exclude this individual as being a child of Nicholas and Alexandra," Coble and Podini report. The mitochondrial DNA profile from these new hairs also fails to match that found in the remains of Empress Alexandra, again excluding any possibility that Anderson had been Anastasia. It does, though, match the sequence established for Karl Maucher by Gill and his colleagues—exactly. When Coble and Podini checked DNA databases in America and in Europe, they found that this mitochondrial DNA shared by Anna Anderson and Maucher remains extremely rare.[29]

These new tests, arriving just as we complete this book, are important. Thanks to Dr. Coble and Dr. Podini, we can now dismiss any idea of contamination, worries about changes in methodology, or hints about possible corruption in the Anna Anderson DNA tests. Having been in Greg King's possession since 1990—before the exhumation of the Romanov grave or the discovery of the Anderson bowel tissue—the

Memorial statue outside the Cathedral on the Blood, Ekaterinburg, depicting the Romanovs descending the staircase to the murder room in the cellar.

hairs, like those belonging to Susan Grindstaff Burkhart, lay waste to any notions of some far-reaching conspiracy. Anna Anderson matches the Maucher profile; she does not match Empress Alexandra.

So it's impossible to impeach the DNA evidence, that uncomfortable and uncompromising string of codes that forever shattered this most persistent of twentieth-century myths. The myth portrayed the recognitions, the asserted memories, the handwriting and photographic comparisons, the alleged matches between her ears and those of Anastasia—all of it as compelling, convincing, plausible. It wasn't. The DNA not only stands in direct opposition to this body of favorable evidence, it also demolishes it, and conclusively so.

And, in a roundabout way, this brings us to the present book. Ours has been a thirty-year journey through the Anna Anderson story, a journey down this long, tangled road that has taken us from belief in her claim to firm conviction that she was indeed Franziska Schanzkowska. It has, in many ways, been a very personal book, a search for resolution, for answers to the very real questions that we, and so many others, had in the wake of the 1994 tests. We had read books and magazines, watched films and documentaries, and most importantly enjoyed extraordinary access to rare unpublished materials and to those personally involved in the case, and it all seemed so convincing. How to reconcile this with the DNA?

This was the power of the myth. It took a full decade for us to wade through the case files assembled by Darmstadt, through the dozens of bound volumes of Hamburg testimony, through the boxes of letters, newspaper clippings, and books that told the story, a story that made us realize just how pervasive the myth had been, how it had distorted the truth, how it had portrayed Gilliard and Doris Wingender as liars, had painted the investigation by Knopf and the *Berliner Nachtausgabe* as unreliable. None of it was true. The world had largely been exposed to only one side of the case, the side that the world preferred, that Anastasia had indeed survived the massacre in Ekaterinburg, and had survived in the person of Anna Anderson. The world had been led to believe that evidence in her favor was overwhelming. How wrong we all were.

And we were wrong, all of us who believed, who bought into the myth. The only way to find the answers we sought, the answers history needed, was to question everything in this case, every piece of evidence, every assertion, every test. All too often, important, lingering questions over Franziska's claim were dismissed on the pretext that the DNA tests resolved the mystery. Such reasoning did nothing to illuminate the case. We needed to understand not just how it had happened but also

The Cathedral on the Blood, Ekaterinburg, built 2000–2003 atop the former site of the Ipatiev House.

why it had happened, so we began in reverse. We spent years pursuing arguments that Anderson was Anastasia, investigating the DNA, poring over hundreds of unpublished documents, only to reject the idea; we then investigated charges that Anderson wasn't Franziska, only to find that she was. But without asking these questions, without investigating these objections and the mass of evidence, we would never have found just how shaky the myth really was, how distorted the story had become, how Franziska had actually managed to seem so convincing. Had it been otherwise, had we been able to discover new and compelling information refuting the DNA tests, or conclusive proof that Anderson was Anastasia, we would have been delighted to challenge history.

Some questions will always remain. No one knows what went on inside Franziska's mind, and her early years are doomed to remain matters of shadowy conjecture. It would be wrong, though, to assume that if some events remain unexplained, some contradiction lingers, that the question of Anderson's identity remains unresolved. It doesn't. Contradiction and coincidence, uncertainties and speculation do not negate the massive accumulation of evidence proving that she was Franziska Schanzkowska. People like their mysteries neatly resolved, with all conflicts explained and all doubts erased; life, though, seldom fits into such a box, and history—and historical mysteries—are always fragmentary in nature. This is the appeal of Franziska's story, the pull of the myth, the hope that somehow, in some way, fate was more humane to Anastasia than the fusillade of Bolshevik bullets that rang out that hot summer night nearly a century ago.

+ + +

So what did really happen in Ekaterinburg? Woken in the middle of the night, a sleepy Anastasia had followed her family down the narrow Ipatiev House stairway, followed Yakov Yurovsky out into the courtyard and back inside the mansion's ground floor, through a warren of corridors to the small storeroom from which there was no escape. They waited, the Romanovs, Dr. Botkin, and the three retainers imprisoned with them, Alexandra sitting in one chair, a sickly-looking Tsesarevich Alexei in another, and the four grand duchesses standing near the back of the room. It was two-thirty in the morning.[30]

And then Yurovsky reappeared, standing with a grim-looking group that filled the room's only exit. There were gasps, low screams, sobs when Yurovsky announced that the Ural Regional Soviet had condemned Nicholas II to death; even in these last few seconds, did the Romanovs believe that only the tsar was to be killed? Yurovsky mercifully said nothing of the rest of the family; then the guns appeared, shining in the light of a single electric bulb hanging from the ceiling, the shots began, and mercy disappeared in a haze of smoke. Nicholas fell under a barrage of bullets; so, too, did valet Alexei Trupp and cook Ivan Kharitonov; Alexandra had time only to cross herself before a shot tore through her skull, knocking her backward, off her chair, and onto the floor where her daughters stood, untouched. Bullets ricocheted around the walls; within a few seconds, smoke from the guns filled the room with a noxious fog that sent the assassins stumbling for air as the cellar echoed with terrified sobs and pleas for help.[31]

Anastasia was still alive, at the back of the room, with her sisters, screaming, when the men came back. Trying to raise himself up from the floor, Dr. Botkin was shot through the head; Alexei sat petrified as the bullets poured into his frail body until he finally collapsed. Then they came for them, the grand duchesses who had flirted with young officers, who had danced across the deck of the imperial yacht, who had walked in white dresses and elegant picture hats before newsreel cameras, who had nursed and tended to wounded soldiers as their father's empire edged toward disaster, and who now stumbled and slipped across a floor slick with their parents' blood. The bullets came now, hitting them, striking the protective layers of jewels concealed beneath their blouses, driving them back but leaving them alive. The men came closer: Olga and Tatiana fell, shot through their heads. And then the men turned on the two youngest daughters, stabbing at them with bayonets as they hurled themselves in vain against a set of locked doors at the back of the room. And still they lived, hidden jewels deflecting the flashing blades. Finally one of the men drunkenly aimed his gun and shot at their heads as the others turned their bayonets on the maid Anna Demidova until the room fell silent.[32]

The silence of death: it lay across the terrible jumble of bodies and blood-spattered walls. But Anastasia was still alive, and Marie, too, for as their bodies were carried to a Fiat truck that stood waiting in the courtyard, first one, then the other, suddenly sat up, coughing blood, moaning, screaming. They were outside now, and the men couldn't shoot them; the bayonets came out, slashing through the air, but the knives struck the hidden jewels. And so someone grabbed a rifle, turned it around, and hammered away at the barely conscious faces, driving the wooden stock down again and again and again.[33] Battered into silence, choking on splintered bone and shattered teeth, drowning in her own blood—this was how Anastasia died.

Two days passed, days in which Anastasia's stiff and bloodied body, stripped naked, was cast down the abandoned Four Brothers mine shaft in the Koptyaki Forest with the rest of the victims; in which it, and the other bodies, was tied with ropes and pulled back out of the shaft, thrown on the ground, and covered with brush; in which it, bruised and bloated in the Siberian summer, was hurled onto the back of a truck and driven through the night until the truck broke down in a forest clearing called Pig's Meadow. Yurovsky's men dug a pit in the rutted roadway and tossed the corpses into the grave—all, that is, except for Anastasia and Alexei, who were dragged some two hundred feet across the wet grass and through the muddy meadow, where a bonfire had been hastily built. First one, then the other was flung atop the glowing timbers, doused with gasoline, consigned to the consuming flames. Two shallow pits received what, after ninety minutes, remained of the charred bodies, covered with dirt and ash, packed down, concealed, hidden for nearly ninety years.[34]

For sixteen years following the 1991 exhumation of the nine sets of remains from the mass grave, geologists, archaeologists, historians, and amateur investigators searched through the Koptyaki Forest, searched for this missing grave, for these missing remains. They mapped every foot of Pig's Meadow, dug it up with shovels and spades and tractors, sifted through the upturned soil for a single bone splinter, a single tooth. It wasn't a question of endless acres of forest: if Yurovsky was telling the truth about burning and burying the two corpses in the meadow, someone, sometime, should have found something. But sixteen years passed, years without a single, identifiable bone fragment. The DNA tests had resolved the Romanov mystery and the identity of Anna Anderson, but history and science could not definitively answer the most intriguing question—the fate of Anastasia.

But then it happened—unlikely; unexpected; perhaps, even, to the more conspiratorially minded, unconvincing: in August 2007, a group of Ekaterinburg historians and archaeologists discovered two shallow pits in a low rise at the edge of Pig's Meadow, two hundred feet from the cross marking the site of the mass grave. Within, they found forty-eight highly fragmented bones, including a piece of skull, a pelvic bone, shattered femurs, seven teeth, ribs, and arm bones: all showed signs of having been burnt, and several bore indications of possible gunshot wounds and possible hacking apart by axes prior to being consigned to the bonfire.[35] Examination established that they came from two separate individuals, a male of between twelve and fifteen years, and a female approximately fifteen to nineteen years old. The Armed Forces DNA Identification Laboratory in Maryland, which had previously worked on the Romanov and Anderson cases, as well as the Institute for Forensic Medicine in Innsbruck, received samples for genetic testing. Analysis by Dr. Michael Coble of the Armed Forces DNA Identification Laboratory and his colleagues revealed, using nuclear DNA testing, that both sets of remains had been Nicholas and Alexandra's children, while mitochondrial tests confirmed their maternal descent from the empress. Only one teenage male, Tsesarevich Alexei, had disappeared, making his identification easiest.

And Anastasia? When the remains of Olga, Tatiana, and Marie were exhumed from the mass grave in 1991, each had their femurs intact; the discovery of a fragmented female femur, as Dr. Coble wryly noted, closed the door to any idea of "Yurovsky taking a portion of the femurs from the first grave and sneakily burying them nearby."[36] The shattered femur, shown to belong to a female, shown to be from a daughter of Nicholas and Alexandra, shown to be a descendant of the empress—this and a few charred bone fragments were all that remained of Russia's most famous Grand Duchess.[37] The myth that Franziska had made seem so convincing, so real, for so many years, was over: Anastasia was no longer missing.

IN 1967, IN AN UNGUARDED MOMENT while speaking with Alexei Miliukov, Franziska spoke of "who I am, and who I pretend to be."[38] It was the second and last time that she admitted her deception, but the remark passed unnoticed. Propelled by favorable assumptions and a shifting prism of truth, Franziska's story spiraled beyond her own control and entered the realm of legend, where the few verifiable facts of her case slipped into obscurity as the myth assumed a life of its own.

Was she victim or villain? The portrait of Franziska that emerges is neither black nor white, neither entirely calculated nor ruled by a confused mind. From a nomadic childhood, a youth of indulgence and unsavory rumors, she developed into a singular young woman of fragile emotions and warring personalities, deprived of maternal affection and bereft of comforting influences. Her experiences in Berlin—the loss of a fiancé, pregnancy, the accident at AEG—shattered whatever stability she had temporarily achieved; a nervous breakdown led to involuntary commitment, to declarations of insanity. She found no comfort in her 1917 return to Hygendorf; attacked at Gut-Friederikenhof, left physically battered, she staggered from crisis to crisis, from impoverished despair to rumors of prostitution until the weight of a hopeless life drove her into the waters of the Landwehr Canal.

And what began as a ploy for a few extra privileges, a few special attentions, this claim to be Anastasia, soon became something more as the possibilities stretched before Franziska, weaving an alluring and ready lifeline to a woman desperately in need of salvation. It all came together in a most extraordinary way, a series of coincidences that coincided with desire. In 1922, when word of her claim spread through émigré circles in Berlin, there wasn't any real evidence proving that Anastasia had perished in Ekaterinburg. Reported sightings, whispers of escape, and persistent rumors all played into Franziska's hands, giving her story a veneer of unlikely plausibility—a situation that wouldn't change until a decade after her death. She found a group of uncertain Russian émigrés still traumatized by the Revolution, a fractured collection of refugees divided by loyalties and beliefs and ruled by hope. Scarred by the loss of their country, their titles, and their fortunes, many were susceptible to any echo from their vanished past. Her claim played upon these dreams, where intriguing possibility joined force with a deeper need, a psychological desire, to make sense of overwhelming loss.

It was a performance so apparently convincing that even after the 1994 DNA tests, no one could answer any of the lingering questions. But Franziska's claim—and her abilities—evolved in a natural fashion as she assimilated information and grew into the role of Anastasia. At first she said little, offering few details to support her claim, but increased exposure to former aristocrats, courtiers, and published materials allowed her to add names and dates to her tale, to recognize faces and places as she built her identity. She understood desire—the desire from those she met, those who wanted to be convinced, and from the world at large. And the world, through the efforts of Harriet von Rathlef-Keilmann, Gleb Botkin, Dominique Auclères, and Peter Kurth, through the sympathetic newspapers and magazines, through the performance of Ingrid Bergman, viewed her as a woman wronged, a tragic figure, the living embodiment of an exotic and brilliant vanished past. Anastasia was an unremarkable young woman when she stepped across the threshold of that cellar room in the Ipatiev House; it was her rumored survival as Anna Anderson that made her extraordinary.

Chance and coincidence aided Franziska, but she was, in her own right, a remarkable woman. Someone of fewer capabilities and dedication, who lacked the mental acumen to absorb the myriad details that came her way, would undoubtedly have failed in the difficult quest she set for herself. Martin Knopf, the detective working for Grand Duke Ernst Ludwig, made an important observation: "There is a difference," he wrote in his report on Franziska, "between being uneducated and incapable of education. She was quite capable of educating herself."[39] It was Franziska's genius and her gift that she understood precisely what was needed to make her claim seem possible; that she knew when to retreat if danger threatened; and that she knew how to deploy her considerable personal charm to best present herself as a viable pretender. That she continues to arouse strong passions is scarcely surprising, given the length of her claim and the extent to which it became a part of twentieth-century popular culture; she still has believers, even in the face of the DNA results, people sincerely troubled—as we once were—by previously unanswered questions in her case. And she has an oddly vocal group of modern critics, those with no connection to the story but who, ruled by sentimental nostalgia for the vanished Romanovs, disdain the very mention of her name, insisting that discussion of her claim somehow insults the memory of the real Anastasia. But those who would confine Franziska to a grudging footnote do history a disservice, ignoring her singular place in the story of the last Romanovs.

If Franziska was coldly calculating, especially after her temporary disappearance in 1922, she also paid a high price for her charade, condemned to forever dwell in a world she could not escape. Hers became a kind of twilight existence: she could never force her claim and risk exposure, nor could she simply abandon the pretense for fear of legal repercussions. She once confessed to Tatiana Botkin that she bore a heavy burden on her conscience, perhaps an acknowledgment that years of deception had taken an emotional toll.[40] Condemned to exist in a netherworld of uncertainty and ambiguity, Franziska could only transform herself into the curious figure of Anna Anderson, a phantom grand duchess forever doomed to haunt the Romanov story.

It is impossible to know if, in the end, Franziska's brain ever crossed that intangible line between fantasy and reality, if she actually, in her last years, came to believe and embrace the lie she had woven over the decades. But in a very real sense, she became Anastasia. It was, after all, a more emotionally satisfying and perhaps even believable life than the one she had so willingly abandoned. Franziska lived for eighty-seven years; of these, she spent sixty-four, three quarters of her life, as the would-be grand duchess. This reality, this purloined life, ironically rescued the real Anastasia from obscurity. Through Franziska, Anastasia survived the execution in Ekaterinburg, appeared before a fascinated public in books and magazines, and gazed out from across time in the motion pictures that kept her story alive. It is the greatest irony in Franziska's tale: the farm girl from an obscure German village turned the real grand duchess, whose name appropriately meant "Resurrection," into a modern legend.

Notes

This book draws on a number of different archival sources and references. In addition to the authors' collection of materials on the case of Anna Anderson, which includes numerous documents, letters, and the audio recordings of her conversations made in the 1960s by Alexei Miliukov, we have drawn on the following:

Nicholas Sokolov Archive: Copies of the multvolume dossier assembled by White Army investigator Nicholas Sokolov during his 1919–1924 inquiry into the murders of the imperial family. These were made available to us during research for our 2003 work *The Fate of the Romanovs*.

Polish State Archives, Warsaw: Census records for Pomerania and West Prussia, registry records from Borok and Sullenschin, and the records from the former German District Registry Offices of Kreis Stolp, Pomerania, and Sullenschin, West Prussia, items and entries referenced within individual source notes.

GARF: Gosudarstvennyi Arkhiv Rossiiskii Federatsii (State Archives of the Russian Federation), Moscow.

APRF: Arkhiv Presidentsii Rossiiskii Federatsii (Archive of the President of the Russian Federation), Moscow.

TsDOOSO: Tsentr Dokumentatsii Obshchestvennykh Organizatsii Sverdlovskoi Oblasti (Center for Documentation of the History and Party Organization of the Sverdlovsk Region), Ekaterinburg.

Ian Lilburn Collection: Archives, documents, and records collected and assembled by Anderson historian Ian Lilburn, and in his private possession in London.

Peter Kurth Collection: Documents and records collected and assembled by Anderson's biographer Peter Kurth, and in his private possession.

Staatsarchiv, Darmstadt: The dossiers, records, depositions, legal notes by Dr. Hans Hermann Krampff and Dr. Gunther von Berenberg-Gossler, and evidence assembled by Grand Duke Ernst Ludwig of Hesse against Anna Anderson's claim, and continued by his surviving son Prince Ludwig of Hesse. Previously kept at the Hessian royal family's estate, Wolfsgarten, this was transferred to Darmstadt following the death of Prince Ludwig's widow, Princess Margaret of Hesse. Most documents in the archive have not yet been assigned formal reference numbers. Where such numbers do exist, we give them in the individual source notes; those materials lacking specific reference numbers have been cited simply as "Staatsarchiv, Darmstadt."

Hamburg: Anastasia Prozess, lodged in the Staatsarchiv, Hamburg (most material also reproduced in the Staatsarchiv, Darmstadt). This is the single largest collection of materials related to Anderson's claim, spanning her thirty-seven-year legal battle to prove that she was Anastasia. Materials from petitions to the Central District Court (Amtsgericht) in Berlin, the High Court (Landesgeriht) in Berlin, and the Court of Appeal (Kammergericht) in Berlin, covering the years 1938–1957, are lodged in Hamburg under the files labeled Bln (for Berlin). When Anderson launched her civil suit against Barbara, Duchess Christian Ludwig of Mecklenburg, the Berlin materials were incorporated into the new record, which covered the trials at the Hanseatic High Court (Landesgericht) in Hamburg, 1957–1961, and the appeal to the Hanseatic Court of Appeals (Oberlandesgericht) in Hamburg, 1964–1967. Material from the 1970 appeal to the West German Federal Supreme Court (Bundesgericht) in Karlsruhe was appended to the existing Berlin and Hamburg records, and is all listed in the Staatsarchiv, Hamburg, under one general heading. To simplify matters, we have referred to all of these materials as "Hamburg," and given the appropriate reference citations within the individual source notes—for example, Hamburg, IV, 470, indicating volume 4, page 470.

Introduction

1. Chavchavadze, 228.
2. See Longworth for further discussion.
3. See Troyat and Troubetskoy for further discussion.
4. Chavchavadze, 233.
5. Tatiana Botkin, affidavit of May 2, 1929, in Hamburg, Bln I/113–127.
6. Notes of Erika von Redern, secretary to Edward Fallows, from records and bulletin of Dalldorf Asylum, May 16, 1929, cited in Kurth, 6; Dr. Karl Bonhoeffer, report of March 18, 1926, quoting Elisabeth Hospital admission report of February 18, 1920, in Hamburg, XIV/2389–2402; See Auclères in Le Figaro, February 5, 1965, and September 24, 1969; Kurth, 330–331.
7. Schiller Report, cited in Kurth, 32; Dr. Theodor Eitel, report of December 22, 1926, in Hamburg, VIII/1394–1402.
8. See Horan, 141.
9. Dr. Serge Rudnev, report of March 1926, in Hamburg, XIV/2485–2488; Dr. Serge Rudnev, affidavit of July 18, 1938, in Hamburg, Bln I/134–138; diary of Faith Lavington, entry of November 15, 1927, in Hamburg, XXXIV/6402–6428.
10. Auclères, 249.
11. See Summers and Mangold, 227–228.
12. See Kurth, 57.
13. Rathlef-Keilmann, 106.
14. Olga Alexandrovna to Anna Anderson (hereafter AA in Notes), undated letter, autumn 1925, in "Application to the Amstgericht Court, Berlin, in the matter of the Estate of Anastasia Nikolaievna Romanov, Case No. 461.VE.733/38," pleading submitted by Paul Leverkuehn and Kurt Vermehren on behalf of AA, October 31, 1938, and lodged in Hamburg under Bln, 33.

1 "My God, What a Disappointment!"

1. Grand Duchess Xenia Alexandrovna, diary entry of June 5/18, 1901, in Maylunas and Mironenko, 206.
2. Nicholas II, diary entry of June 5/18, 1901, in Maylunas and Mironenko, 206.
3. Eagar, 52; details drawn from imperial christenings described in Buxhoeveden, Life and Tragedy, 103–105; Buxhoeveden, Before the Storm, 238–241; and Marie Pavlovna, Education, 66.
4. Buxhoeveden, Life and Tragedy, 103–105; Eagar, 52; Buxhoeveden, Before the Storm, 240; Marie Pavlovna, Education, p. 66.
5. Prince Christopher of Greece, 55.
6. Gilliard, Thirteen Years, 76; Colonel Eugene Kobylinsky, statement of April 6–10, 1919, in Sokolov Archive, vol. 3, doc. 29.
7. Anastasia Nikolaievna, letter to Nicholas II, October 28, 1916 (Old Style), in Maylunas and Mironenko, 406; Anastasia Nikolaievna, letter to Nicholas II, May 8, 1913 (Old Style), in GARF, F. 601, Op. 1, D. 1156; Anastasia Nikolaievna to Nicholas II, letter of September 23, 1914 (Old Style), in Maylunas and Mironenko, 402.
8. Gilliard, Thirteen Years, 93.
9. Buxhoeveden, Life and Tragedy, 150.
10. Vyrubova, 76; Gilliard, Thirteen Years, 62–63.
11. Vyrubova, 77; Buxhoeveden, Life and Tragedy, 157; Dehn, 78; Gilliard, Thirteen Years, 73.
12. Gilliard, Thirteen Years, 75; Buxhoeveden, Life and Tragedy, 158.
13. Gilliard, Thirteen Years, 75.
14. Hough, 265.
15. Gilliard, Thirteen Years, 75; Dehn, 79; Buxhoeveden, Life and Tragedy, 158; Vyrubova, 78.

16. Buxhoeveden, *Life and Tragedy*, 156.
17. Dehn, 78.
18. Buxhoeveden, *Life and Tragedy*, 156.
19. Botkin, *Au Temps des Tsars*, 81; Dehn, 78.
20. Vorres, 111–112; Olga Alexandrovna to Princess Irene of Hesse, Princess Heinrich of Prussia, letter of December 22, 1925 (this letter is misdated 1926), in Hamburg, Bln III, 181–182; Alexandra Feodorovna to Nicholas II, letter of January 8, 1916, in GARF, F. 601, Op. 1, D. 1150.
21. Botkin, *The Woman Who Rose Again*, 23.
22. Vorres, 112; Xenia Georgievna, Mrs. Herman Jud, testimony of February 10, 1958, at the West German consulate, New York City, in Hamburg, IV/ 749–751.
23. Chavchavadze, 57; Xenia Georgievna, Mrs. Herman Jud, testimony of March 16–17, 1959, at the West German consulate, New York City, in Hamburg, VII, 1214–1230.
24. Eagar, 20–21; www.alexanderpalace.org; Dehn, 79.
25. Vyrubova, 77; Dehn, 79; Buxhoeveden, *Life and Tragedy*, 156.
26. Dehn, 78–79; Eagar, 21.
27. Vyrubova, 77–78; Buxhoeveden, *Life and Tragedy*, 157–158.
28. Dehn, 78.
29. Buxhoeveden, *Life and Tragedy*, 157.
30. Vyrubova, 57–58.
31. Eagar, 39; Vyrubova, 58; Volkov, 65–66; Dehn, 46.
32. Gilliard, *Thirteen Years*, 83.
33. Vyrubova, 56–59.
34. Mossolov, 62–64; Voyekov, 216.
35. Eagar, 272.
36. Buxhoeveden, *Before the Storm*, 320–321; Buxhoeveden, *Life and Tragedy*, 150.
37. Gilliard, *Thirteen Years*, 77.
38. Vyrubova, 79.
39. Ibid.
40. Vyrubova, 80; Buxhoeveden, *Life and Tragedy*, 156.
41. Vorres, 112.
42. Grabbe and Grabbe, 69.
43. Mossolov, 241–242.

2 The Imp

1. Grabbe and Grabbe, 69.
2. Gilliard, *Thirteen Years*, 12, 17.
3. Gilliard and Savitch, 14.
4. Ibid.
5. Charles Sidney Gibbes to Alexander Mikhailovich, letter of December 1, 1928, in Hamburg, XXIII, 4403–4404.
6. Alexandra Feodorovna to Margaret Jackson, letter of August 19, 1912, in Buxhoeveden, *Life and Tragedy*, 129.
7. Gilliard, *Thirteen Years*, 77; Vyrubova, 73; Buxhoeveden, *Life and Tragedy*, 156.
8. Gilliard and Savitch, 14.
9. Trewin, 10, 29.
10. Trewin, 13–17; Benagh, 11–18.
11. See Trewin for several examples of Anastasia's later English compositions and her questionable grasp of the written language.
12. Gilliard, *Thirteen Years*, 76–77; Gilliard, in the *Illustrated London News*, July 16, 1927, 102–103; Gilliard and Savitch, 14–18.
13. Verdict of the Bundesgerichthof (West German Federal Supreme Court), Karlsruhe, February 17, 1970, appended to Hamburg, loose.
14. Item No. 8, German Composition Book, "A. Romanova, February 16, 1916, Tsarskoye Selo," receipt dated April 22, 1964, in Hamburg, XX, 3834.
15. Gilliard and Savitch, 18; Gibbes, statement of July 1, 1919, in Sokolov Archive, vol. 5, doc. 31; Buxhoeveden statement of March 12, 1922, in Gilliard and Savitch, 36.
16. Gilliard, *Thirteen Years*, 75, 77.
17. Gilliard and Savitch, 15.
18. Vorres, 112.
19. Trewin, 74; Buxhoeveden, *Life and Tragedy*, 155–156.
20. Botkin, *Real Romanovs*, 179.
21. Rathlef-Keilmann, 51; Olga Alexandrovna to Princess Irene of Hesse, Princess Heinrich of Prussia, letter of December 22, 1925, in Hamburg, Bln III, 181–182; Gilliard and Savitch, 78; statement of Maria von Hesse in Gilliard and Savitch, 141.
22. Gilliard and Savitch, 16.
23. Gilliard, *Thirteen Years*, 75–76; Dehn, 78.
24. Vorres, 112.
25. Vyrubova, 77, 80.
26. Mossolov, 247.
27. Anastasia Nikolaievna to Nicholas II, letter of May 8, 1913 (OS), in GARF, F. 601, Op. 1, D. 1156.

28. Anastasia Nikolaievna to Nicholas II, letter of October 28, 1914 (OS), in Maylunas and Mironenko, 406; Anastasia Nikolaievna to Nicholas II, letter of January 5, 1916 (OS), at www.alexanderpalace.org; Anastasia Nikolaievna to Nicholas II, letter of August 16, 1916 (OS), at www.alexanderpalace .org.
29. Vorres, 110.
30. Buxhoeveden, *Life and Tragedy*, 296.
31. Vyrubova, 46.
32. Fromenko, 15; Vyrubova, 48.
33. See King, *The Court of the Last Tsar*, 276–277; Spiridovich, 1:193.
34. Grabbe and Grabbe, 57.
35. Grabbe and Grabbe, 105–107; Buxhoeveden, *Life and Tragedy*, 119–120; Vyrubova, 18; Gilliard, *Thirteen Years*, 71–74.
36. Nicholas II to Dowager Empress Marie Feodorovna, letter of October 20, 1912, in Bing, 275.
37. Vyrubova, 91.
38. Ibid., 92.
39. Gilliard, *Thirteen Years*, 29; Vyrubova, 93.
40. Naryshkin-Kuryakina, 196.
41. Vyrubova, 93.
42. Prince Sigismund of Prussia, affidavit, July 5, 1938, in Hamburg, Bln I, 113.
43. See Duff, 289.
44. Naryshkin-Kuryakina, 196.
45. Gilliard, *Thirteen Years*, 29.
46. Gilliard, *Thirteen Years*, 29–31; Vyrubova, 93.
47. Vyrubova, 94.
48. Vorres, 130.
49. Spiridovich, 2:234–235; Dzhunkovsky, 2:195–199; Kokovtsov, 169.

3   Into the Abyss

1. Buxhoeveden, *Life and Tragedy*, 185; Gilliard, *Thirteen Years*, 105–106.
2. Marie Pavlovna, *Education*, 162.
3. Buxhoeveden, *Life and Tragedy*, 191–192.
4. See Alexandra Feodorovna to Nicholas II, letter of October 21, 1914, in GARF, F. 601, Op. 1, D. 1065.
5. Dassel, 10–14, 38–39; Marie Nikolaievna, diary entry of December 31, 1916, in Zvereva and Zverev, 238–240.
6. Dassel, 10–15, 36–37; Dassel, affidavit of April 19, 1929, in Hamburg, Bln I,

130–131; I. V. Stepanov, in Zvereva and Zverev, 303–304.
7. I. V. Stepanov, in Zvereva and Zverev, 303–304.
8. Anastasia Nikolaievna to Nicholas II, letter of September 4, 1915 (OS), in Zvereva and Zverev, 130.
9. Protocol of the Duke of Leuchtenberg, Felix Dassel and Otto Bornemann, September 19, 1927, Ian Lilburn Collection; Dassel, 28–29; Dassel, testimony of April 24, 1958, in Hamburg, II, 352–366; Tatiana Botkin, affidavit, May 2, 1929, in Hamburg, Bln I, 113–127.
10. Anastasia Nikolaievna to Nicholas II, letter of October 28, 1914 (OS), in Maylunas and Mironenko, 406.
11. Spiridovich, vol. 2, chap. 18, translated and provided by Rob Moshein.
12. See Nicholas II, diary entry of June 5/18, 1915, in GARF, F. 601, Op. 1, D. 259; Timms, 122, item no. 164.
13. Letter from Vassili Koliubakin to Peter Kondzerovski, August 21, 1928, in Gilliard and Savitch, 118–119.
14. Anastasia Nikolaievna to Nicholas II, letter of September 4, 1915 (OS), in Zvereva and Zverev, 130.
15. Gilliard, *Thirteen Years*, 166; Buxhoeveden, *Life and Tragedy*, 220.
16. Buxhoeveden, *Life and Tragedy*, 221.
17. Gilliard, *Thirteen Years*, 166.
18. Vorres, 138.
19. Grand Duchess Xenia Alexandrovna, diary entry of March 15, 1910 (OS), in Maylunas and Mironenko, 331.
20. See Fuhrmann, 84–92, for details; Maylunas and Mironenko, 331.
21. Alexandra Feodorovna to Nicholas II, letter of December 19, 1916, in GARF, F. 601, Op. 1, D. 1150.
22. In Maylunas and Mironenko, 507.
23. Buxhoeveden, *Life and Tragedy*, 247; Benckendorff, 42; Gilliard, *Thirteen Years*, 209–211; Vyrubova, 204–205; Dehn, 159–160.
24. Dehn, 151–152.
25. Buxhoeveden, *Life and Tragedy*, 254; Benckendorff, 6–9; Dehn, 156.
26. Buxhoeveden, *Life and Tragedy*, 254; Gilliard, *Thirteen Years*, 212; Dehn, 156; Vyrubova, 206–207.
27. Dehn, 158.

28. Ibid.
29. Buxhoeveden, *Life and Tragedy*, 215–216; Dehn, 151–152.
30. Buxhoeveden, *Life and Tragedy*, 186; Benckendorff, 33.
31. Vyrubova, 218.
32. Benckendorff, 33; Buxhoeveden, *Life and Tragedy*, 284.
33. Buxhoeveden, *Life and Tragedy*, 284.
34. Benckendorff, 78–79.
35. Buxhoeveden, *Life and Tragedy*, 297–299; Gilliard, *Thirteen Years*, 228–230.
36. Benckendorff, 71; Buxhoeveden, *Life and Tragedy*, 297–299; Vyrubova, 212–213.
37. Buxhoeveden, *Life and Tragedy*, 299; Gilliard, *Thirteen Years*, 229.
38. Gilliard, *Thirteen Years*, 231–232.
39. Pierre Gilliard, diary entry of June 24, 1917, in Gilliard, *Thirteen Years*, 232–233; Benckendorff, 86–87; Nicholas II, diary entry of June 10/23, 1917, in GARF, F. 601, Op. 1, D. 265.
40. Botkin, *Au Temps des Tsars*, 66.
41. Anastasia Nikolaievna, letter of August 17, 1917, in Trewin, 75.
42. Bulygin and Kerensky, 130.
43. See King and Wilson, 49–50.
44. Ibid., 70.
45. Buxhoeveden, *Life and Tragedy*, 311–312.
46. Olga Nikolaievna to Anna Vyrubova, letter of December 10, 1917, in Vyrubova, 308.
47. Gilliard, *Thirteen Years*, 240.
48. Gilliard, statement of March 5, 1919, in Sokolov Archive, vol. 2, doc. 55.
49. Colonel Eugene Kobylinsky, statement of April 6–10, 1919, in Sokolov Archive, vol. 3, doc. 29.
50. Gibbes, statement of July 1, 1919, in Sokolov Archive, vol. 5, doc. 31.
51. Gilliard, *Thirteen Years*, 240–242.
52. Gibbes, statement of July 1, 1919, in Sokolov Archive, vol. 5, doc. 31.
53. Gilliard, *Thirteen Years*, 244–245.
54. Vyrubova, 309.
55. Buxhoeveden, *Life and Tragedy*, 316.
56. Gleb Botkin, affidavit, July 20, 1938, in Hamburg, Bln I, 101–112; Botkin, *Real Romanovs*, 160, 266–267; Botkin, *Lost Tales*, vii.
57. Alexandra Feodorovna to Anna Vyrubova, letter of December 15, 1917, in Vyrubova, 316.
58. Colonel Eugene Kobylinsky, statement of April 6–10, 1919, in Sokolov Archive, vol. 2, doc. 55; Gibbes, statement of July 1, 1919, in Sokolov Archive, vol. 5, doc. 31.
59. Trewin, 82–83.
60. Gilliard, *Thirteen Years*, 254.
61. Ibid., 255; Buxhoeveden, *Life and Tragedy*, 322–333.
62. Gilliard, statement of March 5, 1919, in Sokolov Archive, vol. 2, doc. 55.
63. Botkin, *Au Temps des Tsars*, 111.

4 "How Little I Suspected I Was Never to See Them Again"

1. Volkov, 122.
2. See King and Wilson, 80–99.
3. Anastasia Nikolaievna to Marie Nikolaievna, letter of May 7, 1918, in Maylunas and Mironenko, 619–620.
4. Bulygin and Kerensky, 232.
5. Alexandra Tegleva, in Sokolov, 105; also letter from Minister of Justice Starynkevich to the Ministry of Foreign Affairs, Executive Board, Omsk, February 19, 1919, original in authors' possession, quoted in King and Wilson, 136.
6. Gilliard, *Thirteen Years*, 264–265; Sokolov, 109.
7. Buxhoeveden, *Life and Tragedy*, 336; Alexandra Tegleva, deposition of July 5–6, 1919, in Sokolov Archive, vol. 5, doc. 36.
8. Volkov, 123–125.
9. Botkin, *Real Romanovs*, 107–108; Gleb Botkin, affidavit, July 20, 1938, in Hamburg, Bln I, 101–112.
10. Nicholas II, diary entry of May 23, 1918, in GARF, F. 601, Op. 1, D. 266.
11. Buxhoeveden, *Left Behind*, 73–75.
12. Bykov, 74; Kobylinsky, testimony of April 6–10, 1919, in Sokolov Archive, vol. 3, doc. 29; Charles Sidney Gibbes, testimony of July 1, 1919, in Sokolov Archive, vol. 5, doc. 31; Volkov, 126; Buxhoeveden, *Life and Tragedy*, 336.
13. Gilliard, *Thirteen Years*, 269–270.
14. Anatoly Yakimov, statement of May 7–11, 1919, in Sokolov Archive, vol. 5, doc. 18; statement of Paul Medvedev, February 21–22, 1919, in Sokolov Archive, vol. 2, doc. 86; see also King and Wilson, 105 passim.

15. Nicholas II, diary entry of May 23, 1918, in GARF, F. 601, Op. 1, D. 266.
16. Alexandra Feodorovna, diary entry of May 27, 1918, in GARF, F. 640, Op. 1, D. 326.
17. Charles Sidney Gibbes, testimony of July 1, 1919, in Sokolov Archive, vol. 5, doc. 31; Paul Medvedev, statement of February 21–22, 1919, in Sokolov Archive, vol. 2, doc. 86; Alexander Nametkin, "Protocol of the Inspection of the Upper Floor of the Ipatiev House," August 2–3 and 6–8, 1918, in Sokolov Archive, vol. 3, doc. 27; Trewin, 148; Nicholas II, diary entry of May 23, 1918, in GARF, F. 601, Op. 1, D. 266.
18. Telberg and Wilton, 212.
19. Ibid., 295.
20. See King and Wilson, chap. 5.
21. Gilliard, *Thirteen Years*, 282.
22. Gilliard, statement of March 5, 1919, in Sokolov Archive, vol. 2, doc. 55.
23. Telberg and Wilton, 295.
24. Anatoly Yakimov, testimony of May 9–10, 1919, in Sokolov Archive, vol. 5, doc. 18.
25. Colonel Eugene Kobylinsky, statement of April 6–10, 1919, in Sokolov Archive, vol. 2, doc. 55; Sokolov, *Enquete*, 130.
26. Telberg and Wilton, 296.
27. Colonel Eugene Kobylinsky, statement of April 6–10, 1919, in Sokolov Archive, vol. 2, doc. 55.
28. Telberg and Wilton, 295.
29. See King and Wilson, chap. 5.
30. Alexander Nametkin, "Protocol of the Inspection of the Upper Floor of the Ipatiev House," August 2–3 and 6–8, 1918, in Sokolov Archive, vol. 3, doc. 27; Ivan Sergeyev, statement on inspection of the Ipatiev House, August 11–14, 1918, in Sokolov Archive, vol. 1, doc. 19; Nicholas Sokolov, statement on inspection of the Ipatiev House, April 15–25, 1919, in Sokolov Archive, vol. 3, doc. 42.
31. Philip Proskuryakov, testimony of April 1–3, 1919, in Sokolov Archive, vol. 5, doc. 17; Avdayev, 202–203.
32. Alexandra Feodorovna, diary entry of June 18, 1918, in GARF, F. 640, Op. 1, D. 326; Yakov Yurovsky, "Memoirs," 1922, in APRF, F. 3, Op. 58, D. 280; Avdayev, 202.
33. Avdayev, 202.
34. Alexandra Feodorovna, diary entry of June 18, 1918, in GARF, F. 640, Op. 1, D. 326.
35. Yurovsky, "Memoirs," 1922, in APRF, F. 3, Op. 58, D. 280.
36. Alexander Strekotin, in Speranski, 56.
37. Ibid.
38. See King and Wilson, 222 passim.
39. Nicholas II, diary entry of June 25–26, 1918, in GARF, F. 601, Op. 1, D. 266; Alexandra Feodorovna, diary entry of June 26, 1918, in GARF, F. 640, Op.1, D. 326.
40. Nicholas II, diary entry of June 26, 1918, in GARF, F. 601, Op. 1, D. 266.
41. See King and Wilson, 251 passim.
42. Yurovsky, "Memoirs," 1922, in APRF, F. 3, Op. 58, D. 280.
43. Father Ioann Vladimirovich Storozhev, in Sokolov, 124–126.
44. Sokolov, 127.
45. Maria Starodumova, statement of November 11, 1918, in Sokolov, 128.
46. Speranski, 118–122.
47. Alexandra Feodorovna, diary entry of July 16, 1918, in GARF, F. 640, Op. 1, D. 326.
48. Sokolov, 138.
49. Alexandra Feodorovna, diary entry of July 16, 1918, in GARF, F. 640, Op. 1, D. 326.
50. Preston, 102.
51. Anatoly Yakimov, testimony of May 9–11, 1919, in Sokolov Archive, vol. 5, doc. 18.
52. Telberg and Wilton, 306; Anatoly Yakimov, testimony of May 9–11, 1919, in Sokolov Archive, vol. 5, doc. 18.
53. Anatoly Yakimov, testimony of May 9–11, 1919, in Sokolov Archive, vol. 5, doc. 18; Paul Medvedev, statement of February 21–22, 1919, in Sokolov Archive, vol. 2, doc. 86; Telberg and Wilton, 309.
54. Anatoly Yakimov, testimony of May 9–11, 1919, in Sokolov Archive, vol. 5, doc. 18.
55. Philip Proskuryakov, testimony of April 1–3, 1919, in Telberg and Wilton, 154.
56. Anatoly Yakimov, testimony of May 9–11, 1919, in Sokolov Archive, vol. 5, doc. 18.

57. Telberg and Wilton, 310.
58. Paul Medvedev, statement of February 21–22, 1919, in Sokolov Archive, vol. 2, doc. 86.
59. Telberg and Wilton, 310.
60. Anatoly Yakimov, testimony of May 9–11, 1919, in Sokolov Archive, vol. 5, doc. 18.
61. Telberg and Wilton, 310.
62. Paul Medvedev, statement of February 21–22, 1919, in Sokolov Archive, vol. 2, doc. 86.
63. Telberg and Wilton, 347–349.
64. Ibid., 349.
65. Ibid., 343.
66. See the *Times*, London, February 18, 1919.
67. Telberg and Wilton, 327.
68. See Gilliard and Savitch, 24.
69. See Summers and Mangold, 190.
70. Gilliard, *Thirteen Years*, 299–300.
71. See Summers and Mangold, 320 passim.
72. Benckendorff, 132.
73. Ibid., 140 and 147.
74. Dehn, 238.
75. Vyrubova, 344.
76. King George V, diary entry of July 25, 1918, in Rose, 216.
77. Queen Marie of Romania to Grand Duchess Xenia Alexandrovna, letter of September 19, 1918, in Hall and Van Der Kiste, 137.
78. Alexander Mikhailovich, *Always a Grand Duke*, 7–8.
79. Hall, *Little Mother*, 342; Alexander Mikhailovich, *Always a Grand Duke*, 212; Marie Pavlovna, *Princess in Exile*, 102.
80. Princess Irene of Hesse, Princess Heinrich of Prussia, to Eleonore, grand duchess of Hesse, letter of August 13, 1918, in Staatsarchiv, Darmstadt.
81. See Vickers, 140–143.
82. Louis, Earl Mountbatten of Burma, to Prince Ludwig of Hesse, letter of November 12, 1958, in Staatsarchiv, Darmstadt.
83. Hough, 326.
84. Summers and Mangold, 196.

5 Resurrection

1. Davis, 19.
2. Blucher, 24.
3. Rosenberg, 90.
4. Blucher, 100.
5. Blucher, 122–127, 136; Davis, 24, 165, and chap. 3.
6. Blucher, 102, 162.
7. Ibid., 256.
8. Ibid., 287.
9. Gill, *Dance*, 57.
10. Friedrich, 82–83.
11. Kurth, 15; Friedrich, 82 passim.
12. Marie Pavlovna, *Princess in Exile*, 131.
13. Berlin Police bulletin of February 18, 1920, in Krug von Nidda, 89.
14. Berlin Police bulletin of February 18, 1920, in Krug von Nidda, 89; Doris Rittmann, née Wingender, testimony of November 16, 1965, in Hamburg, XXVII/5144–5151; *Berliner Nachtausgabe*, Berlin, April 11, 1927; Nicholas von Schwabe, affidavit, June 10, 1922, in Hamburg, XIV, 2519–2534.
15. Berlin Police bulletin of February 18, 1920, in Krug von Nidda, 89.
16. Statement of Dr. Theodor Eitel, December 22, 1926, in Hamburg, VIII, 1394–1402.
17. Undated notes by Rathlef-Keilmann, quoted in Kurth, 3.
18. Berlin Police bulletin of February 18, 1920, in Krug von Nidda, 89; Nicholas von Schwabe, affidavit, June 10, 1922, in Hamburg, XIV, 2519–2534.
19. Hamburg, summary of evidence in *Frau Anna Anderson in Unterlengenhardt v. Barbara, Herzogin Christian Ludwig zu Mecklenburg, Ludwig, Prinz von Hesse und bei Rhein*, May 18, 1967, 30.
20. Auclères, 33.
21. Notes of Erika von Redern, secretary to Edward Fallows, from records of Dalldorf Asylum, May 16, 1929, quoted in Kurth, 7; Bonhoeffer Report, March 18, 1926, quoting Elisabeth Hospital patient admissions report of February 18, 1920, in Hamburg, XIV, 2389–2402; *National Tidende*, Copenhagen, January 16, 1926; *Konigsberg Allgemeine Zeitung*, no. 110, March 7, 1927.
22. Bonhoeffer, report, March 18, 1926, quoting Elisabeth Hospital patient admissions report of February 18, 1920, in Hamburg, XIV, 2389–2402.
23. Notes of Erika von Redern, secretary to Edward Fallows, from records

of Dalldorf Asylum, May 16, 1929, quoted in Kurth, 6; Bonhoeffer, report, March 18, 1926, quoting Elisabeth Hospital patient admissions report of February 18, 1920, in Hamburg, XIV, 2389–2402.

24. *New York Times*, February 14, 1928.

25. Rathlef-Keilmann, 41.

26. AA to Rathlef-Keilmann, June 30, 1925, in Rathlef-Keilmann Notes, in Hamburg, Bln III, loose.

27. Dr. Serge Rudnev, report of March 1926, in Hamburg, Bln I, 134ff, XIV, 2485–2488; Dr. Serge Rudnev, affidavit, July 18, 1938, in Hamburg, Bln I, 134–138.

28. Horan, 137.

29. These medical reports are delineated in "Application to the Amstgericht Court, Berlin, in the Matter of the Estate of Anastasia Nikolaievna Romanov, Case No. 461.VE.733/38," pleading submitted by Paul Leverkuehn and Kurt Vermehren on behalf of AA, October 31, 1938, and lodged in Hamburg under Bln.

30. Bonhoeffer, report, March 18, 1926, quoting Elisabeth Hospital patient admissions report of February 18, 1920, and his own report of March 18, 1926, in Hamburg, XIV, 2389–2402.

31. Dr. Lothar Nobel, statement, March 1926, in Hamburg, XIII, 4417–4426.

32. Dr. Theodor Eitel, statement of December 22, 1926, in Hamburg, VIII, 1394–1402.

33. Opinion concerning Frau Anna Tchaikovsky, Hans Willige, November 5, 1938, in Hamburg, Bln IV, 328–330, and XII, 1985–1994.

34. Dr. Lothar Nobel, statement, March 1926, in Hamburg, XIII, 4417–4426.

35. Dr. Serge Rudnev, report, March 1926, in Hamburg, Bln I, 134ff, XIV, 2485–2488; Dr. Serge Rudnev, affidavit, July 18, 1938, in Hamburg, Bln I, 134–138; Horan, 133; Dr. Theodor Eitel, statement of December 22, 1926, in Hamburg, VIII, 1394–1402; Bonhoeffer, report, March 18, 1926, in Hamburg, XIV, 2389–2402; Kurth, 8; Gilliard and Savitch, 36.

36. Kurth, 85; Rudnev, report, March 1926, in Hamburg, Bln I, 134ff, XIV, 2485–2488; Dr. Serge Rudnev, affidavit,

July 18, 1938, in Hamburg, Bln I, 134–138; Dr. Theodor Eitel, statement of December 22, 1926, in Hamburg, VIII, 1394–1402; opinion concerning Frau Anna Tchaikovsky, Hans Willige, November 5, 1938, in Hamburg, Bln IV, 328–330 and XII, 1985–1994.

37. Bonhoeffer, report, March 18, 1926, quoting Elisabeth Hospital patient admissions report of February 18, 1920, in his report of March 18, 1926, in Hamburg, XIV, 2389–2402; Dr. Theodor Eitel, statement of December 22, 1926, in Hamburg, VIII, 1394–1402.

38. Bonhoeffer, report, March 18, 1926, quoting the Elisabeth Hospital patient admissions report, in his report of March 18, 1926, in Hamburg, XIV, 2389–2402.

39. Dr. Serge Rudnev, affidavit, July 18, 1938, in Hamburg, Bln I, 134–138; Rudnev, report, March 1926, in Hamburg, Bln I, 134ff, and XIV, 2485–2488; Dr. Friedrich Reiche, affidavit of July 19, 1929, in Hamburg, XX, 3781–3783; Bonhoeffer, report, March 18, 1926, quoting Elisabeth Hospital patient admissions report, in Hamburg, XIV, 2389–2402.

40. Dr. Serge Rudnev, affidavit, July 18, 1938, in Hamburg, Bln I, 134–138; Rudnev, report, March 1926, in Hamburg, Bln I, 134ff, and XIV, 2485–2488.

41. Dominique Auclères, in *Le Figaro*, February 5, 1965, and in *Le Figaro*, September 24, 1969.

42. Dr. Theodor Eitel, statement of December 22, 1926, in Hamburg, VIII, 1394–1402; opinion concerning Frau Anna Tchaikovsky, Hans Willige, November 5, 1938, in Hamburg, Bln IV, 328–330, and XII, 1985–1994.

43. Dr. Serge Rudnev, affidavit, July 18, 1938, in Hamburg, Bln I, 134–138; Rudnev, report, March 1926, in Hamburg, Bln I, 134ff, and XIV, 2485–2488.

44. Gilliard and Savitch, 180, citing the records of the Elisabeth Hospital.

45. Inspector Franz Grunberg, letter of June 19, 1925, in Hamburg, XIV, 2540–2545.

46. Bonhoeffer, report, March 18, 1926, quoting the Dalldorf Hospital patient

admissions report, in Hamburg, XIV, 2389–2402.

47. Hamburg, summary of evidence in *Frau Anna Anderson in Unterlengenhardt v. Barbara, Herzogin Christian Ludwig zu Mecklenburg, Ludwig, Prinz von Hesse und bei Rhein*, May 18, 1967, 30–31.

48. Bonhoeffer, report, March 18, 1926, in Hamburg, XIV, 2389–2402; Kurth, 7.

49. Kurth, 6.

50. Report of Dr. Gorz, May 30, 1920, and letter of Dr. Gorz to Dr. Serge Kastritsky, December 15, 1928, quoted in letter of Mme L. Kastritsky-Proce to Dr. Berenberg-Gossler, March 4, 1966, in Hamburg, XXXI, 5718; Hamburg, summary of evidence in *Frau Anna Anderson in Unterlengenhardt v. Barbara, Herzogin Christian Ludwig zu Mecklenburg, Ludwig, Prinz von Hesse und bei Rhein*, May 18, 1967, 170.

51. Report of Dr. Gorz, May 30, 1920, and letter of Dr. Gorz to Dr. Serge Kastritsky, December 15, 1928, quoted in letter of Mme L. Kastritsky-Proce to Dr. Berenberg-Gossler, March 4, 1966, in Hamburg, XXXI/5718; Bonhoeffer, report, March 18, 1926, in Hamburg, XIV, 2389–2402; Gilliard and Savitch, 36.

52. Dr. Serge Rudnev, affidavit, July 18, 1938, in Hamburg, Bln I, 134–138; Rudnev, report, March 1926, in Hamburg, Bln I, 134ff, and XIV, 2485–2488; Horan, 133; Dr. Theodor Eitel, statement of December 22, 1926, in Hamburg, VIII, 1394–1402; opinion concerning Frau Anna Tchaikovsky, Hans Willige, November 5, 1938, in Hamburg, Bln IV, 328–330, and XII, 1985–1994.

53. Statement of Anna (Thea) Chemnitz, née Malinovsky, June 27, 1929, in Hamburg, Bln III, loose; testimony of Anna (Thea) Chemnitz, née Malinovsky, December 17, 1958, in Hamburg, V, 979–981.

54. Testimony of Anna (Thea) Chemnitz, née Malinovsky, December 17, 1958, in Hamburg, V, 979–981.

55. Statement of Anna (Thea) Chemnitz, née Malinovsky, June 27, 1929, in Bln III, loose; testimony of Anna (Thea) Chemnitz, née Malinovsky, December 17, 1958, in Hamburg, V, 979–981.

56. Testimony of Anna (Thea) Chemnitz, née Malinovsky, December 17, 1958, in Hamburg, V, 979–981.

57. Notes of Erika von Redern, secretary to Edward Fallows, from records and bulletin of Dalldorf Asylum, May 16, 1929, cited in Kurth, 7.

58. Statement of Bertha Walz, June 17, 1922, in Hamburg, XXIV, 4479; statement of Emilie Barfknecht, June 12, 1922, in Hamburg, XXIV, 4476–4478; testimony of Anna (Thea) Chemnitz, née Malinovsky, December 17, 1958, in Hamburg, V, 979–981.

59. Statement of Serge Botkin, March 1929, in Peter Kurth collection.

60. Statement of Erna Buchholz, June 17, 1922, in Hamburg, Bln IV, 98, and statement of July 22, 1940, in Hamburg, Bln IV, 98–101.

61. Bonhoeffer, report, March 18, 1926, in Hamburg, XIV, 2389–2402.

62. Kurth, 8, 11; testimony of Anna (Thea) Chemnitz, née Malinovsky, in Hamburg, V, 979–981.

63. Bonhoeffer, report, March 18, 1926, in Hamburg, XIV, 2389–2402.

64. Testimony of Anna (Thea) Chemnitz, née Malinovsky, in Hamburg, V, 979–981.

65. Affidavit of Nicholas von Schwabe, June 10, 1922, in Hamburg, XIV, 2519–2534.

66. See *Berliner Illustrierte Zeitung*, no. 43, vol. 23, October 23, 1921.

67. Statement of Bertha Walz, June 17, 1922, in Hamburg, XXIV, 4479.

68. Statement of Emilie Barfknecht, June 14, 1922, in Hamburg, XXIV, 4476–4478.

69. Statement of Erna Buchholz, June 17, 1922, in Hamburg, Bln IV, 98.

70. Testimony of Anna (Thea) Chemnitz, née Malinovsky, December 17, 1958, in Hamburg, V, 979–981.

71. Ibid.

6 Fraulein Unbekannt

1. In "Application to the Amstgericht Court, Berlin, in the Matter of the Estate of Anastasia Nikolaievna Romanov, Case No. 461.VE.733/38," pleading submitted by Paul Leverkuehn and Kurt Vermehren on behalf of AA, October 31, 1938, and lodged in Hamburg under Bln.

2. Testimony of Anna (Thea) Chemnitz, née Malinovsky, December 17, 1958, in Hamburg, V, 979–981.
3. Affidavit of Nicholas von Schwabe, June 10, 1922, in Hamburg, XIV, 2519–2534; Gilliard and Savitch, 29.
4. Information to the authors from Ian Lilburn.
5. Statement of Marie Clara Peuthert, June 10, 1922, in Hamburg, XIV, 2535–2537.
6. Statement of Emilie Barfknecht, June 14, 1922, in Hamburg, XXIV, 4476–4478.
7. Ibid.
8. Affidavit of Nicholas von Schwabe, June 10, 1922, in Hamburg, XIV, 2519–2534; Gilliard and Savitch, 29; Hamburg, Summary of Evidence in *Frau Anna Anderson in Unterlengenhardt v. Barbara, Herzogin Christian Ludwig zu Mecklenburg, Ludwig, Prinz von Hesse und bei Rhein*, May 18, 1967, 35.
9. Affidavit of Nicholas von Schwabe, June 10, 1922, in Hamburg, XIV, 2519–2534; Gilliard and Savitch, 32, 111.
10. Statement of Emilie Barfknecht, June 14, 1922, in Hamburg, XXIV, 4476–4478.
11. Kurth, 21; Affidavit of Nicholas von Schwabe, June 10, 1922, in Hamburg, XIV, 2519–2534; Hamburg, Summary of Evidence in *Frau Anna Anderson in Unterlengenhardt v. Barbara, Herzogin Christian Ludwig zu Mecklenburg, Ludwig, Prinz von Hesse und bei Rhein*, May 18, 1967, 35.
12. Kurth, 16; Friedrich, 95.
13. Affidavit of Nicholas von Schwabe, June 10, 1922, in Hamburg, XIV, 2519–2534; Zenaide Tolstoy to Baron von Kleist, letter of August 7, 1922, in Gilliard and Savitch, 39.
14. Zenaide Tolstoy to Baron von Kleist, letter of August 7, 1922, in Gilliard and Savitch, 38–39; Botkin, Anastasia, 26.
15. Affidavit of Nicholas von Schwabe, June 10, 1922, in Hamburg, XIV, 2519–2534; Baroness Sophie Buxhoeveden, statement of March 12, 1922, in Gilliard and Savitch, 34.
16. Baroness Sophie Buxhoeveden, statement of March 12, 1922, in Gilliard and Savitch, 34–36.
17. Ibid., 34–35.
18. Louis, Earl Mountbatten of Burma, to Prince Louis of Hesse, letter of

November 12, 1957, in Staatsarchiv, Darmstadt.
19. Baroness Sophie Buxhoeveden, statement of March 12, 1922, in Gilliard and Savitch, 36.
20. Rathlef-Keilmann, 35.
21. Testimony of Anna (Thea) Chemnitz, née Malinovsky, December 17, 1958, in Hamburg, V, 979–981.
22. Gilliard and Savitch, 46.
23. Baroness Marie von Kleist, affidavit of July 5, 1929, entered into evidence May 20, 1958, in Hamburg, III, 569–574.
24. Written request of March 22, 1922, from Baron Arthur von Kleist to the director of Dalldorf Asylum, in Ian Lilburn Collection.
25. Affidavit of Nicholas von Schwabe, June 10, 1922, in Hamburg, XIV, 2519–2534.
26. Baroness Marie von Kleist, affidavit of July 5, 1929, entered into evidence May 20, 1958, in Hamburg, III, 569–574; certificate of release of Fraulein Unbekannt to Baron von Kleist, from Dalldorf patient file 394, signed by Fischer, municipal assistant of Dalldorf, in Ian Lilburn Collection.
27. Hamburg, summary of evidence in *Frau Anna Anderson in Unterlengenhardt v. Barbara, Herzogin Christian Ludwig zu Mecklenburg, Ludwig, Prinz von Hesse und bei Rhein*, May 18, 1967, 39.
28. Auclères, 45; Kurth, 29; testimony of Baroness Gerda von Kleist in Hamburg, November 19, 1965, in Hamburg, XXVII, 5158–5165; affidavit of Baroness Marie von Kleist, July 5, 1929, entered into evidence May 20, 1958, in Hamburg, III, 569–574.
29. Statement of Baron Arthur von Kleist, June 7, 1922, in Gilliard and Savitch, 47; verdict of the Bundesgerichthof (West German Federal Supreme Court), Karlsruhe, February 17, 1970, appended to Hamburg, loose.
30. Affidavit of Baroness Marie von Kleist, July 5, 1929, entered into evidence May 20, 1958, in Hamburg, III, 569–574.
31. Nicholas von Schwabe to Pierre Gilliard, letter of November 17, 1926, in Gilliard and Savitch, 114–115; information to the authors from Robert K. Massie; Gilliard and Savitch, 82; Nicholas von Schwabe to Pierre Gilliard, letter of

December 12, 1926, in Gilliard and Savitch, 110; Hamburg, summary of evidence in *Frau Anna Anderson in Unterlengenhardt v. Barbara, Herzogin Christian Ludwig zu Mecklenburg, Ludwig, Prinz von Hesse und bei Rhein*, May 18, 1967, 166.

32. Nicholas von Schwabe to Pierre Gilliard, letter of November 17, 1926, in Gilliard and Savitch, 113–114.

33. Nicholas von Schwabe to Pierre Gilliard, letter of November 17, 1926, in Gilliard and Savitch, 113–114; affidavit of Baroness Marie von Kleist, July 5, 1929, entered into evidence May 20, 1958, in Hamburg, III, 569–574; Hamburg, summary of evidence in *Frau Anna Anderson in Unterlengenhardt v. Barbara, Herzogin Christian Ludwig zu Mecklenburg, Ludwig, Prinz von Hesse und bei Rhein*, May 18, 1967, 166.

34. Testimony of Baroness Gerda von Kleist, November 19, 1965, in Hamburg, XXVII, 5158–5165.

35. Statement of Baron Arthur von Kleist, June 7, 1922, in Gilliard and Savitch, 47; statement of Baron Arthur von Kleist, June 20, 1922, certified February 1, 1926, in Gilliard and Savitch, 47; affidavit of Baroness Marie von Kleist, July 5, 1929, entered into evidence May 20, 1958, in Hamburg, III, 569–574.

36. Statement of Baron Arthur von Kleist, June 7, 1922, in Gillard and Savitch, 47; verdict of the Bundesgerichthof (West German Federal Supreme Court), Karlsruhe, February 17, 1970, appended to Hamburg, loose; Baroness Marie von Kleist, affidavit of July 5, 1929, entered in Hamburg May 20, 1958, in Hamburg, III, 569–574.

37. Affidavit of Baroness Marie von Kleist, July 5, 1929, entered into evidence May 20, 1958, in Hamburg, III, 569–574; in "Application to the Amstgericht Court, Berlin, in the Matter of the Estate of Anastasia Nikolaievna Romanov, Case No. 461.VE.733/38," pleading submitted by Paul Leverkuehn and Kurt Vermehren on behalf of AA, October 31, 1938, and lodged in Hamburg under Bln, 25.

38. Zenaide Tolstoy, affidavit of May 3, 1929, cited in Kurth, 403, n. 40.

39. Affidavit of Baroness Marie von Kleist, July 5, 1929, entered into evidence May 20, 1958, in Hamburg, III, 569–574.
40. Statement of Baron Arthur von Kleist, June 7, 1922, in Gilliard and Savitch, 46.
41. Ibid., 48.
42. Gilliard and Savitch, 112.
43. Testimony of Baroness Gerda von Kleist, May 20, 1958, in Hamburg, III, 551–562.
44. Ibid.
45. Statement of Baron Arthur von Kleist, June 20, 1922, in Gilliard and Savitch, 48.
46. AA to Rathlef-Keilmann, June 19, 1925, in Rathlef-Keilmann notes, in Hamburg, Bln III, loose.
47. Schiller report, cited in Kurth, 32.
48. Kurth, 399, n.18.
49. Gilliard and Savitch, 38.
50. Ibid.; affidavit of Baroness Marie von Kleist, July 5, 1929, entered into evidence May 20, 1958, in Hamburg, III, 569–574; Zenaide Tolstoy, affidavit of May 3, 1929, quoted in Kurth, 30; Gilliard and Savitch, 70–71.
51. Affidavit of Baroness Marie von Kleist, July 5, 1929, entered into evidence May 20, 1958, in Hamburg, III, 569–574.
52. Testimony of Baroness Gerda von Kleist, November 19, 1965, in Hamburg, III, 551–562; Kurth, 32; affidavit of Baroness Marie von Kleist, July 5, 1929, entered into evidence May 20, 1958, in Hamburg, III, 569–574.
53. Auclères, 234.
54. Krug von Nidda, 92.
55. Cited in Kurth, 55.
56. Affidavit of Baroness Marie von Kleist, July 5, 1929, entered into evidence May 20, 1958, in Hamburg, III, 569–574.
57. Affidavit of Baroness Marie von Kleist, July 5, 1929, entered into evidence May 20, 1958, in Hamburg, III, 569–574; Gilliard and Savitch, 41.
58. *Berliner Nachtausgabe*, April 8, 1927; affidavit of Baroness Marie von Kleist, July 5, 1929, entered into evidence May 20, 1958, in Hamburg, III, 569–574.
59. *Berliner Nachtausgabe*, April 8, 1927; Rathlef-Keilmann, 172; Wilhelm Voller, affidavit, April 29, 1927, in Hamburg, XXII, 4270.

60. Hamburg, summary of evidence in *Frau Anna Anderson in Unterlengenhardt v. Barbara, Herzogin Christian Ludwig zu Mecklenburg, Ludwig, Prinz von Hesse und bei Rhein*, May 18, 1967, 41–42.

61. Affidavit of Baroness Marie von Kleist, July 5, 1929, entered into evidence May 20, 1958, in Hamburg, III, 569–574.

62. See Kurth, 49–50; Hamburg, summary of evidence in *Frau Anna Anderson in Unterlengenhardt v. Barbara, Herzogin Christian Ludwig zu Mecklenburg, Ludwig, Prinz von Hesse und bei Rhein*, May 18, 1967, 41–43.

63. See, for example, comments of Dr. Gunther von Berenberg-Gossler, quoted by John Godl in "Remembering Anna Anderson," part II, at http://www .serfes. org/royal/rememberingAnna Anderson. htm.

7   A Story of Escape

1. AA to Rathlef-Keilmann, notes of June 22, 1925, in Rathlef-Keilmann notes, in Hamburg, Bln III, loose.

2. Affidavit of Baroness Marie von Kleist, July 5, 1929, entered into evidence May 20, 1958, in Hamburg, III, 569–574.

3. Rathlef-Keilmann, 23.

4. Ibid., 89.

5. Statement of Baron Arthur von Kleist, June 20, 1922, in Gilliard and Savitch, 48.

6. Rathlef-Keilmann, 90.

7. Marie Clara Peuthert to Princess Irene of Hesse, Princess Heinrich of Prussia, letter of August 23, 1922, in Gilliard and Savitch, 52.

8. AA to Rathlef-Keilmann, notes of June 30, 1925, in Rathlef-Keilmann notes, in Hamburg, Bln III, loose.

9. Statement of Baron Arthur von Kleist, June 20, 1922, in Gilliard and Savitch, 48.

10. Marie Clara Peuthert to Princess Irene of Hesse, Princess Heinrich of Prussia, letter of August 23, 1922, in Gilliard and Savitch, 51.

11. AA, dictated replies to questions, May 8, 1929, page 8, in Ian Lilburn Collection.

12. Rathlef-Keilmann, 93; see Kurth, 400, n. 33; AA, conversations with Alexei Miliukov, August 20, 1966, in Miliukov tapes.

13. AA to Rathlef-Keilmann, notes of June 20, 1925, in Rathlef-Keilmann notes, in Hamburg, Bln III, loose.

14. Statement of Baron von Kleist, August 4, 1922, in Gilliard and Savitch, 49; Marie Clara Peuthert to Princess Irene of Hesse, Princess Heinrich of Prussia, letter of August 23, 1922, in Gilliard and Savitch, 51–52; AA to Rathlef-Keilmann, notes of June 21, 1925, in Rathlef-Keilmann notes, in Hamburg, Bln III, loose.

15. Statement of Baron von Kleist, August 4, 1922, in Gilliard and Savitch, 49; Marie Clara Peuthert to Princess Irene of Hesse, Princess Heinrich of Prussia, letter of August 23, 1922, in Gilliard and Savitch, 51–52; AA to Rathlef-Keilmann, notes of June 21, 1925, in Rathlef-Keilmann notes, in Hamburg, Bln III, loose.

16. Zenaide Tolstoy to Baron Arthur von Kleist, August 4, 1922, in Gilliard and Savitch, 49; Gertrude Spindler to former Russian ambassador in Bucharest Pokloevsky-Kozell, in Pokloevsky-Kozell letter to Serge Botkin, May 17, 1926, in Gilliard and Savitch, 146; Marie Clara Peuthert to Princess Irene of Hesse, Princess Heinrich of Prussia, letter of August 23, 1922, in Gilliard and Savitch, 52; statement of Dr. Sonnenschein of St. Mary's Hospital, in Ian Lilburn Collection; Rathlef-Keilmann, 91–93.

17. Rathlef-Keilmann, 91.

18. Statement of Baron Arthur von Kleist, June 20, 1922, in Gilliard and Savitch, 48; statement of Baron Arthur von Kleist, quoting Zenaide Tolstoy, August 4, 1922, in Gilliard and Savitch, 49; Marie Clara Peuthert to Princess Irene of Hesse, Princess Heinrich of Prussia, letter of August 23, 1922, in Gilliard and Savitch, 51–52; Pokloevsky-Kozell, letter to Serge Botkin, May 17, 1926, in Gilliard and Savitch, 146; Bonhoeffer report, March 18, 1926, in Hamburg, XIV, 2389–2402.

19. Rathlef-Keilmann, 91–92.

20. Auclères, 235.

21. Rathlef-Keilmann, 31.

22. Rathlef-Keilmann, 94–95; Gertrude Spindler to former Russian ambassador

in Bucharest Pokloevsky-Kozell, in Pokloevsky-Kozell letter to Serge Botkin, May 17, 1926, in Gilliard and Savitch, 146; AA to Rathlef-Keilmann, notes of December 9, 1925, in Rathlef-Keilmann notes, in Hamburg, Bln III, loose.

23. AA, dictated replies to questions, May 8, 1929, p. 7, in Ian Lilburn Collection.

24. Statement of Baron Arthur von Kleist, quoting Zenaide Tolstoy, August 4, 1922, in Gilliard and Savitch, 49.

25. Statement of Dr. Karl Sonnenschein, in Ian Lilburn Collection; AA to Rathlef-Keilmann, notes of December 9, 1925, in Rathlef-Keilmann notes, in Hamburg, Bln III, loose.

26. Statement of Baron Arthur von Kleist, August 10, 1922, in Gilliard and Savitch, 49.

27. Kurth, 34.

28. Statement of Baron Arthur von Kleist, August 10, 1922, in Gilliard and Savitch, 49; Marie Clara Peuthert to Princess Irene of Hesse, Princess Heinrich of Prussia, letter of August 23, 1922, in Gilliard and Savitch, 52; letter of Inspector Franz Grunberg, June 19, 1925, in Hamburg, XIV, 2540–2545.

29. AA to Rathlef-Keilmann, June 30, 1925, in Rathlef-Keilmann notes, in Hamburg, Bln III, loose.

30. Rathlef-Keilmann, 30–31.

31. Affidavit of Agnes Gallagher, December 22, 1930, in Hamburg, XXIV, 4481–4493; statement of Baron Arthur von Kleist, quoting Zenaide Tolstoy, August 4, 1922, in Gilliard and Savitch, 49; statement of Dr. Karl Sonnenschein, in Ian Lilburn Collection.

32. Krug von Nidda, 99.

33. Statement of Baron Arthur Kleist, August 10, 1922, in Gilliard and Savitch, 49–50; Inspector Franz Grunberg, letter of June 19, 1925, in Hamburg, XIV, 2540–2545.

34. Statement of Baron Arthur Kleist, August 10, 1922, in Gilliard and Savitch, 49–50; Marie Clara Peuthert to Princess Irene of Hesse, Princess Heinrich of Prussia, letter of August 23, 1922, in Gilliard and Savitch, 51–52; letter of Inspector Franz Grunberg, June 19,

1925, in Hamburg, XIV, 2540–2545; statement of Dr. Karl Sonnenschein, in Ian Lilburn Collection.

35. Statement of Baron Arthur Kleist, August 10, 1922, in Gilliard and Savitch, 49.

36. Marie Clara Peuthert to Princess Irene of Hesse, Princess Heinrich of Prussia, letter of August 23, 1922, in Gilliard and Savitch, 52.

37. Marie Clara Peuthert to Princess Irene of Hesse, Princess Heinrich of Prussia, letter of August 23, 1922, in Gilliard and Savitch, 52; statement of Baron Arthur von Kleist, quoting Zenaide Tolstoy, August 4, 1922, in Gilliard and Savitch, 49; statement of Baron Arthur von Kleist, August 10, 1922, in Gilliard and Savitch, 50; statement of Dr. Karl Sonnenschein, in Ian Lilburn Collection.

38. Statement of Baron Arthur von Kleist, quoting Zenaide Tolstoy, August 4, 1922, in Gilliard and Savitch, 49.

39. AA to Alexei Miliukov, June 18, 1966, in Miliukov tapes.

40. Gertrude Spindler to former Russian ambassador in Bucharest Pokloevsky-Kozell, in Pokloevsky-Kozell letter to Serge Botkin, May 17, 1926, in Gilliard and Savitch, 147.

41. Bonhoeffer report, March 18, 1926, in Hamburg, XIV, 2389–2402; statement of Dr. Theodor Eitel, December 22, 1926, in Hamburg, VIII, 1394–1402; AA, dictated replies to questions, May 8, 1929, 10, in Ian Lilburn Collection; statement of Dr. Karl Sonnenschein, in Ian Lilburn Collection.

42. Marie Clara Peuthert to Princess Irene of Hesse, Princess Heinrich of Prussia, letter of August 23, 1922, in Gilliard and Savitch, 53.

43. Statement of Baron Arthur von Kleist, quoting Zenaide Tolstoy, August 4, 1922, in Gilliard and Savitch, 49–50; statement of Baron Arthur von Kleist, June 7, 1922, in Gilliard and Savitch, 46.

44. Statement of Baron Arthur von Kleist, June 7, 1922, in Gilliard and Savitch, 46; statement of Baron Arthur von Kleist, June 20, 1922, in Gilliard and Savitch, 48; Gertrude Spindler to former Russian ambassador in Bucharest

Pokloevsky-Kozell, in Pokloevsky-Kozell letter to Serge Botkin, May 17, 1926, in Gilliard and Savitch, 147; Bonhoeffer report, March 18, 1926, in Hamburg, XIV, 2389–2402; Rathlef-Keilmann, 31.

45. Statement of Baron Arthur von Kleist, quoting Zenaide Tolstoy, August 4, 1922, in Gilliard and Savitch, 49.

46. Statement of Baron Arthur von Kleist, June 20, 1922, in Gilliard and Savitch, 48.

47. Rathlef-Keilmann, 32.

48. Rathlef-Keilmann, 32; Marie Clara Peuthert to Princess Irene of Hesse, Princess Heinrich of Prussia, letter of August 23, 1922, in Gilliard and Savitch, 53.

49. Statement of Dr. Theodor Eitel, December 22, 1926, in Hamburg, VIII, 1394–1402.

50. Statement of Dr. Karl Sonnenschein, in Ian Lilburn Collection.

51. Marie Clara Peuthert to Princess Irene of Hesse, Princess Heinrich of Prussia, letter of August 23, 1922, in Gilliard and Savitch, 53.

52. Franz Svoboda, affidavit of November 19, 1928, in Hamburg, Bln IV, 4–47; Svoboda, statement of December 12, 1938, in Hamburg, Bln IV, 41–52; Svoboda, statement of February 21, 1940, in Hamburg, Bln IV, 40.

53. Heinrich Kleibenzetl, statement of July 28, 1965, in Hamburg, XXVI, 4911–4924, 4935–4941.

54. Alexei Golovine, statement of February 25, 1965, in Hamburg, XXIV, 4677–4680; Alois Hochleitner, statement of April 8, 1929, in Hamburg, XXIV, 4465; Olga Vissor, statement in Rathlef-Keilmann, 207; Dr. Gunther Bock, testimony of November 19, 1965, in Hamburg, XXVII, 5159, 5166; Julius Homberg to Rathlef-Keilmann, letter of April 20, 1929, cited in Kurth, 45; Arthur Rohse, testimony of November 20, 1956, in Hamburg, VII, 69–70.

55. Rathlef-Keilmann, 207; Heinrich Kleibenzetl, testimony of July 28, 1965, in Hamburg, XXVI, 4911–4924, 4935–4941; Alois Hochleitner, statement of April 8, 1929, in Hamburg, XXIV, 4465; Auclères, 25–27; Dr. Vladimir Poletyka,

statement of May 23, 1929, in Hamburg, XXIV, 4468–4470.

56. Arthur Rohse, testimony of November 20, 1956, in Hamburg VII, 69–70.

57. Gilliard and Savitch, 24; Count Carl Bonde, statement in letter of October 13, 1952, to Prince Friedrich of Saxe-Altenburg, in Hamburg, Bln V, 96.

58. Sokolov, 155, 158; see Rathlef-Keilmann, 196.

59. Declaration of Constantine Anastasiou, April 8, 1926, in Rathlef-Keilmann, 220–222.

60. Statement of Sarcho Gregorian, quoted in memorandum of Lieutenant General Heroua, Romanian Ministry of the Interior, Criminal and Police Department, Bucharest, May 4, 1927, in Rathlef-Keilmann, 223–224.

61. See Lieutenant Colonel Werner Hassenstein, testimony of May 6, 1955, in Hamburg, XVIII, 3113–3118; Heinrich Dietz, testimony of August 27, 1958, in Hamburg, VIII, 3344.

62. See Rathlef-Keilmann, 217–218; Botkin, *Woman Who Rose Again*, 107; Kurth, 62–63; the reverse of the photograph is in Rathlef-Keilmann, illustration 35, facing p. 209.

63. Pokloevsky-Kozell letter to Serge Botkin dated May 17, 1926, in Gilliard, *False Anastasia*, 145–150.

64. Statement of Baron Arthur von Kleist, quoting Zenaide Tolstoy, August 4, 1922, in Gilliard and Savitch, 49; Pokloevsky-Kozell letter to Serge Botkin, May 17, 1926, in Gilliard and Savitch, 150; Kurth, 402, n. 88.

65. Pokloevsky-Kozell letter to Serge Botkin, May 17, 1926, in Gilliard and Savitch, 150.

66. Princess Ileana of Romania to Brien Horan, 1972, in Horan, 39.

67. Vorres, 177.

8 A Ghost from the Past?

1. Konrad Wahl to Ian Lilburn and Peter Kurth, in Kurth, 54.

2. See Inspector Franz Grunberg, letter dated June 19, 1925, in Hamburg, XIV, 2540–2545.

3. Statement of Serge Botkin, March 1929, in Ian Lilburn Collection.

4. See Inspector Franz Grunberg, letter dated June 19, 1925, in Hamburg, XIV, 2540–2545.

5. Private information to the authors.

6. Inspector Franz Grunberg, letter dated June 19, 1925, in Hamburg, XIV, 2540–2545.

7. Princess Irene of Hesse, Princess Heinrich of Prussia, in Gilliard and Savitch, 43; Princess Irene of Hesse, Princess Heinrich of Prussia, statement of July 31, 1925, in Hamburg, Bln III, 185.

8. Prince Friedrich of Saxe-Altenburg to AA and Alexei Miliukov, March 12, 1967, Miliukov tapes.

9. Testimony of Eleonore von Oertzen, September 16, 1958, in Hamburg, V, 951–953.

10. Inspector Franz Grunberg, letter dated June 19, 1925, in Hamburg, XIV, 2540–2545.

11. Princess Irene of Hesse, Princess Heinrich of Prussia, in Gilliard and Savitch, 43; Princess Irene of Hesse, Princess Heinrich of Prussia, statement of July 31, 1925, in Hamburg, Bln III, 185.

12. Krug von Nidda, 196.

13. AA to Rathlef-Keilmann, June 25, 1925, in Rathlef-Keilmann notes, in Hamburg, Bln III, loose.

14. Inspector Franz Grunberg, letter dated June 19, 1925, in Hamburg, XIV, 2540–2545.

15. AA to Princess Irene of Hesse, Princess Heinrich of Prussia, letter of August 13, 1924, in Ian Lilburn Collection.

16. AA to Princess Irene of Hesse, Princess Heinrich of Prussia, postcard dated August 30, 1924, in Ian Lilburn Collection.

17. Marie Clara Peuthert to Princess Irene of Hesse, Princess Heinrich of Prussia, letter dated September 10, 1924, in Ian Lilburn Collection.

18. Secretary Gaebel to Baroness Marie von Kleist, letter dated September 21, 1924, in Ian Lilburn Collection.

19. Horan, 84.

20. Prince Friedrich of Saxe-Altenburg, quoted in Summers and Mangold, 218.

21. Grand Duke Andrei Vladimirovich to Grand Duchess Olga Alexandrovna, letter dated February 10, 1955, in Hamburg, XIV, 2549.

22. Lyons, Note 52.

23. Nicholas Sablin, quoted in Spiridovich to Gilliard, letter dated December 8, 1928, in Gilliard and Savitch, 39–40.

24. Kurth, 59.

25. Nicholas Sablin, quoted in Spiridovich to Gilliard, letter dated December 8, 1928, in Gilliard and Savitch, 39–40.

26. Baroness Marie von Kleist, affidavit of July 5, 1929, entered into evidence May 20, 1958, in Hamburg, III, 569–574.

27. See Gilliard and Savitch, 37.

28. Kurth, 60–65.

29. Botkin, *Anastasia*, 355.

30. See Botkin, *Real Romanovs*, 262; Botkin, *Woman Who Rose Again*, 77.

31. Rathlef-Keilmann, 18–19; Kurth, 99.

32. Auclères, 70.

33. Rathlef-Keilmann, 19.

34. Gilliard and Savitch, 80.

35. Zahle to Gilliard, letter dated August 4, 1925, and Zahle to Gilliard, letter dated August 26, 1925, in Gilliard and Savitch, 68.

36. Gilliard and Savitch, 73.

37. Dr. Ludwig Berg to Gilliard, letter dated January 13, 1926, in Gilliard and Savitch, 61.

38. Rathlef-Keilmann, 28.

39. Ibid., 129–130.

40. Amy Smith, testimony of December 18, 1965, in Hamburg, XXIX, 5387–5409.

41. Grand Duke Ernst Ludwig of Hesse to Victoria, marchioness of Milford Haven, letter dated February 7, 1927, in Staatsarchiv, Darmstadt.

42. Nancy Leeds Wynkoop to Brien Horan, 1972, quoted in Horan, 49.

43. See Cecilie, crown princess of Prussia, affidavit of October 2, 1953, in Hamburg, XXIV, 4696–4699.

44. Vorres, 173; Rathlef-Keilmann, 47.

45. Rathlef-Keilmann, 18.

46 Kurth, 102.

47. Ibid., 59.

48. Kurth, 99.

49. Rathlef-Keilmann, 48–49.

50. Rathlef-Keilmann, statement of July 1925, in Ian Lilburn Collection; Rathlef-Keilmann, 50–51.

51. Rathlef-Keilmann, 50.

52. Alexei Volkov, quoted in *Posledniye Novosti* 10, no. 1733, January 15, 1926.

53. Rathlef-Keilmann, statement of July 1925, in Ian Lilburn Collection.
54. Rathlef-Keilmann, 52.
55. Ibid., 51–52.
56. Dr. Serge Ostrogorsky, affidavit of May 21, 1929, cited in Kurth, 123.
57. Rathlef-Keilmann, 77.
58. Grand Duchess Olga Alexandrovna to Princess Irene of Hesse, Princess Heinrich of Prussia, letter dated December 22, 1925, in Hamburg, Bln III, 181–182.
59. Grand Duchess Olga Alexandrovna to Alexandra Gilliard, letter dated July 23, 1925, in Gilliard and Savitch, 64.
60. Gilliard and Savitch, 58.
61. Ibid., 65.
62. Rathlef-Keilmann, 57.
63. Gilliard and Savitch, 66; Gilliard to Vladimir Kokovtsov, letter dated July 18, 1926, in Hamburg, II, 281–307; Gilliard to Zahle, letter dated June 13, 1926, in Gilliard and Savitch, 81.
64. Gilliard to Zahle, letter dated June 13, 1926, in Gilliard and Savitch, 81; Rathlef-Keilmann, 57.
65. Gilliard to Zahle, letter dated June 13, 1926, in Gilliard and Savitch, 81.
66. Kurth, 107.
67. Rathlef-Keilmann, 57.
68. Gilliard and Savitch, 67.
69. Gilliard to Kokovtsov, letter dated July 18, 1926, in Hamburg, II, 281–307.

9 Encounter in Berlin

1. Hall, *Little Mother*, 342; Alexander Mikhailovich, *Always a Grand Duke*, 7, 212; Marie Pavlovna, *Princess in Exile*, 102.
2. Xenia Alexandrovna to Michael Thornton, quoted in Thornton to Phenix, letter of January 10, 1998, in Phenix, 237.
3. See Bella Cohen, *New York Times*, March 28, 1926.
4. Olga Alexandrovna to Princess Irene of Hesse, Princess Heinrich of Prussia, letter of December 22, 1925, in Hamburg, Bln III, 181–182.
5. Zahle to Gilliard, letter of October 16, 1925, in Gilliard and Savitch, 69.
6. Rathlef-Keilmann, 105.
7. Gilliard and Savitch, 70.
8. Rathlef-Keilmann, 98.
9. AA (signed as Anastasia Tchaikovsky), affidavit of August 10, 1938, Berlin, in Hamburg, Bln I, 92–100.
10. Cohen in *New York Times*, March 28, 1926.
11. Gilliard and Savitch, 70.
12. Olga Alexandrovna to Anatole Mordvinov, letter of December 4, 1925, in Hamburg, XIII, 2091–2092.
13. Rathlef-Keilmann, 106.
14. Vorres, 174.
15. Rathlef-Keilmann, statement of November 20, 1926, in Hamburg, XIII, 2261–2270; Gilliard and Savitch, 70–71; Olga Alexandrovna to Mordvinov, letter of December 4, 1925, in Hamburg, XIII, 2091–2092.
16. Rathlef-Keilmann, 99.
17. Gilliard and Savitch, 70–72; Vorres, 175.
18. Rathlef-Keilmann, 104.
19. Rathlef-Keilmann to Serge Botkin, letter of August 4, 1926, quoted in Auclères, 72–73; Rathlef-Keilmann, 102.
20. Zahle report, undated, quoted in Auclères, 74.
21. Rathlef-Keilmann, statement of November 20, 1926, in Hamburg, XIII, 2261–2270.
22. Rathlef-Keilmann to Serge Botkin, letter of August 4, 1926, quoted in Auclères, 72–73.
23. Rathlef-Keilmann, 104.
24. Gilliard to Kokovtsov, letter of July 18, 1926, in Hamburg, II, 281–307.
25. Gilliard and Savitch, 72–75.
26. See Nicholas von Schwabe, statement of June 10, 1922, in Hamburg, XIV, 2519–2534; Nicholas von Schwabe to Gilliard, letter of December 12, 1926 in Hamburg, Bln III, 208; Gilliard and Savitch, 72–75; Olga Alexandrovna to Princess Irene of Hesse, Princess Heinrich of Prussia, letter of December 22, 1925, in Hamburg, Bln III, 181–182.
27. Gilliard and Savitch, 75.
28. Olga Alexandrovna to Gilliard, letter of November 1, 1925, quoted in Gilliard to Kokovtsov, letter dated July 18, 1926, in Hamburg, II, 281–307.
29. Gilliard to Kokovtsov, letter dated July 18, 1926, in Hamburg, II, 281–307.

30. Rathlef-Keilmann to Serge Botkin, letter of August 4, 1926, quoted in Auclères, 72–74.
31. Olga Alexandrovna to Mordvinov, letter of December 4, 1925, in Hamburg, XIII, 2091–2092.
32. Rathlef-Keilmann, 106.
33. Gilliard to Zahle, letter of June 13, 1926, in Gilliard and Savitch, 82.
34. Rathlef-Keilmann, 107.
35. Ibid., 106.
36. Olga Alexandrovna to Zahle, letter of October 31, 1925, in Hamburg, XXXII, 6025–6026.
37. Undated letter from Olga Alexandrovna to AA, quoted in "Application to the Amstgericht Court, Berlin, in the Matter of the Estate of Anastasia Nikolaievna Romanov, Case No. 461.VE.733/38," pleading submitted by Paul Leverkuehn and Kurt Vermehren on behalf of AA, October 31, 1938, and lodged in Hamburg under Bln, 33.
38. "Application to the Amstgericht Court, Berlin, in the Matter of the Estate of Anastasia Nikolaievna Romanov, Case No. 461.VE.733/38," pleading submitted by Paul Leverkuehn and Kurt Vermehren on behalf of AA, October 31, 1938, and lodged in Hamburg under Bln, 33–34.
39. Alexandra Gilliard to Lillian Zahle, letter of December 14, 1925, cited in Kurth, 124.
40. *National Tidende*, Copenhagen, January 16, 1926.
41. Gilliard to Kokovtsov, letter dated July 18, 1926, in Hamburg, II/281–307.
42. See Cohen, *New York Times*, March 28, 1926. Cohen claimed to have heard details of the visits not only from Rathlef-Keilmann but also from the Gilliards at the Danish legation, an unlikely assertion that has proved impossible to verify. Aside from erroneously claiming that Frau Tchaikovsky had not been warned in advance of her visitors, and had greeted Olga Alexandrovna by name, Cohen's article inaccurately insisted, among other things, that the patient "bears bullet wounds on her body and scars of a knife on her face and skull"; that Professor Serge Rudnev had

treated Anastasia in 1914; and that while delirious, the patient had spoken in Russian to Professor Rudnev—the latter something that, had it actually occurred, would certainly have been noted by Rathlef-Keilmann.
43. Xenia Georgievna, Mrs. Herman Jud, testimony of February 10, 1958, at the West German consulate in New York City, in Hamburg, IV, 749–751.
44. Grand Duke Andrei Vladimirovich to Serge Botkin, letter of March 14, 1927, quoted in Horan, 104.
45. See Rathlef-Keilmann, 107; Botkin, *Woman Who Rose Again*, 41–42.
46. Tatiana Botkin to Serge Botkin, letter of October 27, 1926, cited in Kurth, 120; information from Ian Lilburn to the authors.
47. Andrei Vladimirovich to Serge Botkin, letter of March 14, 1927, quoted in Horan, 103.
48. Rathlef-Keilmann to Serge Botkin, letter of August 4, 1926, quoted in Auclères, 72–73; Rathlef-Keilmann, 104.
49. Zahle to Serge Botkin, letter of November 26, 1926, in Hamburg, XIII, 2271–2272.
50. Zahle questionnaire, October 31, 1938, in Hamburg, XVIII, 7–16.
51. Rathlef-Keilmann, statement of March 15, 1926, in Hamburg, XVI, 133–137.
52. Rathlef-Keilmann to Serge Botkin, letter of August 4, 1926, quoted in Auclères, 72–73; Rathlef-Keilmann, 104.
53. See Rathlef-Keilmann, 236; affidavit of Dr. Serge Rudnev, April 9, 1929, in Hamburg, XXIV, 4480; affidavit of Dr. Serge Rudnev, July 18, 1938, in Hamburg, Bln I, 134–138; Gilliard and Savitch, 71–76; Cohen, *New York Times*, March 28, 1926. Cohen's article quoted Rudnev directly in stating—falsely—that he had personally treated Anastasia in 1914; apparently, either he or Rathlef-Keilmann had let this "fact" be known in Berlin circles; when Zahle related this to Gilliard, the latter confronted both the surgeon and Rathlef-Keilmann on the claim, and each protested that they had never said such a thing, blaming the other for the error. See Gilliard and Savitch, 75–78.

54. Gilliard to Kokovtsov, letter dated July 18, 1926, in Hamburg, II, 281–307.

55. Gilliard and Savitch, 190.

56. Rathlef-Keilmann to Gilliard, letter of January 16, 1926, in Gilliard and Savitch, 192.

57. Kurth, 408, n. 55. Gilliard burned these papers—his entire dossier on AA's case—after the 1957 verdict against her by a Berlin court, on the presumption that it had come to an end and he would have no need of them in the future. He explained this when he took the witness stand during her civil trial. See Gilliard, testimony of March 29, 1958, in Hamburg, II, 239–247.

58. Private information to the authors.

59. See Auclères, 199–200.

60. Gilliard to Count Schulenberg, letter of December 8, 1925, in Gilliard and Savitch, 191.

61. Alexandra Gilliard to Lillian Zahle, letter of December 14, 1925, cited in Kurth, 124.

62. Gilliard to Zahle, letter of January 11, 1926, in Gilliard and Savitch, 83.

63. Quoted in Kurth, 124.

64. Kurth, 124.

65. Zahle, letter of October 27, 1925, cited in Phenix, 153.

66. Alexandra Gilliard to Rathlef-Keilmann, letter of January 1926, quoted in Welch, 124.

67. Statement of Pierre and Alexandra Gilliard, January 21, 1927, in Hamburg, Bln III, 175–176.

68. Zahle to Serge Botkin, letter of November 26, 1926, in Hamburg, XIII, 2271–2272.

69. Summers and Mangold, 216.

70. Vorres, 177.

71. See notes and postcards of Olga Alexandrovna to AA, autumn 1925, in "Application to the Amstgericht Court, Berlin, in the Matter of the Estate of Anastasia Nikolaievna Romanov, Case No. 461.VE.733/38," pleading submitted by Paul Leverkuehn and Kurt Vermehren on behalf of AA, October 31, 1938, and lodged in Hamburg under Bln, 33–34.

72. Olga Alexandrovna to Mordvinov, letter of December 4, 1925, in Hamburg, XIII, 2091–2092.

73. Gilliard to Kokovtsov, letter dated July 18, 1926, in Hamburg, II, 281–307.

74. Zahle, report to the Danish Foreign Ministry, December 12, 1928, in Hamburg, Summary of Evidence in *Frau Anna Anderson in Unterlengenhardt v. Barbara, Herzogin Christian Ludwig zu Mecklenburg, Ludwig, Prinz von Hesse und bei Rhein*, May 18, 1967, 56.

75. Quoted in Kurth, 124.

76. Olga Alexandrovna to Mordvinov, letter of December 4, 1925, in Hamburg, XIII, 2091–2092.

77. Olga Alexandrovna to Princess Irene of Hesse, Princess Heinrich of Prussia, letter of December 22, 1925, in Hamburg, Bln III, 181–182.

78. Olga Alexandrovna to Tatiana Botkin, letter of August 30, 1926, in Hamburg, XXXIV/6370.

79. Olga Alexandrovna to Mordvinov, letter of January 1, 1927, in Hamburg, XXIII, 4368.

80. Ibid.

81. Phenix, 217.

82. Olga Alexandrovna, testimony of March 23, 1959, at the West German consulate in Toronto, in Hamburg, VII, 1298–1312.

83. See Botkin, *Real Romanovs*, 266; Botkin, *Woman Who Rose Again*, 99.

84. Olga Alexandrovna, testimony of March 23, 1959, at the West German consulate in Toronto, in Hamburg, VII, 1298–1312.

85. Ibid.

86. See Kurth, 309.

87. Vorres, 174.

88. Vorres, 174; Olga Alexandrovna to Mordvinov, letter of December 4, 1925, in Hamburg, XIII, 2091–2092.

89. Vorres, 176.

90. Tikhon Kulikovsky to Kurth, letter of September 2, 1971, in Peter Kurth Collection.

10 "If the Imperial House of Russia Wants to Let One of Its Own Die in the Gutter . . ."

1. Baron Osten-Sacken, letter of February 1926, quoted in Kurth, 129.

2. Olga Alexandrovna to Gilliard, letter of January 16, 1926, quoted in Gilliard

to Kokovtsov, letter of July 18, 1926, in Hamburg, II, 281–307.

3. Olga Alexandrovna to Mordvinov, letter of January 1, 1927, in Hamburg, XXIII, 4368.

4. Gilliard to Kokovtsov, letter dated July 18, 1926, in Hamburg, II, 281–307.

5. See Kurth, 118.

6. Zahle questionnaire, in Hamburg, XVIII, 7–16. King Christian X abruptly terminated Zahle's investigation into the case, and when he retired, the former diplomat handed over all of his notes and files to the Danish Royal Archives. Those interested in Anderson's case have long suspected that the dossiers Zahle turned over to King Christian X held important evidence in her favor. Repeated requests to Queen Margrethe II for access have always been refused, on the grounds that the papers are in the private family archives and thus not subject to ordinary disclosure. (See, for example, *Spectator*, London, July 18, 1992.) Private inquiries, however, now suggest that they remain restricted because the Danish minister was rather too adamant in expressing his own personal opinions of the royal personages involved and discussing private behavior unrelated to the claim that would prove embarrassing to the Romanovs and to their crowned relations.

7. Prince Friedrich Saxe-Altenburg to Brien Horan, December 1973, quoted in Horan, 47.

8. Ernst Ludwig to Victoria, marchioness of Milford Haven, letter dated February 2, 1927, in Staatsarchiv Darmstadt.

9. Serge Botkin to Andrei Vladimirovich, letter of April 1927, quoted in Kurth, 164.

10. Andrei Vladimirovich to P. S. von Kugelgen, letter of July 8, 1928, quoted in Rathlef-Keilmann, 12.

11. Zahle to Serge Botkin, letter of February 5, 1927, quoted in Krug von Nidda, 204–205.

12. Andrei Vladimirovich to Serge Botkin, letter of November 30, 1926, in Hamburg, VIII, 1595–1597.

13. Gilliard and Savitch, 101.

14. Graf, 151.

15. Kurth, 127.

16. Andrei Vladimirovich to Tatiana Botkin, letter of September 2, 1927, quoted in Auclères, 175.

17. Gilliard and Savitch, 102, 195–196.

18. Andrei Vladimirovich to Serge Botkin, March 14, 1927, quoted in Horan, 94.

19. Information from Ian Lilburn to the authors.

20. Rathlef-Keilmann, 126.

21. Combined reports of letters from Rathlef-Keilmann to Serge Botkin, dated June 9, 1926, and from Rathlef-Keilmann to Zahle, dated June 10, 1926, cited in Kurth, 132.

22. Botkin, Anastasia, 335, n. 8.

23. Baron von Osten-Sacken to Serge Botkin, letter of June 29, 1926, in Ian Lilburn Collection.

24. Dr. Serge Rudnev, report of March 1926, in Hamburg, XIV, 2485–2488.

25. Dr. Lothar Nobel, report of March 1926, in Hamburg, XIII, 4417–4426.

26. Ibid.

27. Dr. Karl Bonhoeffer, report of March 18, 1926, in Hamburg, XIV, 2389–2402.

28. Professor Saathof to Duke Georg of Leuchtenberg, letter of December 7, 1927, in Hamburg, XXIV, 4508–4509.

29. Dr. Theodor Eitel, report of December 22, 1926, in Hamburg, VIII, 1394–1402.

30. Tatiana Botkin to Duke Georg of Leuchtenberg, undated letter, in Rathlef-Keilmann, 142–143; Nancy Leeds Wynkoop to Brien Horan, quoted in Horan, 112.

31. Dr. Lothar Nobel, report of March 1926, in Hamburg, XIII, 4417–4426.

32. Dr. Karl Bonhoeffer, report of March 18, 1926, in Hamburg, XIV, 2389–2402.

33. Dr. Theodor Eitel, report of December 22, 1926, in Hamburg, VIII, 1394–1402.

34. Kurth, 153.

35. Rathlef-Keilmann to Tatiana Botkin, letter of March 10, 1927, in Ian Lilburn Collection.

36. Kurth, 159–160; Botkin, *Anastasia*, 155.

37. Tatiana Botkin to Kurth, quoted in Kurth, 159; Rathlef-Keilmann, 14.

11 "A Sort of Weird Charm"

1. AA to Alexei Miliukov, April 23, 1966, in Miliukov tapes.

2. Details from Ob, Berger, and personal visits by the authors.

3. Botkin, *Woman Who Rose Again*, 63.

4. Rathlef-Keilmann, 49; Kurth, 159; Belyakova, 224; *Berliner Nachtausgabe*, April 8, 1927; diary of Faith Lavington, January 31, 1927, in Hamburg, XXXIV, 6402–6428.

5. Botkin, *Woman Who Rose Again*, 64.

6. Botkin, *Woman Who Rose Again*, 48, 65; Belyakova, 41; Kournosoff, 5–7, 46, 63.

7. Botkin, *Woman Who Rose Again*, 65; Belyakova, 227.

8. Botkin, *Woman Who Rose Again*, 48, 65.

9. Belyakova, 222.

10. Botkin, *Woman Who Rose Again*, 45; Gilliard and Savitch, 91.

11. Kurth, 182.

12. Duke Georg of Leuchtenberg to Rathlef-Keilmann, letter of July 7, 1927, cited in Kurth, 184.

13. Kurth, 180; see diary of Faith Lavington, November 21, 1927, in Hamburg, XXXIV, 6402–6428.

14. Rathlef-Keilmann, 111–112.

15. Ibid., 117.

16. Ibid., 111–116.

17. Duke Georg of Leuchtenberg to Olga Alexandrovna, letter of August 26, 1927, in Hamburg, XIV, 2558–2559.

18. Rathlef-Keilmann, 155.

19. Duke Georg of Leuchtenberg to Andrei Vladimirovich, letter of April 17, 1927, quoted in Rathlef-Keilmann, 154.

20. Statement of Duchess Nathalia of Leuchtenberg, Baroness Meller-Zakomelsky, November 3, 1959, in Hamburg, IX, 1623–1630.

21. Statement of Duke Dimitri of Leuchtenberg, March 20, 1959, in Hamburg, VII, 1253–1261; statement of Duchess Catherine of Leuchtenberg, March 20, 1959, in Hamburg, VII, 1261–1264.

22. Maria von Hesse, quoted in Gilliard and Savitch, 141–142.

23. Kurth, 127.

24. Gilliard and Savitch, 34, 77; *Berliner Nachtausgabe*, April 16, 1927.

25. Rathlef-Keilmann, 232.

26. See Bonhoeffer report, March 18, 1926, in Hamburg, XIV, 2389–2402; Gilliard and Savitch, 29, 110; testimony of Anna (Thea) Chemnitz, née Malinovsky, December 17, 1958, in Hamburg, V, 979–981; Baroness Marie von Kleist, affidavit of July 5, 1929, entered into evidence May 20, 1958, in Hamburg, III, 569–574; statement of Nicholas von Schwabe, June 10, 1922, in Hamburg, XIV, 2519–2534; Nicholas von Schwabe to Gilliard, in Gilliard and Savitch, 110; Nicholas von Schwabe to Gilliard, letter of November 17, 1926, quoted in Gilliard and Savitch, 114–115; Hamburg, *Summary of Evidence in Frau Anna Anderson in Unterlengenhardt v. Barbara, Herzogin Christian Ludwig zu Mecklenburg, Ludwig, Prinz von Hesse und bei Rhein*, May 18, 1967, 166.

27. Rathlef-Keilmann, 232–233.

28. Dr. Karl Bonhoeffer report, March 18, 1926, in Hamburg, XIV, 2389–2402; Dr. Lothar Nobel, report of March 1926, in Hamburg, XIII, 4417–4426.

29. Dr. Theodor Eitel, report of December 22, 1926, in Hamburg, VIII, 1394–1402.

30. Testimony of Dr. Theodor Eitel, May 20, 1959, in Hamburg, VIII, 1406–1421.

31. Dr. Lothar Nobel, report of March 1926, in Hamburg, XIII, 4417–4426. This portion of Nobel's statement, not surprisingly, was edited out before Rathlef-Keilmann published it in her book. See her reproduction of Nobel's statement in Rathlef-Keilmann, 238–242.

32. Duke Georg of Leuchtenberg to Olga Alexandrovna, letter of August 26, 1927, in Hamburg, XIV, 2558–2559.

33. Duchess Nathalia of Leuchtenberg, Baroness Meller-Zakomelsky, letter of December 11, 1974, to Brien Horan, quoted in Horan, 139.

34. Duke Dimitri of Leuchtenberg, letter of March 5, 1961, quoted in Vorres, 239–240.

35. Duke Konstantin of Leuchtenberg, quoted in the *Ottawa Citizen*, December 1, 1964.

36. Testimony of Anna (Thea) Chemnitz, née Malinovsky, December 17, 1958, in Hamburg, V, 979–981; Rathlef-Keilmann, 232–233; Dr. Lothar Nobel, report of March 1926, in Hamburg, XIII, 4417–4426.

37. Statement of Rathlef-Keilmann, July 1925, in Ian Lilburn Collection.

38. This point was especially noted in the 1967 verdict of the Hanseatic Court of Appeals that reviewed Anderson's case. See Hamburg, *Summary of Evidence in Frau Anna Anderson in Unterlengenhardt v. Barbara, Herzogin Christian Ludwig zu Mecklenburg, Ludwig, Prinz von Hesse und bei Rhein*, May 18, 1967, 217.

39. Dr. Ludwig Berg, statement of May 10, 1929, cited in Kurth, 86.

40. Affidavit of Tatiana Botkin, May 2, 1929, in Hamburg, Bln I, 113–127; testimony of Dr. Theodor Eitel, May 20, 1959, in Hamburg, VIII, 1410.

41. Duke Georg of Leuchtenberg to Olga Alexandrovna, letter of August 26, 1927, in Hamburg, XIV, 2558–2559; diary of Faith Lavington, September 26, 1927, in Hamburg, XXXIV, 6402–6428.

42. See Rathlef-Keilmann, notes of June 30, 1925, in Hamburg, Bln III loose.

43. Franz Jaenicke, statement of February 27, 1956, in Ian Lilburn collection; Dr. Serge Rudnev, report of March 1926, in Hamburg, XIV, 2485–2488; Rudnev affidavit of July 18, 1938, in Hamburg, Bln I, 134–138.

44. Agnes Gallagher, affidavit of December 22, 1930, in Hamburg, XXIV, 4481–4493.

45. Statement of Serge Botkin, March 1929, in Ian Lilburn Collection.

46. Auclères, 16.

47. Cited in Kurth, 131.

48. Baron Osten-Sacken to Serge Botkin, letter of June 29, 1926, in Ian Lilburn Collection.

49. Dr. Theodor Eitel, report of December 22, 1926, in Hamburg, VIII, 1394–1402.

50. See diary of Vera von Klemenz, August 21, 1927, in Rathlef-Keilmann, 168; affidavit of Agnes Gallagher, December 22, 1930, in Hamburg, XXIV, 4481–4493.

51. Duke Georg of Leuchtenberg to Olga Alexandrovna, letter of August 26, 1927, in Hamburg, XIV, 2552–2557.

52. Diary of Faith Lavington, September 19, 1927, in Hamburg, XXXIV, 6402–6428.

53. Ibid. September 26, 1927.

54. Ibid., November 15, 1927.

55. Ibid.

56. Agnes Wasserschleben, notes of July 28, 1929, in Hamburg, IV, 1017–1024.

57. Diary and notes of Vera von Klemenz, June 17, 1927, in Rathlef-Keilmann, 161.

58. Ibid., June 23, 1927, in Rathlef-Keilmann, 161–162.

59. Ibid., June 24, 1927, in Rathlef-Keilmann, 163.

60. Ibid., July 17, 1927, in Rathlef-Keilmann, 164.

61. Botkin, *Woman Who Rose Again*, 309.

62. Ibid., 69.

63. Diary of Faith Lavington, September 26, 1927, in Hamburg, XXXIV, 6402–6428.

64. Botkin, *Woman Who Rose Again*, 48, 66; Agnes Gallagher, affidavit of December 22, 1930, in Hamburg, XXIV, 4481–4493.

65. Kurth, 166.

66. AA, dictated replies to questions, May 8, 1929, 5, in Ian Lilburn Collection.

67. Kurth, 197.

68. Botkin, *Woman Who Rose Again*, 45.

69. Ibid., 44.

70. Ibid., 45.

71. See Botkin, *Woman Who Rose Again*, 45; Agnes Gallagher, affidavit of December 22, 1930, in Hamburg, XXIV, 4481–4493.

72. Diary of Faith Lavington, February 21, 1928, in Hamburg, XXXIV, 6402–6428.

73. Duke Dimitri of Leuchtenberg, letter of March 5, 1961, quoted in Vorres, 239–240.

74. See diary of Faith Lavington, December 16, 1927, in Hamburg, XXXIV, 6402–6428; Gilliard and Savitch, 99.

75. Diary of Faith Lavington, September 26, 1927, in Hamburg, XXXIV, 6402–6428.

76. Ibid., November 8, 1927.

77. Ibid., November 30, 1927.

78. Ibid., February 21, 1928.

12 The Making of a Myth

1. See Gilliard and Savitch, 138; Madeleine Zanotti, statement of February 9, 1939, in Hamburg, Bln III, 167.

2. Alexander Conrad to Alexander Mikhailovich, letter of December 14, 1928, in Gilliard and Savitch, 140–141.

3. Maria von Hesse, quoted in Gilliard and Savitch, 141.
4. Diary of Faith Lavington, January 31, February 13, and March 9, 1928, in Hamburg, XXXIV, 6402–6428.
5. Ibid., January 31, 1928.
6. Prince Felix Yusupov to Gilliard, letter of December 10, 1928, quoted in Gilliard and Savitch, 144–145; see also Yusupov, 113–114.
7. Prince Felix Yusupov to Andrei Vladimirovich, letter of September 19, 1927, in Kurth, 186.
8. Auclères, 116.
9. AA to Alexei Miliukov, July 11, 1965, in Miliukov tapes.
10. Statement of Anatole Mordvinov, Oberstdorf, August 27, 1928, in Gilliard and Savitch, 94.
11. Gilliard and Savitch, 94–95.
12. Ibid., 93.
13. Ibid., 94.
14. Auclères, 98.
15. Statement of Felix Dassel, April 19–20, 1929, in Hamburg, Bln I, 130–131.
16. Drawn from Summers and Mangold, 227–228.
17. Testimony of Felix Dassel, April 22, 1958, in Hamburg, III, 475–476; protocol of Duke Georg of Leuchtenberg, Felix Dassel, and Otto Bornemann, Munich, September 19, 1927, in Ian Lilburn Collection.
18. Protocol of Duke Georg of Leuchtenberg, Felix Dassel, and Otto Bornemann, Munich, September 19, 1927, in Ian Lilburn Collection; Dassel, 26.
19. Protocol of Duke Georg of Leuchtenberg, Felix Dassel, and Otto Bornemann, Munich, September 19, 1927, in Ian Lilburn Collection.
20. Ibid.
21. Ibid.
22. Testimony of Felix Dassel, April 24, 1958, in Hamburg, II, 352–366.
23. Protocol of Duke Georg of Leuchtenberg, Felix Dassel, and Otto Bornemann, Munich, September 19, 1927, in Ian Lilburn Collection.
24. Protocol of Duke Georg of Leuchtenberg, Felix Dassel, and Otto Bornemann, Munich, September 19, 1927, in Ian Lilburn Collection; Tatiana

Botkin, affidavit of May 2, 1929, in Hamburg, Bln I, 113–127.
25. Dassel, 28–29; testimony of Felix Dassel, April 24, 1958, in Hamburg, II, 352–366.
26. Protocol of Duke Georg of Leuchtenberg, Felix Dassel, and Otto Bornemann, Munich, September 19, 1927, in Ian Lilburn Collection.
27. Dassel, 18–19; protocol of Duke Georg of Leuchtenberg, Felix Dassel, and Otto Bornemann, Munich, September 19, 1927, in Ian Lilburn Collection.
28. Protocol of Duke Georg of Leuchtenberg, Felix Dassel, and Otto Bornemann, Munich, September 19, 1927, in Ian Lilburn Collection.
29. Diary of Faith Lavington, September 19, 1927, in Hamburg, XXXIV, 6402–6428.
30. Diary of Nicholas II (then Tsesarevich Nicholas), April 16/27, 1891, in GARF, F. 601, Op. 1, D. 225.
31. Dassel, 37.
32. Diary of Vera von Klemenz, September 18, 1927, in Rathlef-Keilmann, 169.
33. Dassel, 36–37.
34. Dassel, 38–39; statement of Otto Bornemann, August 8, 1952, in Hamburg, Bln VI, 211–212.
35. Excerpts from the diary of Faith Lavington, September 19, 1927, in Hamburg, XXXIV, 6402–6428.
36. Protocol of Duke Georg of Leuchtenberg, Felix Dassel, and Otto Bornemann, Munich, September 19, 1927, in Ian Lilburn Collection.
37. Dassel, 34–35.
38. Protocol of Duke Georg of Leuchtenberg, Felix Dassel, and Otto Bornemann, Munich, September 19, 1927, in Ian Lilburn Collection.
39. Dassel, 47–48.
40. We are grateful to Tim Welsh for suggesting this last hypothesis.
41. Testimony of Felix Dassel, April 24, 1958, in Hamburg, II, 331–366.
42. Gerda von Kleist, Hamburg, May, 1958
43. Affidavit of Baroness Marie von Kleist, July 5, 1929, entered into evidence May 20, 1958, in Hamburg, III, 569–574.
44. See *Illustrierte Blatt*, Frankfurt, April 4, 1927; Hamburg, Summary of Evidence in *Frau Anna Anderson in Unterlengenhardt*

v. Barbara, Herzogin Christian Ludwig zu Mecklenburg, Ludwig, Prinz von Hesse und bei Rhein, May 18, 1967, 74.

45. Botkin, *Anastasia*, 18.

46. Baron Vassili Osten-Sacken, statement of July 1, 1929, in Hamburg, XXIV, 4512–4516; Tatiana Botkin, affidavit of May 2, 1929, in Hamburg, Bln I, 113–127.

47. Tatiana Botkin, affidavit of May 2, 1929, in Hamburg, Bln I, 113–127.

48. Botkin, *Anastasia*, 23.

49. Baron Vassili Osten-Sacken, statement of July 1, 1929, in Hamburg, XXIV, 4512–4516; Botkin, *Anastasia*, 27.

50. Tatiana Botkin, affidavit of May 2, 1929, in Hamburg, Bln I, 113–127.

51. Ibid.

52. Gilliard, *Thirteen Years*, 209, 213; Gilliard and Savitch, 115.

53. Baron Osten-Sacken, affidavit, July 1, 1929, in Hamburg, XXIV, 4512–4516.

54. Olga Alexandrovna to Tatiana Botkin, letter dated August 30, 1926, in Hamburg XXXIV, 6370.

55. Botkin, *Real Romanovs*, 273.

56. Gleb Botkin, affidavit of July 20, 1938, in Hamburg, Bln I, 101–112.

57. Botkin, *Real Romanovs*, 260–262; private information to the authors.

58. Botkin, *Real Romanovs*, 260.

59. Gleb Botkin, affidavit of July 20, 1938, in Hamburg, Bln I, 101–112.

60. Ibid.

61. See Botkin, *Woman Who Rose Again*, 260–267.

62. Gleb Botkin, affidavit of July 20, 1938, in Hamburg, Bln I, 101–112.

63. Botkin, *Real Romanovs*, 287.

64. Botkin, *Woman Who Rose Again*, 60.

65. Gleb Botkin, affidavit of July 20, 1938, in Hamburg, Bln I, 101–112.

66. Botkin, *Woman Who Rose Again*, 53–54; Rathlef-Keilmann, 183.

67. Rathlef-Keilmann, 183; Botkin, *Real Romanovs*, 286; Gleb Botkin, affidavit of July 20, 1938, in Hamburg, Bln I, 101–112.

68. Botkin, *Real Romanovs*, 286; Gleb Botkin, affidavit of July 20, 1938, in Hamburg, Bln I, 101–112.

69. Gleb Botkin, affidavit of July 20, 1938, in Hamburg, Bln I, 101–112; Rathlef-Keilmann, 183.

70. Klier and Mingay, 152.

71. Private information to the authors.

13 "A Gruesome Impression"

1. See Kurth, 156.

2. See, for example, Rathlef-Keilmann, 112–114, and Kurth, 126 and 276.

3. Botkin, *Woman Who Rose Again*, 147–149; Gleb Botkin, affidavit of July 20, 1938, in Hamburg, Bln I, 101–112.

4. Prince Christopher of Greece, 219.

5. Xenia Georgievna, Mrs. Herman Jud, testimony of March 16–17, 1959, at the West German consulate in New York City, in Hamburg, VII, 1214–1230.

6. Diary of Faith Lavington, February 13, 1928, in Hamburg, XXXIV, 6402–6428.

7. Agnes Gallagher, affidavit of December 22, 1930, in Hamburg, XXIV, 4481–4493.

8. Kurth, 208–209; AA to Alexei Miliukov, April 17, 1965, in Miliukov tapes.

9. Kurth, 210.

10. AA, dictated replies to questions, May 8, 1929, p. 8, in Ian Lilburn Collection.

11. *New York Herald Tribune*, February 10, 1928.

12. Xenia Georgievna, Mrs. Herman Jud, testimony of March 16–17, 1959, in Hamburg, VII, 1214–1230.

13. Ibid.

14. Ibid.

15. Ibid.

16. Margharita Derfelden, affidavit of April 22, 1959, in Hamburg, VII, 1329–1337.

17. See Horan, 141.

18. Ibid.

19. Xenia Georgievna, Mrs. Herman Jud, testimony of March 16–17, 1959, in Hamburg, VII, 1214–1230.

20. Kurth, 217; Chavchavadze, 236.

21. Princess Nina Georgievna to Brien Horan, quoted in Horan, 144–145.

22. Xenia Georgievna, Mrs. Herman Jud, testimony of March 16–17, 1959, in Hamburg, VII, 1214–1230.

23. In *Literary Digest* 98 (July 7, 1928): 37.

24. Hall and Van Der Kiste, 233.

25. Prince Christopher of Greece, 223.

26. See Auclères, 184.

27. Botkin, *Woman Who Rose Again*, 170.

28. Botkin, *Real Romanovs*, 275–276.

29. Andrei Vladimirovich to Serge Botkin, letter of December 25, 1927, in Ian Lilburn Collection.
30. See Kurth, 221–224.
31. Botkin, *Woman Who Rose Again*, 239–244; Gleb Botkin, deposition of July 20, 1938, in Hamburg, Bln I, 101–112; AA, affidavit of August 10, 1938, in Hamburg, Bln I, 92–100.
32. Auclères, 184.
33. Kurth, 224.
34. Ibid., 227.
35. Walter Ruch, statement of May 2, 1961, in Hamburg, XV, 2698–2700.
36. Kurth, 226; private information to the authors.
37. See Clarke, 98–102, for discussion of imperial finances; Alexander Kerensky, in Sokolov, 34–35; Alexandra Feodorovna to Nicholas II, letter of August 27, 1915, in GARF, F. 601, Op. 1, D. 1149; Benckendorff, 89, 125; Vorres, 245.
38. AA, declaration of December 15, 1928, in Botkin, *Woman Who Rose Again*, 203; AA, affidavit of August 10, 1938, in Hamburg, Bln I, 92–100; Gleb Botkin, deposition of July 20, 1938, in Hamburg, Bln I, 101–112.
39. See, for example, Botkin, *Woman Who Rose Again*, 201 passim; and Lovell, 193 passim.
40. Vorres, 179.
41. See Berkman, 149.
42. See Kurth, 233–235.
43. Victoria, marchioness of Milford Haven, to Princess Xenia Georgievna, letter of July 23, 1930, in Hamburg, XXXII, 3276.
44. Gilliard and Savitch, 10; Kurth, 229.
45. Botkin, *Woman Who Rose Again*, 238.
46. Gleb Botkin to Xenia Alexandrovna, letter of October 18, 1928, in Hamburg, VII, 1211–1213.
47. Botkin, *Woman Who Rose Again*, 284–285.
48. Botkin, *Anastasia*, 201–203.
49. Kurth, 231–232.
50. Botkin, *Woman Who Rose Again*, 7.
51. Botkin, *Real Romanovs*, 255, 265; Botkin, *Woman Who Rose Again*, 44, 223–226.
52. Botkin, *Woman Who Rose Again*, 286.
53. Kurth, 232.
54. Ibid., 245–246.
55. Ibid., 250–251.
56. Ibid., 251.
57. Krug von Nidda, 250; Kurth, 252.

14 A Tale of Two Books

1. In Koenigsberg, *Allgemeine Zeitung*, 110, March 7, 1927.
2. See Pierre Gilliard in *Journal de Geneve*, June 15, 1927; in *L'Illustration*, June 25, 1927; and in *Illustrated London News*, July 16, 1927; Rathlef-Keilmann in *Tägliche Rundschau*, October 1927, articles in Hamburg, XVII, 3165–3188.
3. Rathlef-Keilmann, 14.
4. Ibid., 258.
5. Gilliard and Savitch, xi, 70.
6. Ibid., 210.
7. Ibid., xii.
8. Botkin, *Woman Who Rose Again*, 91.
9. Kurth, 128; Auclères, 153.
10. Rathlef-Keilmann, 28.
11. Gilliard and Savitch, 123.
12. Rathlef-Keilmann to Gilliard, letter of January 1, 1926, in Gilliard and Savitch, 123; Rathlef-Keilmann notes, June 30, 1925, in Hamburg, Bln III, loose.
13. Rathlef-Keilmann to Gilliard, letter of January 25, 1926, in Gilliard and Savitch, 116, reproduced on p. 117; Rathlef-Keilmann notes, December 8, 1925, in Hamburg, Bln III, loose.
14. See the diary of Nicholas II, June 5/18, 1915; Timms, p. 122, item 164.
15. Rathlef-Keilmann, 109.
16. Vassili Koliubakin to Peter Kondzerovski, letter of August 21, 1928, in Gilliard and Savitch, 118–119.
17. Rathlef-Keilmann, 85–86.
18. In "Application to the Amstgericht Court, Berlin, in the Matter of the Estate of Anastasia Nikolaievna Romanov, Case No. 461.VE.733/738," pleading submitted by Paul Leverkuehn and Kurt Vermehren on behalf of AA, October 31, 1938, and lodged in Hamburg under Bln, 42.
19. Auclères, 154–156.
20. Diary of Vera von Klemenz, August 16, 1927, in Rathlef-Keilmann, 168.
21. Gilliard and Savitch, 120.
22. Auclères, 15.
23. Botkin, *Woman Who Rose Again*, 108–109.
24. Kurth, 76.
25. Rathlef-Keilmann, 193.

26. Rathlef-Keilmann notes, June 23, 1925, in Hamburg, Bln III, loose.
27. Zahle to Gilliard, letter of November 4, 1925, in Gilliard and Savitch, 125.
28. Gilliard and Savitch, 126.
29. Rathlef-Keilmann notes, June 21, 1925, in Hamburg, Bln III, loose.
30. Rathlef-Keilmann, 76.
31. Rathlef-Keilmann notes, June 20, 1925, and June 21, 1925, in Hamburg, Bln III, loose.
32. Rathlef-Keilmann notes, June 30, 1925, in Hamburg, Bln III, loose.
33. Affidavit of Agnes Gallagher, December 22, 1930, in Hamburg, XXIV, 4481–4493.
34. Kurth, 242.
35. AA, dictated answers to questions, May 8, 1929, 2–8, in Ian Lilburn Collection.
36. Hans Willige, "Opinion Concerning Frau Anna Tchaikovsky," November 5, 1938, in Hamburg, XII, 1985–1994.
37. Information from Robert K. Massie to the authors; Kurth, 275.
38. Information from Robert K. Massie to the authors.
39. AA to Alexei Miliukov, August 18, 1965, in Miliukov tapes.
40. Kurth, 285; Horan, 153.
41. Kurth, 267; Paganuzzi, 16.
42. Kurth, 265.
43. Horan, 155; information from Ian Lilburn to the authors.
44. Cited in Horan, 154–155.
45. King, "Romanovs in Film," 42; Kurth, 241.
46. King, "Romanovs in Film," 43.
47. Maurette, 120.
48. Kurth, 425, Note 29; King, "Romanovs in Film," 44.
49. Cited in Phenix, 216.
50. Lovell, 246.
51. AA to Alexei Miliukov, August 14, 1965, in Miliukov tapes.
52. AA, letter to unknown recipient, November 22, 1954, in authors' collection.

15 Émigrés at War

1. Quoted in Horan, 51.
2. See diary of Faith Lavington, entry of February 7, 1928, in Hamburg, XXXIV/6402–6428.

3. Andrei Vladimirovich to Serge Botkin, letter of February 16, 1928, quoted in Auclères, 178.
4. Andrei Vladimirovich to Olga Alexandrovna, letter of February 4, 1928, in Hamburg, XVII, 3119.
5. Botkin, *Anastasia*, 82.
6. Andrei Vladimirovich to Paul von Kuegelgen, letter of August 1, 1928, quoted in Rathlef-Keilmann, 11–12.
7. Graf, 152.
8. Andrei Vladimirovich to Olga Alexandrovna, letter of February 10, 1955, in Hamburg, XIV, 2549. In 1974, on the death of his son Prince Vladimir Romanov, the dossier compiled by Andrei Vladimirovich on the claimant was taken by Grand Duke Vladimir Kirillovich, only son of Andrei's brother Kirill Vladimirovich. It remains the private property of Vladimir's daughter Grand Duchess Maria Vladimirovna and unavailable to historians. See Horan, 53.
9. Prince Vladimir Andreievich, in *L'Aurore*, Paris, February 23, 1960.
10. Horan, 52–53.
11. Princess Kira Kirillovna, testimony of September 20, 1965, in Hamburg, XXVI, 5003.
12. Ibid.
13. Crown Princess Cecilie of Prussia, affidavit of October 2, 1953, in Hamburg, XXIII, 4411–4412.
14. Princess Kira Kirillovna, testimony of September 20, 1965, in Hamburg, XXVI, 5003.
15. See *Le Figaro*, June 30, 1959, cited in Kurth, 59; Kurth, 257.
16. Ivan Arapov, affidavit of October 1, 1938, cited in Kurth, 275.
17. Paganuzzi, 16.
18. Private information to the authors.
19. Prince Sigismund of Prussia, affidavit of July 5, 1938, in Hamburg, Bln I, 133; Prince Friedrich of Saxe-Altenburg, affidavit of August 1, 1938, in Hamburg, Bln I, 132.
20. See Kurth, 272–273.
21. Prince Sigismund of Prussia, affidavit of July 5, 1938, in Hamburg, Bln I, 133.
22. From the collection of Brien Horan. Horan, a lawyer and a historian of the

Anderson case, explained to the present authors: "In 1974 my friend Prince Friedrich of Saxe-Altenburg allowed me to copy the list of Prince Sigismund's questions. The last time I saw him, in summer 1984, a few months before his death, we discussed the questions again, because he and his sister, the widow of Prince Sigismund, had then come to stay with me in Paris. Although in 1984 he was still of the view that releasing the questions would be unhelpful to Anna Anderson's case, the fact that he allowed me to have a copy of them 'for history' is, in my opinion, an implicit recognition that he envisaged the possibility that future circumstances might make their publication appropriate. I think the time now has certainly come to make them available 'for history,' and I have now decided to do so." Brien Horan to the authors.

23. Anna Vyrubova's memoirs were published as *Glanz und Untergang der Romanows* in Berlin in 1927 by Amalthea Verlag. See also the diary of Faith Lavington, entry of September 19, 1927, in Hamburg, XXXIV, 6402–6428; Agnes Wasserschleben, affidavit of July 28, 1929, in Hamburg, VI, 1017–1024. In Vyrubova could also be found the answers to questions 1, 2, 8, 11, 13, 15, 16, and 17, while Spiridovich also dealt with questions 1, 2, 6, 14, 15, 16, 17, and 18. See Vyrubova, 90–95; Spiridovich, vol. 2, chap. 12, translation provided to the authors by Rob Moshein.

24. Prince Sigismund of Prussia, affidavit of July 5, 1938, Hamburg, Bln I, 133; see also Hamburg, Summary of Evidence in *Frau Anna Anderson in Unterlengenhardt v. Barbara, Herzogin Christian Ludwig zu Mecklenburg, Ludwig, Prinz von Hesse und bei Rhein*, May 18, 1967, 101–102.

25. Prince Friedrich of Saxe-Altenburg, affidavit of August 1, 1938, in Hamburg, Bln I, 132.

26. Hamburg, Summary of Evidence in *Frau Anna Anderson in Unterlengenhardt v. Barbara, Herzogin Christian Ludwig zu Mecklenburg, Ludwig, Prinz von Hesse und bei Rhein*, May 18, 1967, 101.

27. Lord Mountbatten to Prince Ludwig of Hesse, letter of November 12, 1957, in Staatsarchiv, Darmstadt.

28. Summers and Mangold, 192.

29. Thornton, 39.

30. Prince Friedrich of Saxe-Altenburg, affidavit of August 1, 1938, in Hamburg, Bln I, 132.

31. Charles Sidney Gibbes to Alexandra Gilliard, letter of September 17, 1926, in Ian Lilburn Collection.

32 Charles Sidney Gibbes to Alexander Mikhailovich, letter of December 1, 1928, in Hamburg, XXIII, 4403–4404.

33. Charles Sidney Gibbes, affidavit of April 17, 1958, in Hamburg, III, 495–497.

34. Ibid.

35. Rathlef-Keilmann, 70.

36. Welch, 220; AA to Alexei Miliukov, August 14, 1965, in Miliukov tapes.

37. Trewin, 134.

38. Hamburg, Summary of Evidence in *Frau Anna Anderson in Unterlengenhardt v. Barbara, Herzogin Christian Ludwig zu Mecklenburg, Ludwig, Prinz von Hesse und bei Rhein*, May 18, 1967, 102, 122.

39. Lili Dehn, affidavit of November 5, 1957, in Hamburg, I, 28–35.

40. Hamburg, Summary of Evidence in *Frau Anna Anderson in Unterlengenhardt v. Barbara, Herzogin Christian Ludwig zu Mecklenburg, Ludwig, Prinz von Hesse und bei Rhein*, May 18, 1967, 125.

41. Ibid., 125–126; Lili Dehn, affidavit of November 5, 1957, in Hamburg, I, 28–35.

42. Cited in Kurth, 288.

43. Dehn, 152 passim.

44. Lili Dehn, affidavit of November 5, 1957, in Hamburg, I, 28–35; see Dehn, 77–78, and Vyrubova, 62–63, on Tiutcheva, and Rathlef-Keilmann, 167–168, on AA's previous discussion of this fact.

45. Lili Dehn, affidavit of November 5, 1957, in Hamburg, I, 28–35.

46. Ibid.

47. Hamburg, Summary of Evidence in *Frau Anna Anderson in Unterlengenhardt v. Barbara, Herzogin Christian Ludwig zu Mecklenburg, Ludwig, Prinz von Hesse und bei Rhein*, May 18, 1967, 122.

48. Michael Fulda, grandson of Lili Dehn, to Greg King.

49. Lord Mountbatten to Prince Ludwig of Hesse, letter of November 12, 1957, in Staatsarchiv, Darmstadt.

50. Tatiana Botkin to Brien Horan, quoted in Horan, appendix, n.p.

51. Information culled from several letters among Lord Mountbatten; Prince Ludwig of Hesse; and Ludwig's wife, Princess Margaret of Hesse, in Staatsarchiv, Darmstadt.

16 The Trials

1. Copy of Certificate of Inheritance, September 8, 1933, issued by the Central District Court (Amtsgericht) in Berlin, in Hamburg, I, 1–10.

2. Johann Meyer, testimony of December 13, 1956, in Hamburg, XIV, 2349–2354.

3. Decision of the High Court (Landesgericht), Berlin, February 2, 1957; *Time*, February 11, 1957; see also Summers and Mangold, 228–230; Kurth, 294.

4. Kurth, 295.

5. Private information to the authors.

6. Lord Mountbatten to Prince Ludwig of Hesse, letter of November 12, 1957, in Staatsarchiv, Darmstadt.

7. Summers and Mangold, 213.

8. Ian Lilburn to Gleb Botkin, letter of May 1, 1965, in Ian Lilburn Collection.

9. Thornton, 38.

10. Godl.

11. Verdict of the Hanseatic High Court (Landesgericht), Hamburg, issued May 16, 1961, and appended to Hamburg, XXIV loose.

12. Kurth, 319–320, 323.

13. Cited in Horan, 5.

14. Summers and Mangold, 256.

15. Gertrude Lamedin, quoted in "Eine Rettung, die Mutterchen Russlands gelang?" by Gerhard Mauz, in *Der Spiegel*, March 6, 1967.

16. Ian Lilburn to Gleb Botkin, letter of May 1, 1965, in Ian Lilburn Collection.

17. Kurth, 322.

18. Information from Ian Lilburn to the authors.

19. Receipt for nine exercise books, Hanseatic Court of Appeals (Oberlandesgericht), received into evidence April 22, 1964, in Hamburg, XX, 3834; Kurth, 340;

Information from Ian Lilburn to the authors.

20. See Auclères, 240; Ian Lilburn to Alexander Nikitich, letter of October 10, 1965, in Ian Lilburn Collection.

21. Opinion of Georg Dulckheit, in Hamburg, XIII, 2068–2069.

22. See Item 7, "Book for Instruction in the Russian Language, Anastasia Nikolaievna, 1913," with corrections by tutor Peter Petrov, entered into evidence April 22, 1964, in Hamburg XX, 3834.

23. Agnes Gallagher, affidavit of December 22, 1930, in Hamburg, XXIV, 4481–4493.

24. Auclères, 249.

25. Vorres, 174.

26. Baroness Sophie Buxhoeveden, statement of March 12, 1922, in Gilliard and Savitch, 34–36.

27. Buxhoeveden, *Life and Tragedy*, 156.

28. Telberg and Wilton, 57; Gibbes, statement of July 1, 1919, in Sokolov archive, vol. 5, doc. 31.

29. Charles Sidney Gibbes, statement of April 17, 1958, in Hamburg, III, 495–497.

30. Gilliard, *Thirteen Years*, 70.

31. Gilliard and Savitch, 18, 70–71.

32. Gilliard, in *The Illustrated London News*, July 16, 1927, 102–103; Castelot, 416.

33. Item 8, exercise book "A. Romanova, February 16, 1916, Tsarskoye Selo," receipt dated April 22, 1964, in Hamburg, XX, 3834.

34. Timetables for lessons, 1917–1918, from Pierre Gilliard papers, in Hamburg, XXI, 3966.

35. Gleb Botkin to AA, letter of November 10, 1963, in authors' collection.

36. Gleb Botkin to AA, letter of September 3, 1964, in authors' collection.

37. Rathlef-Keilmann, 41.

38. Ibid.

39. Rathlef-Keilmann, 103; report of Dr. Serge Rudnev, March 1926, in Hamburg, XIV, 2485–2488; Dr. Serge Rudnev, affidavit of July 18, 1938, in Hamburg, Bln I, 134–138.

40. Cohen, in *New York Times*, March 28, 1926; Rathlef-Keilmann, 103.

41. Rathlef-Keilmann, 104.

42. AA to Rathlef-Keilmann, June 29, 1925, in Rathlef-Keilmann notes in Hamburg, Bln III, loose.

43. Rathlef-Keilmann, 78; Cohen, in *New York Times*, March 28, 1926.
44. See, for example, Rathlef-Keilmann, 210; Karl Wagner, statement of October 3, 1957, in Hamburg, XXXIV, 6382.
45. Olga Alexandrovna to Princess Irene of Hesse, Princess Heinrich of Prussia, letter of December 22, 1925, in Hamburg, Bln III, 181–182.
46. F. van der Hoeven, statement of October 3, 1927, in Hamburg, Bln III, 78-80; Vorres, 176.
47. See Auclères in *Le Figaro*, February 5, 1965, and *Le Figaro*, September 24, 1969; Kurth, 330–331.
48. Kurth, 331.
49. See, for example, Dr. Serge Rudnev, report of March 1926, in Hamburg, XIV, 2485–2488; Dr. Serge Rudnev, affidavit of July 18, 1938, in Hamburg, Bln I, 134–138; diary of Faith Lavington, entry of November 21, 1927, in Hamburg, XXXIV, 6402–6428.
50. Rathlef-Keilmann, 111.
51. Ibid., 157.
52. See statement of Dr. Serge Kastritsky, February 28, 1928, in Hamburg, X, 1868; Grey, 190.
53. Auclères, 130.
54. Victoria, marchioness of Milford Haven, to Princess Xenia Georgievna, letter of July 23, 1930, in Hamburg, XXXII, 3276.
55. Report of Dr. Volker Kruger, January 18, 1965, in Hamburg, XXIII, 4294–4312. These plaster casts were admitted into evidence by the Hamburg High Court and are now in the court records holdings in the Staatsarchiv, Hamburg. They can be seen in the 1995 German documentary *Anastasia: Zarentochter oder Hochstaplerin?* (*Anastasia: Tsar's Daughter or Imposter?*) by Maurice Philip Remy, an MPR Film und Fernsen Produktion GmbH, in cooperation with NDR Norddeutscher Rundfunk, 1995.
56. Professor Marc Bischoff, Report on the Tchaikovsky Matter, March 9, 1927, in Gilliaird and Savitch, 153–157, and in Hamburg, Kurzbericht Archiv fur Kriminologie Band 88 S., 138–141; also Bischoff study, March 9, 1927, in Hamburg, Bln III, 207 loose.
57. Gilliard and Savitch, 159–161.
58. Rathlef-Keilmann, 173–174; In "Application to the Amstgericht Court, Berlin, in the Matter of the Estate of Anastasia Nikolaievna Romanov, Case No. 461.VE.733/38," pleading submitted by Paul Leverkuehn and Kurt Vermehren on behalf of AA, October 31, 1938, and lodged in Hamburg under Bln, 53; and Rathlef-Keilmann articles in *Tägliche Rundschau*, October 1927, in Hamburg, XVII, 3165–3188.
59. Gilliard and Savitch, 142.
60. Ibid.
61. Victoria, marchioness of Milford Haven, to Princess Xenia Georgievna, letter of July 23, 1930, in Hamburg, XXXII, 3276.
62. Gilliard and Savitch, 78.
63. Sergeant Riesling, *Report on Comparison of Ears in the Matter of the Identity of Grand Duchess Anastasia of Russia*, Darmstadt, April 26, 1927, quoted in Gilliard and Savitch, 164–165, and submitted to Hamburg, in Hamburg, XXIV, 6438–6442.
64. "Study M" by Professor Dr. V. Müller-Hess and Professor Dr. F. Curtius, March 2, 1940, in Hamburg, XIII, 2104–2126.
65. "Study F," report of Dr. Eugen Fischer, June 10, 1941, in Hamburg, XIII, 2175–2203.
66. "Study C," Professor Dr. Karl Clauberg, report of December 29, 1955, in Hamburg, XIII, 2231–2256; also additional report and photo analysis submitted January 30, 1958, in Hamburg, I, 130–133.
67. Report by Eickstadt and Klenke, submitted to Hamburg, July 26, 1958, in Hamburg, IV, 710a; supplemental report, August 7, 1959, by Eickstadt and Klenke, in Hamburg, IX, 1616.
68. Kurth, 314.
69. Report of Professor Otto Reche, May 12, 1959, in Hamburg, IX, 1648–1724. Modern critics have pointed out that Reche was a former Nazi whose discredited racial blood theories had supported the Third Reich's anti-Semitic policies; similar charges, though, could be leveled at many of the other German experts

involved in both sides of Anderson's case. Reche's anthropological work in Anderson's case was unrelated to his serology work with the Nazi regime and, as with the opinions of similar colleagues who testified for and against her claim, must stand or fall on its own merits.

70. Dr. Karl Clauberg, report of May 15, 1959, in Hamburg, VI, 37–42.

71. Lucy Weiszäcker, report of August 11, 1927, in Hamburg, XXXI, 5827.

72. Maurice Delmain, study dated May 16, 1957, in Hamburg, VII, 1–7; Delmain study and comments, June 5, 1958, in Hamburg, IV, 598–602; Hamburg, Summary of Evidence in *Frau Anna Anderson in Unterlengenhardt v. Barbara, Herzogin Christian Ludwig zu Mecklenburg, Ludwig, Prinz von Hesse und bei Rhein*, May 18, 1967, 148.

73. Minna Becker, report of September 5, 1960, in Hamburg, XI, 1909–1950.

74. Hamburg, *Summary of Evidence in Frau Anna Anderson in Unterlengenhardt v. Barbara, Herzogin Christian Ludwig zu Mecklenburg, Ludwig, Prinz von Hesse und bei Rhein*, May 18, 1967, 154; Rathlef-Keilmann notes, June 21, 1925, in Hamburg, Bln III, loose; AA, dictated replies to questions, May 8, 1929, 3, in Ian Lilburn Collection.

75. Amy Smith, testimony of December 18, 1965, in Hamburg, XXIX, 5397–5409.

76. Prince Dimitri Golitsyn, testimony of September 24, 1965, Hamburg, XXXVII, 6595.

77. See Colonel Dimitri von Wonlar-Larsky to Prince Friedrich of Saxe-Altenburg, letter of April 19, 1949, in Hamburg, VIII, 1584–1585; Baroness Marie Pilar von Pilchau, testimony of January 20, 1957, in Hamburg, VII, 299; Elisabeth, infanta of Portugal, Princess Thurn und Taxis, testimony of June 21, 1963, in Hamburg, XVIII, 3658–3660.

78. Crown Princess Cecilie of Prussia, statement of October 2, 1953, in Hamburg XXIV, 4696–4699; Prince Friedrich of Schoenaich-Carolath, testimony of January 11, 1966, in Hamburg, XXXI, 5826–5827, and testimony of November 18, 1966, in Hamburg, XXXII, 5878–5883.

79. Fritz von Unruh, testimony of April 7, 1963, in Hamburg, XX, 3932.

80. Lord Mountbatten to Prince Ludwig of Hesse, letter of November 12, 1957, in Staatsarchiv, Darmstadt.

81. Baron Fabian von Massenbach, affidavit of April 21, 1939, in Hamburg, Bln III, 199–200; Viktoria Luise, 101.

82. "Aus Hessen Haus," in *Der Spiegel*, August 2, 1961; see Kurth, 346–348; diaries of Grand Duke Ernst Ludwig, February 18–March 6, 1916, in Hamburg, XIX, 3735; Grand Duke Ernst Ludwig to Grand Duchess Eleonore, letters of February 18–March 4, 1916, in Hamburg, XIX/3735; Grand Duke Ernst Ludwig to Grand Duchess Eleonore, field postcard of March 12, 1916, in Hamburg, XXXIII, 6061; diaries of Grand Duke Ernst Ludwig, March 5–April 2, 1916, in Hamburg, XXXIII, 6063–6076; Grand Duke Ernst Ludwig to Grand Duchess Eleonore, letters of March 5–April 7, 1916, in Hamburg, XXXIV, 6399.

83. Hamburg, Summary of Evidence in *Frau Anna Anderson in Unterlengenhardt v. Barbara, Herzogin Christian Ludwig zu Mecklenburg, Ludwig, Prinz von Hesse und bei Rhein*, May 18, 1967, 254.

84. The first published mention of the alleged mission came in the March 7, 1927, issue of the German newspaper *Königsberger Allgemeine Zeitung*, two years after Anderson made her controversial statement. It also was mentioned in two Soviet publications, *Monarkhia Pered Khrushenem: Bumagi Nikolaya II I drugie dokumenti 1914–1917*, Moscow/Leningrad: Gosudarstvennoye Izdatelstvo, published in 1927, and in *Romanovy I germanskie vliianiia vo Vremia mirovoi voiny*, Leningrad: Izdatelstvo Krasnaya Gazeta, 1929, both edited by V. P. Semennikov. It also has been alleged that a third book, supposedly published in 1921 prior to Anderson's statement, *Im Angesicht der Revolution*, mentioned the alleged visit. In fact, extensive searches by Dr. Richard Davis, curator of the Russian Archive at Leeds University in Great Britain and by the University of Marburg, including

comprehensive examinations of German national bibliographies, reveal that no such book was published in Germany between 1921 and 1925. Dr. Richard Davis to David Vernall-Downes, e-mail of October 11, 2008, provided to the authors by David Vernall-Downes.

85. Hamburg, Summary of Evidence in *Frau Anna Anderson in Unterlengenhardt v. Barbara, Herzogin Christian Ludwig zu Mecklenburg, Ludwig, Prinz von Hesse und bei Rhein*, May 18, 1967, 281.

86. Report by Eickstadt and Klenke, July 26, 1958, in Hamburg, XIII, 2302–2344.

87. Hamburg, Summary of Evidence in *Frau Anna Anderson in Unterlengenhardt v. Barbara, Herzogin Christian Ludwig zu Mecklenburg, Ludwig, Prinz von Hesse und bei Rhein*, May 18, 1967, 148, 294–295.

88. Maurice Delmain, study dated May 16, 1957, in Hamburg, VII, 1–7; Delmain study and comments, June 5, 1958, in Hamburg, IV, 598–602; Hamburg, Summary of Evidence in *Frau Anna Anderson in Unterlengenhardt v. Barbara, Herzogin Christian Ludwig zu Mecklenburg, Ludwig, Prinz von Hesse und bei Rhein*, May 18, 1967, 148.

89. Verdict of the Bundesgerichthof (West German Federal Supreme Court), Karlsruhe, February 17, 1970, appended to Hamburg, loose.

17   "How Shall I Tell You Who I Am?"

1. "The Case of a New Anastasia," *Life*, October 18, 1963, 111–112.

2. AA to Alexei Miliukov, August 5, 1965, in Miliukov tapes.

3. Gleb Botkin to AA, letter of October 22, 1963, in authors' collection.

4. AA to Alexei Miliukov, February 7, 1968, in Miliukov tapes.

5. Horan, 63–63; information from Ian Lilburn to the authors.

6. *Le Figaro*, September 21, 1967.

7. AA to Alexei Miliukov, September 11, 1965, in Miliukov tapes.

8. AA to Alexei Miliukov, September 12, 1965, in Miliukov tapes.

9. AA to Alexei Miliukov, November 21, 1965, in Miliukov tapes; AA to Alexei

Miliukov, September 26, 1965, in Miliukov tapes.

10. AA to Alexei Miliukov, August 15, 1965, in Miliukov tapes; AA to Alexei Miliukov, September 26, 1965, in Miliukov tapes.

11. AA to Alexei Miliukov, September 12, 1965, in Miliukov tapes.

12. AA to Alexei Miliukov, June 17, 1965, in Miliukov tapes.

13. AA to Alexei Miliukov, September 12, 1965, in Miliukov tapes.

14. Welch, 93–94.

15. Botkin, *Anastasia*, 264–265.

16. Gleb Botkin to AA, letter of July 12, 1963, in authors' collection.

17. Gleb Botkin to AA, letter of June 13, 1964, in authors' collection.

18. Gleb Botkin to AA, letter of June 12, 1965, in authors' collection.

19. AA to Alexei Miliukov, April 15, 1967, in Miliukov tapes.

20. Information from Ian Lilburn to the authors. The chalet is still standing in Unterlengenhardt, and it is privately occupied.

21. Horan, 160; information from Ian Lilburn to the authors.

22. AA to Alexei Miliukov, June 17, 1966, in Miliukov tapes.

23. Information from Patte Barham to Greg King.

24. Ibid.; *Charlottesville Daily Progress*, January 20, 1970; Kurth, 375.

25. *Charlottesville Daily Progress*, January 12, 1968.

26. Ruffin, 64–66.

27. Peter Kurth to Greg King, e-mail of July 16, 2009.

28. Ruffin, 64, 67.

29. Ibid., 68.

30. Ibid.

31. Ibid., 65.

32. Kurth, 379.

33. Chavchavadze, 239.

34. Horan, 141; Chavchavadze, 239.

35. Tucker, 43.

36. Lovell, 333–334.

37. *Richmond Times Dispatch*, September 2, 1978.

38. Summers and Mangold, 198–199.

39. *Richmond Times Dispatch*, September 2, 1978.

40. *Charlottesville Daily Progress*, August 30, 1978.

41. *Richmond Times Dispatch*, September 2, 1978; *Charlottesville Daily Progress*, September 2, 1978.

42. *Charlottesville Daily Progress*, February 28, 1977.

43. *In Search of . . . Anastasia*, Alan Landsberg Productions, syndicated for North American television, 1976.

44. Summers and Mangold, 239.

45. *Charlottesville Daily Progress*, October 28, 1976.

46. She gave this version to her onetime British legal representative Michael Thornton, and to author James Blair Lovell. See Michael Thornton in *London Sunday Express*, "Anastasia: Mystery Remains Unsolved," May 17, 1992; Lovell, 352–355.

47. *Charlottesvile Daily Progress*, October 28, 1976.

48. Ibid., August 6, 1979.

49. Ibid., August 7, 1979.

50. Ibid., August 7, 1979, and June 18, 1981.

51. Rives, 34.

52. Ruffin, 66.

53. Ibid., 69.

54. *Charlottesville Weekly* 6, no. 21 (October 4–10, 1994): 10.

55. Kurth, 389.

56. *Charlottesville Daily Progress*, October 13, 1976.

57. Ruffin, 73.

58. Kurth, 453, 1984 paperback version.

59. Kurth, 453–454, 1984 paperback version; *Charlottesville Daily Progress*, December 3, 1983.

60. Lovell, 370.

61. Lovell, 368–370; Kurth, 455, 1984 paperback version.

62. Information from James Blair Lovell to Greg King; information from Ian Lilburn to the authors; *London Daily Express*, July 29, 1988.

63. Death certificate of Anastasia Nicholaievna Manahan, February 12, 1984, commonwealth of Virginia, certificate of death 203–256.

64. *Charlottesville Daily Progress*, February 15, 1984.

65. Private information to the authors; Lovell, 374.

66. Lovell, 374–375.

67. Prince Friedrich of Saxe-Altenburg, sworn statement of March 12, 1984, notarized by Brien Horan, chief of the Legal Section of Defense Attaché Office at the United States Embassy, Paris, France, in Ian Lilburn Collection.

68. Brien Horan to the authors.

18 The Fairy Tale Crumbles

1. Kurth, 455, 1984 paperback version.

2. Gill, Ivanov, Kimpton, Piercy, Benson, Tully, Evett, Hagelberg, and Sullivan, 130–135; P. Ivanov et al., 417–420.

3. Syd Mandelbaum to Greg King, e-mail of May 29, 2009.

4. Massie, 194–197.

5. Information from James Blair Lovell to Greg King; Massie, 196.

6. Information from Maurice Philip Remy to the authors.

7. Massie, 197; *Charlottesville Daily Progress*, November 16, 1993.

8. *London Daily Mail*, June 24, 1994.

9. *Marina Botkin Schweitzer, Petitioner v. Martha Jefferson Hospital*, Case No. 8021, Sixteenth Judicial Circuit Court of Virginia in the city of Charlottesville, September 30, 1993.

10. *Charlottesville Daily Progress*, November 11, 1993; Massie, 210.

11. *Charlottesville Daily Progress*, June 20, 1994; *London Daily Mail*, June 24, 1994.

12. Information from Peter Kurth to the authors; *Charlottesville Daily Progress*, July 30, 1993; Syd Mandelbaum to Greg King, e-mail of May 29, 2009; Susan Grindstaff Burkhart to Greg King, e-mail of June 14, 2009.

13. Susan Grindstaff Burkhart to Greg King, e-mail of June 14, 2009.

14. Gill, Kimpton, Aliston-Greiner, Sullivan, Stoneking, Melton, Nott, Barritt, et al., 9–10.

15. Ibid.

16. Syd Mandelbaum to Greg King, e-mail of May 29, 2009; Terry Melton to Greg King, e-mail of June 1, 2009.

17. Terry Melton to Greg King, e-mail of June 1, 2009; Gill, Kimpton, Aliston-Greiner, Sullivan, Stoneking, Melton, Nott, Barritt, et al., 9–10.

18. Ibid.

19. Kurth, 217.

20. Gill, Kimpton, Aliston-Greiner, Sullivan, Stoneking, Melton, Nott, Barritt, et al., 9–10.
21. Information from Maurice Philip Remy to the authors; Dietmar Wulff to Greg King, e-mail of May 10, 2001; Dr. Charles Ginther to Maurice Philip Remy, letter of September 30, 1994, quoted in Ginther, e-mail to J. A. Hubert, July 6, 2005, posted on the Alexander Palace Time Machine Discussion Forum, at www.alexanderpalace.org, July 9, 2005; *Sunday Times* of London, October 2, 1994.
22. Gill, Kimpton, Aliston-Greiner, Sullivan, Stoneking, Melton, Nott, Barritt, et al., 9–10.
23. Susan Grindstaff Burkhart to Greg King, e-mail of June 14, 2009.

19 A Girl from the Provinces

1. Lorentz, Fischer, and Lehr-Splawinski, 24–27.
2. Details of 1900 census, at http://pom-wpru.kerntopf.com/ortedetails/ort_borreck.htm; Willi Heidn, *Die Ortschaften des Kreises Karthaus/Westpr.*, at www.westpreussen.de.
3. Charlotte Meyer to Dr. Hans Hermann Krampff, letter of February 14, 1944, in Staatsarchiv, Darmstadt.
4. Davies, 112; Lorentz, Fischer, and Lehr-Splawinski, vii, 4.
5. Lorentz, Fischer, and Lehr-Splawinski, 70–71, 88–89, 109–113.
6. Ibid., 70–71.
7. Registry of baptism, entry 196-A, December 24, 1896, Kreis Karthaus, Sullenschin, West Prussia, District Records Office.
8. Davies, 112; Lorentz, Fischer, and Lehr-Splawinski, vii, 4.
9. The *drobna szlachta* or petty nobility was the lowest of three aristocratic levels in the Polish *szlachta*, or national nobility; the Czenstkowskis were designated as *szlachta zagonowa*, the fourth of eight ranks in the petty nobility, indicating that they had received land from the sovereign. Information from Massie; Brzezinski, 1:6–11; Zamoyski, 1–3; www.ka-na.org; Manteuffel, 963–1194; Zajaczkowski, chap.1.
10. Manteuffel, 963–1194; Zajaczkowski, chap. 1.

11. Richard Meyer, burgomaster of Hygendorf, statement of September 1, 1944, in Staatsarchiv, Darmstadt.
12. Hamburg, Summary of Evidence in *Frau Anna Anderson in Unterlengenhardt v. Barbara, Herzogin Christian Ludwig zu Mecklenburg, Ludwig, Prinz von Hesse und bei Rhein*, May 18, 1967, 177; information from Ian Lilburn to the authors; Richard Meyer, burgomaster of Hygendorf, statement of September 1, 1944, in Staatsarchiv, Darmstadt.
13. Hamburg, Summary of Evidence in *Frau Anna Anderson in Unterlengenhardt v. Barbara, Herzogin Christian Ludwig zu Mecklenburg, Ludwig, Prinz von Hesse und bei Rhein*, May 18, 1967, 177–178. As with her husband's surname, Marianna's maiden name has been variously rendered in official documents as "Wilzke."
14. Dr. Hans Hermann Krampff to Dr. Gunther Berenberg-Gossler, letter of July 16, 1958, quoting Richard Meyer, in Staatsarchiv, Darmstadt.
15. See Gertrude Ellerik, née Schanzkowska, statement of September 8, 1937, in Hamburg, XXIV, 65–70.
16. Dawson, 86–87.
17. Details of the family's movements found in census records of 1900, 1905, and 1910, and in birth certificate of Felix Schanzkowsky, dated February 17, 1903, Glischnitz, Kreis Stolp, register entry C-1844, District Record Office; Gertrude Ellerik, née Schanzkowska, statement of September 8, 1937, in Hamburg, XXIV, 65–70; testimony of Frau Margarethe Kothe, February 18, 1958, quoting her mother, Frau Martha Borkowski, previously Reetz, née Schrock, in Staatsarchiv, Darmstadt; statement of Anna Thrun, née Kruger, May 30, 1958, in Staatsarchiv, Darmstadt.
18. Gertrude Ellerik, née Schanzkowska, statement of September 8, 1937, in Hamburg, XXIV, 65–70; Richard Meyer, burgomaster of Hygendorf, statement of September 1, 1944, in Staatsarchiv, Darmstadt.
19. Lorentz, Fischer, and Lehr-Splawinski, 31–32, 49–61.
20. Davies, 189; Lorentz, Fischer, and Lehr-Splawinksi, 19–22, 74, 99–101; Dawson, 77.

21. Gertrude Ellerik, née Schanzkowska, statement of May 23, 1959, in Hamburg, VII, 1470–1475.

22. Otto Meyer, statement of April 22, 1927, in Ian Lilburn Collection.

23. Gertrude Ellerik, née Schanzkowska, statement of May 23, 1959, in Hamburg, VII, 1470–1475.

24. Richard Meyer, burgomaster of Hygendorf, statement of September 1, 1944, in Staatsarchiv, Darmstadt.

25. Charlotte Meyer to Dr. Hans Hermann Krampff, letter of February 14, 1944, in Staatsarchiv, Darmstadt; Gertrude Ellerik, née Schanzkowska, statement of May 23, 1959, in Hamburg, VII, 1470–1475.

26. Gertrude Ellerik, née Schanzkowska, statement of May 23, 1959, in Hamburg, VII, 1470–1475; Gertrude Ellerik, née Schanzkowska, statement of September 8, 1937, in Hamburg, XXIV, 65–70; Felix Schanzkowsky, statement of November 10, 1937, in Hamburg., XXIV, 74–76; Valerian Schanzkowsky, statement of October 11, 1937, in Hamburg, XXV, 19–21; Hamburg, Summary of Evidence in *Frau Anna Anderson in Unterlengenhardt v. Barbara, Herzogin Christian Ludwig zu Mecklenburg, Ludwig, Prinz von Hesse und bei Rhein*, May 18, 1967, 92. A 1910 census of Borowilhas and Borok recorded that of the 611 residents in the area, 527 declared Kashubian to be their primary language, while only 84 listed German as their principal tongue. See http://pom-wpru.kerntopf.com/ortdetails/ort_borreck.htm.

27. Lorentz, Fischer, and Lehr-Splawinski, 3–11, 351–353.

28. Duke Georg of Leuchtenberg to Olga Alexandrovna, letter of August 26, 1927, in Hamburg, XIV, 2558–2559.

29. http://pom-wpru.kerntopf.com/ortdetails/ort_borreck.htm.

30. Lorentz, Fischer, and Lehr-Splawinski, 3–11, 187–190, 339–345; www.ka-na-org.

31. Gertrude Ellerik, née Schanzkowska, statement of May 23, 1959, in Hamburg, VII, 1470–1475; Felix Schanzkowsky, statement of May 9, 1927, in Hamburg, XIII, 2288–2289.

32. Hamburg, Summary of Evidence in *Frau Anna Anderson in Unterlengenhardt v. Barbara, Herzogin Christian Ludwig zu Mecklenburg, Ludwig, Prinz von Hesse und bei Rhein*, May 18, 1967, 187; Fritz Schuricht, testimony of May 21, 1959, in Staatsarchiv, Darmstadt, doc. 74 0.294/57.

33. Testimony of Anna (Thea) Chemnitz, née Malinovsky, December 17, 1958, in Hamburg, V, 979–981.

34. Gilliard and Savitch, 38.

35. See Massie, 250.

36. Felix Schanzkowsky, statement of May 9, 1927, in Hamburg, XIII, 2288–2289; Rathlef-Keilmann, 232–233; Dr. Lothar Nobel, report of March 1926, in Hamburg, XIII, 4417–4426.

37. Richard Meyer, quoted by Dr. Hans Hermann Krampff to Dr. Gunther Berenberg-Gossler, in letter of July 16, 1958, in Staatsarchiv, Darmstadt.

38. Gertrude Ellerik, née Schanzkowska, statement of May 23, 1959, in Hamburg, VII, 1470–1475.

39. Richard Meyer, quoted by Dr. Hans Hermann Krampff to Dr. Gunther Berenberg-Gossler, in letter of July 16, 1958, in Staatsarchiv, Darmstadt.

40. Richard Meyer, statement of September 1, 1944, in Staatsarchiv, Darmstadt.

41. *Franziska Schanzkowski und ihr Leben*, 4.

42. Richard Meyer, quoted by Dr. Hans Hermann Krampff to Dr. Gunther Berenberg-Gossler, in letter of July 16, 1958, in Staatsarchiv, Darmstadt; Richard Meyer, statement of July 18, 1958, in Staatsarchiv, Darmstadt.

43. Information from Ian Lilburn to the authors.

44. Herman, 267–282; also see Russell for further discussion.

45. Herman, 272–279; Courtois, 203–208; Herman, Perry, and van der Kolk, 492–494; also see Wyatt and Johnson Powell for further discussion.

46. Martha Borkowski, née Schrock, testimony of May 23, 1958, in Hamburg, III, 563–564; also see testimony of Frau Margarethe Kothe, February 18, 1958, in Staatsarchiv, Darmstadt.

47. Richard Meyer, quoted by Dr. Hans Hermann Krampff to Dr. Gunther Berenberg-Gossler, in letter of July 16, 1958, in Staatsarchiv, Darmstadt.

48. Richard Meyer, statement of July 18, 1958, in Staatsarchiv, Darmstadt.

49. Hamburg, Summary of Evidence in *Frau Anna Anderson in Unterlengenhardt v. Barbara, Herzogin Christian Ludwig zu Mecklenburg, Ludwig, Prinz von Hesse und bei Rhein*, May 18, 1967, 184.

50. Gertrude Ellerik, née Schanzkowska, statement of May 23, 1959, in Hamburg, VII, 1470–1475.

51. Heinrich Trapp, quoted by Dr. Hans Hermann Krampff to Dr. Gunther Berenberg-Gossler, in letter of July 16, 1958, in Staatsarchiv, Darmstadt.

52. Hamburg, Summary of Evidence in *Frau Anna Anderson in Unterlengenhardt v. Barbara, Herzogin Christian Ludwig zu Mecklenburg, Ludwig, Prinz von Hesse und bei Rhein*, May 18, 1967, 177.

53. Richard Meyer, quoted by Dr. Hans Hermann Krampff to Dr. Gunther Berenberg-Gossler, in letter of July 16, 1958, in Staatsarchiv, Darmstadt.

54. Richard Meyer, statement of July 18, 1958, in Staatsarchiv, Darmstadt.

55. Fritz Schuricht, testimony of May 21, 1959, in Staatsarchiv, Darmstadt, doc. 74 0.294/57.

56. Marianna Knopf, quoted in Martin Knopf, "Report on Franziska Schanzkowska," 1927, in Staatsarchiv, Darmstadt.

57. These rumors about incest and Marianna's worries over Franziska came to the attention of Anna Anderson's legal team during the Hamburg trials, according to Ian Lilburn, but were never explored or introduced into evidence. Information from Ian Lilburn to the authors.

58. Hamburg, Summary of Evidence in *Frau Anna Anderson in Unterlengenhardt v. Barbara, Herzogin Christian Ludwig zu Mecklenburg, Ludwig, Prinz von Hesse und bei Rhein*, May 18, 1967, 178.

20 The Polish Factory Worker

1. Davis, 2.

2. Dawson, 59–60; Masur, 133.

3. *Berliner Nachtausgabe*, April 16, 1927; Gertrude Ellerik, née Schanzkowska, statement of May 23, 1959, in Hamburg, VII, 1470–1475; "Evolution of Franziska Schanzkowska to Grand Duchess Anastasia," summary prepared by Herr Meyer for Darmstadt, June 24, 1944, in Staatsarchiv, Darmstadt.

4. *Berliner Nachtausgabe*, April 8, 1927.

5. Gertrude Ellerik, née Schanzkowska, statement of May 23, 1959, in Hamburg, VII, 1470–1475; *Berliner Nachtausgabe*, April 8, 1927.

6. Hamburg, Summary of Evidence in *Frau Anna Anderson in Unterlengenhardt v. Barbara, Herzogin Christian Ludwig zu Mecklenburg, Ludwig, Prinz von Hesse und bei Rhein*, May 18, 1967, 178.

7. Davis, 34.

8. Ibid., 175.

9. Rosenberg, 91; Davis, 164–165, 170.

10. Gertrude Ellerik, née Schanzkowska, statement of May 23, 1959, in Hamburg, VII, 1470–1475; Masur, 218.

11. Masur, 272.

12. Gertrude Ellerik, née Schanzkowska, statement of May 23, 1959, in Hamburg, VII, 1470–1475; Davis, 179.

13. Blucher, 133.

14. *London Sunday Times*, October 2, 1994; *Berliner Nachtausgabe*, April 8 and April 16, 1927.

15. *Berliner Nachtausgabe*, April 8, 1927.

16. Robert Crouch to Greg King, e-mail of March 10, 2000.

17. Doris Wingender in *Berliner Nachtausgabe*, April 8 and April 16, 1927; statements of Doris Rittmann, née Wingender, and Luise Fiedler, née Wingender, of May 20, 1958, in Staatsarchiv, Darmstadt, 74 0.294/57.

18. Gertrude Ellerik, née Schanzkowska, statement of May 23, 1959, in Hamburg, VII, 1470–1475.

19. Statements of Doris Rittmann, née Wingender, and Luise Fiedler, née Wingender, of May 20, 1958, in Staatsarchiv, Darmstadt, 74 0.294/57; Doris Rittmann, née Wingender, testimony of November 18, 1965, in Hamburg, XXVII, 5144–5151.

20. *Berliner Nachtausgabe*, April 8, 1927.

21. Doris Rittmann, née Wingender, testimony of November 18, 1965, in Hamburg, XXVII, 5144–5151.

22. Gertrude Ellerik, née Schanzkowska, statement of May 23, 1959, in Hamburg, VII, 1470–1475.

23. See Davis, 165–166.

24. Doris Wingender, quoted in Martin Knopf, "Report on Franziska Schanzkowska," 1927, in Staatsarchiv, Darmstadt

25. Gertrude Ellerik, née Schanzkowska, statement of May 23, 1959, in Hamburg, VII, 1470–1475; Gertrude Ellerik, née Schanzkowska, statement of January 31, 1961, in Staatsarchiv, Darmstadt; Hamburg, Summary of Evidence in *Frau Anna Anderson in Unterlengenhardt v. Barbara, Herzogin Christian Ludwig zu Mecklenburg, Ludwig, Prinz von Hesse und bei Rhein*, May 18, 1967, 178; *Berliner Nachtausgabe*, April 8 and April 16, 1927.

26. Rathlef-Keilmann notes, June 30, 1925, in Hamburg, Bln III, loose.

27. Felix Schanzkowsky, affidavit, May 9, 1927, in Hamburg, XIV, 2380–2384; Hamburg, Summary of Evidence in *Frau Anna Anderson in Unterlengenhardt v. Barbara, Herzogin Christian Ludwig zu Mecklenburg, Ludwig, Prinz von Hesse und bei Rhein*, May 18, 1967, 342; interview with Marianna Knopf, previously Czenstkowski, by Fritz Schuricht, in Fritz Schuricht, testimony of May 21, 1959, in Staatsarchiv, Darmstadt, doc. 74 0. 294/57; Gertrude Ellerik, née Schanzkowska, statement of May 23, 1959, in Hamburg, VII, 1470–1475.

28. Hamburg, Summary of Evidence in *Frau Anna Anderson in Unterlengenhardt v. Barbara, Herzogin Christian Ludwig zu Mecklenburg, Ludwig, Prinz von Hesse und bei Rhein*, May 18, 1967, 178–179.

29. Gertrude Ellerik, née Schanzkowska, statement of May 23, 1959, in Hamburg, VII, 1470–1475; Gertrude Ellerik, née Schanzkowska, statement of January 31, 1961, in Staatsarchiv, Darmstadt.

30. Hamburg, Summary of Evidence in *Frau Anna Anderson in Unterlengenhardt v. Barbara, Herzogin Christian Ludwig zu Mecklenburg, Ludwig, Prinz von Hesse und bei Rhein*, May 18, 1967, 178–179.

31. *Berliner Nachtausgabe*, April 8, 1927.

32. *Berliner Nachtausgabe*, April 7, 1927; Gertrude Ellerik, née Schanzkowska, statement of May 23, 1959, in Hamburg, VII, 1470–1475; Franziska Schanzkowska, hospital records from Berlin-Schöneberg, submitted to Hamburg, March 13, 1958, in Hamburg, II, 214; Hamburg, Summary of Evidence in *Frau Anna Anderson in Unterlengenhardt v. Barbara, Herzogin Christian Ludwig zu Mecklenburg, Ludwig, Prinz von Hesse und bei Rhein*, May 18, 1967, 178; "Evolution of Franziska Schanzkowska to Grand Duchess Anastasia," compiled by Herr Meyer for Darmstadt, June 24, 1944, in Staatsarchiv, Darmstadt; Kurth, 415, n. 93.

33. See Courtois; Herman, Perry, and van der Kolk; and Wyatt and Johnson Powell for further discussion.

34. Blucher, 136; Davis, 165.

35. Davis, 165, 180–184.

36. "Evolution of Franziska Schanzkowska to Grand Duchess Anastasia," summary by Herr Meyer for Darmstadt, June 24, 1944, in Staatsarchiv, Darmstadt; Gertrude Ellerik, née Schanzkowska, statement of May 23, 1959, in Hamburg, VII, 1470–1475.

37. Ibid.

38. Information from Neu-Ruppin hospital records submitted to Hamburg tribunal, March 13, 1958, in Hamburg, II, 214–247; Hamburg, Summary of Evidence in *Frau Anna Anderson in Unterlengenhardt v. Barbara, Herzogin Christian Ludwig zu Mecklenburg, Ludwig, Prinz von Hesse und bei Rhein*, May 18, 1967, 178; *Berliner Nachtausgabe*, April 7, 1927; "Evolution of Franziska Schanzkowska to Grand Duchess Anastasia," summary by Herr Meyer for Darmstadt, June 24, 1944, in Staatsarchiv, Darmstadt.

39. Gertrude Ellerik, née Schanzkowska, statement of May 23, 1959, in Hamburg, VII, 1470–1475; information from Neuruppin hospital records submitted to Hamburg tribunal, March 13, 1958, in Hamburg, II, 214–247; Hamburg, Summary of Evidence in *Frau Anna Anderson in Unterlengenhardt v. Barbara, Herzogin Christian Ludwig zu Mecklenburg, Ludwig, Prinz von Hesse und bei Rhein*, May 18, 1967, 178.

40. Marianna Knopf, quoted in Martin Knopf, "Report on Franziska Schanzkowska," 1927, in Staatsarchiv, Darmstadt.

41. Gertrude Ellerik, née Schanzkowska, statement of May 23, 1959, in Hamburg, VII, 1470–1475; *Berliner Nachtausgabe*, April 6, 1927; *Franziska Schanzkowska und ihr Leben*, 4.

42. Gertrude Ellerik, née Schanzkowska, statement of May 23, 1959, in Hamburg, VII, 1470–1475.

43. Hamburg, Summary of Evidence in *Frau Anna Anderson in Unterlengenhardt v. Barbara, Herzogin Christian Ludwig zu Mecklenburg, Ludwig, Prinz von Hesse und bei Rhein*, May 18, 1967, 184; see Dr. Serge Rudnev, report of March 1926, in Hamburg, XIV, 2485–2488; Dr. Theodor Eitel, report of December 22, 1926, in Hamburg, VIII, 1394–1402; Dr. Hans Willige, statement of November 5, 1938, in Hamburg, XII, 1985–1994; *Berliner Nachtausgabe*, April 8, 1927; Gertrude Ellerik, née Schanzkowska, statement of May 23, 1959, in Hamburg, VII, 1470–1475.

44. Fritz Schuricht, testimony of May 21, 1959, in Staatsarchiv, Darmstadt, doc. 74 0.294/57; Gertrude Ellerik, née Schanzkowska, statement of May 23, 1959, in Hamburg, VII, 1470–1475.

45. Gertrude Ellerik, née Schanzkowska, statement of May 23, 1959, in Hamburg, VII, 1470–1475.

46. "Evolution of Franziska Schanzkowska to Grand Duchess Anastasia," summary by Herr Meyer for Darmstadt, June 24, 1944, in Staatsarchiv, Darmstadt; Gertrude Ellerik, née Schanzkowska, statement of May 23, 1959, in Hamburg, VII, 1470–1475; Martin Knopf, "Report on Franziska Schanzkowska," 1927, in Staatsarchiv, Darmstadt.

47. Gertrude Ellerik, née Schanzkowska, statement of May 23, 1959, in Hamburg, VII, 1470–1475; Doris Rittmann, née Wingender, testimony of November 18, 1965, in Hamburg, XXVII, 5144–5151; information from Robert K. Massie to the authors.

48. "Evolution of Franziska Schanzkowska to Grand Duchess Anastasia," summary by Herr Meyer for Darmstadt, June 24, 1944, in Staatsarchiv, Darmstadt.

49. *Berliner Nachtausgabe*, April 8 and April 16, 1927; "Evolution of Franziska Schanzkowska to Grand Duchess Anastasia," summary by Herr Meyer for Darmstadt, June 24, 1944, in Staatsarchiv, Darmstadt; Luise Fiedler, née Wingender, testimony of November 19, 1965, Hamburg, XXVIII, 5145–5147.

50. "Evolution of Franziska Schanzkowska to Grand Duchess Anastasia," summary by Herr Meyer for Darmstadt, June 24, 1944, in Staatsarchiv, Darmstadt; *Berliner Nachtausgabe*, April 16, 1927.

51. Gertrude Ellerik, née Schanzkowska, statement of May 23, 1959, in Hamburg, VII, 1470–1475.

52. Doris Rittmann, née Wingender, testimony of November 18, 1965, in Hamburg, XXVII, 5144–5151.

53. Doris Wingender, interview of April 23, 1927, in Staatsarchiv, Darmstadt.

54. *Berliner Nachtausgabe*, April 8, 1927.

55. Doris Rittmann, née Wingender, testimony of November 18, 1965, in Hamburg, XXVII, 5144–5151.

56. *Berliner Nachtausgabe*, April 8, 1927.

57. Doris Wingender, interview of April 23, 1927, in Staatsarchiv, Darmstadt.

58. Doris Rittmann, née Wingender, statement of May 20, 1958, in Hamburg, III, 535–546.

59. *Berliner Nachtausgabe*, April 8, 1927.

60. Doris Rittmann, née Wingender, testimony of November 18, 1965, in Hamburg, XXVII, 5144–5151; Gertrude Ellerik, née Schanzkowska, statement of May 23, 1959, in Hamburg, VII, 1470–1475; see also *Berliner Nachtausgabe*, April 16, 1927; Doris Rittmann, née Wingender, statement of May 20, 1958, in Hamburg, III, 535–546; Fritz Schuricht, statement of May 21, 1959, in Staatsarchiv, Darmstadt, doc. 74 0.294/57.

61. Doris Rittmann, née Wingender, testimony of November 18, 1965, in Hamburg, XXVII, 5144–5151.

62. Doris Rittmann, née Wingender, testimony of November 18, 1965, in Hamburg, XXVII, 5144–5151; Luise Fiedler, née Wingender, testimony of November 18, 1965, in Hamburg, XXVIII, 5145–5147; *Berliner Nachtausgabe*, April 8, 1927.

63. Doris Rittmann, née Wingender, testimony of November 18, 1965, in Hamburg, XXVII, 5144–5151.

64. *Berliner Nachtausgabe*, April 8, 1927.

65. Doris Rittmann, née Wingender, testimony of November 18, 1965, in Hamburg, XXVII, 5144–5151.

66. See, for example, Anna (Thea) Chemnitz, née Malinovsky, testimony of December 17, 1958, in Hamburg, V, 979–981; Baroness Marie von Kleist, affidavit of July 5, 1929, entered into evidence at Hamburg May 20, 1958, in Hamburg, III, 569–574; notes of Erika von Redern, secretary to Edward Fallows, from records of Dalldorf Asylum, May 16, 1929, cited in Kurth, 7; Dr. Karl Bonhoeffer, report of March 18, 1926, in Hamburg, XIV, 2389–2402; *National Tidende*, Copenhagen, January 16, 1926; *Königsberg Allgemeine Zeitung* 110, March 7, 1927.

67. Statements of Doris Rittman, née Wingender, and of Luise Fiedler, née Wingender, May 20, 1958, in Staatsarchiv, Darmstadt, 74 0.294/57; *Berliner Nachtausgabe*, April 8, 1927.

68. Doris Rittmann, née Wingender, testimony of November 17, 1965, in Hamburg, XXVII, 5144–5151; Doris Rittmann, née Wingender, statement of May 20, 1958, in Staatsarchiv, Darmstadt, 74 0.294/57.

69. Blucher, 102, 162.

70. *Berliner Nachtausgabe*, April 8, 1927; "Evolution of Franziska Schanzkowska to Grand Duchess Anastasia," summary by Herr Meyer for Darmstadt, June 24, 1944, in Staatsarchiv, Darmstadt; statement of Doris Rittmann, née Wingender, May 20, 1958, in Staatsarchiv, Darmstadt, 74 0.294/57.

71. In *Police von Anfang April und vom June 2, 1927*, in *der Beikate ZK* 83, filed in Hamburg under Tchaikovsky Bln 72, 72R, 75; Summary of Evidence in *Frau Anna Anderson in Unterlengenhardt v. Barbara, Herzogin Christian Ludwig zu Mecklenburg, Ludwig, Prinz von Hesse und bei Rhein*, May 18, 1967, 178.

72. Doris Rittmann, née Wingender, statement of May 23, 1959, in Staatsarchiv, Darmstadt, 74 0.294/57.

21 The Myth Unravels

1. Hamburg, Summary of Evidence in *Frau Anna Anderson in Unterlengenhardt v. Barbara, Herzogin Christian Ludwig zu Mecklenburg, Ludwig, Prinz von Hesse und bei Rhein*, May 18, 1967, 30.

2. *Berliner Nachtausgabe*, April 8, 1927; Martin Knopf, "Report on Franziska Schanzkowska," 1927, in Staatsarchiv, Darmstadt.

3. Ibid.; Doris Rittmann, née Wingender, testimony of November 17, 1965, in Hamburg, XXVII, 5144–5151; Fritz Lucke, testimony of November 17, 1965, in Hamburg, XXVII, 5167; Luise Fiedler, née Wingender, testimony of November 18, 1965, in Hamburg, XXVIII, 5145–5147; Martin Knopf, "Report on Franziska Schanzkowska," 1927, in Staatsarchiv, Darmstadt.

4. *Berliner Nachtausgabe*, April 11, 1927; Luise Fielder, née Wingender, testimony of November 18, 1965, in Hamburg, XXVIII, 5145–5147.

5. Hamburg, Summary of Evidence in *Frau Anna Anderson in Unterlengenhardt v. Barbara, Herzogin Christian Ludwig zu Mecklenburg, Ludwig, Prinz von Hesse und bei Rhein*, May 18, 1967, 178; the Abmeldung, dated March 15, 1920, is listed as BL 73 in ZK 83 in Hamburg.

6. Felix Schanzkowsky, affidavit of May 9, 1927, in Hamburg, XIII, 2288–2289.

7. Gertrude Ellerik, née Schanzkowska, statement of May 23, 1959, in Hamburg, VII, 1470–1475.

8. See, for example, Fritz Schuricht protocol of conversation with a "Commissar X," April 29, 1927, cited in Kurth, 6, on the unproven contention that records of all hospitals and asylums in Berlin were examined.

9. See Berlin police files of *Reichskriminalpolizeiamnt Berlin die Vorgange S 190278=Sch 8623* in Hamburg under Bln IV, 147–150.

10. Anna (Thea) Chemnitz, née Malinovsky, testimony of December 17, 1958, in Hamburg, V, 979–981.

11. Ibid.

12. See Gilliard and Savitch, 31–32.

13. See Anna (Thea) Chemntiz, née Malinovsky, letter in *Berliner Nachtausgabe*, March 5, 1927; Anna (Thea) Chemnitz, née Malinovsky, to Kurt Pastenaci, letter of September 27, 1927, in Rathlef-Keilmann, 180–181; Anna (Thea) Chemnitz, née Malinovsky,

statement of June 27, 1929; in Hamburg, Bln III, loose; Anna (Thea) Chemnitz, née Malinovsky, testimony of December 17, 1958, in Hamburg, V, 979–981; Emilie Barfknecht, statement of June 14, 1922, in Hamburg, XXIV, 4476–4478.

14. Gilliard and Savitch, 29.

15. Emilie Barfknecht, statement of June 14, 1922, in Hamburg, XXIV, 4476–4478.

16. Hamburg, Summary of Evidence in *Frau Anna Anderson in Unterlengenhardt v. Barbara, Herzogin Christian Ludwig zu Mecklenburg, Ludwig, Prinz von Hesse und bei Rhein*, May 18, 1967, 41; Baroness Marie von Kleist, statement of July 5, 1929, entered into evidence in Hamburg May 20, 1958, in Hamburg, III, 569–574.

17. *Berliner Nachtausgabe*, April 7, 1927; Baroness Marie von Kleist, statement of July 5, 1929, entered into evidence in Hamburg May 20, 1958, in Hamburg, III, 569–574.

18. *Berliner Nachtausgabe*, April 8, 1927; Rathlef-Keilmann, 172; Voller statement, April 29, 1927, in Hamburg, XXII, 4270; Rathlef-Keilmann, in *Tägliche Rundschau*, October 1927, in Hamburg, XVII, 3165–3188.

19. Doris Rittmann, née Wingender, statement of May 20, 1958, in Staatsarchiv, Darmstadt, 74 0.294/57.

20. Ibid.; Doris Rittmann, née Wingender, testimony of November 17–18, 1965, in Hamburg, XXVII, 5144–5151; *Berliner Nachtausgabe*, April 7, 1927.

21. Doris Rittmann, née Wingender, May 20, 1958, in Staatsarchiv, Darmstadt, 74 0.294/57; Gilliard and Savitch, 177–178; in "Application to the Amstgericht Court, Berlin, in the matter of the Estate of Anastasia Nikolaievna Romanov, Case No. 461.VE.733/738," pleading submitted by Paul Leverkuehn and Kurt Vermehren on behalf of AA, October 31, 1938, and lodged in Hamburg under Bln 58.

22. *Berliner Nachtausgabe*, April 8, 1927; Doris Rittmann, née Wingender, statement of May 20, 1958, in Staatsarchiv, Darmstadt, 74 0.294/57.

23. See Kurth, 104.

24. *Berliner Nachtausgabe*, April 8, 1927; Fritz Lucke, testimony of November 17, 1965,

in Hamburg, XXVII, 5167; Martin Knopf, "Report on Franziska Schanzkowska," 1927, in Staatsarchiv, Darmstadt.

25. Baroness Marie von Kleist, statement of July 5, 1929, entered into evidence in Hamburg May 20, 1958, in Hamburg, III, 569–574.

26. See Kurth, 166, 308; verdict of the Hanseatic High Court (Landesgericht), Hamburg, issued May 16, 1961, and appended to Hamburg, XXIV, loose.

27. Baroness Marie von Kleist, statement of July 5, 1929, entered into evidence in Hamburg May 20, 1958, in Hamburg, III, 569–574.

28. Dr. Lothar Nobel, report of March 1926, in Hamburg, XIII, 4417–4426.

29. Dr. Karl Bonhoeffer, report of March 18, 1926, in Hamburg, XIV, 2389–2395; Dr. Lothar Nobel, report of March 1926, in Hamburg, XIII, 4417–4426.

30. Duke Georg of Leuchtenberg to Olga Alexandrovna, letter of August 26, 1927, in Hamburg, XIV, 2558–2559.

31. Anna (Thea) Chemnitz, née Malinovsky, testimony of December 17, 1958, in Hamburg, V, 979–981.

32. Dr. Karl Bonhoeffer, report of March 18, 1926, in Hamburg, XIV, 2389–2395; Gilliard and Savitch, 110.

33. Anna (Thea) Chemnitz, née Malinovsky, testimony of December 17, 1958, in Hamburg, V, 979–981.

34. Nicholas von Schwabe to Gilliard, letter of November 17, 1926, in Gilliard and Savitch, 114–115; Gilliard and Savitch, 82; Nicholas von Schwabe to Gilliard, letter of December 12, 1926, in Gilliard and Savitch, 110; information from Robert Massie; Hamburg, Summary of Evidence in *Frau Anna Anderson in Unterlengenhardt v. Barbara, Herzogin Christian Ludwig zu Mecklenburg, Ludwig, Prinz von Hesse und bei Rhein*, May 18, 1967, 166; Martin Knopf, "Report on Franziska Schanzkowska," 1927, in Staatsarchiv, Darmstadt; Marie Clara Peuthert to Gilliard, letter of January 1926, in Gilliard and Savitch, 29.

35. Baroness Marie von Kleist, statement of July 5, 1929, entered into evidence in

Hamburg May 20, 1958, in Hamburg, III, 569–574.

36. Nicholas von Schwabe to Gilliard, letter of November 17, 1926, in Gilliard and Savitch, 113–114; Baroness von Kleist, statement of July 5, 1929, entered into evidence in Hamburg May 20, 1958, in Hamburg, III, 569–574; Hamburg, Summary of Evidence in *Frau Anna Anderson in Unterlengenhardt v. Barbara, Herzogin Christian Ludwig zu Mecklenburg, Ludwig, Prinz von Hesse und bei Rhein*, May 18, 1967, 166.

37. Gilliard to Rathlef-Keilmann, letter of December 30, 1925, in Rathlef-Keilmann, 232; information from Ian Lilburn to the authors.

38. Rathlef-Keilmann, 233.

39. Gilliard and Savitch, 116.

40. Rathlef-Keilmann, 233; Gilliard and Savitch, 115; "Application to the Amtsgericht Court, Berlin, in the Matter of the Estate of Anastasia Nikolaievna Romanov, Case No. 461.VE.733/738," pleading submitted by Paul Leverkuehn and Kurt Vermehren on behalf of AA, October 31, 1938, and lodged in Hamburg under Bln 58, 40.

41. *Berliner Illustrierte Zeitung*, October 23, 1921.

42. Statement of Baron von Kleist according to Tolstoy, August 4, 1922, in Gilliard and Savitch, 49; Marie Clara Peuthert, letter to Princess Irene of Hesse, Princess Heinrich of Prussia, August 23, 1922, in Gilliard and Savitch, 51.

43. Gilliard and Savitch, 110.

44. Botkin, *Anastasia*, 82.

45. Botkin, *Vospominaya*, 4, 8–9; Botkin, *Au Temps*, 81; Tatiana Botkin to Brien Horan, in Horan, 68; Tatiana Botkin to Paul Paganuzzi, in Paganuzzi, 17; Gilliard and Savitch, 90; Gleb Botkin, affidavit of July 20, 1938, in Hamburg, Bln I, 101–112; Botkin, *Real Romanovs*, 160, 286–267.

46. See Tatiana Botkin, affidavit of May 2, 1929, in Hamburg, Bln I, 113–127; Botkin, *Woman Who Rose Again*, 260–267.

22 Into the Pages of History

1. Doris Rittmann, née Wingender, statement of May 20, 1958, in Staatsarchiv,

Darmstadt, 74 0.294/57; affidavit of Doris Rittmann, née Wingender, February 5, 1960, in Hamburg, XIV, 2365; letter of Doris Rittmann, née Wingender, to Hans Hermann Krampff, December 11, 1955, in Hamburg, XIV, 2366–2367; Doris Rittmann, née Wingender, testimony of December 17, 1965, in Hamburg, XXIX, 5346–5356; Doris Rittmann, née Wingender, testimony of November 18–19, 1965, in Hamburg, XXVII, 5144–5151; Doris Rittmann, née Wingender, statement of May 7, 1958, in Hamburg, III, 502–513. The issue of *Die Woche*, dated February 2, 1927, was admitted into evidence at Hamburg, in XXXII, 6029. The clarity of the image, a central point, was raised during the Hamburg trials, as discussed in Kurth, 348–349. Kurth, though, confirms that the photograph was clearly recognizable as Franziska. Information from Peter Kurth to Greg King.

2. Luise Fiedler, née Wingender, testimony of December 17, 1965, in Hamburg, XXIX, 5356–5358; Luise Fiedler, née Wingender, testimony of November 18, 1965, in Hamburg, XXVIII, 5145–5147; Luise Fiedler, née Wingender, statement of May 21, 1958, in Hamburg, III, 542–547.

3. Doris Rittmann, née Wingender, statement of May 20, 1958, in Staatsarchiv, Darmstadt, 74 0.294/57; notes by Dr. Hans Hermann Krampff concerning visit to Frau Maria Kathe Wypyrczyk, née Wingender, and Luise Fiedler, née Wingender, in Hamburg, X, 1861–1862; affidavit of Doris Rittmann, née Wingender, February 5, 1960, in Hamburg, XIV, 2365; letter of Doris Rittmann, née Wingender, to Hans Hermann Krampff, December 11, 1955, in Hamburg, XIV, 2366–2367; Doris Rittmann, née Wingender, testimony of December 17, 1965, in Hamburg, XXIX, 5346–5356; Doris Rittmann, née Wingender, testimony of November 18–19, 1965, in Hamburg, XXVII, 5144–5151; Doris Rittmann, née Wingender, statement of May 7, 1958, in Hamburg, III, 502–513; Luise Fiedler, née Wingender, testimony of December 17,

1965, in Hamburg, XXIX, 5356–5358; Luise Fiedler, née Wingender, testimony of November 18, 1965, in Hamburg, XXVIII, 5145–5147; Luise Fiedler, née Wingender, statement of May 21, 1958, in Hamburg, III, 542–547.

4. Doris Rittmann, née Wingender, statement of May 20, 1958, in Staatsarchiv, Darmstadt, 74 0.294/57; Wilhelm Voller interview with Anna Wingender, statement of May 25, 1927, cited in Hamburg, Summary of Evidence in *Frau Anna Anderson in Unterlengenhardt v. Barbara, Herzogin Christian Ludwig zu Mecklenburg, Ludwig, Prinz von Hesse und bei Rhein*, May 18, 1967, 59–60.

5. Doris Rittmann, née Wingender, testimony of November 18, 1965, in Hamburg, XXVII, 5144–5151; Doris Rittmann, née Wingender, statement of May 20, 1958, in Staatsarchiv, Darmstadt, 74 0.294/57; Doris Rittmann, née Wingender, statement of December 11, 1955, in Hamburg, XIV, 2366–2367; Fritz Lücke, testimony of November 17, 1965, in Hamburg, XXVII, 5167; affidavit of Doris Rittmann, née Wingender, February 5, 1960, in Hamburg, XIV, 2365; Martin Knopf, "Report on Franziska Schanzkowska," 1927, in Staatsarchiv, Darmstadt. The contract stipulated that Doris was to receive 1,000 marks on confirmation of her story, and 500 marks on publication.

6. Andrei Vladimirovich to Serge Botkin, letter of May 13 1927, in Ian Lilburn Collection; information from Ian Lilburn to the authors.

7. See letter from Fritz Spengruber, in *Tägliche Rundschau*, Berlin, October 4, 1927; Duke Georg of Leuchtenberg to Olga Alexandrovna, letter of August 26, 1927, in Hamburg, XIV, 2558–2559; Fritz Lucke, testimony of July 10, 1958, in Hamburg, IV, 666–667; Agnes Wasserschleben, statement of July 28, 1929, in Hamburg, VI, 1017–1024.

8. Hamburg, Summary of Evidence in *Frau Anna Anderson in Unterlengenhardt v. Barbara, Herzogin Christian Ludwig zu Mecklenburg, Ludwig, Prinz von Hesse und bei Rhein*, May 18, 1967, 69.

9. See *Berliner Nachtausgabe*, April 6, 1927; Gilliard and Savitch, 175–176; *Police von Anfang April und vom June 2, 1927*, in Hamburg under der *Keikate ZK 83 Tchaikovsky* Bl 72, 72R, 75.

10. Martin Knopf, affidavit of February 28, 1928, in Hamburg, XIV, 2353–2354; Martin Knopf, "Report on Franziska Schanzkowska," 1927, in Staatsarchiv, Darmstadt.

11. Fritz Lücke, testimony of July 10, 1958, in Hamburg, IV, 666–667; cable from Knopf to Berlin Police of March 26, 1927, in Hamburg under Bl 68, ZK 83, 76–77.

12. *Berliner Nachtausgabe*, April 16, 1927.

13. See Martin Knopf, affidavit of February 28, 1928, in Hamburg, XIV, 2353–2354; Knopf, cable of March 26, 1927, to Berlin Police, in Hamburg under Bl 68 ZK 83, 76–77; Marianna Knopf, quoted in Martin Knopf, "Report on Franziska Schanzkowska," 1927, in Staatsarchiv, Darmstadt; Gertrude Ellerik, née Schanzkowska, statement of May 23, 1959, in Hamburg, VII, 1470–1475.

14. Gertrude Ellerik, née Schanzkowska, statement of May 23, 1959, in Hamburg, VII, 1470–1475.

15. Martin Knopf, affidavit of February 28, 1928, in Hamburg, XIV, 2353–2354; Knopf, cable of March 26, 1927, to Berlin Police, in Hamburg under Bl 68 ZK 83, 76–77; Escaich, 123.

16. Cited in Kurth, 168.

17. *Berliner Nachtausgabe*, April 5, 1927.

18. See *Berliner Nachtausgabe*, April 5–16, 1927.

19. *Berliner Nachtausgabe*, April 8, 1927.

20. See Duke Georg of Leuchtenberg to Olga Alexandrovna, letter of August 26, 1927, in Hamburg, XIV, 2558–2559.

21. Rathlef-Keilmann, 172.

22. Doris Rittmann, née Wingender, statement of May 20, 1958, in Staatsarchiv, Darmstadt, 74 0.294/57; *Berliner Nachtausgabe*, April 11, 1927.

23. Doris Rittmann, née Wingender, statement of May 20, 1958, in Staatsarchiv, Darmstadt, 74 0.294/57; *Berliner Nachtausgabe*, April 11, 1927. There are several variations of this utterance. The duke of Leuchtenberg recalled it as *"Sie muss herausgehen!"* (She must get

out!), while Faith Lavington was told that she shouted the rather less grammatical, *"Dass muss heraus!"* (That must out!). See the duke's account in Rathlef-Keilmann, 171, and the diary of Faith Lavington, entry of February 21, 1928, in Hamburg, XXXIV, 6402–6428.

24. Marianna Knopf, quoted in Martin Knopf, "Report on Franziska Schanzkowska," 1927, in Staatsarchiv, Darmstadt; Martin Knopf, affidavit of February 28, 1928, in Hamburg, XIV, 2353–2354.

25. Doris Rittmann, née Wingender, statement of May 20, 1958, in Staatsarchiv, Darmstadt, 74 0.294/57; Doris Rittmann, née Wingender, affidavit of February 5, 1960, in Hamburg, XIV, 2365.

26. Martin Knopf, "Report on Franziska Schanzkowska," 1927, in Staatsarchiv, Darmstadt; Martin Knopf, affidavit of February 28, 1928, in Hamburg, XIV, 2353–2354.

27. *Berliner Nachtausgabe*, April 11, 1927.

28. Ibid.; see also Martin Knopf, "Report on Franziska Schanzkowska," 1927, in Staatsarchiv, Darmstadt; Martin Knopf, affidavit of February 28, 1928, in Hamburg, XIV, 2353–2354.

29. Diary of Faith Lavington, entry of February 21, 1928, in Hamburg, XXXIV, 6402–6428.

30. Luise Fiedler, née Wingender, testimony of November 19, 1965, in Hamburg, XXVIII, 5145–5147.

31. See *L'Illustration*, Paris, February 18, 1928.

32. Kurth, 170.

33. Rathlef-Keilmann, 174.

34. See Martin Knopf, "Report on Franziska Schanzkowska," 1927, in Staatsarchiv, Darmstadt; Martin Knopf, affidavit of February 28, 1928, in Hamburg, XIV, 2353–2354.

35. Frau Margarethe Kothe, statement of February 18, 1958, in Staatsarchiv, Darmstadt; Dr. Hans Hermann Krampff to Dr. Gunther Berenberg-Gossler, letter of July 16, 1958, quoting Heinrich Trapp, in Staatsarchiv, Darmstadt; Richard Meyer, statement of July 18, 1958, in Staatsarchiv, Darmstadt.

36. Fritz Schuricht, statement of May 21, 1959, in Staatsarchiv, Darmstadt, doc. 74 0.294/57.

37. Frau Margarethe Kothe, statement of February 18, 1958, quoting her mother, Frau Martha Borkowski, previously Reetz, née Schrock, in Staatsarchiv, Darmstadt.

38. Wilhelm Voller, affidavit of May 10, 1927, in Hamburg, XIV, 2380–2384.

39. Diary of Faith Lavington, entry of February 21, 1928, in Hamburg, XXXIV, 6402–6428; Duke Dimitri of Leuchtenberg, statement of April 15, 1958, in Hamburg, III, 521–522; Duchess Nathalie of Leuchtenberg, Baronin Meller-Zakomelski, statement of November 3, 1959, in Hamburg, IX, 1623–1630.

40. Wilhelm Voller, affidavit of May 10, 1927, in Hamburg, XIV, 2380–2384; diary of Faith Lavington, entry of February 21, 1928, in Hamburg, XXXIV, 6402–6428.

41. Diary of Faith Lavington, entry of February 21, 1928, in Hamburg, XXXIV, 6402–6428.

42. Wilhelm Voller, affidavit of May 10, 1927, in Hamburg, XIV, 2380–2384.

43. Duke Dimitri of Leuchtenberg, letter of March 5, 1961, in Vorres, 239–240; Duke Dimitri of Leuchtenberg, statement of April 15, 1958, in Hamburg, III, 521–522; Duchess Catherine of Leuchtenberg, statement of March 20, 1959, in Hamburg, VII, 1261–1264; information from Robert K. Massie to the authors; Hamburg, Summary of Evidence in *Frau Anna Anderson in Unterlengenhardt v. Barbara, Herzogin Christian Ludwig zu Mecklenburg, Ludwig, Prinz von Hesse und bei Rhein*, May 18, 1967, 182.

44. Rathlef-Keilmann, 174; Botkin, *Real Romanovs*, 284.

45. Duchess Nathalia of Leuchtenberg, Baronin Meller-Zakomelski, statement of November 3, 1959, in Hamburg, IX, 1623–1630.

46. Wilhelm Voller, affidavit of May 10, 1927, in Hamburg, XIV, 2380–2384.

47. Felix Schanzkowsky, affidavit of May 9, 1927, in Hamburg, XIII, 2288–2289.

48. Duke Georg of Leuchtenberg to Olga Alexandrovna, letter of August 26, 1927, in Hamburg, XIV, 2558–2559.

49. Botkin, *Woman Who Rose Again*, 85.
50. Ibid., 93–94, 87.
51. Rathlef-Keilmann, 176.
52. Klier and Mingay, 106.
53. Rathlef-Keilmann, 176.
54. Ibid.; Friedrich, 333; Wilson and Pitman, 243–244; *New York Times*, July 6, 1921.
55. *Kriminalpolizei* File 678 IV K 15/27, Case 21.J.266/28, cited in Gilliard and Savitch, 185.
56. Rathlef-Keilmann articles in *Tägliche Rundschau*, Berlin, October 1927, in Hamburg, XVII, 3165–3188.
57. Otto Meyer to Martin Knopf, in Martin Knopf, affidavit of February 28, 1928, in Hamburg, XIV, 2353; Richard Meyer quoted in letter of Dr. Hans Hermann Krampff to Dr. Gunther von Berenberg-Gossler, July 16, 1958, in Staatsarchiv, Darmstadt; Richard Meyer, statement of July 18, 1958, in Staatsarchiv, Darmstadt; Frau Margarethe Kothe, statement of February 18, 1958, quoting mother Martha Borkowski, previously Reetz, née Schrock, in Staatsarchiv, Darmstadt; Doris Rittmann, née Wingender, statement of May 20, 1958, in Staatsarchiv, Darmstadt, 74 0.294/57; affidavit of Doris Rittmann, née Wingender, February 5, 1960, in Hamburg, XIV/2365; Letter of Doris Rittmann, née Wingender, to Dr. Hans Hermann Krampff, December 11, 1955, in Hamburg, XIV, 2366–2367; Luise Fiedler, née Wingender, statement of May 21, 1958, in Hamburg, III, 542–547; file notes by Dr. Hans Hermann Krampf concerning visit to Frau Maria Kathe Wypyrczyk, née Wingender, and Luise Fiedler, née Wingender, in Hamburg, X, 1861–1862. During the Hamburg trial Martha Schrock failed to identify Franziska from a group of photographs; more than thirty years earlier, though, when memories were presumably more vivid, she had unhesitatingly recognized photographs of the claimant as Franziska. See Kurth, 307.
58. *Hessischen Polizeiamt Kriminalzentrale für Hessen-Erkennungsdienst, Darmstadt*, April 26, 1927, in Hamburg, Bln, 11–17 loose; Berlin Police files of Franziska Schanzkowska submitted from *Reichskriminalpolizeiamt Berlin die Vorgange*, 8623, in Hamburg, IV, 147–150; and *Police von Anfang April und vom June 2, 1927*, in Hamburg, under Bln, ZK 83 Tchaikovsky, 72, 72R, 75.
59. Gertrude Ellerik, née Schanzkowska, statement of May 23, 1959, in Hamburg, VII, 1470–1475; Gertrude Ellerik, née Schanzkowska, statement of November 26, 1966, in Hamburg, XXXV, 6148.
60. Emma Mueller Schanzkowsky to Dr. Hans Hermann Krampff, letter of February 10, 1969, in Hamburg, XIV, 2340; Waltraut von Czenstkowski, affidavit of July 23, 1959, in Hamburg, X, 1863, and of January 31, 1961, in Hamburg, XIV, 2388; Gertrude Ellerik, née Schanzkowska, statement of May 23, 1959, in Hamburg, VII, 1470–1475.
61. Hamburg, Summary of Evidence in *Frau Anna Anderson in Unterlengenhardt v. Barbara, Herzogin Christian Ludwig zu Mecklenburg, Ludwig, Prinz von Hesse und bei Rhein*, May 18, 1967, 91.
62. Kurth, 282.
63. Hamburg, Summary of Evidence in *Frau Anna Anderson in Unterlengenhardt v. Barbara, Herzogin Christian Ludwig zu Mecklenburg, Ludwig, Prinz von Hesse und bei Rhein*, May 18, 1967, 177–178; Gertrude Ellerik, née Schanzkowska, statement of May 23 1959, in Hamburg, VII, 1470–1475.
64. Gertrude Ellerik, née Schanzkowska, statement of May 23, 1959, in Hamburg, VII, 1470–1475.
65. Gertrude Ellerik, née Schanzkowska, statement of May 23, 1959, in Hamburg, VII, 1470–1475; Gertrude Ellerik, née Schanzkowska, statement in Hygendorf on September 8, 1937, in Hamburg, XXIV, 65–70; Felix Schanzkowsky, statement of November 10, 1937, in Hamburg, XXIV, 74–76; Valerian Schanzkowsky, statement of October 11, 1937, in Hamburg, XXV, 19–21; report from Criminal State Police, Hannover, July 10, 1938, in Hamburg, I, 44–52.
66. Minutes of meeting of July 9, 1938, Hannover State Police Files, in Hamburg, Bln, II, 69–71; Hannover State Police, memorandum, July 10, 1938, in Hamburg, XIV, 2335–2338; statement of Criminal

Police Commissioner A. W. Paar, July 10, 1938, in Hamburg, I, 71–74; letter of February 17, 1961, from Criminal Police Commissioner A. W. Paar in Hannover to Dr. Gunther von Berenberg-Gossler, in Hamburg, XXII, 4107–4111.

67. Gertrude Ellerik, née Schanzkowska, statement of May 23, 1959, in Hamburg, VII, 1470–1475.

68. Minutes of meeting of July 9, 1938, Hannover State Police Files, in Hamburg, Bln II, 69–71; Hannover State Police memorandum, July 10, 1938, in Hamburg, XIV, 2335–2338; statement of Criminal Police Commissioner A. W. Paar, July 10, 1938, in Hamburg, I, 71–74; letter of February 17, 1961, from Criminal Police Commissioner A. W. Paar in Hannover to Dr. Gunther von Berenberg-Gossler, in Hamburg, XXII, 4107–4111.

69. Hannover State Police memorandum, July 10, 1938, in Hamburg, XIV, 2335–2338; statement of Criminal Police Commissioner A. W. Paar, July 10, 1938, in Hamburg, I, 71–74.

70. Gertrude Ellerik, née Schanzkowska, statement of November 26, 1966, in Hamburg, XXXV, 6148.

71. See letter of Emma Mueller Schanzkowsky to Dr. Hans Hermann Krampff, February 10, 1959, in Hamburg, XIV, 2340, and letter of Waltraut von Czenstkowski to Krampff, July 23, 1959, in Hamburg, XIV, 2388–2394.

72. See Gilliard and Savitch, 175–176; Maurice Delamin study, 1957, Hamburg, 4a-h 8, 1–7.

73. Report of Dr. Otto Reche, May 12, 1959, in Hamburg, IX, 1648–1724.

74. Bruno Grandsitzki, testimony of November 24, 1958, in Hamburg, V, 939–942.

75. Gerhard Mauz, "Eine Rettung, die Mutterchen Russland gelang?," Der Spiegel, June 3, 1967.

76. Auclères, 150.

77. See testimonies of Charlotte Janus, Margarete Binner, and Emma Bezug, October 4, 1966, in Hamburg, XXXI, 5802–5814.

78. Gerhard Mauz, "Eine Rettung, die Mutterchen Russland gelang?," Der Spiegel, June 3, 1967.

79. Verdict of the Hanseatic High Court (Landesgericht), Hamburg, May 16, 1961, appended to Hamburg, loose.

80. Dr. Hans Hermann Krampff to Gertrude Ellerik, née Schanzkowska, letter of April 11, 1959, quoted in Auclères, 146–147.

81. Margarete Ellerik to Felix Schanzkowsky, letter of May 16, 1959, quoted in Auclères, 147.

Epilogue

1. Botkin, Real Romanovs, 265.

2. Charlottesville Daily Progress, October 6, 1994.

3. Ibid., October 7, 1994.

4. See Kurth, "Anna Anderson: Notes on Franziska Schanzkowska"; Rathlef-Keilmann, 175–176.

5. See "Kriminalistik," Der Spiegel, February 13, 1967.

6. Summers and Mangold, 236; Kurth, 384–385.

7. Associated Press report of February 25, 1977; Quick, Germany, February 24, 1977.

8. Victoria, marchioness of Milford Haven, to Xenia Georgievna, letter of July 23, 1930, in Hamburg, XXXII, 3276.

9. See Gilliard and Savitch, 78; Lord Mountbatten to Prince Ludwig of Hesse, letter of November 12, 1957, in Staatsarchiv, Darmstadt.

10. Thornton, 32; London Daily Express, July 29, 1988.

11. Kurth, 387.

12. See In Search of . . . Anastasia.

13. See "Kriminalistik," Der Spiegel, February 13, 1967; see, for example, Popular Science, March 1951, 45; Dr. Andre Moenssens, professor emeritus, University of Richmond, University of Missouri at Kansas City, e-mail of January 8, 2010, to Greg King.

14. Dr. Andre Moenssens, professor emeritus, University of Richmond, University of Missouri at Kansas City, e-mail of January 8, 2010, to Greg King.

15. The Mystery of Anastasia, produced by Julian Nott for Peninsula Films, aired on Channel 4, U.K., October 5, 1994.

16. Dr. Andre Moenssens, at http://www.forensic-evidence.com/site/ID/ID00004_4.html; Dr. Andre Moenssens,

professor emeritus, University of Richmond, University of Missouri at Kansas City, e-mail of January 8, 2010, to Greg King.

17. Dr. Geoffrey Oxlee, Dr. Peter French, and David Ellen in *The Mystery of Anastasia*, produced by Julian Nott for Peninsula Films, aired on Channel 4, U.K., October 5, 1994.

18. Alexander Palace Time Machine discussion forum, at www.alexanderpalace .org, post by J. A. Hubert, July 9, 2005, quoting e-mail from Ginther of July 6, 2005; e-mail from Dietmar Wulff to Greg King, May 10, 2001; Dr. Stefan Sandkuhler to Greg King, May 22, 2000.

19. Information from Maurice Philip Remy to the authors.

20. Letter from Ginther to Remy, September 30, 1994, quoted in Ginther, e-mail to J. A. Hubert, July 6, 2005, on Alexander Palace Time Machine discussion forum, at www.alexanderpalace.org, July 9, 2005; *Sunday Times*, London, October 2, 1994.

21. Dr. Stefan Sandkuhler to Greg King, May 22, 2000; Massie, 234; Ginther, e-mail to J. A. Hubert, July 6, 2005, on Alexander Palace Time Machine discussion forum, at www.alexanderpalace .org, July 9, 2005.

22. See Kurth, "Anna Anderson: Notes on Franziska Schanzkowska."

23. *Charlottesville Daily Progress*, June 20, 1994; *London Daily Mail*, June 24, 1994.

24. Susan Grindstaff Burkhart to Greg King, e-mail of June 14, 2009.

25. Dr. Andre Moenssens, professor emeritus, University of Richmond, University of Missouri at Kansas City, e-mail of January 8, 2010, to Greg King.

26. Dr. Terry Melton to Greg King, e-mail of June 1, 2009.

27. Massie, 245.

28. Susan Grindstaff Burkhart to Greg King, e-mail of June 14, 2009.

29. "Analysis of Hair from Anna Anderson," by Dr. Michael Coble, National Institute of Standards and Technology, and Dr. Daniele Podini, George Washington University, September 9, 2010; reports compiled for the authors; Dr. Michael to Greg King, e-mails of September 3, 6, 9, 17, and 18, 2010.

30. Yakov Yurovsky, "Memoirs," 1922, in APRF, F. 3, Op. 58, D. 280.

31. Yurovsky, 1920 note, in GARF, F. 601, Op. 2, D. 35; "Memoirs," 1922, in APRF, F. 3, Op. 58, D. 280; statement of Alexander Strekotin, 1934, in TsDOOSO, F. 221, Op. 2, D. 849.

32. Yurovsky, 1920 note, in GARF, F. 601, Op. 2, D. 35; "Memoirs," 1922, in APRF, F. 3, Op. 58, D. 280; Yurovsky, notes on talk delivered February 1, 1934, in TsDOOSO, F. 41, Op. 1, D. 151; statement of Alexander Strekotin, 1934, in TsDOOSO, F. 221, Op. 2, D. 849; Viktor Netrebin, "Memoirs of the Destruction of the Imperial Family," in TsDOOSO, F. 41, Op. 1, D. 149.

33. Statement of Alexander Strekotin, 1934, in TsDOOSO, F. 221, Op. 2, D. 849.

34. Yurovsky, 1920 note, in GARF, F. 601, Op. 2, D. 35; "Memoirs," 1922, in APRF, F. 3, Op. 58, D. 280; Yurovsky, notes on talk delivered February 1, 1934, in TsDOOSO, F. 41, Op. 1, D. 151.

35. "Remains Of Czar Heir May Have Been Found," Associated Press report, August 23, 2007; Yuri Zarakhovich, "Playing Politics with the Romanovs," *Times*, London, August 28, 2007; RIA Novosti report, August 24, 2007. The number of bones found was variously reported as forty-four or forty-eight: Dr. Michael Coble, who helped identify the remains, confirms that the latter number is correct, and confusion may have arisen as several small samples were grouped together under single designations. Dr. Michael Coble to Greg King, e-mail of August 16, 2010.

36. Dr. Michael Coble to Greg King, e-mail of August 16, 2010.

37. Coble, M. D., O. M. Loreille, M. J. Wadhams, S. M. Edson, K. Maynard, et al., at http://www.plosone.org/article/ info%3Adoi%2F10.1371%2Fjournal .pone.0004838; Dr. Michael Coble to Greg King, e-mail of August 17, 2010.

38. AA to Alexei Miliukov, June 7, 1967, in Miliukov tapes.

39. Martin Knopf, "Report on Franziska Schanzkowska," 1927, in Staatsarchiv, Darmstadt.

40. Summers and Mangold, 237.

Bibliography

Books and Articles

Alexander Mikhailovich, Grand Duke of Russia. *Always a Grand Duke*. New York: Farrar & Rinehart, 1933.

———. *Once a Grand Duke*. New York: Farrar & Rinehart, 1932.

Auclères, Dominique. *Anastasia, Qui êtes-vous?* Paris: Hachette, 1962.

Avdayev, Alexander. "Vospominanya." *Krasnaia Nov* 5 (1928).

Barbour, Philip. *Dimitry, Called the Pretender Tsar and Great Prince of All Russia, 1605–1606*. London: Macmillan, 1967.

Benagh, Christine. *An Englishman in the Court of the Tsar: The Spiritual Journey of Charles Sidney Gibbes*. Ben Lomond, Calif.: Conciliar Press, 2000.

Benckendorff, Count Paul von. *Last Days at Tsarskoye Selo*. London: William Heinemann, 1927.

Belyakova, Zoia. *Grand Duchess Maria Nikolayevna and Her Palace in St. Petersburg*. St. Petersburg: Ego Publishing, 1994.

Berger, Michael, ed. *1000 Jahre Seeon*. Seebruck, Bavaria: Weissen-Verlag, 1994.

Berkman, Ted. *The Lady and the Law*. Boston: Little, Brown, 1976.

Bing, Edward J., ed. *The Secret Letters of the Last Tsar: Being the Confidential Correspondence between Tsar Nicholas II and the Dowager Empress Marie*. London: Longmans, Green, 1938.

Blucher, Evelyn, Princess. *An English Wife in Berlin*. London: Constable, 1920.

Botkin, Gleb. *The Baron's Fancy*. Garden City, N.Y.: Doubleday, 1930.

———. *The God Who Didn't Laugh*. London: Victor Gollancz, 1929.

———. *Lost Tales: Stories for the Tsar's Children*. New York: Random House, 1996.

———. *The Real Romanovs*. New York: Fleming H. Revell, 1931.

———. *The Woman Who Rose Again*. New York: Fleming H. Revell, 1937.

Botkin, Tatiana. *Anastasia Retrouveé*. Paris: Grasset, 1985.

———. *Au Temps des Tsars*. Paris: Grasset, 1980.

———. *Vospominanya o Tsarskoi Sem'i*. Belgrade: Stefanovich, 1921.

Brzezinski, Richard. *Polish Armies, 1569–1696*. 2 vols. London: Osprey, 1987.

Bulygin, Paul, and Alexander Kerensky. *The Murder of the Romanovs*. London: Hutchinson, 1935.

Buxhoeveden, Baroness Sophie. *Before the Storm*. London: Macmillan, 1938.

———. *Left Behind*. London: Longmans, Green, 1929.

———. *The Tragic Empress: The Life and Tragedy of Alexandra Feodorovna*. London: Longmans, Green, 1928.

Bykov, Paul. *The Last Days of Tsar Nicholas*. New York: International Publishers, 1934.

Castelot, Andre. "Le mystère de la grande-duchesse Anastasie." In *Drames et Tragédies de l'Histoire*. Paris: Librairie Academique Perrin, 1966.

Chavchavadze, Prince David. *Crowns and Trenchcoats*. New York: Atlantic International Publications, 1990.

Clarke, William. *The Lost Fortune of the Tsars*. New York: St. Martin's Press, 1996.

Courtois, Christine A. *Healing the Incest Wound: Adult Survivors in Therapy*. New York: W. W. Norton, 1988.

Dassel, Felix. *Grossfursten Anastasie Lebt!* Berlin: Verlagshaus fur Volksliteratur und Kunst, 1928.

Davies, Norman. *God's Playground: A History of Poland*. 2 vols. Oxford: Oxford University Press, 1986.

Davis, Belinda. *Home Fires Burning: Food, Politics, and Everyday Life in World War I Berlin*. Chapel Hill, N.C.: University of North Carolina Press, 2000.

Dawson, William. *German Life in Town and Country*. London: George Newness, 1901.

Decaux, Alain. *L'Énigme Anastasia*. Paris: La Palatine, 1961.

Dehn, Lili. *The Real Tsaritsa*. London: Thornton Butterworth, 1922.

Duff, David. *Hessian Tapestry*. London: Frederick Miller, 1967.

Dzhunkovsky, Vladimir. *Vospominanya*. 2 vols. Moscow: Progress, 1997.

Eagar, Margaretta. *Six Years at the Russian Court*. London: Hurst & Blackett, 1906.

Escaich, René. *Anastasia de Russie: La Morte Vivante*. Paris: Plantin, 1955.

"Franziska Schanzkowski und ihr Leben." Manuscript prepared for the Staatsarchiv, Darmstadt, 1995.

Friedrich, Otto. *Before the Deluge: A Portrait of Berlin in the 1920s*. New York: Harper & Row, 1972.

Fromenko, Irina. "Krimskii Al'bom Nikolaya II." In *Krymskii Al'bom: Istoriko-kraevedcheskii I literaturno-khudozh*. Sevastopol: Taurida, 1998.

Fuhrmann, Joseph. *Rasputin: A Life*. New York: Praeger, 1990.

Gill, Anton. *A Dance Between Flames: Berlin Between the Wars*. New York: Carroll & Graf, 1993.

Gill, Peter, P. L. Ivanov, C. Kimpton, R. Piercy, N. Benson, G. Tully, I., Evett, E. Hagelberg, and K. Sullivan. "Identification of the Remains of the Romanov Family by DNA Analysis." *Nature Genetics* 6, no. 2 (1994).

Gill, Peter, C. Kimpton, R Aliston-Greiner, K. Sullivan, M. Stoneking, T. Melton, J. Nott, S. Barritt, et al. "Establishing the Identity of Anna Anderson Manahan." *Nature Genetics* 9, no. 1 (1995).

Gilliard, Pierre. *Thirteen Years at the Russian Court*. New York: George H. Doran, 1921.

———. *Das Tragische Schicksal der Zarenfamilie*. Berlin: Berliner-Verlag, 1922.

Gilliard, Pierre, and Konstantin Savitch. *La Fausse Anastasie*. Paris: Payot, 1929.

Grabbe, Paul, and Beatrice Grabbe. *The Private World of the Last Tsar: In the Photographs and Notes of General Count Alexander Grabbe*. Boston: Little, Brown, 1984.

Graf, H. G. *In the Service of the Imperial House of Russia, 1917–1941*. New York: privately published, 1998.

Greece, Prince Christopher of. *Memoirs*. London: Right Book Club, 1934.

Grey, Marina. *Enquête sur la massacre des Romanovs*. Paris: Librairie Academique, 1987.

Hall, Coryne. *Little Mother of Russia*. London: Shepheard-Walwyn, 1999.

Hall, Coryne, and John Van Der Kiste. *Imperial Dancer*. Stroud, Gloucestershire, U.K.: Sutton, 2005.

———. *Once a Grand Duchess: Xenia, Sister of Nicholas II*. Stroud, Gloucestershire, U.K.: Sutton, 2002.

Herman, Judith. *Father-Daughter Incest*. Cambridge, Mass.: Harvard University Press, 1981.

Herman, Judith Lewis, J. Christopher Perry, and Bessel A. van der Kolk. "Childhood Trauma in Borderline Personality Disorder." *American Journal of Psychiatry* 146 (1998).

Horan, Brien. "Anastasia: The Anna Anderson–Anastasia Case." Unpublished manuscript, 1976.

Hough, Richard. *Louis and Victoria: The First Mountbattens*. London: Hutchinson, 1974.

King, Greg. *The Court of the Last Tsar*. Hoboken, N.J.: John Wiley & Sons, 2006.

King, Greg. "The Romanovs in Film." *Atlantis Magazine: In the Courts of Memory* 1, no. 4 (2000).

King, Greg, and Penny Wilson. *The Fate of the Romanovs*. Hoboken, N.J.: John Wiley & Sons, 2003.

Klier, John, and Helen Mingay. *The Quest for Anastasia: Solving the Mystery of the Last Romanovs*. New York: Birch Lane Press, 1995.

Kokovtsov, Count Vladimir. *Out of My Past: The Memoirs of Count Kokovtsov*. Palo Alto, Calif.: Stanford University Press, 1935.

Kournosoff, Mikhail. *What Price Glory: Max Leuchtenberg in Russia*. Rosedale, B.C., Canada: Tlaguna Press, n.d.

Krug von Nidda, Roland, ed. *I, Anastasia*. London: Michael Joseph, 1958.

Kurth, Peter. *Anastasia: The Riddle of Anna Anderson*. Boston: Little, Brown, 1984.

Longworth, Philip. "The Pretender Phenomenon in Eighteenth-Century Russia." *Past and Present*, 66 (February 1975).

Lorentz, Friedrich, Adam Fischer, and Tadeusz Lehr-Splawinski. *The Cassubian Civilization*. London: Faber & Faber, 1935.

Lovell, James Blair. *Anastasia: The Lost Princess*. Washington, D.C.: Regnery, 1991.

Lyons, Marvin, ed. *Diary of Vladimir Mikhailovich Bezobrazov, Commander of the Russian Imperial Guard, 1914–1917*. Boynton Beach, Fla.: Dramco, 1994.

Manteuffel, Tadeusz. *The Formation of the Polish State: The Period of Ducal Rule*. Detroit: Wayne State University Press, 1982.

Marie Pavlovna, Grand Duchess of Russia. *Education of a Princess*. New York: Viking, 1931.

———. *A Princess in Exile*. New York: Viking, 1932.

Massie, Robert K. *The Romanovs: The Final Chapter*. New York: Random House, 1995.

Masur, Gerhard. *Imperial Berlin*. New York: Basic Books, 1970.

Maurette, Marcelle. *Anastasia*. English adaptation by Guy Bolton. New York: Random House, 1955.

Maylunas, Andrei, and Sergei Mironenko. *A Lifelong Passion*. New York: Doubleday, 1997.

Mossolov, Alexander. *At the Court of the Last Tsar*. London: Methuen, 1935.

Naryshkin-Kuryakina, Princess Elizabeth. *Under Three Tsars*. New York: E. P. Dutton, 1931.

Ob, Bezirk, ed. *Kloster Seeon*. Weissenhorn, Bavaria: Anton H. Konrad Verlag, 1993.

Paganuzzi, Paul. *Tschaikowska–Anna Anderson–Manahan: Tsar's Daughter or Impostor? A Historical Critical Essay*. St. Petersburg, Fla.: Privately published, 1987.

Phenix, Patricia. *Olga Romanov: Russia's Last Grand Duchess*. Toronto: Viking, 1999.

Preston, Sir Thomas H. *Before the Curtain*. London: Murray, 1950.

Rathlef-Keilmann, Harriet von. *Anastasia: The Survivor of Ekaterinburg*. New York: Payson & Clarke, 1928.

Rives, Barclay. "Keeping in Touch with John Manahan." *Albemarle* 1, no. 3 (1988).

Rose, Kenneth. *King George V*. New York: Alfred A. Knopf, 1984.

Rosenberg, Arthur. *Die Entstehung der Deutschen Republik*. Frankfurt: Europaische Verlagsantalt, 1931.

Ruffin, Bernard. "The Grand Duchess and Mrs. Manahan." *Atlantis Magazine: In The Courts of Memory* 1, no. 4 (2000).

Russell, Diana E. H. *The Secret Trauma: Incest in the Lives of Girls and Women*. New York: Basic Books, 1986.

Sokolov, Nicholas. *Der Todesweg des Zaren*. Berlin: Berliner-Verlag, 1925.

———. *Enquête Judiciaire sur l'assassinat de la Famille Impériale de Russie*. Paris: Payot, 1924.

Speranski, Valentin. *La Maison à Destination Speciale: La tragédie d'Ekaterinenbourg*. Paris: Payot, 1928.

Spiridovich, Alexandre. *Les Dernières Années de la Cour de Tsarskoie Selo*. Paris: Payot, 1928.

Summer, Anthony, and Tom Mangold. *The File on the Tsar*. New York: Harper & Row, 1976.

Telberg, George Gustav, and Robert Wilton. *The Last Days of the Romanovs*. London: Thornton Butterworth, 1920.

Thornton, Michael. "Anastasia: Has the Mystery Been Solved?" *Royalty Monthly* 13, no. 9 (1989).

Timms, Robert, ed. *Nicholas and Alexandra: The Last Imperial Family of Russia*. New York: Harry N. Abrams, 1998.

Trewin, J. C. *The House of Special Purpose*. New York: Stein & Day, 1975.

Troubestskoy, Alexis. *Imperial Legend: The Mysterious Disappearance of Tsar Alexander I*. London: Arcade Books, 2002.

Troyat, Henri. *Alexander of Russia*. New York: E. P. Dutton, 1982.

Tucker, William O. "Jack & Anna: Remembering the Czar of Charlottesville Eccentrics." *Hook* (Charlottesville), July 5, 2007.

Vickers, Hugo. *Alice, Princess of Greece*. London: Hamish Hamilton, 2000.

Viktoria Luise, Princess of Prussia. *The Kaiser's Daughter*. New York: Viking, 1977.

Volkov, Alexis. *Souvenirs d'Alexis Volkov: Valet de Chambre de la Tsarine Alexandra Feodorovna, 1910–1918*. Paris: Payot, 1928.

Vorres, Ian. *The Last Grand Duchess*. London: Hutchinson, 1964.

Voyekov, Vladimir. *S Tsarem i bez Tsarya*. Moscow: Rodnik, 1994.

Vyrubova, Anna. *Glanz und Untergang der Romanows*. Berlin: Amalthea Verlag, 1927.

———. *Memories of the Russian Court*. New York: Macmillan, 1923.

Welch, Frances. *A Romanov Fantasy: Life at the Court of Anna Anderson*. London: Short Books, 2007.

Wilson, Colin, and Patricia Pitman. *Encyclopedia of Murder*. New York: G. P. Putnam's Sons, 1961.

Wyatt, Gail Elizabeth, and Gloria Johnson Powell, eds. *Lasting Effects of Child Sexual Abuse*. Newbury Park, Calif.: Sage, 1988.

Yusupov, Prince Felix. *En Exil*. Paris: Plon, 1954.

Zajaczkowski, Andrzej. *Szlachta Polska: Kultura i Struktura*. Warsaw: Semper, 1993.

Zamoyski, Adam. *The Polish Way*. London: John Murray, 1987.

Zvereva, N. K., and A. C. Zverev. *Avgusteyshie Sestry Miloserdiya*. Moscow: Izdatel'ski Dom Veche, 2006.

Documentaries

Anastasia, Zarentochter oder Hochstaplerin? Documentary by Maurice Philip Remy, MPR Film and Fernsen Produktion GmbH, in cooperation with NDR Norddeutscher Rundfunk, 1995.

The Mystery of Anastasia. Equinox Production. Produced by Julian Nott for Peninsula Films, U.K., 1994.

In Search of . . . Anastasia. Syndicated television series. Alan Landsberg Productions, produced by Barbara J. Wegher. Season 2, episode 13, 1978.

Web Sites

Alexander Palace Time Machine. Web site and discussion forum at www.alexanderpalace.org.

Coble, M. D., O. M. Loreille, M. J. Wadhams, S. M. Edson, K. Maynard, et al. "Mystery Solved: The Identification of the Two Missing Romanov Children Using DNA Analysis." *PLoS ONE* 4(3): e4838. doi:10.1371/journal.pone.0004838. Michael Hofreiter, ed., Max Planck Institute for Evolutionary Anthropology, Germany. Published: March 11, 2009, at http://www.plosone.org/article/info%3Adoi%2F10.1371%2Fjournal.pone.0004838.

Godl, John. "Remembering Anna Anderson." Parts I and II at http://www.serfes.org/royal/rememberingAnnaAnderson.htm.

www.ka-na.org.

Kurth, Peter. "Anna Anderson: Notes on Franziska Schanzkowska." At http://www.peter-kurth.com/ANNA-ANASTASIA%20NOTES%20ON%20FRANZISKA%20SCHANZKOWSKA.htm.

Moenssens, Professor Andre. At http://www.forensic-evidence.com/site/ID/ID00004_4.html http://pom.

wpru.kerntopf.com/ortdetails/ort_borreck.htm www.westpreussen.de.

Index

Page numbers in *italics* indicate illustrations.

Felix Felixovich Yusupov, Prince, *163*
  Copenhagen statement and, 187
  meeting with Anderson, 163–164
  Rasputin and, 47
Feodorovsky Gorodok, 42
Ferdinand, Prince of Schoenaich-
  Carolath, 234
Figaro, Le, 224
File on the Tsar, The, 250
fingerprint evaluation, for trials, 224–225
Fischer, Eugen, 231
Feodor Alexandrovich, Prince, 187
Forensic Science Service Laboratory (Great
  Britain), 261–266,
  322–323, 324
Four Brothers Mine (Koptyaki Forest), *68,*
  70, 330
Four Winds Rest Home (Katonah, New
  York), 190, 199–200
Franz Ferdinand, Archduke of
  Austria-Hungary, 40
Freedericksz, Count Vladimir de,
  212, 213
French, Peter, 322
Freund, Irmgard, 95
Friedrich Ernst, Prince of
  Saxe-Altenburg, 112, *202*
  Anderson meeting with, *212,* 212–215
  Andrei Vladimirovich and, 210
  post-trial friendship with Anderson, 240,
  242–243, 244–245, 255
  trials and, 221
  Zahle and, 143
Furtmayr, Mortiz, 320–321, 322

Gaida, Rudolf, 72
Gallagher, Agnes, 178–179
Garde Equipage, 26, 48
Garden City Hotel (Long Island, New
  York), 184–189
Georg-August Institute for
  Anthropology, University of
  Göttingen (Germany), 323
Georg Donatus, Prince, *222*
George, Prince, 26, 118, 261
George Mikhailovich, Grand Duke,
  26, 179
George V, King of England, 51, 71,
  73, 74
George Washington University, 326
Gibbes, Charles Sidney
  Anderson and, 215–216
  freed by Provisional Government, 59

Imperial Family remains identified by, 70
Imperial Family's imprisonment and, 50,
  54, 55
trials and, 226
as tutor to Imperial Family, 30
Gienath, Baron Ulrich von, 203
Gill, Peter, 261–266, 324, 326
Gilliard, Alexandra. *See* Tegleva, Alexandra
  "Shura" (Gilliard)
Gilliard, Pierre, 9
  Anderson met by, 121–123, 125–140
  on Anderson's handwriting, 298–299
  Andrei Vladimirovich and, 144–146
  articles written by, 191–193
  Copenhagen statement and, 186–189
  Duke Leuchtenberg and, 160–161
  freed by Provisional Government, 59
  Gleb Botkin and, 174, 189, 312
  Imperial Family remains identified by, 70
  Imperial Family's imprisonment and,
  53, 55, 62
  La Fausse Anastasie, 194–199, 226, 265
  at Livadia, *120*
  memoirs published by, 173
  Poutziado's claims disputed by, 71–72
  Thirteen Years at the Russian Court,
  173, 226
  trials and, 226–227, 230
  views on Anastasia, 28–32, 32–33
  views on grand duchesses, 25
  on World War I and Imperial Family, 46
  Zachle and, 142–144
Ginther, Charles, 265–266, 323
Gish, Lillian, 240
Glischnitz, Pomerania, 271, 272
God Who Didn't Laugh, The (Botkin), 243
Golitsyn, Prince Dimitri, 234
Gorz, Dr., 85
Governor's House (Mogilev), 45
Governor's House (Tobolsk), *52,* 53–54
Grabbe, General Count Alexander
  von, 28
Graefe, Dr., 82–83, 84
Grandanor Corporation, 185–186
Grandsitzki, Bruno, 317
Great Palace (Peterhof), 15–17
Gregorian, Sarcho, 105
Grossman, Georg, 313
Grunberg, Franz, 99, 109–112, 157
Gudunov, Boris, 4–5
Gut-Friederikenhof estate (Schleswig-
  Holstein, Germany), 285, 288, 291
Gut-Retzow (Pomeranian estate), 201